Readings in Economics

Paul A. Samuelson

Institute Professor
Massachusetts Institute of Technology

with the assistance of
Felicity Skidmore

Readings in Economics

Sixth Edition

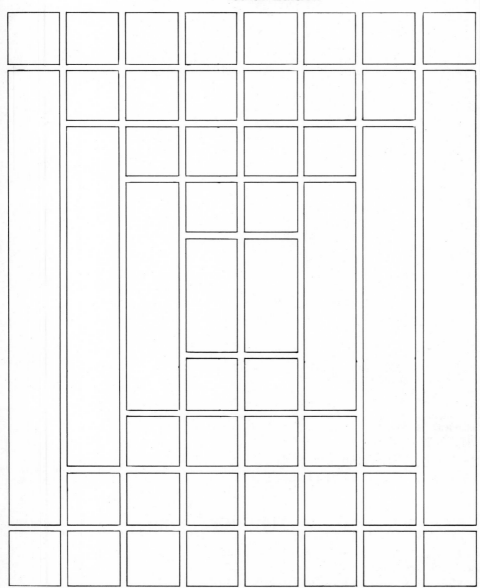

McGraw-Hill Book Company

New York   St. Louis   San Francisco   Düsseldorf   London
Mexico   Panama   Sydney   Toronto

Readings in Economics

Copyright © 1955, 1958, 1964, 1967, 1970 by McGraw-Hill, Inc. All rights reserved. Copyright 1952 by McGraw-Hill, Inc. All rights reserved. Printed in the United States of America. No part of this publication may be reproduced, stored in a retrieval system, or transmitted, in any form or by any means, electronic, mechanical, photocopying, recording, or otherwise, without the prior written permission of the publisher.

Library of Congress Catalog Card Number 76–112844

2 3 4 5 6 7 8 9 0   BABA   7 9 8 7 6 5 4 3 2 1 0

This book was set in Caledonia by Monotype Composition Company, Inc., and printed on permanent paper and bound by George Banta Company, Inc. The designer was Marsha Cohen; the drawings were done by John Cordes, J. & R. Technical Services, Inc. The editors were Gerald C. Spencer and Mary A. O'Callahan. Robert R. Laffler supervised the production.

Preface

This sixth edition of the *Readings in Economics* is by far the largest yet. So many tempting writings in economics have recently become available that I have chosen no less than 97 items—ruthlessly dropping articles of only a few years back, in favor of up-to-date essays by the great economists of our age.

Economics is now in new ferment: although the truly great names of the past—Adam Smith, Keynes, Ricardo, and Marshall—remain ever fresh, the stale anthology of one-time establishment writers will no longer do. Therefore, I have pitted Walter Heller against Milton Friedman in debate on monetarism; Robert Solow against Robin Marris on Galbraithism; Galbraith against the world on the world; Simon Kuznets against Walt Rostow on stages of development; Robert Heilbroner in a sympathetic critique on Marx; Charles Kindleberger against Andrew Shonfield on planning; . . . .

But life is not a who's who. It is the *problems* that count. If an obscure graduate student (such as Robert Fitch) has written a trenchant criticism of Galbraith's *New Industrial State* as a capitalistic apologia, I have sought it out. Where reformer Michael Harrington and businessman Eli Goldston have written the choicest articles on capitalism-to-the-rescue-of-our-cities, I have not asked for their union cards as professional economists. Imperialism (as treated by Paul Baran and Paul Sweezy), race economics (as treated by James Tobin and Arthur Lewis), Yugoslavia's new "middle way" (Anthony Lewis)—these are only samplings of the new winds that are sweeping through modern economics.

To make more papers possible in reasonable compass, something had to give. In this edition I have cut the original texts. Though no new words are put into any author's mouth, some of his throat clearings have been carefully omitted. Since no one should rely on these edited versions for a definitive text of the originals, there has been no need to annoy the reader with those vexing signs of deletions. And the headings and subheadings, useful to punctuate incomplete texts, are generally my handiwork as editor and should not be held against the authors.

Finally, I have written introductions to the essays, provided biographical data about the authors, and supplied questions to guide the readings. Although the order of arrangement has been integrated with the 1970 eighth edition of Samuelson's *Economics,* these *Readings* have been found useful in the past with a variety of alternative texts. (A few intrepid instructors have even built the whole course around them alone.)

My acknowledgments are many. For this edition, Felicity Skidmore (Institute of Research on Poverty, University of Wisconsin) was not available to carry the load; but her name on the title page reflects, inadequately, her contributions carried over from the previous editions. Robert L. (now Dean) Bishop and John C. (now President) Coleman, my earlier collaborators, have left their indelible marks on the work. Mary Anne O'Callahan of McGraw-Hill as editor, Harriet Braunfeld (who supervised permissions), Mary Griffin as free-lance editor, Joan Thompson, my personal secretary—all know my indebtedness to them. But only I know how much I owe to instructors and countless readers for suggestions and criticisms.

Paul A. Samuelson

Contents

Contents by Author

Basic Economic Concepts and National Income 1

The Nature of Economics

Readings 1, 2, and 3

Economics is a social science, and therefore cannot attain the exactitude and precision of the hard physical sciences. In the Reading 1, a modern historian meets head on the ethical problems with respect to indoctrination and objectivity that any professors of the social sciences face.

In the Reading 2, one of the most eminent economists of all time sets down his definition of economics.

Finally in the Reading 3, a prominent modern economist and financial writer explains the virtues and limitations of economics as a science. The fact that economics is both an art and a science, dealing necessarily with problems vital to everyone, constitutes its tremendous importance.

Gordon Wright is head of the history department at Stanford University. Alfred Marshall, gigantic Victorian, long was professor of economics at Cambridge University, England; he trained a whole generation of economists all over the world including Lord Keynes. Henry C. Wallich is professor of economics at Yale University, served on President Eisenhower's Council of Economic Advisers, and is an advisor to the Secretary of the Treasury in the Nixon administration. He writes extensively in the press to present the intelligent case for economic conservatism.

Questions to Guide the Reading

Do you think a professor should avoid "taking sides"? Is it possible for him to do so? Can beginning students be trusted to choose among competing arguments?

Can money measure the important elements of life? Are people spiritually better off when the material basis of life is mismanaged and deficient?

Can economists make controlled experiments? Can astronomers? Can meteorologists? Which do you think is more exact as a science, astronomy or biology?

Reading 1

One Side, All Sides—Or No Sides

Gordon Wright

Some years ago, at the end of my course, I solicited written criticisms from those students who had survived the experience and were still conscious. One of the most intriguing responses ran thus: "During the course I swayed back and forth in my emotions. At first I thought the lectures were provacative [sic]; now I think they are indoctrinary. I am not against freedom of speech; I am glad you have ideas and are consistent, but your lectures are very subtly indoctrinating the class without the class realizing it. . . ." Having delivered this thunderbolt, my anonymous critic offered a constructive suggestion: "Continue as you are, but at the beginning of the course warn the students and state when you express your thesis that it is yours." A somewhat rueful footnote was appended: "I know you did this, but do it oftener."

Perhaps I ought to have shrugged off this

From Gordon Wright, "One Side, All Sides—Or No Sides." Reprinted from *Stanford Today*, Winter, 1965, Series 1, No. 11, © 1966 by the Board of Trustees of Leland Stanford Junior University. Reprinted abridged with kind permission of the author and publisher.

complaint, or consoled myself with the thought that Socrates too had once been accused of surreptitiously corrupting the young. Better still, I might have sought reassurance by challenging my critic's grasp of the nature of history as a discipline. True, he had not fallen into the common error of demanding total objectivity in the classroom; like most of us today, he had abandoned the positivist fallacy that humanists can be as neutral as chemists, and that we can all agree if we simply stick to "verifiable facts." But he did demand something almost as difficult: a clear separation of judgment and fact, with each judgment (like each pack of cigarettes) carefully labeled "DANGEROUS."

I could not quite shake off the feeling that my critic had found a chink in my academic armor, and had drawn a bit of blood. After all, I had always believed that teaching and preaching are two quite different things, and that any attempt to impose one's own value judgments in the classroom is (as the French say) an abuse of confidence. Had I been unwittingly misleading students by a false appearance of objectivity? If some bias is inescapable when man studies man, is it not safer for the teacher to flaunt his prejudices, to preach and proselyte without restraint, so that even the most naïve student will be on guard against "subtle indoctrination"?

This is a plausible thesis; and I know some teachers (at Stanford and elsewhere) who subscribe to it. Indeed, one administrator at a fine California university has frankly set out to staff his sector of the campus with dedicated right-wing doctrinaires on the dubious ground that the rest of the campus is loaded with left-wingers. Presumably these two legions of crusaders, clashing in the free market place of ideas, will fight it out until Truth finally prevails. I am not so sure myself that this is the best way to arrive at Truth, to advance learning, or even to educate students. Certainly the presence of some strong-minded partisans of a given system or idea will add savour to a campus, and ought to frighten nobody. But a faculty heavily loaded with true believers, either of one simon-pure variety or of several rival sects, would be likely to spend most of its energy either in indoctrination campaigns or in civil war.

There is, nevertheless, a real dilemma here; it confronts any teacher whose concern is human behavior, either past or present. If aloof objectivity is impossible and if flagrant partisanship may be destructive, is there any sort of middle ground that might be any better? I myself believe that the answer is affirmative —but only if certain difficult conditions are met.

In the first place, the teacher seeking that middle ground must possess a high degree of that rare trait called intellectual integrity: a willingness to face all the facts, even those that may jolt his own deeply-held beliefs. In the second place, he must really subscribe to the dictum of the late Judge Learned Hand: "The spirit of liberty is the spirit which is not too sure that it is right."

Reading 2

Definition of Economics

Alfred Marshall

Economics is a study of men as they live and move and think in the ordinary business of life. But it concerns itself chiefly with those motives which affect, most powerfully and most steadily, man's conduct *in the business part of his life*.

Everyone who is worth anything carries his higher nature with him into business; and, there as elsewhere, he is influenced by his personal affections, by his conceptions of duty and his reverence for high ideals. And it is true that the best energies of the ablest inventors

From Alfred Marshall, *Principles of Economics* (Macmillan and Co. Ltd., London, 1920), 8th edition. Reprinted by permission of The Macmillan Company, New York and Macmillan & Co., Ltd., London.

and organizers of improved methods and appliances are stimulated by a noble emulation more than by any love of wealth for its own sake. But, for all that, the steadiest motive to ordinary business work is the desire for the pay which is the material reward of work.

The pay may be on its way to be spent selfishly or unselfishly, for noble or base ends; and here the variety of human nature comes into play. But the motive is supplied by a definite amount of money: and it is this definite and exact money measurement of the steadiest motives in business life, which has enabled economics far to outrun every other branch of the study of man.

Just as the chemist's fine balance has made chemistry more exact than most other physical sciences; so this economist's balance, rough and imperfect as it is, has made economics more exact than any other branch of social science. But of course economics cannot be compared with the exact physical sciences: for it deals with the ever changing and subtle forces of human nature.

It is essential to note that the economist does not claim to measure any affection of the mind in itself, or directly; but only indirectly *through its effect.* No one can compare and measure accurately against one another even his own mental states at different times: and no one can measure the mental states of another at all except indirectly and conjecturally by their effects. Of course various affections belong to man's higher nature and others to his lower, and are thus different in kind. But, even if we confine our attention to mere physical pleasures and pains of the same kind, we find that they can only be compared indirectly by their effects. In fact, even this comparison is necessarily to some extent conjectural, unless they occur to the same person at the same time.

Economists watch carefully the conduct of a whole class of people, sometimes the whole of a nation, sometimes only those living in a certain district, more often those engaged in some particular trade at some time and place: and by the aid of statistics, or in other ways, they ascertain how much money on the average the members of the particular group they are watching are just willing to pay as the price of a certain thing which they desire, or how much must be offered to them to induce them to undergo a certain effort or abstinence that they dislike.

The measurement of motive thus obtained is not indeed perfectly accurate; for if it were, economics would rank with the most advanced of the physical sciences; and not, as it actually does, with the least advanced.

Reading 3

Is Economics a Science?

Henry C. Wallich

Economists are having a trying time these days. "Why can't you say how long this recession will go on? Why can't you agree about what ought to be done? What good is your science if people don't know whether they can rely on your predictions and prescriptions?"

Economists have heard this sort of thing before and are acutely aware that they have much to be modest about. They remember Bernard Shaw's observation that if the economists of this world were laid end to end they wouldn't reach a conclusion. They have heard angry young men within their own ranks question economic science on the ground that where it is really scientific it doesn't have much to do with economics, and where it is economics it isn't scientific. They may long for the golden days of economics a hundred and more years ago, when the science was held in awe and the views expressed by economists were received with appropriate respect.

If economists were to take time out to reply

From Henry C. Wallich, "Is Economics a Science? And Can It Be?" *New York Times,* © June 8, 1958 by The New York Times Company. Reprinted with kind permission of the author and publisher.

to today's charges they might say something like this: It is, of course, quite true that economics is not an exact science. But economics can claim a number of important discoveries that have improved our understanding and our economic performance. If economists cannot make reliable forecasts nor always arrive at universally agreed recommendations, the failure is attributable to difficulties of a kind that sciences like physics and biology do not have to face.

Kinds of economists

Note for a moment such progress and accomplishments as can be found in economics. The field is wide—economics is what economists do, it has rightly been said, and economists nowadays do many things that Adam Smith never dreamed of. One can perhaps divide economists into three groups in accordance with their activities, doing about equal violence to each by this arbitrary classification. One group comprises the finders and analysts of facts, the second the theorists, the third the administrators and policy makers. Many economists, of course, qualify as members of more than one group.

Empiricists. The fact-finders have done a very solid job. Time was when economic statistics were in the main a by-product of some primitive counting of noses and pennies that governments conducted for fiscal purposes. Consider, for instance, the national income statistics, which show the total of all incomes received in the country. We know the origin of the national income—how much is contributed by industry, agriculture and services. We know its uses—how much goes for consumption, how much is saved and invested. We know its distribution—how much of the total goes to labor, to capital, to professional people and others. And many of these data come to us at monthly intervals, with a lag of barely one month.

Surely it is worth a good deal to know just where we stand. Without data like these, people with conflicting axes to grind would no doubt inform us, on the same day, that the country was facing bankruptcy and that there was no recession at all. Any effort to make economics a more exact science must begin with statistics.

Another feather in the fact-finder's cap is

the development of data on plans and intentions. Consumer spending plans for durable goods are regularly surveyed now. Business plans for expenditures on new plant and equipment are reported for two and three years ahead. What the fact-finders don't find it easy to anticipate is how people are going to change their minds. But, even without that, the intentions data are helpful in forecasting.

Novel builders. Next, let us look at the achievements of the second group of economists, the theorists. Here we come to the heart of economics. The great names in economics—from Adam Smith to Ricardo, Leon Walras, Marshall and Keynes—all owe their fame principally to their theoretical contributions. But their thoughts, in many cases, have suffered the familiar fate of great ideas: first often regarded as quite wrong, they are later taken in stride as obvious and nothing new. Once an idea has been fully accepted, the original difficulty of reaching it is easily forgotten.

Yet much of what today goes for "common sense" or "what every practical man knows" is the laborious achievement of theorists. Take the case history of fiat money and inflation. For centuries, kings and politicians practiced the gentle arts of clipping coins and debasing their gold or silver contents, as an easy way out of financial embarrassments. Their successors accomplished the same thing even more handily by printing paper money.

Eventually, theoretical economists, Adam Smith among them, demonstrated that a country does not get richer by running a deficit and multiplying the money in circulation. All that this accomplishes is to drive up prices. The economists then preached the gospel of sound money and balanced budgets until every practical man knew it and believed that he had got hold of an obvious law of nature, instead of a proposition in theoretical economics.

Then theoretical economics, under the leadership of Keynes, took a further step forward. It was discovered that while the gospel of the balanced budget was true enough under conditions of prosperity and full employment, such as Adam Smith and his successors had assumed, it suffered exceptions in depressions. When men and machines are idle, Keynes reasoned, deficit spending need not mean "too much money chasing too few goods" and consequent inflation. The idle men and machines could be drawn into production by money-creation and deficit spending. They would increase the supply of goods and thus keep money and goods in balance. Deficit spending, which at full employment is inflationary, in a depression becomes the means to increase production and end the depression.

Keynes' doctrine, after an initial uproar, was soon accepted by most economists for what it was: not a flat denial of the old teachings but a doctrine dealing with an exception—unfortunately a frequent one—from the classical norm of a full employment economy. But among non-economists the classical teachings had done their work only too well. After they were transmuted in popular thinking from the conclusions of economic reasoning to universal truths, belief in them was hard to shake. It took many years of argument and persuasion to gain popular acceptance of the doctrine that, in depressions, the government should run a deficit and finance it by expanding the volume of money. The example of Keynes demonstrates one of the difficulties of progress in economic theory; the findings of theorists become commonplace, depriving economics of the credit it deserves, and they end up by standing in the way of new ideas.

Policymakers. Finally, we come to the third group of economists, the administrators and policymakers. Most economists probably feel that economic thought and research, if they are to justify themselves, must ultimately lead to action. Of course, it is precisely when economists come out into the arena of business or government that the difficulties against which they must struggle become most apparent.

Physical vs. social science

A physicist or a chemist speaking of the achievements of his science would probably sound more self-assured than an economist, and he would have a right to. Economists labor under a series of handicaps from which the exact sciences are usually free. These handicaps are responsible for the frequent uncertainty of our knowledge, and for the unreliability of our forecasts. Let us note the principal ones.

Economists are handicapped, in the first place, because economic reality is complex and

hard to come to grips with. What with billions of people in the world, hundreds of thousands of commodities and prices, trillions of purchases and sales during the year, the man who advised, "Get your facts first," was handing out no small order.

Even more important, economists cannot experiment. Biologists can set up a colony of mice and put this society through its paces under varying controlled conditions. Humanity's ardor for more precise economic knowledge has not been great enough, so far, to supply economists with similar facilities. Economists can, of course, gather experience, including such experience as may be derived from measures taken at their advice. But economists do not deliberately experiment with the fate of a nation, and from the scientist's point of view such experience lacks the decisive ingredient of a real experiment—control of the environment, and repetition.

Statistical tools have been forged that enable economists to trace cause and effect even under the haphazard experimental conditions offered by nature. But they are a poor substitute for the order and simplicity with which many other sciences can arrange their subject-matter. In economics, nothing is certain, anything is possible, and everything depends on everything else. The plain difficulty of understanding what goes on in the economy is the first big handicap faced by economists.

Forecasting and probability

This insufficient understanding naturally adds to the complications of forecasting. If we have a hard time keeping up with people's present actions, how can we appraise their intentions for the future? As a matter of fact, economists may be able to predict people's behavior better than people themselves can. The action of a single individual is quite uncertain, but the behavior of large groups follows the laws of probability. Insurance companies base their calculations upon this rule of large numbers.

Two factors, however, often frustrate economists who would like to avail themselves of the laws of probability. The first is the prevalence of trends and fashions among consumers and business men. Like an epidemic that upsets the mortality tables, sudden trends and fashions upset the economist's probability calculations. The second is the dominant role of a few important decision makers—leaders in politics, business and labor. Their actions cannot be forecast by the laws of large numbers, men in this élite category not being numerous. Yet their decisions, essentially unpredictable, influence the course of events.

It is worth noting also that economic forecasting, to be successful, has to be extraordinarily accurate. Whether business will turn up or down, for instance, depends on a very slim margin. If total demand exceeds total supply by a couple of billions out of about $430 billion of gross national product, business will expand. If demand falls short by a similar sum, business will contract. Economists can easily predict that total demand will be *approximately* $430 billion, but that is not good enough. A difference of two billion either way, less than half of 1 per cent, means the difference between up and down. This applies to most forecasts in economics.

Agreement among economists

After all this, it should be obvious why economists do not always agree. It might be more to the point, however, to emphasize that economists do agree on a great many things that make up the body of their science. Being agreed upon and accepted, these points are just not discussed much. Today a large measure of agreement exists even in formerly controversial fields like the general principles of anti-recession policy.

Lively discussion goes on among economists, naturally, at the frontiers of knowledge, as it does in all fields. Here indeed disagreement is the rule—fortunately so, if economics is not to die from complacency and boredom. Until a few years ago, this kind of argument was sharpened by the Keynesian revolution that had shaken the profession. Other disciplines— even physics and medicine—from time to time experience similar convulsions. In their cases, however, such reversals of old beliefs have usually been interpreted as progress. Economists, who are their own worst press agents, have managed to make each other look needlessly foolish in the process.

Achievements of the science

I have been critical in what I have said of my science, because I believe that economics still has a long way to go. But if I am asked how good economics is, as of now, the unqualified answer is that the plus signs far exceed the minus signs.

Economics, to be sure, must confess to some obvious weaknesses, which I have made no effort to conceal. So, however, must other disciplines. Doctors still can't cure the common cold, yet nobody thinks that medicine is a failure.

But economists can, without immodesty, point to substantial accomplishments. The Great Depression demonstrated that a modern economy cannot operate on *laissez-faire* principles. It needs the stabilizing action of government. Modern economics has provided the principles that underlie stabilization policy. On the basic features of this policy most economists see eye to eye—barring possible disagreement as to objectives. Differences occur mainly over details of procedure and timing. Our stabilization policy, manifested in the Employment Act of 1946, has on the whole worked well. We have avoided major recessions, let alone a catastrophe on the scale of 1932. If it is said that the record nevertheless is very far from perfect, economists can reply that their advice is not always taken.

Final caution

To avoid misunderstanding, I shall close on a note of caution. Economics is not an exact science, and few economists are likely to argue that it ever will be. The reasons lie in the difficulties of understanding and forecasting, which we noted earlier. But progress has been made and more is sure to come. That much can confidently be said. Furthermore, if economists, and those interested in their work, sometimes feel troubled and unsure, they may take comfort in the thought that absolute certainty is vouchsafed to no science and that complete conviction in this world can come only from ignorance.

Population and Resources

Reading 4

Economics is about people. Population relative to natural and man-made resources, and to technical knowledge, is a prime determinant of economic well-being. Here we meet the man and ideas that led Thomas Carlyle to put the persistent stigma of "the dismal science" on economics. The Reverend Thomas Robert Malthus (1766–1834) was a distinguished member of the classical school in economics. Despite his other contributions to the growing science of economics, his fame today rests principally on his gloomy analysis of population trends. He argues in this passage that, in the absence of moral restraint, population must forever tend to outstrip the available means of subsistence. This analysis, which for a time seemed irrelevant to the American scene, is now coming back into the world spotlight.

Questions to Guide the Reading

Do you agree with Darwin and Malthus that, left to herself, Nature would cause species numbers to explode, leading inevitably, through the laws of diminishing returns, to a jeopardization of decent living standards? Just how is the law of diminishing returns involved?

If each couple wants to have three or more children per family, and modern medicine keeps virtually all children alive, what is the prospective long-term population trend? What does this imply for privacy, air and water pollution, and a serene environment in an advanced economy? What would it imply for an impoverished economy?

Population Growth and Poverty

Thomas R. Malthus

In an inquiry concerning the improvement of society, the mode of conducting the subject which naturally presents itself, is,

1. To investigate the causes that have hitherto impeded the progress of mankind towards happiness; and,
2. To examine the probability of the total or partial removal of these causes in future.

The principal object of the present essay is to examine the effects of one great cause intimately united with the very nature of man; which, though it has been constantly and powerfully operating since the commencement of society, has been little noticed by the writers who have treated this subject. The facts which establish the existence of this cause have, indeed, been repeatedly stated and acknowledged; but its natural and necessary effects have been almost totally overlooked; though probably among these effects may be reckoned a very considerable portion of that vice and misery, and of that unequal distribution of the bounties of nature, which it has been the unceasing object of the enlightened philanthropist in all ages to correct.

The cause to which I allude, is the constant tendency in all animated life to increase beyond the nourishment prepared for it.

It is observed by Dr. Franklin, that there is no bound to the prolific nature of plants or ani-

From T. R. Malthus *An Essay on the Principle of Population* (Reeves and Turner, London, 1878), 8th edition.

mals, but what is made by their crowding and interfering with each other's means of subsistence. Were the face of the earth, he says, vacant of other plants, it might be gradually sowed and overspread with one kind only, as for instance with fennel: and were it empty of other inhabitants, it might in a few ages be replenished from one nation only, as for instance with Englishmen.

This is incontrovertibly true. Through the animal and vegetable kingdoms Nature has scattered the seeds of life abroad with the most profuse and liberal hand; but has been comparatively sparing in the room and the nourishment necessary to rear them. The germs of existence contained in this earth, if they could freely develop themselves, would fill millions of worlds in the course of a few thousand years. Necessity, that imperious, all-pervading law of nature, restrains them within the prescribed bounds. The race of plants and the race of animals shrink under this great restrictive law; and man cannot by any efforts of reason escape from it.

Population has this constant tendency to increase *beyond* the means of subsistence, and it is kept to its necessary level by these causes. The subject will, perhaps, be seen in a clearer light, if we endeavour to ascertain what would be the natural increase of population, if left to exert itself with perfect freedom; and what might be expected to be the rate of increase in the productions of the earth, under the most favourable circumstances of human industry.

The potential rate of increase of population. It will be allowed that no country has hitherto been known, where the manners were so pure and simple, and the means of subsistence so abundant, that no check whatever has existed to early marriages from the difficulty of providing for a family, and that no waste of the human species has been occasioned by vicious customs, by towns, by unhealthy occupations, or too severe labour. Consequently in no state that we have yet known, has the power of population been left to exert itself with perfect freedom.

In the northern states of America, where the means of subsistence have been more ample, the manners of the people more pure, and the checks to early marriages fewer, than in any of the modern states of Europe, the population has been found to double itself, for above a

century and a half successively, in less than twenty-five years. In the back settlements, where the sole employment is agriculture, and vicious customs and unwholesome occupations are little known, the population has been found to double itself in fifteen years. Even this extraordinary rate of increase is probably short of the utmost power of population. Sir William Petty supposes a doubling possible in so short a time as ten years.

But, to be perfectly sure that we are far within the truth, we will take the slowest of these rates of increase, a rate in which all concurring testimonies agree, and which has been repeatedly ascertained to be from procreation only.

It may safely be pronounced, therefore, that *population, when unchecked,* goes on doubling itself every twenty-five years, or *increases in a geometrical ratio*.

The potential rate of increase of food production. The rate according to which the productions of the earth may be supposed to increase, it will not be so easy to determine. Of this, however, we may be perfectly certain, that the ratio of their increase in a limited territory must be of a totally different nature from the ratio of the increase of population. A thousand millions are just as easily doubled every twenty-five years by the power of population as a thousand. But the food to support the increase from the greater number will by no means be obtained with the same facility. Man is necessarily confined in room. When acre has been added to acre till all the fertile land is occupied, the yearly increase of food must depend upon the melioration of the land already in possession. This is a fund, which, from the nature of all soils, instead of increasing, must be gradually diminishing. But population, could it be supplied with food, would go on with unexhausted vigour; and the increase of one period would furnish the power of a greater increase the next, and this without any limit.

From the accounts we have of China and Japan, it may be fairly doubted, whether the best-directed efforts of human industry could double the produce of these countries even once in any number of years. There are many parts of the globe, indeed, hitherto uncultivated, and almost unoccupied; but even in new colonies, a geometrical ratio increases with such extraordinary rapidity, that the advantage could not last long. If the United States of America continue increasing, which they certainly will do, though not with the same rapidity as formerly, the Indians will be driven further and further back into the country, till the whole race is ultimately exterminated, and the territory is incapable of further extension.

The science of agriculture has been much studied in England and Scotland; and there is still a great portion of uncultivated land in these countries. Let us consider at what rate the produce of this island might be supposed to increase under circumstances the most favourable to improvement.

If it be allowed that by the best possible policy, and great encouragements to agriculture, the average produce of the island could be doubled in the first twenty-five years, it will be allowing, probably, a greater increase than could with reason be expected.

In the next twenty-five years, it is impossible to suppose that the produce could be quadrupled. It would be contrary to all our knowledge of the properties of land. It must be evident to those who have the slightest acquaintance with agricultural subjects, that in proportion as cultivation extended, the additions that could yearly be made to the former average produce must be gradually and regularly diminishing.

Let us suppose that the yearly additions which might be made to the former average produce, instead of decreasing, which they certainly would do, were to remain the same; and that the produce of this island might be increased every twenty-five years, by a quantity equal to what it at present produces. The most enthusiastic speculator cannot suppose a greater increase than this. In a few centuries it would make every acre of land in the island like a garden.

It may be fairly pronounced, therefore, that, considering the present average state of the earth, *the means of subsistence,* under circumstances the most favourable to human industry, *could not possibly be made to increase faster than in an arithmetical ratio.*

The potential rates of increase of population and food compared. The necessary effects of these two different rates of increase, when brought together, will be very striking. Let us call the population of this island eleven millions; and suppose the present produce equal

to the easy support of such a number. In the first twenty-five years the population would be twenty-two millions, and the food being also doubled, the means of subsistence would be equal to this increase. In the next twenty-five years, the population would be forty-four millions, and the means of subsistence only equal to the support of thirty-three millions. In the next period the population would be eighty-eight millions, and the means of subsistence just equal to the support of half that number. And, at the conclusion of the first century, the population would be a hundred and seventy-six millions, and the means of subsistence only equal to the support of fifty-five millions, leaving a population of a hundred and twenty-one million totally unprovided for.

Taking the whole earth, instead of this island, emigration would of course be excluded; and, supposing the present population equal to a thousand millions, the human species would increase as the numbers 1, 2, 4, 8, 16, 32, 64, 128, 256, and subsistence as 1, 2, 3, 4, 5, 6, 7, 8, 9. In two centuries the population would be to the means of subsistence as 256 to 9; in three centuries as 4096 to 13 and in two thousand years the difference would be almost incalculable.

In this supposition no limits whatever are placed to the produce of the earth. It may increase for ever and be greater than any assignable quantity; yet still the power of population being in every period so much superior the increase of the human species can only be kept down to the level of the means of subsistence by the constant operation of the strong law of necessity, acting as a check upon the greater power.

Of the general checks to population, and the mode of their operation

The ultimate check to population appears then to be a want of food, arising necessarily from the different ratios according to which population and food increase. But this ultimate check is never the immediate check, except in cases of actual famine.

The immediate check may be stated to consist in all those customs, and all those diseases, which seem to be generated by a scarcity of the means of subsistence; and all those causes, independent of this scarcity, whether of a moral or physical nature, which tend prematurely to weaken and destroy the human frame.

These checks to population, which are constantly operating with more or less force in every society, and keep down the number to the level of the means of subsistence, may be classed under two general heads—(i) the preventive, and (ii) the positive checks.

The preventive and positive checks described. (i) The *preventive* check, as far as it is voluntary, is peculiar to man, and arises from that distinctive superiority in his reasoning faculties, which enables him to calculate distant consequences. The checks to the indefinite increase of plants and irrational animals are all either positive, or, if preventive, involuntary. But man cannot look around him, and see the distress which frequently presses upon those who have large families; he cannot contemplate his present possessions or earnings, which he now nearly consumes himself, and calculate the amount of each share, when with very little addition they must be divided, perhaps, among seven or eight, without feeling a doubt whether, if he follow the bent of his inclinations, he may be able to support the offspring which he will probably bring into the world. In a state of equality, if such can exist, this would be the simple question. In the present state of society other considerations occur. Will he not lower his rank in life, and be obliged to give up in great measure his former habits? Does any mode of employment present itself by which he may reasonably hope to maintain a family? Will he not at any rate subject himself to greater difficulties, and more severe labour, than in his single state? Will he not be unable to transmit to his children the same advantages of education and improvement that he had himself possessed? Does he even feel secure that, should he have a large family, his utmost exertions can save them from rags and squalid poverty, and their consequent degradation in the community?

These considerations are calculated to prevent, and certainly do prevent, a great number of persons in all civilised nations from pursuing the dictate of nature in an early attachment to one woman.

If this restraint do not produce vice, it is undoubtedly the least evil that can arise from the principle of population. Considered as a restraint on a strong natural inclination, it must be allowed to produce a certain degree of temporary unhappiness; but evidently slight, compared with the evils which result from any of the other checks to population; and merely of the same nature as many other sacrifices of temporary to permanent gratification, which it is the business of a moral agent continually to make.

When this restraint produces vice, the evils which follow are but too conspicuous. A promiscuous intercourse to such a degree as to prevent the birth of children, seems to lower, in the most marked manner, the dignity of human nature. It cannot be without its effect on men, and nothing can be more obvious than its tendency to degrade the female character, and to destroy all its most amiable and distinguishing characteristics. Add to which, that among those unfortunate females, with which all great towns abound, more real distress and aggravated misery are, perhaps, to be found, than in any other department of human life.

When a general corruption of morals, with regard to the sex, pervades all the classes of society, its effects must necessarily be, to poison the springs of domestic happiness, to weaken conjugal and parental affection, and to lessen the united exertions and ardour of parents in the care and education of their children:—effects which cannot take place without a decided diminution of the general happiness and virtue of the society; particularly as the necessity of art in the accomplishment and conduct of intrigues, and in the concealment of their consequences necessarily leads to many other vices.

(ii) The *positive* checks to population are extremely various, and include every cause, whether arising from vice or misery, which in any degree contributes to shorten the natural duration of human life. Under this head, therefore, may be enumerated all unwholesome occupations, severe labour and exposure to the seasons, extreme poverty, bad nursing of children, great towns, excesses of all kinds, the whole train of common diseases and epidemics, wars, plague, and famine.

On examining these obstacles to the increase of population which I have classed under the heads of preventive and positive checks, it will appear that they are all resolvable into *moral restraint, vice,* and *misery.*

Of the preventive checks, the *restraint from marriage* which is not followed by irregular gratifications may properly be termed moral restraint.

Promiscuous intercourse, unnatural passions, violations of the marriage bed, and improper arts to conceal the consequences of irregular connexions, are preventive checks that clearly come under the head of *vice.*

Of the positive checks, those which appear to arise unavoidably from the laws of nature, may be called exclusively misery; and those which we obviously bring upon ourselves, such as wars, excesses, and many others which it would be in our power to avoid, are of a mixed nature. They are brought upon us by vice, and their consequences are misery.

The mode of operation of preventive and positive checks. The sum of all these preventive and positive checks, taken together, forms the immediate check to population. In every country some of these checks are, with more or less force, in constant operation; yet, notwithstanding their general prevalence, there are few states in which there is not a constant effort in the population to increase beyond the means of subsistence. This constant effort as constantly tends to subject the lower classes of society to distress, and to prevent any great permanent melioration of their condition.

These effects seem to be produced in the following manner. The constant effort towards population, which is found to act even in the most vicious societies, increases the number of people before the means of subsistence are increased. The food, therefore, which before supported eleven millions, must now be divided among eleven millions and a half. The poor consequently must live much worse, and many of them be reduced to severe distress. The number of labourers also being above the proportion of work in the market, the price of labour must tend to fall, while the price of provisions would at the same time tend to rise. The labourer therefore must do more work, to earn the same as he did before.

During this season of distress the discouragements to marriage and the difficulty of rearing a family are so great, that the progress of population is retarded. In the mean time, the cheapness of labour, the plenty of labourers, and the necessity of an increased industry among them, encourage cultivators to employ more labour upon their land, to turn up fresh soil, and to manure and improve more completely what is already in tillage, till ultimately the means of subsistence may become in the same proportion to the population, as at the period from which we set out. The situation of the labourer being then again tolerably comfortable, the restraints to population are in some degree loosened; and, after a short period, the same retrograde and progressive movements, with respect to happiness, are repeated.

One principal reason why this oscillation has been less remarked, and less decidedly confirmed by experience than might naturally be expected, is, that the histories of mankind which we possess are, in general, histories only of the higher classes. We have not many accounts that can be depended upon, of the manners and customs of that part of mankind, where these retrograde and progressive movements chiefly take place.

Reading 5

To many living in the relative affluence of contemporary America, Malthus' gloomy predictions in Reading 4 may seem remote and badly outdated. One does not have to look far away, however, to find that these predictions are all too relevant in describing the grim realities of much of today's world. Our own national interest, as well as a broader concern for mankind in general, compels us to ask the question: Can the underdeveloped economies bring their rapidly rising populations under control and advance their levels of living, or must they see hard-won economic gains eaten up in keeping more and more people alive at subsistence levels?

The Committee on Science and Public Policy of the National Academy of Sciences has studied both past and present population trends in various parts of the world in an attempt to put the current population problem in the proper perspective. As a result of this study, they conclude that an expanded program of research and publicity to promote the effective voluntary control of family size is now an urgent item of world business.

Questions to Guide the Reading

Why should the technically advanced nations of the world concern themselves with the population problems of the less-developed countries?

Is there any reason to believe that the less-developed countries of today will not follow the population pattern exhibited by the economically developed countries as they move increasingly into industrialization and urbanization?

The Growth of World Population

National Academy of Sciences

All nations are committed to achieving a higher standard of living for their people—adequate food, good health, literacy, education, and gainful employment. These are the goals of millions now living in privation. An important barrier to the achievement of these goals is the current rate of population growth. The present world population is likely to double in the next 35 years, producing a population of six billion by the year 2000. If the same rate of growth continues, there will be 12 billion people on earth in 70 years and over 25 billion by the year 2070. Such rapid population growth, which is out of proportion to present and prospective rates of increase in economic development, imposes a heavy burden on all efforts to improve human welfare. Moreover, since we live in an interconnected world, it is an international problem from which no one can escape.

In our judgment, this problem can be successfully attacked by developing new methods of fertility regulation, and implementing programs of voluntary family planning widely and rapidly throughout the world. Although only a few nations have made any concerted efforts in this direction, responsible groups in the social, economic, and scientific communities of many countries have become increasingly aware of the problem and the need for intelligent and forthright action. We recommend that these groups now join in a common effort to disseminate present knowledge on population problems, family planning, and related bio-medical matters, and to initiate programs of research that will advance our knowledge in these fields.

In pursuit of these objectives, many different kinds of institutions in the United States, both public and private, have important contributions to make. Other than the search for lasting peace, no problem is more urgent.

The growth of world population

The population of the world, now somewhat in excess of three billion persons, is growing at about two per cent a year, or faster than at any other period in man's history. While there has been a steady increase of population growth during the past two or three centuries, it has been especially rapid during the past 20 years. To appreciate the pace of population growth we should recall that world population doubled in about 1,700 years from the time of Christ until the middle of the 17th century; it doubled again in about 200 years, doubled again in less than 100, and, if the current *rate* of population increase were to remain constant, would double every 35 years. Moreover, this rate is still increasing.

To be sure, the rate of increase cannot continue to grow much further. Even if the death rate were to fall to zero, at the present level of human reproduction the growth rate would not be much in excess of three and one-half

From *The Growth of World Population* (National Academy of Sciences, Washington, D.C., 1963). Reprinted with kind permission of the publisher.

per cent per year, and the time required for world population to double would not fall much below 20 years.

Although the current two per cent a year does not sound like an extraordinary rate of increase, a few simple calculations demonstrate that such a rate of increase in human population could not possibly continue for more than a few hundred years. Had this rate existed from the time of Christ to now, the world population would have increased in this period by a factor of about 7×10^{16}; in other words, there would be about 20 million individuals in place of each person now alive, or 100 people to each square foot. If the present world population should continue to increase at its present rate of two per cent per year, then, within two centuries, there will be more than 150 billion people. Calculations of this sort demonstrate without question not only that the current continued increase in the rate of population growth must cease but also this long-term prognosis: *Either the birth rate of the world must come down or the death rate must go back up.*

Population growth in different parts of the world

The rates of population growth are not the same, of course, in all parts of the world. Among the industrialized countries, Japan and most of the countries of Europe are now growing relatively slowly—doubling their populations in 50 to 100 years. Another group of industrialized countries—the United States, the Soviet Union, Australia, New Zealand, Canada, and Argentina—are doubling their populations in 30 to 40 years, approximately the world average. The pre-industrial, low-income, and less-developed areas of the world, with two thirds of the world's population—including Asia (except Japan and the Asiatic part of the Soviet Union), the southwestern Pacific islands (principally the Philippines and Indonesia), Africa (with the exception of European minorities), the Caribbean Islands, and Latin America (with the exception of Argentina and Uruguay)—are growing at rates ranging from moderate to very fast. Annual growth rates in all these areas range from one and one-half to three and one-half per cent, doubling in 20 to 40 years.

The rates of population growth of the vari-

ous countries of the world are, with few exceptions, simply the differences between their birth rates and death rates. International migration is a negligible factor in rates of growth today. Thus, one can understand the varying rates of population growth of different parts of the world by understanding what underlies their respective birth and death rates.

The reduction of fertility and mortality in western Europe since 1800

A brief, over-simplified history of the course of birth and death rates in western Europe since about 1800 not only provides a frame of reference for understanding the current birth and death rates in Europe, but also casts some light on the present situation and prospects in other parts of the world. A simplified picture of the population history of a typical western European country is shown in Figure 1. The jagged interval in the early death rate and the recent birth rate is intended to indicate that all the rates are subject to substantial annual variation. The birth rate in 1800 was about 35 per 1,000 population and the average number of children ever born to women reaching age 45 was about five. The death rate in 1800 averaged 25 to 30 per 1,000 population although, as indicated, it was subject to variation because of episodic plagues, epidemics,

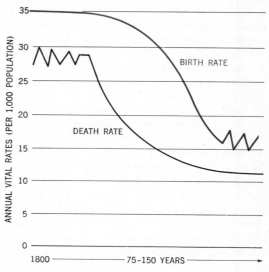

Fig. 1   Schematic presentation of birth and death rates in western Europe after 1800. (The time span varies roughly from 75 to 150 years.)

and crop failures. The average expectation of life at birth was 35 years or less. The current birth rate in western European countries is 14 to 20 per 1,000 population with an average of two to three children born to a woman by the end of childbearing. The death rate is 7 to 11 per 1,000 population per year, and the expectation of life at birth is about 70 years. The death rate declined, starting in the late 18th or early 19th century, partly because of better transport and communication, wider markets, and greater productivity, but more directly because of the development of sanitation and, later, modern medicine. These developments, part of the changes in the whole complex of modern civilization, involved scientific and technological advances in many areas, specifically in public health, medicine, agriculture, and industry. The immediate cause of the decline in the birth rate was the increased deliberate control of fertility within marriage. The only important exception to this statement relates to Ireland, where the decline in the birth rate was brought about by an increase of several years in the age at marriage combined with an increase of 10 to 15 per cent in the proportion of people remaining single. The average age at marriage rose to 28 and more than a fourth of Irish women remained unmarried at age 45. In other countries, however, such social changes have had either insignificant or favorable effects on the birth rate. In these countries—England, Wales, Scotland, Scandinavia, the Low Countries, Germany, Switzerland, Austria, and France—the birth rate went down because of the practice of contraception among married couples. It is certain that there was no decline in the reproductive capacity; in fact, with improved health, the contrary is likely.

Only a minor fraction of the decline in western European fertility can be ascribed to the invention of modern techniques of contraception. In the first place, very substantial declines in some European countries antedated the invention and mass manufacture of contraceptive devices. Second, we know from surveys that as recently as just before World War II more than half of the couples in Great Britain practicing birth control were practicing withdrawal, or *coitus interruptus*. There is similar direct evidence for other European countries.

In this instance, the decline in fertility was not the result of technical innovations in contraception, but of the decision of married couples to resort to folk methods known for centuries. Thus we must explain the decline in the western European birth rates in terms of why people were willing to modify their sexual behavior in order to have fewer children. Such changes in attitude were doubtless a part of a whole set of profound social and economic changes that accompanied the industrialization and modernization of western Europe. Among the factors underlying this particular change in attitude was a change in the economic consequences of childbearing. In a preindustrial, agrarian society children start helping with chores at an early age; they do not remain in a dependent status during a long period of education. They provide the principal form of support for the parents in their old age, and with high mortality, many children must be born to ensure that some will survive to take care of their parents. On the other hand, in an urban, industrialized society, children are less of an economic asset and more of an economic burden.

Among the social factors that might account for the change in attitude is the decline in the importance of the family as an economic unit that has accompanied the industrialization and modernization of Europe. In an industrialized economy, the family is no longer the unit of production and individuals come to be judged by what they do rather than who they are. Children leave home to seek jobs and parents no longer count on support by their children in their old age. As this kind of modernization continues, public education, which is essential to the production of a literate labor force, is extended to women, and thus the traditional subordinate role of women is modified. Since the burden of child care falls primarily on women, their rise in status is probably an important element in the development of an attitude favoring the deliberate limitation of family size. Finally, the social and economic changes characteristic of industrialization and modernization of a country are accompanied by and reinforce a rise of secularism, pragmatism, and rationalism in place of custom and tradition. Since modernization of a nation involves extension of deliberate human control over an increasing range of the environment, it is not surprising that people living in an economy undergoing industrialization should extend the notion of deliberate and rational control to the question of whether or not birth should result from their sexual activities.

As the simplified representation in Figure 1 indicates, the birth rate in western Europe usually began its descent after the death rate had already fallen substantially. (France is a partial exception. The decline in French births began late in the 18th century and the downward courses of the birth and death rates during the 19th century were more or less parallel.) In general, the death rate appears to be affected more immediately and automatically by industrialization. One may surmise that the birth rate responds more slowly because its reduction requires changes in more deeply seated customs. There is in most societies a consensus in favor of improving health and reducing the incidence of premature death. There is no such consensus for changes in attitudes and behavior needed to reduce the birth rate.

Declining fertility and mortality in other industrialized areas

The pattern of declining mortality and fertility that we have described for western Europe fits not only the western European countries upon which it is based but also, with suitable adjustment in the initial birth and death rates and in the time scale, eastern and southern Europe (with the exception of Albania), the Soviet Union, Japan, the United States, Australia, Canada, Argentina, and New Zealand. In short, every country that has changed from a predominantly rural agrarian society to a predominantly industrial urban society and has extended public education to near-universality, at least at the primary school level, has had a major reduction in birth and death rates of the sort depicted in Figure 1.

The jagged line describing the variable current birth rate represents in some instances—notably the United States—a major recovery in the birth rate from its low point. It must be remembered, however, that this recovery has not been caused by a reversion to uncontrolled family size. In the United States, for example, one can scarcely imagine that married couples have forgotten how to employ the contraceptive techniques that reduced the birth rates to a level of mere replacement just before World War II. We know, in fact, that more couples are skilled in the use of contraception today than ever before. (Nevertheless, effec-

tive methods of controlling family size are still unknown and unused by many couples even in the United States.) The recent increase in the birth rate has been the result largely of earlier and more nearly universal marriage, the virtual disappearance of childless and one-child families, and a voluntary choice of two, three, or four children by a vast majority of American couples. There has been no general return to the very large family of pre-industrial times, although some segments of our society still produce many unwanted children.

Population trends in less-developed countries

We turn now to a comparison of the present situation in the less-developed areas with the demographic circumstances in western Europe prior to the industrial revolution. Figure 2 presents the trends of birth and death rates in the less-developed areas in a rough schematic way similar to that employed in Figure 1. There are several important differences between the circumstances in today's less-developed areas and those in pre-industrial Europe. Note first that the birth rate in the less-developed areas is

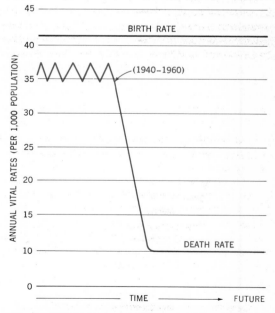

Fig. 2   Schematic presentation of birth and death rates in less-developed countries, mid-20th century. (The steep drop in the death rate from approximately 35 per thousand began at times varying roughly between 1940 and 1960 from country to country.)

higher than it was in pre-industrial western Europe. This difference results from the fact that in many less-developed countries almost all women at age 35 have married, and at an average age substantially less than in 18th century Europe. Second, many of the less-developed areas of the world today are much more densely populated than was western Europe at the beginning of the industrial revolution. Moreover, there are few remaining areas comparable to North and South America into which a growing population could move and which could provide rapidly expanding markets. Finally, and most significantly, the death rate in the less-developed areas is dropping very rapidly—a decline that looks almost vertical compared to the gradual decline in western Europe—and without regard to economic change.

The precipitous decline in the death rate that is occurring in the low-income countries of the world is a consequence of the development and application of low-cost public health techniques. Unlike the countries of western Europe, the less-developed areas have not had to wait for the slow gradual development of medical science, nor have they had to await the possibly more rapid but still difficult process of constructing major sanitary engineering works and the build-up of a large inventory of expensive hospitals, public health services, and highly trained doctors. Instead, the less-developed areas have been able to import low-cost measures of controlling disease, measures developed for the most part in the highly industrialized countries. The use of residual insecticides to provide effective protection against malaria at a cost of no more than 25 cents per capita per annum is an outstanding example. Other innovations include antibiotics and chemotherapy, and low-cost ways of providing safe water supplies and adequate environmental sanitation in villages that in most other ways remain relatively untouched by modernization. The death rate in Ceylon was cut in half in less than a decade, and declines approaching this in rapidity are almost commonplace.

The result of a precipitous decline in mortality while the birth rate remains essentially unchanged is, of course, a very rapid acceleration in population growth, reaching rates of three to three and one-half per cent. Mexico's population, for example, has grown in recent years at a rate of approximately three and one-half per cent a year. This extreme rate is undoubtedly due to temporary factors and would stabilize at not more than three per cent. But even at three per cent per year, two centuries would see the population of Mexico grow to about 13.5 billion people. Two centuries is a long time, however. Might we not expect that long before 200 years had passed the population of Mexico would have responded to modernization, as did the population of western Europe, by reducing the birth rate? A positive answer might suggest that organized educational efforts to reduce the birth rate are not necessary. But there is a more immediate problem demanding solution in much less than two centuries: Is the current demographic situation in the less-developed countries impeding the process of modernization itself? If so, a course of action that would directly accelerate the decline in fertility becomes an important part of the whole development effort which is directed toward improving the quality of each individual's life.

Population trends and the economic development of pre-industrial countries

The combination of high birth rates and low or rapidly declining death rates now found in the less-developed countries implies two different characteristics of the population that have important implications for the pace of their economic development. One important characteristic is rapid growth, which is the immediate consequence of the large and often growing difference between birth and death rates; the other is the heavy burden of child dependency which results from a high birth rate whether death rates are high or low. A reduced death rate has only a slight effect on the proportion of children in the population, and this effect is in a rather surprising direction. The kinds of mortality reduction that have actually occurred in the world have the effect, if fertility remains unchanged, of reducing rather than increasing the average age of the population.

Mortality reduction produces this effect because the largest increases occur in the survival of infants; thus, although the reduction in mortality increases the number of old persons, it increases the number of children even more. The result is that the high fertility found in low-income countries produces a proportion of children under fifteen of 40 to 45 per cent of the total population, compared to 25 per cent or less in most of the industrialized countries.

What do these characteristics of rapid growth and very large proportions of children imply about the capacity to achieve rapid industrialization? It must be noted that it is probably technically possible in every less-developed area to increase national output at rates even more rapid than the very rapid rates of population increase we have discussed, at least for a few years. The reason at least slight increases in per capita income appear feasible is that the low-income countries can import industrial and agricultural technology as well as medical technology. Briefly, the realistic question in the short run does not seem to be whether some increases in per capita income are possible while the population grows rapidly, but rather whether rapid population growth is a major deterrent to a *rapid* and *continuing* increase in per capita income.

A specific example will clarify this point. If the birth rate in India is not reduced, its population will probably double in the next 25 or 30 years, increasing from about 450 million to about 900 million. Agricultural experts consider it feasible within achievable limits of capital investment to accomplish a doubling of Indian agricultural output within the next 20 to 25 years. In the same period the output of the non-agricultural part of the Indian economy probably would be slightly more than doubled if the birth rate remained unchanged. For a generation at least, then, India's economic output probably can stay ahead of its maximum rate of population increase. This bare excess over the increase in population, however, is scarcely a satisfactory outcome of India's struggle to achieve economic betterment. The real question is: Could India and the other less-developed areas of the world do substantially better if their birth rates and thus their population growth rates were reduced? Economic analysis clearly indicates that the answer is yes. Any growth of population adds to the rate of increase of national output that must be achieved in order to increase per capita by any given amount.

To double per capita output in 30 years requires an annual increase in per capita output of 2.3 per cent; if population growth is three per cent a year, then the annual increase in

national output must be raised to 5.3 per cent to achieve the desired level of economic growth. In either instance an economy, to grow, must divert effort and resources from producing for current consumption to the enhancement of future productivity. In other words, to grow faster an economy must raise its level of net investment. Net investment is investment in factories, roads, irrigation networks, and fertilizer plants, and also in education and training. The low-income countries find it difficult to mobilize resources for these purposes for three reasons: The pressure to use all available resources for current consumption is great; rapid population growth adds very substantially to the investment targets that must be met to achieve any given rate of increase in material well-being; and the very high proportions of children that result from high fertility demand that a larger portion of national output must be used to support a very large number of non-earning dependents. These dependents create pressure to produce for immediate consumption only. In individual terms, the family with a large number of children finds it more difficult to save, and a government that tries to finance development expenditures out of taxes can expect less support from a population with many children. Moreover, rapid population growth and a heavy burden of child dependency divert investment funds to less productive uses—that is, less productive in the long run. To achieve a given level of literacy in a population much more must be spent on schools. In an expanding population of large families, construction effort must go into housing rather than into factories or power plants.

Thus the combination of continued high fertility and greatly reduced mortality in the less-developed countries raises the levels of investment required while impairing the capacity of the economy to achieve high levels of investment. Economists have estimated that a gradual reduction in the rate of childbearing, totaling 50 per cent in 30 years, would add about 40 per cent to the income per consumer that could be achieved by the end of that time.

To recapitulate, a short-term increase in per capita income may be possible in most less-developed areas, even if the fertility rate is not reduced. Nevertheless, even in the short run, progress will be much faster and more certain if the birth rate falls. In the longer run, economic progress will eventually be stopped and reversed unless the birth rate declines or the death rate increases. Economic progress will be slower and more doubtful if less-developed areas wait for the supposedly inevitable impact of modernization on the birth rate. They run the risk that rapid population growth and adverse age distribution would themselves prevent the achievement of the very modernization they count on to bring the birth rate down.

Conclusion

This brief statement of population problems indicates the pervasive and depressive effect that uncontrolled growth of population can have on many aspects of human welfare. Nearly all our economic, social, and political problems become more difficult to solve in the face of uncontrolled population growth. It is clear that even in the wealthier nations many individuals and families experience misery and unhappiness because of the birth of unwanted children. The desirability of limiting family size is now fairly generally, though not universally, recognized, particularly among the better-educated and culturally advanced segments of the population in many countries.

Effective voluntary control of family size essentially depends upon the successful interaction of two variables: level or intensity of motivation and the availability and utility of procedures. When motivation is high and sustained, difficult procedures for controlling fertility can be used successfully, but when motivation is weak and erratic, simple procedures that impose few demands are essential. Quite obviously any comprehensive program for solving population problems must work with both

these variables, must seek to enhance motivation and also to improve procedures for voluntary control of fertility.

A broadly based effort to develop clearer understanding of the physiology and biochemistry of the reproductive process is a primary requirement. Work in this area can be effectively strengthened by expansion and coordination of the activities of the few existing laboratories now devoted to basic problems of human reproduction.

There is a parallel need—no less important— for extensive, systematic application of new basic knowledge in the development of new techniques, procedures, devices, and medically active compounds for the regulation of fertility. Inherent in this requirement is the necessity for assurance of safety in techniques and procedures, and freedom from undesirable side-effects from compounds and treatments.

These objectives require extensive studies in chemistry, physiology, and biochemistry, with large animal colonies and clinical facilities for large-scale animal and, subsequently, human tests.

Field surveys and experiments must be enlarged, and new projects of this kind undertaken on a continuing basis in many more parts of the world, making effective use of growing bio-medical knowledge and newly developed devices, techniques, and compounds. The objectives of these projects should be two-fold: (1) to determine the advantages and disadvantages of various techniques, procedures, and devices, and (2) to determine the degree and scope of their acceptability in various societies, cultures, and economies. To reach the objective, the means must be provided and they must be accepted and used.

Reading 6

Overpopulation is a serious concern. To promote the cause of family planning, scientists publicize dire predictions about famine immediately ahead, or just around the corner. But actual, detailed studies of the probable future supply and demand for foodstuffs suggest that you will lose your money if you bet on the side of the alarmists. New hybrid varieties of rice and wheat have, in the last few years, tended to bear out Brandt's general viewpoint.

Dr. Brandt came to the United States from Germany in 1933. Emeritus from the Food Research Institute of Stanford University, he served as a member of President Eisenhower's Council of Economic Advisors and is currently being consulted on international economic developments by decision makers.

Questions to Guide the Reading

How can scientists trained in biology and physics be unreliable when they speak about population and make projections into the future? Does the author's obvious antipathy toward any government's economic *dirigisme* color his own judgment? Since 1965 how much improvement has there been in the food supply of India, Japan, Burma, and China? Could the problem feared by Malthus come back again fifty years from now, if not twenty?

Malthus and the Malthusians Are Wrong

Karl Brandt

During the last few years the discussion of agricultural production and foreign trade has turned toward a new theme. Instead of the old dilemma of an excessive output of food, feed, and fibers resulting in government price supports and subsidized exports, a much greater emergency, if not a genuine disaster, is held to be imminent. The population in the under-developed part of the world, it is claimed, has begun to "explode" while agriculture in those countries is unable to keep pace with the progressively rising demand for food.

These stark conclusions are supported, it is alleged, by a formidable economic and demographic statistical armament that is for all practical purposes complete, accurate and reliable. "Our purpose is not to frighten," intone the pundits, "we know what is going on in the world's food economy, and what we know is menacing in the extreme." But are the experts so knowledgeable and do their projections hold water? The author has reason to doubt both their claims to omniscience and, more importantly, the validity of the central conclusions so stridently and doggedly maintained.

Inaccuracy of population estimates

Consider first the demographic side of the argument. Some demographers, but far more economists, do not hesitate to predict how many people *will be* living not only in scores of backward countries but in all continents by the year 2000, although the historical record of the last 35 years is strewn with the most embarrassing utterly erroneous projections. Many of these projections emphasized exactly the opposite trend that is today in vogue. Not only were there false anticipations of declining population growth, but based on them were serious recommendations that governments ought to use crash programs to prop up birth rates by public premiums and benefits.

Suffice it to note that today nobody can prove whether there are in Red China more than 460 or less than 790 million people. And in an interview in New Delhi, India's Minister of Health and Family Planning warned: "Any Indian vital statistics are not very reliable." But this does not deter the experts from asserting, based on the latest population and fertility data, that the emergency will soon assume such gigantic and disastrous proportions that a crash program of "planned parenthood" must throttle the population explosion, particularly in the developing areas of Asia, Africa, and Latin America.

There are the horror projections of the world's population doubling by the end of the century and hundreds of millions of people starving within 4 or 5 years. Needless to say, ringing the alarm bell may well be justified under certain conditions. But those who ring it ought first to have the integrity to lay bare the evidence and the method by which they arrive at their projections. In this connection they ought particularly to reveal whether they have made earlier projections that miscarried—and why. They ought also to say bluntly whether their calculations are based on the most essential causational factors for which data are available or whether they have given

Excerpted from Karl Brandt, "World Food: Calming the Cassandras," *Columbia Journal of World Business*, Vol. II, No. 4, July–August, 1967. Reprinted with kind permission of the author and publisher.

consideration to major causes that are not quantifiable. Second, they ought to reveal their special vested interest in any one of the solutions which they recommend for avoiding the famine disaster.

Inaccuracy of food estimates

The same cautions are suggested for those who pontificate on the other side of the equation. There is no question that during this century extraordinary progress has been made, particularly in the industrially advanced and in quite a few of the leading agricultural-export countries, in assembling data on production, trade, stockholding, and prices of basic food, feed, and fiber commodities. Of course, many of the data are cumulative guesses. However, even in a number of leading industrial countries the impact of the military logistics of warfare and of governmental planning on the food economy has led to serious deterioration in the reliability of statistical data concerning, particularly, the dynamic processes of the agricultural economy from sowing to harvesting and from farm via wholesale and retail markets to the kitchen and dinner table.

In many densely populated areas of monsoon Asia, particularly in India, reliable knowledge of how much of a multitude of basic food commodities actually has been harvested, stored, or lost in storage remains problematical as to any major degree of accuracy. Exposed even more than the urban population to the hazard of perishing by starvation in case of floods or drought or locusts or other crop-devouring pests, the peasants have a powerful urge to survive and hence tend to keep the facts of their food inventory a closely guarded secret. The same secrecy goes even for the trading of foodstuffs, especially where it is decentralized and transportation is chiefly by beasts of burden, draft animals or fleets of small boats.

Guesstimators run rampant

Neat graphic illustrations of food statistics with little asterisks saying "schematic—not drawn to scale" and tabulated data with a bewildering set of footnotes and fine print suggest an utterly simple structure and an equally simple dynamic functioning of the world's food economy. Yet those of us who have studied that very food economy in depth are overwhelmed

by its utter complexity. Even in those industrially advanced countries that have a uniform geography and a racially and culturally uniform population, quantification of the prospective supply of food is far from simple.

But when large countries with wide differences in climate, topography, soils, and with a racially, culturally and economically differentiated population are under observation, or when the food economy of whole continents is to be evaluated, then the gap between statistical surveys and projections, on one side, and the actual course of events, on the other, becomes embarrassingly larger by leaps and bounds. When military strategy is active on a global scale behind the international grain market, the scenery becomes foggy indeed.

But even if we had real peace, the accountancy of what goes on is largely an art of estimation. The difficulty begins with the values underlying such concepts as "food." One economic analyst may accept a particular set of values while another adheres to a different set, and still others are unaware of the impact of the potentially diverse meanings of terms related to food. In fact, one arrives at quite a little encyclopedic dictionary of such terms as food supply, food demand, food stocks, food production capacity, hunger, famine, malnutrition, starvation. Is it a "disastrous food shortage" when in a state where bananas, sugar cane, coconuts and yams are plentiful, one particular variety of rice is temporarily unavailable?

Free man, free diet

If man is considered as the most highly advanced mammal on earth, defined by Aristotle and ever since as the *zoon politicon,* or a biological unit with certain physiologically minimal requirements of calories, protein, vitamins, and mineral trace elements, it is conceivable to determine the minimum provision for adults of either sex as well as for children under certain conditions of work or leisure.

However, as soon as one begins to consider a society or nation as an association of human beings with the potential quality of human dignity, a yearning for individual freedom in the pursuit of happiness, there is no longer such a simple rationale as an optimum standard food "requirement." Food is no longer only the substance that holds body and soul together but a social and cultural adornment of communication, a far more complex matter than fuel for biological engines. People have the natural right to exercise their preference for the type and the composition of their diets; open to them are a host of vegetarian and omnivorous paths. The latter include scores of kinds of "red meats" of game or domesticated animals like pigs, cattle, buffaloes, water buffaloes, yaks, reindeer, sheep or goats. These diets also comprise the "white meats" of farm birds or their eggs or the milk of many of the ruminants and of equides like horses, donkeys or others. And there is the vast variety of seafood from seawater or fresh water. Neither the state nor any other authority has a legitimate right to determine what sort of food or how much of it the people may eat, except when intoxicating foods or beverages or narcotics beyond certain boundaries are concerned.

Similarly, the principles and values of the humane society, based on respect for the human dignity of free citizens with self-discipline, prohibit the arrogation of the control of population growth by the state. It is the prerogative of citizens to determine whether in their pursuit of happiness they prefer to remain childless in matrimony, or how many children in what sequence they want. The claim that agriculture cannot increase food production per capita at a rate commensurate with the growth of population is phony and demonstrably false.

Famines: statistician-made and government-made

The author's dissent is based not merely on an analysis of the weaknesses of world food statistics and their often seriously misleading cosmetic beautification in charts and diagrams; it derives, more positively, from economic reasoning based on his observation in most parts of the world outside the Soviet Union, Mainland China and the southern part of Africa. The upshot is to raise the question of whether the latest cycle of neo-Malthusian speculation is not a *statistician-made* famine spectrum on the foreign-trade and development-aid sky. Not that such obfuscation is done on purpose; a major part of it, the author is prepared to accept, may very well be innocent delusion fostered by the utter complexity of the international tug-of-war.

It is the good fortune of the world's population that *the capacity to produce an abundance of wholesome food at decreasing costs has grown in this century to such an extent that the Malthusian theorem no longer holds*. With an abundance of energy in the form of solid, liquid or gaseous fuels, wind or hydropower or electric current that can be made available at declining costs in any part of the world, and with falling transportation costs, the potential output of crops and animal products has technically no earthly limits. This incontestable fact derives from the emerging overabundance of petrochemical products like plant nutrients, pesticides, predator- and weed-killers, and sprinkler irrigation water or drainage via minute combustion engines.

If, within certain national boundaries, there are economic limits and *if there is still the possibility of serious food shortage or even mass starvation, it is the result of policies that prohibit the farmers, horticulturalists and fishermen in many developing countries from performing their tasks*. Indeed, I go so far as to say that if there should be widespread famine it will most likely be government-made, irrespective of whether it occurs in India or other parts of Asia or in any part of Africa or Latin America. If anybody doubts this statement he may study the case of enforced meatless days in Argentina several years after the agrarian reform and planned economy of the Perón regime.

In the western world we are today slightly better educated as to how agriculture and the food economy can be state controlled and state operated than we were say 20, 30, or 50 years ago when the Third International Socialist Manifesto was celebrated. Since then such control has been painfully tried out by the most gruesome experimental test in human history, with many hundreds of millions of human beings as the guinea pigs in the USSR and satellite realms—and after that on twice as many people in Red China.

This experiment has conclusively proven two closely correlated facts. With sufficient brute force it is possible to reduce the entire farm population to the function of little cogwheels and parts of the state-controlled machine of collective farms or state-operated machine of state farms. With sufficiently brutal enforcement of regulations it is also possible to keep a whole rapidly industrializing nation as food consumers on a state-controlled ration far below the quality and variety they would want or what they would need for more efficient performance of work.

Revenge of the peasant

But the historical experience of this Eurasian laboratory—a test case of hundreds of millions of people inside a fenced-in area controlled by Stalin, Khrushchev and Brezhnev-Kosygin—has also proven what can simultaneously *not* be done with farmers and an agricultural system under this arrangement. No matter where it is being tried, the (according to Lenin, Stalin and Khrushchev) supposedly pliable, stupid and detestable farmers and their wives have proven to be far less malleable than many intellectual geniuses of the centrally directed computerized economy in quite a few countries still assume them to be. It has been proven beyond any doubt that while one can torture, brainwash, treat like Pavlov's dogs or kill these farmers and obstinate small craftsmen in the villages, one cannot simultaneously earn the benefit of their otherwise intelligent, effective and wealth-creating efforts. Indeed, the leverage exerted by the self-defending passive resistance of the peasants in their powerful urge to survive is enormous. Obviously such resistance was so strong in enduring the pressures of shrewd, cynical, scientific state control that Khrushchev had to give in. In due time Mao or his successors will also have to give in. In the end only psychopaths can dare to continue this craze.

When compared to the enormity of the crimes perpetrated against the farmer by the communist countries and their emulators, the infractions of the U.S. seem just so many peccadillos. Yet, there have been some unwise acts. The goal of income support for small farmers, which had been adopted in the years of the Great Depression, has remained up to this day, in spite of the healthy growth of the national economy, the main social and political motivation of U.S. agricultural policy. The Federal Government has acted to purchase basic agricultural commodities, hold them off the domestic market, and release them primarily as subsidized exports to foreign countries. Other industrial countries as well as the leading agricultural export nations have been engaged even more in similar policies, with the same results. The actual dumping and violation of the principles of a mutually beneficial division of labor and fair competition in international trade were the consequence of price-fixing for four commodities. In order to gain at home and abroad a more effective endorsement for the disposal of surpluses, the Congress inserted into Public Law 480 several authorizations that concern large-scale food aid and donable programs in support of economic development. From 1955 through 1966, out of a total value of $58 billion in U.S. agricultural exports, $17.7 billion were exported under specified government-financed programs, rising from $3.1 billion per year in 1955 to $6.9 billion in 1966.

It is an unwittingly and innocently rendered disservice to less-developed countries, which by definition have a large proportion of their labor force in agriculture and other primary product industries, when industrially advanced countries grant aid in the form of food grants or loans. This has been true for India as well as other recipient nations of PL 480 concessional deals because it has permitted the recipient government to neglect the development of the country's agriculture while investing the capital in often ill-timed, ill-placed, and unprofitable industrial prestige plants.

The agricultural and food economy in many underdeveloped countries has suffered in recent years not only from attempts at price-fixing, with the ensuing misallocation of resources, but from a multitude of popular mystiques and clichés which have misguided many legislative and executive branches of the governments in developing countries. Among them I list a few:

1. So long as the overwhelming majority of the farm population is not fully literate and formally educated there can be no progress in agricultural technology.

2. Rural people tend to be lazy and do not respond to incentives.

3. Farm tenancy is an institution which prevents technological progress.

4. Production credit, the selling of farm inputs, and the marketing of farm products must not be entrusted to private businessmen who derive profit from it but must be given over exclusively to farmer-cooperatives, which are supposed to be nonprofit, noncapitalistic, democratic welfare entities.

5. The land worked by plantations or other large-scale farm enterprises should be redistributed among small farmers.

6. Religions like Buddhism and Hinduism prevent farmers from adopting efficient farming methods.

7. The world's supply of land that is not yet in agricultural use but which could be brought into cultivation without exorbitant costs is practically exhausted.

Every one of these popular clichés or assertions is false and invalid. Indeed, they have become the roadblocks which impede development and agricultural progress in various ways. In the following paragraphs, they are examined one by one in staccato fashion.

Illiteracy and incentives. The author has found in most remote areas on all continents that *farm people are economic men.* The less they rely on printed symbols as means of communication, the more they respond to changes of prices and price relations. It is true that some men among peasants put a higher marginal-utility value on leisure, but it is hard to find a man of any color in any country who does not respond to the incentive of a bicycle, motorcycle, or scooter, or the woman who is immune to the attraction of stylish clothing.

Farm tenancy. The nonsense on this subject was abandoned in Europe in the first decades of this century and in the U.S. after World War II. In many parts of the world, tenants are among the most progressive farm enterprisers.

Cooperative associations. It is the solid experience on both sides of the Atlantic that, if these have any right to exist at all, it is because they are capitalistic business corporations which create or strengthen competition and render better service than would be available without them.

Land redistribution. In many less-developed countries the plantations are the only farm enterprises which have full command of, and use successfully, the latest word in advanced agricultural technology and science. To destroy them is to sabotage progress on farms of all sizes.

Religion. Differences in the performance of farm people of the same faith operating under different political regimes and national economic policies make it at least doubtful that there is a close causal connection between religion and backwardness which appropriate economic arrangements cannot break.

No more frontiers. Finally, there is the canard that the world is so overpopulated that its agricultural frontiers are closed and there is no more land for settlers; this is a ridiculous distortion of the facts—or a sort of magician's trick of making solid objects disappear. Africa is a continent with extreme scarcity of population. The formerly Belgian Congo alone, as large as India, has only 13 million people. In Colombia only 7% of agriculturally usable land is under the plow. On his second trip around the world, the author was so impressed by enormously wide areas that can be brought into cultivation that he was tempted to write a book with the title "This Underpopulated World of Ours."

Exercise in projection

So much for the prevailing clichés. Next let us turn briefly but cautiously to what may happen in the coming years in the world's food economy.

If there should be years of political instability in parts of Southeast Asia, Africa, or South America, or retarded economic development, the rise in the level of living of urban consumers in the leading industrial countries could slow down or stagnate. This would put the brakes on livestock production in the EEC and thus shut the door more tightly to U.S. feedgrain exports. There is the further possibility that high-gluten wheat, of which the U.S. is a leading supplier, could also be offered by countries like Hungary, or Mediterranean countries in North Africa or the Near East.

It is evident that there are excellent opportunities for further intensification of agricultural production in those countries which have so far been the main markets for U.S. agricultural exports. Indeed, it seems that this increased production could occur with gradually declining costs per unit of product by the use of more and more of the latest U.S. technological progress in every phase of agribusiness.

Conclusion

Thus *the author foresees the opposite of what the neo-Malthusian alarmists in our midst envision for the U.S. agricultural-export business.* Instead of a trend toward diminishing per capita production of food in agrarian countries, an expanding demand for United States supplies, and high prices, it would not be surprising if the competition for foreign markets in less-developed countries were strong. Such competition would call for increasing efficiency in the allocation of productive resources in our agriculture. It would dictate the elimination of governmental market controls and subsidies.

In conclusion, rather than the perspective of mass starvation, there are less dramatic trends in the world's food balance, with at least as much of a possibility of downward pressures on the prices of major commodities in what remains of an open world market. Of course there are dangers. Yet, all in all the picture is not such as to elicit the kind of scaremongering that has become almost reflexive in the present environment.

Reading 7

In 1939 all the experts thought that the American population was about to decline. Small family size seemed to be the goal of the middle classes, and the rest of the population was gradually taking on the middle-class pattern. Then came World War II and postwar prosperity. All the experts were confounded when third, fourth, and fifth children began to be common in American families. A veritable population boom followed, quite beyond that seen by any advanced nation before.

In the other modern countries there was a similar wartime upswing in birth rates. But a few years after the war fertility rates subsided. Would the same happen in the United States? Finally in the 1960s the corner was turned. The phenomenally early age of marriage began to change. More important, very large family goals seemed to be in the process of being modified. *Business Week* tells the story.

Questions to Guide the Reading

Why should countries like Italy and Japan, which used to have such high birth rates, move to a lower fertility pattern just when the United States was experiencing an increasing birth rate? If questionnaires show that people still want just about three children, how will changing attitudes and techniques of family planning affect the *actual* size of families in the future?

"Exploding population numbers does not mean for the United States what it would mean for the underdeveloped countries of the world—diminishing returns and poverty. For advanced America it means loss of privacy, despoiled national parks, polluted air, contaminated rivers, and deprivation of serene living." Do you agree?

U.S. Population Stops Exploding

Business Week

The great baby bust—that's the only way to describe what's now happening to population growth in the U.S.

By all the old rules, the steep decline in the birth rate that has occurred so far in the 1960s simply should not have happened. In the past, marriages and births have had much the same unromantic relation to the business cycle as new orders for durable goods, bank clearings outside New York City, and other conventional economic indicators. It is traditional for prosperity to be accompanied by an early upturn in the marriage rate, followed like clockwork by an upturn in the birth rate about a year later.

Over the past five years, the marriage rate has behaved about as expected, increasing from 8.5 per 1,000 population in 1960 to 9.2 per 1,000 in 1965. But instead of rising, the birth rate has declined steeply, from 23.9 per 1,000 in 1960 to 19.6 per 1,000 in 1965.

The break with the past is profound. Even though the actual number of marriages is up 17% from 1960, the number of births has dropped steadily from 4.3-million in 1960 to an estimated 3.6-million this year, a decline of 16%. Moreover, the 18.4 per 1,000 birth rate that demographers expect for 1966 is the lowest since 1936, during the great depression.

The new relation between prosperity and the birth rate has implications that will reach into every nook and cranny of the economy.

Obviously not the product of deep economic distress, the decline in births signals a basic change in the way in which U.S. families —particularly newlyweds—want to live their lives. Some demographers believe the current decline in births means that parents and prospective parents now want completed families that are smaller than those that were fashionable in the 1950s. Others say the decline is due mainly to a desire for better spacing of children, that some of the births that now are being lost will be made up in the future.

Because no one can be certain on exactly what will happen to the birth rate, the U.S. Census Bureau always provides a range for long-term population projections rather than a single set of numbers. However, for businessmen, the important point is that each of these projections, from the highest to the lowest, has been revised downward.

Many demographers think that the Census Bureau's medium low forecast—called Series C —takes the most accurate account of current experience. This series now estimates the 1975 U.S. population at 218-million. In 1958, the official Series C projection was for a 1975 population of 226-million.

Even on the most conservative assumptions,

demographers expect an early reversal of the declining trend in the actual number of births. Because of the great postwar baby boom, more than 42-million women will be between 15 and 44 in 1970, almost 9% above the 1965 total of less than 39-million. So even if most newly wed couples delay having babies, the total number of births is bound to increase. Census Series C predicts a reversal of the trend in 1968 with births increasing to almost 4.6-million in 1975, up 27% over this year's expected 3.6-million.

I. Cause and effect

Any honest population expert will admit that even his own explanation of the slowdown in population growth is controversial. But the experts, nevertheless, agree on some significant points.

Contrary to what might be popular opinion, population authorities deny that the "pill" has much to do with the sinking birth rate of the 1960s. Arthur A. Campbell, chief, natality statistics branch of the U.S. Public Health Service, argues that "the use of contraceptives in the past has followed business cycles."

He estimates that more than 80% of married couples used some form of contraception in 1935 when people couldn't afford to have children. This figure dropped to 70% in a 1955 survey, when the popularity of large families was on the rise, and then jumped back to over 80% in the 1960s, when more couples wanted a lid on family size.

To population experts, the low birth rate of the 1930s is evidence that contraception always has worked, no matter how ineffective earlier methods may seem as compared to the pill. Moreover, despite what seems to be a major break in the old business cycle relationship between prosperity, marriages, and births, demographers generally agree that the birth rate continues to have an economic explanation.

University of Pennsylvania economist Richard A. Easterlin blames the current baby bust on difficulties that young people are having in finding high-paying jobs, in contrast to the 1950s when the baby boom was in full sway.

Easterlin argues that young marrieds are in a hurry to upgrade their standard of living to a level that approaches that of their parents. In the 1950s, when the numerically shy gen-

THE UNITED STATES BIRTH RATE IS CLOSE TO AN HISTORIC LOW...

...AND THE NUMBER OF BIRTHS IS PLUNGING TOO...

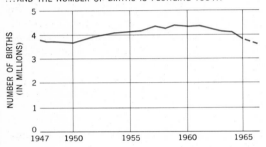

...DESPITE AN UPTURN IN THE MARRIAGE RATE.

Data: U.S. Census Bureau

ples in the mid-1950s—the heyday of the baby boom—had incomes exceeding 80% of the earlier income of their parents.

In Easterlin's analysis, young people have reacted to this unfavorable change by having fewer children. For the 20- to 24-year-old group, the fertility rate—the number of births per 1,000 women—has dropped from around 260 births per 1,000 women during the late 1950s to below 220 births per 1,000 in 1964.

During 1965, the rate may have reached the lowest level since 1946—around 190 births per 1,000. This decline in the number of births among younger women is the major explanation of the over-all slowdown in the population growth rate.

II. Out of the nursery

Just how long the slowdown will last depends on the way current trends affect what demographers call completed fertility—the total number of babies that women have over their lifetime.

One way to find this out is to ask women how many children they intend to have. The Survey Research Center at the University of Michigan did this five times, once in 1955, once in 1960 and again in each year between 1962 and 1964. In 1955 average intended family size was 3.0; in each of the surveys carried out in the 1960s the figure was 3.1. If families in fact carry out these plans over their lifetime, then the birth dip of the first half of the 1960s will prove temporary.

Some demographers insist that they won't. Easterlin thinks that family size will be determined by economic conditions. And Campbell of the Public Health Service insists that there is a cycle in the number of children that women want to have. His hunch is that this figure will be around 2.8 between now and the mid-1970s.

If this is true, then families will get smaller, and the U.S. can look for a persistent decline in population growth.

However, some demographers stick with the figures. Ronald Freedman, director of the Population Studies Center at the University of Michigan, insists on the significance of the surveys showing that women's plans for family size did not change from 1960 to 1964 but held steady at 3.1 children.

According to Freedman, this means that the

eration born in the 1930s was hitting the job market, young workers were scarce and had little trouble finding good-paying jobs. However, as wartime and postwar baby crops began hitting the labor market in the 1960s, good jobs became scarce.

To clinch his point statistically, Easterlin has analyzed the current real income of young people, 14 to 24 years of age, and compared it with the incomes of their parents five years earlier—when children were still at home and their parents were age 35 to 44. His calculations show that young marrieds averaged only 70% to 74% of the earlier earnings of their parents in the 1960s. By contrast, young cou-

current decline in births is due mainly to a desire for better spacing of children among younger women, and a drop in births among the older women who completed their families ahead of schedule in the 1950s. It may be that some of the young marrieds who have thus far postponed having babies may find themselves unable, or unwilling, to have as many children as they originally intended. But if desired family size stays constant, population growth over the long run won't decline very much.

However this argument turns out, the U.S. must learn to live with a lower rate of population growth, at least over the next decade. But modern economists view this prospect with more relief than alarm.

III. Better lives

It's true that more babies mean more demand and that through U.S. history, fast population growth and fast economic growth have gone hand in hand. But, in today's economy, the active use of fiscal policy probably means that declining population growth need no longer lead to declining growth in demand. After all, the great economic boom of the 1960s has oc-curred while the actual number of births declined.

For this reason, U.S. economists now are concentrating on the substantial benefits that the existing population can get from a drop in the rate at which the number of new mouths to feed is growing.

Joseph J. Spengler, a Duke University economist who now is president of the American Economic Assn., estimates that it takes the equivalent of 4% to 5% of national income to support an annual rate of population growth of 1%.

On the basis of this calculation, the 1.2% rate of population growth in 1965 soaked up between $26-billion and $29-billion of the $48-billion increase in gross national product. Thus, $19-billion to $22-billion was left over in GNP to improve the standard of living of the existing population.

So, providing that the level of demand can be kept high, a decline in the birth rate is bound to benefit the living standard of the existing population, mainly by reducing the cost of supporting the sheer increase in population numbers.

Pricing under Capitalism

Reading 8

All economies have one problem in common: relatively limited resources to be allocated among the unlimited wants of their people. Indeed an economic system may be viewed as a way in which a society organizes itself to answer certain fundamental questions: WHAT goods and services shall be produced? How shall they be produced? FOR WHOM shall they be produced? At the core of the American economic system, there is a much-lauded but little understood mechanism for answering these questions: the free marketplace.

The late Sumner H. Slichter, long a professor of economics at Harvard University and a prolific writer on the American economy, in 1928 described how this system relies on the motivations of individual freedom, self-interest, and profit to give it its forward thrust, and how it relies too on the forces of competition to check the accumulation of power in the marketplaces. The picture was a qualified one even at the time of Slichter's writing; it is still more qualified today as we increasingly modify the market mechanisms with one restraint or another. But none of those modifications lets us escape from the necessity of beginning with an understanding of the market system in its purer forms. Society may or may not want to operate in a totally free private-enterprise world; but it must at least know that bench mark if intelligent choices are to be made.

Questions to Guide the Reading

The market mechanism described here was eloquently discussed by an early and towering figure in economics, Adam Smith, in this manner:

> Every individual necessarily labors to render the annual revenue of the society as great as he can. He generally indeed, neither intends to promote the public interest, nor knows how much he is promoting it. . . . he intends only his own security; and by directing that industry in such a manner as its produce may be of the greatest value, he intends only his own gain, and he is in this, as in many other cases, led by an invisible hand to promote an end which was no part of his intention. Nor is it always the worse for the society that it was no part of it. By pursuing his own interest he frequently promotes that of the society more effectually than when he really intends to promote it. I have never known much good done by those who affected to trade for the public good. (*The Wealth of Nations*, Book IV, Chap. II, 1776.)

How does this "Invisible-Hand" mechanism work in, say, getting resources to move where they are most desired by consumers, or arriving at prices that serve to clear the marketplaces?

What is the nature of the system of values on which such a free-market society might be built? To what extent are these values that might be shared by men in the Soviet Union, or in one of the newly developing countries of Africa?

What is the rationale on which we have chosen in our economy to interfere at some points with the workings of the market system? Have we succeeded in finding what Adam Smith could not find, an effective way of pursuing the public good by direct intervention rather than by the use of the free markets?

Free Private Enterprise

Sumner H. Slichter

Possible forms of economic organizations

Every economic system must provide some way of doing three fundamental things: (1) getting goods produced; (2) determining what share each person shall have in the total product; and (3) regulating the consumption of goods, that is, determining who shall consume this good and who that. The manner in which these three basic economic processes are performed stamps the economic system with its most essential characteristics. How does the existing economic order organize and regulate the production, distribution, and consumption of goods?

There are several ways in which these activities *might* be organized and regulated:

1. On the basis of family autonomy. Each family might produce everything which it uses, relying upon others for nothing. In such a society there would be no trade.

2. On a communistic basis. What is produced and what each person does might be determined by the group as a whole and the product might be the property of the group, to be divided in accordance with socially determined rules.

3. On a despotic basis. The things produced and the tasks of each person might be decided

From Sumner H. Slichter, *Modern Economic Society* (Henry Holt and Company, Inc., New York, 1928). Reprinted with kind permission of the publisher.

by a despot or a despotic class, the product in all or in part being the property of the despot to be shared with the others as he saw fit.

4. On the basis of custom and heredity. Instead of choosing his own work or having it selected for him by the group or a despot, each person might be born into his occupation. He might be expected to do the thing which his father did, and other occupations might be closed to him. Likewise the share of each person in the product and the things which he is permitted or forbidden to consume might also be determined by custom.

All of these methods of organizing and controlling economic activities have been more or less prevalent in the past and, indeed, instances of them still exist. They are not, however, the methods which prevail today in the United States. It may seem a strange way of doing, but we organize industry by, in effect, saying to each individual, "Choose your own occupation. Produce what you like. What you do, to whom you sell, what or from whom you buy, the prices you get or give, are all your own concern. You are free, subject to a few restrictions, to produce whatever you wish regardless of whether or not it is needed, regardless of whether or not too much of it already exists. You are likewise free to refrain from engaging in any occupation no matter how acute may be the shortage of goods or how pressing the need for your help. You are free to buy from whoever is willing to sell and to sell to whoever is willing to buy. You are equally free to refuse to buy or sell whenever you please and for any reason or no reason."

This is what we mean by *free private enterprise*. Under it the government confines itself in the main to the suppression of fraud and violence and to the enforcement of contracts. It does not itself engage in or attempt to guide the course of industry. It pursues a "let alone" or "hands off" policy. Let us now see how, under free enterprise, the three fundamental economic processes of production, distribution, and consumption take place.

How free enterprise organizes production

Why does not a system of freedom, in which each person is at liberty to pursue whatever occupation he pleases and to produce whatever he wishes, result in hopeless chaos? Why do not many essential articles fail to get made and why does not the output of many things far exceed the demand for them? How can we get along without a central directing body to discover how much different things are in demand and to tell each of us what to produce?

To put the problem specifically, how does New York City each day obtain about the quantity of milk that it demands? Of the thousands of people engaged in supplying New York with milk, almost none knows either how much the city consumes or how much is being produced. And yet, despite this ignorance, New York each day receives about the amount of milk that it demands. There is neither a great surplus nor a shortage. Milk does not spoil because there is no one to consume it, and babies do not go without it because too small a supply reaches the city on some days. At the same time, other cities in the neighborhood are also receiving their daily supply from the same territory. Each uses a different quantity, yet each receives about the amount it demands.

The guide upon which we rely is the profit in making different goods, which, of course, depends upon the prices which they command and the cost of producing them. Suppose, for example, that New York failed to receive enough milk to satisfy the demand. Rather than go without milk or drink less, many people would be willing to pay more. Consequently the price would promptly rise. This would tend to end the shortage. More milk would be shipped to New York and less to other places. This would continue until there was no greater profit in selling milk in New York than elsewhere.

Just as price regulates the distribution of milk between cities, so it also determines the total amount produced in the country as a whole. Failure of the supply to keep pace with the demand would cause the price to rise. The greater profit to be had from the sale of milk would cause farmers to produce more of it. Some farmers, who had been separating their milk and selling the cream to be made into butter, might turn to the sale of whole milk. Others might abandon raising grain, stock, or fruit and enter dairy farming. As the output of milk increased, the price, of course, would drop. This would continue until producing milk was no more attractive than alternative branches of farming. If, furthermore, the demand for milk were to fall off or the supply to increase faster than the demand, farmers, in order to dispose of their supply, would be compelled to lower the price. Milk production would become a less profitable occupation, men would be deterred from entering it, and some of those already engaged in it might be led to abandon it or at least to reduce their output. And this would continue until the price rose and milk production became no less attractive than alternative occupations.

Price also determines in large measure where and how goods are made. Because living in New York City is expensive, it might seem a poor place in which to locate a factory. But the great stream of immigrants who for many years entered the country at New York and who were reluctant to undertake a long journey through a strange country provided the city with a bountiful supply of cheap labor. To take advantage of this, many industries, such as the needle trades, grew up in or near the East Side. At one time the Genesee valley in western New York was an important wheat region and Rochester, at the falls of the Genesee, was a great milling center. As the urban population in the East has grown, the greater profits in dairying and in fruit and truck raising have driven wheat raising to the West. The same is true of sheep raising. At one time, New York State contained nearly 5,000,000 sheep; now it has less than one-tenth that number. The growth of urban population has made dairying so profitable that most farmers cannot afford to raise sheep in New York.

Whether goods shall be made by hand or by machinery is often a question of money costs. Shall houses be built of wood or brick? As long as our immense forests were far from exhaustion, wooden houses were the almost universal rule. In Europe, where timber is less plentiful, frame dwellings are the exception. We still use timber to a greater extent than do most countries, but the cost of certain woods, such as white pine, has caused us to use cheaper varieties—Norway pine, hemlock, spruce, Douglas fir. Shall land be farmed intensively or extensively? The English obtain about twice as many bushels of wheat per acre as do the Americans, but we obtain about twice as many bushels per man. The reason is that in England, where land is relatively expensive, it is economized by the use of more labor and less land. Here where labor is ex-pensive in comparison with land, labor is economized by the use of more land and less labor.

How shares in the output of industry are determined

In our highly specialized society, each of us, at the best, contributes to industry's output very few things. One man may produce wheat, another wood, another milk, another cattle, another corn. In fact, most men do not contribute even one complete product. Hundreds of workers combine their efforts to make a suit of clothes, a pair of shoes, an automobile, or a telephone.

Although each individual makes a very specialized contribution to the product of society, each wishes to obtain from that output hundreds of articles. The man who produces only wheat desires flour, butter, sugar, clothing, shoes, hats, magazines, furniture, services of doctors, dentists, lawyers, and much else. If he contributes 2,000 bushels of wheat to society's stock of goods, how much is he entitled to withdraw?

Just as prices determine what things are produced, in what proportions, and by what methods, so, under free enterprise, they also determine the share of each person in the output of industry. If our imaginary wheat grower, who has produced a crop of 2,000 bushels, obtains $1.25 for each bushel, he is thereby enabled to purchase articles valued at $2,500. Just how much this is, will depend upon the price of shoes, hats, sugar, and the various other things which he desires. The next year he may work harder and produce 2,400 bushels. In the meantime, however, the price of wheat may drop to 75 cents a bushel. Hence, despite the fact that he has worked harder and raised more wheat, he has only $1,800 to spend for goods. And if, perchance, prices in general have risen, each of his dollars will buy him less than the year before. In a word, what share a man receives in the product of industry is determined by the prices of what he has to sell quite as much as by how industriously and efficiently he labors.

How consumption is regulated under free enterprise

There are many ways in which we might determine what goods each person shall consume.

We might undertake to ascertain the peculiar needs of each and see that he was afforded some special opportunity to obtain the things which would satisfy them. Or we might study the ability of different persons to use goods to the advantage of the rest of us and arrange for men of outstanding ability to receive the things which they require in order to be of greatest service to the community.

To a limited extent, we do regulate consumption upon the basis of either needs or ability to use goods advantageously. Schooling is considered so important that many governments supply a certain amount of it free or below cost. Police and fire protection, parks, playgrounds, and, to some extent, transportation, communication, and insurance are also considered so essential that they are provided by the government. Fellowships and scholarships, awarded to students of special promise, are among the few attempts which we make to place goods within reach of those who can use them to special advantage.

Under a system of free enterprise, however, which permits men to buy whatever they can get on the best terms that they can obtain, neither need nor ability to use goods for the benefit of others necessarily has much to do with determining how goods are consumed. Of far greater importance are the prices of different commodities and the ability of different persons to pay these prices.

In some respects, the control of consumption by price and ability to pay works out very satisfactorily. Suppose, for example, that unfavorable weather or blight made it likely that the potato crop would be exceptionally small. It is obvious that we should need to consume potatoes sparingly, making more than customary use of substitutes. If, on the other hand, the outlook were for a large crop, it would be to our interest to use more potatoes than usual. In each case, price produces the desired effect. If the prospects are for a small crop, the higher price induces sparing consumption; if a large crop seems probable, the low price encourages larger consumption. Because skilled labor is scarce, it is desirable that we economize it by using its products sparingly. The high wages of skilled craftsmen make their products expensive and encourage consumers to avoid wasting them. Commodities which can be made only at great risk of accidental or industrial disease should also be used sparingly. In so far as these hazards cause workmen to demand higher wages, they increase the price of the products and limit their consumption.

Although the regulation of consumption by prices usually encourages the economizing of scarce goods, it does so in a manner not altogether satisfactory. If consumption must be reduced this should perhaps be accomplished by those using less who can do so with the smallest inconvenience and sacrifice. As a matter of fact, the well-to-do, who are best supplied, are least induced by higher prices to curtail their purchases. It is the poor, who can least afford to reduce their consumption, who get along with less when the supply falls short. In periods of severe food shortage, such as often occur during war time, the regulation of consumption by ability to pay works such hardship that it is sometimes superseded by a system of rationing.

Some claims on behalf of free enterprise

Since free enterprise is the principal method by which our economic activities are organized and controlled, our study of modern industrial society must very largely consist of an inquiry into how freedom works under present-day conditions—such as machine industry, huge corporations, and science applied to business. But before we proceed further with our analysis, it will be helpful to become familiar in a general way with some of the claims which have been made in behalf of free enterprise. The "obvious and simple system of natural liberty," as Adam Smith called freedom of enterprise, has been regarded as the one and only way in which men might attain the maximum satisfaction of their desires with a minimum outlay of sacrifice. It is true that this extreme view has been accepted by few economists of repute and that since the middle of the last century, it has been increasingly under attack. Nevertheless it has had and still does have a wide acceptance by the general public and by certain schools of politicians, and it is appealed to frequently in political controversies. And even though we no longer spend much time discussing whether or not we can *always* trust free enterprise to regulate economic activity better than any other method, we are frequently compelled to decide whether or not it is the best way of controlling a specific economic activity under specific circumstances. Consequently the claims which have been made on its behalf are still very live issues.

The reasoning in support of the belief that freedom of enterprise is the maximum of satisfaction at the minimum of cost is very simple. Each individual, it is said, is better able than any one else to judge his own interests. If men are at liberty to spend their money as they choose, they will naturally purchase those things that will yield them the most satisfaction. Consequently the very commodities which give consumers the greatest pleasure are the most profitable for business enterprises to produce. Likewise, if men are free to use such methods of production as they wish, they will select those which involve the least cost per unit of output. With the goods which give the greatest gratification being made by the methods which are least costly, it follows, according to the theory, that there will be the maximum surplus of satisfaction over sacrifice.

Some assumptions of the theory of free enterprise

But if this result is to follow, two things would appear to be necessary: (1) goods must go to the consumers who will derive the greatest pleasure from them, and (2) the tasks of making goods must be assigned to the workers who can perform them with the least sacrifice for each unit of product. Does freedom of enterprise cause either goods or jobs to be distributed in this manner?

We have already seen that under a system of free enterprise goods tend to get into the hands of those who offer the best prices for them. But how then can they be consumed so as to yield the maximum of satisfaction? Are the people who are willing and able to pay most for goods also those who will derive the most satisfaction from using them? If they are not, it would appear possible to increase the surplus of satisfaction over sacrifice by causing goods to be distributed more in accordance with needs and less in accordance with ability to pay. We have no way of comparing the amount of pleasure which two persons derive from consuming an article. And yet it seems ridiculous to assert that ability to derive satisfaction from goods is proportionate to ability to pay for them. Assume that A and B each wish a pair of shoes. A, who is well-to-do, is willing to pay $12; B, who is poor, will offer only $7. Obviously A will get the shoes. But because he is rich and well supplied with shoes, an additional pair is only a slight con-

venience to him. B, poor and scantily supplied, has urgent need for another pair. It seems clear that the sum total of satisfaction would be greater if B obtained the shoes, and yet it seems equally clear that under freedom of enterprise they will go to A.

We are no better able to compare the pains suffered by different persons than we are the pleasures which they enjoy. Nevertheless it does not appear probable that freedom of enterprise necessarily causes jobs to be distributed so as to result in a minimum sacrifice for each unit of output—so that, for example, persons who can do heavy work with least fatigue will be given heavy work. Rather jobs tend to go to those who are willing to do the most work for the least money. Now the fact that X is willing to do a job for a dollar a day less than Y does not necessarily mean that X finds the task less onerous or unpleasant than Y. It may simply mean that he needs the money more and is willing to work at a lower rate in order to get it.

In face of the fact that ability to derive pleasure from goods does not appear to correspond to capacity to pay for them and that jobs are not necessarily given to the men who can do them with the least sacrifice for each unit of product, how can it be asserted that industrial liberty results in a maximum of satisfaction over sacrifice? But the exponents of free enterprise are not without a reply. To interfere with liberty in order to bring about a distribution of goods upon the basis of needs rather than ability to pay, or in order to cause jobs to be assigned to those who perform them with least sacrifice, might have the *immediate* effect of increasing the surplus of satisfaction over sacrifice. But this result, it is said, would be short lived. Men have the greatest incentive to improve their efficiency when they are free to compete for any jobs which they desire and to spend their income as they see fit. Were this incentive diminished by distributing jobs to those who could perform them with the least sacrifice and goods to those who would derive the most pleasure from them, output would inevitably decline. What would be gained by a different distribution of goods and jobs would be lost through smaller production.

The significance of competition

But how is it possible for us to trust business enterprises with so much freedom? In other branches of human relations, laws to regulate conduct seem to be quite essential. Why should industry be an exception to this general rule? If we leave business concerns free to make anything they like by any methods which they see fit, what is to prevent them from supplying the public with poorly made or adulterated goods or from using methods that are cheap in terms of dollars but expensive in terms of human sacrifice? Might not the sum total of pleasure be greater and of pain be less if the state enforced certain standards of quality or prohibited the use of certain methods of production?

The theory of free enterprise does not, it is important to emphasize, assert that restraints upon human selfishness are not needed. It simply assumes that they are provided by *competition*. This, according to the theory, is the great regulative force which establishes effective control over economic activities and gives each of us an incentive to observe the interests of others. Thus business establishments are deterred from furnishing adulterated or poorly made goods by the fear that customers may shift their patronage to rivals. Likewise the enterprises which fail to protect their men against accidents or industrial disease or which work them unusually hard, are penalized by the refusal of laborers to work for them except at a higher wage than other employers pay.

The mere existence of competition, however, is not enough. For it to perform satisfactorily the protective function attributed to it, certain very definite conditions must be present.

To begin with, an appreciable proportion of buyers and sellers must be willing to discriminate against those sellers or buyers who ignore, and in favor of those who take account of, the welfare of others. Otherwise, of course, no one has an economic incentive to pay attention to the well-being of his fellows. Assume, for example, that an enterprise pollutes a stream by dumping refuse and chemicals into it. From the standpoint of the firm, this may be an economical method of production. But from the standpoint of the community it is an expensive one because it kills the fish, spoils the stream for bathing, and makes it foul and ill-smelling. But competition will not stop the pollution unless an appreciable number of consumers, wage earners, or investors refuse to deal with the firm which is responsible—that is, unless a substantial number of consumers refuse to buy from it, or wage earners to work for it, or

investors to put money into it. But if the enterprise charges no more than its rivals for goods of equal grade, offers equally attractive conditions of employment, and pays as high dividends, who has an interest in discriminating against it? Perhaps the very fact that the enterprise pollutes the stream enables it to offer better terms than its rivals. Or take the case of child labor—another method of production cheap in dollars and cents but expensive in terms of human cost. If the firms which employ children are able, *because of that very fact*, to sell for less or to pay higher wages to adults or higher profits to investors, who is going to discriminate against them? Under these circumstances, does not competition positively encourage the employment of children?

But willingness to discriminate between those who consider the interests of others and those who do not is insufficient. Competition protects consumers against inferior ware only when they know good quality from bad; it protects laborers from unguarded machines only when they know which employers have and which have not guarded their machines. In other words, competition is an efficient protective agency only when buyers or sellers have the information necessary to make intelligent choices. It fails, for example, to protect consumers against milk from tubercular cattle because the ordinary buyer of milk has no way of distinguishing the milk of healthy cows from that of diseased.

The information needed for intelligent choices may be available, and yet many buyers or sellers may be too ignorant, too careless, too neglectful of their own interests to use it. If, for example, workmen show no disposition to shun plants which are notoriously dangerous or unsanitary, what incentive have employers to improve conditions?

Some issues raised by free enterprise

The whole theory that industrial liberty results in a maximum net satisfaction rests, it will be recalled, upon the assumption that each individual knows his own interests better than any one else and consequently can make his own decisions better than any one can make them for him. Is this true? May not free enterprise fail to yield the greatest possible satisfaction precisely *because* it results in choices which are molded too much by impulse, habit, prejudice, ignorance, or clever sales talk and too little by reflection, investigation of facts, or comparison of alternative opportunities? Under the system of economic freedom, choices are largely a matter of individual decision. This means that they are usually made in a hurry and by amateurs who have little opportunity to obtain expert advice. This situation may not be inevitable, but it exists. And yet millions of individuals, each attempting to decide for himself about the purchase of scores of articles concerning which he knows little, are an easy prey for ingenious selling and advertising experts. It may be true, as the theory of free enterprise asserts, that each individual knows his own desires better than any one else, but of what good is this if he has time to investigate neither what he is buying nor what he might buy, or if he is prevented by a skillful salesman from reflecting very much as to what he really does wish after all? Hence, when we find the United States spending more for tobacco than for education, the explanation may be, not that we desire tobacco more than education, but simply that the facilities for getting people to buy tobacco are more efficient than those for persuading them to pay for education. A representative body which could employ experts to investigate people's needs and desires and to test products might be able to spend a considerable portion of consumers' money with greater satisfaction to them than they could obtain by spending it themselves.

Role of government

Perhaps the most striking aspect of the theory of free enterprise is its assertion that intervention of the government in economic activities is unnecessary. The theory, as we have said, does not deny that restraints on human selfishness are needed. It simply asserts that we can trust competition to provide them. But closer inquiry reveals that the defenders of free enterprise do not trust competition to do all things. However much they trust it to guard the lives and limbs of workmen against dangerous machinery or to protect consumers against injurious foods, they do not rely upon it to enforce contracts or to prevent fraud. But the same reasoning which is used to prove that the government need not intervene on behalf of wage earners and consumers can be employed to show that laws are not required to guard business men against fraud or breach of con-

tractual obligations. Would not a customer who refused to pay his bills soon experience difficulty in getting dealers to sell to him, and would not an enterprise which violated its contracts find other concerns unwilling to deal with it? Is not the aid of the courts in these matters as superfluous as laws to protect workmen against dangerous machines or consumers against adulterated wares?

This inconsistency in the theory of free enterprise is to be explained by its origin. The theory was invented several hundred years ago to justify the demand of business men for release from oppressive legal restrictions. That the makers of the theory should have had greater faith in the capacity of competition to protect workmen against loss of life or limb than in its capacity to protect business men against bad debts is not surprising. When the rights of business were involved, it seemed quite proper for the government to lend the aid of its courts; only when the interests of consumers or wage earners were at stake did competition become a perfect protective instrument and intervention by the government "paternalistic" and "an unwarranted invasion of private rights."

Because the theory of free enterprise assumes that competition is needed to prevent freedom from being abused, it must also assume that competition is a more economical method of production than monopoly. Otherwise the claim that freedom results in the greatest satisfaction and the least sacrifice could not be correct. In many instances, however, it seems reasonably certain that monopoly is more economical than competition. The clearest cases are the so-called "octopus" industries, such as gas, electric light and power, water, railway, and street railway, which must run wire, pipe, or rails close to each consumer in order to deliver the service. It is the cost of duplicating this part of the plant which makes competition in these industries so uneconomical. In the oil industry, the desire of each landowner to obtain as much of the oil as possible causes him to put down an excessive number of wells along the edge of his property, thus diminishing the pressure under which the oil is held, substantially reducing the quantity which can be recovered, and greatly increasing the cost of getting it. Or consider the wastefulness of competition in distributing milk. With only a few customers in each block, a driver must travel many miles to reach several hundred customers. A study of competitive milk distribution in Rochester, New York, indicated that 2,509 miles of travel were necessary to distribute milk which a monopoly could deliver with 300 miles of travel. Competition required 356 men, 380 horses, and 305 wagons; a monopoly, it was estimated, would need 90 men, 80 horses, and 25 horsedrawn trucks. In most other industries, the case against competition is less clear, but undoubtedly there are many in which monopoly would be more economical.

The exponents of economic freedom answer that, even though monopoly is more economical at any given time, it may be less so in the long run. The search for new and cheaper methods of production needs, it is said, the spur of competition. In other words, competition more than makes up for its wastes by stimulating the development of better techniques.

Although the theory that government intervention in industry is unnecessary presupposes the existence of competition, the very absence of state interference often results in monopoly. This is not surprising. Indeed, it would be strange if business men left at liberty to do as they like, should not frequently combine to exploit the public rather than compete to serve the public. Consequently the government may find itself compelled to intervene either to enforce competition or to regulate monopoly. Either policy, of course, is a departure from the principle of free enterprise.

Reading 9

Widespread agreement could quickly be found for the proposition that we need much capital to sustain and improve our high standard of living in the United States. But what is implied in this approval?

To the economist, "capital" is a word with too many popular meanings. It requires a quite specific meaning if it is to convey a concept with analytical significance in understanding how our economy operates. This definition is found in using the word to refer to either (1) man-made factors of production or (2) goods that have been produced by the economic system not to satisfy present consumption but to aid in further production. In this sense, a nation's stock of *real capital* consists of the improved land, buildings, equipment, and inventories that are used to produce other goods and services. So defined, capital can come into existence only by diverting some of today's scarce resources from the production of "final" goods for present consumption to the production of "intermediate" goods for use in further production. Why would a society choose to follow such an "indirect" or "roundabout" way of satisfying its wants? And why do some societies rely more on capital intensive productive processes than other societies?

The Austrian economist Eugen von Böhm-Bawerk (1851–1914) is best known for his writings on capital and interest. Here he describes how and why capital intensive or "roundabout" methods of production work to man's advantage.

Questions to Guide the Reading

How do other popular uses of the word "capital" relate to the definition employed here?

If capital intensive or roundabout methods of production yield greater results than direct methods, why do we not immediately adopt the most roundabout or the most indirect methods of production available?

Capital and Roundabout Production

Eugen von Böhm-Bawerk

The end and aim of all production is the making of things with which to satisfy our wants; that is to say, the making of goods for immediate consumption, or Consumption Goods. We combine our own natural powers and natural powers of the external world in such a way that, under natural law, the desired material good must come into existence. But this is a very general description indeed of the matter, and looking at it closer there comes in sight an important distinction which we have not as yet considered. It has reference to the *distance* which lies between the *expenditure of human labour* in the combined production and *the appearance* of the desired good. We either put forth our labour just before the goal is reached, or we, intentionally, take a *roundabout* way. That is to say, we may put forth our labour in such a way that it at once completes the circle of conditions necessary for the emergence of the desired good, and thus the existence of the good *immediately* follows the expenditure of the labour; or we may associate our labour first with the more remote causes of good, with the object of obtaining, not the desired good itself, but a proximate cause of the good; which cause, again, must be associated with other suitable materials and powers, till, finally, —perhaps through a considerable number of intermediate members,—the finished good, the instrument of human satisfaction, is obtained.

Enhanced productiveness of roundabout method

The nature and importance of this distinction will be best seen from a few examples. A peasant requires drinking water. The spring is some distance from his house. There are various ways in which he may supply his daily wants. First, he may go to the spring each time he is thirsty, and drink out of his hollowed hand. This is the most direct way; satisfaction follows immediately on exertion. But it is an inconvenient way, for our peasant has to take his way to the well as often as he is thirsty. And it is an insufficient way, for he can never collect and store any great quantity such as he requires for various other purposes.

Second, he may take a log of wood, hollow it out into a kind of pail, and carry his day's supply from the spring to his cottage. The advantage is obvious, but it necessitates a roundabout way of considerable length. The man must spend, perhaps, a day in cutting out the pail; before doing so he must have felled a tree in the forest; to do this, again, he must have made an axe, and so on. But there is still a third way; instead of felling one tree he fells a number of trees, splits and hollows them, lays them end for end, and so constructs a runnel or rhone which brings a full head of water to his cottage. *Here, obviously, between the expenditure of the labour and the obtaining of the water we have a very roundabout way, but, then, the result is ever so much greater.* Our peasant need no longer take his weary way from house to well with the heavy pail on his shoulder, and yet he has a constant and full supply of the freshest water at his very door.

Another example. I require stone for building a house. There is a rich vein of excellent sandstone in a neighbouring hill. How is it to be got out? First, I may work the loose stones back and forward with my bare fingers, and break off what can be broken off. This is the most direct, but also the least productive way. Second, I may take a piece of iron, make a hammer and chisel out of it, and use them on the hard stone—a roundabout way, which, of course, leads to a very much better result than the former. Third method—Having a hammer and chisel I use them to drill a hole in the rock; next I turn my attention to procuring charcoal, sulphur, and nitre, and mixing them in a powder, then I pour the powder into the hole, and the explosion that follows splits the stone into convenient pieces—still more of a roundabout way, but one which, as experience shows, is as much superior to the second way in result as the second was to the first.

The lesson to be drawn from these examples is obvious. It is—that *a greater result is obtained by producing goods in roundabout ways*

From Eugen von Böhm-Bawerk, *Positive Theory of Capital* (1891).

than by producing them directly. Where a good can be produced in either way, we have the fact that, by the indirect way, a greater product can be got with equal labour, or the same product with less labour. But, beyond this, the superiority of the indirect way manifests itself in being the only way in which certain goods can be obtained.

A fundamental law

That roundabout methods lead to greater results than direct methods is one of the most important and fundamental propositions in the whole theory of production. It must be emphatically stated that the only basis of this proposition is the experience of practical life. Economic theory does not and cannot show *a priori* that it must be so; but the unanimous experience of all the technique of production says that it is so. And this is sufficient; all the more that the facts of experience which tell us this are commonplace and familiar to everybody. But *why* is it so?

In the last resort all our productive efforts amount to shiftings and combinations of matter. We must know how to bring together the right forms of matter at the right moment, in order that from those associated forces the desired result, the product wanted, may follow. But, as we saw, the natural forms of matter are often so infinitely large, often so infinitely fine, that human hands are too weak or too coarse to control them. We are as powerless to overcome the cohesion of the wall of rock when we want building stone as we are, from carbon, nitrogen, hydrogen, oxygen, phosphor, potash, etc., to put together a single grain of wheat. But there are other powers which can easily do what is denied to us, and these are the powers of nature. There are natural powers which far exceed the possibilities of human power in greatness, and there are other natural powers in the microscopic world which can make combinations that put our clumsy fingers to shame. If we can succeed in making those forces our allies in the work of production, the limits of human possibility will be infinitely extended. And this we have done.

Nature of capitalist production

The condition of our success is, that we are able to control the materials on which the power that helps us depends, more easily than the materials which are to be transformed into the desired good. Happily this condition can be very often complied with. Our weak yielding hand cannot overcome the cohesion of the rock, but the hard wedge of iron can; the wedge and the hammer to drive it we can happily master with little trouble. We cannot gather the atoms of phosphorus and potash out of the ground, and the atoms of carbon and oxygen out of the atmospheric air, and put them together in the shape of the corn or wheat; but the organic chemical powers of the seed can put this magical process in motion, while we on our part can very easily bury the seed in the place of its secret working, the bosom of the earth. Often, of course, we are not able directly to master the form of matter on which the friendly power depends, but in the same way as we would like it to help us, do we help ourselves against it; we try to secure the alliance of a second natural power which brings the form of matter that bears the first power under our control. We wish to bring the well water into the house. Wooden rhones would force it to obey our will, and take the path we prescribe, but our hands have not the power to make the forest trees into rhones. We have not far to look, however, for an expedient. We ask the help of a second ally in the axe and the gouge; their assistance gives us the rhones; then the rhones bring us the water. And what in this illustration is done through the mediation of two or three members may be done, with equal or greater result, through five, ten, or twenty members. Just as we control and guide the immediate matter of which the good is composed by one friendly power, and that power by a second, so can we control and guide the second by a third, the third by a fourth, this, again, by a fifth, and so on,—always going back to more remote causes of the final result—till in the series we come at last to one cause which we can control conveniently by our own natural powers. This is the true importance which attaches to our entering on roundabout ways of production: every roundabout way means the enlisting in our service of a power which is stronger or more cunning than the human hand; every extension of the roundabout way means an addition to the powers which enter into the service of man, and the shifting of some portion of the burden of production from the scarce and costly labour of human beings to the prodigal powers of nature.

The kind of production which works in these wise circuitous methods is nothing else than what economists call Capitalist Production, as opposed to that production which goes directly at its object. And Capital is nothing but the complex of intermediate products which appear on the several stages of the roundabout journey.

Supply and Demand Pricing

Reading 10

The market system is all around us. We buy and sell, and use money as the medium of exchange, with such ease that we often miss seeing just what functions the market and the exchange medium fulfill for us. Sometimes we need to get an unusual, even artificial perspective on this system in order to understand it. Then perhaps we can come at long last to feel about markets as Monsieur Jourdain came to feel about prose in Molière's *Le Bourgeois Gentilhomme:* "By my faith! for over forty years I've been speaking prose without knowing anything about it."

R. A. Radford found an unusual vantage point from which to view markets in his experiences as a British prisoner of war in Germany during World War II. Here he saw, in microcosm, the emergence of complex markets out of a simple barter system; he saw a medium of exchange—cigarettes—emerge to perform the same functions that less "useful" money performs for us. The very simplicity of the story he tells has made this article a minor classic in economics. To understand its full flavor is to know the world around us better than we knew it before.

Questions to Guide the Reading

Why did a system of exchange develop among the prisoners, and what is the parallel case for exchange in the world outside the prison camp?

What determined how elaborate or simple this prison market system became? What determines the extent to which we develop and use markets in everyday life?

The Economic Organisation of a P.O.W. Camp

R. A. Radford

Introduction

After allowance has been made for abnormal circumstances, the social institutions, ideas and habits of groups in the outside world are to be found reflected in a Prisoner of War Camp. It is an unusual but a vital society.

One aspect of social organisation is to be found in economic activity, and this, along with other manifestations of a group existence, is to be found in any P.O.W. camp. True, a prisoner is not dependent on his exertions for the provision of the necessaries, or even the luxuries of life, but through his economic ac-

From R. A. Radford, "The Economic Organisation of a P.O.W. Camp," *Economica*, Volume XII, 1945. Reprinted with kind permission of the editor.

tivity, the exchange of goods and services, his standard of material comfort is considerably enhanced. And this is a serious matter to the prisoner: he is not "playing at shops" even though the small scale of the transactions and the simple expression of comfort and wants in terms of cigarettes and jam, razor blades and writing paper, make the urgency of those needs difficult to appreciate, even by an ex-prisoner of some three months' standing.

Nevertheless, it cannot be too strongly emphasised that economic activities do not bulk so large in prison society as they do in the larger world. There can be little production; as has been said the prisoner is independent of his exertions for the provision of the necessities and luxuries of life; the emphasis lies in exchange and the media of exchange.

Everyone receives a roughly equal share of essentials; it is by trade that individual preferences are given expression and comfort increased. All at some time, and most people regularly, make exchanges of one sort or another.

Although a P.O.W. camp provides a living example of a simple economy which might be used as an alternative to the Robinson Crusoe economy beloved by the textbooks, and its simplicity renders the demonstration of certain economic hypotheses both amusing and instructive, it is suggested that the principal significance is sociological. True, there is interest in observing the growth of economic institutions and customs in a brand new society, small and simple enough to prevent detail from obscuring the basic pattern and disequilibrium from obscuring the working of the system. But the essential interest lies in the universality and the spontaneity of this economic life; it came into existence not by conscious imitation but as a response to the immediate needs and circumstances. Any similarity between prison organisation and outside organisation arises from similar stimuli evoking similar responses.

The following is as brief an account of the essential data as may render the narrative intelligible. The camps of which the writer had experience were Oflags and consequently the economy was not complicated by payments for work by the detaining power. They consisted normally of between 1,200 and 2,500 people, housed in a number of separate but intercommunicating bungalows, one company of 200 or so to a building. Each company formed a

group within the main organisation and inside the company the room and the messing syndicate, a voluntary and spontaneous group who fed together, formed the constituent units.

Between individuals there was active trading in all consumer goods and in some services. Most trading was for food against cigarettes or other foodstuffs, but cigarettes rose from the status of a normal commodity to that of currency. RMk.s existed but had no circulation save for gambling debts, as few articles could be purchased with them from the canteen.

Our supplies consisted of rations provided by the detaining power and (principally) the contents of Red Cross food parcels—tinned milk, jam, butter, biscuits, bully, chocolate, sugar, etc., and cigarettes. So far the supplies to each person were equal and regular. Private parcels of clothing, toilet requisites and cigarettes were also received, and here equality ceased owing to the different numbers despatched and the vagaries of the post. All these articles were the subject of trade and exchange.

The development and organisation of the market

Very soon after capture people realised that it was both undesirable and unnecessary, in view of the limited size and the equality of supplies, to give away or to accept gifts of cigarettes or food. "Goodwill" developed into trading as a more equitable means of maximising individual satisfaction.

We reached a transit camp in Italy about a fortnight after capture and received ¼ of a Red Cross food parcel each a week later. At once exchanges, already established, multiplied in volume. Starting with simple direct barter, such as a non-smoker giving a smoker friend his cigarette issue in exchange for a chocolate ration, more complex exchanges soon became an accepted custom. Stories circulated of a padre who started off round the camp with a tin of cheese and five cigarettes and returned to his bed with a complete parcel in addition to his original cheese and cigarettes; the market was not yet perfect. Within a week or two, as the volume of trade grew, rough scales of exchange values came into existence. Sikhs, who had at first exchanged tinned beef for practically any other foodstuff, began to insist on jam and margarine. It was realised that a tin of jam was worth ½ lb. of margarine plus something else; that a cigarette issue was worth several chocolates issues, and a tin of diced carrots was worth practically nothing.

In this camp we did not visit other bungalows very much and prices varied from place to place; hence the germ of truth in the story of the itinerant priest. By the end of a month, when we reached our permanent camp, there was a lively trade in all commodities and their relative values were well known, and expressed not in terms of one another—one didn't quote bully in terms of sugar—but in terms of cigarettes. The cigarette became the standard of value. In the permanent camp people started by wandering through the bungalows calling their offers—"cheese for seven" (cigarettes)— and the hours after parcel issue were Bedlam. The inconveniences of this system soon led to its replacement by an Exchange and Mart notice board in every bungalow, where under the headings "name," "room number," "wanted" and "offered" sales and wants were advertised. When a deal went through, it was crossed off the board. The public and semi-permanent records of transactions led to cigarette prices being well known and thus tending to equality throughout the camp, although there were always opportunities for an astute trader to make a profit from arbitrage. With this development everyone, including non-smokers, was willing to sell for cigarettes, using them to buy at another time and place. Cigarettes became the normal currency, though, of course, barter was never extinguished.

The unity of the market and the prevalence of a single price varied directly with the general level of organisation and comfort in the camp. A transit camp was always chaotic and uncomfortable: people were overcrowded, no one knew where anyone else was living, and few took the trouble to find out. Organisation was too slender to include an Exchange and Mart board, and private advertisements were the most that appeared. Consequently a transit camp was not one market but many. The price of a tin of salmon is known to have varied by two cigarettes in 20 between one end of a hut and the other. Despite a high level of organisation in Italy, the market was morcellated in this manner at the first transit camp we reached after our removal to Germany in the autumn of 1943. In this camp—Stalag VIIA at Moosburg in Bavaria—there

were up to 50,000 prisoners of all nationalities. French, Russians, Italians, and Jugo-Slavs were free to move about within the camp; British and Americans were confined to their compounds, although a few cigarettes given to a sentry would always procure permission for one or two men to visit other compounds. The people who first visited the highly organised French trading centre with its stalls and known prices found coffee extract—relatively cheap among the tea-drinking English—commanding a fancy price in biscuits or cigarettes, and some enterprising people made small fortunes that way. (Incidentally we found out later that much of the coffee went "over the wire" and sold for phenomenal prices at black market cafes in Munich: some of the French prisoners were said to have made substantial sums in RMk.s. This was one of the few occasions on which our normally closed economy came into contact with other economic worlds.)

Eventually public opinion grew hostile to these monopoly profits—not everyone could make contact with the French—and trading with them was put on a regulated basis. Each group of beds was given a quota of articles to offer and the transaction was carried out by accredited respresentatives from the British compound, with monopoly rights. The same method was used for trading with sentries elsewhere, as in this trade secrecy and reasonable prices had a peculiar importance, but as is ever the case with regulated companies, the interloper proved too strong.

The permanent camps in Germany saw the highest level of commercial organisation. In addition to the Exchange and Mart notice boards, a shop was organised as a public utility, controlled by representatives of the Senior British Officer, on a no profit basis. People left their surplus clothing, toilet requisites and food there until they were sold at a fixed price in cigarettes. Only sales in cigarettes were accepted—there was no barter—and there was no higgling. For food at least there were standard prices: clothing is less homogeneous and the price was decided around a norm by the seller and the shop manager in agreement; shirts would average say 80, ranging from 60 to 120 according to quality and age. Of food, the shop carried small stocks for convenience; the capital was provided by a loan from the bulk store of Red Cross cigarettes and repaid by a small commission taken on the first transactions. Thus the cigarette attained its fullest currency status, and the market was almost completely unified.

It is thus to be seen that a market came into existence without labour or production. The B.R.C.S. may be considered as "Nature" of the textbook, and the articles of trade—food, clothing and cigarettes—as free gifts—land of manna. Despite this, and despite a roughly equal distribution of resources, a market came into spontaneous operation, and prices were fixed by the operation of supply and demand. It is difficult to reconcile this fact with the labour theory of value.

Actually there was an embryo labour market. Even when cigarettes were not scarce, there was usually some unlucky person willing to perform services for them. Laundrymen advertised at two cigarettes a garment. Battle-dress was scrubbed and pressed and a pair of trousers lent for the interim period for twelve. A good pastel portrait cost thirty or a tin of "Kam." Odd tailoring and other jobs similarly had their prices.

There were also entrepreneurial services. There was a coffee stall owner who sold tea, coffee or cocoa at two cigarettes a cup, buying his raw materials at market prices and hiring labour to gather fuel and to stoke; he actually enjoyed the services of a chartered accountant at one stage. After a period of great prosperity he overreached himself and failed disastrously for several hundred cigarettes. Such large-scale private enterprise was rare but several middlemen or professional traders existed. The padre in Italy, or the men at Moosburg who opened trading relations with the French, are examples: the more subdivided the market, the less perfect the advertisement of prices, and the less stable the prices, the greater was the scope for these operators. One man capitalized his knowledge of Urdu by buying meat from the Sikhs and selling butter and jam in return: as his operations became better known more and more people entered this trade, prices in the Indian Wing approximated more nearly to those elsewhere, though to the end a "contact" among the Indians was valuable, as linguistic difficulties prevented the trade from being quite free. Some were specialists in the Indian trade, the food, clothing or even the watch trade. Middlemen traded on their own account or on commission. Price rings and agreements were suspected and the traders certainly co-

operated. Nor did they welcome newcomers. Unfortunately, the writer knows little of the workings of these people: public opinion was hostile and the professionals were usually of a retiring disposition.

One trader in food and cigarettes, operating in a period of dearth, enjoyed a high reputation. His capital, carefully saved, was originally about 50 cigarettes, with which he bought rations on issue days and held them until the price rose just before the next issue. He also picked up a little by arbitrage; several times a day he visited every Exchange or Mart notice board and took advantage of every discrepancy between prices of goods offered and wanted. His knowledge of prices, markets and names of those who had received cigarette parcels was phenomenal. By these means he kept himself smoking steadily—his profits—while his capital remained intact.

Sugar was issued on Saturday. About Tuesday two of us used to visit Sam and make a deal; as old customers he would advance as much of the price as he could spare us, and entered the transaction in a book. On Saturday morning he left cocoa tins on our beds for the ration, and picked them up on Saturday afternoon. We were hoping for a calendar at Christmas, but Sam failed too. He was left holding a big black treacle issue when the price fell, and in this weakened state was unable to withstand an unexpected arrival of parcels and the consequent price fluctuations. He paid in full, but from his capital. The next Tuesday, when I paid my usual visit, he was out of business.

Credit entered into many, perhaps into most, transactions, in one form or another. Sam paid in advance as a rule for his purchases of future deliveries of sugar, but many buyers asked for credit, whether the commodity was sold spot or future. Naturally prices varied according to the terms of sale. A treacle ration might be advertised for four cigarettes now or five next week. And in the future market "bread now" was a vastly different thing from "bread Thursday." Bread was issued on Thursday and Monday, four and three days' rations respectively, and by Wednesday and Sunday night it had risen at least one cigarette per ration, from seven to eight, by supper time. One man always saved a ration to sell then at the peak price: his offer of "bread now" stood out on the board among a number of "bread Monday's" fetching one or two less, or not selling at all—and he always smoked on Sunday night.

The cigarette currency

Although cigarettes as currency exhibited certain peculiarities, they performed all the functions of a metallic currency as a unit of account, as a measure of value and as a store of value, and shared most of its characteristics. They were homogeneous, reasonably durable, and of convenient size for the smallest or, in packets, for the largest transactions. Incidentally, they could be clipped or sweated by rolling them between the fingers so that tobacco fell out.

Cigarettes were also subject to the working of Gresham's Law. Certain brands were more popular than others as smokes, but for currency purposes a cigarette was a cigarette. Consequently buyers used the poorer qualities and the Shop rarely saw the more popular brands: cigarettes such as Churchman's No. 1 were rarely used for trading. At one time cigarettes hand-rolled from pipe tobacco began to circulate. Pipe tobacco was issued in lieu of cigarettes by the Red Cross at a rate of 25 cigarettes to the ounce and this rate was standard in exchanges, but an ounce would produce 30 home-made cigarettes. Naturally, people with machine-made cigarettes broke them down and re-rolled the tobacco, and the real cigarette virtually disappeared from the market. Hand-rolled cigarettes were not homogeneous and prices could no longer be quoted in them with safety: each cigarette was examined before it was accepted and thin ones were rejected, or extra demanded as a make-weight. For a time we suffered all the inconveniences of a debased currency.

Machine-made cigarettes were always universally acceptable, both for what they would buy and for themselves. It was this intrinsic value which gave rise to their principal disadvantage as currency, a disadvantage which exists, but to a far smaller extent in the case of metallic currency;—that is, a strong demand for non-monetary purposes. Consequently our economy was repeatedly subject to deflation and to periods of monetary stringency. While the Red Cross issue of 50 or 25 cigarettes per man per week came in regularly, and while there were fair stocks held, the cigarette currency suited its purpose admirably. But when

the issue was interrupted, stocks soon ran out, prices fell, trading declined in volume and became increasingly a matter of barter. This deflationary tendency was periodically offset by the sudden injection of new currency. Private cigarette parcels arrived in a trickle throughout the year, but the big numbers came in quarterly when the Red Cross received its allocation of transport. Several hundred thousand cigarettes might arrive in the space of a fortnight. Prices soared, and then began to fall, slowly at first but with increasing rapidity as stocks ran out, until the next big delivery. Most of our economic troubles could be attributed to this fundamental instability.

Price movements

Many factors affected prices, the strongest and most noticeable being the periodical currency inflation and deflation described in the last paragraphs. The periodicity of this price cycle depended on cigarette and, to a far lesser extent, on food deliveries. At one time in the early days, before any private parcels had arrived and when there were no individual stocks, the weekly issue of cigarettes and food parcels occurred on a Monday. The non-monetary demand for cigarettes was great, and less elastic than the demand for food: consequently prices fluctuated weekly, falling towards Sunday night and rising sharply on Monday morning. Later, when many people held reserves, the weekly issue had no such effect, being too small a portion of the total available. Credit allowed people with no reserves to meet their non-monetary demand over the weekend.

The general price level was affected by other factors. An influx of new prisoners, proverbially hungry, raised it. Heavy air raids in the vicinity of the camp probably increased the non-monetary demand for cigarettes and accentuated deflation. Good and bad war news certainly had its effect, and the general waves of optimism and pessimism which swept the camp were reflected in prices. Before breakfast one morning in March of this year, a rumour of the arrival of parcels and cigarettes was circulated. Within ten minutes I sold a treacle ration, for four cigarettes (hitherto offered in vain for three), and many similar deals went through. By 10 o'clock the rumour was denied, and treacle that day found no more buyers even at two cigarettes.

More interesting than changes in the general price level were changes in the price structure. Changes in the supply of a commodity, in the German ration scale or in the make-up of Red Cross parcels, would raise the price of one commodity relative to others. Tins of oatmeal, once a rare and much sought after luxury in the parcels, became a commonplace in 1943, and the price fell. In hot weather the demand for cocoa fell, and that for soap rose. A new recipe would be reflected in the price level: the discovery that raisins and sugar could be turned into an alcoholic liquor of remarkable potency reacted permanently on the dried fruit market. The invention of electric immersion heaters run off the power points made tea, a drag on the market in Italy, a certain seller in Germany.

In August, 1944, the supplies of parcels and cigarettes were both halved. Since both sides of the equation were changed in the same degree, changes in prices were not anticipated. But this was not the case: the non-monetary demand for cigarettes was less elastic than the demand for food, and food prices fell a little. More important however were the changes in the price structure. German margarine and jam, hitherto valueless owing to adequate supplies of Canadian butter and marmalade, acquired a new value. Chocolate, popular and a certain seller, and sugar, fell. Bread rose; several standing contracts of bread for cigarettes were broken, especially when the bread ration was reduced a few weeks later.

In February, 1945, the German soldier who drove the ration wagon was found to be willing to exchange loaves of bread at the rate of one loaf for a bar of chocolate. Those in the know began selling bread and buying chocolate, by then almost unsaleable in a period of serious deflation. Bread, at about 40, fell slightly; chocolate rose from 15; the supply of bread was not enough for the two commodities to reach parity, but the tendency was unmistakable.

The substitution of German margarine for Canadian butter when parcels were halved naturally affected their relative values, margarine appreciating at the expense of butter. Similarly, two brands of dried milk, hitherto differing in quality and therefore in price by five cigarettes a tin, came together in price as the wider substitution of the cheaper raised its relative value.

Enough has been cited to show that any change in conditions affected both the general price level and the price structure. It was this latter phenomenon which wrecked our planned economy.

Paper currency—Bully Marks

Around D-Day, food and cigarettes were plentiful, business was brisk and the camp in an optimistic mood. Consequently the Entertainments Committee felt the moment opportune to launch a restaurant, where food and hot drinks were sold while a band and variety turns performed. Earlier experiments, both public and private, had pointed the way, and the scheme was a great success. Food was bought at market prices to provide the meals and the small profits were devoted to a reserve fund and used to bribe Germans to provide grease paints and other necessities for the camp theatre. Originally meals were sold for cigarettes but this meant that the whole scheme was vulnerable to the periodic deflationary waves, and furthermore heavy smokers were unlikely to attend much. The whole success of the scheme depended on an adequate amount of food being offered for sale in the normal manner.

To increase and facilitate trade, and to stimulate supplies and customers therefore, and secondarily to avoid the worst effects of deflation when it should come, a paper currency was organised by the Restaurant and the Shop. The Shop bought food on behalf of the Restaurant with paper notes and the paper was accepted equally with the cigarettes in the Restaurant or Shop, and passed back to the Shop to purchase more food. The Shop acted as a bank of issue. The paper money was backed 100 per cent. by food; hence its name, the Bully Mark. The BMk. was backed 100 per cent. by food: there could be no over-issues, as is permissible with a normal bank of issue, since the eventual dispersal of the camp and consequent redemption of all BMk.s were anticipated in the near future.

Originally one BMk. was worth one cigarette and for a short time both circulated freely inside and outside the Restaurant. Prices were quoted in BMk.s and cigarettes with equal freedom—and for a short time the BMk. showed signs of replacing the cigarette as currency. The BMk. was tied to food, but not to cigarettes: as it was issued against food, say 45 for a tin of milk and so on, any reduction in the BMk. prices of food would have meant that there were unbacked BMk.s in circulation. But the price of both food and BMk.s could and did fluctuate with the supply of cigarettes.

While the Restaurant flourished, the scheme was a success: the Restaurant bought heavily, all foods were saleable and prices were stable.

In August parcels and cigarettes were halved and the Camp was bombed. The Restaurant closed for a short while and sales of food became difficult. Even when the Restaurant reopened, the food and cigarette shortage became increasingly acute and people were unwilling to convert such valuable goods into paper and to hold them for luxuries like snacks and tea. Less of the right kinds of food for the Restaurant were sold, and the Shop became glutted with dried fruit, chocolate, sugar, etc., which the Restaurant could not buy. The price level and the price structure changed. The BMk. fell to four-fifths of a cigarette and eventually farther still, and it became unacceptable save in the Restaurant. There was a flight from the BMk., no longer convertible into cigarettes or popular foods. The cigarette reestablished itself.

But the BMk. was sound! The Restaurant closed in the New Year with a progressive food shortage and the long evenings without lights due to intensified Allied air raids, and the BMk.s could only be spent in the Coffee Bar—relict of the Restaurant—or on the few unpopular foods in the Shop, the owners of which were prepared to accept them. In the end all holders of BMk.s were paid in full, in cups of coffee or in prunes. People who had bought BMk.s for cigarettes or valuable jam or biscuits in their heyday were aggrieved that they should have stood the loss involved in their restricted choice, but they suffered no actual loss of market value.

Price fixing

Along with this scheme came a determined attempt at a planned economy, at price fixing. The Medical Officer had long been anxious to control food sales, for fear of some people selling too much, to the detriment of their health. The deflationary waves and their effects on prices were inconvenient to all and would be dangerous to the Restaurant which had to carry stocks. Furthermore, unless the BMk. was convertible into cigarettes at about par it had little chance of gaining confidence and of succeeding as a currency. As has been explained, the BMk. was tied to food but could not be tied to cigarettes, which fluctuated in value. Hence, while BMk. prices of food were fixed for all time, cigarette prices of food and BMk.s varied.

The Shop, backed by the Senior British Officer, was now in a position to enforce price control both inside and outside its walls. Hitherto a standard price had been fixed for food left for sale in the shop, and prices outside were roughly in conformity with this scale, which was recommended as a "guide" to sellers, but fluctuated a good deal around it. Sales in the Shop at recommended prices were apt to be slow though a good price might be obtained: sales outside could be made more quickly at lower prices. (If sales outside were to be at higher prices, goods were withdrawn from the Shop until the recommended price rose: but the recommended price was sluggish and could not follow the market closely by reason of its very purpose, which was stability.) The Exchange and Mart notice boards came under the control of the Shop: advertisements which exceeded a 5 per cent. departure from the recommended scale were liable to be crossed out by authority: unauthorised sales were discouraged by authority and also by public opinion, strongly in favour of a just and stable price. (Recommended prices were fixed partly from market data, partly on the advice of the M.O.)

At first the recommended scale was a success: the Restaurant, a big buyer, kept prices stable around this level: opinion and the 5 per cent. tolerance helped. But when the price level fell with the August cuts and the price structure changed, the recommended scale was too rigid. Unchanged at first, as no deflation was expected, the scale was tardily lowered, but the prices of goods on the new scale remained in the same relation to one another, owing to the BMk., while on the market the price structure had changed. And the modifying influence of the Restaurant had gone. The scale was moved up and down several times, slowly following the inflationary and deflationary waves, but it was rarely adjusted to changes in the price structure. More and more advertisements were crossed off the board, and black market sales at unauthorised prices increased: eventually public opinion turned against the recommended scale and authority gave up the struggle. In the last few weeks, with unparalleled deflation, prices fell with alarming rapidity, no scales existed, and supply and demand, alone and unmellowed, determined prices.

Public opinion

Public opinion on the subject of trading was vocal if confused and changeable, and generalisations as to its direction are difficult and dangerous. A tiny minority held that all trading was undesirable as it engendered an unsavoury atmosphere; occasional frauds and sharp practices were cited as proof. Certain forms of trading were more generally condemned; trade with the Germans was criticised by many. Red Cross toilet articles, which were in short supply and only issued in cases of actual need, were excluded from trade by law and opinion working in unshakable harmony. At one time, when there had been several cases of malnutrition reported among the more devoted smokers, no trade in German rations was permitted, as the victims became an additional burden on the depleted food reserves of the Hospital. But while certain activities were condemned as anti-social, trade itself was practised, and its utility appreciated, by almost everyone in the camp.

More interesting was opinion on middlemen and prices. Taken as a whole, opinion was hostile to the middleman. His function, and his hard work in bringing buyer and seller together, were ignored; profits were not regarded as a reward for labour, but as the result of sharp practices. Despite the fact that his very existence was proof to the contrary, the middleman was held to be redundant in view of the existence of an official Shop and the Exchange and Mart. Appreciation only came his way when he was willing to advance the price of a sugar ration, or to buy goods spot and carry them against a future sale. In these cases the element of risk was obvious to all, and the convenience of the service was felt to merit some reward. Particularly unpopular was the middleman with an element of monopoly, the man who contacted the ration waggon driver, or the man who utilised his knowledge of Urdu. And middlemen as a group were blamed for reducing prices. Opinion notwithstanding,

most people dealt with a middleman, whether consciously or unconsciously, at some time or another.

There was a strong feeling that everything had its "just price" in cigarettes. While the assessment of the just price, which incidentally varied between camps, was impossible of explanation, this price was nevertheless pretty closely known. It can best be defined as the price usually fetched by an article in good times when cigarettes were plentiful. The "just price" changed slowly; it was unaffected by short-term variations in supply, and while opinion might be resigned to departures from the "just price," a strong feeling of resentment persisted. A more satisfactory definition of the "just price" is impossible. Everyone knew what it was, though no one could explain why it should be so.

As soon as prices began to fall with a cigarette shortage, a clamour arose, particularly against those who held reserves and who bought at reduced prices. Sellers at cut prices were criticised and their activities referred to as the black market. In every period of dearth the explosive question of "should non-smokers receive a cigarette ration?" was discussed to profitless length. Unfortunately, it was the non-smoker, or the light smoker with his reserves, along with the hated middleman, who weathered the storm most easily.

The popularity of the price-fixing scheme, and such success as it enjoyed, were undoubtedly the result of this body of opinion. On several occasions the fall of prices was delayed by the general support given to the recommended scale. The onset of deflation was marked by a period of sluggish trade; prices stayed up but no one bought. Then prices fell on the black market, and the volume of trade revived in that quarter. Even when the recommended scale was revised, the volume of trade in the Shop would remain low. Opinion was always overruled by the hard facts of the market.

Curious arguments were advanced to justify price fixing. The recommended prices were in some way related to the calorific values of the foods offered: hence some were overvalued and never sold at these prices. One argument ran as follows:—not everyone has private cigarette parcels: thus, when prices were high and trade good in the summer of 1944, only the lucky rich could buy. This was unfair to the man with few cigarettes. When prices fell in the following winter, prices should be pegged high so that the rich, who had enjoyed life in the summer, should put many cigarettes into circulation. The fact that those who sold to the rich in the summer had also enjoyed life then, and the fact that in the winter there was always someone willing to sell at low prices were ignored. Such arguments were hotly debated each night after the approach of Allied aircraft extinguished all lights at 8 P.M. But prices moved with the supply of cigarettes, and refused to stay fixed in accordance with a theory of ethics.

Conclusion

The economic organisation described was both elaborate and smooth-working in the summer of 1944. Then came the August cuts and deflation. Prices fell, rallied with deliveries of cigarette parcels in September and December, and fell again. In January, 1945, supplies of Red Cross cigarettes ran out: and prices slumped still further: in February the supplies of food parcels were exhausted and the depression became a blizzard. Food, itself scarce, was almost given away in order to meet the non-monetary demand for cigarettes. Laundries ceased to operate, or worked for £s or RMk.s: food and cigarettes sold for fancy prices in £s, hitherto unheard of. The Restaurant was a

memory and the BMk. a joke. The Shop was empty and the Exchange and Mart notices were full of unaccepted offers for cigarettes. Barter increased in volume, becoming a larger proportion of a smaller volume of trade. Thus, the first serious and prolonged food shortage in the writer's experience, caused the price structure to change again, partly because German rations were not easily divisible. A margarine ration gradually sank in value until it exchanged directly for a treacle ration. Sugar slumped sadly. Only bread retained its value. Several thousand cigarettes, the capital of the Shop, were distributed without any noticeable effect. A few fractional parcel and cigarette issues, such as one-sixth of a parcel and twelve cigarettes each, led to monetary price recoveries and feverish trade, especially when they coincided with good news from the Western Front, but the general position remained unaltered.

By April, 1945, chaos had replaced order in the economic sphere: sales were difficult, prices lacked stability. Economics has been defined as the science of distributing limited means among unlimited and competing ends. On 12th April, with the arrival of elements of the 30th U.S. Infantry Division, the ushering in of an age of plenty demonstrated the hypothesis that with infinite means economic organisation and activity would be redundant, as every want could be satisfied without effort.

Reading 11

When a book on sex, or on health, or on the Civil War makes the best-seller list, that is not news. But when a book on the stock market—and not a how-to-do-it manual—stays month after month on the best-seller list, that is a testimonial to its quality. *The Money Game*, written by one who signs himself "Adam Smith" (and whom some believe is Harvard- and Oxford-trained George J. W. Goodman), is such a book. It is a modern-day classic. Like many modern paintings, the book looks simple. But as W. Somerset Maugham said about an unforgettable Mondrian abstraction: "It looks as though you had only to take a ruler, a tube of black paint and a tube of red, and you could do the thing yourself. Try!"

Questions to Guide the Reading

Is the lack of interest in money as the ultimate payoff a snobbish pose? Does it matter what motivates the money manager, if the people who hire him and give him chips to play with are themselves motivated by money? Won't those who disregard the money payoff end up with a smaller stake to invest than those who do?

Not For Money, Not For Love . . . The Stock Market

"Adam Smith"

We are taught—at least those of us who grew up without a great deal of it—that money is A Very Serious Business, that the stewardship of capital is holy, and that the handler of money must conduct himself as a Prudent Man. It is all part of the Protestant ethic and the spirit of Capitalism and I suppose it all helped to make this country what it is. Penny saved, penny earned, waste not, want not. Summer Sale Save 10 Percent, and so on. Then I came across this sentence in "Long-Term Expectation" of Keynes' General Theory:

The game of professional investment is intolerably boring and overexacting to anyone who is entirely exempt from the gambling instinct; whilst he who has it must pay to this propensity the appropriate toll.

Game? Game? Why did the Master say Game? He could have said business or profession or occupation or what have you. What is a Game? It is "sport, play, frolic, or fun"; "a scheme or art employed in the pursuit of an object or purpose"; "a contest, conducted according to set rules, for amusement or recreation or winning a stake." Does that sound like Owning a Share of American Industry? Participating in the Long-Term Growth of the American Economy? No, but it sounds like the stock market.

Let us go one step beyond. Drs. John von Neumann and Oskar Morgenstern developed, some years ago, a *Theory of Games and Economic Behavior*. This game theory has had a tremendous impact on our national life; it influences how our defense decisions are made and how the marketing strategies of great corporations are worked out. What is game theory? You could say it is an attempt to quantify and work through the actions of players in a game, to measure their options continuously. Or, to be more formal, game theory is a branch of mathematics that aims to analyze problems of conflict by abstracting common strategic features for study in theoretical models. (You can tell by the phrasing of that last sentence that I have the book before me, so let me go on.) By stressing strategic aspects, i.e., those controlled by the participants, it goes beyond the classic theory of probability, in which the treatment of games is limited to aspects of pure chance. Drs. von Neumann and Morgenstern worked through systems that incorporated conflicting interests, incomplete information, and the interplay of free rational decision and choice. They started with dual games, zero sum two-person games, i.e., those in which one player wins what the other loses. At the other end you have something like the stock market, an infinite, *n*-person game. (*N* is one of the letters economists use when they don't know something.) The stock market is probably temporarily too complex even for the Game Theoreticians, but I suppose some day even it will become a serious candidate for quantification and equations.

The rich man's lottery

I bring this up only because I think the market is both a game and a Game, i.e., both sport, frolic, fun, and play, and a subject for continuously measurable options. If it is a game, then we can relieve ourselves of some of the heavy and possibly crippling emotions that individuals carry into investing, because in a game the winning of the stake is clearly defined. Anything else becomes irrelevant. Is this so startling? "Eighty percent of investors are not really out to make money," says one leading Wall Streeter. Investors not out to make money? It seems almost like a contradiction in terms. What are they doing then? That can be a subject for a whole discussion, and will be, a bit later.

Let us go back to the *illumine*, that the investment game is intolerably boring save to those with a gambling instinct, while those with the instinct must pay to it "the appropriate toll." This really does say it all. We have twenty-four million direct investors in this country, i.e., people who have actually bought stocks. (I say direct investors because indirectly, through insurance companies and pension plans, we have more than a hundred million investors, which is just about everybody except children and the truly poor.) Not all of the twenty-four million are fiercely active, but the number grows all the time, making the stock market a great national pastime. Active investors do not pursue bonds (except convertibles) and preferreds (except convertibles). It isn't that one can't make money with these instruments, it's that they lack romance enough to be part of the game; they are boring. It is very hard to get excited over a bond basis book, where your index finger traces along a column until its gets to the proper degree of safety and yield.

Sometimes illusions are more comfortable than reality, but there is no reason to be discomfited by facing the gambling instinct that saves the stock market from being a bore. Once it is acknowledged, rather than buried, we can "pay to this propensity the appropriate toll" and proceed with reality.

I mean here no more than recognizing an instinct. Dr. Thomas Schelling, a Harvard economist and the author of a number of works on military strategy, goes a lot further. Writing on "Economics and Criminal Enterprise," Dr. Schelling says:

The greatest gambling enterprise in the United States has not been significantly touched by organized crime. That is the stock market. . . . The reason is that the market works too well. Federal control over the stock market, designed mainly to keep it honest and informative . . . makes it a hard market to tamper with.

Sentences like the first one in that excerpt must make the public-relations people at the New York Stock Exchange wake up screaming. For years the New York Stock Exchange and the securities industry have campaigned to correct the idea that buying stocks was gambling, and while there may be some dark corners of this country that persist in a Populist suspicion of Wall Street, by and large they have succeeded. Dr. Schelling's phrasing has to be counted as unfortunate, and in no sense is the stock market a great gambling enterprise like a lottery. But it is an exercise in mass psychology, in trying to guess better than the crowd how the crowd will behave. Sometimes the literature which was produced in order to dispel the pre-1929 suspicions can get in the way of seeing things the way they are.

All this is simply leading up to a pragmatic observation. It has been my fate to know a

number of people in and around markets: investment bankers, economists, portfolio managers of great institutions. I have been through the drill of security analysis—that set me back quite a bit—and in a minor way through portfolio management. (I haven't ever been a broker or sold securities; that is another talent.) During lunch at my own house I have seen "random walk" theoreticians grow apoplectic over their dessert at the thought that there were people who called themselves "technicians" and believed that prices forecast the future, and I have known technicians, backed by computers, who got themselves so wound up into their own systems they forgot what they started with.

It has taken me years to unlearn everything I was taught, and I probably haven't succeeded yet. I cite this only because most of what has been written about the market tells you the way it ought to be, and the successful investors I know do not hold to the way it ought to be, they simply go with what is. If thinking of this fascinating, complex, infinite, n-person process as a Game helps, then perhaps that is the way we should think; it helps rid us of the compulsions of theology.

I'd rather do it myself

If you are a player in the Game, or are thinking of becoming one, there is one irony of which you should be aware. The object of the game is to make money, hopefully a lot of it. All the players in the Game are getting rapidly more professional; the amount of sheer information poured out on what is going on has become almost too much to absorb. The true professionals in the Game—the professional portfolio managers—grow more skilled all the time. They are human and they make mistakes, but if you have your money managed by a truly alert mutual fund or even by one of the better banks, you will have a better job done for you than probably at any time in the past.

But if you have your money managed for you, then you are not really interested, or at least the Game element—with that propensity to be paid for—does not attract you. I have known a lot of investors who came to the market to make money, and they told themselves that what they wanted was the money: security, a trip around the world, a new sloop, a country estate, an art collection, a Caribbean house for cold winters. And they succeeded. So they sat on the dock of the Caribbean home, chatting with their art dealers and gazing fondly at the new sloop, and after a while it was a bit flat. Something was missing. If you are a successful Game player, it can be a fascinating, consuming, totally absorbing experience, in fact it has to be. If it is not totally absorbing you are not likely to be among the most successful, because you are competing with those who do find it so absorbing.

The lads with the Caribbean houses and the new sloops did not, upon the discovery that something was missing, sell those trophies and acquire sackcloth and ashes. The sloops and the houses and the art are all still there, but the players have gone back to the Game, and they don't have a great deal of time for their toys. The Game is more fun. It probably does not make you a better person, and I am not sure it does any good for humanity; the best you can say is what Samuel Johnson said, that no man is so harmlessly occupied as when he is making money.

The irony is that this is a money game and money is the way we keep score. But the real object of the Game is not money, it is the playing of the Game itself. For the true players, you could take all the trophies away and substitute plastic beads or whale's teeth; as long as there is a way to keep score, they will play.

*   *   *

You mean that's what money really is?

"The very bright people," says one of my Wall Street philosopher friends, "know how to worm their way around the Street, and they do very well. And the ones who just buy the stock and put it away probably do all right. But the investors who really follow the market, the ones who call up all the time, ninety percent of them really don't care whether they make money or not."

We will come back to what these eager investors *do* care about, but first, this business about all the investors not wanting to make money; it may just be the healthiest thing we have heard in a long time, if we can believe what money *really* is, at least unconsciously. If the eleven thousand security analysts, the hundred thousand brokers, and all those programs in the IBM 360s are busy looking for

the right set of rational numbers, perhaps we can sneak around the flank for a look at what money may mean to you. If we knew that we might be able to step outside ourselves, as Mister Johnson said, and look back, and if we know something about ourselves and money, at least we can be conscious of the instincts toward it which influence our actions.

The reading list on mass psychology and markets may be brief, but the list on men and money is endless. Norman Brown, whose *Life Against Death* is one of the most brilliant critiques extant, has to run through Alfred North Whitehead, Émile Durkheim, Claude Lévi-Strauss, Marcel Mauss, Freud, Marx, M.J. Herskovits, Laum, Ruskin, and Nietzsche just to get warmed up. All of these learned scholars think money is more than just that green stuff in your wallet. Money has a mystical quality; the markets of antiquity were sacred places, the first banks were temples, and the money-issuers were priests and priest-kings. Gold and silver held a stable relationship through antiquity, based, says one authority, on the astrological ratio of the cycles of their divine counterparts, the sun and moon. (This is in a book called *Wirtschaftsgeschichte des Altertums*, if you want to look it up. I don't. I am reporting this at second hand, and anyway we have busted the old sun-moon business by pegging gold and letting silver go through the roof. There are those that think gold is due to go up—whether or not because of the influence of the sun—but that is another story.)

The point all these learned scholars make is that money is useless; that is, it must literally be useless in order to be money, whether money is the stone cartwheels of Yap island, shells, dogs' teeth, gold stored in Fort Knox, or East African cattle which can't be eaten because that would be—literally—eating up capital. The thread of thought here goes directly against that of Adam Smith the First, who postulated that money was useful and men rational. The invisible hand of the market brought the cobbler's boots to market in exchange for the farmer's cabbages so that, efficiently, the cobbler did not have to farm nor the farmer to cobble. Adam Smith the First's economic man was a rational man, and much of economics assumes that men will always go in the direction of the maximization of profit or of production. But since we are skittering over the idea that men are not always rational, we have to see where the idea that money is useless, or why it is useless, will lead us.

Scorecard for neurotics

At the root of the impulse to pile up this useless money is "the compulsion to work." (Norman Brown here.)

This compulsion to work subordinates man to things. . . . it reduces the drives of the human being to greed and competition (aggression and possessiveness) . . . the desire for money takes the place of all genuinely human needs. Thus the apparent accumulation of wealth is really the impoverishment of human nature, and its appropriate morality is the renunciation of human nature and desires—asceticism. The effect is to substitute an abstraction, *Homo economicus*, for the concrete totality of human nature, and thus to dehumanize human nature.

Wealth is useless stuff that can be condensed and stored. Sandor Ferenczi, a member of Freud's Wednesday Evening Psychological Association, went about as far as you can go in an essay called "On the Ontogenesis of the Interest in Money," in which he equates money with body wastes—"nothing other than odorless dehydrated filth that has been made to shine" —presumably gold, in this case. (Before hooting, remember that we are groping for something on the nonrational level. Aristotle said money-making was an unnatural perversion.) Money has always had overtones of the mystical; for Luther this becomes secular, and therefore demonic—Satan's work.

Why pile up this useless stuff? The surplus labor that produces surplus wealth is from the dammed-up or mischanneled libido (Freud again). Norman Brown goes Freud one further: "The whole money complex is rooted in the psychology of guilt," and gold is the absolute symbol of sublimation. Money is "condensed wealth; condensed wealth is condensed guilt. But guilt is essentially unclean." Thus Christmas gift-giving is a partial expiation for piling up all that condensed guilt during the year. Guilt here is not for anything in particular; it is part of the personality structure. Back to Freud: "One must . . . never allow oneself to be misled into applying to the repressed creations of the mind the standard of reality; this might result in underestimating the importance of fantasies in symptom-formation on the ground that they are not actualities . . . one is bound to employ the currency that pre-

vails in the country one is exploring; in our case it is the neurotic currency." To which Norman Brown adds, "all currency is neurotic currency."

Now it may seem a far cry from the kind of money being cited here to the total wealth of all those liquid pieces of paper, say some $700 billion in common stocks and $600 billion or so in bonds. That money, clearly, is not useless, it is out there building new plants and paying payrolls and producing widgets and so on. But Norman Brown, trying to work interest (i.e., return on capital) into his scheme, even covers this: "Things become the god (the father of himself) that he [man] would like to be; money *breeds* . . . thus money in the civilized economy comes to have a psychic value it never had in the archaic economy." And this is a true infantile wish: to become a father to oneself. All of this leads Norman Brown on into a discussion of the city as related to all that piled-up wealth, and the city as an attempt at immortality, an attempt to beat death. (The inability to accept death is the woof of Brown's fabric.)

All this may seem like peculiar stuff, especially taken cold, but I find it provocative. I have been a bit terse with it, and perhaps have not done it justice. Perhaps our whole Game is outside the realm of money as condensed, useless, and guilt, for if it is a Game, then it is "sport, frolic, fun and play," and presumably on the Life side, not the Death side. (Norman Brown does make me feel sometimes that the only way to spend an afternoon is drinking beer and fishing, so as to escape the accusation of compulsive, guilt-ridden work, but I have the sneaky feeling that while I am fishing he is working on another book.) It is true that you have to work long enough to acquire a surplus enough to buy some chips for the Game, but the money you make playing the Game isn't work, it's play—or are you making it seem like work?

What seems to me missing from Norman Brown is not only the idea of the Game but any concept of the paperness of our paper markets, what we all learned in basic economics as the multiplier. Grant all that compulsive work to make the compulsive money on a one-for-one basis, we slave one hour, we get one white chip for the Game. But three of us form a little company, create stock (paper), earn $50,000, and our public liquid market will give us not $50,000 but a million if we can convince it that the piece of paper is worth twenty times earnings. That is really effortless wealth, and we live in one of the only countries where this can be done.

Come to think of it, the Federal Reserve Board creates money all the time. It just waves its wand of bill purchases and sales, and presto, there is money where there was none before. This is called regulating the money supply, but it works exactly the same as printing bright new greenbacks, and the Fed doesn't even have to take the money from somewhere else in order to put that money into the banking system. On the other hand, maybe the members of the Federal Reserve Board feel guilty as hell.

So, in a logical sense, perhaps all these investors who come to the marketplace *not* to make money are free from the guilt and anxieties of money-making, and that's why they set out not to make money. No? I don't believe it either. If they were really free, they wouldn't have even shown up for the Game. Something else must be bugging them.

I suppose there does have to be a balance in time, so that we do not have, as Keynes said, quoting *Alice*, "a case of jam tomorrow and never jam today," or in Norman Brown's words, "the dynamics of capitalism is postponement of enjoyment to the constantly postponed future." And it is true that many of our most adept Game players never get around to spending the money they have made. But if they had escaped the guilt and tension necessary for the first white chip, they would never have had all the fun of the Game.

❁   ❁   ❁

The purposive investor

Do You Really Want to Be Rich?

The wheel is about to come full circle. We have seen some of the rules of the Game, and some of the players, and some of the reasons the players play. The reasons are not entirely, as we have seen, the ones we learn as catechism in the religion we grow up with, which is the sanctity of property. The most profound reason the players play is in the essence of capitalism, and we will get to it in one moment.

It is part of the ethos of this country that you *ought* to be rich. You ought to be, unless you have taken some specific vow of poverty such as the priesthood, scholarship, teaching, or civil service, because money is the way we keep score. This feeling has been a long time in the making. It goes away sometimes in depressions, when briefly wealth becomes suspect and poverty is not dishonorable. The rest of the time, poverty is very close to criminal. The worst crimes a man can commit, other than the crimes of violence which for one with property would have to be considered irrational, are crimes against capital. A man can break most of the Commandments with impunity, but please, let him not go bust, that will get him ostracized faster than lying, fudging on his income taxes, cheating, adultery, and coveting all the oxes and asses there are.

Duty calls

In times of prosperity, the old feeling that you ought to be rich is very much in the air, It is not new. In a previous period of prosperity, just before the turn of the century, one of the most popular lectures in the country was Russell Conwell's "Acres of Diamonds." Those diamonds were wealth in your own backyard, and "every good man and woman ought to strive for it," thundered Conwell. "I say, get rich! Get rich!" In the same era, William Graham Sumner, a famous professor of Yale, wrote: "There is no reason, at the moment, why every American may not acquire capital by being industrious, prudent, and frugal, and thus become rich." And Bishop Lawrence, the doyen of the Episcopal Church, really did say, "In the long run, it is only to the man of morality that wealth comes. Godliness is in league with riches. Material prosperity makes the national character sweeter, more Christlike." So it is no wonder that when John D. Rockefeller was asked how he came by his vast fortune, he answered, "God gave me my money."

If God is truly on the side of the biggest bank accounts, there will be some who will be offended by the very idea that the management of money is a Game, even though Game these days has been dignified by game theory, mathematics, and computeering. Money, they would say, is serious business, no laughing matter, and certainly nothing that should suggest sport, frolic, fun, and play. Yet it may be that the Game element in money is the most harmless of all the elements present. Is it always to be this way?

A man for all times

Let us go back to the Master who gave us the aphorism, John Maynard Keynes, Baron of Tilton, and leave aside his revolutionary doctrines. For our purposes Keynes is not the Master because he changed the course of economic history. He is the Master because he started with nothing, set out to become rich, did so, part time, from his bed, as a player in the Game, and having become rich, had some thoughts that must be integral to any study of the Game. For what follows, we must acknowledge Keynes' own *General Theory* and *Essays in Persuasion,* and also the stimulating works on Keynes of Sir Roy Harrod and Robert L. Heilbroner.

Even second hand, through his biographers, a certain *joie de vivre* emerges. (None of the biographers mention Keynes' subterranean relationship with Lytton Strachey, and perhaps his proclivities are as irrelevant here as the later uses made of his theories.) Here was an economist and a Cambridge don, yet a man in the center of the Bloomsbury set that included the lights of English art and letters, who married the leading ballerina of Diaghilev's company. At the same time he was the chairman of a life insurance company and the darling of the avant-garde. He disdained inside information. Every morning he gathered his income statements and balance sheets and phoned his orders, using only his own knowledge and intuition, and after his phone calls he was ready for the business of the day. He not only made himself several million dollars, but he became Bursar of Kings College in Cambridge and multiplied its endowment by a factor of ten.

He was a pillar of stability in delicate matters of international diplomacy, but his official correctness did not prevent him from acquiring knowledge of other European politicians that included their mistresses, neuroses, and financial prejudices. He collected modern art long before it was fashionable to do so, but at the same time he was a classicist with the finest private collection of Newton's writings in the world. He ran a theater, and he came to be a Director of the Bank of England. He knew Roosevelt and Churchill and also Bernard Shaw and Pablo Picasso. He played bridge like a speculator, preferring a spectacular

play to a sound contract, and solitaire like a statistician, noting how long it took for the game to come out twice running. And he once claimed that he had but one regret in life—he wished he had drunk more champagne.

(Mr. Heilbroner, who wrote that paragraph, is obviously another admirer.) And what did the Master think of the Game? All purposeful money-making impulses come from the thousands of years of economic scarcity. But wealth is not pursued solely as an answer to scarcity. "He that loveth silver shall not be satisfied with silver; nor he that loveth abundance with increase," wrote Koholeth, the Preacher, Ecclesiastes. What does the purposive investor seek? "Purposiveness," said Lord Keynes, "means that we are more concerned with the remote future results of our actions than with their own quality or their immediate effects on our own environment. The 'purposive' man is always trying to secure a spurious and delusive immortality for his acts by pushing his interest in them forward into time. He does not love his cat, but his cat's kittens; nor, in truth, the kittens, but only the kittens' kittens, and so on forward for ever to the end of catdom. For him jam is not jam unless it is a case of jam tomorrow and never jam today. Thus by pushing his jam always forward into the future, he strives to secure for his act of boiling it an immortality."

Touch wood

You know, in the end, that so deep-seated an impulse could not be merely the amusement that comes with a Game. The compounding of wealth, like the building of the City, is part of the much older game of life against death. The immortality is spurious because that particular wheel is fixed; you do have to lose in the end. That is the way the senior game is set up: You can't take it with you.

In a remarkably prophetic essay, "The Economic Possibilities for our Grandchildren," Keynes has some remarks that would seem to make him the king of the hippies, if hippies could read Keynes, the Master of the flower-children as well as of speculators. He said the problem of the future would be how to use the freedom from pressing economic cares "which science and compound interest will have won . . . to live wisely and agreeably and well." In this millennium, he wrote, "I see us free, therefore, to return to some of the most sure and certain principles of religion and traditional virtue—that avarice is a vice, that the exaction of usury is a misdemeanor, and the love of money is detestable—

that those walk most truly in the paths of virtue and sane wisdom who take least thought for the morrow. We shall once more value ends above means and prefer the good to the useful. We shall honour those who can teach us how to pluck the hour and the day virtuously and well, the delightful people who are capable of taking direct enjoyment in things, the lilies of the field who toil not, neither do they spin.

In this millennium, wealth will no longer be of social import, morals will change, and "we shall be able to rid ourselves of many of the pseudo-moral principles which have hag-ridden us for two hundred years, by which we have exalted some of the most distasteful of human qualities into the position of the highest virtues. We shall be able to afford to dare to assess the money-motive at its true value:

The love of money as a possession—as distinguished from love of money as a means to the enjoyments and realities of life—will be recognised for what it is, a somewhat disgusting morbidity, one of those semi-criminal, semi-pathological propensities which one hands over with a shudder to the specialists in mental disease.

There. Now that you know, do you really want to be rich?

Bon appetit!

In defense of the players, we must note that when Keynes had a heart attack in 1937, he gave up all of his activities but the editorship of the *Economic Journal*—and his daily half-hour of trading. He stayed a player.

"Beware!" he said, after his vision of the millennium. "The time for all this is not yet. For at least another hundred years we must pretend to ourselves and to every one that fair is foul and foul is fair; for foul is useful and fair is not. Avarice and usury and precaution must be our gods for a little longer still. For only they can lead us out of the tunnel of economic necessity into daylight."

Now that you know some of the things as they are and not as they ought to be, perhaps you will know whether to take the Game or leave it alone. You have to make your own choice, and there are many other and more productive outlets for time and energy.

Until daylight, I wish you the joys of the Game.

Business Organization and the Corporate Conscience

Readings 12, 13, and 14

The discussion a book evokes is sometimes as valuable as the work itself. And the second round of a debate may be more valuable than the first. Robert Solow, brilliant professor of economics at M.I.T. and one-time framer of the Kennedy New Frontier policies, wrote a brilliant critique of the *New Industrial State*. Professor John Kenneth Galbraith of Harvard wrote a brilliant reply. Brilliant salvos were going off all over the place. Then Robin Marris, Fellow of King's College, Cambridge, England, who has actually done serious research work on the motives and behavior of the modern corporation, joined in the debate. Reading 12 is his affirmation that Galbraith is on to something new and good; Reading 13 is Solow's evaluation of what Galbraith's contribution adds up to.

Instead of eavesdropping on scholars, let us turn (in Reading 14) to the businessman beast himself to hear what he says he is actually doing. Eli Goldston is a highly successful corporate executive, being President of Eastern Gas and Fuel Associates. Mr. Goldston also finds time to serve on many public-policy commissions and governmental advisory bodies. Thus he was on the Democratic Advisory Council set up by Senator Edward Kennedy in Massachusetts. When Goldston asserts that he and men like him in other large corporations are obsessed with maximizing their company per-share earnings and the future market value of the companies stock price, he is speaking from *inside* observation of the technostructure.

Questions to Guide the Reading

You and your parents buy Fords and Chevrolets, Ivory soap and Tide detergent, RCA and Zenith television sets. Looking back on last year's expenditures, are there any purchases you really regret? Which were merely the result of persuasive advertising and unconscious conditioning? Why did you not buy Edsels when you did buy Mustangs?

If Marris is right and managers become obsessed with the cancer of growth even at the expense of profits, how can we account for the fact that General Mills sold off its animal-food lines in order to conserve capital for more lucrative undertakings? If managers are absolute monarchs, why not dispense with dividends and grow even faster?

If Solow is right, could we get out of a depression by more advertising? Since successful long-run profit maximization will lead to growth in directions of greatest advantage, how can we differentiate such behavior from actions to maximize growth for its own sake?

We know that people often rationalize. Often too, they unconsciously distort reality in this process. On its own merits does the Goldston argument strike you as having the ring of truth or is it self-deception and propaganda?

Reading 12

Galbraith: *Oui*

Robin Marris

I have volunteered to intervene in the Solow-Galbraith controversy, which began in the Fall issue of this journal, because I have some doubts whether, at the end of the day, the lay reader was left clear about the basic issues.

It is true that Galbraith relies largely on assertion (or, shall we say, on persuasive writing) in contrast to large-scale evidence to make his case—especially his case about advertising. It is also true that, by a great deal of hard work and by painstaking development of mathematical and statistical methods, economists over the last twenty years have learned to work more scientifically. But, for reasons which seem to be as much cultural as technical, the leading exponents of the new methods have

chosen largely to confine themselves within the framework of the traditional assumptions. The form of their experiments has tended to preclude answering many of the questions here in debate. The influence of advertising, for example, has not been tested, but when the question arises it is customary to say that the traditional framework, now endowed with statistical flesh, provides a reasonable explanation of observed behavior, so that it is probably unnecessary to worry about Madison Avenue. If asked for a further opinion, exponents of this school usually themselves resort to assertions; specifically, they assert that the effects of large-scale advertising largely cancel themselves out, leaving the broad pattern of

From Robin Marris, "Galbraith, Solow, and the Truth about Corporations," *The Public Interest*, No. 11, Spring, 1968. Copyright © 1968 National Affairs, Inc. Reprinted with kind permission of the author and publisher.

consumer expenditure undisturbed. Solow's review of Galbraith followed this line of argument almost precisely.

If the great majority of applied economists in this country are really so sure that they already know the answer, i.e., they are sure that most advertising results in a stand-off, the profession has clearly been guilty of a grave dereliction of duty to the public. They should have been shouting loudly and with one voice, "Here is an activity that has no significant net economic effect, good or bad; it is a total waste; it should be prohibited like arson." The discussion would then be thrown back into the sociological arena. I personally regard the cultural effects of advertising as debasing to language, to truth, and to logic, and as especially despicable because advertising is known to be most effective where the consumer has the least capacity to obtain the information necessary to evaluate products. There are sociologists who argue that the modern style of advertising (especially television) has a function in integrating the working class into the mass society and that the less well-educated obtain satisfaction from being wooed by advertisers. It is true that it is mostly the educated who scoff at advertising. We know from British experience that the working class positively prefers commercial programs and that BBC's audience is largely confined to the better educated. On the other hand, one has to count the cost of the recent effects in the United States of parading television commercials before people living in squalid conditions who can see no hope of buying many of the goods displayed. These are sorts of questions which economists have not equipped themselves to judge, and here I would align myself with Galbraith (in his rejoinder) in a plea for the broadening of both economics and sociology.

The myth of "consumers' sovereignty"

This said, I must confess that the picture which, in my book, I drew in support of my own theory was more complex than Galbraith's and put considerably less emphasis on the effects of advertising as such. The picture was not strictly confirmed by "hard" evidence, although it is considerably supported by evidence drawn from the work of sociologists and market researchers. I saw the process by which consumer tastes develop as a complicated interaction of personal influence (meaning the influence of consumers on other consumers), greatly helped at critical points by advertising and marketing efforts generally. Sociologists have shown, in rather carefully designed experiments, that consumption decisions are effectively influenced, on the one hand, by a variety of advertising media and, on the other, by the recommendations of other persons known to the individual consumer. Each factor—advertising and personal recommendation—is responsible, very broadly, for about an equal share of the total result. The experiments cannot contribute directly to the present controversy, because they relate to decisions between alternative brands of the same product at given prices; but they remain suggestive.

The implications for the "affluent society" thesis, and for economic theory, are also clear. A complex, dynamic, socio-economic system of this kind must be considered to be something like a biological phenomenon. Chance constellations of small individual factors at a particular time can have a considerable influence on the future direction of a plant's development. The needs, interests, and performance of producers are a particularly potent example of such influence, and one way of reading Galbraith is to take "advertising" as a portmanteau word for all these kinds of effects. In any event, once we accept this kind of picture, the notion of "consumers' sovereignty" becomes vague, to say the least, and we are provided with a virtually complete justification for a wide range of political action to impose social value judgments in the direction of consumption patterns. Here, quite likely, Solow would want to raise his hand and say, "I do not disagree." But the fact remains that the notion of consumers' sovereignty, essentially an *economic* theory, retains very considerable political force in defense of the status quo. Anyone who doubts the close political relationship should take a look at an advertisement in the January 1968 issue of *Fortune* magazine, paid for by the Magazine Publishers' Association. This advertisement pointed to the alleged relative economic failure of East Germany, as compared with West Germany, in a defense of the activity of United States mass media in fostering demand for a wide range of, and variety among, individual consumers' goods (using the example of stuffed olives). A dramatic juxtaposition of a representation of the Berlin Wall was clearly intended to create a mental association between political repression and government intervention in the pattern of consumption.

The large corporation

The other basic issue between Galbraith and Solow concerned the role of the large corporations. Of course it is true that important sectors of the American economy are still traditionally organized. Supermarkets were an important social innovation, and still more important was the discovery that they can be operated successfully by quite small businesses. But does Solow or anyone else *really* believe that these small-business sectors have a significant influence on the speed and pattern of economic development? The drive of our system comes manifestly from the large-scale sector, now increasingly including the government as well as the large "profit-making" corporations.

And there is a major exception that marvelously tests the rule. The temporary visitor to this country cannot help being impressed by the apparently general dissatisfaction with the economic and social performance in the field of urban development, dissatisfaction which ranges from the fact of the existence of slums (and the associated difficulty in providing low-cost housing) to the more general question of the adequacy of city planning, the development of the suburbs, and so on. From overseas, the United States appears so prosperous that the "urban" problem is widely assumed to be no more than a euphemism for the race problem. But is it a coincidence that the production sector must closely concerned (namely the construction industries and the real estate business) happens to represent the most prominent exception to the rule of "managerial" capitalism? In this sector, medium-scale organization is typical, and large-scale organizations are usually owned by traditional capitalists. In particular, the free market in urban land (which is at the bed of this whole sea of troubles) displays one of the purest forms of traditional capitalism still surviving. And the cream of the joke is that most qualified observers of the scene other than economists are asking that the great managerial corporations come to the rescue.

Galbraith, on the other hand, thinks that the "Technostructure" cannot or will not undertake the task, because its performance would lack technical virtuosity. I am not convinced. Although put across with characteristic force, the argument is not in fact very strong. There is not firm evidence that, if money were provided for massive urban projects on a scale comparable with current military and space programs, opportunities for exercising technical virtuosity would not be found or would be rejected, especially if the new programs made liberal use of such labels as "Componentization Research" and "Systems Analysis." Galbraith's later argument (in his chapter on the Cold War), that one reason why this kind of money is not in practice available is the indirect political (and indirectly bellicose) influence of the existing Technostructure, is much more convincing, but was not referred to by Solow.

The real world of the firm

When we reach the core of the debate—i.e., the economic theory of corporate behavior—the truth is that Solow was disingenuous, but that Galbraith had left out vital elements and laid himself open to legitimate attack. What Solow omitted to tell was that my theory implies that *in spite* of the existence of "an important discipline in the capital market," the real-world system almost certainly behaves very differently from the way implied in the conventional theory: the conventional theory would imply that corporations would choose to grow considerably more slowly and reward stockholders significantly better. Galbraith, however, in failing to meet the argument that profits are needed for growth, failed to explain how this divergence can occur. In offering to put the record straight, I am motivated not only by vanity, but also by the conviction that an accurate theory about corporate growth is essential for a correct understanding of a wide range of contemporary problems of economic and social policy. The theory cannot be made simple, but can be summarized as follows.

A growing corporation faces two problems: the problem of creating a growing demand for its products, and the problem of financing the necessary growth of capacity. The corporation may strive to be as efficient as possible, in the sense of squeezing the maximum profit from its existing markets; but the search for (or creation of) *new* markets inevitably costs money (in research, marketing, and losses from failures), and so, as the growth process is accelerated, the average return realized on the *total* assets of the corporation must be *adversely* affected (even if the development expenditure is deployed as efficiently as possible).

Profits and/or growth

A decision by the management to grow at a certain rate, and to choose the consistent retention ratio, must also evidently imply a unique level and expected rate of growth of the dividend; and so, in a rational stock market, the decision must imply a unique current price and prospective capital gain in the corporation's stock. Up to a point, actual or potential stockholders may be content to see increased growth creating prospects of future gain at the expense of current dividends; beyond this point, any further increase in the growth rate chosen by the management must have a depressing effect on the stock price. There is no reason to suppose that a growth-oriented management will always refrain from accelerating beyond this point; and if they go too far they will undoubtedly lay themselves open to a variety of dangers (e.g., a take-over raid). I suggested in my theory that we might describe a typical "managerial" objective as maximum growth subject to a *minimum* on the stock price.

Solow said that my theory, in recognizing the minimum stock-price constraint, "came closer to the conventional view." On the contrary, in the conventional view management exists only to serve stockholders, and the essential technical problem is to find decision rules that would establish the policy which will, in fact, *maximize* the price of the stock. The two theories become "similar" only in the special conditions where the minimum and maximum position lie close together. These conditions are most improbable; in other words, the traditional theory is literally a "special case."

Because large-scale, professional management, not personally owning large supplies of finance, has such predominant technical ad-

vantages in the modern economy; because, although it may *use* stockmarket investors and bankers, it no longer *depends* on them; because the (not insubstantial) true capitalists who remain in our system avoid speculating in large manufacturing businesses unless these are going very cheap (they prefer real estate); because the other potential take-over raiders are typically themselves management-controlled—because of all this and much more, it is inevitable that the safe minimum level of the price of a corporation's stock will be significantly lower, and the safe maximum growth rate correspondingly higher, than the values which would be chosen by a management that really did care only for the welfare of the stockholders. Numerical calculations based on statistical observation suggest that a rather growth-conscious management could typically grow almost twice as fast, setting the stock market value at all times about one-third lower, as compared to the values which would be obtained in an otherwise comparable corporation dominated by stockholders who knew all the facts. Furthermore, the growth-oriented management could safely continue the policy indefinitely, even if there were quite a number of others who chose to behave otherwise. Since the growth-oriented managements will by definition be located in the faster growing corporations, this type of behavior must in time drive out other types—a process which, I suggest, has been going on for some time. The further the process goes, the weaker is the power of the stock market to resist. Since the growth-oriented firms are technically efficient, they display not unattractive levels and growth rates of dividends, the incentive to resistance is dampened, and the latent preference for slower growth and higher current dividends remains unrecognized.

Furthermore, because managements, in fostering growth, also create technical progress, new wants, new goods, and a generally different dynamic environment, the implications of the two types of theory cannot easily be compared. We cannot possibly assert that it would necessarily be in the public interest to compel managements to conform to the traditional norm; we might very likely make many people worse off and few better off. Galbraith, however, imposed the value judgment (the "affluent-society" thesis) that the higher rate of consumer innovation resulting from "managerial" behavior by the corporations is undesirable, because it is biased against the expression of leisure preferences and against the development of "public" goods. He does not, however (as maybe does Solow in saying "it might perhaps be better if companies were forced more often into the capital market") suggest that the remedies lie in the direction of the traditional model.

The conclusion I draw (and it is an implication which I suspect to be one of the causes of the considerable ideological drive of "neoclassical" economics in the United States) would probably be disliked by both parties: namely, that once the classical idealization of capitalism is thus destroyed, there is no *economic* case for its superiority over socialism. Consequently, the attempt to impose capitalism all around the world, in some cases virtually by force, can only be justified on political grounds. The latter, however, seem to get thinner every day. In the miserable developing countries of the "free" world, where we cheerfully give aid to almost any form of dictatorship provided no industries are nationalized (the case of Tito being a historical freak, much disliked by the Congress, I understand), there is no dearth of greedy *profit* maximizers, many living in considerable luxury. What the non-affluent majority of the world's population so badly needs is a much greater number of *growth* maximizers.

The need for "restructuring"

More domestic and less inflammatory implications of the truth about the corporations are varied and pervasive. I will conclude with an example which may be of some topical interest. Suppose it is desired to get the corporations interested in replacing slums with wholesome low-rental dwellings, and suppose that the political conditions for the necessary diversion of national resources have already been created. Suppose federal contracts provide a massive injection of technical stimulus into the construction sector. We would still face the difficulty that low-income housing is an unprofitable line of business. This keeps out the traditionally motivated corporation and also discourages the growth-motivated corporation,

because it means growing in directions that offer a particularly unfavorable relationship between growth and profitability, and consequently, means low "equilibrium" rates of growth in accordance with the theory. Under present conditions, therefore, a growth-oriented management undertaking these desirable activities *will be penalized in terms of its own motives*—a point which, once seen, appears rather obvious, but is not in fact generally well understood, and seems to have been missed by Galbraith.

Solow and many of his colleagues would then say, of course, that here is a perfect example of the traditional assumptions being good enough for policy purposes. On the contrary, it provides an excellent example of the serious practical errors which can result from that attitude. Suppose a certain senator, who may be nameless, proposes a scheme of tax credits to firms which will undertake socially oriented urban renewal projects. On the traditional assumptions, the function of the subsidy is simply to compensate stockholders for a reduced pre-tax rate of return. In my kind of model, the function is to compensate the management for lost growth-opportunity by offsetting the reduction in cash flow. If we follow this through, we will find that the size of the tax credit needed to obtain a given amount of housing would be substantially smaller, and the general political appeal of the project consequently more attractive.

Finally, I would suggest, if we were to "restructure" our economic system so that the units of production were endowed with the social norm of growth maximization (subject to financial constraints), and were freed from the embarrassments of stockholders and other trappings of private property, manipulation of the financial rules to offset various kinds of built-in bias, and generally to foster a good society, would be much easier. We would be freed from the inhibitions and costs resulting from our archaic but powerful custom of assigning a private owner or part owner to most of our means of production. We should be able to concentrate on the task of finding the most efficient ways of organizing all the things we want to do, and to stop wasting our time discussing whether the old corporations did, or were supposed to, "maximize profits." But that is a longer story.

Reading 13

Galbraith: *Non*

Robert M. Solow

Marris comments at length on the influence of advertising in the management of consumer demand, and on the theory of corporate behavior. On the first, he does not endorse Galbraith's view of the utter helplessness of the consumer, but he does agree that the success of salesmanship undermines conventional presumptions about the beneficence of market processes. On the second, he presents a theory which corresponds roughly with Galbraith's more impressionistic sketch, but which, because of its greater precision, offers less freedom to draw picturesque implications. I shall say a word about each subject.

On advertising

Here one must be clear what the question is. No one who believes, as I do, that profit is an important business motive could argue that advertising has no influence on the willingness of consumers to buy a given product at a given price. After all, how could I then account for the fact that profit-seeking corporations regularly spend billions of dollars on advertising? Nor did I exactly "resort to assertion." What I said was: "I have no great confidence in my own casual observations either. But I should think a case could be made that much advertising serves only to cancel other advertising, and is therefore merely wasteful." I should think it obvious that this almost *has* to be true—i.e., that much advertising merely cancels other advertising—for otherwise there would be nothing to stop both the cigarette industry and the detergent industry from expanding their sales to their hearts' desire and to the limits of consumers' capacity to carry debt. And what would stop each individual manufacturer of cigarettes and detergents from doing the same?

No, that is hardly the issue. I have no wish to deny that an individual seller can shift the relation between his sales and the price he charges by incurring advertising or other sell-

ing costs. There is even a lot of conventional theory about that. It is important that the evidence Marris cites relates, as he admits, to consumers' "decisions between alternative brands of the same product at given prices." I suppose, on common sense grounds, that it must be relatively easy to affect such decisions by advertising. That is why essentially all tobacco companies advertise—because each is forced to offset the advertising of any one of their number, or lose sales. It must be harder to influence the consumer's choice between purchases of cigarettes and purchases of beer, and much harder still to influence his distribution of expenditures among such broad categories as food, clothing, automobiles, housing. It is open to legitimate doubt that advertising has any detectable effect at all on the sum total of consumer spending or, in other words, on the choice between spending and saving.

My remarks were directed primarily to this last proposition. I wanted to show how shaky the foundations are for the naïve belief that not only the fortunes of individual companies, but also the viability of capitalism, rests on the success of the Madison Avenue shock troops, because without them the flow of consumer spending would dry up.

I suspect Marris would agree with me on this point. He goes on to ask why, if much advertising is merely wasteful, economists are not in favor of prohibiting it. Well, as a principle, that does seem to border on the tyrannical. But it has sometimes occurred to me that there might be some point in taxing advertising expenditure, and I gather from conversation with other economists that they have had the same thought. If we do not push it very hard, that is perhaps because up to now there have been more important causes to promote, with a considerably greater chance of success.

That leaves the difficult question of the status of the notion of consumers' sovereignty. Once sellers of commodities can influence, even if not control, consumers' preferences among commodities, it becomes a much less persuasive defense of laissez-faire to say that the system caters to consumers' preferences. Since I am not much of a believer in laissez-faire anyway, that doesn't disturb me. But I am not, for a number of reasons, prepared to accept Marris' leap to apparently wholesale political steering of the direction of consumption. In the first place, to the extent that competition induces sellers to offset one another's advertising campaigns, the seriousness of the problem is tempered and we are back again to waste (and the possibility of taxation as a remedy). Second, there is already piecemeal political intervention in the direction of consumption, beginning with pure-food-and-drug legislation, the mild policing of deception in labeling and advertising, and the various other consumer-protection laws recently proposed or enacted. There would seem to be plenty of room for strengthening and extending such devices. Moreover, just because the formation of consumer preferences is inescapably a social process, it is not clear by what standard Marris' proposal is superior to what we have now. Indeed, "collective political action . . . to steer the direction of consumption" might simply centralize taste-making powers in the hands of a government certainly more powerful and probably more nearly monolithic than even the world of large corporations. I am not sure I want exclusive access to the formation of my tastes to rest with the government of an Eisenhower or a Johnson (or a Douglas-Home or a Wilson). Probably neither does Marris, and in practice we might accept the same sort of policies.

On corporate behavior

Marris has summarized, with quite wonderful economy, his own theory of corporate behavior. It is a self-contained determinate theory, with implications that are testable at least in principle. Like any theory, this one raises two questions. Does it tell a true story? And, if it does, what are its larger implications about economic life?

As I mentioned in my review of Galbraith, it is not easy to invent a clear-cut statistical test of the Marris theory of corporate growth against the more standard model of long-run profit maximization anchored by a target rate

of return. I suggested that this is because the two theories do not have drastically different implications. Marris objects; like any student of advertising, he would like to stress the differences between his own product and Brand X. I should have been more precise. The two theories need not have very different implications, but they may. Whether they do depends on the height of the minimum acceptable-rate-of-return (or stock price) in Marris' model. The higher it is, or the closer to the target rate of return, the more similar a Marris economy will be to mine. I am uncertain about the source of Marris' conviction that the differences are in fact large, since so far as I know his theory has not yet been given a large-scale run against the facts. One would like to know, for example, how well it does as a predictor of plant and equipment spending.

In the meanwhile, we are reduced to casual empiricism about the assumptions and implications of the Marris theory. This is hardly the place to discuss the matter in detail. I will simply say that the theory, interesting and attractive as it is, seems to me to rest on two fairly weak assumptions. The first is that for a given corporation in a given environment there must be a well-defined relation between its rate of growth (of output) and its rate of return on capital, independent of the absolute size of the corporation. It is not enough for the theory that, with everything else momentarily given, a corporation's profitability should depend on how rapidly it is trying to expand its sales and its capacity. What is required is that this relation hold for long intervals of time during which the corporation is actually growing. Both at the beginning of the period, when the company is small, and at the end, when it is large, it has to be true that to a particular, more or less steady rate of growth of x per cent a year corresponds the same more or less steady rate of profit of y per cent a year. This is not outlandish, but I think the assumption rests on too simple a view of the business of sales promotion, and on insufficient attention to the production-cost side of the problem.

The second dubious assumption is the one that names growth of sales as the prime object of the corporation. Marris does not simply assert this; he argues it with care and sociological circumstance in his book. He gives two versions: a management may "choose to go for a certain growth rate," or else it may seek "maximum growth subject to a minimum on the stock price." In a more technical statement of the theory he can allow profits and growth to be two separate objectives which have to be weighed against each other. The more weight a corporation attaches to profits and the less to growth, the more nearly it will behave according to the conventional theory.

There is certainly a lot of talk in the business press about growth and expansion. But this, by itself, is hardly support for the Marris-Galbraith doctrine. In the first place, the alternative theory—that corporations maximize long-run profits more or less, and expand whenever they earn more than a target rate of return—also entails that successful companies will be growing most of the time, and will no doubt be talking about it. In the second place, one must keep in mind that the federal government taxes long-term capital gains only half as heavily as dividends, and under some circumstances considerably less than that. Retention and reinvestment of earnings—i.e., internally financed growth—is the obvious way for a corporation to convert dividends into capital gains for its shareholders, including its officers. So devotion to growth is quite consistent with profit-maximization if profit is interpreted as the after-tax return to the stockholder.

Theories that emphasize the separation of ownership and control tend to ignore the fact that, if the common stockholder cannot control the policy of the corporation he owns, he can arrange to own a different corporation by merely telephoning his broker. He can even buy shares in a mutual fund that will tailor a portfolio to his expressed preferences between current dividends and capital gains. Indeed, such theories generally tend to ignore the large-scale institutional investors, whose presence on the other side of the market makes the balance of power between management and owner look a little different.

This would seem to be important, even within the framework of Marris' theory. He admits that some corporations can be more growth-oriented and less profit-oriented than others. If any substantial number of stockholders strongly favors immediate profits over growth, their demands can be mobilized by institutional investors. Corporate managements are sure to be found or created who will be prepared to get their kicks by catering to these demands.

I realize that these casual remarks about the plausibility of assumptions can never be decisive. For that we will have to wait for serious empirical testing. And if I am right that the two theories could turn out to have similar implications, we may have to wait even longer —but of course it will matter less. By the way, Marris' discussion of the problem of getting private firms interested in the construction of low-rent housing seems to me to favor my view of the matter at least as much as it does his. It turns out that low-income housing is now an unattractive business to be in, on the assumptions of either theory. When you get right down to the nitty-gritty, the difference is merely the size of the subsidy needed to obtain a given amount of housing, and there is probably room for more than one opinion about that, too.

On ideology

Marris considers his theory to be subversive of the existing order. Since the consumer is presumably manipulated and the stockholder presumably ignored, no intellectual case remains for capitalism as an efficient economic system. Even leaving aside the question whether this argument applies to the regulated mixed economy of today, it is the damnedest argument for socialism I ever heard. Who would storm the Winter Palace so that units of production could be "endowed with the social norm of growth maximization (subject to financial constraints)" even if "manipulation of the financial rules to offset various kinds of built-in bias . . . would be much easier"?

Marris also suspects that only an ideological drive can explain the persistence with which economists in the United States cling to some (incomplete) confidence in market mechanisms. I would not deny that some academic disputes have a genuine ideological content. But I would also assert that there is far less ideology wrapped up in academic economics in the United States than a man from Cambridge, England, can possibly realize. (One of Cambridge's most distinguished economists, with whom I had been carrying on a rather abstract controversy, once said to me at a party: "You're not a reactionary; so why don't you agree with me?" I thought it was a good question.) In fact, I don't think that my argument with Galbraith and Marris is really ideological in character. My own view is that any economic system can be made to work, if you go at it cleverly. But to do that, you have to get the analysis right. If Marris' theory of the firm turns out to work beter, which is conceivable, I will buy it cheerfully.

Reading 14

The Real Truth about Profit Maximizing

Eli Goldston

Net profit per share is more important to professional managers than many current theorists assume. Observations about business by one immersed in it may lack the breadth and depth of a scholarly inquiry and, above all, its historical perspective. But without endorsing the discredited barnyard aphorism that only a hen can judge a good egg, perhaps an active businessman can add some new knowledge of business to what is usually reported by academic observers.

My comments will apply principally to *big* business—business with substantial *public stock ownership.* Small, proprietary businesses are an important element in the American economy, but they are not likely to be significant in changing the way business generally participates in major social problems. I believe my observations should, however, be pertinent over quite a range of business sizes. Just as styles and manners tend to drift out from Cafe Society or the Jet Set through society columns, so the structure, staffing, procedures, and objectives of *Fortune*'s 500 Largest Industrials spread through the business press to the rest of business. A wise government will make use of this "trickle-down" theory and try first to get the business "influentials" or "opinion leaders" to accept new programs.

Big business firms today often differ from the customary descriptions of American corporate enterprise in a number of ways: ownership, structure, exposure, motivation and measurement, character of decision-makers, objectives, and product. I will emphasize the factors that make for greater participation by private firms in solving social problems.

Characteristics of contemporary American business

Ownership. The degree of *separation between owners and managers* of modern big business has been overstated. So has the alleged ability of incompetent or unaggressive management to survive and even to perpetuate itself by selecting its successors. The number of shareholders in United States corporations has risen from about 6.5 million to over 24 million during the past fifteen years. Those economists who feel that a corporate manager can turn his back on stock prices and no longer feel any real pressure for earnings performance should try coming home to find that the cleaning woman who owns ten shares of his company's stock wants to know if she should buy more. They should try going to a cocktail party that develops into an impromptu shareholders' meeting or attending a dinner party where the hostess has the cleaning woman's question—except that, in addition, she plans to report on the stock to her investment club.

The firms where unaggressive management can relax are typically ones where a founding family is still powerful enough to keep control and affluent enough not to press for profit maximization. Except in such firms, ownership is proving to be an increasingly strong influence on management. Repeated successes in unseating poor managements by "takeovers," "overhead tenders," and "forced mergers" have demonstrated that the owners of a contemporary American business more often than not insist on and can demand growing profits. "Performance-minded" investment trusts have

From Eli Goldston, "New Prospects for American Business," *Daedalus,* Journal of the American Academy of Arts and Sciences, Winter, 1969. Reprinted with kind permission of the author and publisher.

speeded the process, for they no longer automatically vote with incumbent management or sell off their stock. Instead they look for, follow, and even back "raiders" in undervalued situations, convinced that nothing can be bought so cheap as a company under poor management about to be replaced.

Banks are still occasionally reluctant to finance "overhead tenders," but they have raised their sights from the days when it was assumed that about $500,000 for expenses and $50,000,000 in capital was the absolute maximum a "raider" could raise. Managements are no longer safe behind these financial limitations, as witness the takeover of United Gas by Pennzoil in 1966 largely by the use of bank loans. United Gas management, owning 3.3 per cent of a market equity of $442 million, was not safe.

Both the number and value of tender offers have increased spectacularly. In 1960, there were 25 tender offers with a total value of $186 million. By 1965, there were 75 with a total value of $951 million, and 1967 went well over the $1 billion mark. In the first six months of 1968, the 1967 total was exceeded. Not only shareholders, but institutional lenders and public creditors are intent on profitable performance, and they may bring quiet but considerable pressure, the existence or true nature of which is seldom publicly revealed. Those economists who believe that size and inertia provide a safe moat for an incompetent but incumbent management should follow Hodson's "Beauties Between the Balance Sheets" or *Finance Magazine*'s "Wolves of Wall Street," which list companies selling below break-up value. Watching the names of the listed firms disappear suggests that the moat is loaded with amphibian sharks who are not above crawling out to devour those they are intended to defend.

Structure. The degree to which large enterprises can once again be personally directed is not yet fully appreciated. With modern technology, a business enterprise can truly be the shadow of one man. Communication is instant, so rapidly improved that it is difficult to realize that as recently as 1929 even the President of the United States did not have a telephone in his office. Personal transportation makes it possible for any executive group to be assem-

bled anywhere in the world within forty-eight hours. Data-handling technology applied to budgeting, forecasting, accounting by profit centers, and control by variances brings small and early deviations quickly to the attention of top management. The applications of business simulation with third-generation *computers permit the choice of policies to be isolated in a small top-management group working on long-range planning and leaving operations to carefully watched line managers.* The clearer separation between policy and operations permits the elimination of vast clerical staffs and the accompanying middle management, making the corporate apparatus more responsive and personalized. This separation also heightens concern with profit in both policy and operating decision-making; objectives and reasons for decisions cannot remain fuzzy under modern procedures.

Exposure. Greater disclosure requirements by the S.E.C., the growth of security analysis as a profession, and broader public stock ownership have combined since World War II to create what many corporate managements regard as well-nigh indecent exposure. Also of importance have been continuous expansion of commonly accepted accounting principles, increasing detail of reports to regulatory authorities, and the stock exchange dictum: "If in doubt, announce it." Together these forces have released an unprecedented flow of business data, all making up the *public performance scoreboard.*

Security analysts of brokerage firms, institutions, and mutual funds hammer on the doors of management requesting interviews and pressing invitations to speak at their weekly meetings in forty-one cities. Since 1948, the number of security analysts has increased from 1,600 to 11,000, so that there are almost five full-time students for each of the 2,296 companies listed on all United States exchanges. Their findings appear in *The Wall Street Transcript,* a trade publication whose circulation has gone from 500 in 1963 to 7,500 in 1967, and their judgments are summarized in the *Wall Street Journal,* whose circulation has increased from 56,500 in 1945 to over 1 million today. The number of "owners" has also soared, which greatly increases the attention given to all these materials. No manager can publish a report bare of progress and can assume that he is sunning on an isolated beach where his nakedness will be unnoticed.

Motivation and measurement As management feels ownership influence more and more and as its exposure increases, it will be even more concerned with the public scoreboard that records the market value of stock and the price-earnings ratio. This will be reinforced by the trend to greater stock ownership among managers themselves. Managers have become owners in varying degrees—to some extent by ordinary purchases, but more often through stock options granted as a performance incentive. At present, 860 companies listed on the New York Stock Exchange (two thirds of the total) have stock option plans. A recent study indicates that within this group the median number of shares authorized under the plans equals nearly 3 per cent of the outstanding stock. Although this a modest percentage of the total market equity of a company, it usually represents a substantial percentage of the total net worth of management.

For the new manager, the lure of personal financial gain is thus linked to that of publicized good performance; he seeks good results for reasons both of personal gain and of team pride. He realizes a significant part of his compensation through market appreciation and therefore tends to appraise his own performance, even if his functions are non-financial, by the stock exchange scoreboard that operates from 10:00 A.M. to 3:30 P.M. each market day and displays the market opinion of the management team to which he belongs. One should think of big business in the United States as something like a highly competitive professional sport in which the players have intertwined desires for greater personal wealth and for team victory. The teams are organized and guided by coaches who, like athletic coaches, must be smart enough to understand the management of people and the changing rules of a complex game, but also simple-minded enough to regard winning as being terribly important. Government planners might usefully study American professional baseball players.

Character of the decision-makers. Today's typical top-management decision-maker has had advanced professional business education after an A.B. in economics, engineering, or accounting. He is pragmatic and goal-oriented to earnings per share, but he also shares the middle-class American notions of team competition, fair play, observance of the rules of the game, rewards calibrated to results (with some modest recognition of length of service), and the ability of the individual to make himself into pretty much what he wishes. He has a stern regard for honesty and for the importance of paying one's own way. He looks on taxes as an expense and would no sooner think of cheating on them than of cheating a supplier or customer. But he considers taxes an important and controllable expense and is interested in *exploiting all proper allowances, deductions, and exemptions.* This well-trained, law-abiding, profit-motivated entrepreneurial administrator, fully in command of his own operations, can easily be guided by a government that understands him and the game he is playing.

The memory of the electric equipment price fixing case and of General Motors' clash with Ralph Nader is too recent for me to suggest that all professional managers fit this description. But such incidents, which put the machinery of business decision into an opaque box for idealistic bright college graduates, are less likely to happen when some of these young men, with a fresh concept of the role of business in society, mature into top business leadership. I am not suggesting that violations of law or morality will cease or that private enterprise can be moved by social concern to do the uneconomic. Nor will business decisions be based upon uncertain and unquantifiable concerns about the impact of a general urban crisis on a particular firm. But an atmosphere of understanding and commitment can be developed so that reasonable incentives will work.

Summary

With the clear focus of business on a public scoreboard where growth in earnings per share is the major criterion, it is easy to understand that earnings growth has become the consuming objective of American business.

Readings 15 and 16

Critics have damned historic capitalism as being heartless and indifferent to human welfare and suffering. Careful study of the actual operations of competitive markets revealed to economic experts that human welfare in a market system is not necessarily dependent upon the altruistic motivations of businessmen and laborers. Today, however, we live in a mixed economy, not in historic capitalism. And it is persuasively argued by many thinkers that the modern large corporation has developed a soul and a social conscience.

In Reading 15 a brilliant economic analyst and polemicist of the "Chicago" free-market school pooh-poohs the notion that the system relies on, or should rely on, social motivations of even the largest corporations. In Reading 16 a distinguished libertarian philosopher criticizes Galbraith from the right. It is the following Gailbraith views that are criticized by Friedrich Hayek.

Galbraith believes there is a ". . . disparity between our flow of private and public goods and services. . . . The family which takes its mauve and cerise, air-conditioned, power-steered, and power-braked automobile out for a tour, passes through cities that are badly paved, made hideous by litter, blighted buildings, billboards, ... They pass on into a countryside that has been rendered largely invisible by commercial art." He goes on to argue that an increase in private output creates a technological need for complementary public goods—more autos requiring more and better roads; more private goods creating more trash and garbage that must be publicly carried away. In the absence of more public expenditure on police and parks, ". . . comic books, alcohol, narcotics, and switch-blade knives . . ." abound. ". . . in an atmosphere of private opulence and public squalor, the private goods have full sway. . . . An austere community is free from temptation. It can be austere in its public services. Not so a rich one."

He goes on to put forward a more positive case for public services. "By failing to exploit the opportunity to expand public production we are missing opportunities for enjoyment. . . . A community can be as well rewarded by buying better schools or better parks as by buying bigger automobiles. By concentrating on the latter rather than the former, it is failing to maximize its satisfactions." Galbraith does not agree that if a community seems to be making the decisions he criticizes, it is after all getting what it really wants. Galbraith believes that such arguments ignore the crucially important "dependence effect." Here, in a few words (from his pages 204–205), is the nucleus of his argument.

The conventional wisdom holds that the community, large or small, makes a decision as to how much it will devote to its public services. This decision is arrived at by democratic process. . . .

It will be obvious, however, that this view depends on the notion of independently determined consumer wants. In such a world one could with some reason defend the doctrine that the consumer, as a voter, makes an independent choice between public and private goods. But given the dependence effect—given that consumer wants are created by the process by which they are satisfied—the consumer makes no such choice. He is subject to the forces of advertising and emulation by which production creates its own demand. Advertising operates exclusively, and emulation mainly, on behalf of privately produced goods and services. Since management and emulative effects operate on behalf of private production, public services will have an inherent tendency to lag behind.

Jack Hirshleifer is professor of economics at the University of California at Los Angeles. Friedrich Hayek, Austrian economist, economic libertarian, and author of the widely read *Road to Serfdom*, has been professor at the London School of Economics, the University of Chicago, and the University of Freiburg. He questions the idea that just because a want is socially fabricated it can properly be discounted.

Questions to Guide the Reading

Adam Smith said that if people pursued their self-interest in competitive markets, they would be led—as if by an "Invisible Hand"—to secure the maximum of social well-being. Do you think this holds true, with respect to free enterprise in heroin? Advertising expenditures on or off Madison Avenue? Farm production? Sweat-shop labor? How important is the assumption of "perfection of competition"?

Could Hirshleifer be correct about the limited freedom of a small-scale competitor and yet be wrong about the 100 largest corporations? What would happen if a Christ-like altruist became head of a large corporation? Could he change the system?

How do you think a tough Chicago-school writer like Hayek would react to the readings advocating black capitalism and reliance on the large corporations to solve urban and other public problems?

Are people with higher private incomes happier? Do most Americans already have the comfortable income of, say, a Harvard professor? If TV advertising makes us unhappy with our lot and envious of the Joneses' down the street, can the money spent by people really measure their true psychic contentments and well-being?

If our cars are wide and our roads narrow, and if our rivers and atmospheres are polluted and contaminated, may not there be an imbalance of resource use even if the "Dependence-Effect" argument is rejected?

Reading 15

Capitalist Ethics—Tough or Soft?

Jack Hirshleifer

> I have never known much good done by those who affected to trade for the public good. It is an affectation, indeed, not very common among merchants, and very few words need be employed in dissuading them from it.

> Sometimes it is said that man cannot be trusted with the government of himself. Can he, then, be trusted with the government of others?

Few world outlooks have been responsible for greater social mischief than the ideology or social philosophy which might be called "sentimental socialism"—the cluster of ideas centering upon a contrast between the evil capitalist ethic and its supposedly superior socialist counterpart. Sentimental socialists maintain, for one thing, that, since the system of private enterprise for profit rewards pursuit of self-interest, it cannot serve the general interest.

From Jack Hirshleifer, "Capitalist Ethics—Tough or Soft?," *The Journal of Law and Economics*, October, 1959, The University of Chicago Law School. Reprinted with kind permission of the author and publisher.

Consequently, a system banning selfish private enterprise for profit is bound to encourage economic activity in the public interest in the place of the proscribed private interest.

What is sentimental here is the belief that a change in social organization is all that is required to abolish human selfishness. As Mr. Dooley said, "A man that'd expect to train lobsters to fly in a year is called a lunatic; but a man that thinks men can be turned into angels by an election is called a reformer and remains at large." Among sentimental socialists are such disparate modern thinkers as Albert Einstein, Jawaharlal Nehru, and R. H. Tawney. Sentimental or "soft" socialism has an extraordinary appeal to gentle physicists, non-materialistic statesmen, Unitarian ministers, and social workers—to mention just a few vulnerable categories. By way of contrast, it is worth mentioning that Karl Marx was primarily a realistic or "tough" socialist. He despised the Utopians with their proposed ethical reconstitutions of society. Basically, Marx understood both capitalism and socialism as systems of power relations developing out of an ineluctable historical process.

Proponents of capitalism have often, on varying grounds, attacked the beautiful image of beneficent socialism as a false picture. Alternatively, there have been attempts to construct an ideology of capitalism which will be less vulnerable to socialist criticism.

When business preaches

Such an attempt appears in a recent article by James C. Worthy, a vice-president of a leading American corporation, entitled "Religion and Its Role in the World of Business."[1] "Soft socialism" regards the business system as convicted of encouraging selfishness and, consequently, of failing to serve humanity. Speaking before a religious conference, an audience which he may (perhaps wrongly) have suspected of being especially likely to hold a soft view of human nature, Worthy propounded an ideology which might be called "sentimental capitalism" as the answer to sentimental socialism. Admitting that selfishness is socially harmful, Worthy declares that businessmen, despite appearances, are really unselfish. In Worthy's view, the reason for the business-

[1] 31 J. Business 293 (1958).

man's odd behavior is the outmoded theory of laissez faire economics, which justifies and condones "rational" conduct based exclusively on self-interest. Businessmen, influenced by this ideology, feel constrained to explain their behavior in these terms.

There are several interesting things about this defense of capitalism—that capitalists are really not selfish after all. The first is that, as a defense, it is a hopeless failure. There are many reasons why this argument must fail, but perhaps the most conspicuous reason is that it is untrue. Instances of "generous" practice whether or not masked by "selfish" talk may exist, but they are not the characteristic examples that come immediately to mind as representative of business behavior. One doubts, for example, that the cigarette companies are giving serious consideration these days to stopping sales of their product merely because there is a strong suspicion that cigarette smoking causes lung cancer. Industries often ask to be relieved of tax burdens and only rarely that their taxes be increased.

Of course, selfishness is not limited to capitalists, in our society, or in any other. A gentle physicist may rise to wrath when someone steals his ideas or perhaps only disagrees with them; a non-materialistic statesman may call on the troops when the populace of a province prefers another government. Even socialist writers are rarely unconcerned with their royalties—unless, indeed, as is likely in a socialist society, this concern becomes trivial because of the more pressing need to keep head and neck firmly attached.

What does all this prove? Simply that all the world is largely governed by self-interest, and all the world knows it. Consequently, the assertion that capitalists are exempt from this failing is unlikely to win many converts to capitalism.

No need for shame

The second interesting—even amazing—thing about Mr. Worthy's argument is that he, as defender of the capitalist system, completely misunderstands the fundamental nature of that system as viewed by the laissez faire ideology he attacks. Worthy's basic ideas are expressed in the following sentences:

The ideas of fair play and self-restraint are essentially religious. They help keep dog-eat-dog practices in check and enable the economy to operate without strict governmental supervision and control: self-restraint rather than legal restraint is the rule....

The great weakness of laissez faire economics (both the earlier and the later variety) is not so much the reliance on individual freedom and the distrust of government controls but rather the absence—indeed, the explicit denial in official business theory—of any responsibility of the businessman to anyone but himself....

The principle that self-interest is a sufficient guide for personal and public policy (that private vices make for public good) makes the demand for greater public control inevitable....

In other words, the alternatives Worthy recognizes are self-restraint or legal restraint. But the essence of the laissez faire idea is that there is a third form of "restraint" against antisocial practices—not so frail a reed as the hope of self-restraint, nor such a threat to individual freedom as legal restraint. I refer, of course, to the *market* restraint of competition. Under laissez faire, if a business charges high prices, either because of inefficiency or because it is attempting to exploit its position, competitors rush in to serve the public in the place of the firm which is failing to do so. It is competition, not self-interest or the lack of it, which forces businessmen (if they wish to succeed) to give the public what it wants at the lowest attainable price.

The third interesting point in Mr. Worthy's presentation is his implicit acceptance of the ideas of the "new managerialism"—that the corporate manager (the typical "capitalist" of today) should serve the interest of all affected groups (owners, employees, customers, suppliers, and the community) rather than seek profits (i.e., serve stockholders) alone. No one can represent conflicting interests; he can at best mediate among them. Where there are conflicting masters, the servant is responsible to none. In this interpretation "unselfishness" of managers who deal with corporate funds (other people's money) may not be much of a virtue.

Selfishness better than sentiment

On all these grounds, a sentimental defense of capitalism cannot be accepted. Is it possible to give a tough-minded defense of capitalism—that is, to show that, taking people as they really are, capitalism can convert their energies to useful social results more effectively than

other systems? The answer to this question, I believe, is "Yes."

Under the system of private enterprise for profit, men enjoy the opportunity to receive high returns if they provide people with goods and services that people are willing to pay for. The disciplining rod is competition; if some producers do not fill an existing public need or do not fill it well, others can begin to do so. In this system everyone can be selfish—consumers buy what they like, businessmen produce what they can sell, laborers work for whoever pays most—but the market forces them to serve one another's interests, the laborer by working, the employer by paying labor and organizing production, and the consumer by paying for the final product. (Of course, it is not true that everyone *must* be selfish under this system—all who choose to serve others without reward may do so, but the choice is their own.) To be sure, the system has more or less serious failings: among those usually cited are the arbitrariness of the distribution of inherited wealth, and possible divergences between what the public wants and what it ought to have. These and other real objections to the capitalist system can be raised, but it remains to be shown how alternative systems will perform better. Capitalism has the decisive merit, at least, of being based on human motives as they actually are.

If we ask how an actual socialist system would have to cope with the same motives, we see that the consumers, managers, workers, and government officials of a socialist system can on no reasonable ground be assumed to be less selfish than their equivalents in a capitalist society. The distinctive characteristic of the socialist system is that it encourages and gratifies a rather different aspect of human self-interest. The main rewards in capitalism go to those who serve others through providing services and products for which others are willing to pay. In a socialist system, the monopolization of the economic (together with the political) sphere by government eliminates the check of competition. The great rewards will then go not to those who serve the public but to those who control government and thereby *rule* the public.

Checks and balances

Corresponding to the alternative "soft" and "tough" defenses which have been given for the private enterprise system in the economic sphere, it is of interest to note that there are both sentimental and realistic defenses for democracy in the political realm. The sentimental argument runs that the people are "good" (unselfish) and so deserve to rule. The unsentimental argument, in contrast, says that all are humanly selfish—rulers and ruled alike. Democracy is a good system because it sets up a regularized procedure whereby those in the seats of power are held in check by the necessity for election by the people they govern. As in the economic sphere, the test of a desirable social system is not whether the group to whom it grants power constitutes an unselfish class but whether the holders of power are effectively checked in their exercise of it.

Reading 16

The *Non Sequitur* of the "Dependence Effect"

F. A. Hayek

For well over a hundred years the critics of the free enterprise system have resorted to the argument that if production were only organized rationally, there would be no economic problem. Rather than face the problem which scarcity creates, socialist reformers have tended to deny that scarcity existed. Even since the Saint-Simonians their contention has been that the problem of production has been solved and only the problem of distribution remains. However absurd this contention must appear to us with respect to the time when it was first advanced, it still has some persuasive power when repeated with reference to the present.

The latest form of this old contention is expounded by Professor J. K. Galbraith. He attempts to demonstrate that in our affluent society the important private needs are already satisfied and the urgent need is therefore no longer a further expansion of the output of commodities but an increase of those services which are supplied (and presumably can be supplied only) by government.

I believe the author would agree that his argument turns upon the "Dependence Effect." The argument starts from the assertion that *a great part of the wants which are still unsatisfied in modern society are not wants which would be experienced spontaneously by the individual if left to himself, but are wants which are created by the process by which they are satisfied.* It is then represented as self-evident that for this reason such wants *cannot* be urgent or important. This crucial conclusion appears to be a complete *non sequitur* and it would seem that with it the whole argument of the book collapses.

Man a social being

The first part of the argument is of course perfectly true: we would not desire any of the amenities of civilization—or even of the most primitive culture—if we did not live in a society in which others provide them. The innate wants are probably confined to food, shelter, and sex. All the rest we learn to desire because we see others enjoying various things. To say that a desire is not important because it is not innate is to say that the whole cultural achievement of man is not important.

The cultural origin of practically all the needs of civilized life must of course not be confused with the fact that there are some desires which aim, not at a satisfaction derived directly from the use of an object, but only from the status which its consumption is expected to confer. Very few needs indeed are "absolute" in the sense that they are independent of social environment or of the example of others, and that their satisfaction is an indispensable condition for the preservation of the individual or of the species. Most needs which make us act are needs for things which only civilization teaches us exist at all, and

From F. A. Hayek, "The *Non Sequitur* of the 'Dependence Effect,'" *Southern Economic Journal*, April, 1961. Reprinted with kind permission of the author and publisher.

these things are wanted by us because they produce feelings or emotions which we would not know if it were not for our cultural inheritance. Are not in this sense probably all our esthetic feelings "acquired tastes"?

Case apart

How complete a *non sequitur* Professor Galbraith's conclusion represents is seen most clearly if we apply the argument to any product of the arts, be it music, painting, or literature. If the fact that people would not feel the need for something if it were not produced did prove that such products are of small value, all those highest products of human endeavor would be of small value. Professor Galbraith's argument could be easily employed, without any change of the essential terms, to demonstrate the worthlessness of literature or any other form of art. Clearly my taste for the novels of Jane Austen or Anthony Trollope or C. P. Snow is not "original with myself." But is it not rather absurd to conclude from this that it is less important than, say, the need for education? Public education indeed seems to regard it as one of its tasks to instill a taste for literature in the young and even employs producers of literature for that purpose. Is this want creation by the producer reprehensible? Or does the fact that some of the pupils may possess a taste for poetry only because of the efforts of their teachers prove that since "it does not arise in spontaneous consumer need and the demand would not exist were it not contrived, its utility or urgency, ex contrivance, is zero"?

The appearance that the conclusions follow from the admitted facts is made possible by an obscurity of the wording of the argument with respect to which it is difficult to know whether the author is himself the victim of a confusion or whether he skillfully uses ambiguous terms to make the conclusion appear plausible. The obscurity concerns the implied assertion that the wants of consumers are *determined* by the producers. Professor Galbraith avoids in this connection any terms as crude and definite as "determine." The expressions he employs, such as that wants are "dependent on" or the "fruits of" production, or that "production creates the wants" do, of course, suggest determination but avoid saying so in plain terms. After what has already been said it is of course obvious

that the knowledge of what is being produced is one of the many factors on which depends what people will want. It would scarcely be an exaggeration to say that contemporary man, in all fields where he has not yet formed firm habits, tends to find out what he wants by looking at what his neighbours do and at various displays of goods (physical or in catalogues or advertisements) and then choosing what he likes best.

In this sense the tastes of man, as is also true of his opinions and beliefs and indeed much of his personality, are shaped in a great measure by his cultural environment. But though in some contexts it would perhaps be legitimate to express this by a phrase like "production creates the wants," the circumstances mentioned would clearly not justify the contention that particular producers can deliberately determine the wants of particular consumers. The efforts of all producers will certainly be directed towards that end; but how far any individual producer will succeed will depend not only on what he does but also on what the others do and on a great many other influences operating upon the consumer. The joint but unco-ordinated efforts of the producers merely create one element of the environment by which the wants of the consumers are shaped. It is because each individual producer thinks that the consumers can be persuaded to like his products that he endeavours to influence them. But though this effort is part of the influences which shape consumers' tastes, no producer can in any real sense "determine" them. This, however, is clearly implied in such statements as that wants are "both passively and deliberately the fruits of the process by which they are satisfied." If the producer could in fact deliberately determine what the consumers will want, Professor Galbraith's conclusions would have some validity. But though this is skillfully suggested, it is nowhere made credible, and could hardly be made credible because it is not true.

Freedom to emulate

It might be worthwhile briefly to ask what, assuming that some expenditure were actually determined solely by a desire of keeping up with the Joneses, that would really prove? At least in Europe we used to be familiar with a type of persons who often denied themselves even enough food in order to maintain an appearance of respectability or gentility in dress and style of life. We may regard this as a misguided effort, but surely it would not prove that the income of such persons was larger than they knew how to use wisely. That the appearance of success, or wealth, may to some people seem more important than many other needs, does in no way prove that the needs they sacrifice to the former are unimportant. In the same way, even though people are often persuaded to spend unwisely, this surely is no evidence that they do not still have important unsatisfied needs.

Professor Galbraith's attempt to give an apparent scientific proof for the contention that the need for the production of more commodities has greatly decreased seems to me to have broken down completely. With it goes the claim to have produced a valid argument which justifies the use of coercion to make people employ their income for those purposes of which he approves. It is not to be denied that there is some originality in this latest version of the old socialist argument. For over a hundred years we have been exhorted to embrace socialism because it would give us more goods. Since it has so lamentably failed to achieve this where it has been tried, we are now urged to adopt it because more goods after all are not important.

Organized Labor

Reading 17

Human labor is perhaps the most important factor of production. In the modern mixed economy a large fraction of the labor force belongs to the trade union movement which, in contrast to the union movements of the totalitarian countries, really are free to engage in independent collective bargaining. The public at large both approves of, and is uneasy about, organized labor. Here a leading expert on the economics of labor describes the dynamics of the American labor movement.

George W. Taylor, professor of economics at the University of Pennsylvania, has been a leading labor arbitrator, member of the War Labor Board, and adviser on labor matters to presidents of both political parties.

Questions to Guide the Reading

When workers band together to improve their working conditions and wages, why are they any different from collusive monopolists out to improve their own well-being at the expense of the rest of the community? Is labor merely a commodity like anything else? Is bargaining power "equal" in the absence of unions? Why is the right to strike a crucial issue in the realm of collective bargaining?

The Role of Labor Unions

George W. Taylor

It has been said: "Man stands always at the beginning and at the end of an era." The one we presently survey looms as the most heroic of all the epics. In the newest era, the impact of science and technology upon traditional social and economic theory has consequences in

From George W. Taylor, "The Role of Labor Unions," The Benjamin Franklin Lecture Series, 1961–1962, March 29, 1962, University of Pennsylvania Wharton School of Finance and Commerce. Reprinted with kind permission of the author.

many ways as revolutionary as the more widely-recognized effect upon older theories of war and international cooperation. In perspective, however, one sees essentially an intensification of the "normal" propensity of social systems to dissolve and to reform in response to changed environments.

In the Eighteenth Century, Adam Smith created little controversy when he first expounded economic individualism as the key to promotion of national welfare.

Perhaps it was fortunate that even while the "Wealth of Nations" was still a best-seller, economic individualism was giving way to the organization as the dominant institution. A synthetic but powerful "person"—the corporation—was created without benefit of Adam's rib. More and more, the individual had to adjust to the status of a worker for the corporation and, later on, as a member of the union organization. The government might still leave the individual alone, but the organization did not and doubtless could not if its economic function was to be performed. Where was it said: "One trouble about laissez-faire was that nobody ever made clear who was to leave what alone"? At any event, the organizational revolution produced the business corporation and, later as a countervailing power, the labor union.

The notable extent to which the organizational laissez-faire doctrine has become a part of "traditional wisdom" was recently revealed when certain management representatives, who have long opposed the labor union idea, rushed to the ramparts in staunch defense of free collective bargaining. The government had suggested, in a tentative feeling-out move, that under present emergency conditions the public interest would have to be specifically taken into account in private wage and price determinations. Of course, organized labor was also there telling the government to keep its grasping hands off. Here was a stark expression of the creed: "Whatever is good for the corporation and the unions automatically and adequately conserves the national interest."

As the response of a democratic country to the challenges to ideals and safety, leaders in both the public and private sectors have a responsibility to work at inventing new ways and means to create new institutions, or adjust the old ones, in order to assure the mutual compatibility of governmental and private decisions. The definition of the private system which will best enhance the odds for national safety and survival in the current world environment is being formulated. As Barbara Ward put it: "The fundamental question is whether we in the West are able to confront the challenge of our times. And here we face the agonizing difficulty that some of the creative responses we need to make run deeply against the grain of our traditional thinking."

Unions and collective bargaining

This paper will be focused mainly upon the kind of creative responses necessary to make union functions and the process of collective bargaining workable in the new environment. May I propose that in industrial relations, more than in any area, federal policy and private decision-making "come uneasily face to face." These subjects, moreover, are deeply involved in the value determinations that will shape Western civilization.

There is so much prating about the "dignity of man" in the more flashy oratory of the day that the good term unfortunately has become quite shop-worn. One hesitates considerably in even using the phrase. There is still a considerable "bite," however, to the concomitant notion that, in a democracy such as ours, the conditions under which one man becomes subject to the direction of his fellow, for the latter's profit, is an important determinant of the emphasis that is placed upon the conservation of human values.

As a nation we have become increasingly concerned, especially since 1929, about effecting a fair and equitable balance between the conflicting goals of efficiency in production and the preservation of human values. The invisible hand of the market place did not provide compensation for men injured on the job, wages as a matter of right for men out of work, pensions for retired workers, or freedom from unjustified discharges. Much of the strength of this country, I believe, has derived from a strong drive for efficiency in competition moderated, however, by an inherent compassion in the utilization of one factor of production—labor. Here is the really revolutionary idea of the past century.

In the United States, employees in the key sectors of the economy seek to attain their personal objectives through union organization.

The institution is designed primarily to exert a strong bargaining position in the making of labor contracts with the employers. This unique orientation of the labor movement in the United States has elements of the mysterious to labor leaders in other democracies where a far greater reliance is placed upon political action. The importance of the decisions made in the private sector of our economy is matched in no other country in the world. This is in large part the case because of the so-called job-consciousness of the American worker. We are indebted to the late Selig Perlman for observing that in our so-called job-conscious unionism: ". . . the Hegelian dialectic nowhere occurs, nor is cognizance taken of 'labor's historical mission.' What monopolizes attention is labor combating competitive menaces . . . labor bargaining for the control of the job."

It is significant that labor unions did not initiate the current movement in the United States for governmental guides to be used in wage and price determination. And, no more than employers, do unions see any merit in the kind of national bargaining for a general wage policy that is practiced in some other democratic countries. Decentralized private decision-making in the wage and price areas has been our way of life. It is the economists and those in the governmental agencies who are in the van of the national planning movement. In their own ways, they seek to express the national interests vis-a-vis those who make private decisions and to reflect an insistent public demand for protection against inflation. How can national planning needs be provided for under a decentralized decision-making system in which great power resides in the private institutions?

It seems to me that, in their model building, most economists underrate not only the private power centers but the importance of the functions assigned to a labor union in the United States. Its primary responsibility is to the employees directly represented and not to the model builders. The terms of a labor contract with an employer must meet the fundamental expectations of employees—at least the terms must be appraised by them as preferable to a strike. Most labor agreements must be validated by a majority vote of a union meeting.

The script is generally adhered to by most unions. There have been notable deviations, however, such as those recently revealed in the investigations of the Senate Committee headed by Mr. McClelland. The evidence showed how easy it is for the dialogue of collective bargaining to be short-circuited by a dictatorial union leader who, glorifying either "effectiveness" or personal power, views the accommodation process as an unnecessary nuisance. But, the public demands that the script be followed. Accordingly, legislators pass laws to limit the power of all union leaders and to make them more responsive to the demands of the employees they represent. There is some incongruity between that thrust of legislation and the now insistent call upon the unions to exercise restraint in establishing employment terms.

Most unions do seek to carry out the functions so crucial in a democracy of channeling employee dissent to the bargaining table and of dissipating it through negotiated terms accepted by the employees as well as by the employer. Outstanding union leaders are well aware of the mediation element in their jobs. To begin with, they have to moderate the extreme demands of the membership which can't possibly be secured. The question of "democracy in unions," it has always seemed to me, concerns the procedures employed for this purpose and especially for mediating intra-union differences. For example, is priority to be given to the demands of older men for improved pensions rather than the claims of younger men for unemployment benefits? The assignment of priorities becomes more arduous as prospective wage increases are limited. Management also has a stake in "satisfying the men," and the public interest is involved. The efficiency of performance on the job, we believe, is related to the acceptability of employment terms. We differ from the totalitarians on this point but continue to be glad for the difference.

Thus, those calls upon the unions to exercise restraint in the national interest are, in essence, the assignment to union leaders of the responsibility for inducing the employees they represent to moderate their expectations. The reasons have to be clear, convincing and intelligible to "the man on the street," and they have yet to be formulated. In my opinion, the 25-hour week gained in New York by Local 3 of the International Brotherhood of Electrical Workers represents unwarranted, preferred treatment for a select group. It is reported, however, that the membership voted 5,000 to 3 to strike if necessary to gain this objective. Maybe they didn't read the national economic analyses. Even so, a national problem about gold balances is vital to the economists, understandable to most union leaders, but more remote than the moon to most employees. They have all they can do to hold a job, meet installment charges, and keep the crab grass out of the front lawn. They want those high-prized work rules which, so lightly dismissed by the rest of us as featherbedding, make their lives more secure and comfortable. Nor is there anything unusual about all this. People in every walk of life cherish the special vested interest they have staked out for themselves even if only through squatters rights. The state of mind that underlies featherbedding is neither an invention nor a monopoly of organized labor. Professor Aaron has cynically observed: "The popular feeling that there is something immoral about featherbedding may be appropriately described as a selective revulsion to unearned increment not elsewhere observable in the economy." The willingness of employees to give up their featherbedding in the national interest might conceivably be enhanced if the rest of us would lead the way.

The difficult mediation process which begins within the union continues in collective bargaining. Here the expectations of the employees have to be reconciled with the management need to minimize competitive costs and to maintain profits margins sufficient for capital expansion. Just as the employer has an interest in proper performance of the union function, the employees are dependent for their job security upon a proper performance of the management collective bargaining function.

In my opinion, the several steps designed to reconcile diverse objectives in collective bargaining have never been more difficult or exacting. This is because of the acceleration of technological change, the pressures of national and world competition, the claim upon resources for national programs, and the need to stabilize prices—all coming to a head at the same time. Employee demands are not limited to increased standards of living for those likely to keep their jobs, but include increasingly costly provisions for those who will be displaced. A double wage claim has to be dealt with. Competition, and national planning, introduces road blocks to price in-

creases at a time when increased corporate earnings are sought to support the capital formation so vital to sound economic growth. There just isn't enough increased productivity in sight to meet all the demand upon it.

In addition, the strike as a traditional means of inducing agreement in collective bargaining has become less and less tolerable. Not only can strikes interfere with constructive economic growth but the answers fashioned out of trial by economic combat often do not, in this day and age, adequately resolve the issues that caused the work stoppage in the first place.

Clearly, the need is for an agreement based upon analytic processes rather than economic power arbitrament. A much higher standard of performance is thus required of collective bargaining between the labor and management institutions in the 1960's if the country is to survive with freedom and thus to advance the historic mission of Western civilization.

In the process, the standard objectives of collective bargaining have to be modified to the fact of national emergency as a way of life. For, as far ahead as one can project, vast resources will be diverted year after year to maintain a huge military establishment, to assist people in underdeveloped nations to raise their living standards, and to meet relentless Communist pressures throughout the world. A greater share of the Gross National Product doubtless will be absorbed in providing better education "at every level and in every discipline," and improved medical care for more people.

All this means that the overhead costs of keeping the country in business have grown to mammoth proportions. And, these overhead costs have to be met before increases in the production of goods and services can be allocated to the enhancement of our own personal standards of living. Little short of nonsensical is the current tendency to pin responsibility solely upon the hourly-rated workers, especially those in the mass production industries, for becoming more productive and for curbing their expectation. They are truly a part of the picture but no more than the rest of us.

Cooperation between the public and the private sectors

A number of stubborn propositions can be identified: (1) in terms of the virtually unlimited claims upon even mighty resources, ours is not an affluent society at all but one of limited means, (2) the resources we do possess should be fully utilized—idle or ineffectively used plant and service facilities and high rates of employment are incompatible with the needs of the times, (3) accelerated economic growth and higher productivity in all endeavors are a must in order to meet as many pressing needs as is possible, (4) even if economic performance is vastly improved, priorities will still have to be specified, (5) changes are necessary in those existing institutions, including collective bargaining, which now serve essentially to balance conflicting private interests without particular regard for the general welfare.

Particularly in evolving priorities, of which voluntary restraints are a part, close cooperating between decision-makers in the private and public sectors is called for. In other words, the democratic principles of participation, accommodation and consent should be recognized as providing an element of strength not available to the totalitarian nations.

The evolving collective bargaining

The people of this country have had a genius for creating institutional forms to effectuate their value judgments. This has been evident, during the past generation, in the historic transformation of industrial relations in the United States. We have moved in important industries from unilateral decision-making by management toward co-determination by management and organized workers. Substitution of the two-party system for the one-party system for determining conditions of employment was one of the responses made to the devastating depression of the 1930's. Then came World War II and, as a result of agreement between labor and employer representatives, public members served with these parties on the War Labor Board to insure that the national interests were taken into account along with those of employees and management. A temporary three-party system was evolved. The principles of participation and consent were applied during World War II in an unprecedented manner to formulate and administer a national wage policy. When concern about inflation became the dominant national mood, changes in industrial relations were made by enactment of the Taft-Hartley Act in 1947. On the record,

it can be concluded that collective bargaining is an institution adaptable to changing circumstances. The main adaptations now being urged arise from the growing intolerance of strikes and the public interest in the substantive terms of private wage agreements.

The right to the strike

Just why is it that we have adhered so staunchly, even ritualistically, to the notion that in a democratic society the right to strike must be preserved. Considerable costs to everyone can be entailed in the exercise of that right. How can it be argued that the fair and equitable solution to the problems at the workplace can best be found in trial by economic combat?

One can wonder about the efficacy of the strike as a means of bringing about agreement. Yet, even the late Senator Robert Taft, in devising a procedure in 1947 to protect the public interest in public emergency disputes, insisted that while a strike might be temporarily enjoined for 80 days, the employee right to engage in a concerted stoppage should thereafter be reinstated in the absence of a settlement agreement. He accepted the traditional principles that: (1) only by agreement between those directly affected can the terms of employment be established in a democracy and (2) the strike is the only available device for inducing the essential compromise and agreement and (3) it provides an assurance against the terms of employment being imposed by the government.

There is, however, no certainty that the economic and social costs will always be viewed as a fair price to pay in allowing adherence to these principles. During the protracted steel strike of 1959, for instance, the public demand for compulsory arbitration mounted insistently when it seemed as though the complete stoppage of this basic industry could bring the public to its knees before bringing the parties to terms. In the even more exacting recent world moreover, intolerance of the strike has become more general. The need is apparent for a better and less costly means for motivating agreement. A social invention is called for.

To be sure, the total number of strikes has been declining and the average length of a shut-down has been decreasing. Since 1947, strike losses have averaged less than one-third of one percent of total working time. This is probably less than the working hours lost because of layoffs. As is so often the case, the overall statistics don't tell the whole story. A series of short stoppages by a few men on the missile sites do not make big statistics but can impair critical defense programs. By withdrawing their services, a small group of tug-boat operators can bring New York City to its knees in a few days. Little strikes can make big trouble. And, there are the occasional big, industry-wide strikes that may be averaged out in the national statistics but nevertheless have some adverse effect on nearly everybody in the year of occurrence. Some day perhaps, the function now assigned to the strike because of lack of a better technique, will appear no more sensible than bloodletting as an earlier surgical practice.

Whether or not an acceptable substitute for the strike can be designed depends mainly upon those in the private sector although governmental assistance can be accorded to those who are receptive. A considerable recognition of public responsibility is a prerequisite for the formulation of a creative response in this area. A number of initial efforts are encouraging.

An illustration of purposeful experimentation is the procedure for dealing with labor disputes at the missile and space sites. At each location, a Missile Site Labor Relations Committee has been established. It consists of representatives from manufacturing and construction concerns, various labor organizations, contracting agencies along with mediators assigned by the Federal Mediation and Conciliation Service. These committees are to "forecast impending problems, arrange for their settlement before they become acute, using fully all existing voluntary procedures and devising new adequate procedures where none exist." The unions have agreed not to call any strikes. Unauthorized or so-called wild-cat strikes still occur and this has led impatient men to call for compulsory arbitration to fix employment terms. Even the neophytes in industrial relations know, however, that a legislative ban on strikes doesn't eliminate work stoppages. It only makes them illegal. Procedures worked out by the affected parties which are relied upon to resolve disputes ordinarily settled by strikes is the indicated course of action in a democracy.

Significant experimentation is also under

way in having informed outsiders participate in collective bargaining at the invitation of the union and management. The third parties have sometimes been authorized to recommend settlement terms before resort is made to a work stoppage. In its present form, this is a new development. Through private mediation by third-party participants who have the authority to recommend terms, I have no doubt that work stoppages can be minimized. Nor will the substantive terms be any less attentive to the public interest than is presently the case. Indeed, to a limited degree, the public interest will be given a more emphatic expression. Perhaps, it is this very possibility which accounts, in some measure, for the opposition of many companies and unions to third-party participation. Yet, the third-party participants do operate within the limits of the private institution. Any recommendations, if they are to be effective, must be geared to terms which can form the basis for agreement between the union and the management.

In my opinion, there is a strong likelihood that the public interest in avoiding strikes, in an increasingly interdependent society and at a time when the effective utilization of resources is a national necessity, will result increasingly in the designation of third parties to participate in collective bargaining and in their authorization to make recommendations for settlement terms if that becomes necessary. This would be an institutional change short of arbitration and the specification of employment terms by the outsiders. The indicated "voluntary" response of unions and management would be a natural result of an increasing public intolerance of work stoppages with its "or else" implications.

Public interest in the terms of settlement

Collective bargaining conducted without any work stoppages at all might still be inadequate. Negotiated terms fully acceptable to the private parties of direct interest could, nevertheless, be obstructive to the attainment of major national goals. Under present circumstances, it is not safe to look upon all wage and price determinations as exclusively involving private interests. But, in a democracy, neither can they be construed as strictly a governmental affair.

Existing institutional arrangements are not adequate to fix conditions of employment in this context. Over the past 20 years, one President after another has called upon unions and management in general terms to exercise voluntary restraint. One trouble with this approach is in the generality. How much restraint is necessary under varying circumstances? What relative degrees of restraint are to be exercised in wage determination as compared to price determination? Would a likely result be the inclusion of prices and profit margins among the subjects dealt with by collective bargaining in order to determine whether or not a certain wage would require a price increase? And, how can a responsibility for national planning be undertaken by private decision-makers whose job it is to serve the particular interests of constituencies which can dis-elect them? More questions are raised than are answered by the call for restraint in general.

If the public involvement in these private decisions is real, and I believe this is the case, an effective enunciation of the required restraint has to be expressed in micro-economic terms, i.e., for ready insertion into the equation which has to be resolved in the private sector. In World War II, for example, the guide lines were in terms of the relation between wage-rates and the Consumer Price Index, comparative wage-rates and the like. Experience shows, moreover, that to be effective a public wage policy should be created through the cooperative endeavors of public, union and management representatives. It cannot be created by public representatives alone.

Among the obstacles to tackling the problem is the fact that the dimensions of today's challenge are not fully perceived or certainly not publicly admitted, by many important leaders in the private sector. How else can one interpret these recently reported remarks of a steel executive: "From a broad philosophical standpoint, most businessmen feel that in a competitive system, you serve the national interest in pursuing your private interest." Or, the outright rejection by Mr. George Meany, President of the A.F.L.-C.I.O., of Secretary Goldberg's suggestion that "the role of govern-

ment is to assert the national interest." To Mr. Meany, that is an infringement upon "the rights of free people and free society." The institutional laissez-faire policy has become rather thoroughly embedded.

The democratic approach

A recognition of the urgency of today's problems is a prerequisite for purposeful co-operation between governmental and private decision-makers to devise institutional forms for meeting the question: how are the vital goals of national planning to be achieved while the strengths of the private enterprise system are maintained? Devising an adequate answer to the question is a big part of the task of making democracy work in the new world environment.

The old faith in democracy was "simple and confident." It has been described as a belief in "the civilization of the dialogue, where everybody talked with everybody else above everything, where nobody tried to get his way by force or fraud, where everybody was content to abide by the decision of the majority as long as the dialogue could continue." This might have constituted, once upon a time, a fairly reasonable facsimile of the accommodation process. But, that was certainly before the emergence of that complex web of interdependence in which we are enmeshed. Yet, the democratic concept of self-government based upon an accommodation of conflicting interests through reason and persuasion remain "perhaps the most potent idea of modern history." Improved institutional forms provide the best hope for maintaining and furthering the democratic idea in a world in which people are developing a willingness to be told what to do. In the words of Robert M. Hutchins: ". . . if our hopes of democracy are to be realized, the next generation is in for a job of institutional remodeling the like of which has not been seen since the Founding Fathers." One need not go that far while still visualizing institutional adjustments as the most promising way of adapting our negotiating processes, including collective bargaining, to the demands of life in the second half of the Twentieth Century.

Government and Taxation

Readings 18 and 19   A Dialogue on the Proper Economic Role of the State

No question was more hotly debated in the 1960s than the proper economic rule of government. Here is a debate on the subject before a Swarthmore College audience between a conservative and a liberal.

George J. Stigler is Walgreen Professor at the Graduate School of Business of the University of Chicago and a world authority on microeconomics. Though a trifle shorter than J. K. Galbraith, Stigler is considered by some connoisseurs to be even wittier. At times each of the debaters has served as adviser to Republican and Democratic administrations, respectively.

Paul A. Samuelson is Institute Professor at M.I.T. He served as economic adviser to senator, candidate, and president-elect John F. Kennedy.

Questions to Guide the Reading

Since we cannot expect prefection in this world, do you think that Dr. Stigler is being overly critical in pointing out governmental errors? Was the wartime development of the atomic bomb an exception to Stigler's first rule? How does its success affect your judgment on rule 2? Is uniform mistreatment always worse than discrimination? Is it contemptuous of the poor to insist that money which they are given not be badly spent?

From Abraham Lincoln's statement, can you judge what he would think about today's SEC, control of thalydimide, of marijuana, of heroin? Can such problems be settled by aphorisms? How can you measure "freedom" when in the absence of coercive rules you may even have less of it? When one man's freedom is another man's coercion in a tight, little world? Is impersonality always a bad thing? Under centralism there would be one big employer: Is that a good thing? In what ways is a market system coercive?

Reading 18

The Government of the Economy

George J. Stigler

No doubt this is the best of all possible worlds, for the time being. But even in the best of possible worlds, a good many things happen that displease us. Without exception we are shocked when a tranquilizer is sold, and its use by pregnant women leads to tragic deformities in babies. We are all distressed when there is extensive unemployment and personal suffering. Most of us are displeased when a strike closes down a railroad or a port or the airlines. Some of us are deeply annoyed when the price of soybeans falls. A few of us are outraged when an increase is announced in the price of steel, but this particular few is not unimportant.

There was an age when social dissatisfaction was kept in the house. All evils were ancient evils, and therefore necessary evils which served at least to keep men humble and patient. This resignation to imperfection has

From George J. Stigler, "The Government of the Economy," *A Dialogue on the Proper Economic Role of the State*, Selected Paper No. 7, Graduate School of Business, University of Chicago. Reprinted by permission of George J. Stigler.

almost vanished in modern times—the hereafter in which all problems are solved has been moved up to two months after the next election. And government has become the leading figure in almost every economic reform. I propose to discuss what governments can do in economic life, and what they should do.

The question of what governments can do, what they are capable of doing, will strike many Americans, and for that matter most non-Americans, as an easy one. For it is a belief, now widely held and strongly held, that the government can, if it really puts its mind and heart to a task, do anything that is not palpably impossible. The government, we shall all admit, cannot really turn the number π into a simple fraction by legislative mandate, nor can a joint resolution of the houses of Congress confer immortality. But with a will, the government can see to it that fully 85 per cent of the male population, and a few women, are taught several infinite series for calculating π, and with a will, the government can prolong human life appreciably by suitable medical and social insurance programs.

An article of faith

This acceptance of the omnipotence of the state does not represent a generalization of experience; it is not a product of demonstrated effectiveness in bending events to the wise or foolish designs of policy. *On the contrary, the belief is an article of faith, indeed an article of almost desperate faith.* It is not an intrinsically absurd belief; there is no rigorous logical demonstration that the state cannot turn sows' ears into silken purses. There is also no logical demonstration that all men cannot become saints, but the number of saintly men has not yet risen to the level where the census makes it a separate statistical category.

Our faith in the power of the state is a matter of desire rather than demonstration. When the state undertakes to achieve a goal, and fails, we cannot bring ourselves to abandon the goal, nor do we seek alternative means of achieving it, for who is more powerful than a sovereign state? We demand, then, increased efforts of the state, tacitly assuming that where there is a will, there is a governmental way.

Yet we know very well that the sovereign state is not omnipotent. The inability of the state to perform certain economic tasks could be documented from some notorious failures. Our cotton program, for example, was intended to enrich poor cotton farmers, increase the efficiency of production, foster foreign markets, and stabilize domestic consumption. It is an open question whether 28 years of our farm program have done as much for poor cotton farmers as the trucking industry. Again, the Federal Trade Commission is the official guardian of business morals, including advertising morals. I am reasonably confident that more would have been achieved if one of the F.T.C.'s 48 years of appropriations had been devoted to a prize for the best exposé of sharp practices.

That there should be failures of governmental policy is not surprising, nor will the failures lead us to a blanket condemnation of governmental activity in economic life. Invariable success, after all, is found in only a few places. What is surprising is *how little we know about the degree of success or failure of almost all governmental intervention in economic life.* And when I say how little we know, I expressly include the people whose business it should be to measure the achievements, the professional economists.

When we have made studies of governmental controls that are sufficiently varied in scope and penetrating in detail, we may be able to construct a set of fairly useful generalizations about what the state can do. But society will not wait upon negligent scholars before meeting what seem to be pressing issues. The remainder of my talk cannot wait either, so I am driven to present what I consider plausible rules concerning feasible economic controls.

Stigler's laws

What economic tasks can a state perform? I propose a set of rules which bear on the answer to the question, but I shall not attempt a full argument in support of them—it must suffice to give an illustrative case, a plausible argument. It must suffice partly because full proofs have not been accumulated, but partly also because I wish to have time to discuss what the state should do, which is considerably less than what it can do.

RULE 1: The state cannot do anything quickly.

It would be unseemly to document at length the glacial pace of a bureaucracy in double step. A decent respect for due process lies behind some of the procedural delays, and poses a basic issue of the conflicting demands of justice and efficiency in economic regulation. But deliberation is intrinsic to large organizations: not only does absolute power corrupt absolutely; it delays fantastically. I would also note that initiative is the least prized of a civil servant's virtues, because the political process allots much greater penalties for failure than rewards for success.

Size vs. control

RULE 2: When the national state performs detailed economic tasks, the responsible political authorities cannot possibly control the manner in which they are performed, whether directly by governmental agencies or indirectly by regulation of private enterprise.

The lack of control is due to the impossibility of the central authority either to know or to alter the details of a large enterprise. An organization of any size—and I measure size in terms of personnel—cannot prescribe conduct in sufficient detail to control effectively its routine operations: it is instructive that when the New York City subway workers wish to paralyze their transportation system, they can do so as effectively by following all the operating instructions in literal detail as by striking.

Large organizations seek to overcome the frustrating problems of communication and command by seeking and training able executives, who could be described more accurately as able subordinates. But to get a good man and to give him the control over and responsibility for a set of activities is of course another way of saying that it is impossible for the central authorities to control the activities themselves. As the organization grows, the able subordinate must get able subordinates, who in turn must get able subordinates, who in turn must get able subordinates, who in turn—well, by the time the organization is the size of the federal government, the demands for ability begin to outstrip the supply of even mediocre genes.

I estimate, in fact, that the federal government is at least 120 times as large as any organization can be and still keep some control over its general operations. It is simply absurd to believe that Congress could control the economic operations of the federal government; at most it can sample and scream. Since size is at the bottom of this rule, two corollaries are:

1. Political control over governmental activity is diminishing.
2. The control exercised by a small city is much greater than the control exercised over General Motors by its Board of Directors.

Uniformity of treatment

RULE 3: The democratic state strives to treat all citizens in the same manner; individual differences are ignored if remotely possible.

The striving for uniformity is partly due to a desire for equality of treatment, but much more to a desire for administrative simplicity. Thus men with a salary of $100,000 must belong to the Social Security system; professors in New York must take a literacy test to vote; the new automobile and the 1933 Essex must be inspected; the most poorly co-ordinated driver and the most skillful driver must obey the same speed limits; the same minimum wage must be paid to workers of highly different productivities; the man who gives a vaccination for small pox must have the same medical credentials as a brain surgeon; the three-week-old child must have the same whiskey import allowance as a grown Irishman; the same pension must be given to the pilot who flew 100 dangerous missions as to the pilot who tested a Pentagon swivel chair; the same procedure must be passed through to open a little bank in Podunk and the world's largest bank in New York; the same subsidy per bale of cotton must be given to the hillbilly with two acres and the river valley baron with 5,000 acres. We ought to call him Uncle Same.

RULE 4: The ideal public policy, from the viewpoint of the state, is one with identifiable beneficiaries, each of whom is helped appreciably, at the cost of many unidentifiable persons, none of whom is hurt much.

The preference for a well-defined set of beneficiaries has a solid basis in the desire for votes, but it extends well beyond this prosaic value. The political system is not trustful of abstract analysis, nor, for that matter, are most people. A benefit of $50 to each of one million persons will always seem more desirable than a $1 benefit to each of 150 million people, because one can see a $50 check, and hence be surer of its existence.

The suspicion of abstract theory is of course well-founded: most abstract theories recorded in history have been false. Unfortunately it is also an abstract theory, and a silly one, that says one should believe only what he can see, and if the human race had adhered to it we would still be pushing carts with square wheels.

You do not need to be told that someone is always hurt by an economic policy, which is only a special case of the basic economic theorem that there is no such thing as a free lunch. On the other hand, I do not say that all political lunches are priced exorbitantly.

RULE 5: The state never knows when to quit.

One great invention of a private enterprise system is bankruptcy, an institution for putting an eventual stop to costly failure. No such institution has yet been conceived of in the political process, and an unsuccessful policy has no inherent termination. Indeed, political rewards are more closely proportioned to failure than to success, for failure demonstrates the need for larger appropriations and more power. This observation does not contradict my previous statement that a civil servant must avoid conspicuous failure at all costs, for his failure is an unwise act, not an ineffectual policy.

The two sources of this tenacity in failure are the belief that the government must be able to solve a social problem, and the absence of *objective* measures of failure and success.

Let me emphasize as strongly as I can that each of these characteristics of the political process is a source of strength in some activities, as well as a limitation in other activities. If the state could move rapidly, contrary to Rule 1, and readily accepted abstract notions, contrary to Rule 4, our society would become the victim of every fad in morals and every popular fallacy in philosophy. If the state could effectively govern the details of our lives, no tyranny would ever have been overthrown. If the state were to adapt all its rules to individual circumstances, contrary to Rule 3, we would live in a society of utter caprice and obnoxious favoritism. If the state knew

when to quit, it would never have engaged in such unpromising ventures as the American Revolution, not that I personally consider this our best war. But what are virtues in the preservation of our soviety and its basic liberties are not necessarily virtues in fixing the wages of labor or the number of channels a television set can receive.

These rules, and others that could be added, do not say that the state cannot socialize the growing of wheat or regulate the washing of shirts. What the rules say is that political action is social action, that political action displays reasonably stable behavioral characteristics, and that *prescriptions of political behavior which disregard these characteristics are simply irresponsible*. To say, after describing a social economic problem, that the state must do something about it, is equivalent in rationality to calling for a dance to placate an angry spirit. In fact the advantage is with the Indians, who were sure to get some useful exercise. The state can do many things, and must do certain absolutely fundamental things, but it is not an Alladin's lamp.

State's proper economic role

I propose merely to sketch what I believe is the proper treatment of certain classes of important economic problems.

Class 1: monopoly. The fear of monopoly exploitation underlies a vast network of public regulation—the control over the so-called public utilities, including the transportation and communication industries and banking institutions, as well as traditional antitrust policies. The proper methods of dealing with monopoly, in their order of acceptability, are three:

1. The maintenance or restoration of competition by the suitable merger prevention policies, which we now fail to use in areas such as rail and air transport, and by the dissolution of monopolies. This method of once-for-all intervention provides the only really effective way of dealing with monopoly.

It will be said that for technological reasons even a modest amount of competition is unattainable in many areas. I believe these areas are very few in number. Even when a community can have only one electric company, that company is severely limited by the long-run alternatives provided by other communities.

2. Where substantial competition cannot be achieved—and I do not ask for perfect competition—the entry into the field is often controlled by the state—for example the TV channels are allocated by the FCC. Here auctioning off the channels seems the only feasible method of capturing the inherent monopoly gains. The history of regulation gives no promise that such gains can be eliminated.

3. In the few remaining cases in which monopoly cannot be eliminated or sold to the monopolist, monopolies should be left alone, simply because there is no known method of effective control.

Class 2: poverty. A community does not wish to have members living in poverty, whatever the causes of the poverty may be. The maximum level of socially tolerable poverty will vary with the society's wealth, so poor societies will stop short at preventing plain starvation, but Texans will demand, through the oil embargoes that Presidents Eisenhower and Kennedy found expedient to accept, also Cadillacs and psychiatrists in their minimum poverty budget. I consider treatment of poverty a highly proper function of the state, but would propose that it be dealt with according to two principles:

1. Direct aid should take the form of direct grants of money, and only this form. If the poor would rather spend their relief checks on food than on housing, I see no reason for denying them the right. If they would rather spend the money on whiskey than on their children, I take it that we have enforceable laws to protect children.

2. The basic problem of poverty from the social viewpoint, however, is not the alleviation of current need but equipping the people to become self-supporting.

In fact, so-called liberal policies in this area often seem to me to be almost studied in their callousness and contempt for the poor. Many ameliorative policies assume that the poor are much poorer in intelligence than in worldly goods, and must be cared for like children. Few people ask of a policy: What will be the

effects on the poor who are not beneficiaries? If we tear down a slum, and rehouse half the people better at public cost, the only response to a query about the other half will be—we must do this for them too. Much of our welfare program has the macabre humor of a game of musical chairs.

Class 3: economic distress. I define economic distress as experiencing a large fall in income, or failing to share in a general rise, but without reaching some generally accepted criterion of poverty. Here my prescriptions would be:

1. Compensation for losses in the cases in which the distress is clearly and directly caused by governmental policy.

2. Exactly the same kind of treatment of distress as of poverty in other respects: Direct grants in the short-run; policies to foster the mobility of resources in the long-run.

Class 4: consumer and worker protection. Since unpunished fraud is profitable, it must be punished. I doubt whether many people realize how strong are the remedies provided by traditional law, and in particular how effective the actions of people who have been defrauded. I am confident that research in this area would suggest methods of vastly increasing the role of *self-policing* in the economy.

It is otherwise with the alleviation of consumer incompetence. In order to preserve the dignity and freedom of the individual in my society, I shall if I must pay the price of having some fail wholly to meet the challenge of freedom.

We should not, however, accept dramatic episodes as a measure of need; we should not simply assume that there is a useful law for every problem; and we should not lazily accept remedies which take freedom from 97 men in order to give protection to three.

And now I close. I consider myself courageous, or at least obtuse, in arguing for a reduction in governmental controls over economic life. You are surely desirous of improving this world, and it assuredly needs an immense amount of improvement. No method of displaying one's public-spiritedness is more popular than to notice a problem and pass a law. It combines ease, the warmth of benevolence, and a suitable disrespect for a less enlightened era. What I propose is, for most people, much less attractive: Close study of the comparative performance of public and private economy, and the dispassionate appraisal of special remedies that is involved in compassion for the community at large. I would urge you to examine my views in the most critical spirit, if I thought it necessary; I do urge you to attempt the more difficult task of exercising your critical intelligence in an appraisal of the comfortable wishfulness of contemporary policy.

Reading 19

The Economic Role of Private Activity

Paul A. Samuelson

Introduction: matter and antimatter

Thoreau, disapproving of the Mexican War, would not pay his taxes and was put in jail for civil disobedience. His Concord neighbor, Emerson, went to visit him down at the hoosegow and called out: "Henry, what are you doing in there?" Thoreau replied, "Waldo, what are you doing out there?" You will have perceived my point. One way of approaching the question, "What is the proper role of Government?" is to ask, "What is the proper role of non-Government?"

Abraham Lincoln is supposed to have said somewhere:

I believe the government should do only that which private citizens cannot do for themselves, or which they cannot do so well for themselves.

One would think this is supposed to be saying something. Let us try it in its converse form.

I believe the private economy should be left alone to do those activities which, on balance after netting out all advantages and disadvantages, it can best do.

Obviously what I have stated is an empty tautology. It is no more helpful than the usual answer from Dorothy Dix to a perplexed suitor that merely says, "Look into your own heart to see whether you truly love the girl. And then after you have made up your mind, I am sure it will be the right decision."

But are these mere tautologies? Do the two Lincolnesque statements say exactly the same thing? There is a certain literal sense in which they can be interpreted to be saying the same thing. But we all bring to the words we hear certain preconceptions and attitudes.

I think Lincoln meant to imply in his formulation that *there is needed a certain burden of proof that has to be established by anyone who proposes that the government do something.* The balance of advantage in favor of the government must be something substantial or you should stand with the *status quo* of private enterprise.

Why? Lincoln does not say. But he takes it for granted that his listeners will understand that "personal liberty" is a value for its own sake and that some sacrifice of "efficiency" is worth making at the optimal point where activity is divided so as to maximize the total net advantage of "efficiency *cum* liberty" and vice versa.

Overture to the program

So much for introduction. My Act I has prepared the way for what is to follow. In Act II, I want to examine the conditions under which efficiency is realizable by free enterprise or *laissez faire*. This is familiar ground, but too familiar and needs reexamination.

Then in Act III, I want to raise some questions about the notion that absence of government means increase in "freedom." Is "freedom" a simply quantifiable magnitude as much libertarian discussion seems to presume?

From Paul A. Samuelson, "The Economic Role of Private Activity," *A Dialogue on the Proper Economic Role of the State*, Selected Paper No. 7, Graduate School of Business, University of Chicago. Reprinted by permission of Paul A. Samuelson.

In case the clock catches me somewhere in Act II, let me give you a hint of the kind of thing I have in mind: Traffic lights coerce me and limit my freedom, don't they? Yet in the midst of a traffic jam on the unopen road, was I really "free" before there were lights? And has the algebraic total of freedom, for me or the representative motorist or the group as a whole, been increased or decreased by the introduction of well-engineered Stop Lights? Stop Lights, you know, are also Go Lights.

Then I shall conclude on what may seem a *nihilistic* note, but which I hope is actually a *liberating* one.

Technical requirements for competitive optimality

My friend George Stigler points out certain defects of government action. By itself, that is like pointing out certain defects of marriages. What we need to know is, "What are the alternatives? Celibacy? Cold baths? Violent exercise?" Jesting aside, Professor Stigler obviously hopes that the market can undertake most tasks "efficiently" and "equitably." I, too, so hope. But what are the strict conditions for optimal performance by private markets? Here are a bit of heroic assumptions:

1. Each person's tastes (and values) depend only upon his separable consumptions of goods. I.e., there must be no "consumption externalities."
2. Strict constant-returns-to-scale prevails.
3. Perfect competition, in senses too numerous to list here, prevails.
4. The interpersonal distribution of property (inclusive of personal attributes) is ethically correct initially or is to be made so by ideal lump-sum transfers of a perfectly nondistorting type.

Then, and only then, has it been rigorously proved that perfect competitive equilibrium is indeed optimal. So strict are these conditions that one would have thought that the elementary consideration that a line is infinitely thinner than a plane would make it *a miracle for these conditions to be met*. Real life optimality, or an approach to it, would seem to cry out—not merely for departure from *laissez faire*—but for never having been remotely near to *laissez faire*.

And note this. We each belong to many circles: The U.S.A., the Elks, the Samuelson family, the office pool, etc. In almost none of these relationships is the organizing principle that of decentralized competitive pricing. Let the descendants of Abraham Lincoln ponder over that one.

Division of responsibilities

It is a lucky accident that so much of economic life can be performed reasonably well by markets. But a long list of important cases arises where economics suggests that government should intervene:

1. Monopoly needs to be fought tooth and nail.
2. "Externalities"—the pollution of our environment, the rubbing of our elbows together —cry out for laws, zoning ordinances, concise rules of the road, taxes and subsidies.
3. The distribution of income and of opportunity—as between white and black, rich and poor, genetically lucky and unlucky—cries out for governmental measures to reduce inequality. Professor Stigler says the poor should be taught to get prosperous by their own efforts. He overlooks the fact that extensive statistical study shows that much of poverty—perhaps more than half today—is hopeless poverty. The old can never become young; the lame can never become whole; the disadvantaged 21-year-old—and perhaps 3-year-old—will never in his lifetime overcome his handicaps. An affluent society can afford to treat its underdogs humanely—just as tycoons and kings have been able to provide well for their incompetent and mediocre offspring.

All this is commonplace and obvious today. And Abraham Lincoln—reborn in 1975 or 1984 —would be the first to proclaim it.

The nature of freedom

But enough of these technicalities. Let me repeat some reflections on freedom that I presented recently at a conference on Individualism in Twentieth Century.

Adam Smith, our patron saint, was critical of state interference of the pre-Nineteenth Century type. And make no mistake about it: Smith was right. Most of the interventions into economic life by the State were *then* harmful both to prosperity and freedom. What Smith said needed to be said. In fact, much of what Smith said still needs to be said: *Good intentions by government are not enough;* acts do have consequences that had better be taken into account if good is to follow. (Thus, the idea of a decent real wage is an attractive one. So is the idea of a low interest rate at which the needy can borrow. None the less the attempt *by law* to set a minimum real wage at a level much above the going market rates, or to set a maximum interest rate for small loans at what seem like reasonable levels, inevitably does much harm to precisely the people whom the legislation is intended to help. Domestic and foreign experience—today, yesterday and tomorrow—bears out the Smithian truth. Note that this is not an argument against *moderate* wage and interest fiats, which may improve the perfection of competition and make businessmen and workers more efficient.)

Smith himself was what we today would call a pragmatist. He realized that monopoly elements ran through *laissez faire.* When he said that Masters never gather together even for social merriment without plotting to raise prices against the public interest, he anticipated the famous Judge Gary dinners at which the big steel companies used to be taught what every oligopolist should know. Knowing the caliber of George III's civil service, Smith believed the government would simply do more harm than good if it tried to cope with the evil of monopoly. Pragmatically, Smith would, if he were alive today, favor the Sherman Act and stronger anti-trust legislation, or even public utility regulation generally.

The Invisible Hand again

One hundred per cent individualists skip these pragmatic lapses into good sense and concentrate on the purple passage in Adam Smith where he discerns an Invisible Hand that leads each selfish individual to contribute to the best public good. Smith had a point; but he could not have earned a passing mark in a Ph.D. oral examination in explaining just what that point was. Until this century, his followers—such as Bastiat—thought that the doctrine of the Invisible Hand meant one of two things: (a) that it produced maxi-

mum feasible total satisfaction, somehow defined; or (b) that it showed that anything which results from the voluntary agreements of uncoerced individuals must make them better (or best) off in some important sense.

Both of these interpretations, which are still held by many modern libertarians, are wrong. They neglect Assumption 4 of my earlier axioms for non-government. This is not the place for a technical discussion of economic principles, so I shall be very brief and cryptic in showing this.

First, suppose some ethical observer—such as Jesus, Buddha, or for that matter, John Dewey or Aldous Huxley—were to examine whether the total of social utility, (as that ethical observer scores the deservingness of the poor and rich, saintly and sinning individuals) was actually maximized by 1860 or 1962 *laissez faire.* He might decide that a tax placed upon yachts whose proceeds go to cheapen the price of insulin to the needy might increase the total of utility. Could Adam Smith prove him wrong? Could Bastiat? I think not.

Of course, they might say that there is no point in trying to compare different individuals' utilities because they are incommensurable and can no more be added together than can apples and oranges. But if recourse is made to this argument, then the doctrine that the Invisible Hand maximizes total utility of the universe has already been thrown out the window. If they admit that the Invisible Hand will truly maximize total social utility *provided the state intervenes so as to make the initial distribution of dollar votes ethically proper,* then they have abandoned the libertarian's position that individuals are not to be coerced, even by taxation.

In connection with the second interpretation that anything which results from voluntary agreements is in some sense, *ipso facto,* optimal, we can reply by pointing out that when I make a purchase from a monopolistic octopus, that is a voluntary act: I can always go without Alka-seltzer or aluminum or nylon or whatever product you think is produced by a monopolist. Mere voluntarism, therefore, is not the root merit of the doctrine of the Invisible Hand; what is important about it is the system of checks and balances that comes under perfect competition, and its measure of validity is at the technocratic level of efficiency, not at the ethical level of freedom and individualism. That this is so can be seen from the fact that such socialists as Oscar Lange and A. P. Lerner have advocated channeling the Invisible Hand to the task of organizing a socialistic society efficiently.

The impersonality of market relations

Just as there is a sociology of family life and of politics, there is a sociology of individualistic competition. It need not be a rich one. Ask not your neighbor's name; enquire only for his numerical schedules of supply and demand. Under perfect competition, no buyer need face a seller. Haggling in a Levantine bazaar is a sign of less-than-perfect competition. The telephone is the perfect go-between to link buyers and sellers through the medium of an auction market, such as the New York Stock Exchange or the Chicago Board of Trade for grain transactions. Two men may talk hourly all their working lives and never meet.

These economic contacts between atomistic individuals may seem a little chilly or, to use the language of winetasting, "dry." This impersonality has its good side. Negroes in the South learned long ago that their money was welcome in local department stores. Money can be liberating. It corrodes the cake of custom. Money does talk. Sociologists know that replacing the rule of status by the rule of contract loses something in warmth; it also gets rid of some of the bad fire of olden times.

Impersonality of market relations has another advantage, as was brought home to many "liberals" in the Joseph McCarthy witch-hunting era of American political life. Suppose it were efficient for the government to be the one big employer. Then if, for good or bad, a person becomes in bad odor with government, he is dropped from employment, and is put on a black list. He really then has no place to go. The thought of such a dire fate must in the course of time discourage that freedom of expression which individualists most favor.

Many of the people who were unjustly dropped by the federal government in that era were able to land jobs in small-scale private industry. I say small-scale industry because large corporations are likely to be chary of hiring names that appear on anybody's black list.

Wheat growers anonymous

Many conservative people, who think that such men should not remain in sensitive government work or in public employ at all, will still feel that they should not be hounded into starvation. Few want for this country the equivalent of Czarist Russia's Siberia, or Stalin Russia's Siberia either. It is hard to tell on the Chicago Board of Trade the difference between the wheat produced by Republican or Democratic farmers, by teetotalers or drunkards, Theosophists or Logical Positivists. I must confess that this is a feature of a competitive system that I find attractive.

We have seen how a perfect model of competitive equilibrium might behave if conditions for it were perfect. The modern world is not identical with that model. As mentioned before, there never was a time, even in good Queen Victoria's long reign, when such conditions prevailed.

Whatever may have been true on Turner's frontier,[1] the modern city is crowded. Individualism and anarchy will lead to friction. We now have to coordinate and cooperate. Where cooperation is not fully forthcoming, we must introduce upon ourselves coercion. When we introduce the traffic light, we have by cooperation and coercion, although the arch individualist may not like the new order, created for ourselves greater freedom.

The principle of unbridled freedom has been abandoned. It is now just a question of haggling about the terms! On the one hand, few will deny that it is a bad thing for one

---

[1] Density of population produces what economists recognize as external economies and diseconomies. These "neighborhood effects" are often dramatized by smoke and other nuisances that involve a discrepancy between private pecuniary costs and social costs. They call for intervention: zoning, fiats, planning, regulation, taxing, and so forth. But too much diluteness of the gas also calls for social interfering with *laissez faire* individualism. Thus, the frontier has always involved sparse populations in need of "social overhead capital." In terms of technical economics jargon this has the following meaning: when scale is so small as to lead to unexhausted increasing returns, free pricing cannot be optimal and there is a *prima facie* case for cooperative intervention.

man, or a few men, to impose their wills on the vast majority of mankind, particularly when that will involves terrible cruelty and terrible inefficiency. Yet where does one draw the line? At a 51 per cent majority vote? Or, should there be no actions taken that cannot command unanimous agreement—a position which such modern exponents of libertarian liberalism as Professor Milton Friedman are slowly evolving toward. Unanimous agreement? Well, virtually unanimous agreement, whatever that will come to mean.

The principle of unanimity is, of course, completely impractical. My old friend Milton Friedman is extremely persuasive, but not even he can keep his own students in unanimous agreement all the time. Aside from its practical inapplicability, the principle of unanimity is theoretically faulty. It leads to contradictory and intransitive decisions. By itself, it argues that just as society should not move from *laissez faire* to planning because there will always be at least one objector—Friedman if necessary—so society should never move from planning to freedom because there will always be at least one objector. Like standing friction, it sticks you where you are. It favors the *status quo*. And the *status quo* is certainly not to the liking of arch individualists. When you have painted yourself into a corner, what can you do? You can redefine the situation, and I predicted some years ago that there would come to be defined a privileged *status quo*, a set of natural rights involving individual freedoms, which alone requires unanimity before it can be departed from.

At this point the logical game is up. The case for "complete freedom" *has been begged, not deduced.* So long as full disclosure is made, it is no crime to assume your ethical case. But will your product sell? Can you persuade others to accept your axiom when it is in conflict with certain other desirable axioms?

Not by reasoning alone

The notion is repellant that a man should be able to tyrannize over others. Shall he be permitted to indoctrinate his children into any way of life whatsoever? Shall he be able to tyrannize over himself? Here, or elsewhere, the prudent-man doctrine of the good trustee must be invoked, and in the last analysis his

peers must judge—*i.e.*, a committee of prudent peers. And may they be peers tolerant as well as wise!

Complete freedom is not definable once two wills exist in the same interdependent universe. We can sometimes find two situations in which choice A is more free than choice B in apparently every respect and at least as good as B in every other relevant sense. In such singular cases I will certainly throw in my lot with the exponents of individualism. But few situations are really of this simple type; and these few are hardly worth talking about, because they will already have been disposed of so easily.

In most actual situations we come to a point at which choices between goals must be made: do you want this kind of freedom and this kind of hunger, or that kind of freedom and that kind of hunger? I use these terms in a quasi-algebraic sense, but actually what is caled "freedom" is really a vector of almost infinite components rather than a one-dimensional thing that can be given a simple ordering.

Where more than one person is concerned the problem is thornier still. My privacy is your loneliness, my freedom to have privacy is your lack of freedom to have company. Your freedom to "discriminate" is the denial of my freedom to "participate." There is no possibility of unanimity to resolve such conflicts.

The notion, so nicely expounded in a book I earnestly recommend to you, Milton Friedman, *Capitalism and Freedom* (Chicago, 1962), that it is better for one who deplores racial discrimination to try to persuade people against it than to do nothing at all—but, failing to persuade, it is better to use no democratic coercion in these matters—such a notion as a *general* precept is arbitrary and gratuitous. Its arbitrariness is perhaps concealed when it is put abstractly in the following form: If free men follow Practice X that you and some others regard as bad, it is wrong in principle to coerce them out of that Practice X; in principle, all you ought to do is to try to persuade them out of their ways by "free discussion." One counter-example suffices to invalidate a general principle. An exception does not prove the rule, it disproves it. As a counter-example I suggest we substitute for

"Practice X" the "killing by gas of 5 million suitably-specified humans." Who will agree with the precept in this case?

Only two types would possibly agree to it: (1) those so naive as to think that persuasion can keep Hitlers from cremating millions; or (2) those who think the *status quo*, achievable by what can be persuaded, is a pretty comfortable one after all, even if not perfect. When we are very young we fall into the first category; when old and prosperous, into the second; perhaps there is a golden age in between. *The notion that any form of coercion whatever is in itself so evil a thing as to outweigh all other evils is to set up freedom as a monstrous shibboleth.* In the first place, absolute or even maximum freedom cannot even be defined unambiguously except in certain special models. Hence one is being burned at the stake for a cause that is only a slogan or name. In the second place, as I have shown, coercion can be defined only in terms of an infinite variety of arbitrary alternative *status quo*.

The precept "persuade-if-you-can-but-in-no-case-coerce" can be sold only to those who do not understand what it is they are buying. This doctrine sounds a little like the "Resist-Not-Evil" precepts of Jesus or Gandhi. But there is absolutely no true similarity between the two doctrines, and one should not gain in palatability by being confused with the other.

Marketplace coercion, or the Hegelian freedom of necessity

Libertarians fail to realize that *the price system is, and ought to be, a method of coercion.* Nature is not so bountiful as to give each of us all the goods he desires. We have to be coerced out of such a situation, by the nature of things. That is why we have policemen and courts. That is why we charge prices, which are high enough relative to limited money to limit consumption. The very term "rationing by the purse" illustrates the point. Economists defend such forms of rationing, but they have to do so primarily in terms of its efficiency and its fairness. Where it is not efficient—as in the case of monopoly, externality, and avoidable uncertainty—it comes under attack. Where it is deemed unfair by ethical observers, its evil is weighed pragmatically against its advantages

and modifications of its structure are introduced.

Classical economists, like Malthus, always understood this coercion. They recognized that fate dealt a hand of cards to the worker's child that was a cruel one, and a favorable one to the "well-born." John Stuart Mill in a later decade realized that mankind, not Fate with a capital F, was involved. Private property is a concept created by and enforced by public law. Its attributes change in time and are man-made, not Mother-Nature-made.

Nor is the coercion a minor one. Future generations are condemned to starvation if certain supply-and-demand patterns rule in today's market. Under the freedom that is called *laissez faire*, some worthy men are exalted; and so are some unworthy ones.[2] Some unworthy men are cast down; and so are some worthy ones. The Good Man gives the system its due, but reckons in his balance its liabilities that are overdue.

Anatole France said epigrammatically all that needs to be said about the coercion implicit in the libertarian economics of *laissez faire*. "How majestic is the equality of the Law, which permits both rich and poor alike, to sleep under the bridges at night." I believe no satisfactory answer has yet been given to this. It is certainly not enough to say, "We made our own beds and let us each lie in them."[3] For once Democracy rears its pretty head, the voter will think: "There, but for the Grace of God and the Dow-Jones averages, go I." And he will act.

The whole matter of proper government policy involves issues of ethics, coercion, administration, incidence, and incentives that cannot begin to be resolved by semantic analysis of such terms as "freedom," "coercion," or "individualism."

---

[2] "I am kept from attending college because my family is —————." To discern the coercion implicit in a competitive pricing system, note that any of the following can be substituted into the blank space: Negro, bourgeois, Jewish—*or poor.*

[3] If one disagrees with Malthus and France and thinks that we all had equal opportunities and *have* made the beds we are to lie in, our judgment of *laissez faire* improves—as it should. But note it is because of its fine welfare results, and *not because the kind of freedom embodied in it is the end-all of ethics.*

A final law

At the end I must lay down one basic proposition. If you remember only one thing of what I say, let it be this. If you don't remember anything of what I say, let this be the last thing you forget.

There are no rules concerning the proper role of government that can be established by a priori reasoning.

This may seem odd to you: for to state the rule that there are no rules may sound like a self-contradiction, reminiscent of the breakfast cereal box that contains an exact picture of itself . . . of itself . . . of itself. . . . However, no Bertrand Russell theory of types is involved here. For, my proposition—call it Samuelson's Law if you like—does not claim to be established by Reason, but merely to be a uniformity of experience. Whose experience? My experience, and that of every (I mean, almost every) man of experience.

If I am wrong it will be easy to prove me wrong: namely, by stating one valid non-trivial proposition about the proper role of government derived by cogent a priori reasoning alone. After I have digested it, I shall have no trouble in eating my own words.

Let me illustrate by a few rules that have been proposed and that will pass neither the test of experience nor of logic.

JEFFERSON'S LEMMA: That government is best which governs least.

I waive the formal objection that there exists no least positive real number. Just as the only good Injun is alleged to be a dead one, this says that the best government would be one which committed suicide. By a social compact and constitution, anarchy would be proclaimed.

Taken *literally,* no one—certainly not Jefferson—will buy this dictum of zero government. Such sweeping rules are like soap bubbles: Literally take them and you find nothing in your hands to take. In this they differ from the Pythogorean or other theorem about Euclidean space derived by logic: Imagine saying "I believe the three angles of a plane triangle add up to 180°—but of course, not to the degree of taking the belief literally."

Here is another proposed law.

ACTON'S CONJECTURE: "All power corrupts, and absolute power corrupts absolutely."

Of course Lord Acton didn't say quite this in his letter to Bishop Creighton; nor did he profess to deduce it a priori. Yet, since Lord Acton was unfamiliar with the anthropology of the Samoan islands, neither he nor anyone else, with the possible exception of Margaret Mead, can testify to its universal correctness. Even within the experience of the history known to 19th Century Cambridge Dons, this cannot be established unless the words "corrupt" and "power" be defined tautologically. The Spearman rank correlation coefficient between the power of rulers and their abusive rulings is certainly not $+1$; to say the correlation is positive in a wide sampling of history is to say something interesting, but this is the kind of non-sweeping *empirical* uniformity which I am pleading for in this lecture as against dogmatic arguments from the nature of things.

Here is another branch whose graft never took on the tree of wisdom.

COLIN CLARK'S LAW: The role of government must be held below a ceiling of 25 per cent of the national income.

This is not a two-halves truth or even, I fear, a 25 per cent truth. A number of nations whom we all point to as having accomplished miracles in the last decade never had the erudition to know of Clark's Law or the instinctive good sense to desist from violating it. That Western Germany, the showplace of free enterprise, should collect 34 per cent of her national income for taxes is as shocking and thoughtless a violation of Clark's natural law as that a column of mercury should, after 30 vertical inches, neglect to remember that Nature abhors a vacuum.

I could go on. But why do so? My point is made: No *a priori* reasoning has yet been found to demarcate the role of non-government and of government. However, I must not be dogmatic. Having found cause to reject laws of Jefferson, Acton, and Clark, I must out of courtesy and caution reserve judgment on any laws that Professor Stigler may unveil. For, as I learned when our friendship began long ago, George Stigler can do almost anything—anything but be boring.

Reading 20

Since modern man works a few months of the year to pay his taxes, the equity and efficiency of the tax system present a major economic problem. Although our tax structure is so often damned, America actually has one of the best tax systems ever contrived.

Dr. Joseph A. Pechman, director of research at the nonprofit Brookings Institution, is a leading fiscal expert, who has played a pivotal role in the U.S. Treasury Department, the Committee for Economic Development (a liberal business group), and in the academic field of public finance.

Questions to Guide the Reading

Why is it a key feature of our tax system that we depend to such an extent upon the so-called "progressive" income taxes levied against personal and corporate incomes? If Congress were to close loopholes, which are now in the law for noble and ignoble reasons, could tax rates be lowered, efficiency and incentives promoted, and greater equity achieved? Justify your answer.

Best Tax System Yet

Joseph A. Pechman

The taxpayer's reluctance to part with his hard-earned money is perfectly understandable, but much of the grumbling heard around April 15 is not only intemperate but wrong. The fact is that the United States has one of the best tax systems in the world—if not the best. It rates high by all main criteria: productivity, fairness, consistency with economic goals, and ease of compliance and administration. No one can question the system's productivity. Last year, federal, state and local government revenues amounted to about $185 billion.

Yet our taxes are by no means the world's highest. Taxes range between 30 and 35 per cent of gross national product in Germany, France, Italy, the Netherlands, Sweden, and the United Kingdom as compared with about 27 per cent for the United States.

Judgments about fairness are highly personal, and there is disagreement on this point. Our system places great weight on individual and corporation income taxes which are progressive, that is, they place the largest burden on those who have the greatest ability to pay. The major criticism of the system is that it provides special advantages that reduce taxes for some people and businesses and not for others in the same economic circumstances.

The economic potency of the tax system can hardly be disputed. In 1964, the Federal Government reduced taxes by $11 billion ($15 billion at present income levels) in a successful attempt to stimulate private spending. If needed, taxes will be raised this year or next to reduce spending and help avoid inflation.

Such heavy reliance on income taxes would be impossible without good compliance and administration. Few countries can equal our record in this respect. Out of every Federal individual income tax return filed, 3 out of every 4 have no errors. Only about 6 per cent of the income that should be reported does not show up on tax returns, and the Internal Revenue Service picks up quite a bit of this unreported income. The entire Federal tax machinery costs less than 1 per cent of the amount collected. State and local tax administration is not as good as Federal, but it is improving.

If the tax system scores so well, why does it generate so much controversy, dissatisfaction, and emotion? Part of the grumbling reflects the natural distaste for paying taxes, but there are

From Joseph A. Pechman, "Tax System Good, But Needs Key Reforms," *Washington Post*, April 10, 1966. Reprinted with kind permission of the author and publisher.

also real and deep-seated differences of opinion about tax policy. The issues involve difficult, technical questions of law, accounting, and economics, with important implications for the welfare of every citizen and for the vitality of the economy.

Individual income tax

The Nation's biggest and best source of revenue is the individual income tax. The close association between a man's taxpaying ability and his income is commonly accepted.

The main trouble with the present tax is that large amounts of income have been allowed to escape taxation by means of various special provisions and deductions.

The accompanying chart shows the practical effect of erosion. If the total income reported by taxpayers were subject to the statutory rates, taxes would begin at 14 per cent on the first dollar of income and rise to 70 per cent in the top brackets. But nobody pays these rates. After allowing for all special provisions, the maximum average rate in any income class is less than 30 per cent.

Exemptions are most important in the lowest classes, deductions at the top. The capital

gains provisions are also most important at the top, while income splitting gives the largest benefits to persons with incomes between $20,000 and $100,000.

An ideal personal income tax is easy to define, but unlikely to be enacted. Every modification would touch a tender nerve. Some who would scream the loudest are not the "fatcats" caricatured in the cartoons: many of the most expensive eroding features of the law favor the lower and middle-income classes. Nevertheless, reforms that broadened the base of taxation would make it possible to reduce tax rates for all and improve the fairness of the tax.

The most irrational and expensive provisions are the deductions for contributions, interest, medical expenses, taxes, and other personal expenditures that cut out billions of dollars from the tax base. Deductions for state income taxes protect taxpayers against excessive rates. There is also some justification for continuing the deduction for sales and income taxes as a device to encourage further state use of these taxes to raise the revenues they desperately need. But there is no excuse for deducting gasoline taxes, which are levied to pay for benefits received by highway users. The present method of computing the deduction for

EFFECT OF TAX LAW PROVISIONS ON ACTUAL RATES PAID

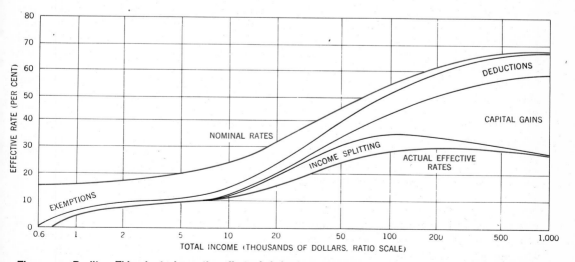

Theory vs. Reality This chart shows the effect of deductions, exemptions, and other special provisions of the tax law on actual tax rates. For example, where the nominal rate on income in the $20,000–$25,000 bracket is 32 per cent, the actual effective rate is only about 15 per cent. The differences are much larger in the top brackets where capital gains are important. At $1,000,000 the theoretical rate is 68½ per cent, the actual about 27 per cent.

charitable contributions is highly questionable. Limiting the deduction to contributions in excess of, say 2 or 3 per cent of income would encourage larger than average gifts to charity and save close to $2 billion of revenue each year.

Capital gains

Revision of capital gains treatment is the most urgent business on the tax reform agenda. Profits from sale of assets held more than 6 months are taxed at only half the regular rates up to a maximum of 25 per cent, but even this tax may be avoided indefinitely if the assets are transferred from one generation to another through bequests. In the case of gifts, capital gains are taxed only if the assets are later sold by the recipient. As a result, billions of dollars of capital gains are subject to low rates or are never taxed.

Capital gains receive favored treatment for two reasons: first, full taxation of a large realized gain accumulated over many years would be unfair unless the impact of the graduated rates were moderated; second, too high a rate on capital gains might lock most security holders into their present portfolios. The first of these problems could be solved by averaging capital gains over the period they were held. The "lock-in" effect would be moderated by such an averaging provision and also by taxing capital gains when assets are transferred, either by gift or at death. Both changes would reduce the advantages of holding onto assets whose values had risen.

Treatment of aged and poor

The Federal income tax has been particularly solicitous of the aged. Taxpayers over 65 years of age have an additional exemption of $600, pay no tax on their social security or railroad retirement pensions, and receive a tax credit on other retirement income (if their earnings are below $1524).

There is every reason to help the aged through public programs, but the tax system is a bad way to do this. It would be better to eliminate these deductions and use the revenue to increase social security benefits for all aged persons.

The present $600 per capita exemption has not been altered since 1948, when consumer

prices were 25 per cent lower. In 1964, a minimum standard deduction was added, providing $300 for the taxpayer and $100 for each additional exemption up to a maximum of $1000, but the starting levels of taxation are still below the official poverty levels.

Policy makers hesitate to raise exemptions because this would be expensive. An increase from $600 to $700 per capita would cost $3 billion per year; an increase to $800 would cost $5.5 billion. An alternative might be to double the minimum standard deduction, which would help those in greatest need at an annual cost of less than $2 billion.

Negative income tax

The negative income tax is a new subject of public discussion, although it has been discussed by economists and social welfare experts for many years. An individual would add up his income and subtract his exemptions and deductions: if the result were negative, he would be entitled to a payment from the Government.

Because the various Government and private welfare programs do not reach all the poor, the negative income tax would be an excellent method of supplementing them. Its major advantage is that it would not discourage the poor from seeking income-earning activities as much as present welfare programs often do.

Many people still regard the negative income tax as a radical innovation, and a number of difficult problems need to be resolved before it becomes feasible. Not the least of these is its relationship with the positive income tax, and with the present welfare programs. However, the concept is worth serious attention and is being given close study in Washington.

Corporate income tax

The corporation income tax produces a large amount of revenue (about $30 billion this year) that would be hard to replace with any other tax. Without it, a substantial part of the individual income would be permanently lost from the tax base through retention of earnings by corporations.

Opponents contend that it reduces corporate saving, encourages debt at the expense of equity financing, and discourages the use of corporate capital. However, the share of the national income originating in the corporate sector has risen from 58 per cent in 1929 to almost 70 per cent in recent years.

The so-called double taxation of dividends is a baffling issue. In theory, income earned by corporations is taxed under the corporation income tax and again under the individual income tax when it is paid out in dividends. This double taxation exists only if the corporation income tax is not shifted in the form of higher prices.

Even if it is agreed that double taxation exists, there is no easy solution. Currently, individuals are not taxed on the first $100 of dividend income, but this is a makeshift arrangement which satisfies no one. The best solution would be to lower corporation income tax rates when circumstances permit. This would automatically reduce the double taxation of dividends equally for all stockholders regardless of their other incomes, and would not complicate the tax law.

The toughest issue involves percentage depletion for oil, gas, and other minerals industries. These allowances are similar in many respects to depreciation. The difference is that the amounts written off as depreciation are limited to the cost of the asset, but percentage depletion can—and does—exceed the amount invested by substantial amounts. In addition, an immediate write-off is permitted for certain capital costs incurred in exploration and development, providing a double deduction for capital invested in these industries. Almost all the experts who have studied the matter have concluded that present allowances are far too generous.

Consumption taxes

Consumption taxes are not popular in the United States. General sales taxes are used by state and local governments, but even when they are taken into account, consumption taxes are less important here than anywhere else in the world.

The Federal Government has relied exclusively on selected excises for consumption tax revenues. These taxes are among the first to be raised in a national emergency, and they linger on and do considerable damage to the economy for years afterward. Excises are bad taxes because they discriminate arbitrarily against consumption of the taxed commodities. The only defensible excises are sumptuary taxes, which help offset the social costs of certain articles of consumption, like liquor and tobacco, and user charges, which compensate for special identifiable benefits received by individuals and firms from public services.

If consumption taxes are needed for revenue purposes, a general tax such as the retail sales tax would make more sense than selective excises. But consumption taxes are most burdensome for low-income taxpayers and have less automatic flexibility than the income tax.

A new method of taxing consumption that has attracted interest of late is the value added tax, which is imposed at a flat rate on the "value added" by each firm (gross receipts less the cost of materials purchased from other firms). It is similar to a retail sales tax, except that it is collected piecemeal as the commodity makes its way through the channels of production and distribution.

Basically the issue is the degree of progression in the tax system. Proponents of a Federal sales tax or of a value added tax wish to reduce progression. My own view is that the general consumption tax should not be used by the Federal Government unless the potential of the income taxes has been exhausted, which is unlikely if the base is broadened and the rates are further reduced.

Payroll taxes

Payroll taxes were introduced during the 1930s to pave the way for the social security system. The tax for old age, survivors, disability, and hospital insurance now amounts to 4.2 per cent each on employers and employes on earnings up to $6600, and will reach 5.65 per cent by 1987. This type of tax was used to emphasize the element of "contribution" by the employe.

Social security is a tremendous achievement, but the use of payroll taxes to finance it is increasingly being questioned. These taxes, which now exceed $20 billion a year, are regressive and discourage the use of labor.

The simplest method of correcting some of the inequity would be to raise the limit on earnings subject to tax and eventually to remove it entirely. The tax would then be a flat percentage of earnings, which would still be regressive with respect to total income but much less than under present law.

Unemployment insurance

Unemployment insurance is financed by a 3.1 per cent tax on payrolls of employers of 4 or more persons up to $3000 per employe. State trust funds are set up from which benefits are paid, but these funds are inadequate in some states during recessions. Provision should be made for Federal assistance to extend benefits automatically when unemployment becomes serious. This can be accomplished through increases in the Federal tax or through contributions from the general fund. Preferably, the entire system should be financed out of general taxes because individual firms have little control over employment.

Estate tax

The federal Government levies an estate tax with rates that go up to 77 per cent and a gift tax which is set at three quarters of the estate tax rates. The exemptions are $60,000 under the estate tax and $30,000 for all gifts during an individual's lifetime plus $3000 per donee per year.

In theory, estate and gift taxes are excellent taxes. In practice, their yield is disappointing —only a little over 2 per cent of Federal cash receipts—and they have little effect on the distribution of wealth. They can be avoided by distributing gifts at the lower gift tax rates, by setting up trusts, and by other methods.

The estate and gift tax rates are high enough: a complete overhaul is needed to eliminate the avenues of escape and to tax equal amounts of transfers equally.

State and local taxes

The state and local segment of the national tax structure is its most dynamic element. Before the Vietnam buildup, state and local expenditures were 60 per cent of Federal cash expenditures and more than twice as much as nondefense expenditures. Whereas the Federal Government reduced tax rates 15 per cent between 1961 and 1965, state and local tax rates increased sharply and are continuing to go up. State and local governments will continue to be hard-pressed as their financial needs continue to grow.

Most of the additional revenue will be raised by the states and local governments themselves. Long-standing traditions against moderate income and sales taxes are breaking down, and 26 states now have both. The recent adoption in three states of a credit against the income tax for sales tax paid suggests that regressivity of the sales tax can be moderated effectively. Deductibility from the Federal income tax should make income taxation at the state level more acceptable. However, states that permit the deduction of Federal taxes from their own state income tax bases lose much more revenue than their taxpayers save.

The crisis in city finances is dramatically illustrated by the plight of New York City. Cities will have to raise their own taxes, but they will also need all the help they can get from the state and Federal governments. In many parts of the country, administration of the property tax—the mainstay of local tax systems—remains weak; but experience has shown that state governments, if they take a strong hand, can force improvements in the quality of local assessment practices and procedures.

Federal aid to states and localities

Whatever their own efforts, states and local governments will continue to rely on Federal assistance which already provides 15 per cent of their revenues. Most of this aid comes from conditional grants for welfare, housing, urban renewal, pollution control, and other programs in which the Federal Government has a vital interest. But additional aid will be required to close the gap between their growing needs and their fiscal capacity.

General purpose grants to the states have been suggested as a means of providing additional Federal help. Details of the proposals differ, but in general they would return a fixed percentage of the Federal individual income tax base to the states, with the understanding that these growing revenues would be shared with the local governments. The funds would be disbursed on a per capita basis, with a small percentage reserved for special distribution to the poorest states.

Such general purpose grants are strongly opposed by those who wish to control the allocation of Federal funds in great detail because they have little faith in the willingness or ability of state governments to use the funds wisely. However, in a tax system which restricts the states and local governments to the least desirable and responsive tax sources, a general-purpose Federal grant system makes good sense as a supplement to conditional grants.

Tax reform and the New Economics

I reserve for last a discussion of the relationship between tax reform and the new economics. The basic proposition of the new economics is that fiscal policy—which includes both tax and expenditure policy—must be used vigorously and promptly to achieve the basic goals of full employment, a high rate of economic growth, and stable prices.

The most serious obstacle to the use of fiscal policy in this way has been the legislative process. Passage of major tax bills may take the better part of a year or longer. Many tax experts and nonpartisan citizens groups have recommended that the President be authorized to make temporary changes in tax rates. Presi-

dents Kennedy and Johnson made such a proposal (limited to tax cuts), but Congress has resisted any such infringement on its constitutional taxing powers. It is clear, in the current situation, that if the power had been given, the President might well have used it already to fight inflation.

The United States tax system is a good one, as tax systems go, but substantial reforms are needed. Such reforms would make the system more equitable and also permit a significant reduction in tax rates for all taxpayers. For example, individual income tax rates could be lowered by at least a third if a broad definition of taxable income were adopted. Such reforms would pave the way for more vigorous and effective use of tax policy to maintain full employment, price stability, and dynamic economic growth.

Reading 21

Government expenditure does much to help those with low incomes. Graduated income taxation further helps to equalize economic opportunity and mitigate the extremes of economic inequality.

Along with these conventional programs against poverty, a new program has captured the imagination of economists—the "negative income tax," which actually has the government pay out money to the poor, rather than collect it from them.

Conservative candidate Barry Goldwater, as well as Yale's Kennedy New Frontiersman James Tobin, agree on the need to explore this new idea.

Questions to Guide the Reading

If people with low incomes receive payments from the government as a matter of right, will that hurt their pride? Blunt their economic incentives? Can we afford the negative income tax without raising tax rates on the middle- and high-income groups?

The Negative Income Tax

James Tobin

Assuring living standards in the absence of earning capacity

People who lack the capacity to earn a decent living need to be helped, but they will not be helped by minimum wage laws, trade union

wage pressures, or other devices which seek to compel employers to pay them more than their work is worth. The more likely outcome of such regulations is that the intended beneficiaries are not employed at all.

A far better approach is to supplement earn-

From James Tobin, "On Improving the Economic Status of the Negro," *Daedalus,* Journal of the American Academy of Arts and Sciences, Fall, 1965. Reprinted with kind permission of the author and publisher.

ings from the public fisc. But assistance can and should be given in a way that does not force the recipients out of the labor force or give them incentive to withdraw. Our present system of welfare payments does just that, causing needless waste and demoralization. This application of the means test is bad economics as well as bad sociology. It is almost as if our present programs of public assistance had been consciously contrived to perpetuate the conditions they are supposed to alleviate.

The welfare mess

These programs apply a strict means test. The amount of assistance is an estimate of minimal needs, less the resources of the family from earnings. The purpose of the means test seems innocuous enough. It is to avoid wasting taxpayers' money on people who do not really need help. But another way to describe the means test is to note that it taxes earnings at a rate of 100 per cent. A person on public assistance cannot add to his family's standard of living by working. Of course, the means test provides a certain incentive to work in order to get off public assistance altogether. But in many cases, especially where there is only one adult to provide for and take care of several children, the adult simply does not have enough time and earning opportunities to get by without financial help. He, or more likely she, is essentially forced to be both idle and on a dole. The means test also involves limitations on property holdings which deprive anyone who is or expects to be on public assistance of incentive to save.

In a society which prizes incentives for work and thrift, these are surprising regulations. They deny the country useful productive services, but that economic loss is minor in the present context. They deprive individuals and families both of work experience which could teach them skills, habits, and self-discipline of future value and of the self-respect and satisfaction which comes from improving their own lot by their own efforts.

Public assistance also encourages the disintegration of the family. The main assistance program, Aid for Dependent Children, is not available if there is an able-bodied employed male in the house. In most states it is not available if there is an able-bodied man in the house, even if he is not working. All too often

it is necessary for the father to leave his children so that they can eat. It is bad enough to provide incentives for idleness but even worse to legislate incentives for desertion.

The bureaucratic surveillance and guidance to which recipients of public assistance are subject undermine both their self-respect and their capacity to manage their own affairs. In the administration of assistance there is much concern to detect "cheating" against the means test and to ensure approved prudent use of the public's money. Case loads are frequently too great and administrative regulations too confining to permit the talents of social workers to treat the roots rather than the symptoms of the social maladies of their clients. The time of the clients is considered a free good, and much of it must be spent in seeking or awaiting the attention of the officials on whom their livelihood depends.

A better plan

The defects of present categorical assistance programs could be, in my opinion, greatly reduced by adopting a system of basic income allowances, integrated with and administered in conjunction with the federal income tax. In a sense the proposal is to make the income tax symmetrical. At present the federal government takes a share of family income in excess of a certain amount (for example, a married couple with three children pays no tax unless their income exceeds $3700). The proposal is that the Treasury pay any family who falls below a certain income a fraction of the shortfall. The idea has sometimes been called a negative income tax.

The payment would be a matter of right, like an income tax refund. Individuals expecting to be entitled to payments from the government during the year could receive them in periodic installments by making a declaration of expected income and expected tax withholdings. But there would be a final settlement between the individual and the government based on a "tax" return after the year was over, just as there is now for taxpayers on April 15.

A family with no other income at all would receive a basic allowance scaled to the number of persons in the family. For a concrete example, take the basic allowance to be $400 per year per person. It might be desirable and equitable, however, to reduce the additional basic allowance for children after, say, the fourth. Once sufficient effort is being made to disseminate birth control knowledge and technique, the scale of allowances by family size certainly should provide some disincentive to the creation of large families.

A family's allowance would be reduced by a certain fraction of every dollar of other income it received. For a concrete example, take this fraction to be one third. This means that the family has considerable incentive to earn income, because its total income including allowances will be increased by two-thirds of whatever it earns. In contrast, the means test connected with present public assistance is a 100 per cent "tax" on earnings. With a one-third "tax" a family will be on the receiving end of the allowance and income tax system until its regular income equals three times its basic allowance.

Families above this "break-even" point would be taxpayers. But the less well-off among them would pay less taxes than they do now. The first dollars of income in excess of this break-even point would be taxed at the same rate as below, one-third in the example. At some income level, the tax liability so computed would be the same as the tax under the present income tax law. From that point up, the present law would take over; taxpayers with incomes above this point would not be affected by the plan.

Pictures of a plan

The best way to summarize the proposal is to give a concrete graphical illustration. On the horizontal axis of Figure 1 is measured family income from wages and salaries, interest, dividends, rents, and so forth—"adjusted gross income" for the Internal Revenue Service. On the vertical axis is measured the corresponding "disposable income," that is, income after federal taxes and allowances. If the family neither paid taxes nor received allowance, disposable income would be equal to family income; in the diagram this equality would be shown by the 45° line from the origin. Disposable income above this 45° line means the family receives allowances; disposable income below this line means the family pays taxes. The line OAB describes the present income tax law for a married couple with three

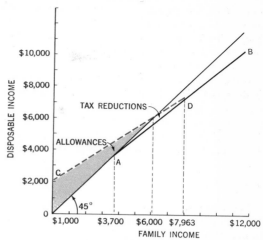

Fig. 1   Illustration of Proposed Income Allowance Plan (married couple with three children)

children, allowing the standard deductions. The broken line CD is the revision which the proposed allowance system would make for incomes below $7963. For incomes above $7963 the old tax schedule applies.

Beneficiaries under Federal Old Age Survivors and Disability Insurance would not be eligible for the new allowances. Congress should make sure that minimum benefits under OASDI are at least as high as the allowances. Some government payments, especially those for categorical public assistance, would eventually be replaced by basic allowances. Others, like unemployment insurance and veterans' pensions, are intended to be rights earned by past services regardless of current need. It would therefore be wrong to withhold allowances from the beneficiaries of these payments, but it would be reasonable to count them as income in determining the size of allowances, even though they are not subject to tax.

Prudent cost

Although the numbers used above are illustrative, they are indicative of what is needed for an effective program. It would be expensive for the federal budget, involving an expenditure of perhaps fifteen billion dollars a year. Partially offsetting this budgetary cost are the savings in public assistance, on which governments now spend five and six-tenths billion dollars a year, of which three and two-tenth billion are federal funds. In addition, savings are possible in a host of other income maintenance programs, notably in agriculture. The program is expensive, but it need not be introduced all at once. The size of allowances can be gradually increased as room in the budget becomes available. This is likely to happen fairly rapidly.

I sometimes refer to programs which make up for lack of earning capacity as stopgaps, but that is not entirely fair. Poverty itself saps earning capacity. The welfare way of life, on the edge of subsistence, does not provide motivation or useful work experience either to parents or to children. A better system, one which enables people to retain their self-respect and initiative, would in itself help to break the vicious circle.

Determination of National Income and Its Fluctuation 2

Modern Theories of Income Determination and Forecasting

Readings 22 and 23

"We are all post-Keynesians now" is a slogan that reflects the gradual ac-
ceptance of the modern theory of income determination. It was not always so.
The late President Hoover used to refer, in his retirement, to the doctrines of
"Keynes and Marx" as if they were more or less synonymous.

In Reading 22, Galbraith describes the slow penetration of Keynesian techniques of thought. In Reading 23, Henry Hazlitt rejects the scientific validity
of Keynesian analysis.

Henry Hazlitt long wrote an economic column for *Newsweek*.

Questions to Guide the Reading

Is it unhealthy for radically new doctrines to be first regarded with suspicion
and hostility, with the burden of proof being put against them? How can you
reconcile Lord Keynes' liking for individualism and the middle classes with his
insistence that laissez faire would have to be modified by the macroeconomic
programs of fiscal and monetary policy if full employment and reasonable
price stability were to be attained?

Could a conservative, primarily interested in business profits and hostile to
the working classes, find modern theories of income determination helpful to
his cause?

Reading 22

How Keynes Came to America

John Kenneth Galbraith

> "I believe myself to be writing a book on economic theory which will largely
> revolutionize—not, I suppose, at once but in the course of the next ten years—the way
> the world thinks about economic problems."   Letter from J. M. Keynes to George
> Bernard Shaw, New Year's Day, 1935.

The most influential book on economic and social policy so far in this century, *The General
Theory of Employment, Interest and Money*,
by John Maynard Keynes, was published
twenty-nine years ago last February in Britain
and a few weeks later in the United States. A
paper-back edition is now available in the
United States for the first time, and quite a
few people who take advantage of this bargain will be puzzled at the reason for the
book's influence. Though comfortably aware
of their own intelligence, they will be unable
to read it. They will wonder, accordingly, how
it persuaded so many other people—not all of
whom, certainly were more penetrating or
diligent. This was only one of the remarkable
things about this book and the revolution it
precipitated.

By common, if not yet quite universal agreement, the Keynesian revolution was one of the
great modern accomplishments in social design. It brought Marxism in the advanced
countries to a total halt. It led to a level of
economic performance that now inspires bitter-
end conservatives to panegyrics of unexampled
banality. Yet those responsible have had no
honors and some opprobrium. For a long while,
to be known as an active Keynesian was to
invite the wrath of those who equate social
advance with subversion. Those concerned de-

John Kenneth Galbraith, "How Keynes Came to America," *New York Times Book Review*, May, 1965.
© 1965 by The New York Times Company. Reprinted with kind permission of the author and publisher.

veloped a habit of reticence. As a further consequence, the history of the revolution is, perhaps, the worst told story of our era.

It is time that we knew better this part of our history and those who made it, and this is a little of the story. Much of it turns on the almost unique unreadability of "The General Theory" and hence the need for people to translate and propagate its ideas to government officials, students and the public at large. As Messiahs go, Keynes was deeply dependent on his prophets.

A modern classic

"The General Theory" appeared in the sixth year of the Great Depression and the fifty-third of Keynes's life. It is a measure of how far the Keynesian revolution has proceeded that its central thesis now sounds rather commonplace. Until it appeared, economists, in the classical (or non-socialist) tradition, had assumed that the economy, if left to itself, would find its equilibrium at full employment. Increases or decreases in wages and in interest rates would occur as necessary to bring about this pleasant result. If men were unemployed, their wages would fall in relation to prices. With lower wages and wider margins, it would be profitable to employ those from whose toil an adequate return could not previously have been made. It followed that steps to keep wages at artificially high levels, such as might result from the ill-considered efforts by unions, would cause unemployment. Such efforts were deemed to be the principal cause of unemployment.

Movements in interest rates played a complimentary role by insuring that all income would ultimately be spent. Thus, were people to decide for some reason to increase their savings, the interest rates on the now more abundant supply of loanable funds would fall. This, in turn, would lead to increased investment. The added outlays for investment goods would offset the diminished outlays by the more frugal consumers. In this fashion, changes in consumer spending or in investment decisions were kept from causing any change in total spending that would lead to unemployment.

Keynes argued that neither wage movements nor changes in the rate of interest had, necessarily, any such agreeable effect. He focused attention on the total of purchasing power in the economy—what freshmen are now taught to call aggregate demand. Wage reductions might not increase employment; in conjunction with other changes, they might merely reduce this aggregate demand. And he held that interest was not the price that was paid to people to save but the price they got for exchanging holdings of cash, or its equivalent, their normal preference in assets, for less liquid forms of investment. And it was difficult to reduce interest beyond a certain level. Accordingly, if people sought to save more, this wouldn't necessarily mean lower interest rates and a resulting increase in investment. Instead, the total demand for goods might fall, along with employment and also investment, until savings were brought back into the line with investment by the pressure of hardship which had reduced saving in favor of consumption. The economy would find its equilibrium not at full employment but with an unspecified amount of unemployment.

What to do

Out of this diagnosis came the remedy. It was to bring aggregate demand back up to the level where all willing workers were employed, and this could be accomplished by supplementing private expenditure with public expenditure. This should be the policy wherever intentions to save exceeded intentions to invest. Since public spending would not perform this offsetting role if there were compensating taxation (which is a form of saving), the public spending should be financed by borrowing —by incurring a deficit. So far as Keynes can be condensed into a few paragraphs, this is it.

Before the publication of "The General Theory," Keynes had urged his ideas directly on President Roosevelt, most notably in a famous letter to *The New York Times* on December 31, 1933: "I lay overwhelming emphasis on the increase of national purchasing power resulting from government expenditure which is financed by loans." And he visited F.D.R. in the summer of 1934 to press his case, although the session was no great success; each, during the meeting, seems to have developed some doubts about the general good sense of the other.

In the meantime, two key Washington officials, Marriner Eccles, the exceptionally able Utah banker who was to become head of the

Federal Reserve Board, and Lauchlin Currie, a former Harvard instructor who was director of research and later an economic aide to Roosevelt (and later still a prominent victim of McCarthyite persecution), had on their own account reached conclusions similar to those of Keynes as to the proper course of fiscal policy. When "The General Theory" arrived, they took it as confirmation of the course they had previously been urging.

Paralleling the work of Keynes in the thirties and rivaling it in importance, though not in fame, was that of Simon Kuznets and a group of young economists and statisticians at the University of Pennsylvania, the National Bureau of Economic Research and the United States Department of Commerce. They developed the now familiar concepts of National Income and Gross National Product and their components and made estimates of their amount. Included among the components of National Income and Gross National Product was the saving, investment, aggregate of disposable income and the other magnitudes of which Keynes was talking. As a result, those who were translating his ideas into action knew not only what needed to be done but how much. And many who would never have been persuaded by the Keynesian abstractions were compelled to belief by the concrete figures from Kuznets and his inventive colleagues.

The "other Cambridge"

However, the trumpet—if the metaphor is permissible for this particular book—that was sounded in Cambridge, England, was heard most clearly in Cambridge, Massachusetts. Harvard was the principal avenue by which Keynes's ideas passed to the United States.

In the late thirties, Harvard had a large community of young economists, most of them held there by the shortage of jobs that Keynes sought to cure. They had the normal confidence of their years in their ability to remake the world and, unlike less fortunate generations, the opportunity. They also had occupational indication of the need. Massive unemployment persisted year after year. It was degrading to have to continue telling the young that this was merely a temporary departure from the full employment norm, and that one need only obtain the needed wage reductions.

Paul Samuelson of M.I.T., who, almost

from the outset, was the acknowledged leader of the younger Keynesian community, has compared the excitement of the young economists, on the arrival of Keynes's book, to that of Keats on first looking into Chapman's Homer. Here was a remedy for the despair that could be seen just beyond the Yard. It did not overthrow the system but saved it. To the non-revolutionary, it seemed too good to be true. To the occasional revolutionary, it was. The old economics was still taught by day. But in the evening, and almost every evening from 1936 on, almost everyone discussed Keynes.

This might, conceivably, have remained a rather academic discussion. As with the Bible and Marx, obscurity stimulated abstract debate. But in 1938, the practical instincts that economists sometimes suppress with success were catalyzed by the arrival at Harvard from Minnesota of Alvin H. Hansen. He was then about fifty, an effective teacher and a popular colleague. But most of all he was a man for whom economic ideas had no standing apart from their use.

The economists of established reputation had not taken to Keynes. Faced with the choice between changing one's mind and proving that there is no need to do so, almost everyone opts for the latter. So it was then. Hansen had an established reputation, and he did change his mind. Though he had been an effective critic of some central propositions in Keynes's "Treatise on Money," an immediately preceding work, and was initially rather cool to "The General Theory," he soon became strongly persuaded of its importance.

He proceeded to expound the ideas in books, articles and lectures and to apply them to the American scene. He persuaded his students and younger colleagues that they should not only understand the ideas but win understanding in others and then go on to get action. Without ever seeking to do so or being quite aware of the fact, he became the leader of a crusade. In the late thirties Hansen's seminar in the new Graduate School of Public Administration was regularly visited by the Washington policy-makers. Often the students overflowed into the hall.

The officials took Hansen's ideas, and perhaps even more his sense of conviction, back to Washington. In time there was also a strong migration of his younger colleagues and students to the capital. Among numerous others were Richard Gilbert, now a principal architect of Pakistan's economic development, who was a confidant of Harry Hopkins; Richard Musgrave, now of Princeton, who applied Keynes's and Hansen's ideas to the tax system; Alan Sweezy, now of California Institute of Technology, who went to the Federal Reserve and the W.P.A.; George Jaszi, who went to the Department of Commerce; Griffiths Johnson, who served at the Treasury, National Resources Planning Board and the White House; and Walter Salant, now of the Brookings Institution, who served in several Federal agencies. Keynes himself once wrote admiringly of this group of young Washington disciples.

Washington learns

The discussions that had begun in Cambridge continued through the war years in Washington. One of the leaders, a close friend of Hansen's but not otherwise connected with the Harvard group, was Gerhard Colm of the Bureau of the Budget. Colm, a German refugee who made the transition from a position of influence in Germany to one of influence in the United States in a matter of some five years, played a major role in reducing the Keynesian proposals to workable estimates of costs and quantities. Keynesian policies became central to what was called post-war planning and designs for preventing the re-emergence of massive unemployment.

Meanwhile, others were concerning themselves with a wider audience. Seymour Harris, another of Hansen's colleagues and an early convert to Keynes, became the most prolific exponent of the ideas in the course of becoming one of the most prolific scholars of modern times. He published half a dozen books on Keynes and outlined the ideas in hundreds of letters, speeches, memoranda, Congressional appearances and articles. Professor Samuelson, mentioned above, put the Keynesian ideas into what became (and remains) the most influential textbook on economics since the last great exposition of the classical system by Alfred Marshall. Lloyd Metzler, now of the University of Chicago, applied the Keynesian system to international trade. Lloyd G. Reynolds, at a later stage, gathered a talented group of younger economists at Yale and made that

university a major center of discussion of the new trends.

Business chimes in

Meanwhile, with the help of the academic Keynesians, a few businessmen were becoming interested. Two New England industrialists, Henry S. Dennison of the Dennison Manufacturing Company in Framingham and Ralph Flanders of the Jones and Lamson Company of Springfield, Vermont (and later United States Senator from Vermont) hired members of the Harvard group to tutor them in the ideas. Before the war they had endorsed them in a book, in which Lincoln Filene of Boston and Morris E. Leeds of Philadelphia had joined, called "Toward Full Employment." In the later war years, the Committee for Economic Development, led in these matters by Flanders and the late Beardsley Ruml, and again with the help of the academic Keynesians, began explaining the ideas to businessmen.

In Washington during the war years the National Planning Association had been a center for academic discussion of the Keynesian ideas. At the end of the war Hans Christian Sonne, the imaginative and liberal New York banker, began underwriting both N.P.A., and the Keynesian ideas. With the C.E.D., in which Sonne was also influential, N.P.A. became another important instrument for explaining the policy to the larger public. (In the autumn of 1949, in an exercise of unparalleled diplomacy, Sonne gathered a dozen economists of strongly varying views at Princeton and persuaded them to sign a specific endorsement of Keynesian fiscal policies. The agreement was later reported to the Congress in well-publicized hearings by Arthur Smithies of Harvard and Simeon Leland of Northwestern University.)

The Full Employment Act

In 1946, ten years after the publication of "The General Theory," the Employment Act of that year gave the Keynesian system the qualified but still quite explicit support of law. It recognized, as Keynes had urged, that unemployment and insufficient output would respond to positive policies. Not much was said about the specific policies but the responsibility of the Federal Government to act in some fashion was clearly affirmed. The Council of Economic Advisers became, in turn, a platform for expounding the Keynesian view of the economy and it was brought promptly into use.

Those who nurture thoughts of conspiracy and clandestine plots will be saddened to know that this was a revolution without organization. All who participated felt a deep sense of personal responsibility for the ideas; there was a varying but deep urge to persuade.

Something more was, however, suspected. And there was some effort at counter-revolution. Nobody could say that he preferred massive unemployment to Keynes. And even men of conservative mood, when they understood what was involved, opted for the policy—some asking only that it be called by some other name. The Committee for Economic Development, coached by Ruml on semantics, never advocated deficits. Rather it spoke well of a budget that was balanced only under conditions of high employment. Those who objected to Keynes were also invariably handicapped by the fact that they hadn't (and couldn't) read the book. It was like attacking the original Kama Sutra for obscenity without being able to read Sanskrit.

Reaction on the Charles River

Harvard, not Washington, was the principal object of attention. In the fifties, a group of graduates of mature years banded together in an organization called the Veritas Foundation and produced a volume called "Keynes at Harvard." It found that "Harvard was the launching pad for the Keynesian rocket in America." But then it damaged this not implausible proposition by identifying Keynesianism with socialism, Fabian socialism, Marxism, Communism, Fascism and also literary incest, meaning that one Keynesian always reviewed the works of another Keynesian. More encouragingly, the authors also reported that "Galbraith is being groomed as the new crown prince of Keynesism (sic)." The university was unperturbed, the larger public sadly indifferent. The book evidently continues to have some circulation on the more thoughtful fringes of the John Birch Society.

Another and more influential group of graduates pressed for an investigation of the Depart-

ment of Economics, employing as their instrument the visiting committee that annually reviews the work of the department on behalf of the Governing Boards.

It was conducted by Clarence Randall, then the exceptionally articulate head of the Inland Steel Company, with the support of Sinclair Weeks, a manufacturer, former Senator and tetrarch of the right wing of the Republican Party in Massachusetts. In due course, the committee found that Keynes was, indeed, exerting a baneful influence on the Harvard economic mind and that the department was unbalanced in his favor. The department, including the members most skeptical of Keynes's analysis—no one accepted all of it and some very little—unanimously rejected the committee's finding. So did President James Bryant Conant. There was much bad blood.

In ensuing years there was further discussion of the role of Keynes at Harvard and of related issues. But it became increasingly amicable, for the original investigators had been caught up in one of those fascinating and paradoxical developments with which the history of the Keynesian (and doubtless all other) revolutions is replete. Shortly after the committee reached its disturbing conclusion, the Eisenhower Administration came to power.

Mr. Randall became a Presidential assistant and adviser. Mr. Weeks became Secretary of Commerce and almost immediately was preoccupied with the firing of the head of the Bureau of Standards over the question of the efficacy of Glauber's salts as a battery additive. Having staked his public reputation against the nation's scientists and engineers on the issue (as the late Bernard De Voto put it) that a battery could be improved by giving it a laxative, Mr. Weeks could hardly be expected to keep open another front against the economists. But much worse, both he and Mr. Randall were acquiring a heavy contingent liability for the policies of the Eisenhower Administration. And these, it soon developed, had almost as strong a Keynesian coloration as the department at Harvard.

Eisenhower retreat

President Eisenhower's first Chairman of the Council of Economic Advisers was Arthur F. Burns of Columbia University and the National Bureau of Economic Research. Mr.

Burns had credentials as a critic of Keynes. In his introduction to the 1946 annual report of the National Bureau, called "Economic Research and the Keynesian Thinking of Our Times," he had criticized a version of the Keynesian underemployment equilibrium and concluded a little heavily that "the imposing schemes for governmental action that are being bottomed on Keynes's equilibrium theory must be viewed with skepticism." Alvin Hansen had replied rather sharply.

But Burns was (and is) an able economist. If he regarded Keynes with skepticism, he viewed recessions with positive antipathy. In his 1955 Economic Report, he said, "Budget policies can help promote the objective of maximum production by wisely allocating resources *first between private and public uses;* second, among various government programs." (Italics added.) Keynes, reading these words carefully, would have strongly applauded. And, indeed, a spokesman for the N.A.M. told the Joint Economic Committee that they pointed "directly toward the planned and eventually the socialized economy."

After the departure of Burns, the Eisenhower Administration incurred a deficit of no less than $9.4 billions in the national income accounts in the course of overcoming the recession of 1958. This was by far the largest deficit ever incurred by an American Government in peacetime; it exceeded the *total* peacetime expenditure by F.D.R in any year up to 1940. No administration before or since has given the economy such a massive dose of Keynesian medicine. With a Republican Administration, guided by men like Mr. Randall and Mr. Weeks, following such policies, the academic Keynesians were no longer vulnerable.

The new conventional wisdom

Presidents Kennedy and Johnson have continued what is now commonplace policy. Advised by Walter Heller, a remarkably skillful exponent of Keynes's ideas, they added the new device of the deliberate tax reduction to sustain aggregate demand. And they abandoned, at long last, the doubletalk by which advocates of Keynesian policies combined advocacy of measures to promote full employment and economic growth with promises of a promptly balanced budget. "We have recognized as self-defeating the effort to balance our budget too quickly in an economy operating well below its potential," President Johnson said in his 1965 report. Now, as noted, Keynesian policies are the new orthodoxy. Economists are everywhere to be seen enjoying their new and pleasantly uncontroversial role.

We have yet to pay proper respect to those who pioneered the Keynesian revolution. Everyone now takes pride in the resulting performance of the economy. We should take a little pride in the men who brought it about. It is hardly fitting that they should have been celebrated only by the reactionaries. The debt to the courage and intelligence of Alvin Hansen is especially great. Next only to Keynes, his is the credit for saving what even conservatives still call capitalism.

Reading 23

Keynesian and Other Present-day Heresies

Henry Hazlitt

Shortly after the appearance of John Maynard Keynes's *General Theory of Employment, Interest, and Money* in 1936, the doctrines enunciated in it conquered the academic world and have dominated it ever since. But in the decade beginning in 1955 a frontal counterattack was launched. In 1959 the present writer published *The Failure of the "New Economics,"* with the subtitle, *An Analysis of the Keynesian Fallacies;* a year later I brought

From Henry Hazlitt, "The Development of Economic Thought," *National Review*, New York, November, 1965. Reprinted with kind permission of the author and publisher.

together in an anthology, *The Critics of Keynesian Economics,* articles written by some twenty distinguished economists over the preceding twenty-four years which directly or indirectly refuted the Keynesian contentions. Then, in 1963, Professor W. H. Hutt, Dean of the Faculty of Commerce at the University of Cape Town, published his brilliant and thoroughgoing *Keynesianism—Retrospect and Prospect.*

Retreat

There are now, at long last, definite signs of a crack-up of the Keynesian ideology. I wish I could report that this is the result of recent criticisms of its internal confusions and contradictions, but the plain truth seems to be that it is cracking up because the remedies based on it are so obviously not working as advertised. What is happening is precisely the result predicted by Jacob Viner in the same year the *General Theory* appeared: "In a world organized in accordance with Keynes's specifications there would be a constant race between the printing press and the business agents of the trade unions."

It would be wrong to give the impression that retreat from the pure Keynesian ideology on the part of the leading Keynesians has been open and avowed. But it can be detected by the shrewd analyst. In an article in *The South African Journal of Economics* of last June, W. H. Hutt pointed out that Samuelson and half a dozen other Keynesians have quietly abandoned Keynes's crucial concept of an "unemployment equilibrium." It was precisely this, however, that they had originally hailed as "the shattering new insight" that had "wrought a revolution in thought." Instead, they are now explaining unemployment as chiefly the result of "money wage rates that are sticky and resistant to downward price movements." In brief, they have returned to the old "classical" explanation of unemployment.

Fellow travelers

I would be misleading the reader if I implied that the bulk of economic discussion in the last decade has circled around the books I have mentioned. Vance Packard and others have enjoyed the greatest sales and attention—for books which give the reader the impression that American industry is chiefly engaged in turning out, wastefully and irrationally, all sorts of silly products that the American public does not need but can be hornswoggled into believing that it wants. And the most discussed and most influential economics book in the last decade has been J. K. Galbraith's *The Affluent Society* (1958). Where the older socialists told us that the trouble with capitalism was that it couldn't produce the goods, Galbraith told us that its trouble was that it was producing altogether too many, but they were all the wrong goods. Therefore, we should tax the "private sector" even more onerously to force it to support an even bigger "public sector"—i.e. still more public spending, more welfare-statism and more socialism.

At the same time, those who were endorsing the Galbraith theme saw no inconsistency in also supporting the theme that the American economy was not "growing" fast enough. In any case, their remedy was the same—various forms of government inflation and other interventions to achieve this faster growth. W. W. Rostow's *The Stages of Economic Growth* was a typical product of this forced-growth mania.

Requiem

The economic theory and practice of a decade cannot be judged merely from its books. Almost every non-Communist government in the world was, and is, practicing Keynesian policies to the accompaniment of Keynesian rationalizations. These policies consist of continuous currency and credit expansion, artificially low interest rates, increased government spending, and budget deficits. When such policies result in inflation, in balance of payments deficits, and in rising prices and wages, the remedy adopted is not to abandon the policies, but to try to offset them by such devices as further import restrictions, penalties and prohibitions on foreign investment, price controls, "wage policies," and "income policies" —in brief, to further government controls that move in the totalitarian direction. And this is the current direction of government economic policy the world over.

Reading 24

Granted that business cycles are not so regular as the oscillations of physics and astronomy, economic science has made some progress toward accurate forecasting. Prediction is important, not simply to make money for speculators, but also as a guide for policy programs of government and business.

The raw materials of every science are its data. It is important to be able to evaluate the accuracy and limitations of economic statistics. The present generation of economists would be the envy of earlier writers because of the great improvement in information now quickly available.

Paul A. Samuelson, Institute Professor at M.I.T., has for years made annual forecasts of the American economy for the *London Financial Times.* He is past president of the Econometric Society, the American Economic Association, and the International Economic Association.

Questions to Guide the Reading

Why is it true that good scientific method may be needed more by an investigator into smoking and cancer or into business-cycle developments than by a physicist working in his laboratory?

What gaps in our economic statistical data relating to unemployment and price indices do you think the government ought to try to fill?

Economic Forecasting and Science

Paul A. Samuelson

If prediction is the ultimate aim of all science, then we forecasters ought to award ourselves the palm for accomplishment, bravery, or rashness. We are the end-product of Darwinian evolution and the payoff for all scientific study of economics. Around the country, students are grinding out doctoral theses by the use of history, statistics, and theory—merely to enable us to reduce the error in our next year's forecast of GNP from $10 billion down to $9 billion.

What prediction means

Actually, though, I am not sure that the ultimate end of science is prediction—at least in the sense of unconditional prediction about what is likely to happen at a specified future date. Students are always asking of professors, "If you are so smart, how come you ain't rich?" Some of our best economic scientists seem to be fairly poor forecasters of the future. One of our very best economists, in fact, couldn't

even correctly foresee the results of the last election. Is it legitimate to ask of a scholar: "If you are so scientific and learned, how come you are so stupid at predicting next year's GNP?"

I think not, for several different reasons. In the first place, a man might be a brilliant mathematician in devising methods for the use of physicists and still be a very poor physicist. Or he might be a genius in devising statistical methods while still being rather poor at conducting statistical investigations. Let us grant then at the beginning, that a person might be poor himself at *any* predictions within a field, and still be a useful citizen. Only we would then call him a mathematician —rather than simply a physicist, statistician, or economist.

The late Sir Ronald Fisher, for instance, was a genius, as we all gladly acknowledge. And perhaps he did good empirical work in the field of agronomy and applied fertilizer. But I must say that his work on genetics—in which

From Paul A. Samuelson, "Economic Forecasting and Science," *Michigan Quarterly Review,* October, 1965. Reprinted with kind permission of the publisher.

he blithely infers the decline of Roman and of all civilizations from the dastardly habit infertile heiresses have of snatching off the ablest young men for mates, thereby making them infertile—seems awfully casual statistical inference to me. And I can't think Fisher covered himself with immortal glory at the end of his life when he doubted that cigarette smoking and inhaling has anything to do with reducing longevity.

A good scientist should be good at *some* kind of prediction. But it need not be flat prediction about future events. Thus, a physicist may be bad at telling you what the radioactivity count in the air will be next year, but be very good at predicting for you what will be the likely effects on air pollution of a given controlled experiment involving fissionable materials. If he is a master scientist, his hunches about experiments never yet performed may be very good ones.

Similarly, a good economist has good judgment about economic reality. To have good judgment means you are able to make good judgments—good predictions about what will happen under *certain specified conditions.* This is different from having a model that is pretty good at doing mechanical extrapolation of this year's trends of GNP to arrive at respectable guesses of next year's GNP. Time and again your naïve model may win bets from me in office pools on next year's outcome. But neither of us would ever dream of using such a naïve model to answer the question, "What will happen to GNP, compared to what it would otherwise have been, when the Kennedy-Johnson massive tax cut is put into effect?" The mechanical, naïve model does not have in it, explicitly, the parameter tax rates. And if we insist upon differentiating the result with respect to such a parameter, we will end up with a zero partial derivative and with the dubious conclusion that massive tax cuts cannot have any effect on GNP. The model that I use, which is perhaps very nonmechanical and perhaps even non-naïve, may be bad at predicting unconditionally next year's GNP, and still be very good at answering the other-things-equal question of the effect of a change in tax rates or in some other structural parameter of the system.

What I have been saying here can be put in technical language: to make good year-to-year predictions, you need not necessarily have accomplished good "identification" of the various structural relations of a model.

The how and why

Is it possible to have everything good?—to be able to make good annual predictions as well as good predictions of identified structural relationships? The best economists I have known, in the best years of their lives, were pretty good at making just such predictions. And that is what I call good judgment in economics.

Obviously, they have to be men of much experience. In the last analysis, empirical predictions can be made only on the basis of empirical evidence. But it is an equal empirical truth that the facts do not tell their own story to scientists or historical observers, and that the men who develop topnotch judgment have an analytical framework within which they try to fit the facts. I should say that such men are constantly using the evidence of economic time series; the evidence of cross-sectional data; the evidence of case studies and anecdotes, but with some kind of judgment concerning the frequency and importance of the cases and instances. And they are even using conjectures of the form, "What if I were no smarter than these businessmen and unionists? What would I be likely to do?"

We all know the great statistical problems involved in the small samples economic statisticians must work with. We have few years of data relevant to the problem at hand. Maybe the data can be found by months or by quarters; but since there is much serial correlation between adjacent monthly data, we can by no means blithely assume that we have increased our degrees of freedom twelve-fold or more by using monthly data. Nature has simply not performed the controlled experiments that enable us to predict as we should wish.

This means that the master economist must piece together, from all the experience he has ever had, hunches relevant to the question at hand. In short, we begin to accumulate "degrees of freedom" from the first moment we draw breath and begin to take in observations of the world around us. Indeed, we could perhaps begin the integral of experience even before birth.

At any rate, just as there is a time for remembering, there is a time for forgetting. Economics is not a stationary time-series. Getting a year's extra data for 1864 is not worth nearly so much as getting extra data for 1964. We must learn both to regard experience and to disregard it. I've known men who paid dearly for every thousand dollars of profits they made from selling short in 1929–1932. They never recovered from being bears —even in 1946–1955!

But if economics does not deal with a stationary time-series, neither is ignorance bliss in our profession. There are thousands of ways for the really uninformed man to be wrong in the field of forecasting. Today will not simply repeat yesterday. But to think that the laws of the universe were born anew this morning when you opened your eyes is pitiful nonsense. The essence of science is mastering the art of filtering out the obsolete patterns of the past and filtering in the patterns of persistence.

If science becomes a private art, it loses its characteristic of reproducibility. Here is an example. Sumner Slichter, from 1930 to his death in the late 1950's, was a good forecaster. Dr. Robert Adams of Standard Oil (New Jersey), comparing different methods of forecasting, found that "being Sumner Slichter" was then about the best. But how did Slichter do it? I could never make this out. And neither, I believe, could he. One year he talked about Federal Reserve policy, another year about technical innovation. Somehow the whole came out better than the sum of its parts. Now what I should like to emphasize is that the private art of Sumner Slichter died with him. No less-gifted research assistant could have had transferred to him even a fraction of the Master's skill. And thus one of the principal aims of science was not achieved —namely, reproducibility by any patient person of modest ability of the empirical regularities discerned by luck or by the transcendental efforts of eminent scholars.

The models of Klein, Goldberger, Tinbergen, and Suits have at least this property. Take away Frankenstein and you still have a mechanical monster that will function for awhile. But unlike the solar system, which had to be wound up by Divine Providence only once, any economic model will soon run down if the breath of intelligent life is not pumped into it. When you see a 7094 perform well in a good year, never forget that it is only a Charlie McCarthy; without an Edgar Bergen in the background it is only a thing of paint and wood, of inert transistors and obsolescing matrices.

Only the best there is

How well can economists forecast? The question is an indefinite one, and reminds us of the man who was asked what he thought about his wife, and had to reply, "Compared to what?"

When I say that as an economist I am not very good at making economic forecasts, that sounds like modesty. But actually, it represents the height of arrogance. For I know that bad as we economists are, we are better than anything else in heaven and earth at forecasting aggregate business trends—better than gypsy tea-leaf readers, Wall Street soothsayers and chartist technicians, hunch-playing heads of mail order chains, or all-powerful heads of state. This is a statement based on empirical experience. Over the years I have tried to keep track of various methods of forecasting, writing down in my little black book what people seemed to be saying before the event, and then comparing their prediction with what happened. The result has been a vindication of the hypothesis that there is no efficacious substitute for economic analysis in business forecasting. Some maverick may hit a home run on occasion; but over the long season, batting averages tend to settle down to a sorry level when the more esoteric methods of soothsaying are relied upon.

What constitutes a good batting average? That depends on the contest. In baseball these days, .300 or 300-out-of-1,000, is very good. In economic forecasting of the direction of change, we ought to be able to do at least .500 just by tossing a coin. And taking advantage of the undoubted upward trend in all modern economies, we can bat .750 or better just by parrot-like repeating, "Up, Up." The difference between the men and the boys, then, comes between an .850 performance and an .800 performance. Put in other terms, the good forecaster, who must in November make a point-estimate of GNP for the calendar year ahead, will, over a decade, have an average error of perhaps one per cent, being in a range of $12 billion dollars, with reality being $6 billion on either side of the estimate. And a rather poor forecaster may, over the same period, average an error of 1½ per cent. When we average the yearly results for a decade, it may be found that in the worst year the error was over 2 per cent, compensated by rather small errors in many of the years not expected to represent turning points.

Irreducible error?

In a sense this is a modest claim. But again I must insist on the arrogance underlying these appraisals. For I doubt that it is possible, on the basis of the evidence now knowable, a year in advance, to do much better than this. An expert owns up to the limits of his accuracy, but goes on arrogantly to insist that the result cannot be bettered. His range of ignorance is, so to speak, based on experience. It is ignorance based on knowledge, not ignorance based on ignorance. It reminds one a little bit of Heisenberg's Uncertainty Principle in quantum mechanics. According to it, an observer cannot simultaneously determine both the position and the velocity of a particle: if he arranges his observational experiment so as to get an accurate fix on position, his recording instruments will make the velocity indeterminate with a range; and if he rearranges the observational instruments so as to get an accurate fix on velocity, the cost he must pay is giving up knowledge of position.

I do not mean to imply that this is fixed for all time. Once our profession got new surveys of businessmen's intentions to invest, of their decisions as to capital appropriations, and of consumers' responses to random polling, the critical level of imprecision was reduced. In all likelihood, the critical level of uncertainty is a secularly declining one. But is its asymptote (for forecasting a year ahead, remember) literally zero? I do not know how to answer this question. Although it may seem pessimistic to give a negative answer, I am tempted to do so. For remember, you cannot find what is in a person's mind by interrogation, before there is anything in his mind. That is why preliminary surveys of the McGraw-Hill type, taken in October before many corporations

have made their capital-budgeting decisions, are necessarily of limited accuracy—which does not deny that they are of some value to us.

Probability spread

The imprecision inherent in forecasting raises some questions about the propriety of making simple point-estimates. If you twist my arm, you can make me give a single number as a guess about next year's GNP. But you will have to twist hard. My scientific conscience would feel more comfortable giving you my subjective probability distribution for all the values of GNP.[1] Thus, I might reckon the rough probability to be one-half that GNP will be at most $655 billion in 1965; one-quarter that it will be at most $650 billion; and three-quarters that it will be at most $662 billion. Actualy, it is a pain in the neck to have to work out the whole probability distribution rather than to give a single point-estimate. But satisfying one's scientific conscience is never a very easy task. And there is some payoff for the extra work involved.

For one thing, just what does a point-estimate purport to mean? That is often not clear even to the man issuing it. Do I give the number at which I should just be indifferent to make a bet *on either side*, if forced to risk a large sum of money on a bet whose side can be determined by an opponent or by a referee using chance devices? If that is what I mean in issuing a point-estimate, I am really revealing the *median* of my subjective probability distribution. Other times estimators have in the back of their mind that over the years they will be judged by their mean-square-error, and hence it is best for them to reveal the *arithmetic mean* of their subjective distribution.

I have known still others who aimed, consciously or unconsciously, at the mode of their distribution—sometimes perhaps using the modal value of forecasts among all their friends and acquaintances as the way of arriving at

[1] Six months after I made this speech (i.e., in April, 1965), new evidence caused me to raise all the GNP numbers by 5 billion, itself an interesting fact.

Taking account of statistical revisions this was revealed in 1966 to have been luckily near the mark.

their own mode. Warning: the distribution of all point-estimates issued from a hundred different banks, insurance companies, corporations, government agencies, and academic experts is usually more bunched than the defensible *ex ante* subjective probability distribution any one of them should use in November. This is illustrated by a story I heard Roy Blough once tell at a Treasury Meeting. He said: "Economic forecasters are like six eskimos in one bed; the only thing you can be sure of is that they are all going to turn over together." Blough is right. In a few weeks time one often sees all the forecasts revised together upward or downward.

The difference between median, mean, and mode is not very significant if our expected distributions are reasonably symmetrical. But often they are not: often it will be easier to be off by $15 billion through being too pessimistic rather than too optimistic. Making your soothsayer provide you with a probability range may seem to be asking him to be more pretentiously accurate than he can be. But that is not my interpretation: using the language of arithmetical probability is my way of introducing and emphasizing the degree of uncertainty in the procedure, not its degree of finicky accuracy. There is a further advantage of using probability spreads rather than single point-estimates. One of the whizziest of the Whiz Kids in the Pentagon told me that they get better point estimates from Generals and Admirals if they make them always give high and low estimates. Before, you could never be sure whether some conservative bias or discount was not already being applied to data. Henri Theil of Rotterdam has studied how well forecasters perform and has found a similar tendency toward conservative bias in economic forecasters.

Suppose we think that GNP is likely to rise, say by $30 billion. If we issue the forecast of a rise of $20 billion, we shall certainly have been in the right direction. And we shall be in the ball park with respect to general magnitude. Why be hoggish and try for better? Particularly since GNP might go down, and then you would be standing all alone out there in right field, more than $30 billion off the mark. "Better be wrong in good company, than run the risk of being wrong all alone" is a slogan that every Trustee knows to represent wisdom for his actions.

Science rather than fun and fame

But here I am talking about science, not about gamesmanship for the forecaster. Gamesmanship introduces a whole new set of considerations. Many forecasters, particularly amateurs, don't really care whether they turn out to be wrong or by how much they turn out to be wrong. They want to tell a good story. They want to back the longshot of possible success when their wild forecasts that depart from that of the fashionable mob might just possibly happen to be right. Then their prescience will be noted and remembered, whereas if they turn out to be woefully wrong, who is going to be there to remind people of that? If that is how you want to play the game, then naturally you should do what the rational entrant in an office pool on the election does. He does not place his bet at 61 per cent of the popular vote for Johnson, even if that is his best belief. Why not? Because there are people who are picking numbers all around that. Instead, he looks for the open spaces—measured of course in his probability metric—where few entrants in the pool have selected their estimates. Why is this rational? Because to amateurs it usually does not matter by how much you are wrong. The only prize is to be at the top. In science and in real economic life, it is terribly important not to be wrong by much. To be second-best year after year in a stock-portfolio competition would be marvelous for a mutual fund manager, and especially where the first-place winners are a shifting group of crap-shooters who stake all on one whim or another.

As an economic scientist, I take economic forecasting with deadly seriousness. I hate to be far wrong. Every residual is a wound on my body. And I'd rather make two small errors, than be right once at the cost of being wrong a second time by the sum of the two errors. The reason is not vanity—because forecasting serves a purpose: each dollar of error costs something in terms of corporate or national policy; and if the "loss function" or "social welfare function" is a smooth one in the neighborhood of its optimum, it will be the square of the error of forecast that gives a rough measure of local error.

If we use mean-square-error as our criterion of fit, I think it will be found that forecasters have another persistent bias, namely a tendency to be too pessimistic. This is different from the conservatism that makes forecasters shade both their upward and downward forecasts below the true magnitude. Why is there this downward bias? First, because it is never easy to know where next year's dollar is going to come from, and many forecasters try to build up their total by adding up the elements that they can see. There is a second, perhaps more defensible, reason for erring on the downward or pessimistic side in making a forecast. The social consequences of unemployment and underproduction may be deemed more serious than those of over-full-employment and (mild) demand inflation. I once shocked the late John Maurice Clark at a meeting in Washington by saying, "Although the chance of a recession next year is only one-third, for policy purposes we should treat it as if it were two-thirds." He thought that a contradiction in terms. But in terms of his colleague Wald's loss-function concept, I could make sense of my statement by postulating that each dollar of deflationary gap had social consequences more serious than each dollar of inflationary gap.

Often a forecaster is forced to give a single point-estimate because his boss or consumers cannot handle a more complicated concept. Then he must figure out for himself which point-estimate will do them the most good, or the least harm. Years ago one of the publishing companies used to have every staff member make a prediction of the sales each textbook would enjoy. If people tried to play safe and guess low figures, the President of the company would penalize them for having too little faith in the company's sales staff and authors. (Incidentally, the sales manager used to come up with the least inaccurate predictions, odd as that may sound.)

Calling turns

A good speech should tell the audience something that it already knows to be true. Then having gained their good approval for soundness, it should tell them something they didn't previously know to be true. I don't know whether I have been able to complete the second part of this recipe, but I want to add a third requirement for a good speech. It should call attention to some problem whose true answer is not yet known. Let me conclude, therefore, by raising an unanswered question.

Naïve models based upon persistence, momentum, or positive serial correlation do rather well in economics as judged by least-square-error of predictions. An extreme case is one which merely projects the current level or the current direction of change. Yet such models do badly in "calling turning points." Indeed, as described above, such naïve models are like the Dow System of predicting stockmarket prices, which never even tries to call a turning point in advance and is content to learn, not too long after the fact, that one has actually taken place.

Forecasters regard models which merely say, "Up and up," or "more of the same," as rather dull affairs. When I once explained to editors of a financial magazine that one disregarded this continuity only at one's risk, they said: "Professor, that may be good economic science, but it's darn dull journalism." But are we forecasters here to have a good time? Dullness may be part of the price we must pay for good performance. More than that. Are we here to cater to our own vanity? One hates to be wrong; but if one's average error could be reduced at the cost of being more often wrong in direction, is that not a fair bargain?

I don't pretend to know the answer to these questions. But they do have a bearing on the following issue. Often an economist presents a model which he admits does worse than some more naïve model, but which he justifies for its better fit at the turning points. Is this emphasis legitimate? That question I leave open.

Is policy action most important at the turning points? Is policy action most potent at the turning points? Is a correct guess about turning points likely to lead to correct guesses for the next several quarters? And if so, why doesn't this importance of accuracy of the turning points already get duly registered in the minimum-squared-error criterion? The whole notion of a turning point would be changed in its timing if we shifted, as many dynamic economies in Europe have to do, to changes in direction of trend-deviations rather than changes in absolute direction as insisted on by the National Bureau. Does this lack of invariance cast doubt on the significance of turning points?

Finally, is it possible that public preoccupation with economics is greatest at the turning point and that we are essentially catering to our own vanity and desire for publicity when we stress accuracy at such times?

Learning from experience

But for all that, to the scientific forecaster I say, "Always study your residuals." Charles Darwin, who lived before the age of Freud, made it a habit to write down immediately any arguments *against* his theory of evolution, for he found that he invariably tended to forget those arguments. When I have steeled myself to look back over my past economic forecasts in the London *Financial Times*, they have appeared to be a little less prescient than I had remembered them to be. Janus-like, we must look at the past to learn how to look into the future.

After I had made some innocent remarks like this in my 1961 Stamp Memorial Lecture at the University of London, I ran into Professor Frank Paish, himself one of England's best economic forecasters.

"Great mistake ever to look back," he quipped, "you'll lose your nerve."

This is almost precisely what the great Satchel Paige of baseball said. "Never look backward. Somebody may be gaining on you."

Like Sir Winston, I bring you blood, sweat, and tears. The way of the scientific forecaster is hard. Let Lot's wife, who did look back, be your mascot and guide. What Satch Paige didn't mention is that "they may be gaining on you anyway." Know the truth—and while it may not make you free—it will help rid you of your amateur standing.

Inflation

Readings 25 and 26

Inflation, which means a general rise in the price level, may be mild or severe. The United States has not experienced what most observers would call a severe inflation for many years. Yet the widespread concern over Vietnam price rises of better than 5 per cent per annum suggests that the fears of runaway inflation may have a powerful grip on American thought.

Certainly the stories of what much more rapid inflations have done to creditors and debtors, to different groups of income receivers, and to political and social institutions in other times and places deserve our careful attention. How do men accommodate themselves to periods of unrestrained price rises? And what is left in the wake of such periods?

Here are two case reports on severe inflations. Frank D. Graham, former professor of economics at Princeton University, describes the burdens placed upon the German society by one of the most spectacular inflations in history —the post-World War I German inflation of 1919–1923.

Internal monetary reform and a revised plan for German reparations (the Dawes Plan, adopted in 1924) finally halted the German inflation but the case of Chile offers the unusual experience of a nation struggling decade after decade with substantial price increases almost constantly eroding the purchasing power of the currency. Yet this prolonged inflation has not developed into the type of galloping hyperinflation that has wrought havoc in other countries. This puzzling experience is described by Joseph Grunwald, expert on Latin America.

Questions to Guide the Reading

What common characteristics are there in the two inflations described?

What lessons are there in these case studies for the United States today?

Reading 25

Hyperinflation: Germany 1919–1923

Frank D. Graham

Germany, in common with other warring countries, departed from the gold standard at the outbreak of hostilities in 1914. On November 20, 1923, the German paper mark, after having fallen to an infinitesimal fraction of its former value, was made redeemable in the newly introduced rentenmark at a trillion to one. The rentenmark, after a short but honorable existence during which its gold value remained substantially stable at that of the original gold mark, was supplemented by the present [1930] standard reichsmark.

The regime of inconvertible and depreciating paper money thus ran for a little less than a decade. The progress of depreciation was, however, very unevenly distributed over these ten years. During most of the war period the exchange value of the mark did not fall greatly from par with the dollar and if, when the issue of the conflict was no longer in doubt, it sank heavily, it was still quoted in December 1918 at more than twelve American cents. During the peace negotiations, however, German exchange continued to fall fast. This downward movement persisted till February 1920 when the descent was checked at just a shade below one cent per mark, that is, at about ¼₄ of its pre-war value. A quick recovery then set in which carried the rate to nearly 3¢ in May. Though there was some reaction from this figure relative stability at a level of from 1½ to 2¢ was attained in June. By early 1920 the period of immediate adjustment to post-war conditions may therefore be considered to have been completed. Not until September 1921 did the value of the mark again fall below one American cent and as late as June 1922 it still sold for about ⅓ of a cent. From then onward the decline was vertiginous till the final collapse in November 1923. At the latter date forty-two billion (42,000,000,000) marks were worth but a single American cent. Without a complete ouster of the currency concerned, no corresponding depreciation appears in the long and varied annals of monetary history. Never

before had a paper money fallen at so rapid a rate over such an extended period.

Reparations or scapegoat

While the payments of cash reparations in 1921 undoubtedly played an important part in promoting the decline in the currency, and while the sanctions imposed on Germany in 1923 led to the ultimate collapse, this is, of course, by no means the whole story. Reparations gravely affected public finances but the fiscal difficulties were far from being solely due to this cause. It is true that, if a more soundly conceived and executed reparations policy had been adopted by the creditor Powers, inflation of the currency might perhaps have been stayed by the vigorous measures of reform of the public finances initiated in Germany in 1920. But inflation had none the less proceeded far before any cash reparations whatever had been paid and it was accelerated after they had been entirely suspended. Its roots went back into the early war period and it was, in many German quarters, nurtured rather than repressed. The war administration had looked with a much too friendly eye on inflationary policies. The initial impetus thus given was never checked and long after the war was over the Reichsbank was entirely too pliable in its attitude toward both governmental and private borrowing.

The attitude of the Reichsbank was but one aspect of a fairly general complacency toward currency depreciation. The burden of the great internal government debt, piled up during and immediately after the war, meant exceedingly high taxes unless it should be lightened by a decline in the value of the counters in which it was expressed. Though currency depreciation meant confiscation of the property of holders of the government debt it was the line of least resistance for the Treasury and was thus not unwelcome in official circles. The policy of in-

From Frank D. Graham, *Exchange, Prices and Production in Hyper-Inflation Germany, 1920–1923* (Princeton University Press, Princeton, New Jersey, 1930). Reprinted with kind permission of the publisher.

flation had, in addition, powerful support from influential private quarters.

Inflation was therefore combated but half-heartedly at best. Though several of the administrations of the years 1920 to 1923 made valiant attempts to arrest its progress they could not summon the sustained powers necessary to success. It may well be doubted whether a stable standard could in any case have been set up while immense reparations debts were plaguing the situation. But this must remain an open question. So long as wealth and income were being merely transferred by the decline in the value of the monetary unit and not, as a sum, diminished, so long as scapegoats could be found to assume the burdens and yield of their substance to those who knew how to profit from the situation, projects of reform were treated cavalierly. It was only when enterprisers, instead of surely profiting from inflation as they long did, were suddenly plunged into a sea of uncertainties, only when business activity passed from the stage of exhilaration to panic, only when resistance to a further assumption of losses on the part of the public at large became general, that influential opinion veered to a conviction of the necessity of restoring a stable standard. The pass to which matters had then come is shown in Table 1.

The masses of the urban population were living from hand to mouth, nay, had nothing in their hands but worthless bits of paper which the farmers would no longer accept in exchange for grain. Food riots were general. Political dissolution was in imminent prospect and armed revolt had already raised its head. Affairs were indeed so black that it is clear, in retrospect, that they actually facilitated the reform by imbuing the people with the resolution of despair.

Inflation and social upheaval

Inflation had shaken the social structure to its roots. The changes of status which it caused were profound. No such shifting of property rights, in time of peace, had ever before taken place. Great numbers of families of long established wealth and position were reduced to beggary at the very time that new or additional fortunes of staggering magnitude were being accumulated. The old middle class well-nigh disappeared and a new group came into prominence. There was less change in the condition of the masses—they had not so much to lose—but the wiping out of savings, insurance, and pensions pressed heavily upon the worker even if his losses did not parallel those of some of the better-to-do social classes.

The drama, and particularly the tragedy, of the time have left an indelible impression of the evils of inflation on the minds of the generation which lived through it. The most striking effects were in the realm of the distribution of wealth rather than in production but there were periods, principally in the final stages of depreciation, when the great majority of the population was in extreme want and perhaps even more distressing uncertainty. When prices were rising hourly by leaps and bounds, when the purchasing power of present and prospective receipts of money was vanishing before it could be spent, or would even be acquired, the population of a so highly specialized exchange society as Germany, was subjected to a well-nigh intolerable strain.

Reading 26

Chronic Inflation: Twentieth-century Chile

Joseph Grunwald

There is some evidence that Chile's price inflation started as far back as the late 1870s. Since the beginning of the official consumer price index in 1928, there have been only about four years, but not consecutive ones, during which it may be said that relative price stability existed.

Chile's very severe depression of the 1930s and the influence of the war years of the forties brought a very erratic pattern of price

From Joseph Grunwald, "The 'Structuralist' School of Price Stabilization and Economic Development: The Chilean Case," in Albert O. Hirschman (ed.), *Latin American Issues* (The Twentieth Century Fund, New York, 1961). Reprinted with kind permission of the publisher.

Table 1 Treasury Bills Discounted by the Reich, Issues of Paper Currency, Index of Wholesale Prices, and Index of Dollar Exchange Rates against Paper Marks: 1919–1923 (value figures in millions of marks)

End of month	Total amount of Treasury bills discounted by the Reich*	Total issues of paper currency (except emergency currency)	Index of wholesale prices† 1913 = 1	Index of dollar exchange rates in Berlin‡ 1913 = 1
1919 Dec.	86,400	50,065	8.03	11.14
1920 June	113,200	68,154	13.82	9.17
Dec.	152,800	81,387	14.40	17.48
1921 June	185,100	84,556	13.66	17.90
Dec.	247,100	122,497	34.87	43.83
1922 June	295,200	180,169	70.30	89.21
July	308,000	202,626	100.59	159.60
Aug.	331,600	252,212	192.00	410.91
Sept.	451,100	331,876	287.00	393.04
Oct.	603,800	484,685	566.00	1,071.94
Nov.	839,100	769,500	1,154.00	1,822.30
Dec.	1,495,200	1,295,228	1,475.00	1,750.83
1923 Jan.	2,081,800	1,999,600	3,286.00	11,672.00
Feb.	3,588,000	3,536,300	5,257.00	5,407.00
Mar.	6,601,300	5,542,900	4,827.00	4,996.00
April	8,442,300	6,581,200	5,738.00	7,099.00
May	10,275,500	8,609,700	9,034.00	16,556.00
June	22,019,800	17,340,500	24,618.00	36,803.00
July	57,848,900	43,813,500	183,510.00	262,030.00
Aug.	1,196,294,700	668,702,600	1,695,109.00	2,454,000.00
Sept.	46,716,616,400	28,244,405,800	36,223,771.00	38,113,000.00
Oct.	6,907,511,102,800	2,504,955,700,000	18,700,000,000.00	17,270,129,000.00
Nov.	191,580,465,422,100	400,338,326,400,000	1,422,900,000,000.00	1,000,000,000,000.00
Dec.	1,232,679,853,100	496,585,345,900,000	1,200,400,000,000.00	1,000,000,000,000.00

* Practically all government borrowing after 1919 was in the form of discounted Treasury bills. The figure for November 1923 is as of the 15th of that month.

† In the index number of wholesale prices from December 1919 to December 1922 inclusive the figures represent monthly averages. From January to June, 1923, statistics are available for specific days three times a month, and from July to December, 1923, weekly. The figures in the table are for the latest available date in each month.

‡ The December 1919 figure for the index number of exchange rates is a monthly average. All other figures for this index are end-of-month quotations.

SOURCES OF DATA: (1) *Zahlen zur Geldentwertung in Deutschland 1914 bis 1923*; Statistisches Reichsamt, Verlag von Reimar Hobbing, Berlin, 1925, pp. 6–10, 16–18, 46–7. (2) *Germany's Economy, Currency and Finance*. Zentral-Verlag G.m.b.H., Berlin, 1924, p. 63.

movements during those two decades. On the average, the yearly price increase was roughly 10 per cent during the thirties and 20 per cent during the forties. The inflation rate increased somewhat during the first years of the fifties, but in the middle of 1953 a price explosion took place which brought the yearly inflation rate to over 80 per cent by 1955. With the 1956 anti-inflation program the inflation rate dropped to 38 per cent in 1956 and 17 per cent in 1957. Price increases were higher in 1958 and 1959, reaching about 35 per cent annually, but since the end of 1959 a relative stability has been attained.

Inflation became a way of life and was institutionalized into the legal and socio-economic structure of the country, each sector of the economy constructing its own defense apparatus.

The wage and salary sectors achieved the right to legal wage readjustments in some relation to the cost-of-living index. These income adjustments applied not only to wages and salaries but also to pensions, retirement and other social security incomes. The other mechanism for the salaried classes was price control and subsidized imports of certain basic consumer items.

The self-employed and profit-earning groups defended themselves first through anticipating the inflation by increasing their prices even before the annual wage adjustments came around, and following this up by further price increases after the wage adjustments were given. Second, the credit mechanism also served as an inflation defense for the more substantial businesses. Increases in costs due to wage adjustments and price increases of raw materials were readily absorbed through relatively easy access to credit for the privileged groups, while for others credit was sharply rationed or unavailable.

The government sector defended itself against inflation through the printing press. It is clear that deficit spending became unavoidable as government revenues were based upon the previous period's assessments compared to current pricing for government expenditures.

Nearly all of the sectors of the community hedged through the building up of inventories. This applied also to consumer groups, who bought consumer goods for storage rather than for use.

It is not surprising that this inflation spirit developed a finesse and cleverness in handling the pressures of price increases in all sectors. Although most of the defense mechanisms employed were in themselves quite inflationary, there is little doubt that they brought a certain self-confidence to the community which helped to stave off panic.

The curious aspect of Chile's inflation history of close to a century is that the country never experienced runaway inflation. One would think that, once a country reaches such high rates of price increases as Chile did, hyperinflation would follow almost automatically. There is no satisfactory answer to this. The fact is that not enough money was printed for hyperinflation to develop. But if the forces that made the authorities "print money" were so strong as to maintain a 20 or more per cent yearly inflation for many years, what stopped those forces from compelling a snowballing monetary expansion? Probably the social pressures were not strong enough, and perhaps public confidence was greater than is generally thought. But if among the factors of hyperinflation is public panic, then the defense mechanisms which the Chilean community has built up over the years have helped to avoid it—no matter how inflationary these mechanisms may be in themselves.

Readings 27 and 28

The American record in the 1950s was one of moderate or "creeping" inflation. The impact of this was widely and emotionally discussed throughout the decade, but the concern reached a peak when prices continued to rise even in the midst of a mild recession in 1958. Was this a portent of inevitable inflation even when jobs were scarce? Did it mean that more severe inflation must follow as soon as employment picked up once again? And what difference did inflation make?

Creeping inflation's critics were numerous. Its defenders were rarer. One of the most articulate defenders was the late Sumner H. Slichter, professor of economics at Harvard University. His view that a modest amount of inflation was both inevitable and healthy in any economy committed to high levels of employment and growth attracted considerable attention, and drew forth the rebuttal in Reading 28 by Jules Backman, professor of economics at New York University. The main issue with which they are concerned was somewhat eclipsed in the early 1960s by the stability of prices which appeared to stem from too high a rate of unemployment. But an economy that sought a way back to a point near full employment had to ask itself once again after 1965: Can we have stable prices too? See Readings 79 and 80 by Burns and Eckstein for a debate on wage-price guideposts.

Questions to Guide the Reading

Have there been significant changes in the American economy in the 1960s to lend greater weight to one side or the other in this debate on inflation?

How might Americans be able to protect themselves against a steady inflation that hovered around 2 per cent per annum? How adequate are the assurances that inflation will not be likely to go much beyond that point in the near future?

Reading 27

The Case for Creeping Inflation

Sumner H. Slichter

The principal economic issue dividing the American people today is the issue of growth of the economy vs. stability of the price level. Mr. Eisenhower has declared that a stable price level "is an indispensable condition for achieving vigorous and continuing economic growth" and has placed strong emphasis on the prevention of inflation in his State of the Union message, his budget message, and his economic report.

His critics accuse him of discouraging growth in order to stabilize the price level. The A.F.L.-C.I.O. Economic Policy Committee has charged that Mr. Eisenhower's program is "a sure-fire prescription for stagnation." The Joint Congressional Economic Committee, under the chairmanship of Senator Paul H. Douglas of Illinois, is about to start hearings on the problem of reconciling full employment, an "adequate" rate of growth and price stability.

Is it true, as Mr. Eisenhower says, that there is no conflict between vigorous economic growth and a stable price level? Or must permanent inflation be accepted as a necessary condition to maximum growth? And if maximum growth entails creeping inflation, what will be the consequences for the economy? Will the United States price itself out of world markets? Will confidence in the dollar be undermined and will there be a disastrous flight from the dollar with creeping inflation developing into a gallop? Will creeping inflation produce great suffering among recipients of fixed incomes? Or are the consequences of creeping inflation greatly exaggerated?

The inflation of the 1950's in the United States has been caused by a mixture of strong demand for goods and a strong upward push of costs, but the principal reason the price level has increased and slow inflation must be expected to continue more or less indefinitely is the strong tendency for labor costs to rise

From Sumner H. Slichter, "Argument for 'Creeping' Inflation," *New York Times Magazine*, March 8, 1959. Reprinted with kind permission of the publisher.

faster than output per man-hour. During the past ten years, for example, hourly compensation of employes in private industry outside agriculture has risen more than twice as fast as output per man-hour.

The unions explain this by asserting that wages were simply chasing prices up, but the facts refute the claims of the union spokesmen. In *every one* of the past ten years the percentage rise in the hourly compensation of workers exceeded the percentage rise in the consumer price index. Furthermore, in nine out of the past ten years, the rise in hourly compensation of workers exceeded the rise in the wholesale prices of finished goods. Wages were not chasing prices up; on the contrary, prices were chasing wages, and were falling behind each year.

The tendency for wages to outrun output per man-hour is bound to occur in an economy of private enterprise and powerful trade unions whenever the demand for goods is strong— that is, whenever the conditions are favorable for rapid growth. Wages could be prevented from outrunning output per man-hour if the bargaining power of unions were weakened and the bargaining power of employers strengthened by the maintenance of a fairly high rate of unemployment.

Some members of the Board of Governors of the Federal Reserve System, some members of the Council of Economic Advisers and some private economists have proposed that tight credit policies be used to create the amount of unemployment necessary to keep wages from rising faster than productivity and to keep the price level steady. The amount of unemployment needed would vary with the phase of the business cycle, the vigor of foreign competition and the year-to-year fluctuation in the size of crops, but recent experience indicates that an unemployment rate of 5 to 8 per cent would be required.

Stagnation vs. growth

Fostering unemployment in order to keep wages from outrunning productivity, however, would mean retarding the growth of the economy. Hence the conflict between maximum growth and stable prices is real—the community must decide which it prefers. There is little doubt which way the decision will go because the loss to the community from a retarded rate of growth would increase at a compound rate and would soon become intolerably burdensome. Suppose that the economy, which is capable of increasing its productive capacity at the rate of 4 per cent a year, were held to a growth of only 2 per cent a year in order to keep the price level steady. At the end of ten years the economy would have a productive capacity more than 26 percentage points less than it would have had at the greater rate of growth.

What about the long run effects of creeping inflation? Would not creeping inflation bring frequent recessions, so that in the long run more real growth would be achieved under a stable price level? There is no doubt that rapid growth entails the risk of recession, but the occasional recessions that accompany a high rate of growth need not be severe. Much progress has been made in building up resistance of the economy to contraction. The recession of 1958 illustrates this progress. The drop in business investment and the liquidation of inventories were moderately severe, but personal income and retail sales remained remarkably steady. As a result, the recession was both mild and short. In view of the growing capacity of the economy to resist contraction, one must reject the view that a stable price level is a necessary condition to the maximum rate of growth.

Best of two worlds?

Are not changes possible in our institutions, policies, or business practices that would enable us to avoid creeping inflation and at the same time realize our maximum growth potential? There are many changes that would diminish the tendency for prices to rise, but none of them would assure that unions would not push up wages faster than industry could raise output per man-hour in the strong sellers' markets that would characterize a rapidly growing economy.

The *possibility of price and wage controls may be dismissed,* partly because the people would not tolerate controls in time of peace and partly because controls are easily evaded by changing the quality of goods and by introducing substitute goods. Strong public hostility to excessive union wage claims will have some effect on wages, but not much. Union members expect their officers to get all that they can for the members and would displace officers whom they suspected of failing to represent them faithfully. Union members, however, are not immune to public opinion, and strong public hostility to excessive demands will tend to weaken by a small amount the upward pressure of unions on wages.

What about the possibility of *curbing the power of the trade unions by organization on the part of employers, by depriving unions of some of their present privileges and immunities, or by imposing new restrictions on unions?* More organization among employers would help, but too much should not be expected from it. The employers are organized for dealing with unions in the steel industry, the coal industry, the railroad industry, and at the local level in many of the building trades, but in none of these industries have employers been able to prevent wages from outrunning output per man-hour.

Depriving unions of some of their present extraordinary privileges, such as the use of coercive picketing to force people to join or the conscription of neutrals in labor disputes, would remove some glaring injustices, but would have little effect upon the bargaining power of most unions. Breaking up some of the large unions, as has been suggested by George Romney and others, would have consequences that are hard to predict. Unions would lose some of their present ability to support strikes by some members while other members work and pay special assessments into a strike fund. Nevertheless, the new unions might drive hard bargains. There would be rivalries among them and each would have a strong desire to make a good showing.

Thus, if there were three or four unions in the automobile industry, each might feel a strong urge to make a better settlement than any of the others. Hence, breaking up the unions might increase their militancy and make reasonable settlements with them more difficult.

Promoting productivity

But whatever the possible results of the breaking up of unions, that step is not going to be taken. The American workers want their unions, and any effort to destroy or seriously weaken organized labor would cause the work-

ers to rally to the support of the unions and make them stronger and more aggressive than ever.

The most promising methods of checking the tendency of rising labor costs to push up prices are new methods of management that enlist the ingenuity and imagination of the men at the machines and benches in reducing the ratio of labor costs to income from sales. Experience in more than a score of plants shows that amazing things begin to happen when workers share in a plant-wide bonus, based upon their success in narrowing the ratio of labor costs to income from sales, and are given good opportunities to discuss their ideas regularly with management. The common interest that everyone in the plant has in reducing labor costs produces an almost startling degree of teamwork and cooperation.

The new methods of management were introduced a few years ago by the late Joseph Scanlon, and his work is being carried out by his followers. But a generation or more will probably be required to spread the new methods throughout industry and adapt them to enterprises of various sizes and kinds. Eventually American industry will drastically modify its methods of handling labor and draw on the great capacity of rank and file workers to contribute to improvements in technology. The new methods of management may or may not be adequate to prevent wages from outrunning productivity, but they hold more promise for checking rising labor costs than any device that has yet been developed.

If a generation or so will be required for new methods of management to check the rise in labor costs, what will happen in the meantime? Fears that the United States will be priced out of world markets are far-fetched. Prices in most other important industrial countries have been rising in recent years even faster than in the United States. Between 1950 and 1957, for example, the increase in the index of wholesale prices in Britain was more than twice as large as in the United States. In Sweden and Norway it was more than three times as large, in France almost three times as large, in West Germany almost twice as large, in Austria four times as large.

No one knows, of course, whether prices in other industrial countries will continue to rise faster than in the United States. Since the principal industrial countries are in competition with one another and since they all are more or less subject to the same influences (such as powerful trade unions and an insistent popular demand for social services that precludes important reductions in taxes), all of the industrial countries are likely to experience about the same movement of the price level.

The competitive position of the United States is very strong, especially in manufacturing. This is indicated by the fact that our exports of finished manufactures are nearly three times as large as our imports. But if important industrial countries were to succeed in underselling us on a broad scale, that would not be a calamity for us. On the contrary, it would help us check inflation by stiffening the resistance of American employers to union demands and by encouraging employers to cut prices.

Also ill-founded are fears that creeping inflation will precipitate a flight from the dollar and that creeping inflation will sooner or later become a gallop. Every country in Europe has had creeping inflation during the past ten years. The idea has become pretty well accepted that a continued drop in the purchasing power of money is to be expected. And yet in virtually all countries the rise in prices between 1953 and 1957 was considerably less than in the period 1948 to 1953.

As for a general flight from the dollar, the practical question arises: "Where is the money to go?" Other currencies have limited attractiveness because almost any country one might name has economic and political problems as formidable as those confronting the United States. Flight into commodities is not satisfactory because the future price of each commodity depends upon specific market conditions (supply, demand, competition of substitutes) far more than on what happens to the general price level. Some shifting of investment is bound to occur and already has occurred, but the process tends to limit itself.

For example, if the price level is expected to rise 2 per cent a year, a good bond yielding nominally 5 per cent has a true yield of 3 per cent. Such a bond may be as attractive as a stock that has been bid up so that it yields only 2.5 per cent.

Adjusting to the inevitable

Our conclusion is that there is no immediate prospect that conflict can be avoided in advanced industrial countries between the desire for the maximum possible economic growth on the one hand and a stable price level on the other hand. This conflict is created by the rise of the relatively new institution of collective bargaining which is too well established and produces too many important benefits to be disturbed simply because it produces creeping inflation.

But the prospect that we shall be living under creeping inflation does call for various common sense adaptations and adjustments. Efforts should be made to speed the adoption of the new methods of management that automatically reward workers for helping reduce the ratio of labor costs to sales income. Pension plans, including the Federal old-age and survivors' insurance plan, should be adapted to creeping inflation. This means that they should either be fitted with escalator clauses or revised every now and then to compensate for the rise in the price level.

People should review their investment policies and should not hold long-term bonds or other long-term fixed-income investments unless the yield is sufficient to compensate them for the probable annual loss in purchasing power. Long-term wage contracts should contain escalator clauses. But in general, people should realize that living under creeping inflation in the future will not be essentially different from living under creeping inflation in the past—in fact, prices will probably rise considerably less in the next ten years than in the past ten.

Most important of all, people should realize that the alternative to creeping inflation is a fairly substantial amount of chronic unemployment. The problems of creeping inflation are a small price to pay for avoiding the much greater problems of unemployment and a rate of growth that falls far short of our potential.

Reading 28

The Case against Creeping Inflation

Jules Backman

There is a general agreement that economic growth is indispensable for a strong America. However, there has been considerable public debate about the ideal rate of growth and how to achieve it.

One school of thought asserts that "an inescapable cost" of a desirable rate of growth is creeping inflation. It holds that the alternatives are "creeping inflation and economic growth" or "price stability and unemployment." In this way, creeping inflation is given "respectability by association," while price stability is subject to "guilt by association."

The second school of thought holds not only that we can have both a desirable rate of growth and stable prices, but that we can maintain our growth only by keeping prices stable.

Creeping inflation refers to a price rise of 2 per cent or 3 per cent a year. Prof. Sumner Slichter, one of the exponents of the first school, states that this type of "slow inflation must be expected to continue more or less indefinitely." Such an annual rate of increase does not seem to be very large, but an annual rise of 2 per cent will wipe out half of the purchasing power of the dollar in thirty-five years, and a 3 per cent rate will result in a similar reduction in less than twenty-five. This is the simple arithmetic of creeping inflation.

Nevertheless, apologists for creeping inflation argue that it is unavoidable if we are to achieve the rate of economic growth which is necessary to enable us to attain our aspirations at home and to meet the threat from Russia. They explain that it is inevitable because labor costs rise more rapidly than output per man-hour. According to this argument, trade unions are so powerful that these excessive increases in wages and other labor costs could be stopped only by stringent governmental monetary and fiscal controls. The result of such curbs would be large-scale unemployment, which would limit economic growth. We are told that we must, therefore, accept creeping inflation as a lesser evil.

There is no disagreement concerning objectives between the creeping inflationists and those who are opposed. We are agreed that our goal is a maximum achievable rate of economic growth. We are agreed that unemployment is undesirable and exacts a high social cost. We are agreed that inflation—creeping or any other kind—is not desirable as a way of life. We disagree as to the means by which we may achieve our goals. The creeping inflationists say that we cannot achieve all three goals, that we much choose among them. The anti-creeping inflationists say we can achieve growth, a minimum level of unemployment *and* price stability.

The arguments against creeping inflation may be summarized as follows: (1) it slows long-term economic growth; (2) it makes recessions worse; (3) it hurts fixed-income groups and savers; (4) not everyone can be protected against it by "escalator clauses"; (5) it leads to galloping inflation; (6) it is not inevitable in an expanding economy.

(1) Creeping inflation slows long-term economic growth

There is general agreement that to meet the threat of the expanding Russian economy our own economy must continue to grow as rapidly as possible. Some say we must step up our rate of growth to about 5 per cent a year as compared with our long-term record of about 3 per cent. While the difference between 3 per cent and 5 per cent appears to be small, it becomes enormous with the passage of time. With a growth rate of 3 per cent, total output of goods and services in our economy increases fourfold in about fifty years. With a 5 per cent rate of increase, on the other hand, total output in a half century would be more than ten times as large as it is at present.

Everyone is in favor of the highest possible rate of economic growth. But there are practical limits to expansion which must be faced.

From Jules Backman, "The Case against Creeping Inflation," *New York Times Magazine*, May 3, 1959. Reprinted with kind permission of the author and publisher.

When we exceed these limits the pressures for inflation become intensified. President Eisenhower properly has pointed out that a stable price level is "an indispensable condition" for achieving the maximum growth rate in the long run.

History does not support the assumption that economic growth must be accompanied by rising prices. Economic growth has occurred in many periods of stable or declining prices. Two such major periods in the nineteenth century—the Eighteen Twenties and Eighteen Thirties and the last third of the century—were periods of declining prices. During the Nineteen Twenties, when prices remained relatively stable, national output rose about 4 per cent a year. On the other hand, from 1955 to 1957, when prices crept upward almost 3 per cent a year, national output rose less than 2 per cent annually.

Two major factors have contributed to economic growth in this country: higher productivity and an expanding population. Two-thirds of our 3 per cent annual rate of growth has been accounted for by rising output per man-hour, about one-third by increasing population. Increases in productivity, therefore, provide the key to future economic growth. Output per man-hour is affected by many factors but the most important has been the investment in new machines and equipment. The magnitude of such investments depends upon the level of savings. Savings will be discouraged by creeping inflation, and thus long-term economic growth will be stultified.

Confronted by creeping inflation, savers are more interested in speculating—to protect themselves against losses in purchasing power —than in providing capital for industry. There is ample evidence of this tendency in the rampant speculation now taking place in stocks. If inflation should continue to be a threat, more and more persons would try to protect themselves in this manner. The result would be a speculative binge which would ultimately collapse. Such a development could only act to retard economic growth.

To stimulate economic growth it is necessary to create an environment in which savings will be encouraged and business will be willing to convert those savings into new plant and equipment. Price stability encourages savings, while tax incentives could be used to induce

new investments. This is the road to greater economic growth.

Creeping inflation also interferes with business planning. When protection against price rises becomes a dominant factor, business men are not likely to plan boldly for expansion. One result is an adverse impact on job creation.

(2) Creeping inflation makes recessions worse

It is true that fear of higher prices may give a temporary stimulus to the economy. But this development induces speculation in inventories. Eventually, the inventories become burdensome, then the economy experiences a setback. The 1948–49 downturn properly has been described as an inventory recession. Inventory liquidation also was significant in the 1953–54 and 1957–58 recessions.

When protection against tomorrow's higher costs becomes a major factor in industry decisions to expand capacity today, the net result tends to be overexpansion—followed by a sharp decline in new investment in plant and equipment. The current lag in the capital goods industries reflects the aftermath of the overexpansion of 1955–57. Thus, creeping inflation means more cyclical unemployment. It is not an alternative to unemployment; it is a significant cause of unemployment. And it is little solace to those who become unemployed that they may have received overtime pay during the boom.

We normally anticipate that there will be 2.5 to 3 million workers unemployed even when the economy is operating at full speed. This frictional unemployment usually is short-term, representing individuals changing jobs or seasonally unemployed (as in the construction, apparel or retail trades). Therefore, when we have a total of 4.3 million unemployed, our real problem is how to create about 1.5 million jobs. The economic cost of unemployment must be measured in terms of this smaller figure.

The hardships attending unemployment should not be minimized. The price in terms of broken homes, loss of self-respect, loss of national output, and related developments is a heavy one indeed. This is why every effort must be directed to adopting the proper policies to reduce unemployment.

Creeping inflation exacts a double toll: first, a loss in the buying power of our money; second, added unemployment. It carries a high price tag.

(3) Creeping inflation hurts fixed-income groups and savers

Persons with fixed or relatively fixed incomes —those who live on proceeds of life-insurance policies, pensioners, those who work for non-profit organizations, government employes and bondholders—are hardest hit by any cut in the purchasing power of money. Ask the pensioner who planned his retirement twenty years ago how he gets along today with the dollars that buy less than half of what they bought then.

With an increasing number of senior citizens in our population, and with the growth of private pension plans, this is a matter of serious national concern. The hardships experienced by these persons can be just as tragic as those suffered by the unemployed.

In addition, families with savings accounts, United States Savings Bonds and other types of savings find their purchasing power steadily eroding. These various forms of savings aggregate about $400 billions. Every increase of 1 per cent in the price level, therefore, wipes out $4 billions in purchasing power.

This problem cannot be evaluated in terms of one-year or two-year results. As we noted earlier, creeping inflation could cut the total value of savings in half within twenty-five to thirty-five years. This is a heavy cost and cannot be ignored.

Nor can workers escape the adverse effects of creeping inflation. Higher prices cut the purchasing power of wages and benefits received under security programs. The part of a wage increase which is excessive is taken away —in whole or in part—by price inflation. Reduced profits mean reduced incentives to invest in new plant and equipment; one result is fewer job opportunities. And unemployment, which thus may attend excessive labor-cost increases, means that those who hold their jobs obtain part of their higher real earnings at the expense of those who lose their job or who fail to obtain jobs.

(4) Not everybody can be protected against creeping inflation by "escalator clauses"

It is significant that not even the apologists for creeping inflation regard it as something to be encouraged. Rather, we are told it is an evil which must be tolerated and to which adjustment must be made. One suggestion is that "escalator clauses," such as those now contained in many union contracts, might be extended to pensioners, insurance beneficiaries, bondholders and the like. This proposal acknowledges the ill effects of inflation, but suggests that the burden could be neutralized.

But not everybody can ride the escalator. It is the height of folly to imagine that we can inflate without some groups paying the price.

Professor Slichter has suggested that under the conditions of creeping inflation people "should not hold long-term bonds or other long-term fixed-income investment unless the yield is sufficient to compensate them for the probable annual loss in purchasing power." What would happen to our financial system if bondholders should attempt to liquidate their investments en masse? The basic weakness of the apology for creeping inflation is reflected in the recognition of the problem in this area.

(5) Creeping inflation leads to galloping inflation

Psychology plays an important role in economic decisions. As the purchasing power of money steadily erodes, more and more persons will seek to protect themselves against future price rises. The resulting flight from money into goods would accelerate the rate of increase in prices. Creeping inflation could then become galloping inflation, and finally runaway inflation.

It is true that such a development would require support from monetary and fiscal inflation. But that this support would be forthcoming seems probable as long as we persist in tolerating wage inflation and insist upon full employment.

(6) Creeping inflation is not inevitable in an expanding economy

Many factors are at work today to raise or hold up prices. They include the agricultural support program, the high level of Federal, state and local government spending, the increases in various sales and excise taxes, featherbedding and make-work rules, controls affecting imports and the steady expansion in private debt.

The primary cause of creeping inflation, however, as Professor Slichter has pointed out, is wage inflation—labor costs rising faster than ouput per man-hour. When wage inflation abates, price inflation also is moderated. It is noteworthy that, despite business recovery in the past year, consumer prices have remained stable and wholesale prices have risen only fractionally. This temporary stability reflects the likelihood that output per man-hour has risen more rapidly than the long-term rate (a typical recovery performance), and that, as a result, wage inflation has been at a minimum —perhaps even nonexistent—for the economy as a whole during this period.

The basic problem, then, is to counteract wage inflation. Two factors make this difficult. One is the national objective to maintain full employment, the other is the growth of powerful labor unions.

The full-employment policy makes it difficult to impose those stringent monetary and fiscal checks to rising prices which would create deflation and unemployment. The national concern over unemployment has assured union leaders that their wage policies will be underwritten by new inflationary measures when necessary. In other words, full-employment policies have increased the bargaining strength of the unions.

The problem of wage inflation could be ameliorated if union leaders and the workers they represent accepted the fact that our average standard of living cannot rise faster than national productivity. Only as we produce more can we obtain more goods and services, or more leisure, or some combination of both.

However, since it is the job of union leaders to get as much for their members as fast as they can, there is little point in criticizing them for taking full advantage of the present situation.

We can make more progress by taking action on two fronts:

First, the power of the unions must be curbed. There is little agreement on how this

may be accomplished. Some students of the problem have suggested applying the antitrust laws to limit unions' monopoly power. Others have proposed more drastic remedies, such as limiting the power to strike, or curbing the size of unions.

Each of these proposals involves serious difficulties which must be carefully evaluated. Possibly some other solution will be forthcoming. However, unless some means is found to curb excessive union power and its abuse, this source of pressure for creeping inflation will continue.

Second, the Employment Act of 1946 should be amended to include the goal of stabilizing the purchasing power of the dollar as well as the goal of maintaining high-level employment. This would provide a guide against which to measure proposed policies. It would not mean wage or price controls. Individual prices would continue to fluctuate as at present but public policy would have as one objective the prevention of marked changes in the general price level.

Uncertainty would be substituted for the present certainty that inflationary wage increases will be supported by governmental actions. The new element of uncertainty might impose some restraint upon unions. It might also make industry less willing to grant excessive wage increases because it would make their recovery through higher prices less certain.

One important caution must be noted. There is no magic in a stable price level. Stability of prices during the Nineteen Twenties did not prevent the most catastrophic depression in modern history. Stability of prices from 1952 to early 1956 did not prevent the 1954 recession—or the 1955–1957 boom. General price stability may conceal important disparities in price relationships or in cost-price relationships which in turn upset the effective functioning of the economy. In other words, general price stability is not a cure-all for the problem of the business cycle.

Nevertheless, if these limitations are kept in mind, the inclusion of the goal of price stability in the Employment Act will focus national attention on inflation and its causes. The public will be made aware of the dangers that are inherent in monetary and fiscal inflation with their impact upon total demand, wage inflation with its impact on costs, and other policies which act to raise or hold up prices. And, certainly, full awareness of the sources—and evils—of creeping inflation is an indispensable step in mobilizing public opinion against inflationary policies.

Monetary and Federal Reserve Policy

Reading 29

The total money supply is manufactured out of the monetary base, i.e., from "currency held by the public plus the reserves held by the commercial banks and upon which their deposit-component-of-the-money-supply is based (as modified by changes in legal reserve requirements)." If the Federal Reserve is to control the money supply, it must contrive the right total of this high-power money base.

The Federal Reserve Bank of St. Louis is sometimes regarded as the single captured province of the Chicago school of monetarism. In any case, analysts rely on it for up-to-date statistics bearing upon modern macroeconomics. This particular reading was originally written by staff members Leonall C. Andersen and Jerry L. Jordan of the St. Louis Reserve Branch.

Questions to Guide the Reading

You can lead a horse to water but you can't make him drink. That old saying is sometimes used to argue that controlling the monetary base is not enough. Excess reserves may pile up and thwart you. Do you think that this explains what happened in the Great Depression of 1929 to 1933 when the monetary base was made to grow but when the total money supply actually declined much in consequence of the fact that people were pulling their money out of the banks? But is such a recurrence likely in a modern mixed economy?

The Monetary Base—Explanation and Analytical Use

Federal Reserve Bank of St. Louis

The monetary base recently has achieved prominence as a measure of monetary influence on the economy. Other aggregates often used are the money stock defined as currency plus demand deposits held by the nonbank public, money plus time deposits at commercial banks, member bank reserves, bank credit, liquid assets, and total credit. Other frequently used measures of monetary actions include market interest rates and so-called marginal reserve measures such as member bank excess reserves, borrowings from Reserve banks, and free reserves.

Those who find the monetary base to be a measure of monetary influence give two reasons for doing so. First, there is a significant body of monetary theory which incorporates the monetary base as an important link between Federal Reserve monetary actions and their ultimate impact on income, output, and prices. Second, among all the variables cited above as measures of monetary actions, the monetary

From "The Monetary Base—Explanation and Analytical Use," Federal Reserve Bank of St. Louis, August, 1968. Reprinted with kind permission of the publisher.

authorities have the most complete control over the monetary base, and the base reflects the actions of these authorities more directly than the other measures do.

The article explains the monetary base concept, and then discusses its role in monetary analysis, briefly developing some of the arguments for using the base as a measure of monetary actions.

Monetary base concepts

Three concepts are used in this article to compute the monetary base. These are the "source base," "reserve adjustments," and the sum of these two, called the "monetary base."

The source base. The "source base" is derived from a consolidated monetary balance sheet of the Federal Reserve System and the United States Treasury.[1] Table 1 presents this consolidated balance sheet. According to column one of this table, the source base is the sum of Federal Reserve credit (Federal Reserve holdings of U.S. Government securities, member bank borrowing from Reserve banks, and Federal Reserve float), the nation's gold stock, and U.S. Treasury currency outstanding *less*

[1] The term "source base" used in this article is the same magnitude which Friedman-Schwartz-Cagan call "high-powered money," and which Brunner-Meltzer call the "monetary base."

Treasury deposits at Reserve banks, Treasury cash balances, and other deposits and accounts at Reserve banks.

For ease of computation, the source base is [also] frequently measured by summing the monetary liabilities of the Federal Reserve and the Treasury. These liabilities, consisting of member bank deposits (reserves) at Reserve banks and currency held by banks and the nonbank public, are referred to as *uses of the base* and are listed in column two of Table I. These uses of the base are equal to the source.

Reserve adjustments. Because of changes in laws and regulations and in the distribution of deposits among banks subject to different regulations, adjustments must be made in the source base in order to maintain comparability over time. "Reserve adjustments" allow for the effects of changes in reserve requirements on member bank deposits, and for changes in the proportion of deposits subject to different reserve requirements (reserve city member banks versus country member banks versus nonmember banks, demand deposits versus time deposits, and recently the over and under $5 million reserve requirement differentials on both demand and time deposits). These reserve adjustments are expressed as dollar amounts which are positive when average reserve requirements fall and negative when they rise.

Table 1   Calculation of the Source Base—June 1968—Monthly Averages of Daily Figures* (millions of dollars)

Sources of base		Uses of base	
Federal Reserve credit:		Member bank deposits	
Holdings of securities	+51,396†	at Federal Reserve	+21,350
Discounts and advances	+ 705	Currency held by banks	+ 5,566
Float	+ 1,712	Currency held by the public	+41,900
Gold stock	+10,369		
Treasury currency outstanding	+ 6,744		
Treasury deposits at Federal Reserve	− 960		
Treasury cash holdings	− 973		
Other deposits and other			
Federal Reserve accounts	− 177		
Source Base	68,816		68,816

* Data are not adjusted for seasonal variation.
† Includes acceptances of $90 million not shown separately.
SOURCE: Board of Governors of the Federal Reserve System, Federal Reserve *Bulletin*. The sources and uses of the base are a rearrangement of data contained in the first table appearing in the Financial and Business Statistics section of the *Bulletin*—"Member Bank Reserves, Federal Reserve Bank Credit, and Related Items."

The monetary base. The monetary base is defined in this article as the source base plus reserve adjustments. In deriving a seasonally-adjusted time series for the monetary base, the source base was first seasonally adjusted and then the month's reserve adjustment amount was added to this magnitude. There are no discernible seasonal movements in the latter. The first chart presents a weekly time series since January 1967, and the second chart presents the time series for the monetary base since January 1947.

Analytical use of the monetary base

This section discusses factors influencing the supply of the monetary base and the demand for the base. It concludes with a brief discussion of the adjustment process by which the amount of the base demanded is brought into equilibrium with the amount supplied by monetary authorities. This adjustment process establishes the monetary base as a strategic economic variable for monetary management and for interpreting actions of such management.

Supply of the monetary base. The supply of the monetary base is substantially under the complete control of the Federal Reserve System. Recent studies [by Brunner and others] have found that movements in Federal Reserve credit dominate movements in other sources

of the source base, and therefore determine most of the movements of the monetary base.[2] Evidence has also been presented that Federal Reserve open market operations are able to offset, to a high degree, seasonal and irregular movements in other components of the source base. Consequently, the Federal Reserve, if it so chooses, is able to achieve desired levels of the monetary base for purposes of economic stabilization.

Demand for the monetary base. Demand for the monetary base consists of the demand of *commercial banks* for excess reserves and required reserves and the demand of the nonbank public for currency (Table I, Column 2). Banks' demand for required reserves is a derived demand reflecting the demands for private demand deposits, Government demand deposits, net interbank deposits, and time deposits. Demand for the monetary base consequently reflects economic decisions made by commercial banks, the nonbank *public*, and the *Government*. Therefore, all of the factors influencing the decisions of each of these sectors influence the demand for the monetary base.

[2] Although member bank borrowing from Reserve banks and changes in the gold stock and float are not under the direct control of monetary authorities, it is generally believed that open market operations may be used to offset short-term changes in these and other accounts in order to achieve a desired level of the monetary base.

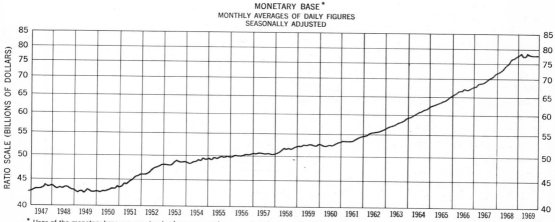

MONETARY BASE *
MONTHLY AVERAGES OF DAILY FIGURES
SEASONALLY ADJUSTED

RATIO SCALE (BILLIONS OF DOLLARS)

* Uses of the monetary base are member bank reserves and currency held by the public and non member banks. Adjustments are made for reserve requirement changes and shifts in deposits among classes of banks. Data are computed by this bank. Percentages are annual rates of change between periods indicated. They are presented to aid in comparing most recent developments with past "trends."
Latest data plotted: June preliminary.

Some of the factors influencing each of these sectors are discussed below:

Total demand. Total demand for the monetary base is the summation of sector demands; it is therefore influenced by the factors determining individual sector demands. Consequently total demand for the base (given wealth, interest rates paid on time deposits and other forms of savings accounts, and the Federal Reserve discount rate) is positively related to economic activity and prices of real assets, and negatively related to a wide variety of short-term market interest rates.

The adjustment process. Most recent developments in monetary theory, which pertain to the determination of economic activity, stress the role of assets, both financial and real, and the market adjustment of asset holdings through the relative price mechanism. The monetary base, according to some economists, is an asset which monetary authorities supply to the economy. Since the supply of this asset can be controlled by the Federal Reserve System, banks and the nonbank public must adjust their holdings of real and other financial assets so as to bring the amount demanded of the monetary base equal to the amount supplied. In the process of adjustment, economic activity, prices of real assets, and interest rates are changed.

There is a "weak" and a "strong" view regarding the role of the monetary base. The weak view embodies the process just outlined and goes no further. The strong view also adopts this adjustment process, but then extends the analysis with additional hypotheses and empirical tests. It holds that the monetary base is the main determinant of the money stock, which, in turn, is *a good indicator of the thrust of monetary forces.* Furthermore, according to the strong view the monetary base is the proper measure of Federal Reserve monetary actions. Whichever view one adopts, changes in the monetary base are held as ultimately leading to changes in the growth of total demand for goods and services.

There are differences between the two views regarding *the strength and predictability of the influence of monetary forces on economic activity.* The weak view holds that other factors, such as *fiscal actions, or shifts in the demand for goods and services,* also influence to a considerable degree changes in economic activity. As a result, the influence of monetary forces is not very predictable. The strong view recognizes these other influences on economic activity, but maintains that monetary forces are the dominant influence and that their influence is highly predictable.

According to the strong view, if the monetary base were to expand at a trend rate of 6 per cent, total demand would adjust to vary around a trend rate consistent with, but not necessarily the same as, the rate of expansion in the base. If the rate of growth in the monetary base were reduced by monetary authorities, total demand would slow and vary around a lower trend rate. Sources of variations around an established trend in economic activity result from changes in fiscal actions and other independent forces.

Summary

The monetary base can be controlled by the Federal Reserve System and is directly influenced by its actions, even though other economic variables are used as guides by monetary managers. Moreover, reliable data for the source base, the main component of the monetary base, are readily available from the balance sheets of the Federal Reserve System and the Treasury. Monetary managers, therefore, have up-to-date information on the major factors affecting movements in the monetary base. Such knowledge makes it possible for them to offset, by open market operations, movements in these other factors in order to achieve a change in the monetary base appropriate for economic stabilization.

Interpretations of movements in the monetary base are not obscured by short-run movements in Government demand deposits or movements between demand and time deposits. Such movements frequently lead to disagreements among monetary analysts regarding the proper interpretation of changes in the money stock, money plus time deposits, and bank credit. Movements in market interest rates and marginal reserve measures are also subject to these same problems of interpretation.

Whether one takes the weak or the strong view, the Federal Reserve System, by varying the supply of the monetary base, causes commercial banks and the nonbank public to adjust their spending on real and financial assets so as to bring the amount demanded of the base into equilibrium with the amount supplied. In the course of these adjustments, the pace of economic activity is affected.

Three points should be noted: the monetary base is under the *direct control of the Federal Reserve System,* it may be *changed by monetary managers* in a predictable manner, and such changes have *an important influence on output, employment, and prices.* These considerations lead to the conclusion that the monetary base is an important magnitude for those interested in monetary management.

Reading 30

Since biblical times there has been antipathy toward charging interest. As a vestige of this feeling we still have state ceilings on small-loan interest rates and Federal Reserve interest-rate ceilings on time deposits. Demand deposits themselves have a zero ceiling, as it has been illegal since the 1930s to pay explicit interest on checkable demand deposits.

This reading, as discussed in a bank publication, shows that the consequences of such regulations may be other than biblical writers had foreseen. The present account, while informative, gives only one side of the issue. Constructively the following considerations are in favor of interest ceilings: It is well known that overall credit restraint hits housing and construction particularly hard. If you forgo specific controls and rely on only one aggregative quantitative weapon, you cannot hope simultaneously to achieve two distinct goals. If you have two weapons at your disposal, you may be able to accomplish two goals, namely keeping down the total of investment spending but ensuring that housing gets a larger share. Deposit-rate ceilings provide you with the second weapon. Suppose you keep a tighter ceiling on what the commercial banks in the East can pay than the ceiling kept on savings and loan associations in the South and West. Then tight money will not cause withdrawals from the savings and loans, and in this way you are "protecting" the housing industry. Because of current and future housing shortages, it is argued, this is defensible.

Questions to Guide the Reading

Is it fair that, under Regulation Q, a rich man with more than $100,000 to invest should get a higher interest rate on his deposits than the poor and less affluent can get? If interest ceilings are placed on the banks, can you guess how this will lead to "disintermediation"—i.e., corporations and families may take their money out of the bank and put it directly into the government-bond and commercial-paper markets? How would you weigh the arguments against Regulation Q with those given in the above introduction for it?

Regulation Q: A Selective Credit Control

Chase Manhattan Bank

For months, the Federal Reserve has been pursuing policies of intensive monetary restraint. The objective is to slow the growth in demand and bring inflation under control gradually without pushing the economy into a recession.

One of the more debatable techniques utilized in this policy has been the maintenance

From "Regulation Q: A Selective Credit Control," *Business in Brief,* Chase Manhattan Bank, August, 1969. Reprinted with kind permission of the publisher.

of a fixed ceiling on rates banks can pay on large denomination time deposits under Regulation Q. Since the ceiling has been below rates available on other money market instruments [treasury bills, commercial paper, etc.], it has *dried up* this source of funds for banks and shifted resources to financial markets not directly controlled by the monetary authorities. Banks have been forced to resort to unusual measures to offset the drain, causing distortions in other markets and producing a number of other adverse consequences.

A blunt instrument

Under Regulation Q, the interest rates that commercial banks are permitted to pay have been held to a maximum of 6¼% on 180-day-or-longer CDs $100,000 or more, and to somewhat lower rates for shorter maturities. These limits were maintained despite the dramatic rise in market interest rates. As a consequence, the ceilings have for some time been significantly below rates on comparable instruments. In mid-July [1969] the 6¼% CD rate competed with rates of 7% or more on Treasury bills and nearly 9% on commercial paper and bankers' acceptances.

By maintaining current ceilings without a change since April 1968, the Federal Reserve has intentionally brought about a reduction in commercial bank time deposits. Commercial banks have been unable to prevent the loss of close to $10 billion in highly interest-sensitive negotiable CDs since late last year, and the outflow is continuing.

This has had an adverse impact on banking's role as a *financial intermediary*. In addition, the CD outflow imposed very significant reserve pressures on banks. When CD funds are withdrawn, the bank pays the CD holder by creating a demand deposit. Thus, a CD runoff is, in effect, a shift from time to demand deposits. Since the top reserve requirement on demand deposits is 17.5% instead of the 6% on negotiable CDs, reserves needed against these funds almost tripled. This intensified the impact of general Federal Reserve policies—restrictive open market operations and a rise in reserve requirements—and significantly increased reserve pressures, especially on major banks [as it was intended to do].

Regulation Q as a selective control

Regulation Q ceilings are shifting the emphasis of Federal Reserve monetary policy from general to a form of selective credit control. One of the time-honored virtues of general monetary restraint is that it leaves to market forces the task of allocating limited supplies of credit among competing uses. Experience shows that such a procedure has worked reasonably well. Such approaches avoid the market dislocations that selective controls often impose.

Rigid Regulation Q ceilings, on the other hand, represent an attempt by the Federal Reserve to apply selective credit controls through a blunt and little-tested device. The ceilings—directed against one type of time deposit, the CD—are not necessary in order to control the over-all supply of money.

Disruption of markets

The attempt to impose a selective control through Regulation Q has had a disruptive impact on credit markets, contributing to the rise in interest rates.

The funds which would normally flow into bank negotiable CDs (and which in part represent business savings) are being diverted into other markets—especially commercial paper, Eurodollars [borrowing of dollars from abroad], Treasury bills or other money market instruments, all of which are free to carry higher interest rates. The commercial paper market alone has swelled by $5 billion or 25% in the short space of five months.

Hard-hit by the run-off in CDs, banks have been forced to make radical adjustments. The banks have sought funds in the Eurodollar market, sold Treasury bills, reduced purchases of municipal securities, sold participations in loan portfolios and, in some instances, issued commercial paper through holding companies.

All of this has brought about a *churning* in credit markets which has placed greater upward pressures on interest rates than might otherwise have been the case. Pressures have been particularly acute in the Eurodollar market, where rates have soared as high as 13%[!]. This strong demand for funds, of course, attracted flows from other financial markets, leading to a general escalation of European interest rates. At the same time, high rates in both the Eurodollar and other European markets pulled some funds from the United States, adding to the deficit in this country's over-all balance of payments.

Distortion of credit flows

These developments have drastically curtailed the ability of the commercial banking system to perform its usual role of *intermediation*. At mid-year, total deposits of major banks, on a seasonally adjusted basis, plus takings from the Eurodollar market showed little if any increase from December 1968.

While the negotiable CD outflow affected banks in all sections of the country, *the impact has been concentrated on larger banks,* and particularly money market center banks. New York City banks' negotiable CD outflow accounted for well over one-half of the country-wide decline. The impact of monetary policy has thus fallen primarily on the larger banks.

Regulation Q controls also raise the prospect of an unbalanced allocation of funds among borrowers. A substantial amount of the CD funds that left the banks were invested in commercial paper. The $5 billion of additional credit in this market all flowed to *larger* corporations, for they alone can qualify for funds in that market. This cannot help but have an adverse impact on funds available for small and medium size businesses, which depend primarily on the commercial banks for financing. Moreover, it acts to increase the volume of lending which lies outside the direct control of the monetary authorities, thus reducing the potential effectiveness of changes in monetary policy.

Long-range implications

In addition to these immediate consequences, the long-range implications of using Regulation Q ceilings as a tool of Federal Reserve policy are also disquieting. Such a selective control subjects the commercial banks to discrimination through a shifting of funds and customers to competitive markets.

Demand deposits have grown very slowly through the postwar period—at only about one-

As Yields on Competing Instruments Rose above the Regulation Q Ceiling, Outstanding CDs Declined $10 Billion

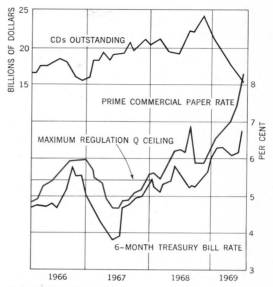

Data: Federal Reserve Board

third the rate of GNP expansion. Even including time deposits, total commercial bank deposits have increased at only about two-thirds the rate of growth of GNP. This growth has been inadequate for banking to maintain its share of financial markets. For some years now, the commercial bank share of total assets held by financial intermediaries has been declining.

Regulation Q policies limit the long-term growth prospects especially for CDs—the dy-

Regulation Q Ceilings Have Restrained the Growth of Commercial Banks' Deposits

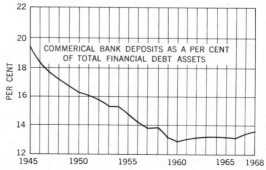

Data: Federal Reserve Board

namic element in time deposits in recent years —and create uncertainties which seriously undermine that market. Banks which had been successful in acquiring CDs may tend to reduce their exposure to the risk of similar outflows in the future. Unless they are permitted to compete effectively for time deposits, it is unlikely that commercial banks can reverse the long-term downtrend in their share of financial markets—thus, narrowing the base of Federal Reserve policies. Moreover, the threat of continued use of Regulation Q with the consequent vulnerability of time deposits can be expected to dampen bank lending policies even in easy money periods. As a result of these factors, the efficiency of Federal Reserve

policies in periods of both tight and easy money may well be diminished.

All these adverse consequences—both short-term and long-term—suggest that *the use of rigid interest ceilings on large denomination time deposits is not an equitable or desirable instrument for implementing monetary policy.* Certainly it should be abandoned over the longer-run. Indeed, the monetary authorities would do well to begin moving in that direction in the immediate future. If there is any lingering concern that such action might divert funds from savings banks and savings and loans, the minimum size of CDs to which higher rates might apply could be raised from $100,000 to $500,000 or more.

Reading 31

In the history of the Federal Reserve System three men have stood out. First there was Governor Strong of the 1920s when the New York Federal Reserve Bank was much more important than the Washington Board of Governors. Then there was Marriner Eccles who was Franklin Roosevelt's appointee during the New Deal days of the Depression and during World War II. Finally, because of his length of service covering almost two decades, William McChesney Martin, Jr. will receive a prominent place in monetary history. During the 1950s he and his board were largely obsessed with inflation and must bear some of the blame for the stagnation years of the Eisenhower era. But also some of the credit for the unprecedentedly long economic expansion of the 1960s must go to Chairman Martin and the Kennedy-Johnson appointees to the Fed. Will Nixon's appointee of 1970, Dr. Arthur F. Burns, do as well?

Chairman Martin is the son of a one-time president of the Federal Reserve Bank of St. Louis. Scarcely out of Yale, he won fame in Wall Street and was the first paid president of the New York Stock Exchange, a position from which he was called to military service. Although a Democrat, Martin was long the object of attack by Congressman Wright Patman and other populists who were "agin' the bankers" and who thought the only good interest rate was a low one.

Questions to Guide the Reading

How would keeping a pegged price for government bonds after World War II have resulted in making the Fed "an engine to create money" and hence inflation? Do you think that a central bank can or should be free of coordinated control by the elected administration? Suppose in full-employment times the Fed increases money and credit and thereby lowers interest rates in the short run. If that sets off a boom and a price inflation, how might the result be (1) an upward shift in the demand for money so that (2) in the end interest rates would actually have to rise in order to contain within them some premium to protect against inflation?

Reminiscences and Reflections: Two Decades at the Federal Reserve Helm
William McChesney Martin, Jr.

This will be my last appearance before this group as chairman of the Board of Governors of the Federal Reserve System. As many of you are aware, my term of office expires next January and I must confess that I'm looking forward to that day.

The more things change . . .

I might say that I have found my more than 18 years as chairman of the Federal Reserve Board an extremely interesting experience also. These years have been some of the most absorbing in our nation's history. And, ironically, my term as chairman is ending on a note reminiscent of its beginning. *It began with a mighty effort by the Federal Reserve to control the inflation that accompanied the Korean conflict.* It is ending with another mighty effort—against the background of another land war in Asia—*to control the current inflation and expectations of further inflation.*

We all have a tendency to say that present times are the most difficult that the country has ever seen. It seems to me we are always in difficult times. Indeed, I can hardly remember when, in the last four decades, you couldn't have gotten up and said, amid widespread agreement, that "these are the most difficult times we have had." Chances are it has always been like that.

War and postwar pegging

I remember when we were plunged into World War II and the Federal Reserve joined in the war effort by adopting a policy of pegging the prices of Government bonds.

By that means, the Federal Reserve saw to it that the banking system was supplied with lendable reserves *ample enough to provide the Government with the war financing funds that it could not raise through taxation and through borrowing people's savings.*

It did so by buying outstanding Government securities on a huge scale. The Federal Reserve's payments for these securities wound up in bank reserves. In turn, the banking system used these additional reserves to purchase new securities that the Treasury was issuing to finance the war effort.

To keep the process going, the Federal Reserve in effect maintained *a standing offer* to buy Government securities in unlimited amount at relatively fixed prices, set high enough to assure that their yields would remain at predetermined low levels—which, for 90-day Treasury bills, meant ⅜ of 1 per cent. When no one else would buy the Government's securities at the prices that went with that, the Federal Reserve did so. And in so doing, it financed the war.

The process was successful for its emergency purpose. But the procedure of pegging Government securities at high prices and low yields entailed a price of its own that the economy—the people and the Government alike—would later have to pay. The results were two-fold:

1. The market for Government securities became *artificial*. The price risks normally borne by participants in that market were eliminated: bonds not payable for 20 years or more became the equivalent of interest-bearing cash since they could be turned into cash at par value—at any time—at the option of the owners.

2. *Money was created rapidly and continually*, in effect setting a time bomb for an ultimate inflationary explosion. For a while, the immediate consequences were held down more or less by a system of direct control over prices, wages, manpower, materials and consumer goods. But eventually, the explosion occurred. And finally, in 1950, the outbreak of hostilities in Korea and the inflation crisis that accompanied it brought matters to a head, setting the stage for the Treasury-Federal Reserve Accord that was to put an end to the price-pegging practice, make it possible to regain effective control over the creation of new money, and open the way to restoring financial stability in the decade of the 1950's.

From William McChesney Martin, Jr., "Reminiscences and Reflections: Two Decades at the Federal Reserve Helm," 1969.

Restoring freedom to the Fed

I remember the day the Accord came into being—March 4, 1951. It may seem strange now that the practice of pegging Government security prices remained in effect for nearly ten years. But discontinuance was slow in coming, largely because of fear that, without Federal Reserve support, the market would collapse.

Let me acknowledge that I was terribly worried myself when President Truman asked me, at about that time, to take the chairmanship of the Federal Reserve. I am a great admirer of President Truman, but I don't think he and I had the same understanding of the market process. I had a talk with him, telling him why I didn't think we could prop Government bond prices further at prevailing prices, and why I thought the country couldn't afford the monetary results of trying to do it.

The President was very patient with me. He explained to me very nicely how in World War I he had bought some Liberty Bonds and they went down to 82, and he said: "You wouldn't ever let that happen again, would you?" I said, "Mr. President, I don't *want* that to happen again, but it is more important to maintain fiscal and monetary responsibility, and maintaining it may mean there is no way to avoid something like that." And I made to him for the first time an observation that some of you have heard me use on a number of occasions since: that markets will not wait upon kings, prime ministers, presidents, secretaries of the Treasury—or chairmen of the Federal Reserve Board.

Then President Truman said maybe he didn't understand market processes fully, and all he wanted from me was assurance that— whatever might happen—"you'll do the best that you can." So I said yes, Mr. President, I'll do the best I can, but if the prices of the Government's securities are to stay up, you'll have to help on budgetary and fiscal policy.

So we went ahead and unpegged the Government securities market, and after a while Government bond prices did drop. Then the press went to the President—by now, the bonds were down to 97½—and they asked: What happened to your man Martin? What's he doing? And President Truman was wonderful. He said, "He's doing the best he can."

Changing administrations

Well, that's about what I've been doing ever since, and I wouldn't want to claim much for it. I think the other Presidents besides Mr. Truman with whom I've served—Messrs. Eisenhower, Kennedy, Johnson and Nixon—have also been generous in recognizing that my efforts have been genuine and undertaken in good faith, even though we haven't always agreed on everything. For my part, I can truthfully say I've enjoyed working with them all, and I am completely convinced that each in his way has sought earnestly to do the very best that he could for his country.

Over these years, our economy—and the standard of living of our people as a whole— have made sizable gains. This has not been an unbroken rise, nor have these been untroubled years. We have been buffeted by inflation in much of this time, but we have been buffeted by deflation also for briefer periods. And we have enjoyed, in the first half of the 1960's, at least one prolonged spell of relatively steady prices and vigorous economic growth, after laying the base for it when the back of another dangerous period of inflation— and mounting expectations of continued inflation—was broken in the late 1950's.

Encounter with President Johnson

I've mentioned days in 1931, 1941, and 1951, so I'll mention just one more in a period closer to the present—in December 1965—when we raised the discount rate. The raise was only from 4 to 4½ per cent, which seems like a bargain basement rate these days, but it won me a trip to Texas for a chat with another President.

Early in his Administration, we had a good talk in which he told me he came from a part of the country that liked low interest rates, and he thought that's the way interest rates should be—*low*.

Well, that wasn't exactly the point of difference between us: it was more subtle than that. I, too, like to see interest rates as low as conditions of inflation, deflation, or stability (which is my preference) permit them to be. But President Johnson liked them to be low— all the time. And he told me so, freely and frankly.

So I said, Mr. President, I want to tell you how you can have low interest rates, and the *only* way you can have low interest rates. It is with *budgetary responsibility*, both in respect to Government spending and taxing, and a fiscal policy that makes that responsibility plain. If you will see to that, you can have moderate interest rates—maybe not as low as Mr. Patman likes, but you can have them low. And I want to add right now that I still think we could, and can, have them that way, on that basis.

Vietnam inflation

But that, of course, wasn't the way things went. The war in Vietnam began to escalate sharply around mid-1965, when we were also embarking on many new, sizable and worthy welfare programs, and we became increasingly over-committed and over-extended, especially because nothing was being done about taxes even though expenditures were mounting.

I tried to set out that situation to President Johnson in another discussion we had in that period, and to impress on him my belief that we were getting into trouble on the budget, and we were going to have inflationary problems—which of course would bring higher interest rates—if we didn't do something about taxes and expenditures to head off a wage-cost-price spiral. I remember him saying to me, "Well, yes, I think so too, but we can't do it now. We'd risk overkill." That was the first time I'd heard that expression used, but I've heard it plenty over the years since, when all the while the economy—and inflationary pressures as well—were burgeoning.

What King Canute can't do

Nothing in the background or history of the Federal Reserve Act indicates any misunderstanding by its framers of the laws of supply or demand, or any belief that a Federal System could control or *successsfully manipulate, for long, supply and demand forces.* For whenever we ignore the working of the market we do so at our peril, and ultimately must pay the piper.

Reading 32

For centuries philosophers and economists have noted as no coincidence that vast increases in the supply of money have been accompanied by tremendous increases in the price level. This doctrine became known as the "Quantity Theory of Money." Like many basic ideas, the Quantity Theory became so familiar and began to seem so simple that a later generation of economists became inclined to disparage its significance. In this lecture, Professor Milton Friedman of the University of Chicago reasserts in an emphatic manner the merits of the Quantity Theory. Professor Friedman, who is a leading spokesman for the University of Chicago "school" of libertarian economists, is well known for the brilliance of his analytical and empirical researches; Candidate Barry Goldwater called upon him for economic counsel in the presidential campaign of 1964, and so did Richard Nixon in 1968.

Questions to Guide the Reading

What is the testimony of some of the great galloping inflations of history concerning the role of money? Why does the author doubt that inflation is necessary to promote economic development and growth?

Since total spending depends upon the velocity with which money circulates, what is the evidence that velocity tends to be constant as people hold the same number of weeks' stock of money?

The Quantity Theory of Money Vindicated

Milton Friedman

Like an old-fashioned preacher delivering a Sunday sermon, I can provide the audience with texts for my talks. The text for this talk is "Cherchez la monnaie." By inflation, I shall mean a steady and sustained rise in prices. I shall deal primarily with open inflation, which is to say, an inflationary process in which prices are permitted to rise without being suppressed by Government price controls or similar techniques.

It is widely asserted that inflation is inevitable in a country that is trying to force the pace of development. The argument generally runs something like this. A country that is trying to force the pace of development places heavy pressure upon the available resources. The pressure upon the resources means an increase in demand which can be met only by a rise in prices. In consequence, it is said, the process of development will surely force a rise in prices. This argument, however, confuses *physical* magnitudes with *money* magnitudes. The pressure on resources during the course of development affects relative prices. It tends to make the prices of those things for which the demand is particularly great in the course of development, high compared with the prices of other things. It need not, however, affect the absolute price level.

Everything depends on how the real resources, which are employed in the course of development, are acquired. If the real resources are acquired by Government, for example, through taxes or through borrowing from the public, or if the real resources are acquired by private enterprises and individuals by using their own savings for the purpose of investment, there will be no pressure of monetary demand. There will be a shift of demand away from certain things towards other things, and this will produce the shift in physical resources required. On the other hand, if the printing press, or any of its more sophisticated modern variants, is used to try to acquire resources, then, of course, there will tend to be inflation and price rise. The view that development makes inflation inevitable is misleading and arises from confusing physical magnitudes in the economy with monetary magnitudes.

The phenomenon of prices changing by more than the difference between the change in output and the change in money stock is often observed and the reason is not far to seek. When prices are going down, money becomes a more desirable way in which to hold assets; its value is increasing day by day; hence people have a strong tendency, if they expect the price decline to continue, to hold a larger fraction of their wealth in the form of money. On the other side of the picture, when prices are going up, money becomes a less desirable form in which to hold assets. In consequence, people tend to economise on their money balances; velocity tends to increase. How much velocity will change depends on whether the fall in prices or the rise in prices is anticipated. Generally, when inflation has started after a period of roughly stable prices, people initially do not expect prices to continue rising. They regard the price rise as temporary and expect prices to fall later on. In consequence, they have tended to increase their monetary holdings and the price rise has been less than the rise in the stock of money. Then as people gradually become wise to what is going on, they tend to re-adjust their holdings. Prices then rise more than in proportion to the stock of money. Eventually people come to expect roughly what is happening and prices rise in proportion to the stock of money.

Progress with prices falling

Numerous examples can be cited to demonstrate that inflation is not inevitable in the course of economic development, that it has little or nothing to do with the pressure on real resources, but rather with monetary institutions and the monetary policies which are followed. One of the most dramatic goes back nearly a century to the fifteen years following the Civil War.

From Milton Friedman, *Inflation: Causes and Consequences* (Asia Publishing House, New York, 1963). Copyright by the Council for Economic Education, Bombay, India. Reprinted with kind permission of the author and publisher.

During the Civil War itself (1861–65), Government resorted to printing money in order to finance the war—the famous "greenbacks"—with the result that by the end of the war, the price level had more than doubled. The United States wanted to return to the gold standard at the pre-war parity. In order to do this, prices had to be cut in half to bring them into line with prices in the rest of the world. And they were in fact cut in half. The decline owed little to deliberate policies followed by the Government. It was the result rather of an extraordinarily high rate of economic growth in that 15-year period. By all the statistical evidence available, that 15-year period saw a more rapid rate of economic growth than almost any other period in the whole history of the United States. According to the estimates which Simon Kuznets has constructed of income in the United States since 1869, the decade of the 1870s shows a higher rate of growth than any decade from 1869 to 1959. Kuznets himself thinks, and I agree with him, that his estimates over-state the rise in the early decades. But whatever index you look at, whether the expansion of railroads, increase in traffic on railroads and canals and so on, shows that period to have been a period of very rapid growth. Output considerably more than doubled; and since the stock of money rose only a trifle, prices were cut in half.

I do not cite this example to suggest that declines in prices promote economic growth. I cite it rather because it is such an extreme example to contradict the widely believed notion that a price rise is somehow inevitable, or, if not inevitable, at any rate highly desirable, in order to promote economic growth. In the American case, I do not believe that the decline in prices produced economic growth. On the contrary, it was the economic growth, which had its origin in very different sources, which produced the decline in prices. Neither do I mean to suggest that this experience is a model for anybody to follow. The fall in prices created real difficulties. It stimulated political discontent and controversy; there was a long recession from 1873 to 1879 and so on. Very likely, the economic growth would have been the same if a monetary policy had been followed which would have meant stable prices, and other difficulties would have been less. Yet the fact remains that economic growth was entirely consistent with falling prices.

Other less dramatic examples are ready at hand. In the United States from 1879, when the U.S. went back on gold, to 1896, prices fell at the rate of something like 2 to 3 per cent a year. From 1896 to 1913, prices rose at the rate of something like 2 to 3 per cent a year. Yet these two periods show almost precisely the same rate of economic growth as judged by the growth in national product. Again, in the same period from 1870 to 1890 or 1895, prices were falling in the United Kingdom; from 1890 or 1895 to 1913 prices were rising. Yet the estimates of real national output constructed some years ago show that the rate of increase in output was faster during the period of falling prices than during the period of rising prices. In more recent times, since the end of the second World War, countries like Italy and West Germany have had very rapidly rising outputs with roughly constant or mildly rising prices. Since something like 1953 or 1954, Greece has had a very rapid rate of economic growth with highly stable prices. In the early years after the War, Japan had a substantial price rise and also a substantial rise in output. Since then, the rise in output has continued but prices have been roughly stable.

I hasten to add that examples can also be cited when rises in prices went along with expansion of output. What I am arguing is not that falling prices are inevitable in the course of economic expansion but only that rising prices are not inevitable, though they may occur. For example, in addition to the cases in the United States and the United Kingdom that I have given, there is the great period of the price revolution in Europe in the 15th and 16th centuries, to which I shall return in another connection. That was a period when the pace of economic development quickened throughout Europe along with a steady and long continued rise in prices. Or again, to take the recent post-war experience, over the past 10 years or so, Israel has been experiencing a rate of price rise of roughly 10 per cent a year—not a negligible rate of price rise by anybody's calculation. Yet it has also experienced a rate of rise in real income of the order of something like 10 per cent a year. So clearly, while inflation is not an inevitable accompaniment of development, neither does it necessarily prevent development. The basic forces making for economic growth are much more fundamental than the question of whether prices are rising or falling.

False causes of inflation

I should like to spend a bit more time examining analytically the causes of inflation because the emphasis I have just been placing on the stock of money as the culprit is widely regarded as old-fashioned and out of date. Most modern writers today attribute inflation to very different kinds of causes. They say it is the result of attempted investment exceeding desired savings; or of a wage push on the part of employees; or of a profit push on the part of employers and entrepreneurs; or of the inability to increase the output of food as rapidly as the increase in output of other things; and so on in infinite variety and diversity. Now these explanations may, in one sense, be correct. If any of these factors produces a rise in the stock of money, it will produce inflation. But if it does not produce a rise in the stock of money, it will not produce inflation.

The reasons why these explanations are so popular are not far to seek. There are, I think, two main reasons. The first is the natural tendency to confuse what is true for the individual with what is true for the society as a whole. The most interesting and important thing about economics as a science is precisely that almost everything that is true for the individual is wrong for the society and almost everything that is true for the society as a whole is wrong for the individual. One individual can affect the price of hardly anything he buys. Yet, all individuals together make the price what it is. In the particular case of inflation, to each individual separately, the price rise is not in any way connected with the fact that somehow or other a printing press has been turning out those loose pieces of paper we like to carry around in our pockets. The individual entrepreneur raises his prices because, on the one hand, his costs have gone up and, on the other, he finds he can still sell his product at higher prices. We never see the fact that that higher price in turn is ultimately the result of the creation of more money. That is one reason. A second and equally important reason is that, so far as the printing of money is concerned, in modern days, the Government has a near-monopoly.

Nobody likes to blame himself for bad things that occur. Though many people like inflation because it helps them personally, nonetheless almost everyone thinks it is a bad thing on the whole and nobody likes to admit that he is responsible for inflation. It is far easier for Government to attribute inflation to the profiteers, or the bad trade unions that insist on pushing up the wages, or the intractability of agricultural producers who are unable to expand food than it is for Government or government officials to say, *mea culpa*.

Keynesian fallacies

Though these are the two main reasons why inflation tends to be attributed to everything except money, there is a third supplementary reason which has been especially important in the last 20 years or so. That is something that happened purely in the intellectual sphere, namely, the Keynesian revolution in economic thought in the 1930s, which led many economists to reduce the role assigned to money. The reason why I think that it is not really a basic explanation is because the emphasis on non-monetary explanations is not a new thing. One can go back one or two thousand years and more and find that every time there is inflation, two explanations are offered. One explanation is that the amount of money has increased. The other explanation is that something special has happened: wage-earners have pushed up their wages; profiteers have been active; there has been a blockade of the country and as a result supplies could not come in; and so on and on.

As I have already noted, these two separate explanations are not necessarily contradictory. The non-monetary factors may, on some occasions, be the cause of the monetary expansion.

One thing is clear from the historical record. The actual sources of monetary expansion have been very different at different times and in different places. Hence, if a theory of inflation is going to deal not with the expansion of the stock of money but with what brought it about, it will be a very pluralistic theory which will have many possible sources of inflation. For example, in the early days, when actual coin was the medium of circulation, inflations tended to be produced by such devices as sweating and clipping.

A modern technological invention has largely put an end to that particular source of inflation, the invention being the milling of coins. In addition, the use of pieces of paper, bank notes, instead of actual coins, has also reduced opportunities for that kind of inflation. Another source of expansion in the nominal stock of money has been what the history books always refer to as "crying up" or "crying down" the nominal value of money. Again, a major source of inflation in the past has been discovery of new sources of gold or of silver, or technological changes which have increased the possibility of extracting silver or gold from ores. Printing money to pay for war has always been one of the major sources of inflation. Full employment policy is, however, a modern invention for producing inflation.

Cherchez la monnaie

Whenever these or other factors have led to a substantially greater expansion in the stock of money than the current rate of increase in output, they have led to inflation. If you are going to regard them as causes, you will, as I said, be fated to have many explanations. I know of no exception to the proposition that there has been a one to one relation between substantial rises in prices and substantial rises in the stock of money.

Why should money be so critical a factor in price level behaviour? Why should it occupy such a central role in the process? The key to an answer is the difference between the *nominal* quantity of money, the quantity of money expressed in terms of rupees, dollars, or marks or what have you, and the *real* quantity of money, the quantity of money expressed in terms of the goods and services it will buy or the number of weeks of income it is equal to.

People seem to be extraordinarily stubborn about the real amount of money that they want to hold and are unwilling to hold a different amount, unless there is a real incentive to do so. This is true not only over time but over space. Let me give a few striking figures. I shall refer only to currency in circulation, excluding deposits, since currency is more comparable among the countries I want to deal with.

In India, the amount of currency that is held by people amounts to roughly seven weeks' in-come. That is to say, if you calculate the aggregate income received by all Indians during a seven weeks' period, the resulting sum is roughly equal to the amount of currency that is held by all the people and all the business enterprises in India.

Let us now turn to Yugoslavia, a country that is vastly different in many respects from India. Yugoslavia has a Communist Government and extensive centralised control over economic activity. It has a different kind of agriculture, different social customs and traditions. Yet the people of Yugoslavia hold in the form of currency something like 6¼ weeks' income, remarkably close to the figure for India.

Greece is a royalist country with a king and queen and a very different economic structure from either Yugoslavia or India. Yet its people hold in the form of currency almost the same amount as in Yugoslavia, a little over 6 weeks' income. In Turkey, they hold a little over 5 weeks' income. In the United States, they hold about 4¼ weeks' income in the form of currency. In Israel they hold about 4¼ weeks' income also, although the level of income in Israel is one-third or one-quarter of that in the United States. Here we have countries with every variety of economic system, with real incomes varying over a range of 15 or 20 to one and yet currency holdings, expressed in terms of weeks' income, vary over a range of decidedly less than 2 to 1.

How money affects prices

Given that people are so stubborn about the amount they hold in the form of money, let us suppose that, for whatever reasons, the amount of money in a community is higher than people want to hold at the level of prices then prevailing. They find that although on the average they would like to hold, let us say, the 7 weeks' income that they hold in India, they are actually holding, say, 8 weeks' income. What will happen? Here again it is essential to distinguish between what happens to the individual and what happens to the community. Each individual separately thinks he can get rid of his money and he is right. He can go out and spend it and thereby reduce his cash balances. But for the community as a whole the belief that cash balances can be reduced is an optical illusion. The only reason I can reduce my cash balances in nominal terms is because somebody else is willing to increase his. One man's expenditures are another man's receipts. People as a whole cannot spend more than they as a whole receive. In consequence, if everybody in the community tries to cut the nominal amount of his cash balances, they will on the average be frustrated. The amount of nominal balances is fixed by the nominal quantity of money in existence and no game of musical chairs can change it. But people can and will try to reduce their cash balances and the process of trying will have important effects. In the process of trying to spend more than they are receiving, people will bid up the prices of all sorts of goods and services. Nominal incomes will rise and real cash balances will indeed be reduced, even though nominal balances are not affected. The rise in prices and incomes will bring cash balances from 8 weeks' income to 7 weeks' income. People will succeed in achieving their objective, but by raising prices and incomes rather than by reducing nominal balances. In the process, prices will have risen by about an eighth. This in a nutshell is the process whereby changes in the stock of money exert their influence on the price level.

Reading 33

Prior to the 1970 edition of the author's textbook, the space given to monetarism was quite limited. The present discussion shows why this topic now deserves ample investigation. Indeed, later Readings 81 and 82 by Friedman and Heller, along with 83 by Samuelson, carry forward the discussion. Reading 32, which gives a more detailed report on the views and findings of Professor Friedman, should be considered along with the present readings.

Since the issues dealt with here are quite technical, not every reader can be expected to master every last nuance of the discussions. Intermediate and advanced courses are the places for more exhaustive inquiry into these disputed matters.

Questions to Guide the Reading

Check the reasons for the eclipse and comeback of money. Summarize in your words the crucial dispute between monetarists and eclectic post-Keynesians. Could crude Keynesianism be right in 1938 but quite wrong in 1970? Could the crude monetarist position be right at one time and wrong at another?

What are the causal links between Fed action and GNP? Does it matter if V is a constant, or if it is speeded up by higher interest rates? What effects on V would withdrawal of government bonds as result of open-market Fed purchase make? Give an example of a hill of evidence to show M has an effect. Does that mean other actions have no effect? In plain words, what does the St. Louis study claim to show? Can controlled experiments decide between competing theories? Why not? If the 1969 tax surcharge was slow and weak in having effects, is that cogent reason to adopt the rule of a constant rate of growth of the M supply? Do the later Friedman and Heller readings change your opinions about the debate here?

Monetarism Objectively Evaluated

Paul A. Samuelson

There are fashions within science. Nowhere is the oscillating pendulum of opinion more marked in the field of economics than in the area of money. By the end of the 1930s, after the so-called Keynesian revolution, courses and textbooks continued to be devoted to money. But in fact money had almost completely dropped out of them and the emphasis had shifted to analysis of income determination in terms of such Keynesian concepts as the multiplier and the propensity to consume.

Comeback of money

If the market quotation for monetary theory sagged in the decade after 1936, by the early 1950s there were unmistakable signs of a comeback. It was Professor Howard S. Ellis of the University of California who coined in those years the expression, "the rediscovery of money." And the famous Accord of 1951, which gave back to the Federal Reserve its freedom to pursue an autonomous monetary policy independently of the needs and desires of President Truman's Treasury, was the objective counterpart of the reappearance of money in the theoretical models of academic scholars.

Of course, we cannot expect recovery to take place at the same time in all markets. Within Britain, the historic home of central banking, the news of the revival of money was late in coming; and even later in being believed. As recently as 1959 the prestigious Radcliffe Report, technically known as the Committee on the Working of the Monetary System, devoted upwards of 3½ million words to the subject. Yet the unanimous conclusion of this distinguished group of British academics and men of finance was, in the end, that money as such did not matter.

Often, if a stock goes down too far in *price*, in reaction it may subsequently go up too far. There is danger of this in the case of monetary theory. A crude monetarism is now stalking the land. In the present article I wish to provide a scientifically objective evaluation of the issues and a balanced history of the oscillations in monetary doctrines.

Friedman and the Chicago School

Undoubtedly the popularity of monetarism can be traced in large part to one man, namely Professor Milton Friedman of the University of Chicago. His monumental *Monetary History of the United States, 1867–1960*, written with Mrs. Anna Schwartz, is the bible of the movement; and let me say as an infidel that it is a classic source of data and analysis to which all scholars will turn for years to come. In addition to this scholarly work, Professor Friedman has published numerous statistical studies in learned economic journals. He has testified before Congress and lectured before lay groups. His influential columns in *Newsweek* and writings for the financial press have hammered away at one simple message:

It is the rate of growth of the money supply that is the prime determinant of the state of aggregate dollar demand. If the Federal Reserve will keep the money supply growing at a steady rate—say 4 to 5 percent by one or another definition of the money supply, but the fact of steadiness being more important than the rate agreed upon—then it will be doing all a central bank can usefully do to cope with the problems of inflation, unemployment, and business instability.

Fiscal policy as such has no independent, systematic effect upon aggregate dollar demand. Increasing tax rates, but with the understanding that money growth remains unchanged, *will have no effect* in lessening the degree of inflation; it will have no *independent* effect in increasing the level of unemployment in a period of deflation; changes in public expenditure out of the budget (it being understood that the rate of growth of the money supply is held unchanged) will also have *no lasting effects on inflationary or deflationary gaps.*

In the past, budgetary deficits and budgetary surpluses have often been accompanied by central bank creation of new money or deceleration of growth of new money. Therefore, many people have wrongly inferred that fiscal deficits and surpluses have *predictable* expansionary and contracting effects upon the total of aggregate spending.

But this is a complete confusion. *It is the changes in the rate of growth of the money supply which alone have substantive effects.* After we have controlled or allowed for monetary changes, fiscal policy has negligible independent potency.[1]

This is my summary of the Friedman-type monetarism. No doubt he would word things somewhat differently. And I should like to emphasize that there are many qualifications in his scientific writing which do not logically entail the *simpliste* version of monetarism outlined above. Indeed it is one of the purposes of this article to demonstrate and emphasize the point that the weight of the evidence on money, theoretical and empirical, does not imply the correctness of crude monetarism.

Among the central bankers of the world, financial journalists, statesmen and politicians, business and academic economists, and men of affairs generally, monetarism seems almost paradoxically simple and perverse. Can President Nixon really suppose that it makes no difference for the control of the 1969–70 American inflation, whether or not he proposes to extend into 1970 the tax surcharge? Professor Friedman is but one of his advisers, and it is evident that Paul McCracken, Chairman of the Council of Economic Advisers, and Arthur F. Burns, the new chairman of the Federal Reserve Board named by Nixon, do *not* see eye to eye with Friedman in this matter.

Yet Professor Friedman does not stand alone. His mountains of data, cogency of reasoning, and formidable powers of patient persuasion have raised unto him a host of followers. Graduates of the Chicago workshops in monetary theory carry to new universities the mes-

[1] Professor Friedman is careful to specify that fiscal policy does have important effects upon the *composition* of any given total of gross national product. Thus increases in government expenditures will pull resources out of the private sector into the public. John Kenneth Galbraith might like this but Milton Friedman does not. Also, increasing taxation relative to public expenditure, although having no independent effect on aggregate demand, will tend to lower consumption and reduce interest rates. This contrived increase in thriftiness will move the mix of full-employment output in the direction of more rapid capital formation; it will speed up the rate of growth of productivity and real output, and will increase the rate of growth of real wages. If the trend of the money supply remains unchanged, this will tend toward a lower price level in the future or a less rapidly rising one. (See the introduction to the Reading 82 for Friedman's exact wording.)

sage. A number of other scholars, such as Professors Allan Meltzer at Carnegie-Mellon University in Pittsburgh and Karl Brunner of Ohio State University, have also produced research in support of monetarism. Professor Harry Johnson leads the campaign to export monetarism to the British Isles. One of our twelve regional Federal Reserve Banks, that of St. Louis, has carried the torch for monetarism, providing up-to-date numerical information on the vagaries of the money supply, and promoting quantitative research on the lagged potency of money. Distinguished graduates of the University of Chicago, such as Dr. Beryl Sprinkel of the Harris Trust Company Bank in Chicago, and Dr. James Meigs, of the First National City Bank of New York, profess to be monetarists who improve the accuracy of their business forecasts by concentrating primarily on money. At one time or another the editorial pages of the influential *Washington Post* and *New York Times* have become permeated by monetarism. Finally, the Joint Economic Committee of Congress, when it was under the chairmanship of Senator William Proxmire, reacted strongly against the use of fiscal policy as a stabilization device, and recommended to the Federal Reserve Board that it never permit the money supply to grow at rates widely different from some agreed-upon constant.

Keynes and Keynesians

Thus monetarism is a movement to reckon with. I believe monetarism could be deemed fruitful, to the degree that it has pushed economists away from a *simpliste* Keynesian model, popular in the United States during the Great Depression and still lingering on in Britain, and made economists more willing to recognize that monetary policy is an important stabilization weapon, fully coordinate with fiscal policy as a macro-economic control instrument. However, my reading of the development of modern economic doctrine does not suggest to me that the post-Keynesian position that I myself hold, and of which Professor James Tobin of Yale and Franco Modigliani of M.I.T. are leading exponents, has been materially influenced by monetarism. Indeed, speaking for myself, the excessive claims for money as an exclusive determinant of aggregate demand would, if anything, have slowed down and delayed my appreciation of money's true quantitative and qualitative role.[2]

Keynes vs. Keynesians

Although the neglect of money is often said to be a characteristic of Keynesian economists and a heritage of the analysis in Keynes' 1936 classic *General Theory of Employment, Interest and Money,* it is doubtful that Keynes himself can be properly described as ever having believed that "money does not matter." If one writes down in the form of equations or graphs the boney structure of the *General Theory,* he sees that money enters into the liquidity-preference function in such a way that an increase in the money supply lowers interest rates, thereby inducing an increase in investment, and through multiplier mechanism causes a rise in employment and production, or, if employment is already full and output at capacity levels, causes upward pressure on the price level.

For a quarter of a century before 1936, Keynes was the principal exponent of monetary theory and the inheritor of the Cambridge tradition of Marshall and Pigou. Although the *General Theory* did represent the repudiation of some of the doctrines Keynes espoused in his 1930 *Treatise on Money,* it represented a continuation and culmination of many of those monetary doctrines. At frequent intervals in the last decade before Keynes' death in 1946, he affirmed and reaffirmed in print and private correspondence his faith that, if the long-term interest rate could be brought down low enough, monetary policy could play an effective role in curing depression and stagnation.[3]

[2] To clarify my point, let me state my belief that Professor Friedman has been a force of the first magnitude in getting economists generally to realize the desirability of flexible exchange rates. He, and Professors Frank Knight and Henry Simons at Chicago before him, deserve an honored place in the history of economic thought in influencing economists to appreciate the merits of market pricing as against direct government interventions. But I do not believe that the positions today of the Tobins and Modiglianis of the modern scene would be very different if a Chicago School had never existed.

[3] When an author writes as much as did Keynes, it is inevitable that certain of his passages might seem to contradict others. There are *some* of his paragraphs written in the 1930s that do seem to play down the quantitative potency of monetary policy in times of deep depression. And those many

Post-Keynesianism

How is it that some Keynesians should ever have become identified with the doctrine that money does not matter? Most converts to Keynesianism became converts during the slump years of the late 1930s. Then the deep-depression polar case did seem to be the realistic case. It is a sad fact about many scholars that they learn and unlearn nothing after the age of 29, so that there exist in chairs of economics around the world many economists who still live mentally in the year 1938. For 1938, when the interest rate on Treasury Bills was often a fraction of a fraction of a fraction of a percent, even a monetarist might despair of the potency of central bank monetary policy.

As one who lived through those times, I can testify by recall how money got lost so that it could later be rediscovered. First, multiple correlation studies by people like Jan Tinbergen, of the Netherlands, who pioneered for the League of Nations macrodynamic models of the business cycle, invariably found that such variables as interest rates turned up with *zero or perversely-signed weights in their estimating equations.* Second, case studies at the Harvard Business School and elsewhere invariably registered the result that *the cost and availability of credit was not a significant determinant of business behavior and investment.* Third, large-scale questionnaire surveys, like those emanating from Oxford and associated with the names of Sir Robert Hall, Sir Hubert Henderson, Sir Roy Harrod, Charles Hitch, and Phillip Andrews, uniformly recorded answers denying the importance of interest rates and monetary conditions. Fourth, as Professor Alvin Hansen and other contemporary writers noted, the inflow to the States of billions of dollars of gold resulting from distrust of Hitler's

writers, such as Sir John Hicks, Sir Roy Harrod, Professor James Meade, and the late Oskar Lange, who have codified the *General Theory* in the form of simple equations and graphs, are able to formulate a "deep-depression" polar case in which money does not matter (either because the liquidity-preference schedule displays infinite elasticity at a "liquidity trap," or the marginal efficiency schedule of investment displays complete inelasticity to interest rate changes). But note that this is not the general case of the *General Theory,* but only a special polar case, just as the classical quantity theory of money is the special case at the opposite pole.

Europe, produced almost a controlled experiment in which the reserves of the banking system were vastly expanded and yet no commensurate expansion in business activity or even in the total money supply was achieved. Finally, it was fashionable in those days for theorists to argue that interest was a negligible cost where short-term investment projects were involved, and where long-term projects were involved the irreducible uncertainties of expectations served to dwarf the importance of the interest rate as a controlling variable.

However realistic it may have been in the 1930s to denigrate the importance of money, and with hindsight I do believe that even this may have been overdone, still in the high-employment epoch that is characteristic of the post-World-War-II years there was little excuse to remain frozen in an archaic denial of money. This is not the place to sketch in detail the evolution of post-Keynesian analysis. Already in the war years, Professor Modigliani in a justly famous article had shown the logical need for placing greater emphasis upon stocks as against flows than had been done by the *General Theory* and its first commentators.

Professor Pigou, in a handsome recantation of his first rejection of the *General Theory,* supplied in the 1940s an important influence of the real money stock as it acts directly on the propensity to consume even in the absence of the interest rate effects that had been recognized in the *General Theory.* Recognition of this "Pigou effect" served to reconcile the deep cleavage between neoclassical theory and the Keynesian revolution: theoretically a sufficiently large decline in the wage rate and the price level could, with a fixed quantum of money, restore full employment; practically no one—and certainly not Pigou—advocated such hyper-deflation as a practicable program to combat unemployment.

How it works

By the 1950s and 1960s a body of analysis and data had been accumulated which led to a positive, strong belief that open-market and discount operations by the central bank could have *pronounced macroeconomic effects upon investment and consumption spending in the succeeding several months and quarters.* One of the principal preoccupations of the post-Keynesian economists, which is to say of the ruling orthodoxy of American establishment economics, has been to trace out the *causal* mechanisms whereby monetary and fiscal variables produce their effects upon the total of spending and its composition.

Thus, an open-market purchase of Treasury bills by the Fed first bids up bond prices and lowers their yield; this spreads to *a reduction in yields* on competing securities, such as longer-term government bonds or corporate bonds or home mortgages. The lowering of interest costs will typically be accompanied by *a relaxation in the degree of credit rationing,* and this can be expected *to stimulate investment spending* that would otherwise not have taken place. The lowering of interest rates generally also brings about an *upward capitalization of the value of existing assets,* and this increase in the money value of wealth can be expected to have a certain *expansionary influence on consumer spending,* and in a degree on business spending for investment. As a limit upon the stimulus stemming from money creation by orthodox open-market operations, must be reckoned the fact that as the central bank pumps new money into the system, it is in return taking from the system *an almost equal quantum of money substitutes* in the form of government securities. In a sense the Federal Reserve or the Bank of England is merely a dealer in second-hand assets, contriving transfer exchanges of one type of asset for another, and in the process affecting the interest rate structure that constitutes the terms of trade among them.

What needs to be stressed is the fact that one cannot expect money created by this process of central-bank open-market operations *alone,* with say the fiscal budget held always in balance, to have at all the same functional relationship to the level of the GNP and of the price index that could be the case for money created by gold mining or money created by the printing press of national governments or the Fed and used to finance public expenditures in excess of tax receipts. Not only would the creation of these last kinds of money involve a flow of production and spendable income in their very *act of being born,* but in addition the community would be *left permanently richer* in its ownership of monetary wealth. In money terms the community *feels* richer, in money terms the community *is* richer. And this can be expected to **reflect** itself in a higher price level or a lower rate of unemployment or both.

By contrast, money created through conventional central-bank operations quite divorced from the financing of fiscal deficits or the production of mining output does not entail an equivalent permanent increase in net wealth as viewed by people in the community. Post-Keynesians emphasize that extinguishing the outstanding interest-bearing public debt, whether by a capital levy or by open-market purchase of it, does rationally make the community *feel poorer* than would be the case if the same amount of money existed and the public debt had been unreduced. All men are mortal. Most men do not concern themselves with the wellbeing of their remote posterity. Hence, government bonds as an asset are not completely offset in their minds by the recognition of the liability of paying in perpetuity taxes to carry the interest on those bonds. Only if people live forever, foreseeing correctly the tax payments they (or the posterity as dear to them in the most remote future as is their own lifetime wellbeing) must make on account of the perpetual future interest payments on government bonds—only then would it be true to say that retirement of public debt would have no substantive effects upon the reckoning of wealth, the levels of spending, and the level of prices generally. Rejecting such a perpetual-life model as extreme and unrealistic, we must debit against an increase in money through open-market operations a partial offset in the form of retirement of some of the outstanding public debt.

Finally, to clarify the significant difference between the post-Keynesian analysis which most modern economists believe to be plausible as against the tenets of monetarism, I must point out that even when the money supply is held constant:

1. Any significant changes in thriftiness and the propensity to consume can be expected to have systematic independent effects on the money value of current output, affecting average prices or aggregate production or both.

2. Likewise an exogenous burst of investment opportunities or animal spirits on the part of business can be expected to have systematic effects on total GNP.

3. Increases in public expenditure, or reductions in tax rates—and even increases in public expenditure balanced by increases in taxation—can be expected to have systematic effects upon aggregate GNP.

All these tenets of the modern eclectic position are quite incompatible with monetarism. (Indeed that is the differentiating definition by which we distinguish the Chicago School monetarism from the post-Keynesian positions with which it has so much overlap.) The eclectic position is incompatible with monetarism, but it is not incompatible with a *sophisticated* version of the Quantity Theory of Money. For as soon as one follows the logic of neoclassical analysis (expecting that less of any kind of inventory will be held if, other things equal, the cost of holding it has gone up) and postulates that the *velocity of circulation of money is a rising function of the interest rate,* the post-Keynesian (and even the simple Keynesian) model becomes compatible with the Quantity Theory. One way of looking at Keynesian liquidity preference is as *a theory of the velocity of circulation.*

Faulty logic

When post-Keynesians study recent economic history, they find that interest rates and money do enter into their estimating equations and with the theoretically expected algebraic signs. Case studies bear out the importance for investment decisions of the cost and availability of credit. Properly phrased questionnaires to business elicit answers that point in the same direction. And plausible theories to explain how businessmen make their investment decisions and how they ought to also bear out the fact that monetary policy does matter. So there is simply no excuse for living in a 1938 dream world in which money does not matter.

The bearing of all this on monetarism is well illustrated by an incident a few years ago at an American Bankers Association symposium where leading academic economists were commenting upon Professor Friedman's writings. Professor James Tobin went to the blackboard and wrote down three sentences:

1. MONEY DOES NOT MATTER.
2. MONEY MATTERS.
3. MONEY ALONE MATTERS.

He went on to say: Professor Friedman produces evidence to prove that the first proposition, Money doesn't matter, is false: he purports to have demonstrated from this that the third proposition, Money alone matters, is true; whereas the correct logical conclusion is that the second proposition, Money does matter, is all that follows. And on that there is no quarrel among leading modern macroeconomic economists.

Power and cogency of relevant evidence. I think there is much wisdom in this. When Professor Friedman defends monetarism, as for example in a late-1968 debate at New York University with new economist Walter Heller [see Reading 82], he refers to a mountain of evidence that supports monetarism. But how many members of the thousands in the overflow crowd attending that debate were able to appraise that evidence to see whether it supports the proposition 2, that money matters, rather than the central tenet of monetarism, that (when it comes to predictable systematic effects on aggregate demand and on inflationary or deflationary gaps) money alone matters? Sir Ronald Fisher, the greatest statistician of our age, pointed out that replication a thousandfold of an inconclusive experiment does nothing to add to its value. In terms of the language of statistics, most of the evidence compiled about money has little or no power to differentiate between propositions 2 and 3. Let me illustrate.

Anecdotes about incidents. A typical bit of historical evidence put forth to support monetarism goes like the following. "In 1919, after World War I, the U.S. Treasury wished to stabilize the interest rate. Keeping the Discount Rate constant resulted in a great increase in the money supply and in strong inflation. Then, early in 1920 on an identifiable date, the Treasury changed its policy; there followed a sharp reduction in the growth of the money supply; there followed a collapse of prices and the Recession of 1920–21. Ergo monetarism is true." But surely, for our purpose, this is a complete *non sequitur*. If we accept the chronology as given, it should indeed give pause to some witness before the Radcliffe Committee who argues that money never matters. But a whole range of mountains of evidence of this type does not tell us whether other factors—

such as fiscal policy—may not also have an independent influence on the pace of inflation. Replicating a refutation does not add commensurately to its weight, so I shall forebear from giving other examples of similar reasoning.

Cyclical leads and lags. But let me mention a different kind of evidence sometimes adduced for monetarism. The rate of change of the money supply precedes by 16 months or so, on the average but with great variance, the turndowns in the business cycle. Now it is easy to show that this set of facts fits in as well with an ultra-Keynesian model as with an ultra-Friedman model. Indeed in an unpublished paper, Professor Tobin has shown that the kind of Keynesian model that only a Radcliffe Committee member could still believe in does *better* than the monetarist model in fitting those facts. And let me add that those facts on timing are not very impressive facts. Those who play seriously the game of looking for leading indicators to predict business activity find the money-change series only one of many straws to indicate the way the wind is blowing. And not one of the more useful straws. Moreover, according to the most thorough studies, those by Dr. Geoffrey Moore of the National Bureau of Economic Research and Dr. Julius Shiskin of the U.S. Census Bureau, the money-change indicator has been scoring less well in recent decades than in earlier times.

Actually, in the 50 years since Warren Persons of Harvard initiated these leads and lags studies, the stock of money always tended to be one of the laggards rather than leaders in business cycle findings. Instead of turning up in the A group of leaders, money and interest rates tended to appear in the C group of laggards. Subsequent work by Arthur F. Burns and Moore at the National Bureau tended to confirm this finding. Indeed it is only in recent years that research is beginning to show signs that Money itself turns down and up as early as, or before, general GNP does—and, ironically, I believe this is probably to be explained by the fact that the Federal Reserve has been disregarding the advice of the monetarists and has tried to do some advance forecasting so that it can lean against the winds of recession before they begin to blow very hard.

What does a monetarist do when confronted with the fact that his causal factor, money, does not empirically lead his response factor, general business? One desperate artifice is to change his focus from the *stock* of money to its *time derivative,* its *rate of growth.* It is a mathematical fact that any periodic fluctuation that behaves a bit like a sine curve will have its derivative turndown a quarter cycle before itself; so if money itself does not lag business by as much as one quarter, one cannot help but get some lead at turning points by using the rate of change of money. But by that kind of frivolous action, one could use the derivative of production, its rate of change, to predict the turning points of the stock of money: or, with recognition of noise in the data, use production's own rate of change to predict its turning points.

Dimensional traps. Obviously, we have to find the reason for using dM/dt, the rate of change of money, rather than M, the stock of money, as our causal variable. One ridiculous argument for using the former is dimensional: both the level of GNP and the rate of growth of the money supply are measured in terms of dollars *per year.* Therefore, relate GNP and dM/dt, not GNP and M. This argument is ridiculous because the whole basis of the quantity theory of money is that V, the velocity of circulation of money or its reciprocal, is the dimensional constant that exists to relate the stock of money and the flow of national product. Professor Friedman, more than any other modern economist, has sloshed through the mountains of Yugoslavia to demonstrate that every peasant holds seventeen-weeks purchasing power in his pockets. The whole demand-for-money concept is for the purpose of making hypotheses about how that number 17 will change when interest rates, branch banking, or price expectations change. Moreover, there is involved a profound misunderstanding of how dimensional analysis is to be used in any science. The behavioral equation of a simple pendulum has for its very purpose the relating of two dimensionally different magnitudes—the position of the pendulum as measured in centimeters or dimensionless angular degrees and its acceleration as measured in centimeters per time squared. Nor is this a special example: Newton's universal law of gravitation, the greatest system of the world produced by man's thoughts, relates dimensionally different magnitudes in precisely the way that Dr. Friedman criticizes.

Trial by simple correlation. Let me mention one last kind of evidence that allegedly bears out the position of monetarism. Dr. Friedman, with the collaboration of Dr. David Meiselman, prepared for our Commission on Money and Credit a comparison of which does better for prediction: a simple correlation of money with GNP, or a simple correlation of some kind of Keynesian multiplicand with GNP or a related measure. They end up with a somewhat larger Pearsonian correlation coefficient for money. Ergo, monetarism is correct; Keynesianism has been defeated in a trial of honor. In my view this is simply silly. I waive the fact that the choice of variables and periods selected for the study has been subject to much criticism and debate. The post-Keynesian position which I adhere to does not believe in either of the simple theories set up as straw men, and is not particularly interested in which has the higher simple correlation coefficient. Even the St. Louis Federal Reserve Bank, a bastion of monetarism, when it came to compare either simple theory with an eclectic combination of both—which was still, in my eyes, an overly simple model and not one optimally formulated at that—they found that there was a statistically significant reduction in unexplained variance from a combination of the two simple theories.

The St. Louis Fed studies

I do not wish to conclude with the impression that there is no possible evidence that would convert me to monetarism. Its tenets are clear cut and are operationally refutable in principle. Thus, a November 1968 study by the St. Louis Federal Reserve Bank, using what is technically called a reduced-form 4-quarter lagged regression model, found that money had a significant positive effect on GNP in the 1952–68 sample period. Tax-rate changes had no significant effect. Public-expenditure changes had weak positive effects for two quarters, followed by weak negative effects two quarters later that wiped out any net steady-state effect. Now I do not believe that such a reduced form analysis correctly specifies the macroeconomic model that needs to be estimated. But if it were not for this fundamental and fatal objection, I would say that evidence like this does have a bearing on whether proposition 3 of the monetarists or proposition 2 of the post-Keynesians is more correct. Although space does not permit a proper evaluation of the St. Louis study here, I shall devote a few words to it because it is the only part of the mountains of evidence that are advanced in favor of monetarism that would, if it were correct, have power and relevance in favor of the monetarist position that the money supply alone matters. As already seen, all the other evidence is germane only to the nondisputed issue as to whether it is true that money does not at all matter.

First, it is at first blush impressive that by money alone one can at least retroactively "explain" in the usual multiple-correlation sense about half the total variance in the change in GNP. But when one examines the whole sample, inclusive of the fifties and the sixties, one sees that all the good fit is in the sixties. The multiple-correlation coefficient (R^2 to be technical) is not at all large in the fifties. We thus are confronted essentially with only one epoch, one experiment upon which to base our new monistic faith in monetarism. And those of us who know the 1960s, who were part of the decisions made and who have a much more intimate feel for the causations than can be given in one crude statistical time series, cannot in accordance with the best modern theories of Bayesian inference believe that the 1960s are best understood in terms of a "money only matters" model. (Specifically, our cross-sectional judgmental data suggest that if Kennedy had frozen the budget at a low balanced level and then made the M supply grow as it did, the vector of economic development would have been very different—in contrast to a crude use of the St. Louis reduced-form equations.)

Second, the so-called reduced-form technique of the St. Louis multiple correlation cannot hope to identify correctly the true causal role of fiscal and monetary policy. I have used that technique on fabricated examples in which money did not alone matter, and it has given the false answer that money does alone matter. Gramlich, Gramley, Davis, and a number of other writers have criticized it on this account and have suggested alternatives. Not all the

criticisms prove to be telling, but I believe that when all the record is in the eclectic position will be the only tenable one.

Third, it is a logical corollary of the monetarist interpretation of events itself that the St. Louis study should exaggerate the potency of money. Friedman, Meiselman, Meltzer, and Brunner, numerous St. Louis Fed writers have all insisted that the Federal Reserve tends to commit the crime of trying to stabilize interest rates rather than the rate of growth of the money supply. Ad nauseam they charge the Fed with an excessive preoccupation with the false criterion of net free reserves. Well, let us take them at their word. As Tobin says, they cannot have it both ways. What would be the consequence of applying the St. Louis reduced-form technique to a model in which the Fed committed the crime of increasing M whenever an exogenous upthrust in GNP tended to destabilize interest rates? Suppose we contrive a model in which money doesn't matter at all but in which the Fed has a criminal fascination for net free reserves and all the other magnitudes that the monetarists abhor and warn against? The answer is this: "Where M does not matter, the St. Louis technique will infer that it really does matter! Where M matters a little, the St. Louis methods will be biased toward the verdict that M matters much, or exclusively." I myself do not conclude from this that the St. Louis studies are of no interest. Indeed they are the only fresh evidence I have seen in 15 years: the rest is persuasive rehash of what has not been in doubt in sophisticated circles. But all the evidence leads me to the prediction that mechanisms like those in the FRB-MIT model of Professor Modigliani will prove to be most useful for description and policy.

Crucial tests in 1966–1967 and 1968–1969

Personally, as a scientist, I would cheerfully accept *any hypothesis that would deliver the goods and explain the facts.* As a fallible human being, I do not relish having to change my mind but if economists had to hang from the ceiling in order to do their job, then there would be nothing for it than to do so. But monetarism does not deliver the goods. I could make a fortune giving good predictions to large corporations and banks based on monetarism if it would work. But I have tried every version of it. And none do.

To this there are two standard answers. The first is that nothing works well. Fine tuning is an illusion. There is much "noise" in the data. No one can claim that monetarism would enable the Federal Reserve to iron out all the variation in the economy. All we can say for it is that stabilizing the growth rate of money is the best policy that the ingenuity of man can ever arrive at. All this involves what I call the chipmunk syndrome. The nimble monetarist sticks his neck out in an occasional prediction: that prediction is not always free of ambiguity, but it does seem to point qualitatively in one direction, often a direction counter to the conventional wisdom of the moment: then if subsequent events do seem to go in the indicated direction, the prediction is trumpeted to be a feather in the cap of monetarism. If, as is happening all the time, events do not particularly go in that direction—or if as happens often, events go somewhat in a direction that neither competing theory has been subjected to a test of any resolving power—the chipmunk pulls in his head, saying that there is no way of fine tuning the economy or making completely accurate predictions.

The other argument against the view that monetarism simply does not work is the assertion, "Monetarism does work. So and so at the Blank bank uses it and he beats the crowd in batting average." I believe this to be a serious and important subject for investigation. Let me therefore, because of space limitations, confine myself to a few observations based upon preliminary investigations of the matter.

1. Those analysts who use their monetarism *neat* really do *not* perform well.

2. A number of bank economists, who give great weight to the money factor but who *also* pay attention to what is happening to defense spending and inventories and a host of other factors, seem to me to have compiled an excellent record at forecasting. Not a perfect record. Who has a perfect record? And not, as far as quantitative studies known to me suggest, a better record than the best macroeconomic forecasters who do not consciously put special stress on the money factor (but who do not neglect it either!). In short, it is impossible to separate "flair" in forecasting from success attributable primarily to use of money-supply variables.

3. The years 1966–67 are often referred to as years of a crucial test in which monetarism defeated Keynesianism. I have gone over all the main forecasts used by both schools during that period and I must report that this is a misapprehension. There was *wide range* of forecasts by practitioners of both schools: there was a *wide overlap* between these two ranges. On the whole, the monetarists averaged better and *earlier* in their perception of the slowdown beginning to be seen in late 1966 in consequence of the money crunch of 1966. And one would expect this to be the case from an eclectic viewpoint since the independent variable of money received the biggest alteration in *that* period. But many of the monetarists went overboard in predicting a recession in 1967 of the National Bureau type: indeed some of the more astute monetarists warned their brethren against following the logic of the method, lest it discredit the method! And some of the largest squared errors of estimate for 1967 that I have in my files came from dogmatic monetarists who did not heed the warning from inside their own camp.

4. Again, the year 1969 is thought by some to provide a test of some power between the two theories. Yet I, who am an eclectic, have my own GNP forecast for the year nicely bracketed by the two banks that have been most successful in the past in using monetarism in their projections. And though I must admit that the last part of 1968 was stronger than those who believe in the potency of fiscal policy and the mid-1969 tax surcharge to be, I do not interpret that extra strength as being a negation of any such potency or as due solely or primarily to the behavior of money during the last 12 months. Without the tax surcharge, I believe the GNP would have surprised us by soaring even faster above predictions. Since history cannot be rerun to perform controlled experiments, I cannot prove this. But the weight of all the evidence known to me does point in this direction. In a soft science like economics, that is all even the best practitioner can say.

Conclusion

The bulk of my remarks have been critical of an overly simple doctrine of monetarism. But they must not be interpreted as supporting the view that money does not matter. There are parts of the world, particularly in Britain and the Commonwealth, where it might be better to believe in overly simple monetarism than in overly simple denial of the role of money.

In the *Sunday Telegraph* (London, December 15, 1968) I was able to invert the Tobin syllogisms to isolate the fatal flaw in the reasoning of the Radcliffe Report. The Radcliffe Committee heard much convincing testimony to show that there existed no invariable velocity of circulation of money to enable one to predict GNP accurately from the money

supply alone. In effect then, Radcliffe established the falsity of Tobin's third proposition, Money alone matters. And, in a *nonsequitur*, they concluded the truth of his first proposition, that Money does not matter. For all their talking around the subject of liquidity as a substitute concept for money alone, they and the fossil-Keynesians who hailed their report should have recognized the fact that both theory and experience give to money (along with fiscal and other variables) an important role in the macroeconomic scenario of modern times.

Deficits and the Public Debt

Readings 34, 35, and 36

There is no subject in political economy more interesting to people than the public debt. And there is no subject on which the mythology of the man in the street is more misinformed than that of the public debt and deficit financing. Fortunately, in the 1960s progress was made in public understanding and acceptance of the scientific aspects of the matter. But these readings remind us that endemic in the minds of uninformed laymen remain tragic illusions.

Reading 34 is by the late Harry F. Byrd, long a Democratic Senator from Virginia, an unreconstructed believer in orthodox finance and limited government. Reading 35 is by Maurice Stans, a certified public accountant, Eisenhower's Director of the Bureau of the Budget, and Secretary of Commerce in the Nixon administration. Reading 36 is by one of the world's most eminent economic scientists, Professor James Tobin, Sterling Professor of Economics at Yale and member of President Kennedy's first Council of Economic Advisers.

Questions to Guide the Reading

Why are analogies between private and public finance misleading? In particular, if the ability of the government to bear the interest costs of the public debt depends primarily upon the taxable incomes of the nation, why should not the burden of the public debt be a manageable one even if it were to grow by more per year than the largest peacetime deficit we have ever had— $12 billion in 1959, during Eisenhower's term, which is less than a growth rate of 4 per cent per annum in an economy that has a money GNP growth rate of 6 or more per cent per annum?

If the real assets of a nation are to grow, how much can debt grow without impairing the ratios of a healthy society? Why is failure to have GNP grow the greatest danger that a society with debt can ever face?

Reading 34

The Evils of Deficit Spending

Senator Harry F. Byrd

As I see it, balancing the budget without resorting to legerdemain or unsound bookkeeping methods is certainly in the category of our No. 1 problems.

Beginning with 1792, the first fiscal year of our Federal Government, and through 1916, Federal deficits were casual and usually paid off in succeeding years. In this 124-year period there were 43 deficit years and 81 surplus years. As late as July 1, 1914, the interest-bearing debt was less than $1 billion.

In Andrew Jackson's administration the public debt was paid off in toto, an achievement in which President Jackson expressed great pride.

It can be said for this first 124 years in the life of our Republic we were on a pay-as-you-go basis. In that period I think it can be accurately said that we laid the foundation for our strength today as the greatest nation in all the world.

It is disturbing these days to hear some economists argue the budget should not be balanced and that we should not begin to pay off the debt because, they allege, it will adversely affect business conditions. Have we yielded so far to the blandishments of Federal subsidies and Government support that we have forgotten our Nation is great because of individual effort as contrasted to state paternalism?

Evils of deficit spending

Here are some of the evils of deficit spending:

The debt today is the debt incurred by this generation, but tomorrow it will be debt on our children and grandchildren, and it will be for them to pay, both the interest and the principal.

It is possible and in fact probable that before this astronomical debt is paid off, if it ever is, the interest charge will exceed the principal.

Protracted deficit spending means cheapening the dollar. Cheapened money is inflation.

Inflation is a dangerous game. It robs creditors, it steals pensions, wages, and fixed income. Once started, it is exceedingly difficult to control. This inflation has been partially checked but the value of the dollar dropped slightly again in the past year. It would not take much to start up this dangerous inflation again.

Public debt is not like private debt. If private debt is not paid off, it can be ended by liquidation, but if public debt is not paid off with taxes, liquidation takes the form of disastrous inflation or national repudiation. Either is destructive of our form of government.

Today the interest on the Federal debt takes more than 10 percent of our total Federal tax revenue. Without the tremendous cost of this debt our annual tax bill could be reduced 10 percent across the board.

Budget reform?

Proposals have been advocated changing our budgetary system. There are two which recur with persistency, and I want to warn you of them.

First, there is the proposal for a cash budget. Those who advocate the cash budget are suggesting that the Government pay its routine bills with savings of the citizens who have entrusted protection of their old age and unemployment to the guardianship of the Federal Government. These trust funds were established from premiums paid by participants in social security, unemployment insurance, bank deposit insurance programs, etc. Not a cent of these funds belongs to the Government.

Second, some are advocating a capital budget which means that so-called capital expenditures should not be considered as current expenditures in the budget.

Those who advocate the so-called capital budget must start out with the fallacious assumption that the Government is in business to make a profit on its citizens. To my knowledge the Federal Government has never made

From a speech by Senator Harry F. Byrd reprinted in *Congressional Record*, vol. 101, pt. 4, 84 Congress, 1 Session, May 4, 1955.

a bona fide profit on any Government operation.

They must assume that debt contracted by a Federal agency is not a debt of the Federal Government and a burden on all of the taxpayers.

I am an old-fashioned person who believes that a debt is a debt just as much in the atomic age as it was in the horse and buggy days.

A capital budget must assume that Government manufacturing plants, such as atomic energy installations, are in commercial production for a profit, and that Government stockpiles are longtime investments for profit instead of precautions against emergencies when they would be completely expendable with no financial return.

Likewise, it must assume that the agriculture surplus program is primarily a long range investment deal instead of a prop for annual farm income to be used when needed on a year-by-year basis.

While the vastness and complexity of the Federal Government of the United States necessarily makes budgeting difficult, the so-called conventional budget currently in use offers the best approach to orderly financing with fullest disclosure.

What is needed for a better fiscal system is fuller disclosure of Federal expenditures and responsibility for them—not less, as inevitably would be the case with so-called cash and capital budgets.

With full disclosure of the Federal expenditure situation, the American people then would have an opportunity to decide whether they wanted to recapture control and bring the rate of spending into balance with the rate of taxing and thus reduce the tremendous Federal debt burden we are now bearing.

At home we can get along without Federal usurpation of individual, local, and State responsibilities, and we can get along without Federal competition in business whether it be hotels, furs, rum, clothing, fertilizer, or other things.

The Bible says if thine eye offend thee pluck it out. I say if the Federal Government should not engage in such activities, we should first stop new invasions and then gradually, if not abruptly, eliminate the old intrusions. When we do these things we shall balance the budget, for lower taxes and reduced debt. There will be no further need for trick budgets and debt-ceiling evasions and hiding taxes. The Government will be honest in itself, and honest with the people.

Reading 35

The Need for Balanced Federal Budgets

Secretary of Commerce Maurice H. Stans

The federal government should have a balanced budget; its expenditures, especially in times like these, should not exceed its income. Of this I am deeply convinced.

As a matter of fact, I find it difficult to understand why there are still some people who do not seem to agree. Even though I have now been an official of the government almost four years and know by hard experience that there are at least two sides to all public questions, on this one the facts speak eloquently for themselves. And the arguments that are marshalled in opposition to show that a balanced budget is unimportant—or that it can be safely forsaken for lengthy periods of time—certainly seem unsound. It is true that we as a nation have been extremely fortunate in maintaining our fundamental strengths thus far despite the heavy deficit spending of the past thirty years. But we cannot count on being lucky forever; and more and more the consequences of past profligacy are now catching up with us.

Let us look at some of the facts:

1. It is a fact that in 24 of the last 30 years (i.e., up to 1959) the federal government has spent more than it has received.

From Maurice H. Stans, "The Need for Balanced Federal Budgets," *Annals of the American Academy of Political and Social Science,* 1959. Reprinted with kind permission of the author and publisher.

2. It is a fact that last fiscal year (1958) the federal government had a deficit (12.5 billion dollars) larger than ever before in time of peace.

3. It is a fact that the federal government debt is now 290 billion dollars (in 1959) and that the annual cost of carrying that debt is more than 10 per cent of the budgeted income of the government—and has been going up.

4. It is a fact that our economy is operating at a higher rate of activity than it ever has before and that the standard of living it is producing for all America is far beyond that of any other country in the world.

5. It is a fact that in times of high economic activity there is competition among business, consumers, and government for the productive resources of the country; if government, by indulging in high levels of spending in such times, intensifies that competition, it openly invites inflation.

6. It is a fact that with an unbalanced budget, federal borrowings to raise the money to spend more than income tend to add to the money supply of the country and therefore are inflationary.

7. It is a fact that the purchasing power of the dollar has declined more than 50 per cent in the last twenty years. Today we spend more than $2.00 to get what $1.00 would buy in 1939.

8. And finally, it is a fact that all too often in history inflation has been the undoing of nations, great and small.

True, there are many people who still feel that a bit of inflation is a tolerable, if not a good, thing. I think they fail to see that a bit of inflation is an installment on a lot of inflation—a condition in which nobody can hope to gain.

Those of our citizens who believe that inflation is not undesirable simply overlook the history of nations. Inflation is an insidious threat to the strength of the United States. Unless we succeed in exercising a tighter rein over it than we have been able to up to this point, I am afraid that we will all lose—as individuals, as a nation, and as a people.

In my view, the facts that I have recited clearly demonstrate the need for:

1. Containing federal expenditures within federal income—which means balancing the budget—in fiscal years 1960 and 1961.

2. Establishing the principle of a balanced budget—including some surplus for reduction of the national debt—as a fiscal objective for the prosperous years ahead.

These are the standards on which fiscal integrity for the nation should rest. These are the standards by which the force of inflation induced by reckless fiscal policy can be averted. Yet in 24 of the last 30 years we have not been able to attain them.

Let us look at some of the circumstances which have caused heavy federal spending in the past and have, perhaps, made us insensitive to the dangers of deficits.

Looking back

Over the last three decades the federal government has spent 264 billion dollars more than it has received. The six years in which there was an excess of income over expense produced negligible surpluses in relation to the deficits of the other years.

We need hardly be reminded of the cause of most of those deficits. In the earlier years it was depression; in the middle years it was war; in recent years it has been war again and then recession.

In the depression years it was not possible to balance the budget; while government services and costs were growing by popular demand, federal revenues declined as a result of economic inactivity. The efforts made to balance the budget by increasing tax rates in 1930 and 1932 and in 1936 and 1938 were apparently self-defeating.

As for the expenditure side of the budget, the decade of the 1930's produced a great deal of talk about "pump-priming" and "compensatory spending"—federal spending which would compensate in poor times for the decline in business and consumer demand and thus lend balance and stability to the economy. The theory was, of course, for the federal government to spend proportionately larger amounts during depression times and proportionately smaller amounts during good times—to suffer deficits in poor years and enjoy surpluses in prosperous years, with the objective of coming out even over the long pull.

Then, in the early 1940's came World War II. During the war years, the federal government's expenditures vastly exceeded its income, and huge further deficits were piled up. In retrospect, most students of wartime economic developments now agree that we did not tax ourselves nearly enough. We did not pay enough of the costs of war out of current income. We created a large debt while suppressing some of its inflationary consequences with direct economic controls, but the suppression was only temporary.

Depression and war, although major factors, were not the only reasons for increased federal expenditures and deficits during the past thirty years. It was more complex than that. In the 1930's the national philosophy of the responsibilities of the federal government underwent a major change. The country's needs for economic growth and social advancement were gradually given increased recognition at the federal level.

The aim of economic growth, of social advancement, and of "compensatory" economic stability became intertwined. Many federal activities of far-reaching implications were established in ways which affected federal expenditures for very long periods of time—if not permanently. Social security, greatly increased support for agriculture, rural electrification, aids to home owners and mortgage institutions, public housing, public power developments like the Tennessee Valley Authority and other multipurpose water resource projects, and public assistance grants are just a few examples. All of them, however, remained as federal programs after World War II. And we were actually fighting in that war before federal spending for work relief could be stopped.

The immediate postwar period was marked by dramatic demobilization. Nevertheless, many of the major costs of war lingered on. The maintenance in the postwar period of even the reduced and relatively modest structure of our Armed Forces was far more costly than anything that existed in the way of the machinery of war prior to 1940. The war also left us with greatly increased expenditure commitments for interest on public debt, for veterans, and for atomic energy. The Marshall Plan and the mutual security program followed in succession. It became obvious next, that the cold war was going to be expensive. Then, with the Korean aggression, it became necessary to rearm and, even after the shooting stopped, the peacetime striking force and defensive machinery we had to maintain continued expenditures at levels that far exceeded in cost anything we had earlier imagined.

Thus, the postwar growth of the budget has been partly in the area of national security, partly deferred costs of World War II, and partly the inheritance of activities and ways of thinking that characterized the depression of the 1930's. We have now learned that many of the programs the federal government initiated in the 1930's were neither temporary nor "compensatory" in character. Moreover, we have not only retained many of them, but we have also greatly expanded them in the postwar period. Since World War II we have seen large increases in federal expenditures for urban renewal, public health, federal aid for airports and highways, new categories and a higher federal share of public assistance grants, aid to schools in federally impacted areas, great liberalization in aid to agriculture, as well as new programs for science, education, and outer space.

The present

What can we conclude from all of this?

It seems to me that in the first place we must recognize that the compensatory theory of federal spending has failed thus far and offers little hope for the future unless we exert a more forceful and courageous determination to control the growth of federal spending. The major spending programs which originated in the depression years have in most cases persisted in the following decades. A work relief project could be turned off when we started to fight a war, but most of the programs established in the 1930's developed characteristics of a far more permanent sort.

An example can be found in the program of the Rural Electrification Administration (REA). This program was started in 1936 when only a minority of farm families enjoyed the benefits of electricity. Today, 95 per cent of our farms receive central station electric service. We have invested 4 billion dollars in this program, at 2 per cent interest. Nonetheless, indications are that future demands for federal funds will be even greater as the REA cooperatives continue to grow.

The startling fact is that three out of four new users currently being added are nonfarm users. About one-half of REA electric power goes to industries, communities, or nonfarm families. The reasonable approach is that rural electric cooperatives should now be able to get some of their financing from other than government sources, especially for nonfarm purposes that compete with taxed private industry.

Inability to turn off expenditures is not all that is wrong with the compensatory theory of the prewar period. Initially, it deals largely with the spending side of the fiscal equation whereas the income side now appears to be playing a more important part. Today—with corporate income tax rates at 52 per cent—any substantial reduction of corporate earnings produces an immediate proportionate and large loss to the federal treasury. Personal income taxes also respond, though less sharply, to a fall in national production and employment. Thus, when times take a turn for the worse, federal revenues decline promptly and substantially.

Couple this with enlarged social obligations in times of recession or depression—unemployment compensation, public assistance, and so on—and you have substantial leverage of a more or less automatic character for the production of federal deficits in times of depressed economic activity. To do more than this—to deliberately step up expenditures still more, for public works and other construction—runs grave risks. There is, first, the risk that an anti-recession expenditure program cannot be turned off after the recession, but instead represents a permanent increase in the public sphere at the expense of the private. Second, it is difficult to start programs quickly, so the major impact may come long after the need for the economic stimulation has passed. Both of these risks mean that anti-recession actions can well represent an inflationary danger for the post-recession period. The danger is there even if, as some believe, positive governmental intervention is required to counter recessions. It is more grave, however, if—and I believe this was proved true in 1958–59—the economy is vigorous and resilient enough to come out of a temporary recession and to go on through a revival period to new prosperous peaks without any direct financial federal interference.

I think we may conclude that it is inevitable that our nation will be faced with large budgets in the years ahead. This is particularly true for the defense obligations which our country has assumed, for its international un-

dertakings to provide economic and military assistance to other free nations, and as a result of many programs which have been started over the years—major programs for water resource development, agriculture, veterans' benefits, low-cost housing, airways modernization, and space exploration—all these and many others have taken on a permanent quality which makes it clear that federal budgets will be large budgets in our lifetimes.

There is still another conclusion which springs from this short recitation of the history of the last thirty years. It is that the federal government has assumed more and more responsibility for activities which formerly were regarded as being under the jurisdiction of state and local governments. More and more the federal government has assumed responsibility for public assistance, housing, urban renewal, educational aid to areas with federal installations, and many other programs that are now supported by federal grants-in-aid to the states. All this, of course, contributes to the conclusion that these federal programs are not only large at the present time, but have a built-in durability—a staying power with which we must reckon as a fact of life.

I think these thoughts are well summarized in the words of Mr. Allen Sproul, former President of the New York Federal Reserve Bank, who recently said:

Government, in our day, touches upon the economic life of the community in an almost bewildering variety of ways, but its overall influence comes into focus in the consolidated cash budget and, in a subsidiary way, in the management of the public debt. When we abandoned the idea of taxation for revenue only and admitted, as we must, a more important role of Government in economic affairs, we thought up a tidy little scheme called the compensatory budget. This envisaged a cash budget balanced in times of real prosperity, in deficit in times of economic recession and in surplus in times of inflationary boom. What we have got is a budget that may throw up a shaky surplus in times of boom, but that will surely show substantial deficits in times of recession. The bias, over time, is toward deficits, with only wobbly contracyclical tendencies.

Looking ahead

It seems to me that as we move into another decade it will be essential to recognize that unless we have a more positive program for operating our federal government within its income, the forces that have gained such tremendous momentum in the past will perpetuate the tradition of deficits—to the great disadvantage of the country as a whole.

Assuming a continuous, but not uninterrupted, economic growth for the country, accompanied by ever-increasing, but not uninterrupted, growth of federal revenues, we should nevertheless expect that the growth of programs started in the past will have a strong tendency to absorb the expected additional revenues—unless aggressive controls are exercised by an alert administration and a statesmanlike Congress during those years.

On those occasions when the economy recedes from its way of growth, we must expect great leverage to be exerted toward the building up of additional deficits. We must learn to live with recession-induced deficits as a matter of necessity, but we should not take un-needed actions which mortgage our nation's future with both more debt and an inflationary potential.

Conclusions

It seems to me to follow from these facts and analyses that it should be the policy of the federal government to strive determinedly for a balanced budget at all times, for, clearly, if it does not, the forces at work to upset financial stability will surely prevail as a matter of momentum.

As we move into the next decade we have the lessons of the three past decades to guide us:

1. Federal programs persist and in most cases grow. As demand expands, the programs expand. It is extremely difficult to curtail them. Their growing costs—and a growing economy—must be reckoned with realistically. This means that actions should be taken to reduce or to end them as they accomplish the purposes for which they were initiated (eighteen such proposals were made in President Eisenhower's budget message for the fiscal year 1960).

2. In times of recession, it is important to avoid doing things as temporary expedients which will become longer range programs and create major problems later on. We have plenty of these as carry-overs from earlier days; we should avoid creating new ones for the years ahead.

3. We must, of course, learn to live with deficits when major national emergencies threaten or exist in our country. But we should resolve to create equivalent surpluses later on to offset such deficits.

The lesson is clear. We should pay as we go, and if we are to look for debt reduction or tax reduction on a sound footing—as we should —we must do more than this. We must plan for substantial budgetary surpluses in good years—or we will surely contribute to further dangerous inflation in the years ahead.

Reading 36

Deficit, Deficit, Who's Got the Deficit?

James Tobin

For every buyer there must be a seller, and for every lender a borrower. One man's expenditure is another's receipt. My debts are your assets, my deficit your surplus.

If each of us was consistently "neither borrower nor lender," as Polonius advised, no one would ever need to violate the revered wisdom of Mr. Micawber. But if the prudent among us insist on running and lending surpluses, some of the rest of us are willy-nilly going to borrow to finance budget deficits.

In the United States today one budget that is usually left holding a deficit is that of the federal government. When no one else borrows the surpluses of the thrifty, the Treasury ends up doing so. Since the role of debtor

From James Tobin, *National Economic Policy* (Yale University Press, New Haven and London, 1966). Reprinted with kind permission of the author and publisher.

and borrower is thought to be particularly unbecoming to the federal government, the nation feels frustrated and guilty.

Unhappily, crucial decisions of economic policy too often reflect blind reactions to these feelings. The truisms that *borrowing is the counterpart of lending* and *deficits the counterpart of surpluses* are overlooked in popular and Congressional discussions of government budgets and taxes. *Both guilt feelings and policy are based on serious misunderstanding of the origins of federal budget deficits and surpluses.*

Private surpluses

American *households* and *financial institutions* consistently run financial surpluses. They have money to lend, beyond their own needs to borrow. Figure 1 shows the growth in their combined surpluses since the war; it also shows some tendency for these surpluses to rise in periods of recession and slack business activity. Of course, many private households have financial deficits. They pay out more than their incomes for food, clothing, cars, appliances, houses, taxes, and so on. They draw on savings accounts, redeem savings bonds, sell securities, mortgage houses, or incur installment debt. But deficit households are far outweighed by surplus households. As a group American *households* and *nonprofit institutions* have in recent years shown a net financial surplus averaging about $15 billion a year—that is, households are ready to lend, or to put into equity investments, about $15 billion a year more than they are prepared to borrow. In addition, *financial institutions* regularly generate a lendable surplus, now of the order of $5 billion a year. For the most part these institutions—banks, savings and loan associations, insurance companies, pension funds, and the like—are simply intermediaries which borrow and relend the public's money. Their surpluses result from the fact that they earn more from their lending operations than they distribute or credit to their depositors, shareowners, and policyholders.

Who is to use the $20 billion of surplus funds available from households and financial institutions? *State and local governments* as a group have been averaging $3–4 billion a year of net borrowing. Pressures of the expanding

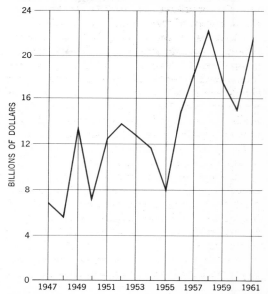

Fig. 1   Financial surpluses of consumers, non-profit institutions, and financial institutions, 1947–61.

Source: Board of Governors of the Federal Reserve System

populations of children, adults, houses, and automobiles, plus the difficulties of increasing tax revenues, force these governments to borrow in spite of strictures against government debt. *Unincorporated businesses*, including farms, absorb another $3–4 billion. To the rest of the world we can lend perhaps $2 billion a year. We cannot lend abroad—net—more than the surplus of our exports over our imports of goods and services, and some of that surplus we give away in foreign aid. We have to earn the lendable surplus in tough international competition. Recent experience shows clearly that when we try to lend and invest too much money abroad, we either have to borrow it back or else pay in gold.

These borrowers account for $8–10 billion. The remainder—some $10–12 billion—must be used either by *nonfinancial corporate business* or by the *federal government*. Only if corporations as a group take $10–12 billion of external funds, by borrowing or issuing new equities, can the federal government expect to break even. This is, moreover, an understatement of what is required to keep the federal debt from rising, for the federal government itself provides annually $3 to $4 billion of new lending; the Treasury would have to borrow to finance these federal lending programs even if the government absorbed no *net* funds from the economy. It is *gross* federal borrowing that offends the conservative fiscal conscience, whether or not the proceeds are used to acquire other financial assets.

Which is it to be?

The moral is inescapable, if startling. If you would like the federal deficit to be smaller, the deficits of business must be bigger. Would you like the federal government to run a surplus and reduce its debt? Then business deficits must be big enough to absorb that surplus as well as the funds available from households and financial institutions.

That does not mean that business must run at a loss—quite the contrary. Sometimes, it is true, unprofitable businesses are forced to borrow or to spend financial reserves just to stay afloat; this was a major reason for business deficits in the depths of the Great Depression. But normally it is businesses with good profits and good prospects that borrow or sell new shares of stock, in order to finance expansion and modernization. As the President of American Telephone and Telegraph can testify, heavy reliance on outside funds, far from being a distress symptom, is an index and instrument of growth in the profitability and worth of the corporation. The incurring of financial deficits by business firms—or by households and governments for that matter —does not usually mean that such institutions are living beyond their means and consuming their capital. Financial deficits are typically the means of accumulating nonfinancial assets —real property in the form of inventories, buildings, and equipment.

When does business run big deficits? When do corporations draw heavily on the capital markets? The record is clear: when business is very good, when sales are pressing hard on capacity, when businessmen see further expansion ahead. Though corporations' internal funds—depreciation allowances and plowed-back profits—are large during boom times, their investment programs are even larger.

The facts of experience

Figure 2 shows the financial deficits or surpluses of corporate business and of the federal government since the war. Three facts stand out. First, the *federal government has big deficits when corporations run surpluses or small deficits and vice versa*. Second, *government surpluses and business deficits reach their peaks in periods of economic expansion*, when industrial capacity is heavily utilized, as in 1947–48, 1951–52, and 1956–57. Third, the combined deficit of corporate business and the federal government is greater now than in the early postwar years; this is the counterpart of the upward trend in available surpluses shown in Figure 1.

Recession, idle capacity, unemployment, economic slack—these are the enemies of the balanced government budget. When the economy is faltering, households have more surpluses available to lend, and business firms are less inclined to borrow them.

The federal government will not succeed in cutting its deficit by steps that depress the economy, perpetuate excess capacity, and deter business firms from using outside funds. Raising taxes and cutting expenses seem like obvious ways to balance the budget. But because of their effects on private spending, lending, and borrowing, they may have exactly the contrary result. Likewise, lowering taxes and raising government expenditures may so stimulate private business activity and private borrowing that the federal deficit is in the end actually reduced.

Misleading parables

This may seem paradoxical, and perhaps it is. Why is it that the homely analogy between family finance and government finance, on which our decisive national attitudes toward federal fiscal policy are so largely based, misleads us? If John Jones on Maple Street is spending $8,700 a year but taking in only $8,000, the remedy is clear. All Mr. Jones need do to balance the family budget is to live resolutely within his income, either spending some $700 less or working harder to increase his earnings. Jones can safely ignore the impact of either action on the incomes and expenditures of others and the possible ultimate feedback on his own job and income. The situation of the President on Pennsylvania Avenue, spending $87 billion a year against tax revenues of $80 billion, is quite different. Suppose that he spends $7 billion less, or tries

through higher tax rates to boost federal revenues by $7 billion. He cannot ignore the
inevitable boomerang effect on federal finances.
These measures will lower taxpayers' receipts,
expenditures, and taxable incomes. The federal deficit will be reduced by much less than
$7 billion; perhaps it will even be increased.

Incidentally, many of the very critics who
are most vocal in chiding the government for
fiscal sin advocate policies that would make
fiscal virtue even more elusive. They want
to keep private borrowing in check by the use
of tight credit policies and high interest rates.
They want to increase corporations' *internal*
flow of funds by bigger depreciation allowances and higher profit margins, making business still less dependent on external funds to
finance investment, even in boom times. When
these apostles of sound finance also tell the
government to shun external finance, have
they done their arithmetic? If everyone is self-
financing, who will borrow the surpluses?

The price we pay

The nation is paying a high price for the
misapplied homely wisdom that guides federal fiscal policy. The real toll is measured by
unemployment, idle capacity, lost production,
and sluggish economic growth. But fiscal conservatism is also self-defeating. It does not
even achieve its own aim, the avoidance of
government deficits. Federal fiscal and mone-

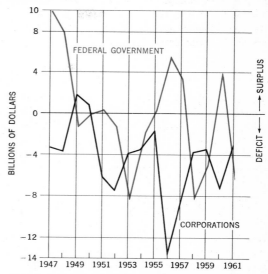

Fig. 2   Net financial surpluses and deficits of the federal government and of nonfinancial corporations, 1947–61.

Source: Board of Governors of the Federal Reserve System

tary policies consciously and unashamedly
designed to stimulate the economy would
have sufficient justification in economic expansion itself. But they might well "improve" the
federal budget too—by inducing business to
use the private surpluses that now have no
destination other than a rising federal debt.

The Composition and Pricing of National Output 3

Microeconomic Pricing

Reading 37

It is a far cry from graphs of supply and demand to actual workings of a competitive price market. Some economics textbooks (e.g., Samuelson, *Economics*, Eighth Edition, Appendix to Chapter 21) explain how speculation works. The present little gem is written by "Adam Smith," whom we have already met in Reading 11 and who is the author of the best seller *The Money Game*. Those who know, say this account has the ring of truth.

Questions to Guide the Reading

Is it not clear that many of the people who are buying and selling cocoa futures are uninformed gamblers? But does that rule out the possibility that the price is ultimately set by shrewder men who utilize the best possible information about supply and demand? By having better information and acting on it, these speculators make money for themselves at the expense of the uninformed gamblers. At the same time they are moving the crop from regions where it is plentiful to those where it is scarce, and are doing the same thing in time——moving supplies from seasons of glut to seasons of scarcity. Also if there are some people who are willing to gamble, will that not make it possible for candy manufacturers to lay off some of the irreducible risks onto such people by means of "hedging"? Can you interpret the following: After studying wheat and other market prices for a lifetime, Professor Holbrook Working of Stanford's Food Research Institute concluded that competitive markets do perform the function of reducing price instability and effecting a rational pattern of crop carryover in time and space.

The Cocoa Caper
"Adam Smith"

The further we come along, the more apparent becomes the wisdom of the Master in describing the market as a game of musical chairs. The most brilliant and perceptive analysis you can do may sit there until someone else believes it too, for the object of the game is not to own some stock, like a faithful dog, which you have chosen, but to get to the piece of paper ahead of the crowd. Value is not only inherent in the stock; to do you any good, it has to be value that is appreciated by others. (Analysts at White, Weld walk around repeating "I have always preferred recognition to discovery" because that is an aphorism of one of the partners.)

It follows that some sort of sense of timing is necessary, and you either develop it or you don't. You could have a chapter on how to swim, but it wouldn't teach you a tenth as much as getting tossed into the water.

The best chapter written on this problem of timing was done by an unknown second-century author who wrote under the pen name of Koholeth, or the Preacher. What survives of Koholeth is not much, but it says all there is to say on this subject. (If you seem to hear a faint rock beat behind what follows, it is because Pete Seeger made a song, "Turn, Turn, Turn," out of this passage of Koholeth and the Byrds made a hit record of it.) In later versions of the Old Testament, Koholeth appears as Ecclesiastes, so you have the best chapter on timing right there on your shelf already.

To everything there is a season,
And a time to every purpose under the heaven:
A time to be born, and a time to die;
A time to plant, and a time to pluck up that which
    is planted;

A time to break down, and a time to build up;
A time to mourn, and a time to dance;
A time to cast away stones, and a time to gather
    stones together;

A time to keep, and a time to cast away;
A time to rend, and a time to sew;
A time to keep silence, and a time to speak;

and so on.

There isn't anything else to say. There are some markets that want cyclical stocks; there are some that do a fugal counterpoint to interest rates; there are some that become as stricken for romance as the plain girl behind the counter at Woolworth's; there are some that become obsessed with the future of technology; and there are some that don't believe at all.

If you are in the right thing at the wrong time, you may be right but have a long wait; at least you are better off than coming late to the party. You don't want to be on the dance floor when the music stops.

If what you are doing doesn't seem to be working, the game may not be on even, though the brokers continue to mail out recommendations, and the pundits say things are getting fatter than ever, and the customers' men are busy with smooth reassurances.

It may be all very well to say: *When there's no game, don't play,* but the Propensity is very strong among those who have been playing. I once got involved in another game because the main game was not on, and the best I can say is that it kept me out of the main game at the right time. This particular cautionary tale is slightly afield, but since it contains international intrigue, lust, greed, piracy, power, valor, racism, witchcraft, and mass psychology, I am including it.

At that time the Dow-Jones average was pointing for 1,000, and all over Wall Street, the lads were so busy calling their customers with buy recommendations that their index fingers were beginning to bleed from all the dialing. I was sitting in the Great Winfield's seedy office, the same Great Winfield who hired the Kids. We were both watching the stock tape chug by, lazily, like two Alabama sheriffs in a rowboat watching the catfish on a hot spring day.

"They ain't movin' right," said the Great Winfield, crossing one cowboy boot over the other. Years ago, as an earnest and sincere young man, I saw the Great Winfield wear suits from Paul Stuart and Tripler, back when he was trying to be a good boy on Wall Street. Then he made some money and bought a ranch and figured that if the Establishment

didn't like him (and it didn't), why should he like the Establishment. So he gave away his Establishment clothes and came down to his office in corduroy coats and cowboy boots, his ranch identity, you see, coffee perkin' in an iron pot—as I said before, the whole Marlboro country commercial bit.

The Great Winfield does not bother with real facts. They only confuse things. He just watches the tape, and when he sees something moving, he hops aboard for a while, and when it stops moving, he gets off, just like a bus. This is good for about a million dollars a year.

Tape traders like the Great Winfield develop a feel for how these stock symbols "act," whether Polaroid is feeling bouncy or whether KLM wants to lie down and go to sleep for a while. The tape tells the story, they say, and they sniff and inhale the atmosphere and proceed on what their Indian-guide awareness tells them.

"No, sir, they ain't bitin', it's time to go home," said the Great Winfield. Now, with hindsight this looks pretty acute, because there was the market near its all-time peak, so a lot of people were obviously buying, and there was the Great Winfield packing up, because the tape was telling him the game was not afoot any more.

Where the action is

"We should all go away for a year and come back fresh, just as everybody is fatigued from riding the market down and watching it rally," said the Great Winfield. "But we can't do nothing for a whole year, so I have us something that will give us ten times our money in six months."

I began to tune in—$1,000 in January becomes $10,000 in July wins my attention any time.

"Cocoa," said the Great Winfield. "There isn't any cocoa. The world is just about out of it."

Now all I know about cocoa is that it comes in little red cans in Gristedes, and as far as I could see there were a lot of little red cans on the shelves.

But the Great Winfield was warming up, in hypnotic tones. He does this with each little discovery, sort of hypnotizes himself. Then he can generate practically infinite enthusiasm for it.

"My boy," said the Great Winfield, "when the world is just about out of something that it wants, the price goes up. The Cocoa Exchange is unregulated. A three-cent rise in cocoa doubles your money. It's going to be wild. Come along for the party."

What the price of cocoa is depends on how much cocoa there is. The main crop is picked from October to March, so along about February or March every year, with the current crop in the bag, the speculation starts about the next year's crop. Now starts the political and international intrigue.

"My informants in Ghana tell me things are in a bad way," said the Great Winfield, sounding like M giving 007 a new assignment. My informants in Ghana, he said. Usually his informant is one company treasurer, but now suddenly he is far-reaching and international.

"The Redeemer, Mr. Kwame Nkrumah, has built himself palaces and a socialist state. The socialist state is printing forms; bureaucrats are supposed to go out and count the cocoa and fill in the forms so the Ghana Marketing Board knows what it is doing. But under the Redeemer, the bureaucrats do not go out and count the cocoa because if they fill in the wrong numbers it throws the five-year plan out of kilter and they are executed. So they find out what the numbers are supposed to be and they fill in those numbers. Consequently, no one knows how much cocoa there is. And my informants tell me there isn't any."

It is impossible to resist: international intrigue, the mockery of socialism, the chance to profit by the tides of history. "Tell me the game," I said.

"You buy a contract on the New York Cocoa Exchange," said the Great Winfield. "The seller promises to deliver to you, say next September, thirty thousand pounds of cocoa at the current price, twenty-three cents. Ten-percent margin, an unregulated market. One contract, one thousand dollars. Cocoa goes up three cents and you double your money. Cocoa goes up six cents, and you triple your money."

"Cocoa goes *down* three cents, I lose *all* my money," I said.

"How can cocoa go down?" said the great Winfield. "Cocoa is going to forty cents. *Minimum.* Six times your money. With some luck, cocoa is going to fifty cents, nine times your money. In 1954, cocoa went to seventy cents."

Anyone can buy or sell cocoa in New York—just the way you can buy and sell flax, hides, silver, wheat, and just about any other commodity. Just bring money to your broker. These contracts for future delivery enable the producers and consumers to hedge their operations and they lubricate the flow of commerce.

Rapid calculation showed me a repeat of 1954 would bring $15,000 for every $1,000 contract. I went away, called a broker I knew who had never heard of the Great Winfield, just to get another pipeline open, and pretty soon for only $5,000 somebody was going to deliver me 150,000 pounds of cocoa in September.

Any number can play

Very heady stuff, being an international cocoa speculator. All of a sudden I was meeting guys I had never met before, fellow members of the International Cocoa Cabal. I met a tweedy consultant type whose business takes him to West Africa. We bought each other drinks.

"I do believe," said the consultant, "that our dark brothers have fabricated the figures. There is no cocoa."

Two weeks later the Redeemer, Mr. Kwame Nkrumah, was paying a social call in Peking when the Opposition took the country away from him—all but the $25 million the Redeemer has stashed somewhere—and the afternoon papers had eight-column headlines, REVOLUTION IN GHANA. My phone rang. It was the Great Winfield's assistant.

"The Great Winfield," he said, "wanted you aboard in the cocoa game because you are a Communicator and you know people. So call up somebody in West Africa and find out who took over Ghana and what does it mean for cocoa."

The Great Winfield had $3 million worth of cocoa, and by hypnotizing me into five contracts he had an intelligence service. But now I wanted to know myself, so there I was on the phone at midnight with a CBS correspondent I once met, his voice fading and burbling from Accra in distant Ghana. The situation was confused, he said. I wanted to know were the new fellows from a cocoa-producing tribe or not. The CBS man said he didn't know, but he thought some of the new cabinet was from the interior, where they produce the cocoa.

Now people I don't know were calling me

out of the blue, saying, "You don't know me, but what do you hear from Ghana? Is the new government pro-cocoa or not?"

Cocoa went to twenty-five cents. Now without putting up any more money I could buy two more contracts.

There was a dinner for the cocoa industry and a man from Hershey gave a speech and said there was plenty of cocoa for everybody. The next day, faced with this vast surplus, cocoa plummeted—cocoa is an unregulated market—so fast they had to shut up the trading. At the bottom the man from Hershey steps in and buys from the panickers. This confuses me. Why should he buy if there is going to be plenty later?

Now I suddenly realized there were three lions in the middle of this ring called Hershey, Nestle, and M&M, and we were all mice trying to cast them in a net. Hershey has only to lean on the market and the mice are mouse pâté. Hershey, Nestle, and M&M have to buy the real cocoa down the road somewhere, and meantime they were hedging themselves with millions of dollars, buying and selling cocoa contracts.

The object of the game is for the mice to keep the cocoa away from the lions so that the lions have to pay up for it when it comes time to make the chocolate bars. However, if the lions catch the mice, they skin them and take their cocoa contracts away, and then they can pay the going rate for cocoa. In their pockets they have the mice's contracts.

After the Hershey speech there was a mouse panic, cocoa dropped to twenty-two cents, and I got a margin call and several rolls of Tums. Happily, cocoa bounced to twenty-four cents immediately and I was saved.

The Great Winfield was on the phone, soothing. "Hershey and M&M are trying to get cheap cocoa contracts, panicking the speculators," he said. "Well, we don't panic. *They* know there isn't any cocoa, that's why they're trying this. The farmers aren't spraying the trees. They're leaving the farms. This crop is already bad. If next year's crop is bad, we'll see cocoa at forty cents, at fifty cents, at sixty cents. The chocolate people will be screaming for cocoa, their backs to the wall."

Cocoa went to twenty-five cents, and now I was beginning to get reports from brokers saying cocoa should be going up soon. That

should have warned me, but it didn't. The phone rang. It was the Great Winfield's assistant.

"I am distressed to report violence in the cocoa-producing country of Nigeria," he said, and the Great Winfield picked up the extension.

"Civil war!" he said happily. "Civil war! The Hausas are murdering the Ibos! Tragedy! I don't see how they can get the crop in, do you?"

I didn't. Of course, a little research would have shown that the trouble between the Ibos and Hausas was in the East and North and the cocoa was in the West, where the Yorubas live, but there we were, a part of every headline. Now the bulletins came thick and fast.

"I am grieved to report," said the Great Winfield's assistant, that General Ironsi, head of Nigeria, has been murdered. Civil war. No cocoa."

Cocoa went up to twenty-seven cents.

"I am grieved to report," said the Great Winfield's assistant, "that the main rail line to the coast was blown up this morning. The Great Winfield had nothing to do with it, no matter what they are saying in London. We abhor violence. We love truth. Truth is that there is no cocoa, and that Hershey will be screaming for it at sixty cents."

"Seventy cents!" cried the Great Winfield, on the extension. "Not bad, making a couple million when the stock market is falling apart, eh?"

Now I heard a rumor from another quarter that the Great Winfield was asking his friends in the drug industry if there was any way of injecting a tree so it would catch Black Pod, a dreaded cocoa disease.

"Wait a minute," I said. "You told me there wasn't any cocoa, the trees haven't been sprayed in five years, the farmers are leaving the farms, civil war, riot, chaos, no cocoa. Now all of a sudden there's cocoa out there and we need a plague so it won't grow and the price will go up."

Into each life

"Don't worry about it," said the Great Winfield. "The crop is going to be very bad. A little rain now, a little outbreak of Black Pod, and we've got 'em. You ever see cocoa trees with all their pods turning a horrible black? A terrible thing to behold, terrible. I think we'll get seventy cents for our cocoa."

I heard another rumor: A doctor walked into the Philadelphia warehouse where the cocoa comes in and discovered rats. Rats! He was shocked. He embargoed the warehouse. The doctor was a friend of the Great Winfield's and had bought five contracts. Two hours later the Hershey doctor arrived at the warehouse and un-embargoed it, and the rats were all gone. I had no way of checking the story. I was building up my own set of anxieties: We needed rain, heavy rain, to encourage the Black Pod. If only torrential rains would burst from the heavens over Ghana, we had a chance for a Black Pod epidemic and sixty-cent cocoa. It was so much on my mind that I introduced myself to a Ghanaian diplomat at a cocktail party.

"Tell me, sir," I said, *"is it raining in your country now?"*

"It always rains in August," he said.

"I know," I said, "but is it raining *hard? Torrentially?"*

The Ghanaian diplomat stared at me as if I were some kind of nut and walked away.

Newton's law

Meanwhile, to an old tape-trader, cocoa was not acting well. It had faltered at twenty-seven cents. The volume was huge. It was drifting down, and no one knew whether there was any cocoa or how big the crop would be. The Great Winfield decided we must send our man to West Africa to find out if it was raining and whether the Dreaded Black Pod Disease was spreading and whether indeed there was any cocoa crop at all. The Great Winfield picked Marvin from Brooklyn, a busted cocoa trader. Marvin usually bought a few cocoa contracts, pyramided them, made a lot of money, then got killed, went broke, and then hustled around for odd jobs trying to get a stake to get back in the game. At the time, Marvin was in the broke stage, so he could perform the mission. Marvin weighs 240 pounds, wears glasses, and had never been west of the Catskills or north of Hartford, and as far as I could tell, he didn't know a cocoa tree from a elderberry bush. To him cocoa was a piece of paper traded on Wall Street, but

Marvin was Our Man in West Africa. I went up to Abercrombie & Fitch with him. The Great Winfield had $3 million worth of cocoa at stake, and he was paying Marvin $500 and expenses.

As Marvin got togged out in his safari suit, I was beginning to get vague feelings this was no investment but a chapter from some early Waugh.

Marvin bought a hunting knife, a compass, a kit that kept the martinis cold, a waterproof cover for the cards. We spent a serious hour talking to a salesman about a Wesley Richards .475. That is an elephant gun.

"You're not going to run into any elephants, you're going to count cocoa," I said.

"You never can tell what you need," Marvin said, taking a careful bead on the elevator of Abercrombie & Fitch, the barrels wavering uncertainly.

Then we went to a drugstore where Marvin got pills for dysentery, jaundice, snake bite, yellow fever, ragweed allergy, poison ivy, and constipation. He also got 100 Meprobamate, a tranquilizer. Then we went to Kennedy, and Marvin hefted himself and his kits into a Pan American jet. He gave a gallant wave of his hand and was gone. Only twenty-four hours later we got our first intelligence.

RAINING OFF AND ON
   MARVIN

Back to our man in Ghana went a cable:

GET PRODUCTION FORECAST BASED NUMBER TREES WHAT WEATHER HOW MANY TREES DISEASED WHAT PRICE TO FARMERS
   WINFIELD

Back came a cable:

BRITISHER IN HOTEL SAYS SAME NUMBER OF TREES AS LAST YEAR AND CAPSID FLY UNDER CONTROL

"Capsid fly? Capsid fly?" I said.

"Eats cocoa trees," said the Great Winfield's assistant.

"Dammit, I didn't send him there to sit in the hotel," roared the Great Winfield. "Tell him to get out and check the cocoa warehouses, the major plantations, find out about the crop. I got three million bucks in this and cocoa is down to twenty-six cents."

"Maybe he doesn't feel safe without that

elephant gun," I said. Cocoa was down to 25.5 cents. Somebody knew something we didn't know, or perhaps the lions were frightening the mice again, no way to tell. The next cable was not much help.

BRITISHER HERE SAYS SOME BLACK POD IN ASHANTI REGION LEAVING FOR ASHANTI REGION TOMORROW STOP IT HAS STOPPED RAINING
MARVIN

In the next two days, cocoa dropped a hundred points to 24.5 cents. I got a margin call and they sold two of my contracts. The Great Winfield scowled and wondered where the hell Marvin was. I visualized Marvin, in his inimitable way, going up to a Ghanaian outside a warehouse, asking, "Say boy, any cocoa in there?" And the Ghanaian saying, "Nosuh, boss, no cocoa in deah." And then, as Marvin trudges off, the Ghanaian, who had been to the London School of Economics, goes back in the warehouse, chock-full of cocoa, puts his Savile Row suit back on, gets on the phone to the next warehouse, and says in crisp British tones, "Marvin heading north by northwest."

That was the last we heard from Marvin for some time. Apparently it happened this way: Marvin rents a car and a driver. The road turns into a mud track and the mud track becomes impassable, so the driver goes ahead to get some help. The driver doesn't return and Marvin sets forth by himself, gets lost, finds himself stumbling through the dark humid jungle, gnats and flies buzzing around his head, the laughter of howling monkeys overhead. Leeches six inches long fasten themselves to his legs. His safari suit is soaked through.

Hours later, frantic and nearly out of his mind, Marvin stumbles to a clearing, to find himself surrounded by grinning citizens pointing spears at him. The grinning citizens seize him and strip him of his clothes. Marvin lets out a great scream.

Meanwhile on the other side of the world cocoa has plummeted another hundred points and the Great Winfield sent another cable:

NO NEWS EXYOU LONDON REPORTS CROP AT LEAST FAIR CABLE AT ONCE
WINFIELD

The grinning citizens have now laid down their spears and are hoisting Marvin into a big vat of oil heated by a fire. Marvin is bellowing like a steer on the way to the steak house.

Baknum's law

In New York, the panicked speculators were unloading their cocoa and the price plummeted to twenty cents. At that price the gentlemen from Hershey and M&M were at the Cocoa Exchange buying. Cocoa had gone down three cents from the original twenty-three cents and M&M got all my cocoa contracts. The Great Winfield was unavailable. Brooding, said his assistant.

It turns out the grinning citizens with the spears are friendly. They know when a visitor comes through the jungle with leeches, a bath of warm oil soothes the hurt. So they are doing Marvin a favor by stripping him and plunking him in the warm oil, and as a matter of fact, after a few more bellows Marvin stops screaming when he finds out the oil is not boiling. He is a rather delectable morsel at 240 pounds, but the citizens dry him off and feed him and trot him along to a police outpost, and eventually to a government cocoa station, where his own driver is waiting to be paid.

There were revolutions in Nigeria and Ghana and outbreaks of Black Pod, and railroads blown up, but apparently something like this happens almost every year and there is still a cocoa crop.

So there was a cocoa crop. Not big. Not small. Medium.

The morning after

But the cocoa crop was less than consumption, so going into next year's crop there will be very small supplies.

I was busted and the Great Winfield's assistant was busted. The Great Winfield himself lost about half his contracts and kept half. "If you can't make it one way, you make it another," he said cavalierly, and went off to chase the shorts in KLM and Solitron Devices, and made his cocoa loss back in the chase.

Marvin has been back a while now. The warm oil really did heal his leech bites, and he is willing to go back to Ghana or Nigeria any time anyone will send him. Just give him a stake to get back in the game and he will have his safari suit packed.

Every once in a while, I glance at cocoa

quotations. Nigeria has broken up into real civil war. Ghana has devalued its currency. Black Pod is everywhere. A bad crop and cocoa could beat fifty cents. Every year the world uses up more cocoa than is produced, and yet the price of cocoa seems to stay in the same range. It doesn't make sense, so I have

to assume that in this game the lions are too far ahead of the mice. I know which side I am on, and the next time someone says there is nothing going on in the stock market, but an interesting situation has come up in commodities, I am going off to some mouse beach and wait in the sun until it all blows over.

Reading 38

How does the auto industry stand up to Galbraith's charge that much money and ingenuity are spent today in making the consumer want not geinuine transportation efficiency and comforts, but mere emulative conspicuous and invidious consumption? This reading is a careful calculation of the costs that could have been avoided if the 1949 American car had been stabilized.

Franklin Fisher is a professor of econometrics at M.I.T.; Zvi Griliches is a professor of economics at the University of Chicago; and Carl Kaysen, long a professor at Harvard, is now Director of the Institute of Advanced Studies at Princeton.

Questions to Guide the Reading

If people want variety and novelty, should they get it, provided they can afford it? What would one propose be done with the money—and, more important, the resources—saved by having less frequent changes in automobile models?

The Costs of Automobile Model Changes Since 1949

Franklin M. Fisher, Zvi Griliches, and Carl Kaysen

This paper reports estimates of the costs to the economy of the changes in private automobile specifications that took place during the fifties. In such costs are included not only the costs to the automobile manufacturers themselves of special retooling for new models but also the direct costs of producing larger, heavier, and more powerful cars, as well as the costs of automatic transmissions, power brakes, and the like. Finally, we include the secondary costs not paid out by the automobile companies but paid nevertheless by the consuming public in the form of increased

expenditures for gasoline necessitated by the "horsepower race."

Throughout, we concentrate on the cost of the resources that would have been saved had cars with the 1949 model lengths, weights, horsepowers, transmissions, etc., been produced in every year. As there was technological change in the industry, we are thus assessing not the resource expenditure that would have been saved had the 1949 models themselves been continued but rather the resource expenditure that would have been saved had cars with 1949 specifications been continued

From Franklin M. Fisher, Zvi Griliches, and Carl Kaysen, "Abstract and the Costs of Automobile Model Changes since 1949," *American Economic Review*, May, 1962. Reprinted with kind permission of the authors and publisher.

but been built with the developing technology as estimated from actual car construction cost and performance data.

In thus assessing the costs of automobile model change, we do not mean to deny that such changes also brought benefits. Indeed, it is quite clear that most or all of the changes involved were in fact desired by the consuming public (perhaps after advertising) and that the automobile companies were satisfying such desires. Nevertheless, the costs estimated seem so staggeringly high that it seems worth while presenting the bill and asking whether it was "worth" it, in retrospect.

The consumer pays

The largest component of the cost of model changes since 1949 turns out to be the higher costs of automobile construction (as measured by automobile prices) attendant on higher horsepowers, greater lengths, greater weights, and so forth. As the cost of a given specification varies with technological change (in particular, that of horsepower clearly declines over time), such costs were estimated by a series of cross-section regressions of the list prices of a given year's models on the specifications thereof. From these regressions, estimates of the cost of construction of the average 1949 car in each successive year (given the retooling expenditures which actually took place) were constructed and compared with the average list price of actual models. Optional equipment was separately costed, as were advertising expenditures. The results showed an average cost per car (in current prices) over 1956–60 of $454 for size and horsepower plus about $116 for optional equipment and $14 for advertising. The total estimated costs of such items thus averaged about 3.3 billion dollars per year for the same period.

These estimates, however, make no allowance for the retooling expenditures which would have been saved had 1949 specifications actually been continued; they merely estimate the saving from producing cars with such specifications given the actual retooling expenditures. Accordingly, we next estimated the saving in retooling expenditure that would have occurred in the absence of model change, basing our estimates on the expenditures for special tools reported by the automobile companies to the Securities and Exchange Commission and charged by them to profit and loss. We concluded that, again in current prices, such savings would have averaged about $99 per car over the 1956–60 period, total savings coming to about 560 million dollars per year.

The total costs of model change as estimated so far came to about $700 per car (more than 25 per cent of purchase price) or about 3.9 billion dollars per year over the 1956–60 period. However, unlike the costs so far considered, there are other costs of model changes which are not exhausted with the construction of the car but are expended over its life. Chief among these (and the only one estimated by us) is the additional gasoline consumption due to changes in transmissions and especially to increases in horsepower.

This part of the study was broken into halves. First, we estimated the relation between over-all gasoline mileage as reported by *Consumer Reports* and the "fuel economy factor" reported by the same source. This analysis was divided by type of transmission and number of forward speeds. We then proceeded (much as in our analysis of direct costs) to analyze the technologically changing relationship between advertised horsepower and displacement (the principal component of the fuel economy factor) by means of a series of cross-section regressions using the engines produced in successive model years. We interpreted the results in terms of engine redesign to secure higher horsepower at given displacement and used them to compute the displacement that could have been secured for the 1949 model horsepowers. We then used the relation between displacement and gasoline consumption via the fuel economy factor to estimate the gasoline consumption that would have been obtained with 1949 horsepowers. The result showed that whereas actual gasoline mileage fell from 16.4 miles per gallon in 1949 to 14.3 miles per gallon ten years later, then rising to about 15.3 in 1960 and 1961, the gasoline mileage of the average 1949 car would have *risen* to 18.0 miles per gallon in 1959 and 18.5 in 1961. This meant that the owner of the average 1956–60 car was paying about $40 more per 10,000 miles of driving (about 20 per cent of his total gasoline costs) than would have been the case had 1949 models been continued.

We then utilized these results to compute the cost of such additional gasoline consumption by the car stock, estimating this to average about 968 million dollars per year over the 1956–60 period in current prices. Moreover, since such additional expenditure continues over the life of the car, we estimated that even if 1962 and all later model years were to see a return to 1949 specifications, the 1961 present value (in 1960 prices) of additional gasoline consumption by cars already built through 1961 discounted at 10 per cent would be about 7.1 billion dollars.

Bill and bill of indictment

We thus estimated costs of model changes since 1949 to run about 5 billion dollars per year over the 1956–60 period with a present value of future gasoline costs of 7.1 billion. If anything, these figures are underestimates because of items not included. As stated at the outset, most of these costs were stated in the price of the car and it is difficult not to conclude that car owners thought the costs worth incurring at the time of purchase. Whether, in retrospect, this means that they were in fact worth incurring is a question we do not attempt to answer.

Reading 39

In a perfectly competitive market, no one producer can have any sizable impact upon the quantities produced or the prices charged. The market is impersonal; Producer A has no occasion to think about what any specific Producer B may do, simply because there are hundreds or even thousands of B's in the market. But in cases of oligopoly (few sellers), every producer if he is wise will think long and hard about the actions of the remaining few producers. Producer A knows—and sometimes fears—Producer B. The structure of prices in such a market is often a fascinating study in mutual trust and, sometimes, distrust.

One of the landmark cases under the Sherman Antitrust Act resulted in the Supreme Court's order to break up the giant American Tobacco Company in 1911. What emerged thereafter was an industry of few sellers. There has been no evidence of collusion or overt contact among the successor firms to the original American Tobacco Company. But the handful of producers have been keenly aware of one another's presence.

William H. Nicholls, professor of economics at Vanderbilt University, discusses some of the more interesting features of pricing in this industry. The price leadership picture which he draws with such fine detail is an invaluable supplement to textbook discussions of oligopoly.

Questions to Guide the Reading

From the point of view of the consumer, what is gained by having oligopoly and price leadership in the cigarette industry in contrast with the near-monopoly of the pre-1911 era?

What are likely to be the most critical considerations entering into any one cigarette manufacturer's decision to go along with or to hold out against a price change elsewhere in the industry? What then are the preconditions for effective price leadership?

Price Leadership: The Case of the Cigarette Industry

William H. Nicholls

Evolution is not a force but a process. . . .
John Viscount Morley

This is a summary and appraisal of cigarette price policies since the Tobacco Trust was dissolved by Court action in 1911. After a brief summary of the principal trends in the cigarette market during 1911–50, we try to analyze the process by which present cigarette policy evolved. We shall be primarily concerned with the means by which the uncertainties inherent in the circular interdependence of a non-collusive, oligopolistic market structure were resolved.

A. Principal trends in the cigarette market, 1911–50

The most important single characteristic of the American cigarette market has been the highly dynamic nature of the demand for cigarettes. During 1911–50, cigarette production in the United States increased from 10 to 393 billions and per capita consumption increased nearly twentyfold. Furthermore, these trends were almost wholly uninterrupted, production falling below previous levels only during 1920–21, 1931–33, and 1949. With the demand curve for cigarettes shifting so steadily upward, each of the four major successor firms to the Tobacco Trust (American Tobacco, Reynolds Tobacco, Liggett and Myers, and Lorillard) could, in considerable part, direct large advertising outlays to extending the aggregate market to its own advantage rather than to taking

old customers away from its principal rivals. Their combined advertising expenditures not only contributed to the expansion of total cigarette consumption, but, during most of the period, greatly strengthened their position relative to the rest of the industry. Thus, having inherited 80 per cent of the nation's cigarette business from the Trust, the four successor companies had achieved a market position of perhaps 97 per cent by 1925 and controlled 98 per cent as late as 1931 (Table 1). During the 1930's, the development of the first significant independent competition since the dissolution reduced the position of the successor companies to 74 per cent, more than half of their loss being attributable to the rise of lower-priced "economy" brands, which had taken over 15 per cent of the domestic market by 1939. However, by 1950—thanks largely to the virtual disappearance of the economy brands—the successor companies' position had recovered to 82 per cent. The three major brands alone (Lucky Strike, Camel, Chesterfield)—which have always received the bulk of the industry's advertising outlays—increased their relative importance from 82 to 86 per cent during 1925–31, fell back sharply to 66 per cent in 1939, and accounted for 68 per cent by 1950.

Among the four successor firms, the relative distribution of cigarette sales has fluctuated widely since the dissolution (Table 1). The

Table 1   Summary of Market Positions of Principal Cigarette Companies, Selected Years, 1911–50

	Total sales as per cent of U.S. cigarette production										Total U.S. production (billions)
Year	Amer.	L.&M.	Rey.	Lor.	4 Co's.	BW	PM	All other	3 major brands	Economy brands	
1911	37.1	27.8	0	15.3	80.2	. . .	. . .	19.8	. . .	. . .	10
1925	21.2	32.0	41.6	1.9	96.7	. . .	. . .	3.3	82	. . .	82
1931	39.4	22.7	28.4	7.0	97.6	0.2	0.3	1.9	86	0.3	117
1939	22.7	21.6	23.7	5.7	73.7	10.6	7.0	8.7	66	14.8	181
1950	30.9	18.7	26.9	5.5	82.0	6.1	11.0	1.8	68	0.9	393

From William H. Nicholls, *Price Policies in the Cigarette Industry* (Vanderbilt University Press, Nashville, Tennessee, 1951). Reprinted with kind permission of the author and publisher.

years 1911–25 were characterized by the rise of Reynolds (which had received no cigarette business from the Trust) to a position of dominance (45 per cent in 1923) to the precipitous decline of Lorillard. During 1925–31, American rapidly pushed far into the lead (39 per cent in 1931)—largely at the expense of Reynolds—while Lorillard for the first time showed some vitality. Between 1931 and 1939, all four companies suffered important setbacks, with American showing the greatest loss of relative position, Liggett & Myers the least. While continuing to show a decline in relative position, Reynolds held a slight lead (with 24 per cent) in the latter year. Since 1939, American has again definitely taken over first place (31 per cent in 1950) although Reynolds has also experienced a relative gain.

Since 1927 (with the exception of 1934 and 1944), Liggett & Myers has never ranked higher than third place in the American cigarette market. Even prior to that time, Liggett & Myers followed a conservative, non-aggressive price and advertising policy, with Reynolds largely setting the pace. After 1927, either Reynolds or American took the lead in most basic policy decisions and their relative positions have fluctuated widely over the years, in contrast with Liggett & Myers' more stable market percentage. Throughout most of the period since the dissolution, Lorillard has been of relatively minor importance in the cigarette market, not having produced more than 8 per cent of the nation's cigarettes since well before 1925. Of the five principal independents which grew to significant size—during the 1930's, two (Brown & Williamson and Philip Morris) outranked Lorillard by 1939. Since the latter date, Philip Morris has continued to expand its market position considerably but the other principal independents (including Brown & Williamson) have rapidly lost ground.

Since the dissolution, the list prices of the major cigarette brands have been relatively inflexible. During the 38 years 1913–50 inclusive, the price of Camel cigarettes was changed 20 times, exclusive of 5 increases (two of them by amounts greater than the tax) resulting from changes in federal cigarette taxes and one upward adjustment in OPA's cigarette price ceiling not related to a tax increase. The list price of Camels ranged from $4.00 to $8.00 per thousand over this period. Had the tax been constant at its present rate throughout

1913–50, however (and had earlier list prices been increased by exactly the amount of the difference in tax rates), the range would have been narrowed to $6.00–$8.50, the lowest price falling in 1933 and the highest in 1919–21. During 1913–23—before virtually identical list and net prices of the three major brands became the rule—the list price of Camels (adjusted to present tax rates) ranged from $6.25 to $8.50, with 9 price changes not associated with tax increases. During the much longer period of virtual list-price identity 1923–50, however, the range (at present tax rates) was $6.00–$8.00, with only 11 price changes (plus one OPA increase) unrelated to tax increases. Thus, during the 27 years of virtual list-price identity the number of price changes only slightly exceeded that during the earlier 11-year period and the range of prices was somewhat less.

Because of the large and fixed federal cigarette tax, however, even these relatively inflexible list prices have resulted in more flexible net prices to manufacturers after dealer discounts and tax. Thus, the range in the net price of Camels during 1913–50 was $1.85 (1933) to $4.05 (1919–21). During 1913–23, the range was $2.28–$4.05 and, during 1923–50, $1.85 to $3.56 (1950), or 3.4 cents a package. If one eliminates two special periods of price-cutting—that of 1928–29 within the Big Four and that of 1933–36 directed against independent competition—and the wartime period of price controls, the range in net prices is narrowed to $2.51–$3.56, or 2.1 cents a package, during a total period of 17 years since 1923. These data underline the barriers which the large federal tax has imposed against price competition, the extreme severity of the 1933 price cuts, and the more moderate price policy which the major firms have followed since 1937.

The price history of the three major brands during 1912–23 reflected many of the characteristics which one associates with the concept of competitive price behavior. Diverse price differentials did exist among the three brands as they were introduced, and the timing and extent of changes in prices and discounts varied considerably from one brand to another. While Reynolds' influence on the price policies of its two major competitors was already discernible, the latter companies did sometimes take independent action in price changes. Despite the frequent diversity of list prices among the three brands, discounts were usually adjusted openly or secretly to bring net prices fairly closely in line—a result still consistent with a process of price competition.

When the three major firms moved to virtual list and net price identity in August 1923, however, any resemblance to competitive price behavior disappeared.

Combined net profits of the three major companies grew from 50 to 106 million dollars during 1923–31, a period in which they accounted for 90 per cent or more of total cigarette production. During the same period, their rates of earnings on net worth increased from 15–20 per cent to 17–22 per cent. Their loss of business to independents, and the resulting severe price reductions of 1933, cut their net profits in half and their earnings to 8–13 per cent in that year. By 1940, their net profits had recovered to 73 million dollars and their earnings to 13–17 per cent, despite a continued loss of relative market position. The coming of price controls brought a tremendous increase in their absolute and relative sales but by 1943 had resulted in a reduction in their combined net profits to 57 million dollars (just above their 1933 low) and earnings of 10–13 per cent. With the price increases of 1946–50, their combined profits at last passed the previous peak of 1933, amounting to 108–111 million dollars in 1948–50, when they earned 12–16 per cent on net worth. This rate of earnings approached their 1932–39 average of 13–17 per cent but still fell short of their average earnings of 18–21 per cent during 1924–31. Nonetheless, it is clear that the three major companies have consistently enjoyed earnings well above normal competitive levels and that the effects of potential and actual competition over many years have not been sufficient to eliminate significant amounts of monopoly profits.

B. The process of revising incorrect anticipations under oligopoly

Since 1911, the American cigarette market has been characterized by oligopoly. Because the great bulk (68–91 per cent) of the nation's cigarettes has been produced and sold by three successor firms, no one of them could ignore the influence of its own price decisions upon the sales (hence price policies) of the other firms or, in turn, the influence of their resultant price policies upon its own sales. Even the smallest of the three major firms, Liggett & Myers, recognized this circular interdependence clearly in stating that its cigarette prices depend "to a considerable extent upon what its chief competitors are doing and what they are likely to do in respect of price changes." Such recognition did not spring full-blown from the dissolution decree. But during 1917–23—after the three major brands had been introduced—each of the three firms certainly came to realize that circular interdependence did exist. It then became incumbent upon each firm to try to judge correctly the nature of this interdependence. For, until it knew what assumptions to make as to the extent and timing of any interactions which it might set in motion by a change in its own policies, it could not correctly assess the probable *ultimate* effects of this change upon its own profits. The simplest way to have eliminated these oligopolistic uncertainties would have been outright merger or formal collusion. But, operating under the shadow of the recent dissolution decree, the successor firms could hardly avail themselves of these alternatives. Hence, a policy of experimentalism—by which the three companies tried out different price differentials and different timings of price changes (and responses to price changes)—was forced upon them.

There is ample evidence in the price history of 1917–23 that the major firms' original anticipations of rival reactions were incorrect. This was especially true during the earlier part of the period when price *increases* were the order of the day. An outstanding example of incorrect anticipations was American's unsuccessful attempt to lead in a price increase in September 1918. It is obvious that American expected its major rivals to follow upward and seriously underestimated the costliness (in loss of sales) of its policy in the event that they failed to do so. Out of this experience, American apparently revised its anticipations of rival reactions, becoming understandably reluctant to initiate price changes thereafter. While Reynolds was less unfortunate in leading price increases during 1918–19 even its success was mixed, with American once following upward all the way, once only in part. In the latter case, Reynolds then cut below American, which (through secret discounts) moved to the same level as Reynolds. Reynolds used similar techniques in following Liggett & Myers' one initial price *increase* only part way, and in following American's single initial price *decrease* by an even larger price cut, in each case thereby establishing the price level to which the original price leader then moved. Obviously, each of these price changes again reflected uncertainty as to what rival reactions would be. But, by its own choice of policies, Reynolds made it clear that a failure to follow its lead completely would result in its returning to lower prices but created a serious doubt as to whether it would itself follow its rivals' leads. While the latter doubts might have led to new conflicts and uncertainties, these were resolved by an increasing willingness of the other firms to concede a position of price leadership to Reynolds.

Uncertainties regarding probable rival reactions to initial price *cuts* were more easily diminished. During the period of price decreases 1921–22, American and Reynolds both discovered that the other would promptly meet price cuts in full, thereby making it possible for each to anticipate correctly the other's reaction to a price decrease. Although reluctant to conform with this policy, Liggett & Myers' resistance to price cuts during 1921–22 probably revealed the costliness of such a policy and brought it around to the same point of view. Experience with secret rather than open price differentials was apparently found to be an unsatisfactory technique (probably because they did not remain secret) of increasing sales, being little used after 1919.

The market situation of 1917–23 had all the elements which, according to general theory, would result in a highly unstable or even chaotic outcome. Unquestionably, each of the three major firms was originally extremely uncertain as to the extent and timing of its rivals' reactions to a price change. Furthermore, the fact that each firm at times tried to initiate price changes (Table 2) implies that each aspired to a position of price leadership in order that it might set that price which would correspond most closely to its own maximum-profit position. Yet, while there were indeed elements of instability during this period, the impressive fact is the pattern of order which rather quickly emerged. Such an outcome—particularly in view of the fact that there was apparently no formal collusion of any kind—is in itself remarkable and stands in sharp contrast with theoretical predictions of extreme instability. This outcome would suggest that anticipations as to rival reactions, while initially incorrect, can be gradually revised with experience until they become both correct and compatible. While it is impossible to predict, on purely theoretical grounds, that such revisions will converge or the paths by which conver-

Table 2   Summary of Price Leadership among the Three Major Cigarette Companies, 1917–50

Time period	Company initiating price change	Number of successful leads			Number of unsuccessful leads		
		Upward	Downward	Total	Upward	Downward	Total
1917–23	Reynolds	2	2	4	0	0	0
	American	0	1	1	1	0	1
	Liggett & Myers	1	0	1	0	0	0
	Uncertain	2	0	2	0	0	0
1924–39	Reynolds	4	1	5	0	0	0
	American	0	2	2	0	0	0
	Liggett & Myers	0	0	0	0	0	0
1940–50 (ex. OPA)	Reynolds	2	0	2	0	0	0
	American	2	0	2	1	0	1
	Liggett & Myers	0	0	0	2	0	2
1917–50 (ex. OPA)	Reynolds	8	3	11	0	0	0
	American	2	3	5	2	0	2
	Liggett & Myers	1	0	1	2	0	2
	Uncertain	2	0	2	0	0	0

gence may be reached, the concrete fact in the cigarette industry is that they did so.

Although American and Liggett & Myers subordinated their aspirations for price leadership to Reynolds' claims only reluctantly, Reynolds meanwhile enforced its own claims with considerable restraint. As a result of this element of "give and take," price competition (such as there was) was keep within reasonable bounds. And, reluctance and restraint notwithstanding, Reynolds' position of price leadership—particularly in the more uncertain area of price *increases*—was gradually recognized, reinforced by its steadily growing strength in the cigarette market. Once this became true, remaining uncertainties could be (and were in August 1923) easily resolved by standardizing dealer discounts—so that identical list prices automatically produced the identical net prices to manufacturers which had tended to result anyway—and by making responses to changes in the leader's price, whether upward or downward, complete and immediate.

We may conclude that the crucial step in eliminating oligopolistic uncertainty in the cigarette industry was the mutual recognition that one of the three firms was to act as price leader, particularly on price increases. For this step eliminated the problem of a "kinked" demand curve which would otherwise have faced each of the three firms. Such a discontinuous demand curve would result if each oligopolist believed that "rivals will quickly match price reductions but only hesitatingly and incompletely (if at all) follow price increases." Under this pattern of expected behavior, the demand curve for the product of each oligopolist would have a kink at the existing price. The part above the kink would be more elastic, indicating the given firm's loss of business if it should raise its price, other prices remaining unchanged at the old level. The lower part would be more inelastic, showing the given firm's gains of business if its price cuts were at all times matched by its rivals.

American's unsuccessful efforts to bring about a general price increase in 1918 and its experience with matched price cuts during 1921–22 were undoubtedly such as to convince it of the reality of the "kink." Had the other two firms (especially Reynolds) had precisely the same experience, any one of them would have been extremely reluctant to lead in a price increase because of the belief (verified by experience) that the others would not follow upward. Under such circumstances, cigarette prices would have been highly insensitive to changes in cost or demand, hence extremely rigid. Furthermore, unless the existing price was initially at the level which would maximize their joint profits, the final price would also have to be below that level. Thus, the advantages of mutual recognition of one (*any one*) of the oligopolists as price leader become obvious. For, once the price leader (Reynolds) could correctly anticipate that its price increases would be followed, the "kink" in its demand curve disappeared and it could raise prices with impunity. What the other firms lost in initiative was far more than offset by the gains in certainty as to the "rules of the game" on price increases, which made greater joint profits possible.

C. Factors favoring a policy of cigarette-price identity

A striking characteristic of cigarette policies after 1923 was that a policy of price identity (rather than differential prices) among the major brands evolved.

Between August 1923 and May 1951, there was a total of only 15 days on which the list (and net) prices of the three major brands differed because of a rival's delay in responding to an initial price change on one of the brands. At all other times (except 1923–28 and 1946–49, when minute price differences of 3–5 cents a thousand existed among them), the three major brands had (apart from what was apparently a small amount of price-shading) absolutely identical list prices, dealer discounts and net prices. The fourth major successor-company brand (Old Gold), while probably never important enough to have upset the common price policy had Lorillard shown more independence, also conformed fully with the policy of price-identity except for a small 10-cent-per-thousand differential during 1928–29. Thus, the prices of the three (or four) brands moved together, either upward or downward, with an almost perfect harmony of amplitude and timing. The same was true for the major standard brands of Philip Morris and Brown & Williamson after 1940, by which time these two independents had successfully established themselves in the standard-brand field.

To be sure, substitution (though imperfect) in consumption established certain narrow limits upon the extent to which price differentials might be profitable. But at least, within these limits, they became possible. Hence, a policy of price identity or price differentials among the several brands became a matter of deliberate choice, based upon expectations of the relative profitability of alternative courses of action. Why, then, was it a policy of price *identity*, and not one of price differentials, which emerged?

First, at the time the three major brands were introduced, there was already certain "customary" retail-price classes (10, 15, and 20 cents a package) which the three companies apparently felt it necessary to respect. These "customary" price classes introduced a very strong element of discreteness into price policies and favored pricing for identical retail prices as compared with so great a minimum price differential as 5 cents. (During the years since 1930, the rapid increase in odd-cents state taxes has effectively destroyed such discreteness in cigarette prices. But, in the early history of the industry, "customary" or "convenient-coin" prices undoubtedly exercised an important influence on cigarette price policies.)

Second, the concentration of advertising on the three brands served to set them apart (in the minds of consumers) as a particular class of product differing from non-advertised minor brands. The effect of such advertising was probably such as to diminish the elasticity of demand for the three brands as a class, while tending to break down the imperfections of substitution within the product class. As a consequence, the elasticity of demand for any one of the three brands was probably increased —a result further enhanced by the steadily growing increment of new, unattached smokers. Because of the small number of firms, sensitivity to the prices of rival products was greatly increased, thereby reducing the likelihood that any given firm could successfully maintain a significant price differential below other brands. Again, therefore, a strong tendency toward identical prices would have been expected.

Third, the tendency of consumers to judge quality by price created a further barrier to departures from price identity among the three brands. We have argued that the existence of discrete price classes, with advertising concentrated upon a single price class, encouraged price identity within that class. But it is equally probable that, as they became accustomed to price identity among the major advertised brands, consumers increasingly judged the extent to which the three brands were close substitutes (in terms of quality) by their common price. Because of this perverse psychology created by product differentiation, an unmatched price cut on one major brand might cause consumers to associate the lower price with lower quality—particularly if the lower price forced a significant reduction in the firm's advertising outlays—so that they would remain with (or soon shift back to) the higher-priced brands. While this factor favoring price identity among the major advertised brands can easily be exaggerated, it is noteworthy that the two principal independent brands (Philip Morris, Raleigh) which finally succeeded in attaining volume sales in the standard-brand price class, did so by initially selling in a *higher* price class, lowering their prices only after they had become established. On the other hand, with minor exceptions, none of the economy brands has yet entered the standard-brand price class after becoming established at lower prices, which made significant advertising outlays prohibitive.

Fourth, the growth of cigarette taxes has increasingly diminished the prospect of gains from unmatched price cuts below other brands and favored even unmatched price increases. Since the dissolution, federal, state and local governments have pyramided taxes upon cigarettes. These taxes have almost invariably been specific rather than graduated or *ad valorem*, and have now reached so high a proportion (50 per cent or more) of the retail price as to make even an unmatched price cut (a price differential below competing brands) of questionable value. Thus—in a state levying a three-cent-per-package cigarette tax in addition to the seven-cent federal tax—suppose that the manufacturer of any one of the major brands of cigarettes had been successful in establishing an unmatched price cut of one cent a package at retail at 1949 prices. To achieve this 5-per cent reduction in the retail price, he would have had to reduce his own final net price by 12 per cent. The effect of present taxes upon the economy-brand manufacturer is even more severe—a 15-per cent reduction in net price would have been required to reduce the retail price by 5 per cent, and an 18-per cent reduction to reduce the retail price by a full cent. Thus, combined cigarette taxes—being so large and unrelated to retail price—have been an increasingly important factor favoring continued price identity.

The effect of these various factors was undoubtedly to strengthen the tendency of oligopolistic competition to result in a policy of price-identity. Given this tendency, absolute price identity was obviously superior to small departures from price identity as a means of eliminating the uncertainties of oligopoly. Even small and variable differences in list prices, discounts and net prices might arouse suspicions that rivals were not living up to the mutually-recognized "rules of the game." Prices and discounts, being the most precisely measurable and most fully publicized variables of market policy, could also be reduced to foolproof "rules" more easily than quality of product (blend, packaging, etc.) and quantity of advertising.

But none of these reasons is enough to explain fully the acceptance of price leadership among the major producers. Why, in particular, were the other firms always willing to follow Reynolds' price *increases*? Because, on balance, they recognized the advantages to themselves in doing so. In most instances, they were "glad to follow" because they "saw the opportunity to make some money," "to reinstate . . . our earnings," or "to increase income." Again, counsel for Liggett & Myers stated it most clearly. "The opportunity to increase sales by not following [was] illusory," since such an action was certain to force "the others . . . to return to the lower figure." Hence, if it is believed that "the higher price will not adversely affect public buying of this type of product, or invite new competition into the field, obviously each has the most natural and legitimate of reasons for following the increase." Even so, why was recognition of a *single* price leader among the dominant firms necessary? The answer lies in the elimination of the kink in the demand curves of the oligopolists. Obviously, no one of the three firms was sufficiently dominant to establish prices to which its rivals would react purely competitively because, individually, they had no influence over price. Rather, their circular interdependence was so great that—

unless the kink was eliminated by mutual acceptance of a common leader for price increases—prices might be frozen despite significant increases in costs or demand. If so, it would become impossible to readjust to changing market conditions in such a way as to hope to achieve and maintain a position of maximum joint profits for the dominant group.

Hence, while Reynolds may at times have turned its position as price leader somewhat to its own advantage, its declining market position after 1923 increasingly put upon it the burden of establishing for the group a price policy which rather promptly reflected changing market conditions, if its position of leadership was to be maintained. American's price cuts of 1933 indicate its belief that, at that time, Reynolds had failed to do so since 1931. On the other hand, Reynolds' price increases of 1929, 1934 and 1937 undoubtedly did represent appropriate adjustments to increased demand and costs, enhancing the willingness of the others to follow. Significantly, there is no evidence that, during 1924–39, American even considered leading in a price increase, higher costs or otherwise. And, while frequently justifying its willingness to follow upward on the basis of costs, Liggett & Myers admitted that trends in costs merely determined "whether we followed gladly or whether we followed reluctantly." Even rising costs did not cause Liggett & Myers to give any thought to leading in a price increase because, as "third seller," it did not wish "to take a chance" on doing so. In any case, the high relative importance of selling costs to total costs probably forced the price leader to give his principal attention to changing demand factors rather than to changing production costs.

Since the direction (if not identical amplitude and timing) of all other price increases of 1924–39 might have been expected in terms of changing market conditions, it was the 1931 price increase which provided the acid test for the common price policy. If ever there was a time when a refusal to follow a price increase might have appeared likely to pay off in increased relative sales, it was then. Yet in 1931, as well as at other times, American and Liggett & Myers apparently believed that their retention of the lower price would result only in temporary gains since Reynolds would then restore its price to its previous lower level, whereas their gains would be permanent if they matched Reynolds' increase. American confirmed this by saying that—in conjunction with a lower price policy on its cigarette substitutes (roll-your-own and pipe tobacco)—it "naturally saw the opportunity to make some money" and "reserve[d] the right to make price changes downward" if its expectations were not fulfilled.

On the other hand, Liggett & Myers officials thought the increase "was a mistake" and "ill-advised." Why, then, did Liggett & Myers follow—especially if it really believed that its current sales position was so weak that it was, for once, "doubtful of its ability to force the [other two] manufacturers . . . to cancel their increases"? Why shouldn't such a doubt have encouraged rather than discouraged an independent price policy? Both American and Liggett & Myers replied that their failure to follow would have given Reynolds a sufficient increment of advertising funds to prevent them from substantially increasing their sales at the lower price. Such an argument is wholly unconvincing and completely inconsistent with their belief in the absolute necessity of fully matching price decreases.

In view of past experience—reinforced by the depressed economic conditions of 1931—it seems absurd to suppose that the failure of either American or Liggett & Myers to follow Reynolds' price increase would not have forced a cancellation of that increase. Hence, the former companies must have believed that the possibility of increased joint profits at the higher common price was sufficiently great to warrant the experiment, while the possible gains from resisting the change were temporary, hence "illusory." By following upward, as

Liggett & Myers clearly recognized, each firm ran "the risk of retaliation by consumers, but that retaliation [would], based on price, be visited on all rivals equally. . . . For a manufacturer to suffer with other manufacturers a loss of sales may be unpleasant but it is not fatal; one of the leading sellers will presumably readjust its price as soon as the effects of the excessive price are obvious." Of course, the real risk was that the aggregate elasticity of demand for cigarettes had been underestimated by the price leader—that is, that the "retaliation of consumers" would be *so great* that profits would be diminished rather than increased. It was recognized, however, that—if experience led to a diminution of profits—a joint price reduction could correct the situation.

According to Liggett & Myers, had it refused to follow the 1931 price increase, it would have run the greater risk "of losing [its] relative] position in the market . . . which [as of the fate of Lorillard shows, it might] never be able to regain." While fully applicable to a failure to follow a price decrease, such a statement is obviously invalid with regard to a price increase (Liggett & Myers' arguments to the contrary notwithstanding). Nonetheless, Liggett & Myers was undoubtedly correct in its belief that "the inertia of custom, plus extensive advertising, tend to assure a well established manufacturer his existing share of the market provided he does not permit his competitors to do anything drastically different from himself." To be sure, in an oligopolistic market situation, "imitation minimizes risk"— the risk of oligopolistic price uncertainties. By the elimination of this risk, the maximization of the dominant firm's joint profits was largely assured.

Reading 40

At first the technical concepts of theoretical economics seem esoteric and difficult. But actually they are no more than codified common sense. An excellent example is provided by the economist's concept of marginal or incremental cost. If you can get some business that will more than cover the incremental cost it occasions for you, you are better off to take it than refuse it— provided you would otherwise lose the business. Is this merely a matter of impractical theory? Not at all, as the meteoric success of Continental Airlines demonstrates.

Questions to Guide the Reading

How does marginal cost differ from average cost? From average variable cost? Can you see that marginal, incremental, and extra are all names for the same concept?

Airline Takes the Marginal Route

Business Week

Continental Air Lines, Inc., last year filled only half the available seats on its Boeing 707 jet flights, a record some 15 percentage points worse than the national average.

By eliminating just a few runs—less than 5%—Continental could have raised its average load considerably. Some of its flights frequently carry as few as 30 passengers on the 120-seat plane. But the improved load factor would have meant reduced profits.

For Continental bolsters its corporate profits by deliberately running extra flights that aren't expected to do more than return their out-of-pocket costs—plus a little profit. Such marginal flights are an integral part of the over-all operating philosophy that has brought small, Denver-based Continental—tenth among the 11 trunk carriers—through the bumpy postwar period with only one loss year.

Marginalism to the rescue

This philosophy leans heavily on marginal analysis. And the line leans heavily on Chris F. Whelan, vice-president in charge of economic planning, to translate marginalism into hard, dollars-and-cents decisions.

Getting management to accept and apply the marginal concept probably is the chief contribution any economist can make to his company. Put most simply, marginalists maintain that a company should undertaken any activity that addes more to revenues than it does to costs—and not limit itself to those activities whose returns equal average or "fully allocated" costs.

The approach, of course, can be applied to virtually any business, not just to air transportation. It can be used in consumer finance, for

instance, where the question may be whether to make more loans—including more bad loans —if this will increase net profit. Similarly, in advertising, the decision may rest on how much extra business a dollar's worth of additional advertising will bring in, rather than pegging the advertising budget to a percentage of sales—and, in insurance, where setting high interest rates to discourage policy loans may actually damage profits by causing policy-holders to borrow elsewhere.

Whelan finds all such cases wholly analo-gous to his run of problems, where he seeks to keep his company's eye trained on the big objective: net profit.

Whelan's work is a concrete example of the

Marginal analysis in a nutshell

Problem:	Shall Continental run an extra daily flight from City X to City Y?
The facts:	Fully-allocated costs of this flight $4,500
	Out-of-pocket costs of this flight $2,000
	Flight should gross $3,100
Decision:	Run the flight. It will add $1,100 to net profit—because it will add $3,100 to revenues and only $2,000 to costs. Overhead and other costs, totaling $2,500 [$4,500 minus $2,000], would be incurred whether the flight is run or not. Therefore, fully-allocated or "average" costs of $4,500 are not relevant to this business decision. It's the out-of-pocket or "marginal" costs that count.

From "Airline Takes the Marginal Route," *Business Week*, April 20, 1963. Reprinted with kind permission of the publisher. © 1963, McGraw-Hill, Inc.

truth in a crack by Prof. Sidney Alexander of MIT—formerly economist for Columbia Broadcasting System—that the economist who understands marginal analysis has a "full-time job in undoing the work of the accountant." This is so, Alexander holds, because the practices of accountants—and of most businesses—are permeated with cost allocation directed at average, rather than marginal, costs.

In any complex business, there's likely to be a big difference between the costs of each company activity as it's carried on the accounting books and the marginal or "true" costs that can determine whether or not the activity should be undertaken.

The difficulty comes in applying the simple "textbook" marginal concept to specific decisions. If the economist is unwilling to make some bold simplifications, the job of determining "true" marginal costs may be highly complex, time-wasting, and too expensive. But even a rough application of marginal principles may come closer to the right answer for business decision-makers than an analysis based on precise average-cost data.

New methods

Proving that this is so demands economists who can break the crust of corporate habits and show concretely why the typical manager's response—that nobody ever made a profit without meeting all costs—is misleading and can reduce profits. To be sure, the whole business cannot make a profit unless average costs are met; but covering average costs should not determine whether any particular activity should be undertaken. For this would unduly restrict corporate decisions and cause managements to forgo opportunities for extra gains.

Whelan's approach is this: He considers that the bulk of his scheduled flights have to return at least their fully allocated costs. Overhead, depreciation, insurance are very real expenses and must be covered. The out-of-pocket approach comes into play, says Whelan, only after the line's basic schedule has been set.

"Then you go a step farther," he says, and see if adding more flights will contribute to the corporate net. Similarly, if he's thinking of dropping a flight with a disappointing record, he puts it under the marginal microscope: "If your revenues are going to be more than

your out-of-pocket costs, you should keep the flight on."

By "out-of-pocket costs" Whelan means just that: the actual dollars that Continental has to pay out to run a flight. He gets the figure not by applying hypothetical equations but by circulating a proposed schedule to every operating department concerned and finding out just what extra expenses it will entail. If a ground crew already on duty can service the plane, the flight isn't charged a penny of their salary expense. There may even be some costs eliminated in running the flight; they won't need men to roll the plane to a hanger, for instance, if it flies on to another stop.

Most of these extra flights, of course, are run at off-beat hours, mainly late at night. At times, though, Continental discovers that the hours aren't so unpopular after all. A pair of night coach flights on the Houston-San Antonio-El Paso-Phoenix-Los Angeles leg, added on a marginal basis, have turned out to be so successful that they are now more than covering fully allocated costs.

Whelan uses an alternative cost analysis closely allied with the marginal concept in drawing up schedules. For instance, on his 11:11 p.m. flight from Colorado Springs to Denver and a 5:20 a.m. flight the other way, Continental uses Viscounts that, though they carry some cargo, often go without a single passenger. But the net cost of these flights is less than would be the rent for overnight hangar space for the Viscount at Colorado Springs.

And there's more than one absolute-loss flight scheduled solely to bring passengers to a connecting Continental long-haul flight; even when the loss on the feeder service is considered a cost on the long-haul service, the line makes a net profit on the trip.

Continental's data handling system produces weekly reports on each flight, with revenues measured against both out-of-pocket and fully allocated costs. Whelan uses these to give each flight a careful analysis at least once a quarter. But those added on a marginal basis get the fine-tooth-comb treatment monthly.

The business on these flights tends to be useful as a leading indicator, Whelan finds, since the off-peak traffic is more than normally sensitive to economic trends and will fall off sooner than that on the popular-hour flights. When he sees the night coach flights turning in consistently poor showings, it's a clue to lower his projections for the rest of the schedule.

Odd problems that remain

There are times, though, when the decisions dictated by the most expert marginal analysis seem silly at best, and downright costly at worst. For example, Continental will have two planes converging at the same time on Municipal Airport in Kansas City, when the new schedules take effect.

This is expensive because, normally, Continental doesn't have the facilities in K.C. to service two planes at once; the line will have to lease an extra fuel truck and hire three new hands—at a total monthly cost of $1,800.

But, when Whelan started pushing around proposed departure times in other cities to avoid the double landing, it began to look as though passengers switching to competitive flights leaving at choicer hours, would lose Continental $10,000 worth of business each month. The two flights will be on the ground in K.C. at the same time.

Reading 41

Economists, properly, put stress on marginal-cost pricing. In this reading an eminent economist, who has spent a good deal of time with the electricity authorities in Britain, discusses some of the practical difficulties in applying marginal-cost pricing.

Ralph Turvey achieved fame as a scholar at the London School of Economics while still very young. He left his post as Reader there to go into government service and is currently Joint Deputy Chairman of the National Board for Prices and Incomes.

Questions to Guide the Reading

What if marginal-cost curves are very irregular and wavy? Or suppose a firm produces many heterogeneous products. Is it easy to make controlled experiments to determine what the incremental effects on total cost are of changes in particular outputs? Is a crude approximation to marginal cost still not better than old-fashioned reliance on average costs? What are the problems of losses that you may encounter if you do adhere to marginal-cost pricing, and what thorny problems for subsidization does this entail?

Practical Problems of Marginal-cost Pricing

Ralph Turvey

Let us assume that the management of a public utility is firmly convinced of two things: that marginal-cost pricing leads to efficient resource allocation and that efficient resource allocation is something which they ought to strive to achieve. We shall not ask whether they are right in holding these twin beliefs. We simply

enquire what there is to stop them from introducing full-blooded marginal-cost pricing in the course of the next couple of years.

I shall talk about four important difficulties and obstacles, one after the other. I shall not argue that they are insuperable but merely that they exist.

From Ralph Turvey, "Practical Problems of Marginal-cost Pricing in Public Enterprise: England," in Almarin Phillips and Oliver E. Williamson (eds.), *Prices: Issues in Theory, Practice, and Public Policy* (University of Pennsylvania Press, Philadelphia, 1968). Reprinted with the kind permission of the author and publisher.

1. Ignorance

The first obstacle is *the difficulty of estimating the marginal cost* of any specified item of output. The accountants may well be ready to use their cost allocations to produce an answer. If, as frequently happens, they have allocated joint costs between products and have not treated bygones as bygones, it is necessary to disregard the answer they give. This requires tact. It is then necessary to do one or both of two things:

1. Go back to the *raw* accounting data, add to them if necessary, and *analyze them*.
2. Get the engineers *to plan and cost* the finite increment in capacity necessary to produce a finite increment in output and divide the cost by the size of the increment.

These are the approaches of *statistical cost analysis* and *engineering cost analysis* respectively.

There are no major difficulties in statistical cost analysis—assuming that the necessary skilled staff is available—but there are hundreds of minor ones! Thus, take the simple problem of estimating the marginal cost of meter-reading by a cross-section regression of meter-readers' wages against the number of meters read. The facts are there, of course, but getting them out can be a big job.

As another example, consider the problem of estimating the cost of periodical vehicle maintenance. Job-time records may provide information about labor cost, but what about spare parts? If detailed information is available about the stocks of hundreds of different parts, an enormous amount of labor is necessary to work out average spare-part cost per overhaul.

Now it may be urged, quite rightly, that these are small cost items. Quite so, but the sum of a large number of small cost items may constitute an appreciable fraction of the relevant total.

A good description of a very large-scale costing exercise undertaken by the 2 Canadian railways has been provided in a recent paper. Just to measure the yard-switching minutes required in handling any particular category of traffic, one of many variables, required that each of the 2 railways employed "a team of from *eight to ten men* with yard experience working *for a six-month period* to analyze only the yards in Western Canada."

In view of the difficulties of this analysis, it is natural to turn to engineering cost analysis so far as capacity costs are concerned. What we would like to know is the capital cost of reinforcing the distribution system to meet anticipated load growth. The key word here is "reinforce." It is fairly easy to construct an abstract model of a new distribution system of given topology to meet a load uniformly distributed over a virgin plain. Such models are constructed in order to examine the optimum choice of voltage levels, transformer ratings, and cable sizes as a function of equipment costs and of load density. But such models tell us very little either about the costs of providing for a specified new load at a particular point, given the existing distribution system, or about average incremental costs over a whole administrative area.

An analytical approach to incremental distribution capital costs is thus not possible. Reinforcement is an *ad hoc* business. On the whole, it is rarely called for purely as a result of cost-minimization. A transformer, for instance, is hardly ever replaced because the saving in expected future running costs will outweigh the capital cost of the changeover. The effective impulse to capital expenditure is usually either thermal overloading or a need to avoid voltage drop. In either case, what matters is the fact that load growth has caused (or will soon cause) certain physical limits to be passed. Cost calculations only come in when it is not obvious which is the cheapest of several alternative methods of reinforcement.

2. Complexity

Electricity may be supplied to consumers at several voltage levels and, since it cannot be stored, is a different commodity in each hour of the year. An [ideal, administrative costs aside] tariff would reflect differences of both kinds. It would also have to vary geographically, since costs do so, and its general level would depend on the degree of system reliability of supply offered, this being an aspect of quality which cannot be differentiated between consumers.

Even this statement is an oversimplification. It nevertheless serves to show that "pure" marginal-cost pricing is nonoperational. Prices have to reflect a *weighted average* of marginal costs over periods of time, over geographical areas, and so on. The gain from more accurate cost-reflection in a tariff must be weighed against the costs of greater accuracy in choosing the optimal point.

Being a platitude, this last statement is not helpful. There is thus a real problem to be faced in applying marginal-cost pricing, namely, the problem referred to above of specifying the items of output. A simple example of the problem is to be found in urban transport; in London underground train rides are *priced according to distance*, while New York subway rides are priced *at a flat rate,* but Professor Vickrey (of Columbia) proposed pricing them *by time of day.* Thus here we have two alternative multiple-output specifications and one simple one from which to choose.

Clearly the choice cannot be made unless we know how the consumer reacts to the change in tariff structure. Thus a knowledge of night and day demand elasticities with respect to both night and day prices is required even when, as assumed here, marginal costs are constant. Yet it is difficult to see how this knowledge can be obtained; in the probable absence of ready-made cross-section data for econometric analysis, the only way of acquiring the necessary information seems to be by experiment. The difficulties of this need no emphasis.

Although these examples leave out many of the factors involved in tariff-making, they suffice to display the difficulties of marginal-cost pricing in practice. It is laborious and expensive to obtain detailed statistical information about the load curves of a sample of consumers. Any tariff can only be approximately correct and the choice of it necessitates a great deal of judgment. This is so even when the only relevant considerations are the matters dealt with so far. We shall now go on to examine some other considerations which make matters even more difficult.

3. Financial objectives

Privately owned public utilities presumably want to make profits—subject to any ceiling imposed by public authorities—while publicly owned public utilities are frequently required to aim at some minimum level of profits. In either case this creates an obstacle to marginal-cost pricing if the revenue it would provide is less than total accounting costs, including the ceiling or target level of profits.

It is tempting (to economists) to say that this obstacle arises only if there are *economies of scale so that long-run marginal cost is below long-run average cost.* Now Vinerian long-run average-cost curves show whether or not the total cost of a new firm built from scratch is greater or less than x per cent of what the total cost of that firm would have been if it had been built x per cent as large. Since public utilities are not built from scratch at one set of relative prices and with a given technology, but grow through time with changing relative prices and improving technology, the concept is wholly inappropriate. To attempt to cram the analysis into the Procrustean boot of a single cost curve is to confuse matters right at the start.

The point is that total accounting costs are a complicated time-integral of a *historical dynamic* process and that expansion costs may depend not only upon present prices and technology but also upon the stock of capital inherited from the past. Thus in an integrated system, the operating mode of new plant, and hence incremental system costs, will depend on how it fits in with existing plant.

Whatever the reasons for it, an excess of total accounting costs over the revenue from marginal-cost pricing obviously constitutes an obstacle to marginal-cost pricing. So what can be done? There are three possibilities: (1) reduce accounting costs; (2) raise the average cost to consumers of output without raising the marginal cost to them; (3) give up marginal-cost pricing.

The first way involves either a subsidy or a capital reconstruction. An example of the latter, though not one inspired by a desire for marginal-cost pricing, is *the writing off* by the British government of £400 million of the National Coal Board's debt to the Exchequer of £960 million. This kind of thing would obviously be rather unpopular among the stockholders of investor utilities, however. Like subsidies, it takes the discussion beyond the framework of decision-making by the public utility itself, so I shall not pursue the matter here.

The second way, in its pure form, involves eating into consumer surplus without affecting resource allocation. *Thus the fixed charge paid by telephone subscribers can be raised while the charge per call is left equal to marginal cost per call.* The trouble is that the scope for this kind of behavior is limited, both by distributional considerations (to which I refer in the next section) and by the circumstance that such a fixed charge is, in effect, the sale to consumer of a license to buy. Now the price attached to this license must be uniform for each class of consumers, and somewhere within each class there will be consumers who are at the margin. An annual subscription for the right to travel on a rapid transit system would shift the odd out-of-town customer to cabs. A higher fixed charge for a telephone would put off a few potential consumers. Thus, in many cases, setting a stiff price on the license to buy will involve a departure from marginal-cost pricing.

This, then, brings us to the third way. Instead of pricing so as to maximize the sum of consumers' and producer's surpluses, i.e., setting prices at marginal cost all along the line, we now price so as to maximize this sum subject to the constraint that the producer's surplus shall be sufficient for his total receipts to cover his total accounting costs.

But this brings us from practice to theory, so, rather than confirming whether this is the right maximand from the point of view of optimal resource allocation, and rather than deducing its implications for the price to marginal-cost ratios for different outputs, I merely note that financial considerations can generate a real obstacle to marginal-cost pricing and pass on to the next item in my list.

4. Political considerations

Deviations from marginal-cost pricing may be freely chosen by the management of a public utility, or forced upon them, in order to achieve or avoid particular results. It is convenient to call these "political" factors, meaning by this merely that they raise issues outside the professional expert competence of the management, involving issues of public policy.

Not all political considerations interfere with marginal-cost pricing. A prohibition on the import of cheap fuel or the requirement that a proportion of new transmission be under-grounded for amenity reasons would both raise marginal costs without impeding marginal-cost pricing. But in other cases, where pricing itself raises political issues, the ability to reflect marginal costs in prices may be reduced.

This can often happen where it is felt that *the consumers who would be adversely affected by the introduction of marginal-cost pricing are particularly deserving.* Old-age pensioners, farmers, the inhabitants of remote areas and newspaper readers provide examples. Of course, economists are in the habit of recommending that such deserving groups should receive an explicit subsidy from the taxpayer in preference to an implicit cross-subsidy from other consumers of the same products. But though this position may sometimes win some support, it usually does not. A classic example of this is the requirement that railways continue to run their urban commuter services at a loss, being permitted neither to raise the fares nor to cut down on the service. Similarly, bus undertakings have often been required to provide unremunerative rural routes as a condition of getting the profitable routes through densely populated areas. The United States Post Office charges extremely low rates for second-class mail, largely on the grounds that newspapers provide a very valuable public service, and charges nothing for reading matter for the blind. Similarly, Greek members of parliament do not pay for their telephone calls and telegrams (with the result that their constituents visiting Athens frequently ask to use their telephone), the parents of large families in France pay extra low rail fares and Swedish university students pay concessionary prices at the state opera. In none of these cases, so far as I know, is the motive that of a monopolist seeking to exploit different elasticities of demand.

The costs of electricity distribution are a decreasing function of load density. This suggests that marginal-cost pricing would involve higher electricity tariffs in less-developed parts of a country. In fixing their tariff for bulk supplies, the *tarif vert*, Electricité de France concluded, however, that such tariffs would jeopardize development in the underdeveloped "departments". It was therefore decided, "as a matter of policy, to assign to all the departments which are not yet industrialized—practically two-thirds of the national territory—a fictitious consumption density, which "anticipates the later development" of consumption. Distribution costs have thus been lowered, over two-thirds of the country, to the level observed in the departments which have already become industrialized.

None of the 12 area boards in England and Wales charges a higher tariff to rural consumers in any given consumer class than to urban consumers in the same class. It may be that a desire to aid rural consumers played some part in this, but I fancy that practical administrative considerations are much more important. The problem of drawing and constantly revising a defensible dividing line between urban and rural areas in a small country is enough to deter anyone who is not totally insensitive to public relations.

Finally, there is a major difficulty in introducing marginal-cost pricing which, though in a sense the most trivial political obstacle, can nevertheless not be neglected. This is that unless a public utility is in the happy situation where all costs are falling rapidly, any change in its tariff structure is bound to make some consumers worse off. These consumers will complain, while those who are made better off will keep quiet. Even if those adversely affected do not constitute a group "politically" deemed worthy of special treatment, the mere fact that they will complain is significant.

A management sufficiently devoted to the ideal of marginal-cost pricing might be ready to weather the storm. But complainants can lobby their representatives in the legislature, raise their grievance with consultative councils, petition regulatory commissions, call for public enquiry, refuse to pay their bills, go on strike, and kick up a shindig in a myriad of ways. Now this upsets other people even if, as we are assuming for the sake of argument, it fails to upset the management. But the other people who get upset may succeed in transmitting the shock to the management. In the end, then, even the purest of mortals has to keep an ear to the ground and, like us of coarser clay, include a quiet life as one of the variables in his objective function.

Imperfect Competition and Antitrust Policy

Reading 42

Conventional views of competition in our economy tend to look at the practices of different firms in the same industry or product market. But one of the most challenging views on markets has been that which looked beyond an industry or a product to the end use and found competition in the whole process of innovations to meet that end need through new products or processes. That view makes it abundantly clear that, just as competition is dynamic, so too is our understanding of its workings.

The late Joseph Schumpeter was professor of economics at Harvard University and is the major name associated with this view. Here he argues that certain of the most criticized aspects of capitalism are in fact essential features in its record of progress. The literature of economics has few pieces to stand alongside the work of Schumpeter.

Questions to Guide the Reading

Is the Schumpeter view of competition at odds with or complementary to the view of, say, Slichter?

Are there important prerequisites in order for the process of "creative destruction" to be operative? Are those conditions met with in all or most of the American economy?

What are the implications of the Schumpeter view for current antitrust policy in the United States?

Capitalism and Economic Progress

Joseph A. Schumpeter

We have a considerable body of statistical data descriptive of a rate of "progress" [under capitalism] that has been admired even by very critical minds. On the other hand, we have a body of facts about the structure of the economic system and about the way it functioned. We wish to know whether that type of economy was favorable, irrelevant, or unfavorable to the performance we observe.

Profits vs. welfare?

Unlike the class of feudal lords, the commercial and industrial bourgeoisie rose by business success. Bourgeois society has been cast in a purely economic mold. Prizes and penalties are measured in pecuniary terms. Going up and going down means making and losing money. This, of course, nobody can deny. But I wish to add that, within its own frame, that social arrangement is, or at all events was, singularly effective. The promises of wealth and the threats of destitution that it holds out, it redeems with ruthless promptitude. Wherever the bourgeois way of life asserts itself sufficiently to dim the beacons of other social worlds, these promises are strong enough to attract the large majority of supernormal brains and to identify success with business success. They are not proffered at random; yet there is a sufficiently enticing admixture of chance: the game is not like roulette, it is more like poker. Spectacular prizes much greater than would have been necessary to call forth the particular effort are thrown to a small minority of winners, thus propelling much more efficaciously than a more equal and more "just" distribution would, the activity of that large majority of businessmen who receive in return very modest compensation or nothing or less than nothing, and yet do their utmost because they have the big prizes before their eyes and overrate their chances of doing equally well. Similarly, the threats are addressed to incompetence. But though the incompetent men and the obsolete methods are in fact eliminated, sometimes very promptly, sometimes with a

lag, failure also threatens or actually overtakes many an able man, thus whipping up *everyone*, again much more efficaciously than a more equal and more "just" system of penalties would. Finally, both business success and business failure are ideally precise. Neither can be talked away.

He who innovates

In most cases the man who rises first *into* the business class and then *within* it is also an able businessman and he is likely to rise exactly as far as his ability goes. This fact, so often obscured by the auto-therapeutic effort of the unsuccessful to deny it, is much more important than anything that can be gleaned from the pure theory of the capitalist machine.

But is not all that we might be tempted to infer from "maximum performance of an optimally selected group" invalidated by the further fact that it aims at maximizing profits instead of welfare? Outside of the bourgeois stratum, this has of course always been the popular opinion. Economists have sometimes fought and sometimes espoused it.

The so-called classical economists disliked many things about the social institutions of their epoch and about the way those institutions worked. They fought the landed interest and approved of social reforms—factory legislation in particular—that were not all on the lines of *laissez faire*. But they were quite convinced that within the institutional framework of capitalism, the manufacturer's and the trader's self-interest made for maximum performance in the interest of all. Confronted with the problem we are discussing, they would have had little hesitation in attributing the observed rate of increase in total output to relatively unfettered enterprise and the profit motive.

It is exceedingly difficult, at this hour of the day, to do justice to these views. They were of course the typical views of the English bourgeois class, and bourgeois blinkers are in evidence on almost every page the classical

From Joseph A. Schumpeter, *Capitalism, Socialism, and Democracy* (Harper & Brothers, New York, 1942). Reprinted with kind permission of Mrs. Joseph A. Schumpeter and the publisher.

authors wrote. No less in evidence are blinkers of another kind: the classics reasoned in terms of a particular historical situation which they uncritically idealized and from which they uncritically generalized. Most of them, moreover, seem to have argued exclusively in terms of the English interests and problems of their time. This is the reason why, in other lands and at other times, people disliked their economics, frequently to the point of not even caring to understand it. But it will not do to dismiss their teaching on these grounds. A prejudiced man may yet be speaking the truth. Propositions developed from special cases may yet be generally valid. And the enemies and successors of the classics had and have only different but not fewer blinkers and preconceptions; they envisaged and envisage different but not less special cases.

From the standpoint of the economic analyst, the chief merit of the classics consists in their dispelling, along with many other gross errors, the naïve idea that economic activity in capitalist society, because it turns on the profit motive, must by virtue of that fact alone necessarily run counter to the interests of consumers.

This later analysis we will take in two strides—as much of it, that is, as we need in order to clarify our problem. Historically, the first will carry us into the first decade of this century, the second will cover some of the postwar developments of scientific economics. Frankly I do not know how much good this will do the non-professional reader; like every other branch of our knowledge, economics, as its analytic engine improves, moves fatally away from that happy stage in which all problems, methods, and results could be made accessible to every educated person without special training. I will, however, do my best.

The profit motive under perfect competition

The first stride may be associated with two great names revered to this day by numberless disciples—so far at least as the latter do not think it bad form to express reverence for anything or anybody, which many of them obviously do—Alfred Marshall and Knut Wicksell. Their theoretical structure has little in common with that of the classics, but it conserves the classic proposition that in the case of perfect competition the profit interest of the producer tends to maximize production. It even supplies almost satisfactory proof. It can be shown that firms which cannot by their own individual action exert any influence upon the price of their products or of the factors of production they employ will expand their output until they reach the point at which the additional cost that must be incurred in order to produce another small increment of product (marginal cost) just equals the price they can get for that increment. And this can be shown to be as much as it is in general "socially desirable" to produce. Where this is so, there exists a state of equilibrium in which all outputs are at their maximum and all factors fully employed. This case is usually referred to as perfect competition.

The profit motive under monopolistic competition

Let us take the second stride. The classics recognized cases of "monopoly," and Adam Smith himself carefully noticed the prevalence of devices to restrict competition and all the differences in flexibility of prices resulting therefrom. But they looked upon those cases as exceptions and, moreover, as exceptions that could and would be done away with in time. If we look more closely at the conditions that must be fulfilled in order to produce perfect competition, we realize immediately that outside of agricultural mass production there cannot be many instances of it. A farmer supplies his cotton or wheat in fact under those conditions: from his standpoint the ruling prices of cotton or wheat are data, though very variable ones, and not being able to influence them by his individual action he simply adapts his output; since all farmers do the same, prices and quantities will in the end be adjusted as the theory of perfect competition requires. But this is not so even with many agricultural products—with ducks, sausages, vegetables and many dairy products for instance. And as regards practically all the finished products and services of industry and trade, it is clear that every grocer, every filling station, every manufacturer of gloves or shaving cream or handsaws has a small and precarious market of his own which he tries to build up and to keep by price strategy, quality strategy, "product differentiation," and advertising. Thus we get a completely different pattern which there seems to be no reason to expect to yield the results of perfect competition. In these cases we speak of Monopolistic Competition. Their theory has been one of the major contributions to [recent] economics.

The work of oligopoly

There remains a wide field of substantially homogeneous products such as steel ingots, cement, cotton gray goods and the like—in which the conditions for the emergence of monopolistic competition do not seem to prevail. This is so. But in general, similar results follow for that field inasmuch as the greater part of it is covered by largest-scale firms which, either individually or in concert, are able to manipulate prices even without differentiating products—the case of Oligopoly.

As soon as the prevalence of monopolistic competition or of oligopoly or of combinations of the two is recognized, many of the propositions which economists used to teach with the utmost confidence become either inapplicable or much more difficult to prove. The "beneficial" competition of the classic type seems likely to be replaced by "predatory" or "cutthroat" competition or simply by struggles for control in the financial sphere. These things are so many sources of social waste, and there are many others such as the costs of advertising campaigns, the suppression of new methods of production (buying up of patents in order not to use them) and so on. And most important of all: under the conditions envisaged, equilibrium no longer guarantees either full employment or maximum output in the sense of the theory of perfect competition. It *may* exist without full employment; it is *bound* to exist, so it seems, at a level of output below that maximum mark, because profit-conserving strategy, impossible in conditions of perfect competition, now not only becomes possible but imposes itself.

Well, does not this bear out what the man in the street (unless a businessman himself) always thought on the subject of private business? Has not modern analysis completely refuted the classical doctrine and justified the popular view? Is it not quite true after all, that there is little parallelism between producing for profit and producing for the consumer and that private enterprise is little more than a device to curtail production in order to extort profits which then are correctly described as tolls and ransoms?

These conclusions are in fact almost completely false. Yet they follow from observations that are almost completely true. But economists and popular writers have once more run away with some fragments of reality they happened to grasp. These fragments themselves were mostly seen correctly. But no conclusions about capitalist reality as a whole follow from such fragmentary analyses.

Most important of all, the modern standard of life of the masses evolved during the period of relatively unfettered "big business." If we list the items that enter the modern workman's budget and from 1899 on observe the course of their prices not in terms of money but in terms of the hours of labor that will buy them —i.e., each year's money prices divided by each year's hourly wage rates—we cannot fail to be struck by the rate of the advance which, considering the spectacular improvement in qualities, seems to have been greater and not smaller than it ever was before. If we economists were given less to wishful thinking and more to the observation of facts, doubts would immediately arise as to the realistic virtues of a theory that would have led us to expect a very different result. Nor is this all. As soon as we go into details and inquire into the individual items in which progress was most conspicuous, the trail leads not to the doors of those firms that work under conditions of comparatively free competition but precisely to the doors of the large concerns—which, as in the case of agricultural machinery, also account for much of the progress in the competitive sector—and a shocking suspicion dawns upon us that big business may have had more to do with creating that standard of life than with keeping it down.

The process of creative destruction

The essential point to grasp is that in dealing with capitalism we are dealing with an evolutionary process. It may seem strange that anyone can fail to see so obvious a fact which moreover was long ago emphasized by Karl Marx.

Capitalism is by nature a form or method of economic change and not only never is but never can be stationary. And this evolutionary character of the capitalist process is not merely due to the fact that economic life goes on in a social and natural environment which changes. Nor is this evolutionary character due to a quasi-automatic increase in population and capital or to the vagaries of monetary system. The fundamental impulse that sets and keeps the capitalist engine in motion comes from the new consumers' goods, and new methods of production or transportation, the new markets, the new forms of industrial organization that capitalist enterprise creates.

The contents of the laborer's budget, say from 1760 to 1940, did not simply grow on unchanging lines but they underwent a process of qualitative change. Similarly, the history of the productive apparatus of a typical farm, from the beginnings of the rationalization of crop rotation, plowing and fattening to the mechanized thing of today—linking up with elevators and railroads—is a history of revolutions. So is the history of the productive apparatus of the iron and steel industry from the charcoal furnace to our own type of furnace, or the history of the apparatus of power production from the overshot water wheel to the modern power plant, or the history of transportation from the mail-coach to the airplane. The opening up of new markets, foreign or domestic, and the organizational development from the craft shop and the factory to such concerns as U.S. Steel illustrate the same process of industrial mutation—if I may use that biological term—that incessantly revolutionizes the economic structure *from within*, incessantly destroying the old one, incessantly creating a new one. This process of Creative Destruction is the essential fact about capitalism. It is what capitalism consists in and what every capitalist concern has got to live in.

Long-run progress vs. short-run efficiency

Since we are dealing with a process whose every element takes considerable time in revealing its true features and ultimate effects, there is no point in appraising the performance of the process [as] of a given point of time; we must judge its performance over time, as it unfolds through decades or centuries. A system that at *every point* of time fully utilizes its possibilities to the best advantage may yet in the long run be inferior to a system that does so at *no* given point of time, because the latter's failure to do so may be a condition for the level or speed of long-run performance.

Second, since we are dealing with an organic process, every piece of business strategy acquires its true significance only against the background of that process and within the situation created by it. It must be seen in its role in the perennial gale of creative destruction; it cannot be understood irrespective of it or, in fact, on the hypothesis that there is a perennial lull.

But economists look at the behavior of an oligopolist industry—an industry which consists of a few big firms—and observe the well-known moves and countermoves within it that seem to aim at nothing but high prices and restrictions of output. They accept the data of the momentary situation as if there were no past or future to it and think that they have understood what there is to understand if they interpret the behavior of those firms by means of the principle of maximizing profits with reference to those data. In other words, the problem that is usually being visualized is how capitalism administers existing structures, whereas the relevant problem is how it creates and destroys them.

In capitalist reality as distinguished from its textbook picture, competition which counts [is] the competition from the new commodity, the new technology, the new source of supply, the new type of organization (the large-scale unit of control for instance)—competition which commands a decisive cost or quality advantage and which strikes not at the margins of the profits and the outputs of the existing firms but at their foundations and their very lives. This kind of competition is so much more important that it becomes a matter of comparative indifference whether competition in the ordinary sense functions more or less promptly; the powerful lever that in the long run expands output and brings down prices is in any case made of other stuff.

It is hardly necessary to point out that competition of the kind we now have in mind acts not only when in being but also when it is merely an ever-present threat. It disciplines before it attacks. The businessman feels himself to be in a competitive situation even if he is alone in his field. In many cases, though not in all, this will in the long run enforce behavior very similar to the perfectly competitive pattern.

Many theorists take the opposite view which is best conveyed by an example. Let us assume that there is a certain number of retailers in a neighborhood who try to improve their relative position by service and "atmosphere" but avoid price competition and stick as to methods to the local tradition—a picture of stagnating routine. As others drift into the trade that quasi-equilibrium is indeed upset, but in a manner that does not benefit their customers. The economic space around each of the shops having been narrowed, their owners will no longer be able to make a living and they will try to mend the case by raising prices in tacit agreement. This will further reduce their sales and so, by successive pyramiding, a situation will evolve in which increasing potential supply will be attended by increasing instead of decreasing prices and by decreasing instead of increasing sales.

Such cases do occur, and it is right and proper to work them out. But as the practical instances usually given show, they are fringe-end cases to be found mainly in the sectors furthest removed from all that is most characteristic of capitalist activity. Moreover, they are transient by nature. In the case of retail trade the competition that matters arises not from additional shops of the same type, but from the department store, the chain store, the mail-order house and the supermarket which are bound to destroy those pyramids sooner or later. Now a theoretical construction which neglects this essential element of the case neglects all that is most typically capitalist about it; even if correct in logic as well as in fact, it is like *Hamlet* without the Danish prince.

Monopolistic practices

Both as a fact and as a threat, the impact of new things considerably reduces the long-run scope and importance of practices that aim, through restricting output, at conserving established positions and at maximizing the profits accruing from them. We must now recognize the further fact that restrictive practices of this kind, as far as they are effective, acquire a new significance in the perennial gale of creative destruction, a significance which they would not have in a stationary state or in a state of slow and balanced growth. In either of these cases restrictive strategy would pro-

duce no result other than an increase in profits at the expense of buyers. But in the process of creative destruction, restrictive practices may do much to steady the ship and to alleviate temporary difficulties. This is in fact a very familiar argument which always turns up in times of depression and, as everyone knows, has become very popular with governments and their economic advisers—witness the NRA. While it has been so much misused and so faultily acted upon that most economists heartily despise it, those same advisers who are responsible for this invariably fail to see its much more general rationale.

Robin Hood to protect the innovators

Practically any investment entails, as a necessary complement of entrepreneurial action, certain safeguarding activities such as insuring or hedging. Long-range investing under rapidly changing conditions, especially under conditions that change or may change at any moment under the impact of new commodities and technologies, is like shooting at a target that is not only indistinct but moving—and moving jerkily at that. Hence it becomes necessary to resort to such protecting devices as patents or temporary secrecy of process. But these protecting devices which most economists accept as normal elements of rational management are only special cases of a larger class comprising many others which most economists condemn although they do not differ fundamentally from the recognized ones.

If for instance a war risk is insurable, nobody objects to a firm's collecting the cost of this insurance from the buyers of its products. But that risk is no less an element in long-run costs if there are no facilities for insuring against it, in which case a price strategy aiming at the same end will seem to involve unnecessary restriction and to be productive of excess profits. Similarly, if a patent cannot be secured or would not, if secured, effectively protect, other means may have to be used in order to justify the investment. Among them are a price policy that will make it possible to write off more quickly than would otherwise be rational. Again, means may have to be devised in order to tie prospective customers to the investing firm.

In analyzing such business strategy [as] of a given point of time, the investigating economist or government agent sees price policies that seem to him predatory and restrictions of output that seem to him synonymous with loss of opportunities to produce. He does not see that restrictions of this type are, in the conditions of the perennial gale, incidents, often unavoidable incidents, of a long-run process of expansion which they protect rather than impede. There is no more of paradox in this than there is in saying that motorcars are traveling faster than they otherwise would *because* they are provided with brakes.

Creators not crooks

This stands out most clearly in the case of those sectors of the economy which at any time happen to embody the impact of new things and methods on the existing industrial structure. The best way of getting a vivid and realistic idea of industrial strategy is indeed to visualize the behavior of new concerns or industries that introduce new commodities or processes (such as the aluminum industry) or else reorganize a part or the whole of an industry (such as, for instance, the old Standard Oil Company).

As we have seen, such concerns are aggressors by nature and wield the really effective weapon of competition. Their intrusion can only in the rarest of cases fail to improve total output in quantity or quality, both through the new method itself—even if at no time used to full advantage—and through the pressure it exerts on the preexisting firms. On the one hand, largest-scale plans could in many cases not materialize at all if it were not known from the outset that competition will be discouraged by heavy capital requirements or lack of experience. Even the securing of advantages that run counter to the public's sense of fair play—railroad rebates—move, as far as long-run effects on total output alone are envisaged, into a different light; they *may* be methods for removing obstacles that the institution of private property puts in the path of progress. In a socialist society that would be no less necessary. They would have to be secured by order of the central authority.

On the other hand, enterprise would in most cases be impossible if it were not known from the outset that exceptionally favorable situations are likely to arise which if exploited by price, quality and quantity manipulation will produce profits adequate to tide over exceptionally unfavorable situations. Again this requires strategy that in the short run is often restrictive. In the majority of cases, however, it is so successful as to yield profits far above what is necessary in order to induce the corresponding investment. These cases then provide the baits that lure capital on to untried trails. Their presence explains in part how it is possible for so large a section of the capitalist world to work for nothing: in the midst of the prosperous twenties just about half of the business corporations in the United States were run at a loss, at zero profits, or at profits which, if they had been foreseen, would have been inadequate to call for the effort and expenditure involved.

Ideology refuted

All this is of course nothing but the tritest common sense. But it is being overlooked with a persistence so stubborn as sometimes to raise the question of sincerity. And it follows that, within the process of creative destruction, there is another side to industrial self-organization than that which these theorists are contemplating. "Restraints of trade" of the cartel type as well as those which merely consist in tacit understandings about price competition may be effective remedies under conditions of depression. As far as they are, they may in the end produce not only steadier but also greater expansion of total output than could be secured by an entirely uncontrolled onward rush that cannot fail to be studded with catastrophes.

Even as now extended, however, our argument does not cover all cases of restrictive or regulating strategy, many of which no doubt have that injurious effect on the long-run development of output which is uncritically attributed to all of them. And even in the cases our argument does cover, the net effect is a question of the way in which industry regulates itself in each individual case. It is certainly as conceivable that an all-pervading cartel system might sabotage all progress as it is that it might realize, with smaller social and private costs, all that perfect competition is supposed to realize. This is why our argument does not amount to a case against state regulation. It does show that there is no general case for indiscriminate "trust-busting" or for the prosecution of everything that qualifies as a restraint of trade. Rational as distinguished from vindictive regulation by public authority turns out to be an extremely delicate problem which not every government agency, particularly when in full cry against big business, can be trusted to solve. But our argument, framed to refute a prevalent *theory* and the inferences drawn therefrom about the relation between modern capitalism and the development of total output, yields another outlook on facts and another principle by which to interpret them. For our purpose that is enough.

Reading 43

An earlier selection (page 176) told of price leadership in an industry of few sellers. Stability was maintained in the cigarette industry without overt collusion. But, the law notwithstanding, producers in some industries have participated in direct but secret conspiracies to bring price stability into their businesses. Few recent instances have been as dramatic as the one involving some of the nation's largest manufacturers of electrical equipment. Here were big names and big stakes caught up in an economic drama that produced both angry finger-pointing and quieter soul-searching in and out of the business world.

John Brooks, novelist and free-lance writer on business subjects, goes well beyond the traditional economist's approach to this famous law case. The economic issues are here, but so too are the moral issues and above all the communications issues raised by this critical and puzzling chapter in our business history.

Questions to Guide the Reading

What light does the case throw on the difficulties in maintaining stability in oligopolistic markets in the absence of direct collusion? From the public point of view, are the results here substantially different from those to be expected under conditions of legal and effective price leadership?

What are our most effective defenses against a recurrence of this type of conspiracy?

Communication and Collusion:
The Case of the Electrical Industry

John Brooks

Among the greatest problems facing American industry today, one may learn by talking with any of a large number of industrialists who are not known to be especially given to pontificating, is "the problem of communication." This preoccupation with the difficulty of getting a thought out of one head and into another is something the industrialists share with a substantial number of intellectuals and creative writers, more and more of whom seem inclined to regard communication, or the lack of it, as one of the greatest problems not just of industry but of humanity. (A few avant-garde writers and artists have given the importance of communication a backhanded boost by flatly and unequivocally proclaiming themselves to be against it.) As far as the industrialists are concerned, I admit that in the course of hearing them invoke the word "communication"—often in an almost mystical way—over the past few years I have had a lot of trouble figuring out exactly what they meant. The general thesis is clear enough; namely, that everything would be all right, first, if they could get through to each other within their own organizations, and, second, if they, or their organizations, could get through to everybody else. What has puzzled me is how and why, in this day when the foundations sponsor one study of communication after another, individuals and organizations fail so consistently to express themselves understandably, or how and why their listeners fail to grasp what they hear.

Recently, I acquired a two-volume publication of the United States Government Printing Office entitled *Hearings Before the Subcommittee on Antitrust and Monopoly of the Committee on the Judiciary, United States Senate, Eighty-seventh Congress, First Session, Pursuant to S. Res. 52*, and after a fairly diligent perusal of its 1,459 pages I think I begin to see what the industrialists are talking about. The hearings, conducted in April, May, and June, 1961, under the chairmanship of Senator Estes Kefauver, of Tennessee, had to do with the now famous price-fixing and bid-rigging conspiracies in the electrical-manufacturing industry, which had already resulted, the previous February, in the imposition by a federal judge in Philadelphia of fines totaling $1,924-500 on twenty-nine firms and forty-five of their employees, and also of thirty-day prison sentences on seven of the employees. Since there had been no public presentation of evidence, all the defendants having pleaded either guilty or no defense, and since the records of the grand juries that indicted them were secret, the public had had little opportunity to hear about the details of the violations, and Senator Kefauver felt that the whole matter needed a good airing. The transcript shows that it got one, and what the airing revealed—at least within the biggest company involved—was a breakdown in intramural communication so drastic as to make the building of the Tower of Babel seem a triumph of organizational rapport.

Verdict rendered

In a series of indictments brought by the government in the United States District Court in Philadelphia between February and October, 1960, the twenty-nine companies and their executives were charged with having repeatedly violated Section 1 of the Sherman Act of 1890, which declares illegal "every contract, combination in the form of trust or otherwise, or conspiracy, in restraint of trade or commerce among the several States, or with foreign nations." (The Sherman Act was the instrument used in the celebrated trust-busting activities of Theodore Roosevelt, and along with the Clayton Act of 1914 it has served as the government's weapon against cartels and monopolies ever since.) The violations, the government alleged, were committed in connection with the sale of large and expensive pieces of apparatus of a variety that is required chiefly by public and private electric-utility companies (power transformers, switchgear assemblies, and turbine-generator units, among many others), and were the outcome of a series of meetings attended by executives of the supposedly competing companies—beginning at least as early as 1956 and continuing into 1959—at which noncompetitive price levels were agreed upon, nominally sealed bids on individual contracts were rigged in advance, and each company was allocated a certain percentage of the available business. The government further alleged that, in an effort to preserve the secrecy of these meetings, the executives had resorted to such devices as referring to their companies by code numbers in their correspondence, making telephone calls from public booths or from their homes rather than from their offices, and doctoring the expense accounts covering their get-togethers to conceal the fact that they had all been in a certain city on a certain day. But their stratagems did not prevail. The federals, forcefully led by Robert A. Bicks, then head of the Antitrust Division of the Department of Justice, succeeded in exposing them, with considerable help from some of the conspirators themselves, who, after an employee of a small conspirator company saw fit to spill the beans in the early fall of 1959, flocked to turn state's evidence.

The economic and social significance of the whole affair may be demonstrated clearly enough by citing just a few figures. In an average year, a total of more than one and three-quarter billion dollars is spent to purchase machines of the sort in question, nearly a fourth of it by federal, state, and local governments (which, of course, means the taxpayers), and most of the rest by private utility companies (which are inclined to pass along any rise in the cost of their equipment to the public in the form of rate increases). To take a specific example of the kind of money involved in an individual transaction, the list price of a 500,000-kilowatt turbine-generator —a monstrous device for producing electric power from steam power—may be something like sixteen million dollars. Actually, manufacturers have sometimes cut their prices by as much as 25 percent in order to make a sale, and therefore, if everything is aboveboard, it may be possible to buy the machine at a saving of four million dollars; if representatives of the companies making such generators hold a single meeting and agree to fix prices, they may, in effect, increase the cost to the customer by the four million. And in the end, the customer is almost sure to be the public.

Caught red-handed

In presenting the indictments in Philadelphia, Bicks stated that, considered collectively, they revealed "a pattern of violations which can fairly be said to range among the most serious, the most flagrant, the most pervasive that have ever marked any basic American industry." Just before imposing the sentences, Judge J. Cullen Ganey went even further; in his view, the violations constituted "a shocking indictment of a vast section of our economy, for what is really at stake here is the survival of . . . the free-enterprise system." The prison sentences showed that he meant it; although there had been many successful prosecutions for violation of the Sherman Act during the seven decades since its passage, it was rare indeed for executives to be jailed. Not surprisingly, therefore, the case kicked up quite a ruckus in the press. The *New Republic*, to be sure, complained that the newspapers and magazines were intentionally playing down "the biggest business scandal in decades," but the charge did not seem to have much foundation. Considering such things as the public's apathy toward switchgear, the woeful blood-

lessness of criminal cases involving antitrust laws, and the relatively few details of the conspiracies that had emerged, the press in general gave the story a good deal of space, and even the *Wall Street Journal* and *Fortune* ran uncompromising and highly informative accounts of the debacle; here and there, in fact, one could detect signs of a revival of the spirit of old-time anti-business journalism as it existed back in the thirties. After all, what could be more exhilarating than to see several dignified, impeccably tailored, and highly paid executives of a few of the nation's most respected corporations being trooped off to jail like common pickpockets? It was certainly the biggest moment for business-baiters since 1938, when Richard Whitney, the president of the New York Stock Exchange at the time, was put behind bars for speculating with his customers' money. Some called it the biggest since Teapot Dome.

To top it all off, there was a prevalent suspicion of hypocrisy in the very highest places. Neither the chairman of the board nor the president of General Electric, the largest of the corporate defendants, had been caught in the government's dragnet, and the same was true of Westinghouse Electric, the second-largest; these four ultimate bosses let it be known that they had been entirely ignorant of what had been going on within their commands right up to the time the first testimony on the subject was given to the Justice Department. Many people, however, were not satisfied by these disclaimers, and instead, took the position that the defendant executives were men in the middle, who had broken the law only in response either to actual orders or to a corporate climate favoring price-fixing, and who were now being allowed to suffer for the sins of their superiors. Among the unsatisfied was Judge Ganey himself, who said at the time of the sentencing, "One would be most naïve indeed to believe that these violations of the law, so long persisted in, affecting so large a segment of the industry, and finally, involving so many millions upon millions of dollars, were facts unknown to those responsible for the conduct of the corporation. . . . I am convinced that in the great number of these defendants' cases, they were torn between conscience and approved corporate policy, with the rewarding objectives of promotion, comfortable security, and large salaries."

Scapegoats needed

The public naturally wanted a ringleader, an archconspirator, and it appeared to find what it wanted in General Electric, which—to the acute consternation of the men endeavoring to guide its destinies from company headquarters, at 570 Lexington Avenue, New York City—got the lion's share of attention both in the press and in the Subcommittee hearings. With some 300,000 employees, and sales averaging some four billion dollars a year over the past ten years, it was not only far and away the biggest of the twenty-nine accused companies but, judged on the basis of sales in 1959, the fifth-biggest company in the country. It also drew a higher total of fines ($437,500) than any other company, and saw more of its executives sent to jail (three, with eight others receiving suspended sentences). Furthermore, as if to intensify in this hour of crisis the horror and shock of true believers—and the glee of scoffers—its highest-ranking executives had for years tried to represent it to the public as a paragon of successful virtue by issuing encomiums to the free competitive system, the very system that the price-fixing meetings were set up to mock. In 1959, shortly after the government's investigation of the violations had been brought to the attention of G.E.'s policymakers, the company demoted and cut the pay of those of its executives who admitted that they had been involved; one vice-president, for example, was informed that instead of the $127,000 a year he had been getting he would now get $40,000. (He had scarcely adjusted himself to that blow when Judge Ganey fined him four thousand dollars and sent him to prison for thirty days, and shortly after he regained his freedom, General Electric eased him out entirely.) The G.E. policy of imposing penalties of its own on these employees, regardless of what punishment the court might prescribe, was not adopted by Westinghouse, which waited until the judge had disposed of the case and then decided that the fines and prison sentences he had handed out to its stable of offenders were chastisement enough, and did not itself penalize them at all. Some people saw this attitude as evidence that Westinghouse was condoning the conspiracies, but others regarded it as a commendable, if tacit, admission that management at the highest level in the conniving companies was responsible—morally, at least—for the whole mess and was therefore in no position to discipline its erring employees. In the view of these people, G.E.'s haste to penalize the acknowledged culprits on its payroll strongly suggested that the firm was trying to save its own skin by throwing a few luckless employees to the wolves, or—as Senator Philip A. Hart, of Michigan, put it, more pungently, during the hearings—"to do a Pontius Pilate operation."

Embattled days at 570 Lexington Avenue! After years of cloaking the company in the mantle of a wise and benevolent corporate institution, the public-relations people at G.E. headquarters were faced with the ugly choice of representing its role in the price-fixing affair as that of either a fool or a knave. They tended strongly toward "fool." Judge Ganey, by his statement that he assumed the conspiracies to have been not only condoned but approved by the top brass and the company as a whole, clearly chose "knave." But his analysis may or may not have been the right one, and after reading the Kefauver Subcommittee testimony I have come to the melancholy conclusion that the truth will very likely never be known. For, as the testimony shows, the clear waters of moral responsibility at G.E. became hopelessly muddied by a struggle to communicate—a struggle so confused that in some cases, it would now appear, if one of the big bosses at G.E. *had* ordered a subordinate to break the law, the message would somehow have been garbled in its reception, and if the subordinate *had* informed the boss that he was holding conspiratorial meetings with the competitors, the boss might well have been under the impression that the subordinate was gossiping idly about lawn parties or pinochle sessions. Specifically, it would appear that a subordinate who received a direct oral order from his boss had to figure out whether it meant what it seemed to or the exact opposite, while the boss, in conversing with a subordinate had to figure out whether he should take what the man *told* him at face value or should attempt to translate it out of a secret code to which he was by no means sure he had the key. That was the problem in a nutshell, and I state it here thus baldly as a suggestion for any potential beneficiary of a foundation who may be casting about for a suitable project on which to draw up a prospectus.

How could it happen?

For the past eight years or so, G.E. has had a company rule called Directive Policy 20.5, which reads, in part, "No employee shall enter into any understanding, agreement, plan or scheme, expressed or implied, formal or informal, with any competitor, in regard to prices, terms or conditions of sale, production, distribution, territories, or customers; nor exchange or discuss with a competitor prices, terms or conditions of sale, or any other competitive information." In effect, this rule is simply an injunction to G.E.'s personnel to obey the federal antitrust laws, except that it is somewhat more concrete and comprehensive in the matter of price than they are. It is almost impossible for executives with jurisdiction over pricing policies at G.E. to be unaware of 20.5, or even hazy about it, because to make sure that new executives are acquinted with it and to refresh the memories of old ones, the company formally reissues and distributes it at intervals, and. all such executives are asked to sign their names to it as an earnest that they are currently complying with it and intend to keep on doing so. The trouble—at least during the period covered by the court action, and apparently for a long time before that as well —was that some people at G.E., including some of those who regularly signed 20.5, simply did not believe that it was to be taken seriously. They assumed that 20.5 was mere window dressing; that it was on the books solely to provide legal protection for the company and for the higher-ups; that meeting illegally with competitors was recognized and accepted as standard practice within the company; and that often when a ranking executive ordered a subordinate executive to comply with 20.5, he was actually ordering him to violate it. Illogical as it might seem, this last assumption becomes comprehensible in the light of the fact that, for a time, when some executives orally conveyed, or reconveyed, the order, they were apparently in the habit of accompanying it with an unmistakable wink. In May of 1948, for example, there was a meeting of G.E. sales managers during which the custom of winking was openly discussed. Robert Paxton, an upper-level G.E. executive who later became the company's president, addressed the meeting and delivered the usual admonition about antitrust violations, where-

upon William S. Ginn, then a sales executive in the transformer division, under Paxton's authority, startled him by saying, "I didn't see you wink." Paxton replied firmly, "There was no wink. We mean it, and these are the orders." Asked by Senator Kefauver how long he had been aware that orders issued at G.E. were sometimes accompanied by winks, Paxton replied that he had first observed the practice way back in 1935, when his boss had given him an instruction along with a wink or its equivalent, and that when, some time later, the significance of the gesture dawned on him, he had become so incensed that he had with difficulty restrained himself from jeopardizing his career by punching the boss in the nose. Paxton went on to say that his objections to the practice of winking had been so strong as to earn him a reputation in the company for being an antiwink man, and that he, for his part, had never winked.

Although Paxton would seem to have left little doubt as to how he intended his winkless order of 1948 to be interpreted, its meaning failed to get through to Ginn, for not long after it was issued, he went out and fixed prices to a fare-thee-well. (Obviously, it takes more than one company to make a price-fixing agreement, but all the testimony tends to indicate that it was G.E. that generally set the pattern for the rest of the industry in such matters.) Thirteen years later, Ginn—fresh from a few weeks in jail, and fresh out of a $135,000-a-year job—appeared before the Subcommittee to account for, among other things, his strange response to the winkless order. He had disregarded it, he said, because he had received a contrary order from two of his other superiors in the G.E. chain of command, Henry V. B. Erben and Francis Fairman, and in explaining why he had heeded their order rather than Paxton's he introduced the fascinating concept of degrees of communication— another theme for a foundation grantee to get his teeth into. Erben and Fairman, Ginn said, had been more articulate, persuasive, and forceful in issuing their order than Paxton had been in issuing his; Fairman especially, Ginn stressed, had proved to be "a great communicator, a great philosopher, and frankly, a great believer in stability of prices." Both Erben and Fairman had dismissed Paxton as naïve, Ginn testified, and, in further summary of how he had been led astray, he said that "the people who were advocating the Devil were able to sell me better than the philosophers that were selling the Lord."

It would be helpful to have at hand a report from Erben and Fairman themselves on the communication techniques that enabled them to prevail over Paxton, but unfortunately neither of these philosophers could testify before the Subcommittee, because by the time of the hearings both of them were dead. Paxton, who was available, was described in Ginn's testimony as having been at all times one of the philosopher-salesmen on the side of the Lord. "I can clarify Mr. Paxton by saying Mr. Paxton came closer to being an Adam Smith advocate than any businessman I have met in America," Ginn declared. Still, in 1950, when Ginn admitted to Paxton in casual conversation that he had "compromised himself" in respect to antitrust matters, Paxton merely told him that he was a damned fool, and did not report the confession to anyone else in the company. Testifying as to why he did not, Paxton said that when the conversation occurred he was no longer Ginn's boss and that, in the light of his personal ethics, repeating such an admission by a man not under his authority would be "gossip" and "talebearing."

Smoke-filled rooms

Meanwhile, Ginn, no longer answerable to Paxton, was meeting with competitors at frequent intervals and moving steadily up the corporate ladder. In November, 1954, he was made general manager of the transformer division, whose headquarters were in Pittsfield, Massachusetts—a job that put him in line for a vice-presidency. At the time of Ginn's shift, Ralph J Cordiner, who has been chairman of the board of General Electric since 1949, called him down to New York for the express purpose of enjoining him to comply strictly and undeviatingly with Directive Policy 20.5. Cordiner communicated this idea so successfully that it was clear enough to Ginn at the moment, but it remained so only as long as it took him, after leaving the chairman, to walk to Erben's office. There his comprehension of what he had just heard became clouded. Erben, who was head of G.E.'s distribution group, ranked directly below Cordiner and directly above Ginn, and according to Ginn's testimony, no sooner were they alone in his

office than he countermanded Cordiner's injunction, saying, "Now keep on doing the way that you have been doing, but just be sensible about it and use your head on the subject." Erben's extraordinary communicative prowess again carried the day, and Ginn continued to meet with competitors. "I knew Mr. Cordiner could fire me," he told Senator Kefauver, "but also I knew I was working for Mr. Erben."

At the end of 1954, Paxton took over Erben's job and thereby became Ginn's boss again. Ginn went right on meeting with competitors, but, since he was aware that Paxton disapproved of the practice, didn't tell him about it. Moreover, he testified, within a month or two he had become convinced that he could not afford to discontinue attending the meetings under any circumstances, for in January, 1955, the entire electrical-equipment industry became embroiled in a drastic price war—known as the "white sale," because of its timing and the bargains it afforded to buyers—in which the erstwhile amiable competitors began fiercely undercutting one another. Such a manifestation of free enterprise was, of course, exactly what the intercompany conspiracies were intended to prevent, but just at that time the supply of electrical apparatus so greatly exceeded the demand that first a few of the conspirators and then more and more began breaking the agreements they themselves had made. In dealing with the situation as best he could, Ginn said, he "used the philosophies that had been taught me previously"—by which he meant that he continued to conduct price-fixing meetings, in the hope that at least *some* of the agreements made at them would be honored. As for Paxton, in Ginn's opinion that philosopher was not only ignorant of the meetings but so constant in his devotion to the concept of free and aggressive competition that he actually enjoyed the price war, disastrous though it was to everybody's profits. (In his own testimony, Paxton vigorously denied that he had enjoyed it.)

Within a year or so, the electrical-equipment industry took an upturn, and in January, 1957, Ginn, having ridden out the storm relatively well, got his vice-presidency. At the same time, he was transferred to Schenectady, to become general manager of G.E.'s turbine-generator division, and Cordiner again called him into headquarters and gave him a lecture on 20.5. Such lectures were getting to be a routine with Cordiner; every time a new employee was assigned to a strategic managerial post, or an old employee was promoted to such a post, the lucky fellow could be reasonably certain that he would be summoned to the chairman's office to hear a rendition of the austere creed. In his book *The Heart of Japan*, Alexander Campbell reports that a large Japanese electrical concern has drawn up a list of seven company commandments (for example, "Be courteous and sincere!"), and that each morning, in each of its thirty factories, the workers are required to stand at attention and recite these in unison, and then to sing the company song ("For ever-increasing production/Love your work, give your all!"). Cordiner did not require his subordinates to recite or sing 20.5—as far as is known, he never even had it set to music—but from the number of times men like Ginn had it read to them or otherwise recalled to their attention, they must have come to know it well enough to chant it, improvising a tune as they went along.

Remorse and doubt

This time, Cordiner's message not only made an impression on Ginn's mind but stuck there in unadulterated form. Ginn, according to his testimony, became a reformed executive and dropped his price-fixing habits overnight. However, it appears that his sudden conversion cannot be attributed wholly to Cordiner's powers of communication, or even to the drip-drip-drip effect of repetition, for it was to a considerable extent pragmatic in character, like the conversion of Henry VIII to Protestantism. He reformed, Ginn explained to the Subcommittee, because his "air cover was gone."

"Your what was gone?" Senator Kefauver asked.

"My air cover was gone," replied Ginn. "I mean I had lost my air cover. Mr. Erben wasn't around any more, and all of my colleagues had gone, and I was now working directly for Mr. Paxton, knowing his feelings on the matter. . . . Any philosophy that I had grown up with before in the past was now out the window."

If Erben, who had not been Ginn's boss since late in 1954, had been the source of his air cover, Ginn must have been without its protection for over two years, but, presumably,

in the excitement of the price war he had failed to notice its absence. However that may have been, here he now was, a man suddenly shorn not only of his air cover but of his philosophy. Swiftly filling the latter void with a whole new set of principles, he circulated copies of 20.5 among his department managers in the turbine-generator division and topped this off by energetically adopting what he called a "leprosy policy"; that is, he advised his subordinates to avoid even casual social contacts with their counterparts in competing companies, because "once the relationships are established, I have come to the conclusion after many years of hard experience that the relationships tend to spread and the hanky-panky begins to get going." But now fate played a cruel trick on Ginn, and, all unknowing, he landed in the very position that Paxton and Cordiner had been in for years—that of a philosopher vainly endeavoring to sell the Lord to a flock that declined to buy his message and was, in fact, systematically engaging in the hanky-panky its leader had warned it against. Specifically, during the whole of 1957 and 1958 and the first part of 1959 two of Ginn's subordinates were piously signing 20.5 with one hand, and with the other, briskly drawing up price-fixing agreements at a whole series of meetings—in New York; Philadelphia; Chicago; Hot Springs, Virginia; and Skytop, Pennsylvania, to name a few of their gathering places.

It appears that Ginn had not been able to impart much of his shining new philosophy to others, and that at the root of his difficulty lay that old jinx, the problem of communicating. Asked at the hearings how his subordinates could possibly have gone so far astray, he replied,

I have got to admit that I made a communication error. I didn't sell this thing to the boys well enough. . . . The price is so important in the complete running of a business that, philosophically, we have got to sell people not only just the fact that it is against the law, but . . . that it shouldn't be done for many, many reasons. But it has got to be a philosophical approach and a communication approach. . . . Even though . . . I had told my associates not to do this, some of the boys did get off the reservation. . . . I have to admit to myself here an area of a failure in communications . . . which I am perfectly willing to accept my part of the responsibility for.

In earnestly striving to analyze the cause of

the failure, Ginn said, he had reached the conclusion that merely issuing directives, no matter how frequently, was not enough; what was needed was "a complete philosophy, a complete understanding, a complete breakdown of barriers between people, if we are going to get some understanding and really live and manage these companies within the philosophies that they should be managed in."

Senator Hart permitted himself to comment, "You can communicate until you are dead and gone, but if the point you are communicating about, even though it be a law of the land, strikes your audience as something that is just a folklore . . . you will never sell the package."

Ginn ruefully conceded that that was true.

The concept of degrees of communication was further developed, by implication, in the testimony of another defendant, Frank E. Stehlik, who had been general manager of the G.E. low-voltage-switchgear department from May, 1956, to February, 1960. (As all but a tiny minority of the users of electricity are contentedly unaware, switchgear serves to control and protect apparatus used in the generation, conversion, transmission, and distribution of electrical energy, and around $125 million worth of it is sold annually in the United States.) Stehlik received some of his business guidance in the conventional form of orders, oral and written, and some—perhaps just as much, to judge by his testimony—through a less intellectual, more visceral medium of communication that he called "impacts." Apparently, when something happened within the company that made an impression on him, he would consult a sort of internal metaphysical voltmeter to ascertain the force of the jolt that he had received, and, from the reading he got, would attempt to gauge the true drift of company policy. For example, he testified that during 1956, 1957, and most of 1958 he believed that G.E. was frankly and fully in favor of complying with 20.5. But then, in the autumn of 1958, George E. Burens, Stehlik's immediate superior, told him that he, Burens, had been directed by Paxton, who by then was president of G.E., to have lunch with Max Scott, president of the I-T-E Circuit Breaker Company, an important competitor in the switchgear market. Paxton said in his own testimony that while he had indeed asked Burens to have lunch with Scott, he had instructed him categorically not to talk about

prices, but apparently Burens did not mention this caveat to Stehlik; in any event, the disclosure that the high command had told Burens to lunch with an archrival, Stehlik testified, "had a heavy impact on me." Asked to amplify this, he said, "There are a great many impacts that influence me in my thinking as to the true attitude of the company, and that was one of them." As the impacts, great and small, piled up, their cumulative effect finally communicated to Stehlik that he had been wrong in supposing the company had any real respect for 20.5. Accordingly, when, late in 1958, Stehlik was ordered by Burens to begin holding price meetings with the competitors, he was not in the least surprised.

Wages of sin

Stehlik's compliance with Burens' order ultimately brought on a whole new series of impacts, of a much more crudely communicative sort. In February, 1960, General Electric cut his annual pay from $70,000 to $26,000 for violating 20.5; a year later Judge Ganey gave him a three-thousand-dollar fine and a suspended thirty-day jail sentence for violating the Sherman Act; and about a month after *that* G.E. asked for, and got, his resignation. Indeed, during his last years with the firm Stehlik seems to have received almost as many lacerating impacts as a Raymond Chandler hero. But testimony given at the hearings by L. B. Gezon, manager of the marketing section of the low-voltage-switchgear department, indicated that Stehlik, again like a Chandler hero, was capable of dishing out blunt impacts as well as taking them. Gezon, who was directly under Stehlik in the line of command, told the Subcommittee that although he had taken part in price-fixing meetings prior to April, 1956, when Stehlik became his boss, he did not subsequently engage in any antitrust violations until late 1958, and that he did so then only as the result of an impact that bore none of the subtlety noted by Stehlik in his early experience with this phenomenon. The impact came directly from Stehlik, who, it seems, left nothing to chance in communicating with his subordinates. In Gezon's words, Stehlik told him "to resume the meetings; that company policy was unchanged; the risk was just as great as it ever had been; and that if our activities were discovered, I personally would be dismissed or disciplined [by the company], as well as punished by the government." So Gezon was left with three choices: to quit, to disobey the direct order of his superior (in which case, he thought, "they might have found somebody else to do my job"), or to obey the order, and thereby violate the antitrust laws, with no immunity against the possible consequences. In short, his alternatives were comparable to those faced by an international spy.

Although Gezon did resume the meetings, he was not indicted, possibly because he had been a relatively minor price-fixer. General Electric, for its part, demoted him but did not require him to resign. Yet it would be a mistake to assume that Gezon was relatively untouched by his experience. Asked by Senator Kefauver if he did not think that Stehlik's order had placed him in an intolerable position, he replied that it had not struck him that way at the time. Asked whether he thought it unjust that he had suffered demotion for carrying out the order of a superior, he replied, "I personally don't consider it so." To judge by his answers, the impact on Gezon's heart and mind would seem to have been heavy indeed.

The other side of the communication problem—the difficulty that a superior is likely to encounter in understanding what a subordinate tells him—is graphically illustrated by the testimony of Raymond W. Smith, who was general manager of G.E.'s transformer division from the beginning of 1957 until late in 1959, and of Arthur F. Vinson, who in October, 1957, was appointed vice-president in charge of G.E.'s apparatus group, and also a member of the company's executive committee. Smith's job was the one Ginn had held for the previous two years, and when Vinson got *his* job, he became Smith's immediate boss. Smith's highest pay during the period in question was roughly $100,000 a year, while Vinson reached a basic salary of $110,000 and also got a variable bonus, ranging from $45,000 to $100,000. Smith testified that on January 1, 1957, the very day he took charge of the transformer division—and a holiday, at that—he met with Chairman Cordiner and Executive Vice-President Paxton, and Cordiner gave him the familiar admonition about living up to 20.5. However, later that year, the competitive going got so rough that transformers were selling

at discounts of as much as 35 percent, and Smith decided on his own hook that the time had come to begin negotiating with rival firms in the hope of stabilizing the market. He felt that he was justified in doing this, he said, because he was convinced that both in company circles and in the whole industry negotiations of this kind were "the order of the day."

By the time Vinson became his superior, in October, Smith was regularly attending price-fixing meetings, and he felt that he ought to let his new boss know what he was doing. Accordingly, he told the Subcommittee, on two or three occasions when the two men found themselves alone together in the normal course of business, he said to Vinson, "I had a meeting with the clan this morning." Counsel for the Subcommittee asked Smith whether he had ever put the matter more bluntly—whether, for example, he had ever said anything like "We're meeting with competitors to fix prices. We're going to have a little conspiracy here and I don't want it to get out." Smith replied that he had never said anything remotely like that—had done nothing more than make remarks on the order of "I had a meeting with the clan this morning." He did not elaborate on why he did not speak with greater directness, but two logical possibilities present themselves. Perhaps he hoped that he could keep Vinson informed about the situation and at the same time protect him from the risk of becoming an accomplice. Or perhaps he had no such intention, and was simply expressing himself in the oblique, colloquial way that characterized much of his speaking. (Paxton, a close friend of Smith's, had once complained to Smith that he was "given to being somewhat cryptic" in his remarks.) Anyhow, Vinson, according to his own testimony, had flatly misunderstood what Smith meant; indeed, he could not recall ever hearing Smith use the expression "meeting the clan," although he did recall his saying things like "Well, I am going to take this new plan on transformers and show it to the boys." Vinson testified that he had thought the "boys" meant the G.E. district sales people and the company's customers, and that the "new plan" was a new marketing plan; he said that it had come as a rude shock to him to learn—a couple of years later, after the case had broken—that in speaking of the "boys" and the "new plan," Smith had been referring to competitors and a price-fixing scheme. "I think Mr. Smith is a sincere man," Vinson testified. "I am sure Mr. Smith . . . thought he was telling me that he was going to one of these meetings. This meant nothing to me."

The bliss of ignorance

Smith, on the other hand, was confident that his meaning had got through to Vinson. "I never got the impression that he misunderstood me," he insisted to the Subcommittee. Questioning Vinson later, Kefauver asked whether an executive in his position, with thirty-odd years' experience in the electrical industry, could possibly be so naïve as to misunderstand a subordinate on such a substantive matter as grasping who the "boys" were. "I don't think it is too naïve," replied Vinson. "We have a lot of boys. . . . I may be naïve, but I am certainly telling the truth, and in this kind of thing I am sure I am naïve."

SENATOR KEFAUVER: Mr. Vinson, you wouldn't be a vice-president at $200,000 a year if you were naïve.

MR. VINSON: I think I could well get there by being naïve in this area. It might help.

Here, in a different field altogether, the communication problem again comes to the fore. Was Vinson really saying to Kefauver what he seemed to be saying—the naïveté about antitrust violations might be a help to a man in getting and holding a $200,000-a-year job at General Electric? It seems unlikely. And yet what else could he have meant? Whatever the answer, neither the federal antitrust men nor the Senate investigators were able to prove that Smith succeeded in his attempts to communicate to Vinson the fact that he was engaging in price-fixing. And, lacking such proof, they were unable to establish what they gave every appearance of going all out to establish if they could: namely, that at least some one man at the pinnacle of G.E.'s management— some member of the sacred executive committee itself—was implicated. Actually, when the story of the conspiracies first became known, Vinson not only concurred in a company decision to punish Smith by drastically demoting him but personally informed him of the decision—two acts that, if he had grasped Smith's meaning back in 1957, would have denoted a remarkable degree of cynicism and hypocrisy. (Smith,

by the way, rather than accept the demotion, quit General Electric and, after being fined three thousand dollars and given a suspended thirty-day prison sentence by Judge Ganey, found a job elsewhere, at ten thousand dollars a year.)

This was not Vinson's only brush with the case. He was also among those named in one of the grand jury indictments that precipitated the court action, this time in connection not with his comprehension of Smith's jargon but with the conspiracy in the switchgear department. On this aspect of the case, four switchgear executives—Burens, Stehlik, Clarence E. Burke, and H. Frank Hentschel—testified before the grand jury (and later before the Subcommittee) that at some time in July, August, or September of 1958 (none of them could establish the precise date) Vinson had had lunch with them in Dining Room B of G.E.'s switchgear works in Philadelphia, and that during the meal he had instructed them to hold price meetings with competitors. As a result of this order, they said, a meeting attended by representatives of G.E., Westinghouse, the Allis-Chalmers Manufacturing Company, the Federal Pacific Electric Company, and the I-T-E Circuit Breaker Company was held at the Hotel Traymore in Atlantic City on November 9, 1958, at which sales of switchgear to federal, state, and municipal agencies were divvied up, with General Electric to get 39 percent of the business, Westinghouse 35 percent, I-T-E 11 percent, Allis-Chalmers 8 percent, and Federal Pacific Electric 7 percent. At subsequent meetings, agreement was reached on allocating sales of switchgear to private buyers as well, and an elaborate formula was worked out whereby the privilege of submitting the lowest bid to prospective customers was rotated among the conspiring companies at two-week intervals. Because of its periodic nature, this was called the phase-of-the-moon formula—a designation that in due time led to the following lyrical exchange between the Subcommittee and L. W. Long, an executive of Allis-Chalmers:

SENATOR KEFAUVER: Who were the phasers-of-the-mooners—phase-of-the-mooners?

MR. LONG: As it developed, this so-called phase-of-the-moon operation was carried out at a level below me, I think referred to as a working group. . . .

MR. FERRALL: [counsel for the Subcommittee]: Did they ever report to you about it?

MR. LONG: Phase of the moon? No.

Vinson told the Justice Department prosecutors, and repeated to the Subcommittee, that he had not known about the Traymore meeting, the phase-of-the-mooners, or the existence of the conspiracy itself until the case broke; as for the lunch in Dining Room B, he insisted that it had never taken place. On this point, Burens, Stehlik, Burke, and Hentschel submitted to lie-detector tests, administered by the F.B.I., and passed them. Vinson refused to take a lie-detector test, at first explaining that he was acting on advice of counsel and against his personal inclination, and later, after hearing how the four men had fared arguing that if the machine had not pronounced them liars, it couldn't be any good. It was established that on only eight business days during July, August, and September had Burens, Burke, Stehlik, and Hentschel all been together in the Philadelphia plant at the lunch hour, and Vinson produced some of his expense accounts, which, he pointed out to the Justice Department, showed that he had been elsewhere on each of those days. Confronted with this evidence, the Justice Department dropped its case against Vinson, and he has stayed on as a vice-president of General Electric. Nothing that the Subcommittee elicited from him cast any substantive doubt on the defense that had impressed the government prosecutors.

Above the madding crowd

Thus, the uppermost echelon at G.E. came through unscathed; the record showed that participation in the conspiracy went fairly far down in the organization but not all the way to the top. Gezon, everybody agreed, had followed orders from Stehlik, and Stehlik had followed orders from Burens, but that was the end of the trail, because although Burens said he had followed orders from Vinson, Vinson denied it and made the denial stick. The government, at the end of its investigation, stated in court that it could not prove, and did not claim, that either Chairman Cordiner or President Paxton had authorized, or even known about, the conspiracies, and thereby officially ruled out the possibility that they had resorted

to at least a figurative wing. Later, Paxton and Cordiner showed up in Washington to testify before the Subcommittee, and its interrogators were similarly unable to establish that they had ever indulged in any variety of winking.

After being described by Ginn as General Electric's stubbornest and most dedicated advocate of free competition, Paxton explained to the Subcommittee that his thinking on the subject had been influenced not directly by Adam Smith but, rather, by way of a former G.E. boss he had worked under—the late Gerard Swope. Swope, Paxton testified, had always believed firmly that the ultimate goal of business was to produce more goods for more people at lower cost. "I bought that then, I buy it now," said Paxton. "I think it is the most marvelous statement of economic philosophy that any industrialist has ever expressed." In the course of his testimony, Paxton had an explanation, philosophical or otherwise, of each of the several situations related to price-fixing in which his name had earlier been mentioned. For instance, it had been brought out that in 1956 or 1957 a young man named Jerry Page, a minor employee in G.E.'s switchgear division, had written directly to Cordiner alleging that the switchgear divisions of G.E. and of several competitor companies were involved in a conspiracy in which information about prices was exchanged by means of a secret code based on different colors of letter paper. Cordiner had turned the matter over to Paxton with orders that he get to the bottom of it, and Paxton had thereupon conducted an investigation that led him to conclude that the color-code conspiracy was "wholly a hallucination on the part of this boy." In arriving at that conclusion, Paxton had apparently been right, although it later came out that there had been a conspiracy in the switchgear division during 1956 and 1957; this, however, was a rather conventional one, based simply on price-fixing meetings, rather than on anything so gaudy as a color code. Page could not be called to testify because of ill health.

Paxton conceded that there had been some occasions when he "must have been pretty damn dumb." (Dumb or not, for his services as the company's president he was, of course, remunerated on a considerably grander scale than Vinson—receiving a basic annual salary of $125,000, plus annual incentive compensation of about $175,000, plus stock options designed to enable him to collect much more, at the comparatively low tax rate on capital gains, if General Electric's stock should go up.) As for Paxton's attitude toward company communications, he emerges as a pessimist on this score. Upon being asked at the hearings to comment on the Smith-Vinson conversations of 1957, he said that, knowing Smith, he just could not "cast the man in the role of a liar," and went on:

When I was younger, I used to play a good deal of bridge. We played about fifty rubbers of bridge, four of us, every winter, and I think we probably played some rather good bridge. If you gentlemen are bridge players, you know that there is a code of signals that is exchanged between partners as the game progresses. It is a stylized form of playing. . . . Now, as I think about this—and I was particularly impressed when I read Smith's testimony when he talked about a "meeting of the clan" or "meeting of the boys"—I began to think that there must have been a stylized method of communication between these people who were dealing with competition. Now, Smith could say, "I told Vinson what I was doing," and Vinson wouldn't have the foggiest idea what was being told to him, and both men could testify under oath, one saying yes and the other saying no, and both be telling the truth. . . . [They] wouldn't be on the same wavelength. [They] wouldn't have the same meanings. I think, I believe now that these men did think that they were telling the truth, but they weren't communicating between each other with understanding.

Here, certainly, is the gloomiest possible analysis of the communications problem.

Chairman Cordiner's status, it appears from his testimony, was approximately that of the Boston Cabots in the celebrated jingle. His services to the company, for which he was recompensed in truly handsome style (with, for 1960, a salary of just over $280,000, plus contingent deferred income of about $120,000, plus stock options potentially worth hundreds of thousands more), were indubitably many and valuable, but they were performed on such an exalted level that, at least in antitrust matters, he does not seem to have been able to have any earthly communication at all. When he emphatically told the Subcommittee that at no time had he had so much as an inkling of the network of conspiracies, it could be deduced that his was a case not of faulty communication but of no communication. He did not speak to the Subcommittee of philosophy or philosophers, as Ginn and Paxton had done, but from his past record of ordering

reissues of 20.5 and of peppering his speeches and public statements with praise of free enterprise, it seems clear that he was *un philosophe sans le savoir*—and one on the side of selling the Lord, since no evidence was adduced to suggest that he was given to winking in any form. Kefauver ran through a long list of antitrust violations of which General Electric had been accused over the past half-century, asking Cordiner, who joined the company in 1922, how much he knew about each of them; usually, he replied that he had known about them only after the fact. In commenting on Ginn's testimony that Erben had countermanded Cordiner's direct order in 1954, Cordiner said that he had read it with "great alarm" and "great wonderment," since Erben had always indicated to him "an intense competitive spirit," rather than any disposition to be friendly with rival companies.

Throughout his testimony, Cordiner used the curious expression "be responsive to." If, for instance, Kefauver inadvertently asked the same question twice, Cordiner would say, "I was responsive to that a moment ago," or if Kefauver interrupted him, as he often did, Cordiner would ask politely, "May I be responsive?" This, too, offers a small lead for a foundation grantee, who might want to look into the distinction between being responsive (a passive state) and answering (an act), and their relative effectiveness in the process of communication.

Guilt denied

Summing up his position on the case as a whole, in reply to a question of Kefauver's about whether he thought that G.E. had incurred "corporate disgrace," Cordiner said, "No, I am not going to be responsive and say that General Electric had corporate disgrace. I am going to say that we are deeply grieved and concerned. . . . I am not proud of it."

Chairman Cordiner, then, had been able to fairly deafen his subordinate officers with lectures on compliance with the rules of the company and the laws of the country, but he had not been able to get all those officers to comply with either, and President Paxton could muse thoughtfully on how it was that two of his subordinates who had given radically different accounts of a conversation between them could be not liars but merely poor communicators. Philosophy seems to have reached a high point at G.E., and communication a low one. If executives could just learn to understand one another, most of the witnesses said or implied, the problem of antitrust violations would be solved. But perhaps the problem is cultural as well as technical, and has something to do with a loss of personal identity that comes from working in a huge organization. The cartoonist Jules Feiffer, contemplating the communication problem in a nonindustrial context, has said, "Actually, the breakdown is between the person and himself. If you're not able to communicate successfully between yourself and yourself, how are you supposed to make it with the strangers outside?" Suppose, purely as a hypothesis, that the owner of a company who orders his subordinates to obey the antitrust laws has such poor communication with himself that he does not really know whether he wants the order to be complied with or not. If his order is disobeyed, the resulting price-fixing may benefit his company's coffers; if it is obeyed, then he has done the right thing. In the first instance, he is not personally implicated in any wrongdoing, while in the second he is positively involved in *right*doing. What, after all, can he lose? It is perhaps reasonable to suppose that such an executive might communicate his uncertainty more forcefully than his order. Possibly yet another foundation grantee should have a look at the reverse of communication failure, where he might discover that messages the sender does not even realize he is sending sometimes turn out to have got across only too effectively.

Expensive retribution

Meanwhile, in the first year after the Subcommittee concluded its investigation, the defendant companies were by no means allowed to forget their transgressions. The law permits customers who can prove that they have paid artificially high prices as a result of antitrust violations to sue for damages—in most cases, triple damages—and suits running into many millions of dollars soon began piling up. (By January, 1962, they had piled up so high that Chief Justice Warren set up a special panel of federal judges to plan how they should all be handled.) Needless to say, Cordiner was not allowed to forget about the matter, either; indeed, it would be surprising if he was allowed a chance to think about much else, for in addition to the suits, he had to contend with active efforts by a minority group of stockholders to unseat him. Paxton retired as president in April, 1961, because of ill health dating back at least to the previous January, when he underwent a major operation. As for the executives who pleaded guilty and were fined or imprisoned, most of those who had been employed by companies other than G.E. remained with them, either in their old jobs or in similar ones. Of those who had been employed by G.E., none remained there. Some retired permanently from business, others settled for comparatively small jobs, and a few landed big ones—most spectacularly Ginn, who in June, 1961, became president of Baldwin-Lima-Hamilton, manufacturers of heavy machinery. And as for the future of price-fixing in the electrical industry, it seems safe to say that what with the Justice Department, Judge Ganey, Senator Kefauver, and the triple-damage suits, the impact on the philosophers who guide corporate policy has been such that they, and even their subordinates, are likely to try to hew scrupulously to the line for quite some time. Quite a different question, however, is whether they have made any headway in their ability to communicate.

Reading 44

In case anyone should be carried away by Galbraithian eloquence in favor of the modern corporation and in criticism of antitrust policy, let him read the following account of the kind of scandal we would meet with every day were we not to have antitrust prosecutions. The present piece speaks for itself, and it is not at all atypical of what goes on abroad or of what used to go on in the shameless days prior to the Sherman Act.

Questions to Guide the Reading
Who caused these monopolists more trouble—the public, government, or cutthroat rivalry among themselves? How did they rig bidding so as to bilk the government? Did our domestic antitrust legislation perhaps do some good internationally in helping to break up this predatory operation?

The Quinine "Convention": A Case Study of an International Cartel

Introduction

Beginning in November 1959 all of the world's producers of quinine, with the sole exception of the Bandoeng factory of the Indonesian Government, entered into a series of restrictive agreements designed to control prices, distribution and production in every aspect of the quinine industry. A key objective was the elimination of competition among the various producers in securing the U.S. stockpile. This grouping of producers, referred to by its members as a "Convention", had been preceded by an earlier cartel agreement between the two largest producers, the Dutch firm, N. V. Nederlandsche Combinatie voor Chemische Industrie (referred to as "Nedchem" or "Combinatie") and the German company, C. F. Boehringer & Söhne G. m. b. H. (referred to as "Boehringer" or "Waldhof"). When the Dutch brought the Convention to an end in November 1962, the earlier cartel agreement appears to have continued in effect.

This is only the latest chapter in a history of cartel control of quinine and quinidine prices which extends over a period of three-quarters of a century. The first agreement was recorded in 1892 between Dutch and German quinine processors. In 1913 a full-fledged cartel was organized by agreement between the European quinine manufacturers and producers of Javanese bark, largely at the instigation of the Netherlands Indies Government. A secretariat, the Kina Bureau, was established at Amsterdam to implement the agreement. The Kina Bureau had "full power to allot supplies of cinchona bark and fix prices of quinine in all the markets of the world."

At a series of meetings starting late in 1959

a new "Convention" was formed which wove a web of restrictions, made up of four different agreements:

1. a stockpile agreement,
2. an export agreement,
3. a gentlemen's agreement, and
4. a barkpool agreement.

The first provided that the Dutch member, Nedchem, would be the sole bidder on behalf of the group for the U.S. stockpile, which would then be shared among them on a *pro rata* basis in terms of previously established quotas. The second fixed prices and imposed other restraints in world markets *outside* the U.S. and the countries of the European Economic Community (Germany, Holland, France, Belgium and Italy). The third, which applied to countries *within* the EEC as well as the United Kingdom, fixed prices, reserved for each of the producers their home markets (except Great Britain), fixed sales quotas for each member, established a regularized system by which those who undersold their quotas would receive adjustments from those who had oversold, designated certain favored buyers to receive specified rebates or discounts, limited the right to manufacture quinidine to the Dutch and German producers, put into effect a method of eliminating competition (though not its appearance) on government bids, and imposed a variety of other restrictions. Finally, the barkpool agreement, which represented an effort to hold down the price for the raw material, set selling prices for cinchona bark and made some efforts toward pooling purchases.

The Convention held a series of meetings beginning on December 2, 1959 and ending at

From U.S. Senate, 90th Congress, 1st Session, Hearings before the Subcommittee on Antitrust and Monopoly of the Committee on the Judiciary, *Prices of Quinine & Quinidine, Pt. 2*, March 1967; (Statement of Dr. John M. Blair), pp. 180–223.

Brussels in October 1962. Detailed minutes of these meetings were kept and circularized to the various members, one of whom was the British concern, Carnegies of Welwyn Limited. In recent months the Subcommittee learned that during the life of the Convention this firm was a wholly-owned subsidiary of Rexall Drug Company Limited of Great Britain, which in turn is a wholly-owned subsidiary of Rexall Drug and Chemical Company of the United States. The minutes of these meetings, as well as related correspondence and memoranda, were produced pursuant to a subpoena served on the U.S. parent corporation.

To facilitate understanding, there are presented below the names of the participating companies and of their officials who customarily attended the meetings. In addition the following listing shows the places and dates at which the Convention held its meetings:

The world price and the stockpile. Early in the Convention's history the members began to grapple with still another dilemma concerning the stockpile, which was to plague them for months to come. Should they raise the world price of quinine, thereby increasing their immediate profits, or should they keep it at its existent and relatively low level, thereby making it possible for them to purchase the stockpile at a lower price? To the Dutch one of the great advantages of a Convention was that they could immediately raise the price—an objective fervently supported by the British:

Mr. van der Spek: Now if we make a convention and put up the price by say Hfl. 3,— that means a million guilders a year, which we let go if we do not make a convention to better our chances to get the stockpile. To quote the immortal Omar: "I'll take the cash and let the profit go."
Dr. Buchler remains of opinion that it is not wise

England:	Rexall Drug Co. Ltd.	Mr. J. R. Lumley
	Carnegies of Welwyn Ltd.	Mr. F. Chapman
	Lake & Cruickshank Ltd.	Mr. G. M. Cruickshank
France:	Société Nogentaise de Produits Chimiques	M. L. Augustins
		M. P. Jacob
	Pointet Girard	M. L. Girard
		M. A. Pointet
		M. J. R. Roques
Germany:	C. F. Boehringer & Söhne G.m.b.H.	Mr. G. Tessmar
	Buchler & Co.	Dr. W. Buchler
Holland:	N. V. Nederlandsche Combinatie voor Chemische Industrie	Mr. C. N. van der Spek
		Mr. C. W. van Heeckeren van der Schoot

December 2, 1959	Plaza Hotel, Brussels
January 7, 1960	Plaza Hotel, Brussels
February 4, 1960	offices of Ets. J. R. Roques, Paris
March 2, 1960	Plaza Hotel, Brussels
April 7, 1960	Amstel Hotel, Amsterdam
August 17, 1960	Plaza Hotel, Brussels
October 26, 1960	Atlantic Hotel, Hamburg
January 26, 1961	Homestead Court Hotel, Welwyn Garden City
April 20, 1961	offices of Ets. J. R. Roques, Paris
April 21, 1961	offices of Ets. J. R. Roques, Paris
June 29, 1961	Amstel Hotel, Amsterdam
October 5, 1961	Hotel Europäischer Hof, Heidelberg
January 12, 1962	Plaza Hotel, Brussels
February 23, 1962	Plaza Hotel, Brussels
May 2, 1962	office of M. Roques, Paris
July 19, 1962	Selsdonpark Hotel, London
September 21, 1962	Gewandhaus, Braunschweig
October 26, 1962	Brussels (no minutes, but reference in letter of Nedchem 11/2/62)

to make a convention just now. We must wait for the stockpile to be disposed of.

Mr. van der Spek asks when this will be; the stockpile came up in 1956 and only now a decision has been taken. It may be a long time before anything is decided. There is much truth in Dr. Buchler's argument, but Mr. van der Spek should prefer to agree with Omar: the price increase is the certain "cash", getting the stockpile is uncertain, therefore hardly "the profit."[1]

At their meeting in Paris on July 19, 1962 all members joined in applauding the Dutch for their success in securing more than four-fifths of the stockpile at an average price of slightly over 21 cents.

Export agreement and gentlemen's agreement

The heart of the price-fixing arrangements of the Convention is to be found in two documents—the Export Agreement and the Gentlemen's Agreement—which, by their nature, must be considered together. The first of these agreements was to serve, in effect, as a cover for the Convention's activities, while the second provides a much more comprehensive picture of its real operations.

The Export Agreement was a contract of dubious but possible legality. Originally negotiated between the Dutch and Boehringer in July 1959, it was extended to include Buchler in March 1960 and the British and French producers on April 7, 1960. With its implementing Rules ("Richtlinien"), it established *for export markets only* a quota for each member and a uniform system of prices, delivery conditions, and payment terms binding on all members. There was also some reservation of export markets, e.g., East Germany to the German producers, Dutch overseas territories to the Dutch, and certain French colonies and former colonies to the French firms.

Sales quotas. An essential feature of any cartel can be found in the market-sharing arrangements accepted by the membership. Some system of marketing quotas, whether overt or carefully hidden, must underlie any price-fixing agreement. The price level for any given product can be maintained above the competitive market level only if the producers are willing to restrict their own sales to a point where the supply offered by the group as a whole is not so great as to depress prices.

[1] Minutes of meeting, February 4, 1960, pp. 2–3.

The importance of a quota arrangement inevitably makes it one of the major areas of bargaining and contention among the member firms. While the possibility of increasing prices above the competitive level is the principal attraction of cartel affiliation to the individual firm, the concomitant responsibility to resist any temptation to sell as much as possible at the higher prices (or slightly below them) arouses considerably less enthusiasm. Each member firm, therefore, feels that it has a vital interest in the basis upon which quotas are established, the markets to which they apply, the method by which each member is informed of the performance of others, and the means by which violations of quotas will be handled.

The allocation of geographic markets. In quinine, as in most international cartels, certain geographic markets were made the exclusive preserve of one or more producers. For example, the various producers were usually granted an exclusive monopoly in their home countries. In this way the "deterioration" of markets resulting from sales by outsiders was brought to an end. The English had been exporting to West Germany and, along with Buchler, to France. The Boehringer representative complained that "since the English sell to Germany, the German home-market price has deteriorated. . . ." The French, in turn, explained that they could not meet prices on imported quinine since, under French price controls, this might encourage their Government to lower the official ceiling prices.

The parties agree to work together in the spirit outlined above and in particular to be guided by their conviction that their co-operative intention can only have effect if all parties, each of its own accord, strive to overcome the practical and legal difficulties that are going to arise. This applies most especially to the punctual fulfillment of the obligation to effect egalisation (vide note about egalisation of February 19th, 1960) and *the protection of the National markets*.

Restriction of production. In addition to reserving geographic markets for designated producers, the Convention also imposed restraints on the manufacture of designated products. Thus, a plant in the Congo originally built by Belgian interests to process Kivu bark and owned by Boehringer was prohibited from exporting quinine and quinidine; in exchange the Congolese market for these products was reserved for Boehringer. All present agree to this procedure.

Government tenders. The Convention addressed itself at an early stage to the question of bidding on government contracts. A method was developed to ensure an "equitable" non-competitive distribution of this business in a manner which would avoid the appearance of collusion in the form of identical bids: "Mr. van der Spek does not like equal bids, they clearly point to a price understanding."[2] Van der Spek suggested another way to handle government orders. The method, in other words, was for the Convention to designate the "successful" bidder, who would grant an agreed-upon discount off the world price, while other members would offer a scatter of "competitive" bids over a range of higher prices. This would avoid the twin dangers of either having only one bidder for each tender or alternatively having several bidders offering identical prices.

A second reason for "taking it in turns" was that government tenders and other unusually large orders offered a partial solution to the equalization problem. This business could be assigned to the under-deliverers as a means of bringing their sales into closer balance with their quotas.

The question of government tenders was made the first point on the agenda of the October 1961 meeting. A firm agreement was reached giving Nedchem the power, subject to Convention approval, to assign government tenders and special orders to particular companies, based generally on their under- or over-delivery positions:

Mr. van der Spek points out that it is traditional that tenders should go to under-deliverers because it is one of the objects of a convention to see that everyone gets his share.
Mr. Chapman while agreeing to this principle, feels that there are no clear cut rules about the subject. . . .

Finally it is decided:

a. All business for which the convention decided pragmatically that a special price is indi-

cated is to come under the description of "tender or large order".
b. The secretariat will in each case propose who is to get the business, the basis for such a proposal will—in general—be the sales position.
c. On this proposal a vote will be taken and members abstaining, within the time-limit set (dependent on when bid should be entered but no longer than 14 days), are considered to have voted for the proposal.
d. Rules b. and c. are considered to be in force for six months to see how they work.[3]

The cartel and the Bandoeng factory. Sales below the established price by "outsiders" can doom any cartel or price-fixing arrangement. Since each of the producers abiding by the price agreement fears that the other parties may reduce *their* price to meet the outsider's competition and that therefore he'd better do likewise, the quantities involved need not be very large. As Dr. Buchler put it, ". . . one outsider can ruin the entire market.[4] At the first meeting of the Convention Dr. Buchler remarked on the impossibility of a price agreement while "outsiders" existed; he was reassured by the representative of Boehringer:

Mr. Tessmar is of opinion that this is a consequence of concluding a cartel while there still are outsiders, but if the manufacturers assembled around this table come to an agreement, he does not see any outsiders.[5]

There were, nevertheless, three potential sources of market disturbance from "outside" sources of supply. One consisted of the U.S. stockpile. A first order of business of the Convention was to eliminate competitive rivalry, both among themselves and from outsiders, for this huge source of bulk quinine. A second potential source was the Pharmakina plant in the Belgian Congo, which enjoyed preferred access to Congolese bark; Pharmakina was successfully neutralized through its acquisition by Boehringer.

There still remained, however, the large—though old—quinine factory at Bandoeng, Indonesia. Originally established by cinchona planters in 1894 to counteract the efforts of

---

[2] Minutes of meeting, October 5, 1961, p. 2.

[3] Minutes of meeting on October 5, 1961, pp. 1, 2.
[4] Minutes of meeting on December 2, 1959, p. 8.
[5] Ibid., p. 7.

the earliest (1892) Dutch–German cartel, Nederlandsche Bandoengsche Kininefabriek provided effective competition to the European firms until it, too, was brought into the cartel in 1913 and later acquired by Nedchem. For years the Dutch had deliberately refrained from exploiting the potential capacity of the plant–which, according to van der Spek, was far more than enough to supply the entire world–and resisted efforts of the Indonesian Government to develop export markets for native quinine.

By limiting the output of the Bandoeng plant, the Dutch were also limiting its input of cinchona bark, leaving that much more available for export to the Netherlands. Throughout the Convention, Dutch strategy was to prevent the Bandoeng factory from exporting finished quinine in order to free up bark supplies for export. To this end members were not to purchase quinine from Indonesia.

The illegality of the convention

From the very outset the members of the Convention were fully aware of the existence of antitrust statutes in most of the major industrialized countries. They were fully aware that what they were doing was in violation of the antitrust laws of the United States, West Germany and the European Economic Community; they also devised various stratagems to avoid detection by the various antitrust agencies.

At the Convention's first meeting on December 2, 1959 the Dutch representative outlined the need for both an Export Agreement (which he thought was permissible and could be registered with the E. E. C.) and a Gentlemen's Agreement (which he knew very definitely could not be):

The Dutch and Germans can make a legal cartel, as long as the Common Market is not concerned and as for the British market, a cartel is allowed as long as the British market is not concerned. *Mr. Chapman* replies that any agreement in England comes under the Restrictive Trade Practices Act and if an arrangement is made for export-markets only, this can be done with other British firms or foreign manufacturers. The Board of Trade should be informed, but the cartel is not subject to approval. *Mr. van der Spek* says that this means that a legal arrangement can be made for all countries except for the Common Market and the U.K. For these markets there should be a Gentlemen's Agreement.

Although of all the European countries, West Germany has, in the words of one of the members, the "strictest anti-cartel regulations", the German producers evidenced little concern over the anti-cartel legislation of their own country as long as the clearly illegal provisions did not have to be put down in writing.

Earlier the smaller German producer, Dr. Buchler, had emphasized in a letter of February 15, 1960 that adjudication of complaints which might arise among the members should be before a private body, the International Chamber of Commerce, as, "There will be certain arrangements in our convention the Germans should better not discuss before a court of justice". He went on to add, "In a certain difference with us the Nedchem did not agree to respect the special German position. After this experience we cannot accept decisions of a court".

The members were most circumspect with regard to the U.S. antitrust laws, using a variety of strategies to avoid the appearance of collusion. The Dutch, in particular, always had in mind their experience as a defendant in the Sherman Act case of 1928 and their inclusion in the resultant permanent consent order. Thus, in the Convention's third meeting on February 4, 1960 the representative of Nedchem described one of the devices by which the U.S. order had been evaded, proferring the necessary information to the others so that they ". . . can export to the U.S. at the same basis".

As to America, *Mr. van der Spek* says that the Dutch sell fob because of the legal trouble they had in 1928.
Mr. Tessmar adds that it is dangerous to sell cif to the U.S. or to hold stocks there.[6]

The break-up of the convention

On November 2, 1962 the life of the Convention was terminated by unilateral action on the part of the Dutch.

What possible reasons could have led the Dutch to demolish that which they had been the leading force in creating? Although it is always hazardous to speculate about motivations, the paradox of an enterprise deliberately undoing two years of the hardest form of co-

[6] Minutes of meeting on February 4, 1960, p. 8.

operative work is so striking as to demand some attempt at explanation.

One possible explanation is that the Dutch had undergone a conversion to the righteousness of competition. Another possible explanation is that the Convention had already served its primary purpose, which was to eliminate competition, by other producers for the U.S. stockpile. Certainly the facts are that the Dutch did end up with physical possession of the stockpile.

Reading 45

Economists recognize that perfect competition is a good thing and deviations from it bad. Since, however, the real world rarely meets the strictest requirements of perfect competition as defined by the economist, the cause of antitrust needs more than these generalities to be useful and effective. The authors in this reading propose a positive and practical approach to the subject. They do not believe laissez faire can itself provide an approximation to workably perfect competition. They do think economic analysis furnishes guides for legislation, prosecution, and adjudication, and for business conduct itself.

When a top-notch economist and a top-notch lawyer collaborate on the problem of antitrust, the result should be of interest. Adding to the importance of these views is the fact that Donald Turner took leave from the Harvard Law School to head President Johnson's Antitrust Division in the Justice Department. Carl Kaysen left the Harvard Economics Department to become Director of the Institute for Advanced Study in Princeton. He combines government service with scholarship and had the opportunity to be the first economist to serve as a "clerk" to a judge in an important antitrust case: Judge Charles Wyzanski Jr. made history when he forced the United Shoe Company to sell, as well as to rent, its machinery.

Questions to Guide the Reading

Why would significant and never-ending economies of large-scale production tend, under laissez faire, to be destructive of competition? What optimistic evidence do the authors give in this regard?

What acts tend to enhance the market power of sellers? What penalties and attitudes do the authors propose to help limit market power?

A Policy for Antitrust Law

Carl Kaysen and Donald F. Turner

This analysis of United States antitrust policy has two aims: the proposal of a strengthened antitrust policy, worked out in enough detail to indicate the changes in law and administration necessary to apply it; and a statement of the logic of the policy proposal—in terms of the presumptions, factual judgments, and analytical reasoning on which it rests—in such a

From Carl Kaysen and Donald F. Turner, *Antitrust Policy*, pp. 3–10, 44–49 (Harvard University Press, Cambridge, 1959). Copyright, 1959, by the President and Fellows of Harvard College. Reprinted with kind permission of the publisher.

way that it will be useful even to those who disagree with the value judgment inevitably involved in it.

Some underlying assumptions

Certain broad propositions must be taken as true to warrant any antitrust policy. We make these explicit here, in part to indicate our justification of them, in part to set bounds to the scope of our discussion.

As the context of our discussion we take for granted the present mixed economy, in which the largest part is organized on the decentralized lines of private property and private enterprise. The market is thus the central institution regulating economic activity. The use to a significantly greater extent than at present of other methods of economic organization—including nationalization, direct government control in detail of individual firms, consumer cooperation, or worker-manager guild organization—is ruled out as a real policy alternative. Indeed, only in this context is it worth while to place much emphasis on antitrust policy.

Further, we assume that the sectors of the economy in which government monopoly, or private monopoly controlled in more or less detail by government (to which antitrust policy is not applicable), are limited, and are not growing rapidly relative to the rest of the economy. Thus we posit a market-controlled sector and a distinct and identifiable government-controlled sector, in the first of which antitrust policy is the primary form of extra-market regulation, while in the second various kinds of more specific controls apply. Although the boundaries between the two sectors cannot be easily specified in general terms, we must be able to say of any specific industry or industrial activity that it falls on one or the other side of the boundary. We further assume that the size of the government-controlled sector and its interrelations with the market-controlled one are not, and will not become, such as to make a successful antitrust policy impossible. This is by no means an obvious truth. The government-regulated sector is not so large in a crude sense as to leave no room for market forces, but the problem of interrelations between regulation in the one area and competition in the other is more complex. Here we can only point out the difference between the existence of regulated monopoly in an industry

like electric power, which does not affect the structure or market operations of power-users, although it does affect their costs; and the kind of regulation involved in crude-oil prorationing, or in collective bargaining as now established, which may have powerful impacts on industrial markets, in the first case in the oil industry, in the second case, generally.

We assume that some kind of antitrust policy is necessary or desirable. Again, though this proposition is often taken as obvious, it is not necessarily so. Other industrial nations, with few exceptions, have not had such policies in the past, although in recent years interest in them has grown. Belief in the need for a procompetitive public policy rests on two propositions. First, there is some minimum level of competition which it is necessary to achieve in the market-controlled sector if that sector is to be allowed to remain a market-regulated rather than a government-controlled one. Second, this level is not self-maintaining: in the absence of antitrust, the level of competition will sink below the minimum. While there are substantial economic arguments for the first proposition, it rests basically on a political judgment. In our democratic, egalitarian society, large areas of uncontrolled private power are not tolerated. The continued freedom of most industries from detailed government regulation rests on their subjection to the control of market forces. This means some level of competition, sufficient to prevent at least the accumulation of visible, unchecked private economic power. A complete absence of positive public policy would lead to a drastic decline in the competitiveness of business. A much more widespread pattern of growth by merger, an efflorescence of collusive arrangements of all sorts, and the use of various exclusionary, and otherwise anticompetitive practices now forbidden would all follow on the abandonment of a procompetitive public policy. In general, these changes in the structure of markets and the conduct of business firms would lead to declining economic efficiency and shifts in income distribution of a sort which are usually viewed as undesirable.

Next, we assume that enforcement of some kind of anti-trust policy is worth its cost. This means that the level of competition which would persist in the absence of any policy is far enough away from what could be achieved so that the administrative, political, and economic costs of government intervention involved in a pro-competitive policy are worth incurring. One way of justifying this assumption is to point to the present antitrust policy, and its application—in changing ways—over the past sixty years. It is fairly clear from the cases that the antitrust law sets a standard of business conduct in respect to anticompetitive practices that is more stringent than would exist in its absence.

Bigness not necessarily better

At a deeper level, the assumption that an effective antitrust policy is worth while involves several complex judgments of fact. First, economies of scale under present technology do not indicate the desirability of a radically *greater* concentration of output in a small number of large firms, so that antitrust policy is not hopelessly at variance with the underlying cost situation. Several kinds of evidence support this conclusion.

First is the importance of mergers in explaining the present relative size distribution of industrial firms. Second is the fact that all of the technical economies of scale are achieved at the level of the plant rather than of the firm, and the greatest part of the size difference between very large and large firms (say $500 million and over assets in the first class, and $50 to $500 million in the second) lies in the number of plants they operate rather than in the size of the plants themselves. Technical economies of scale are not the only kind; economies at the level of the firm in selling, advertising, research, production planning, personnel recruitment, etc., are also possible. Third is the large variation in size within the group of "large" firms with modern management organizations, highly developed research and marketing activities, multiplant and multimarket activity. Among integrated steel producers the range is ten to one; among "major" oil producers, twenty to one; among chemical manufacturers it is perhaps fifty to one. This variation shows no tendency to diminish over time; giant firms are not generally outcompeting smaller ones, by any tests now available.

What is now true must be expected to continue in the future: no sharp change in technology, including the introduction of large-scale rapid computation and automatic control techniques, will in the near future dictate a substantial increase in concentration among market-controlled firms. The truth of this is, of course, a speculative matter; inventions not now foreseen may lead to radical changes in all our ideas. But insofar as we have any basis of speculation, there appears to be no reason to expect any radical change in the character of scale economies.

Need for competition

In singling out the relation between size and efficiency for discussion, we are acknowledging that competition requires the existence of competitors, in the plural. The vexing question is "how many?" We begin exploring this question by observing that the rigorous model of the perfectly competitive market is the appropriate starting point of any definition, but it cannot be the end of any practically useful one. The model provides us with two important notions: first, a market in which each seller acts as if his own decisions had no influence on any significant market variable —price, supply, the number of other sellers and their sales, etc.; second, a definition of economic efficiency in terms of the relations between costs and prices characteristic of the model. The second result, the efficient use of resources in meeting the demands of consumers, depends on the first and on the logic of profit maximization. In the model, the first result comes about because sellers are many in number and individually of insignificant size relative to the total market, the product of any seller is a perfect substitute for that of any other, and new sellers enter and old ones leave freely and quickly in response to profits and losses. In real markets—with very few exceptions—these conditions do not hold. The existence of significant economies of scale at both the plant and the firm level over some size range means that firms are not generally insignificant in relation to the market. The geography of production and consumption reinforces this result: for many products there are local or regional markets in which the number of sellers is relatively small, and which are to a substantial extent isolated from other local and regional markets by the barriers of transport cost. The outputs of one seller are usually only imperfect substitutes for the outputs of another: product differentiation, advertising, and locational differences among sellers which bring about this result must be taken as permanent features of the economy, answering in some measure to real preferences of consumers. Neither entry nor exit is universally free and speedy. All sorts of barriers to entry, from large capital requirements to high advertising costs and closely held patented technology, are widely characteristic of the economy, though in varying measure in different industries. Frictions, and the influence of uncertainty and risk aversion on business decisions, mean that entry and exit often take place with substantial lags after the changes in profitability which occasion them.

Concentration and market power

Nonetheless, though the model of competitive market structure is not usable as such in our definition of competition, other concepts of the model are. Where firms can persistently behave over substantial periods of time in a manner which differs from the behavior that the competitive market would impose on competitive firms facing similar cost and demand conditions, they can be identified as possessing market power. Conversely, where, on the average and viewed over long periods of time, the relations of prices, costs, outputs, capacities, and investments among a group of rivalrous firms are such as would be expected in a competitive model, then it can be inferred that the market does constrain the scope of the individual firm's decisions sufficiently to be called competitive. The existence of such constraints depends on many features of a market. In general, numbers and conditions of entry are the most important of these features. There is a high correlation between concentration of output in the hands of a small number of large producers and the existence of firms with significant degrees of market power. This is the basic reason for singling out the relation between size and efficiency for rather extended discussion at this point. Were they such as to dictate a very small number of sellers—two, three, four—in most markets, antitrust policy would make little sense.

On the same ground, we must be concerned with differences in the levels of cost curves among enterprises. We must assume that it is not the case that a few firms, managed by men of superior gifts, can and will continue to attract the small number of superior managers,

and thus will be enabled to outperform all rivals in all fields, were they permitted and motivated to do so. This proposition implies something about the distribution of business ability in the population at large and the nature of business activity. On the first point it is assumed that first-grade managerial talent exists sufficient to man a few hundred companies such as Du Pont, General Motors, Standard Oil of New Jersey, etc.: there is a chairman of the board's gavel in the attaché case of every division manager. On the second, it is assumed that where a particular firm does have an advantage in men and methods, rivals can and will copy the methods and hire away the men, and that incentives of pay and promotion will suffice to do so, in that employee loyalties to particular firms will not prove so strong as to make this impossible. It is hard to support this proposition with concrete evidence, and, while we believe it accords with experience, others have expressed different views. Perhaps it is best to label this assumption as an article of democratic faith and leave it at that.[1]

[1] Some light is cast on the general subject by an examination of an American Institute of Management survey of excellently managed firms, entitled "Manual of Excellent Managements." The 1955 edition lists 389 firms, of which 199 are in manufacturing. The size distribution of these was examined by comparison with the FTC list of 1000 largest manufacturing corporations (1948). The results showed that, while there was a significant correlation between size and the proportion of excellently managed firms, the largest firms were not all listed, nor were all those listed giants. The distribution by groups of 50 was:

The 1000 largest manufacturing firms, by size	Number of excellently managed firms (AIM)
1st 50	26
2nd	31
3rd	20
4th	26
5th	17
6th	11
7th	15
8th	9
9th	7
10th	5
11th	35
12th	2
13th	4
14th	2
15th	4
16th	11
17th	4

Finally, we must assume that the dependence of business initiative and vigor on the degree of *laissez faire* is not so intimate and important that variations in the amount of government intervention and supervision of the kind involved in antitrust policy will significantly affect it. This is not to say that particular antitrust measures will not vary in their effects on business incentives, and that such variation is not relevant to the choice among them. Rather it is an assertion that over-all we need not fear that the possibility of any effective antitrust policy is foreclosed because of unfavorable repercussions on business vigor. This proposition is broadly supported by the history of the last three (or the last seven) decades, which have witnessed a progressive increase in the scope and detail of federal government intervention in business decisions with no worth-while evidence that over-all business effort has been noticeably diminished.

A policy for antitrust law

Antitrust policy may serve a variety of ultimate aims. We can divide the aims against which any policy proposal may be tested into four broad classes: (1) limitation of the power of big business; (2) performance (efficiency and progressiveness); (3) "fair dealing"; and (4) protection of competitive processes by limiting market power. For reasons to be set forth in detail hereafter, we select (4) as the most desirable and feasible guide, though willy-nilly and by design, the others will necessarily play some part.

18th	2
19th	1
20th	3

A variance analysis of the distribution by groups of 10 among 250 firms showed no correlation between size and the proportion of excellently managed firms over this part of the size range. The assets of the 10th firm on the list were about $1150 million, of the 50th firm, $288 million; the 100th, $139 million; the 200th, $68 million; the 250th, $54 million; the 500th, $23 million; and the 1000th, $9 million.

These figures are compatible with the hypothesis suggested above that rational management practices historically began in large corporations, but have been spreading to smaller and smaller ones. (We do not think it necessary to examine the content of the AIM definition of "excellent management" for the present purposes.)

A review of existing antitrust law indicates what to us are some important gaps in coverage. Since the existing law is primarily oriented toward conduct, it does not effectively deal—or at least has not effectively dealt in the past—with undue market power that cannot be associated with bad or unduly restrictive conduct. It seems clear that there now exist significant concentrations of undue market power, some individually held, some collectively "shared" in the sense that the members of the industry behave nonrivalrously for mutual benefit. It also seems clear to us that present law (1) has not been and cannot be fairly construed to cover the mere nonrivalrous actions of members of a noncompetitive industry, i.e., the "parallel" behavior of firms in a classic oligopoly is not "conspiracy"; and (2) may not cover all situations of individual market power that could be attacked without upsetting competitive goals. In addition, we believe that the law on conduct should be tightened in several respects if the prevention of undue market power is taken as a central guiding light.

In sum, we are suggesting that the primary goal of antitrust policy be the limitation of undue market power to the extent consistent with maintaining desirable levels of economic performance. To carry this out, we propose amendments of the antitrust laws that would (1) enable a direct attack on undue market power without regard to the presence or absence of conspiracy in the legal sense, and (2) severely limit forms of conduct that contribute to, or are likely to contribute to, the creation of undue market power.

The policy goals

Almost any policy proposal resolves itself into a statement of a hierarchy of ends, ordered to indicate which should prevail in situations where they conflict. In proposing that the primary goal of antitrust policy be the limitation of market power, we do not make it our sole goal; we also give great weight to the achievement of desirable economic performance. Indeed, in so far as reduction of market power is incompatible with efficiency and progressiveness, we subordinate the first goal to the second. If, for example, the efficient scale of operation in a particular market is so large in relation to the size of the market that efficient firms are so few in number as to make their possession of market power likely, and the reduction of market power cannot be achieved except at the cost of a substantial loss in efficiency, our policy would call for no action against the power itself. But where market power exists and can be reduced without sacrifices in performance, then such action is desirable without reference to the question of how good over-all performance may have been.

The other two of the broad classes of goals—promoting "fair" business conduct and the redistribution of social power between large and small business—occupy a much lower position in our hierarchy of policy aims. We expect that some degree of regulation of business conduct in the interest of "fair dealing" may be necessary. As we have already indicated, the policy of limiting market power will not be pressed to the point of reducing it to negligible dimensions everywhere (and indeed, this is not possible, even if it were viewed as desirable). Thus there may be some case for limiting the way in which residual market power is used. To the extent that some methods of using market power will be controlled on grounds that they are likely to contribute to the perpetuation of market power or to its increase, the area of regulation on pure "fair dealing" grounds will be correspondingly narrowed. But some kinds of conduct which will require such regulation do exist, and where it can be achieved without too high a price in efficiency, we deem it desirable. The following is a brief summary of our recommendations.

Limitation of market power. 1. We propose statutory authorization for the reduction of undue market power, whether individually or jointly possessed; this to be done normally by dissolution, divorcement, or divestiture. We would except market power derived from economies of scale, valid patents, or the introduction of new processes, products, or marketing techniques.

2. We suggest, in the alternative, that the program be either (a) a permanent feature of antitrust policy, thus applying both to existing concentrations of market power and to concentrations that may later arise through inadequacies in the law, or in enforcement of the law, concerning conduct; or (b) a program

limited to the time required to deal with existing undue concentrations of market power.

3. With respect to either of the above alternatives, we suggest that the policy might be carried out either (a) under a statute in which market power is defined in general terms, requiring a fairly extensive economic inquiry for determination of each case; or (b) under a statute in which market power is more arbitrarily defined, which would facilitate the disposition of cases and more clearly identify the "targets," but could possibly be applied to firms that, in fact, lacked market power.

Limitations on conduct contributing to market power. 1. *Mergers.* Particularly if the proposals as to market power are deemed unwise or undesirable, and perhaps in any event, we propose tightening the law on mergers. Some means of making enforcement more effective than it now is seems of paramount importance. We propose, as one step in this direction, a requirement of advance reporting of all mergers involving firms of more than a certain absolute size in assets or more than a certain share of any market in which they operate. We also suggest the possibility of a more arbitrary standard for illegality, in line with the similar suggestion as to market power stated above.

2. *Price-fixing or price-influencing agreements.* Regarding trade association and similar activities, we propose specific statutory prohibition of agreements:

(a) to abide by reported list prices,

(b) to report offers at which no sales are made,

(c) to inform each other of the individual buyers and sellers in all transactions,

(d) to refuse to make reports, submitted to each other, available to buyers or buyers' trade associations,

(e) to submit books and accounts to the inspection of any member of the group or representative thereof; or

(f) to report transactions to each other, or to a representative of the group, within a period of seven days or less after said transactions take place.

3. *Collective refusals to deal.* Apart from those incidentally resulting from productive joint ventures, we would make collective refusals to deal illegal per se.

4. *Patents and patent licensing.* Proceeding

on the basic premise that patentees' realizable rewards can be lowered without significantly reducing the flow of useful inventions and innovations, we propose:

(a) that the patent laws be revised to create a class of "petty" patents, with monopoly rights for five years only, and to raise the standard of invention for seventeen-year patents;

(b) that on restrictive clauses in patent licensing agreements,

(1) price-fixing clauses be made illegal per se,

(2) clauses providing for grant-backs of new patents or exclusive licenses thereunder be made illegal per se,

(3) covenants not to contest patent validity be invalid in any licensing agreement containing restrictions in addition to a uniform royalty provision,

(4) cross-licensing and pooling agreements contain no restrictions beyond that for a uniform royalty charge on each patent from all licenses (except that the owner may restrict the use), and

(5) all licensing agreements be registered with the Federal Trade Commission (but not made public);

(c) that Section 7 of the Clayton Act be revised to cover acquisitions of patents from individuals as well as from corporations.

5. *Price discrimination.* We propose that the Robinson-Patman Act be repealed, in favor of a statute dealing separately with (a) price discrimination directed against competing sellers and (b) price discrimination that harms particular buyers. In each case, we would make some substantive changes in the existing law. In both cases, we would liberalize the "cost" defense and specifically exclude from the law all geographic price discrimination that is accounted for entirely by differences in transportation cost.

Procedural and related recommendations.

1. We propose that criminal penalties be limited to the so-called per se offenses.

2. We propose that treble damages also be limited to the per se offenses; that no private suit be maintainable under a market power statutory provision; and that judgment under the market power provision would not constitute prima facie proof of anything under Section 5 of the Clayton Act.

3. We suggest the creation of a special court for adjudicating monopoly cases and other Sherman Act cases in which divestiture is part of the relief sought. For an extended program against undue market power, we propose a special court, with the prosecuting function placed in the hands of a new administrative agency. We also propose certain procedural steps designed to clarify and speed the trial of economic issues of fact.

Our reasons for giving primary emphasis to the fourth of the general goals of policy stated above and for making the above recommendations are partly positive and partly negative. Our positive reasons rest ultimately on a value judgment. The most important aspect of the competitive process is that it is self-controlling with regard to private economic power. For all the important qualifications and limitations of the doctrine of the invisible hand which modern economic analysis has produced, that doctrine remains the basic political justification for an enterprise economy in which major economic decisions are compelled and coordinated through the market. It is the fact that the competitive market *compels* the results of its processes which is the ultimate defense against the demand that economic decisions be made or supervised by politically responsible authorities. Without such market compulsion, that demand appears ultimately irresistible in a society committed to representative government. It is our preference for the kind of autonomy in economic life which a market-organized society makes possible that forms the particular judgment we make.

Our negative reasons are more objective, and less subject to dogmatic acceptance or rejection. In essence, they amount to the proposition that the alternative standards present definitional and administrative problems of such magnitude that consistent and sensible enforcement would be well-nigh impossible. While similar difficulties would attend the carrying out of a market power standard, we conclude that they would be much less severe. Moreover, we believe it is possible to formulate arbitrary tests designed to reduce administrative problems under a market power standard with considerably more confidence in the results than if similar steps were taken in order to carry out the other designated goals.

Readings 46, 47, and 48

No one is surprised when right-wing writers defend the corporation. Recall for example the Schumpeter Reading 42. But when the liberal critic Galbraith comes to defend the corporation and to play down the role of antitrust prosecution, that is a more surprising fact and one with which experts in that field disagree vociferously.

In the first of these three readings, Dr. Galbraith provides the Senate committee on small business with a lecture on the new industrial state. Then, in a continuation of the discussion, Professor Walter Adams of Michigan State University (and one-time acting president there) comes out strongly against Galbraith's contentions. In the third reading Professor E. T. Grether of the University of California at Berkeley (and formerly dean of the School of Business Administration there) argues that industrial organization is too important a subject to leave to nonexperts.

Questions to Guide the Readings

Would you agree that Dr. Galbraith is offering a false choice when he says either accept the modern large corporation or break it up? Can't one agree that the large corporation is here to stay and still advocate militant enforcement of antitrust legislation? Does Galbraith perhaps confuse "what is" with "what is right"? Even if the large corporation does do some good things, couldn't it be made to do even better things by vigorous antitrust enforcement? Recall Reading 44 giving the horrible details of the quinine monopoly to remind Galbraith of what might be the shape of things to come if people fell for his advice to go easy in antitrust policy.

Do you think that Professors Adams and Grether would agree with the implied criticisms of the Galbraith view that were expressed in the last paragraph.

Reading 46

In My New Industrial State Trust Busting Not Needed

J. Kenneth Galbraith

I am very happy to be here this morning. I have long been a close and admiring student of [Assistant] Attorney General Turner's writings, as equally those of Professor Adams. As will become evident, Mr. Turner's position, fully explored, provides comprehensive and much appreciated support for mine. In the lectures that precipitated this discussion and the book I have just published [*The New Industrial State 1967*], I took it for granted that American business has become very big.

The element of surprise in this conclusion is very small; I doubt that this conclusion will be much disputed. There are still a large number of small firms and small farms in the United States. They are, however, no longer characteristic of the American economy. In 1962, the

five *largest* industrial corporations in the United States, with combined assets in excess of $36 billion, possessed *over 12 percent* of all assets used in manufacturing. The *50 largest* corporations had *over a third* of all manufacturing assets. The *500 largest* corporations had well *over two-thirds*. Corporations with assets in excess of $10 million, some 2,000 in all, accounted for about 80 percent of all the resources used in manufacturing in the United States.

In the mid-1950's, 28 corporations provided approximately 10 percent of all employment in manufacturing, mining, and retail and wholesale trade. Twenty-three corporations provided 15 percent of all the employment in manufacturing. In the first half of that decade

From U.S. Senate, 90th Congress, 1st Session, Hearing before Subcommittees of the Select Committee on Small Business, June 29, 1967.

—June 1950–June 1956—a hundred firms received two-thirds by value of all defense contracts; 10 firms received one-third. In 1960 four corporations accounted for an estimated 22 percent of all industrial research and development expenditure. Three hundred and eighty-four corporations employing 5,000 or more workers accounted for 85 percent of these research and development expenditures; 260,000 firms employing fewer than 1,000 accounted for only 7 percent.

If I might continue this somewhat exaggerated dose of statistics for just a minute, in 1965, three industrial corporations, General Motors, Standard Oil of New Jersey, and Ford Motor Co., had more gross income than *all* of the farms in the country. This is relevant to my statement that these are the typical, characteristic parts of the economy. The income of General Motors, of $20.7 billion, about equalled that of the 3 million smallest farms in the country—around 90 percent of all farms. The gross revenues of each of the three corporations just mentioned far exceed those of any single State. The revenues of General Motors in 1963 were 50 times those of Nevada, eight times those of New York, and slightly less than one-fifth those of the Federal Government.

These figures, like all statistics, are subject to minor query on matters of detail. As orders of magnitude they are not, I believe, subject to any serious question. Nor are the consequences.

Bigness brings market power

The large firms that dominate the nonservice and nonagricultural sector of the economy have extensive power over their prices. They have large influence over the prices that they pay—at least those costs that are important to their operations. And also the wages they pay. They supply themselves with capital; some three-quarters of all savings now come from the retained earnings of corporations, which is to say that the latter have largely exempted themselves from dependence on the capital market. And, with varying degrees of success, firms with the resources to do so go beyond the prices that they set *to persuade their customers as to what they should buy.* This is a persuasion that, in various and subtle ways, extends to the State [the "military-industrial" complex]. There is great room for difference of opinion, and accordingly for debate, on how

decisive are these several manifestations of power. But nearly all will agree that "There is a large correlation between the concentration of output in the hands of a small number of large producers and the existence of firms with significant degrees of market power." The observation just cited is that of Carl Kaysen and Donald F. Turner in their authoritative volume, "A Policy for Antitrust Law."

They add, as would I, that a policy that deals with "the existence and significance of market power is not aimed at merely marginal or special phenomena, but at phenomena spread widely through the economy."

In my own volume I have gone on, at no slight length, to argue that this trend to the large corporation and this resulting exercise of substantial power over the prices, costs, wages, capital sources, and consumers is part of the broad sweep of economic development. Technology; the extensive use of capital; affluent and hence *malleable customers;* the imperatives of organization [the techno-structure]; the role of the union; the requirements imposed by public tasks, including arms development and space exploration, have all weakened the authority of the market. At the same time, these developments have both enabled and required firms to *substitute planning with its management of markets* for a simple response to the market. Bigness and market power, in other words, are but one part of a much larger current of change. To see them in isolation from other change is artificial. In part it is what results when a social discipline passes however partially from the custody of scholars to that of specialists and mechanics.

I have also been concerned in this book with the problem of how we are to survive, and in civilized fashion, in a world of great organizations which, not surprisingly, impose both their values and their needs on the society they are assumed to serve [the military-industrial complex]. But these further matters are not directly at issue this morning. In any case they do not directly involve the question of the antitrust laws.

The issue of the antitrust laws arises in response to a prior question. That question is whether we can escape the concentration and the attendant market control and planning which I have outlined and whether the antitrust laws, as now used, are an effective instrument for this escape. The present hearings materialized when I urged the contrary—

when *I* said that the trend to great size and associated control was immutable, given our desire for economic development, and that the present antitrust efforts to deal with size and market power were a charade. *I* noted that the antitrust laws legitimatize the real exercise of market power on the part of the large firms by a rather diligent harassment of those who have less of it. Thus, they serve to reassure us on the condition they are assumed to correct.

The facts which lead to the foregoing conclusions are not at all obscure. Nor are they matters of great subtlety. They are accepted by most competent economists and lawyers, including the very distinguished men here this morning. Only the rather obvious conclusions to be drawn from these facts encounter a measure of resistance. This, no doubt, is purely temporary, but while it persists it does cause a measure of confusion.

To him who hath

The most effective manifestation of economic power, all must agree, is simply the big firm. To be big in general and big in an industry is by far the best way of influencing prices and costs, commanding capital, having access to advertising, and selling resources, and possessing the other requisites of market power. And, as we have seen, by common agreement the heartland of the industrial economy is now dominated by large firms. The great bulk of American business is transacted by very large corporations.

And here enters the element of charade in the antitrust laws. If a firm is *already* large it is substantially immune under the antitrust laws. If you *already* have the basic requisite of market power, you are safe. The assistant Attorney General in Charge of the Antitrust Laws [Donald F. Turner, since 1968 at the Harvard Law School] argues that the market power of the large firm should *now* be made subject to the antitrust laws. This indeed is the main thrust of Mr. Turner's and Mr. Kaysen's book. And in responding to the questions of this committee on May 2 of this year he affirmed the point, if in slightly more cautious language:

It is more difficult under present law to bring a case attacking *existing* concentration in an industry than to prevent further concentrations which firms attempt to realize through merger.

But this we see is no minor qualification. If firms are already large—if concentration is already great—if the resulting power, to use Mr. Turner's own words, is not "merely marginal" but is "spread widely through the economy" as he says, then it means that all so favored have won immunity or virtual immunity from the antitrust laws. And this, of course, is the case.

Meanwhile, the antitrust laws are effective in two instances where the firms do not have market power but are seeking to achieve it. Where firms are few and large they can, without overt collusion, establish and maintain a price that is generally satisfactory to all participants. Nor is this an especially difficult calculation, this exercise of power. This is what we economists with our genius for the neat phrase have come to call oligopolistic rationality. And this market power is *legally immune* or very nearly so. It is everyday practice in autos, steel, rubber, and virtually every other industry shared or dominated by, relatively, a few large firms. But if there are 20 or 30 or more significant firms in the industry, this kind of tacit pricemaking—this calculation as to what is mutually advantageous but without overt communication—becomes more difficult, maybe very difficult. The same result can only be achieved by having a meeting or by exchanging information on prices and costs and price intentions. But this is illegal. It is also legally vulnerable. And it is, in fact, an everyday object of prosecution as the Department of Justice will confirm. *What the big firm in the concentrated industry can accomplish legally and effortlessly because of its size, the small firm in the unconcentrated industry does at the pain of civil and even criminal prosecution. Moreover, with this my colleagues will, I believe, agree.*

The second manifestation of the charade has to do with mergers. If a firm is *already* large, it has as a practical matter nothing to fear under antimerger provisions of the Clayton Act. It will not be demerged. It can continue to grow from its own earnings; if discreet, it can even, from time to time, pick up a small and impecunious competitor, for it can reasonably claim that this does little to alter the pattern of competition in the industry. But if two medium-sized firms unite in order to deal more effectively with this giant, the law will be on them like a tiger. Again if large, you are exempt. If you seek to become as large, or even if you seek to become somewhat larger, although still much smaller, you are in trouble.

Here we have the nature of modern antitrust activity. *It conducts a fairly effective war on small firms which seek the same market power that the big firms already, by their nature, possess.* Behind this impressive facade the big participants who have the most power bask in nearly total immunity. And since the competitive market, like God and a sound family life, is something that no sound businessman can actively oppose, even the smaller entrepreneurs who are the natural victims of this arrangement do not actively protest. It is possible that they do not know how they are being used.

My defense of bigness

As I say all of this is agreed—or at least is supported by the past writings and speeches of participants in this discussion. All I have done —I wish I could lay claim to greater novelty— is to state the rather disagreeable conclusion flowing from this agreement. The antitrust laws give the impression of protecting the market and competition by attacking those who exercise it most effectively. I wonder if the committee thinks that charade is an unjust word?

Now let me clear up two or three secondary matters which may seem to affect this discussion but really do not. The first requires me, I think for the first time—in substance as distinct from terminology—to quit company with Attorney General [sic] Turner. Mr. Turner, while conceding that the law is largely helpless in attacking achieved as distinct from aspired-to power, holds that it is important to act *preventatively* to keep smaller firms from getting larger. This he has emphasized in his responses to this committee. It will surely have occurred to the committee, as it must have occurred to Mr. Turner, that this does not meet the issue of gross discrimination as between those who already have and those who aspire to market power. Nor, one imagines, can a major law officer of the Government be entirely happy about such discrimination. It condones professional and accomplished wrongdoing, as it were, but stresses the importance of cracking down on amateur wickedness. Surely this is bad law. Also, given the size and market power that has already been achieved, and given its immunity, it will be evident that

this justification amounts to locking the stable door not alone after the horse has been stolen but after the entire stud has been galloped away.

Next, I must correct a misapprehension of Attorney General Turner. His responses to the committee and his extremely interesting lecture attacking my general position in London convey the impression that I am concerned with making the economic case for the large corporation. I am, he suggests, especially concerned to defend its efficiency and technical virtuosity. To this he responds by arguing that, while the big corporation is more efficient than the small firm, there is no great difference between the big corporation and the giant corporation. He doesn't make altogether clear, incidentally, how big a big as distinct from a giant corporation is. All would, I imagine, be among the five hundred or thousand firms that dominate industrial activity. But I have a more fundamental objection. He attacks me on a point that concerns me little and which is of no importance for my case.

I am not concerned with making the case for big business. Nor am I especially concerned about its efficiency or inefficiency. Doubtless efficiency is worth having. But, like truth, regular bathing and better traffic regulation, it has an adequate number of exponents. I have always thought it unwise to compete with the commonplace. Mr. Turner may be correct in his conclusions about the giants. I am content to argue that we have big business, and that the antitrust laws notwithstanding we will continue to have it, and that they give an impression of alternative possibilities that do not exist.

I conclude also that while big business and giant business may not be more efficient, their market power as manifested only on what they sell and what they buy and over buyers does *give them advantages in planning their own future and insuring their own survival.* Since big business is inevitable and will not be affected by the antitrust laws, I naturally go on to consider how we may come to terms with it. Much of my book is concerned with that. If my colleagues this morning disagree, as is their right, they must tell you how the antitrust laws are to be brought effectively to bear on the large corporation. Otherwise—and here let me interpolate an important point—there is no escape from the conclusion that the antitrust laws, so far from being a threat to business are a facade behind which it operates with yet greater impunity. They create the impression, the antitrust laws, that the market is a viable control. Then, if a drug firm has exorbitant profits, it can say this is what the market allows. Or if an automobile firm does not want to install safety appliances, it can say that the market does not demand it. Or if there is resistance to Government price guideposts to prevent inflation, it can be said that these interfere with the market.

In each case, the antitrust laws effectively protect the large business from social pressure or regulation by maintaining the myth that the market does the regulating instead.

Finally, I agree that the antitrust laws have purposes other than those related to the structure of industry and the resulting power and planning. I agree in particular they are a code of what is deemed fair and decent as between seller and buyers. They exclude the resort to activities—naked aggression, as in the case of the old Standard Oil Co. in the last century—based on superior economic resources, favoritism, surreptitious and unfair discounts, numerous other practices which the civilized commercial community holds in disesteem. I have no complaint about these aspects of the antitrust laws. On the contrary, I consider them serviceable. But only in the most marginal fashion do they thus affect the structure of industry. They are, in large part, a separate matter and do not affect the discussion here.

Put up or shut up

To what then does this all lead? It is possible that my distinguished colleagues here this morning will call for an all-out attack on achieved market power along the lines which Attorney General Turner has adumbrated in his book, which Prof. Walter Adams has long favored, and which I have just said would be necessary if they disagree with my conclusions on the inevitability of market power. This means action, including enabling legislation leading to all-out dissolution proceedings against General Motors, Ford, the oil majors, United States Steel, General Electric, IBM, Western Electric, Du Pont, Swift, Bethlehem, International Harvester, North American Aviation, Goodyear, Boeing, National Dairy Products, Procter & Gamble, Eastman Kodak, and all of comparable size and scope. For there

can be no doubt: All are giants. All have market power. All enjoy an *immunity* not accorded to those who merely aspire to their power. Such an onslaught, tantamount, given the role of the big firms in the economy as I described it, to declaring the heartland of the modern economy illegal, would go far to make legitimate the objections to my position. It would mean that achieved market power was subject to the same legal attack as that which is only a matter of aspiration.

But I will be a trifle surprised if my distinguished colleagues from the Government are willing to proclaim such a crusade. I am frank to say I would not favor it myself; as I indicated at the outset, I do not think that the growth of the modern corporation can be isolated from other and intricately related changes in modern economic development. I doubt that one can operate on one part of this fabric. The political problems in proclaiming much of the modern economy illegal will also strike many as impressive.

If this crusade is not to be launched, then my good friends have no alternative but to agree with me. They are good men; they cannot acquiesce in a policy which by their own admission attacks the small man for seeking what the big firm enjoys with impunity.

The great myth

I readily concede that it would be quixotic to ask the repeal of the antitrust laws although other industrial countries function quite competently without them. But the antitrust laws are part of the American folklore: They receive strong support from the legal profession and vice versa. They have a reserve value for dealing with extreme and sanguinary abuse of power as occasionally occurs. I would be content were we simply to withdraw our faith from the antitrust laws—were we to cease to imagine that there is any chance that they will affect the structure of American industry or its market power and, having in mind the present discrimination in their application, were we then to allow them quietly to atrophy. Then we would face the real problem, which is how to live with the vast organizations—and the values they impose—that we have and will continue to have. This being so, nostalgia will no longer be a disguise for that necessity.

Reading 47

Galbraith Wrong, in Fact and Policy

Walter Adams

Time precludes more than a cursory tribute to an eminently civilized and literate political economist—a leader in that small but brave army of men who "prefer to see the truth imperfectly and obscurely rather than to maintain error, reached indeed with clearness and consistency and by easy logic, but based on hypotheses inappropriate to the facts." It is Galbraith's cardinal virtue to focus on real problems and vital issues. His questions are invariably to the point. Regrettably, his answers are sometimes wrong.

In *The New Industrial State,* Galbraith once again examines the reality of corporate giantism and corporate power, and outlines the implications for public policy. He finds that the giant corporation has achieved such dominance of American industry, that *it can control its environment and immunize itself from the discipline of all exogenous control mechanisms—especially the competitive market.* Through separation of ownership from management it has emancipated itself from the control of stockholders. By reinvestment of profits (internal financing), it has eliminated the influence of the financier and the capital market. By *brainwashing* its clientele, it has insulated itself from consumer sovereignty. By possession of market power, it has come to dominate both suppliers and customers. By *judicious identification with, and manipulation of the state,* it has achieved autonomy from government control. Whatever it cannot do for itself to assure survival and growth, a compliant government does on its behalf—assuring the maintenance of full employment; eliminating the risk of, and subsidizing the investment in, research and development; and assuring the supply of scientific and technical skills required by the modern technostructure.

In return for this privileged autonomy, *the industrial giant performs society's planning function.* And this, according to Galbraith, is not only inevitable (because technological imperatives dictate it); it is also good. The

market is dead, we are told; and there is no need to regret its passing. The only remaining task, it seems, is to recognize the trend, to accept it as inexorable necessity, and, presumably, not to stand in its way.

Mr. Chairman, here is a blueprint for technocracy, private socialism, and the corporate state. The keystone of the new power structure is the giant corporation, freed from all traditional checks and balances, and subject only to the countervailing power of the intellectual in politics—those Platonic philosopher-kings who stand guard over the interests of the Republic. Happily, this blueprint need not cause undue alarm: first, because *Galbraith's analysis rests on an empirically unsubstantiated premise;* and second, even if this analysis were correct, *there would be more attractive public policy alternatives than Galbraith suggests.*

Galbraith's contention that corporate giantism dominates American industry requires no adumbration. On that there is consensus. But Galbraith fails to prove that this dominance is the inevitable response to technological imperatives, and hence beyond our control. Specifically, he offers little evidence to demonstrate that Brobdingnagian size is the prerequisite for, and the guarantor of—

1. operational efficiency
2. invention, innovation, and technological progress
3. effective planning in the public interest

Let me comment briefly on each of these points, and in so doing indicate that the competitive market need not be condemned to the euthanasia which Galbraith thinks is inexorable, and perhaps even desirable.

Bigness not efficient

In the mass-production industries, firms must undoubtedly be large, but do they need to

From U.S. Senate, 90th Congress, 1st Session, Hearing before Subcommittees of the Select Committee on Small Business, June 29, 1967.

assume the dinosaur proportions of some present-day giants? The unit of technological efficiency is the plant, not the firm. This means that there are undisputed advantages to large-scale integrated operations at a single steel plant, for example, but *there is little technological justification for combining these functionally separate plants into a single administrative unit*. United States Steel is nothing more than several Inland Steels strewn about the country, and no one has yet suggested that Inland is not big enough to be efficient. A firm producing such divergent lines as rubber boots, chain saws, motorboats, and chicken feed may be seeking conglomerate size and power; it is certainly not responding to technological necessity. *In short, one can favor technological bigness and oppose administrative bigness without inconsistency.*

Two major empirical studies document this generalization. The first, by Dr. John M. Blair, indicates a significant divergence between plant and company concentration in major industries dominated by oligopoly. It indicates, moreover, that between 1947 and 1958, there was a general tendency for plant concentration to decline, which means that in many industries technology may actually militate toward optimal efficiency in plants of "smaller" size.

The second study, by Professor Joe Bain, presents engineering estimates of scale economies and capital requirements in 20 industries of above-average concentration. Bain finds that—

concentration by firms is in every case but one greater than required by single-plant economies, and in more than half of the cases very substantially greater.

In less precise language, many multiplant industrial giants have gone beyond the optimal size required for efficiency. Galbraith acknowledges the validity of Bain's findings, but dismisses them by saying:

The size of General Motors is in the service not of monopoly or the economies of scale, but of planning. And for this planning . . . there is no clear upper limit to the desirable size. It could be that the bigger the better.

If size is to be justified, then, this must be done on grounds other than efficiency. I shall return to this point in a moment.

The uninventive giants

As in the case of efficiency, there is no strict correlation between giantism and progressiveness. In a study of the 60 most important inventions of recent years, it was found that more than half came from independent inventors, less than half from corporate research, and even less from the research done by large concerns. Moreover, while some highly concentrated industries spend a large share of their income on research, others do not; within the same industry, some smaller firms spend as high a *percentage* as their larger rivals. As Wilcox points out:

The big concern has the ability to finance innovation; it does not necessarily do so. There is no clear relationship between size and investment in research.

Finally, as this committee well knows, roughly two-thirds of the research done in the United States is financed by the Federal Government, and in many cases the research contractor gets the patent rights on inventions paid for with public funds. The inventive genius which ostensibly goes with size would seem to involve socialization of risk and privatization of profit and power.

The U.S. steel industry, which ranks among the largest, most basic, and most concentrated of American industries, certainly part of the industrial state that Professor Galbraith speaks of, affords a dramatic case in point. It spends only 0.7 percent of its revenues on research and, in technological progressiveness, the giants which dominate this industry lag behind their smaller domestic rivals as well as their smaller foreign competitors. Thus, the basic oxygen furnace—considered the "only major breakthrough at the ingot level since before the turn of the century" was invented in 1950 by a miniscule Austrian *firm* which was less than one-third the size of a single *plant* of the United States Steel Corp. The innovation was introduced in the United States in 1954 by McLouth Steel which at the time had about 1 percent of domestic steel capacity—to be followed some 10 years later by the steel giants: United States Steel in December 1963, Bethlehem in 1964, and Republic in 1965. Despite the fact that this revolutionary invention involved an average operating cost saving of $5 per ton and an investment cost saving of $20 per ton of installed capacity, the steel giants during the 1950's according to Business Week, "bought 40 million tons of the wrong capacity—the open-hearth furnace" which was obsolete almost the moment it was put in place.

Only after they were subjected to actual and threatened competition from domestic and foreign steelmakers in the 1960's did the steel giants decide to accommodate themselves to the oxygen revolution. Thus, it was the cold wind of competition, and not the catatonia induced by industrial concentration, which proved conducive to innovation and technological progress.

Planning for whom?

Modern technology, says Galbraith, makes planning essential, and the giant corporation is its chosen instrument. This planning, in turn, requires the corporation to eliminate risk and uncertainty, to create for itself an environment of stability and security, and to free itself from all outside interference with its planning function. Thus, it must have enough size and power not only to produce a "mauve and cerise, air-conditioned, power-steered, and power-braked automobile"—unsafe at any speed—but also enough power to brainwash customers to buy it. In the interest of planning, producers must be able to sell what they make—be it automobiles or missiles—and at prices which the technostructure deems remunerative.

Aside from the unproved premise—and I keep coming back to this: technological necessity—on which this argument rests, it raises crucial questions of responsibility and accountability. By what standards do the industrial giants plan, and is there an automatic convergence between private and public advantage? Must we, as a matter of inexorable inevitability, accept the proposition that what is good for General Motors is good for the country? What are the safeguards—other than the intellectual in politics—against arbitrary abuse of power, capricious or faulty decision making? Must society legitimatize a self-sustaining, self-serving, self-justifying, and self-perpetuating industrial oligarchy as the price for industrial efficiency and progress?

This high price need not and should not be paid. The competitive market is a far more efficacious instrument for serving society—and far more viable—than Galbraith would have us believe. Let me illustrate:

1. In the electric power industry, a network of local monopolies, under Government regulation and protection, was long addicted to the belief that the demand for electric power was inelastic—that rates had little to do with the quantity of electricity used. It was not industrial planning, carried on by private monopolists under public supervision, but the yardstick competition of TVA which demonstrated the financial feasibility of aggressive rate reductions. It was this competitive experiment which proved that lower electric rates were not only possible but also profitable—both to the private monopolists and to the customers they served.

2. In the airline oligopoly, also operating under the umbrella of Government protectionism, the dominant firms long suffered from the same addiction. They refused to institute coach service on the grounds that it would eliminate first-class service and—through a reduction in the rate structure—bring financial ruin to the industry. Again it was the force and discipline of competition—from the small, nonscheduled carriers, operating at the margin of the industry—which proved that the giants and their overprotective public regulators were wrong. As this committee observed, it was the pioneering and competition of the nonskeds which "shattered the concept of the fixed, limited market for civil aviation. As a result, the question is no longer what portion of a fixed pie any company will get, but rather how much the entire pie can grow."

Again, a bureaucracy-ridden, conservative, overcautious, overprotected industry was shown to have engaged in defective planning—to its own detriment as well as the public's.

3. In the steel industry, after World War II, oligopoly planning resulted in truly shabby performance. There was an almost unbroken climb in steel prices, in good times and bad, in the face of rising or falling demand, increasing or declining unit costs. Prices rose even when only 50 percent of the industry's capacity was utilized. Technological change was resisted and obsolete capacity installed. Domestic mar-

kets were eroded by substitute materials and burgeoning imports. Steel's export-import balance deteriorated both in absolute and relative terms; whereas the industry once exported about five times as much as it imported, the ratio today is almost exactly reversed, and steel exports are confined almost exclusively to AID-financed sales guaranteed by "Buy American" provisos. We may be confident that if this deplorable performance is to be improved, it will come about through the disciplining force of domestic and foreign competition, and not through additional planning or an escalation of giant size. It will come about through an accommodation to the exigencies of the world market, and not by insensitive monopolist pricing, practiced under the protectionist shelter of the tariffs which the industry now seeks.

Without multiplying such examples, it is safe to say that *monopoloid planning is done in the interest of monopoly power. Seldom, if ever, is society the beneficiary.*

Verdict against

In conclusion, I would note that industrial giantism in America is not the product of spontaneous generation, natural selection, or technological inevitability. In this era of "Big Government," it is often the end result of unwise, manmade, discriminatory, privilege-creating governmental action. Defense contracts, R. & D. support, patent policy, tax privileges, stockpiling arrangements, tariffs, subsidies, etc., have far from a neutral effect on our industrial structure. Especially in the regulated industries—in air and surface transportation, in broadcasting and communications—the writ of the State is decisive. In controlling

these variables the policy maker has greater freedom and flexibility than is commonly supposed; the potential for promoting competition and dispersing industrial power is both real and practicable.

It seems to me that Professor Galbraith keeps coming back to the charade of antitrust, but a competitive society is the product not simply of negative enforcement of the antitrust laws; it is the product of a total integrated approach on all levels of government—legislative, administrative, and regulatory. An integrated national policy of promoting competition—and this means more than mere enforcement of the antitrust laws—is not only feasible but desirable. No economy can function without built-in checks and balances which tend to break down the bureaucratic preference for letting well enough alone—forces which erode, subvert, or render obsolete the conservative bias inherent in any organization devoid of competition. Be it the dictates of the competitive market, the pressure from imports or substitutes, or the discipline of yardstick competition, it is these forces which the policymaker must try to reinforce where they exist and to *build into* the economic system where they are lacking or moribund. The policy objective throughout must be to promote market *structures* which will *compel* the conduct and performance which is in the public interest.

The disciplining force of competition is superior to industrial planning—by the private or public monopolist, the benevolent or authoritarian bureaucrat. It alone provides the incentives and compulsions to pioneer untried trails, to explore paths which may lead to dead ends, to take risks which may not pay off, and to try to make tomorrow better than the best.

Reading 48

Antitrust Policy Still Vital

E. T. Grether

Professor Galbraith's *The New Industrial State* is another provocative, witty best seller in the tradition of his previous works. In review after review admiration is expressed for style, wit,

elegance and stimulation—and, typically, strong dissent as to much of the substance along with complaints of factual gaps and lacks. *The New Industrial State* can be viewed from many

From E. T. Grether, "Galbraith Versus the Market: A Review Article," *Journal of Marketing*, vol. 32, January, 1968, pp. 9–13. Reprinted with kind permission of the author and publisher.

vantage points. My vantage point will be that of markets and marketing in Galbraith's analysis.

Summary of Galbraith-land

Galbraith, like Berle, is concerned with the "world of the great corporation" which he defines as "The Industrial System." He visualizes this world as comprising about 50% of the economy in terms of the G.N.P., but much more than 50% in terms of role, impacts on social goals and politics, and visibility. His Industrial System is the "heartland" of our economy and contains the showpieces of our society. His ultimate concern is lest the economic goals and requirements of the powerful corporations in the heartland-industrial system dominate those of the state and of society. His hope and prediction are that the large, or as he calls it, "mature," corporation will eventually become part of the complex embracing both the Industrial System and the State where it will be "responsive to the larger purposes of society."

In a sense, Galbraith's fears about the possible dominance of the great corporation over society and its goals are similar to those of critics of the 19th Century market system. In Galbraith, the Industrial System of mature corporations has replaced the market and market system in modern industrial societies. Throughout this volume, as in his others, he heaps disdain on his professional colleagues for their disregard and lack of knowledge of the real world as opposed to the world of theoretical models. At the center of his disdain is the model of the self-regulating market economy.

In Galbraith, *planning has replaced or must replace the market* so far as The Industrial System is concerned. And this is, or must be so, in *all* modern industrial societies. Hence, he envisages the *convergence of industrial societies whether so-called capitalistic, socialistic, or communistic.* The basic unit is the mature corporation which must be large, organized, and autonomous. Size, organization, and autonomy *require* that the mature corporation be free of the market both in its inputs and in final product markets. Such a corporation at the input level increasingly develops its own internal sources of capital and of many other factor inputs. There is no suggestion, however,

of owned sources for labor-inputs, but the training of the labor and technical supply is done by the State for the corporations. In final product markets, *the mature corporation manages both specific demand and prices* while the State regulates aggregate demand for the benefit of all members of The Industrial System. Corporations have become so large and powerful and ownership so diffused that *they are no longer responsible to shareholders internally*[1] or to any external forces, especially the market.

Similarly, they have become so "organized" and complex and dependent upon advancing science and technology and specialized skills that no single individual is able to manage or control them. Instead, the dominant internal force arises out of the members of the so-called "technostructure" of professional experts who provide both the technical know-how and the basis of action through group decision-making. Within the corporation, as in society as a whole, group action increasingly replaces that of individuals.

In these processes, individuals develop difficult problems of motivation and of identification—especially the elite members of the technostructure. A basic outcome within the mature corporation, is to *shift the goals of the corporation from profit maximization*, the presumed required goal under the regulating market system, *toward growth and security*—chiefly because these goals serve the interests of the members of the technostructure. A further outcome is an endeavor to *identify the goals of the corporation with those of the society*, since the professional members of the technostructure are not profit seekers or takers. Galbraith's professed optimism for the long-run future of our society stems in large part from his belief that these well-educated, elite members of the technostructure and their counterparts in universities, research and scientific pursuits, and in government will ultimately insist upon social and aesthetic goals instead of insisting upon specifically economic goals. The mature corporation will be "autonomous," especially it will be free of "the market," but the "autonomy" will be exercised within a framework of unexplained social goals emerging out of the

[1] In agreement with the familiar Berle-Means thesis. But see the Goldston reading (p. 64) for persuasive counter arguments.

larger administrative complex associated with the State.

Markets and the market system

A quick and undoubtedly short count indicated that Galbraith used the term "market" 265 times in his volume, even though the members of his Industrial System are allegedly free of the market. The mature corporation allegedly is free from the market in two senses: first, the classical fictional one of static, general equilibrium analysis in the self-adjusting economy, and, second, the kind of basic force that this model is supposed to represent in western market societies. That is, Galbraith denies that the market performs a disciplinary, allocative, and regulative role in the world of the great mature corporation. Throughout his book he contrasts time and again the relationship of a Wisconsin dairy farmer to the market and that of a large corporation, such as General Motors. He grants that the market has a role in the other half of our economy but focuses attention only on the industrial heartland in which the market allegedly has lost its power.

Consequently, too, *Galbraith is scornful of antitrust endeavors to maintain or enhance competition.* Antitrust for him is largely a charade which protects the entrenched positions of mature corporations at the expense of smaller ones that are denied the opportunity to grow by merger, etc. Actually, in Galbraith's terms The Industrial System would eventually be comprised of a relatively small number (say 200 to 600) of highly integrated corporations which would have under their ownership, control, and management all functional aspects of production and marketing at all levels, including the factors of production. Such integrated corporations would become "little economies" or economic societies within the great society, or perhaps feudalistic blocs or baronies, according to one reviewer.

But there still would be the problems of relations as among the "mature" corporations and between them and their suppliers and customers and the remaining allegedly 50% of the economy. Presumably these relations would be through some form of market mechanism.

Clearly, Galbraith, probably with tongue in the cheek, with his concept of the "mature corporation" with its ill-defined autonomy, is *perpetrating the type of oversimplification* of

which he accuses the adherents of the self-adjusting market model. In fact, he admits this, for he states "there is no such thing as *a* corporation. Rather there are several kinds of corporations all deriving from a common but very loose framework. Some are subject to the market; others reflect varying degrees of adaptation to the requirements of planning and the needs of the technostructures." Further, he has put his best foot forward in terms of factual interpretation.

The issues and also differences in interpretation of the factual evidence were highlighted in a seminar discussion conducted by Senator Wayne Morse's subcommittee of the Select Committee on Small Business of the United States Senate on June 29, 1967. The participants were Galbraith, Professor Walter Adams, Dr. Willard F. Mueller, Chief Economist of the Federal Trade Commission, and the Honorable Donald F. Turner, Assistant Attorney General, Department of Justice. Galbraith contended that antitrust cannot and does not basically affect the structure of American industry. The other members of the seminar stressed that Galbraith's Industrial System is the source at most of only about 20%–25% of the national income instead of his alleged 50%. All of them defended antitrust and the efforts to maintain and enhance the areas of competitive regulation while admtting that there are many problems and problem areas that must require action by the State in relation to or outside the market system. They denied categorically that the market has lost its regulatory viability for most of the economy.

Galbraith's reply and continuing refrain was that antitrust will not and cannot bring actions for the all-out dissolution of General Motors and other great corporations. He finally asked Professor Adams bluntly, "Would you be in favor of breaking up General Motors and do you think it likely that General Motors will be broken up?" He answered his own question as follows: "You know as well as I do that nobody is going to break up General Motors and Ford and Standard Oil and duPont."

At issue in these polemics are the character and effectiveness of our antitrust policy to maintain and promote competition in our market system, especially in the area of Big Business. Most likely, Drs. Adams, Mueller, Turner, and many others, including this writer, will go along with Galbraith's condemnation of the overemphasis of the fictional model of the classical self-regulating market society in which the market system and economy were synonymous. But it does not follow that the market and market system in general have lost their regulatory and disciplinary force under current conditions. Galbraith's critics in the symposium do believe that competition under the market system is sufficiently effective, or can be made so, to be preferable to alternatives. Galbraith in *The New Industrial State* denies this in words that cannot be misunderstood; namely, "Only professional defenders of the free enterprise system, members of a lowly and poorly paid craft, still argue for the rule of competition."

Thus, Galbraith is squarely in opposition not only to professional antitrusters but to the Supreme Court of the United States in the Philadelphia Bank case in which it was stated: "Subject to narrow qualifications, it is surely the case that competition is our fundamental national economic policy, offering as it does the only alternative to the cartelization or governmental regimentation of large portions of the economy."

Galbraith is also in opposition to his own positions expressed in 1956 in the revised edition of *American Capitalism: The Concept of Countervailing Power*. In this instance he argued that the original market power of sellers tended to produce a self-generating countervailing power which supported the role of competition as a regulator ("the growth of countervailing power strengthens the capacity of the economy for autonomous self-regulation and thereby lessens the amount of overall government control or planning that is required.") In a discussion of the role of decentralized decision he concluded that "in a parliamentary democracy with a high standard of living there is no administratively acceptable alternative to the decision-making mechanism of capitalism." The exercise of private authority by the American businessman "is made tolerable by the restraints imposed by countervailing power and by competition."

In terms of time span, *The New Industrial State*, however, follows not *American Capitalism* of 1956 but *The Affluent Society* of 1958. In *The Affluent Society*, Galbraith endeavored to break the hold of economic ideas and attitudes forged in a world of poverty and substitute thinking and approaches appropriate to

a world of wealth and affluence. But he has not been able to make this transition himself so far as his view of the market and functioning of the market system are concerned. The market which he continually discards is the haloed classical model developed under and for the simpler conditions of an earlier period. He characterizes this period as a world of poverty because of low incomes and standards of living and the dominance of staple, homogeneous goods essential for subsistence with only a modicum of the comforts and luxuries characteristic of our period. It is admittedly a grievous mistake to approach and appraise the United States today in 19th Century terms, despite our great poverty areas.

But this brings us to the heart of the whole matter. There really *never* has been a truly self-adjusting market economy or a truly unregulated market. There has been and *always will be a continuing interaction between the regulation of markets by external forces including government and the discipline and "regulation" of the market itself.* All economies. capitalistic, socialistic, communistic, or mixed have and do rely upon market mechanisms for many diverse purposes, including communication, coordination, motivation, incentive, greater efficiency, the better adjustment of the production of goods to wants and desires, and especially the avoidance of a burdensome unduly-centralized governmental bureaucracy in favor of decentralized decision-making. In fact, as noted, the Galbraith of 1956 was thinking along these lines.

Probably the chief contribution of the reflective thinking behind *The Affluent Society* upon *The New Industrial State* was to sharpen and heighten his concern about the overemphasis of goods as such, and often, from his point of view, the wrong goods in contrast with the public services. That is, ultimately what is at stake for Galbraith are our basic social values and his *romantic* belief that these are determined very largely by Madison Avenue serving the mature corporation. Thus, "the further a man is removed from physical need the more open he is to persuasion—or management—as to what he buys. That is, perhaps, the most important consequence for economics of increasing affluence." And the persuasive influence of advertising and selling is so effective that specific demand is brought "under substantial control" and also "provides, in the aggregate a relentless propaganda on behalf of goods in general." Thus, *consumer sovereignty, and even limited consumer sovereignty, is denied,* and the so-called "marketing concept" of recent marketing literature represents merely self-serving rationalization for the rising importance of marketing management under declining market discipline.

But in the earlier *American Capitalism* Galbraith seemed to be much more relaxed about all of this. He chided his professional colleagues in the economics profession for their worries "about partially monopolized prices or excessive advertising and selling costs for tobacco, liquor, chocolates, automobiles, and soap in a land which is already suffering from nicotine poisoning and alcoholism . . . and which is dangerously neurotic about body odors." Economists, so he said, "have brought the mentality of nineteenth-century poverty to the analysis of twentieth-century opulence, . . . anything that denies the community additional goods and services, is the greatest of sins."

The next book?

Perhaps by now, it is already too late to influence the book that will follow *The New Industrial State.* It is not too much to hope, however, that it will assume that the fictional self-regulating all-encompassing market has been laid to rest. Along these lines, Galbraith might even be willing to join forces with intelligent, sophisticated antitrusters and Justices of the United States Supreme Court in a forthright endeavor to maintain an open-ended, viable, and competitive market system appropriate to our society of affluence and our changing mores.

Following the publication of Galbraith's *American Capitalism: The Concept of Countervailing Power,* Professor John Perry Miller of Yale interpreted the role of competition in the American scene. He discarded both the model of perfect or pure competition and that of self-interest *spontaneously* inducing rivalry which narrowly circumscribes power. Then he went on to say:

But if we mean a carefully contrived system which facilitates the process of innovation and adaptation through time, in which individual self-interest is given wide play in a carefully structured field, in which the opportunity for initiative and the level of initiative are high, in which there is a constant striving to add to the body of knowledge and resources, in which the system of communication of economic information is operating well, and in which the market positions of firms is consequently insecure, then I believe competition is an important element in the contemporary American economy. Competition in this sense is a complex process of many dimensions.[2]

Competition so interpreted can provide the basic force and mechanism through the general market system and appropriate governmental regulation for linking Galbraith's *Industrial System* with the other 75% of our economic society. As an open-ended flexible system it will continue to be responsive to social values and social goals, and it can be made even more responsive. The members of Galbraith's *Industrial System* in such an environment should also be more responsive and socially responsible than they would be in the great *State-Industrial System Complex.* Often *the appropriate solution might well be the shared rule of competition and of special governmental regulation or jurisprudence.* Galbraith is critical of the avoidance of seeing *The Industrial System* as a whole, or as a system. He tries to beat critics to the punch by stating, "it will be urged, of course, that the industrial system is not the whole economy . . . all this I concede. And this part of the economy is not insignificant. It is not, however, the part of the economy with which this book is concerned. It has been concerned with the world of the large corporation . . . and it is more deeply characteristic of the modern industrial scene than the dog laundry or the small manufacturer with a large idea."

The true issue is whether the small manufacturer with a large idea and say, General Motors, can live together in the same world. Much of sophisticated antitrust enforcement is intended to guarantee this outcome.

[2] John Perry Miller, "Competition and Countervailing Power: Their Roles in the American Economy," *American Economic Review,* Vol. XLIV (May, 1954), p. 22.

Distribution of Income 4

The Nation's Production Function

Reading 49

Output depends on labor, land, and capital—as determined by technical knowledge. Pessimists think economic growth cannot be stimulated. Uninformed optimists go to the other extreme and talk of long-term U.S. growth rates of 5, 6, and even larger percentages per annum.

Dr. Edward F. Denison, now of the Brookings Institution, formerly served as economist for the U.S. Department of Commerce and the Committee for Economic Development. He estimates numerically the realistic growth goals suggested by our historical experiences.

Questions to Guide the Reading

Do you agree that a country which starts out from a position of much unemployment and unused capacity can be made initially to grow at a much faster rate than it can permanently grow once it has achieved (and maintains) full employment?

How fast can manpower grow? Land acreage? Capital goods? What are likely limits on technical change?

Sources of United States Economic Growth

Edward F. Denison

It is absolutely essential to distinguish between the growth of the nation's "potential" production, its ability or capacity to produce marketable goods and services, and changes in the ratio of actual production to "potential" production. The growth of potential production depends on changes in the quantity and quality of available labor and capital, the advance of knowledge, and similar factors, while the ratio of actual to potential production is governed mainly by the relationship between aggregate demand and potential production.

The fact that the growth of actual national product since 1956 or 1957 has fallen short of our average past record stems from the partial failure of United States business cycle or economic stabilization policy, not in policies affecting the growth of our productive potential. Since 1956 or 1957 our ability to produce has increased at least as fast as it did, on the average, in the past. Moreover, it is now clear that this failure is not related in significant degree to any change in the rate of technological progress or any structural change in the economy. It is a failure in meeting the old problem of equating changes in aggregate demand with changes in productive potential and unit costs. I am convinced that, given appropriate fiscal and monetary policy, the maintenance of high employment need not be made more difficult in this country by the rate at which productive potential advances; rather, if there is any connection, rapid growth of output per man eases the problem by allowing a more rapid advance of wage rates without inflation.

We should move vigorously to reduce unemployment and use our productive capacity fully, and to continue to do so in the future. The loss of income and other costs imposed upon those unemployed or working short hours, upon proprietors and others dependent on profits, is ample reason to do so. The main

From "United States Economic Growth" by Edward F. Denison, *Journal of Business*, Vol. XXXV, No. 2, April, 1962. Reprinted with kind permission of the author and publisher, The University of Chicago Press. Copyright 1962 by the University of Chicago. All rights reserved. Published January, April, October, 1962.

tools open to the federal government are fiscal and monetary policy, and I believe they are adequate.

Past growth

What are the sources of our past growth? From 1929 to 1957 the real national income or product increased at an average annual rate of 2.93 percent. I have tried to break this rate down among its sources. The results, shown in Table 1, are rough estimates, and their derivation required some strong assumptions, but I think they provide correct perspective.

The table distinguishes broadly between the contribution of increases in factor inputs and increases in output per unit of input. To derive the former, I start (in the left-hand columns of Table 1) with estimates of the share breakdown of the national income. I estimate that in the 1929–57 period, the earnings of labor (including the labor of proprietors) represented 73 percent of the national income; earnings of land, 4.5 percent; and earnings of reproducible capital, 22.5 percent. The last amount is divided in the table among types of capital.

The center section of the table provides estimates of the rate at which the various factor inputs increased, computed from indexes of their amount. The most familiar number here is that shown for employment on line 7. The series used, the Office of Business Economics estimates of persons engaged in production, increased at an average annual rate of 1.31 percent from 1929 to 1957. Over the same period, as shown on line 9, annual hours of work declined at an average rate of 0.73 percent a year. All the other entries under labor represent an attempt to adjust for changes in its quality.

The quantity of *land* available for use did not change during the period considered and, therefore, appears with a zero growth rate in line 14.

More and better capital

Capital input, which is restricted to privately owned capital, is measured in five parts. Input of structures and equipment other than residences is shown in line 17 to have increased at an average annual rate of 1.85 percent, much less than the national product.

Line 16 and lines 18–20 measure the growth rates of the deflated value of the gross stock of residences, of the deflated value of inventories, of the deflated value of United States owned investments abroad, and of foreign-owned investments in the United States.

The right side of the table gives the number of percentage points in the total growth rate that I estimate was contributed by each source of growth. Except for three small refinements, the upper portion of the right side of Table 1, referring to the increase in inputs, could be derived from the left and center sections by simple multiplication.

Most of the possible sources considered do not appear in the table at all, either because they appeared not to have changed over the period or because their effect on the growth rate was calculated at less than 0.01. In a few cases it was impossible to decide whether changes were favorable or unfavorable to growth. Also, some changes that might affect a "truer" measure of national income or product do not affect the national product as it is actually measured.

Various private and governmental restrictions prevent the optimum allocation and most efficient use of resources. Most did not change appreciably over the period, but some cost us more output in 1957 than in 1929. I estimate that they subtracted 0.07 points from the growth rate over that period, as shown in line 22. Line 23 refers to the fact, or what I believe to be the fact, that labor nominally employed but ineffectively utilized in agriculture was a smaller fraction of all labor, though a larger fraction of farm labor, in 1957 than in 1929. Line 24 arises because, even after eliminating excessive resources from the computation, resources in agriculture earned less than resources of equal quality in the rest of the economy in the base year of the real product estimates, 1954, because they were in oversupply. The shift out of agriculture thus contributed to a statistical rise in the national product estimated at 0.05 points in the growth rate.

Skip now to the last line, economies of scale associated with the growth of the national market. In the absence of any satisfactory procedure to arrive at a figure statistically, my effort here was to set down a number representing a sort of norm of expert opinion. I assume—and this is the third major assumption

Table 1   Sources of Growth of Real National Income

Line	Source of growth	Share of national income (percent distribution)		Growth rates (percent per year)		Contribution to growth rate of real national income (percentage points)	
		1909–29	1929–57	1909–29	1929–57	1909–29	1929–57
1	Real national income	100.0	100.0[1]	2.82[2]	2.93	2.82[2]	2.93
2	Increase in total inputs, adjusted	—	—	2.24	1.99	2.26	2.00
3	Adjustment	—	—	−0.09	−0.11	—	—
4	Increase in total inputs, unadjusted	—	—	2.33	2.10	—	—
5	Labor, adjusted for quality change	68.9	73.0	2.30	2.16	1.53	1.57
6	Employment and hours	—	—	1.62	1.08	1.11	0.80
7	Employment	—	—	1.58	1.31	1.11	1.00
8	Effect of shorter hours on quality of a man-year's work	—	—	0.03	−0.23	0.00	−0.20
9	Annual hours	—	—	−0.34	−0.73	−0.23	−0.53
10	Effect of shorter hours on quality of a man-hour's work	—	—	0.38	0.50	0.23	0.33
11	Education	—	—	0.56	0.93	0.35	0.67
12	Increased experience and better utilization of women workers	—	—	0.10	0.15	0.06	0.11
13	Changes in age-sex composition of labor force	—	—	0.01	−0.01	0.01	−0.01
14	Land	7.7	4.5	0.00	0.00	0.00	0.00
15	Capital	23.4	22.5	3.16	1.88	0.73	0.43
16	Nonfarm residential structures	3.7	3.1	3.49	1.46	0.13	0.05
17	Other structures and equipment	14.6	15.0	2.93	1.85	0.41	0.28
18	Inventories	4.8	3.9	3.31	1.90	0.16	0.08
19	United States owned assets abroad	0.6	0.7	4.20	1.97	0.02	0.02
20	Foreign assets in United States (an offset)	0.3	0.2	−1.85	1.37	0.01	0.00
21	Increase in output per unit of input	—	—	0.56	0.92	0.56	0.93
22	Restrictions against optimum use of resources	—	—	—	—	[3]	−0.07
23	Reduced waste of labor in agriculture	—	—	—	—	[3]	0.02
24	Industry shift from agriculture	—	—	—	—	[3]	0.05
25	Advance of knowledge	—	—	—	—	[3]	0.58
26	Change in lag in application of knowledge	—	—	—	—	[3]	0.01
27	Economies of scale—independent growth of local markets	—	—	—	—	[3]	0.07
28	Economies of scale—growth of national market	—	—	—	—	0.28	0.27

[1] For 1930–40 and 1942–46, interpolated distributions rather than the actual distributions for these dates were used. Estimates are 1929–58 averages.
[2] This rate, like that for 1929–57, derives from Department of Commerce estimates. Estimates by John W. Kendrick, based on adjustment to Department of Commerce concepts of estimates by Simon Kuznets, yield a growth rate of 3.17, which would result in a figure for output per unit of input (line 21) of 0.91.
[3] Not estimated.

of the study—that in the 1929–57 period, economies of scale added 10 percent to the increment to output that would otherwise be provided by all other sources. Consequently, I allocate one-eleventh of the total growth rate in the 1929–57 period, or 0.27 percentage points, to this source. I use a slightly higher fraction in the earlier period since economies of scale presumably decline as the size of the economy increases.

Much, probably most, of this contribution, of course, is the result of the expansion of local and regional markets that automatically accompanies the growth of the national economy. In addition, however, local markets grew independently as a result of increasing concentration of population and especially of the adaptation of the trade and service industries to the general ownership of automobiles. The contribution of this independent development is represented in line 27.

Invention and technical productivity

Finally, we come to the contribution to growth of the advance of knowledge and the speed with which it is incorporated into production. I believe that, as indicated in line 26, the change in the lag of the average practice behind the best known was of negligible importance.

The estimate in line 25 for the contribution of the advance of knowledge is obtained as a residual, and has the usual weakness of a residual. It is intended to measure the contribution to the growth rate of the advance of knowledge of all types relevant to production, including both managerial and technological knowledge. Many will find the contribution of 0.58 percentage points, or 20 percent, of the total 1929–57 growth rate that I attribute to the advance of knowledge surprisingly small.

If expectation of a larger figure is based on previous studies, there is no basis for surprise. The term "technological progress" has often been applied to all the sources of growth except changes in man-hours, land, and capital. That definition would embrace everything in Table 1 except lines 7, 9, 14, and 15. These accounted for only three-tenths of the growth rate, so my estimates would leave seven-tenths of total growth for attribution to "technological

progress" if that broad definition were used. If the calculation were confined to the private economy, the fraction would be still larger. The main object of these calculations has been to divide up the contribution to growth of what has been vaguely termed technological progress.

Nevertheless, the figure for the contribution of knowledge is rather small even if expectations are based on a priori observation. The explanation is that much of what usually is thought of as the fruits of technological progress is simply not caught in the growth rate of the national product as measured because of the character of the price indexes used in deflation.

In general, the advance of knowledge can contribute to the measured growth rate only by reducing production costs for already existing final products, or through improvements in business organization at levels other than those serving the final purchaser.

Once these characteristics of the output measure are understood, it is not, I think, surprising that the contribution of the advance of knowledge to the measured growth rate is not larger.

Summary of past growth

Space limitations prohibit extended discussion of the results of this part of the study, but the table speaks for itself. In summary, from 1929 to 1957 five sources contributed an amount equal to 101 percent of the growth rate, out of a total of 109 percent contributed by all sources making a positive contribution. These were: increased employment (34 percent); increased education (23 percent); increased capital input (15 percent); the advance of knowledge (20 percent); and economies of scale associated with the growth of the national market (9 percent). The reduction of working hours accounted for −7 percent of the total "contribution" of −9 percent to the growth rate provided by sources adverse to growth, and increased restrictions against the optimum use of resources for the remainder.

The breakdown in the 1909–29 period was, of course, different. Increases in capital and in employment contributed more than in the period after 1929, and improvements in the quality of the labor force, much less.

But whatever period we examine, it is clear that economic growth, occurring within the general institutional setting of a democratic, largely free-enterprise society, has stemmed and will stem mainly from an increased labor force, more education, more capital, and the advance of knowledge, with economies of scale exercising an important, but essentially passive, reinforcing influence. Since 1929 the shortening of working hours has exercised an increasingly restrictive influence on the growth of output.

Future rate of growth

The second question is: *What rate of growth can we reasonably anticipate in the future?* Opinions on this vary, as they must, because the future is inherently uncertain. My own projection, derived by summing estimates of the contribution anticipated from each of the sources affecting past growth, is that if we are reasonably successful in maintaining high employment, avoid a major war, and otherwise maintain existing policies and conditions in fields affecting growth importantly, we can look forward to a growth rate in our productive potential of 3.33 percent over the period from 1960 to 1980. The rate is about 3.5 percent if we start the calculation from the recession-reduced actual national product in 1960 and assume 1980 will be a prosperous year. The 3.33 percent rate for productive potential is almost one-seventh above the actual rate from 1929 to 1957. It implies an average annual percentage increase in potential output per person employed of 1.62 percent per year, just slightly above that experienced from 1929 to 1957, and of 2.17 in output per man-hour.

The third question is: *Will the projected growth rate be high enough?* This obviously cannot be answered without establishing criteria, which I shall not attempt, but three things can be said.

First, the growth rate projected would yield a large improvement in living standards unless the proportion of output required for defense increases enormously. If the fraction of national product devoted to consumption does not change, per capita consumption in 1980 would be above 1960 by 38–46 percent on the basis of the two middle population projections of the Census Bureau.

Second, if it should be considered necessary or desirable to increase expenditures for defense and other essential public purposes, they could be doubled in twenty years without changing the proportion of national product they absorb, and by changing the proportion such expenditures could be enormously increased while still allowing a sizable advance in living standards.

Third, a growth rate of 3.33 or 3.5 percent is not likely to win any statistical growth race with the Soviet Union or any other industrial country that is presently substantially behind us in productivity and that has established institutional conditions equally favorable to growth. Mainly this is because the possibilities open to us of quick gains by imitation are so much more limited. Whether a statistical growth race is important to impress world opinion is a matter of dispute. But for us to accept a challenge for a growth-rate race with Russia or Japan would be as sensible as for Roger Bannister, the day he ran the four-minute mile, to have wagered a promising high-school sophomore on which of them could reduce his best time by the larger percentage.

Policy implications

I come now to the last and most interesting of the four questions that I shall consider. *Should we try to change the future growth rate, and if so what courses are open to us?*

This is a real and legitimate issue. A large national product in the future is desirable, but measures to raise the growth rate significantly involve costs. Certainly, a democratic society is *entitled* to make a collective decision to use the instruments of government and other institutions to promote rapid growth, and there are many steps that might be taken. But to say that a democratic society *can* decide to accelerate growth is not the same as to say that it would be wise for it to do so. If such a decision is to represent a rational choice, it must be based on a comparison of the benefits with the costs that are imposed.

What choices are open to us if we wish to raise the growth rate over the next twenty years above what it would otherwise be? I shall indicate what I conclude would be necessary to raise the growth rate by 0.1 percentage point, as from 3.3 to 3.4 percent. Such a change would yield a national product in 1980 higher than otherwise by about 2 percent or $20 billion. Put the other way around, to change the growth rate over the next twenty years by 0.1 of a percentage point requires some action that will make the 1980 national product 2 percent larger than it would be in the absence of that action.

This requires that we increase either the quantity or quality of the total input of labor, land, and capital into the productive system or else increase its productivity.

To raise the national product 2 percent by increasing inputs would require slightly less than a 2 percent increase in total inputs because of the existence of economies of scale. I estimate total input in 1980 would have to be increased about 1.83 percent. One way to do this would be to increase all kinds of input by 1.83 percent. The other would be to increase only one kind of input by a larger percentage. I estimate that in 1954–58 labor comprised 77 percent of total input, capital 20 percent, and land 3 percent. It follows that we could raise *total* input by 1.83 percent in 1980 if we could raise labor input alone by 2.4 percent over what it would otherwise be, or capital input alone by 9.3 percent, or land alone by 61.0 percent.

Suppose we wish to add 0.1 to the growth rate by increasing the quantity or the average quality of *labor* input in 1980 by 2.4 percent, over and above what it would otherwise be. This could be done if we wished, and could find ways to achieve any of the following changes:

Prevent half the deaths that will otherwise occur from 1960 to 1980 among individuals less than sixty-five years of age; or

Cut in half time lost from work because of sickness and accidents; or

Draw into the labor force one-tenth of all ablebodied persons over twenty years of age who will not otherwise be working in 1980; or

Double the rate of net immigration over the next twenty years; or

Operate with a work week one hour longer than otherwise; or

Eliminate two-thirds of the loss of work resulting from seasonal fluctuations in non-farm production; or

Reduce cyclical unemployment below what it

would be otherwise by 2 percent of the labor force—an impossibility unless the total unemployment rate would otherwise be above 4 percent; or

Add one and a half years to the average time that would otherwise be spent in school by everyone completing school between now and 1980, or make an equivalent improvement in the quality of education.

To raise the growth rate one-tenth of a percentage point by increasing the *capital stock* more rapidly would require devoting an additional 1 percent of the national income to net saving and investment throughout the next twenty years. This would be an increase of about one-sixth in the nation's net saving rate.

To increase *land* input offers no significant possibilities.

The alternative to increasing the quantity or quality of inputs is to increase productivity by accelerating the advance of knowledge or the efficiency with which the economy works. One important source of increase in productivity, the economies of scale that occur when the economy grows for other reasons, cannot be affected directly. I have taken it into account in estimating the yield from increasing inputs, and will also do so in examining other ways of increasing productivity. Let us consider the others.

My projection assumes the advance of knowledge will contribute 0.8 to the 1960–80 growth rate, more than in 1929–57. We could thus add 0.1 to the growth rate if we could raise by one-eighth the rate at which knowledge relevant to production advances. But many discoveries and inventions originate abroad, and many are not the result of deliberate research. On possible assumptions, we would have to increase by one-half the annual increment to knowledge that originates in the United States and is subject to being affected by deliberate action.

We could also add 0.1 to the growth rate over the next twenty years if we could reduce the lag of average production practices behind the best known by two and two-thirds years, in addition to any reduction that would otherwise take place. This would be a huge reduction in the world's most advanced country.

There are a number of smaller possibilities

which we could combine to add 0.1 to the growth rate.

Thus, we might eliminate all the misallocation and wasteful use of resources that results from barriers to international trade (which I estimate costs us 1.5 percent of the national income) *and* misallocation resulting from private monopoly in markets for products.

Or we might eliminate state resale price maintenance laws *and* racial discrimination in hiring. (I estimate these cost us 1 percent and 0.8 percent of the national income, respectively.)

Or we might shift to other uses of resources going into the production of unwanted or little-wanted farm products *and* also eliminate unemployment and underemployment resulting from long-term declines in individual industries and areas by re-employing workers immediately upon their becoming surplus.

Or we might eliminate all formal obstacles imposed by labor unions against use of the most efficient production practices *and* also consolidate local school districts and firms in regulated industries, particularly the railroads, wherever this would reduce unit costs.

There are, of course, other possibilities but they appear small.

Doubts and debits

It is not at all clear that we know *how* to do some of these things; and even where we do, they involve costs. Some, such as those leading to more investment in private or public capital, or to a faster rate of advance in knowledge through more research, require that the nation consume less than it otherwise could. Others, such as diversion of resources to provide more education or better medical care, which are classified as consumption in the national product, require that the nation consume less in other forms. Still others, such as longer hours of work or enlargement of the labor force, require that more work be done. Except for increasing immigration, all of the changes that would permanently raise the growth rate by any considerable amount impose costs of one of these types.

Costs of this kind are not imposed by changes that would make the economy operate more efficiently with given resources and given

knowledge. Also, the means by which such changes could be brought about are frequently obvious, often simply requiring the repeal of existing laws that prevent the best allocation and use of resources. From a broad standpoint, such changes consequently are particularly attractive, even though their possible stimulus to long-term growth is temporary and rather small. Even these, however, require some real or imagined sacrifice on the part of some members of society. Were it not so, these changes would already have been made.

Decisions on whether or not to try to affect the growth rate by any of the means I have suggested cannot sensibly be made without full consideration of their costs.

Almost any policy to affect growth also has other consequences. Some of these consequences, such as improvement of health, or a better educated citizenry, will be widely accepted as desirable. Others, especially any appreciable sacrifice of individual freedoms, will be as widely regarded as undesirable. Still others, including notably changes in the distribution of income, will be regarded as desirable by some individuals and undesirable by others. Among all the policies that might be adopted that would affect growth, there are few indeed where the effect on growth is, or should be, the primary consideration in their appraisal.

A serious effort to stimulate growth significantly would not, in my opinion, concentrate on one or two approaches but would be broadly based. This view is reinforced in the case of steps to increase factor inputs by the phenomenon of diminishing returns. Large increases in either labor or capital input, but especially the latter, without increases in the other, would yield a proportional increase in the growth rate smaller than is implied by calculations used to arrive at the results I have just presented.

If there is one point to be stressed above all, it is that faster growth is not a free good, not something that can be achieved by wishing or by speeches. To change the growth rate requires that something be done differently, and this entails costs in every significant case. Whether the gain is worth the cost can be judged only by careful consideration of each particular proposal.

Land Rent

Reading 50

What accounts for the share of income going to the use of land? One classic answer to this question came from one of the towering figures in the history of economic thought, David Ricardo (1772–1823). Son of a merchant-banker and himself a phenomenal success in business and the stock market, Ricardo brought a gloomier view to British economics than his predecessor, Adam Smith, had done.

   This brief excerpt offers the fundamental logic of Ricardo's answer to the rent question. In this view, rent is the return paid to the landlord for the original, indestructible powers of the soil. Land is fixed in quantity, but varies in quality, since the less productive land is brought into use by an expanding population, and extra return necessarily accrues from farming on the best lands. This extra return goes not to the laborer, nor to the capitalists, but rather to the landlords who are the beneficiaries of the land distribution system.

   The argument here is historically important for two reasons. It gave rise to the school of thought, most often associated with Henry George in the United States, that wanted to place all of society's taxes on the landlords to offset their gains from rent. And it represented an early model of abstract, elegant, but somewhat difficult reasoning in economics.

Questions to Guide the Reading

How does the concept of rent here compare with the current usage of the term when a tenant pays rent to his landlord or a driver rents a car from an agency?

Building on the Ricardian argument, followers of Henry George argue that taxes placed on land to recover for society the extra returns from more desirable land will not have a disincentive effect. A man cannot, for example, withdraw his land from the market without suffering zero returns. Is this argument valid, and does it support the wisdom of moving to heavier reliance on land taxes today rather than on buildings, machinery, or labor?

On Rent

David Ricardo

Definition

Rent is that portion of the produce of the earth, which is paid to the landlord for the use of the original and indestructible powers of the soil.

   It is often, however, confounded with the interest and profit of capital and, in popular language, the term is applied to whatever is annually paid by a farmer to his landlord. If, of two adjoining farms of the same extent, and of the same natural fertility, one had all the conveniences of farming buildings, and, besides, were properly drained and manured, and advantageously divided by hedges, fences, and walls, while the other had none of these

From David Ricardo, *Principles of Political Economy and Taxation* (George Bell and Sons, London, 1891, 3d edition).

advantages, more remuneration would naturally be paid for the use of one, than for the use of the other; yet in both cases this remuneration would be called rent. But it is evident, that a portion only of the money annually to be paid for the improved farm, would be given for the original and indestructible powers of the soil; the other portion would be paid for the use of the capital which had been employed in ameliorating the quality of the land, and in erecting buildings. In the future, then, whenever I speak of the rent of land, I wish to be understood as speaking of that compensation, which is paid to the owner of land for the use of its original and indestructible powers.

Land scarcity and rent

On the first settling of a country, in which there is an abundance of rich and fertile land, a very small proportion of which is required to be cultivated for the support of the actual population, or indeed can be cultivated with the capital which the population can command, there will be no rent; for no one would pay for the use of land, when there was an abundant quantity not yet appropriated, and, therefore, at the disposal of whosoever might choose to cultivate it.

On the common principles of supply and demand, no rent could be paid for such land, for the reason stated why nothing is given for the use of air and water, or for any other of the gifts of nature which exist in boundless quantity. In the same manner the brewer, the distiller, the dyer, make incessant use of the air and water for the production of their commodities; but as the supply is boundless, they bear no price. If all land had the same properties, if it were unlimited in quantity, and uniform in quality, no charge could be made for its use, unless where it possessed peculiar advantages of situation.

It is only, then, because land is not unlimited in quantity and uniform in quality, and because in the progress of population, land of an inferior quality, or less advantageously situated, is called into cultivation, that rent is ever paid for the use of it. When in the progress of society, land of the second degree of fertility is taken into cultivation, rent immediately commences on that of the first quality, and the amount of that rent will depend on the differ-ence in the quality of those two portions of land.

When land of the third quality is taken into cultivation, rent immediately commences on the second, and it is regulated as before, by the difference in their productive powers. At the same time, the rent of the first quality will rise, for that must always be above the rent of the second, by the difference between the produce which they yield with a given quantity of capital and labour. With every step in the progress of population, which shall oblige a country to have recourse to land of a worse quality, to enable it to raise its supply of food, rent, on all the more fertile land, will rise.

Diminishing returns

It often, and, indeed, commonly happens, that before No. 2, 3, 4, or 5, or the inferior lands are cultivated, capital can be employed more productively on those lands which are already in cultivation. It may perhaps be found, that by doubling the original capital employed on No. 1, though the produce will not be doubled, it may be increased by [more than] what could be obtained by employing the same capital on land No. 3.

If, then, good land existed in a quantity much more abundant than the production of food for an increasing population required, or if capital could be indefinitely employed without a diminished return on the old land, there could be no rise of rent; for rent invariably proceeds from the employment of an additional quantity of labour with a proportionally less return.

Rent not price determining

The most fertile, and most favourably situated, land will be first cultivated, and the exchangeable value of its produce will be adjusted in the same manner as the exchangeable value of all other commodities, by the total quantity of labor necessary in various forms from first to last, to produce it, and bring it to market. When land of an inferior quality is taken into cultivation, the exchangeable value of raw produce will rise, because more labour is required to produce it.

The reason then, why raw produce rises in comparative value, is because more labour is employed in the production of the last portion obtained, and not because a rent is paid to the landlord. The value of corn is regulated by the quantity of labour bestowed on its production on that quality of land, or with that portion of capital, which pays no rent. Corn is not high because a rent is paid, but a rent is paid because corn is high; and it has been justly observed, that no reduction would take place in the price of corn, although landlords should forego the whole of their rent. Such a measure would only enable some farmers to live like gentlemen, but would not diminish the quantity of labour necessary to raise raw produce on the least productive land in cultivation.

If the high price of corn were the effect, and not the cause of rent, price would be proportionally influenced as rents were high or low, and rent would be a component part of price. But that corn which is produced by the greatest quantity of labour is the regulator of the price of corn; and rent does not and cannot enter in the least degree as a component part of its price.

Competitive Wages and Collective Bargaining

Reading 51

"The road to hell is paved with good intentions." So argues Milton Friedman of Chicago. Although minimum wages are favored by liberals and unions in order to help the poor who need help most, Dr. Friedman argues that they will hurt precisely this group by excluding them from jobs altogether. In his brief and trenchant remarks, this leading exponent of economic libertarianism and laissez faire does not list both the pros and cons of the subject: e.g., the argument that all the low-paid who *continue* to hold jobs will receive more adequate incomes; the argument that what this group gains may, if the demand for labor is inelastic rather than elastic, more than make up for the wage loss from lower employment; the argument that the higher wage may enable the worker to be better fed, better motivated, and hence, so much more productive that both he and the employer (and, we may add, society) will be better off; the argument that imposing higher wage rates may have a "shock effect" on the employer's efficiency in the use of labor, making the company, the consumer, and the worker all better off; finally, the argument that in our affluent society no one should have to work below some decent wage, even if that means that society must help provide him with minimum income, or better training or (through more aggressive fiscal and monetary policies) greater job opportunities.

Whatever the merits of these pros, the fundamental fact remains that economists of widely differing political opinions agree that the higher the minimum wage is set in comparison with the supply- and demand-level set by the market, the more powerful become the harmful effects on the groups most in need.

Questions to Guide the Reading

If a "decent wage" is $3 an hour, why stop at $1.60? Why not $4 or $5? Why do many experts favor a minimum wage just a bit above the market, as a spur, but not as too great a deterrent?

Since black youth unemployment did not rise to 30 per cent, is the author's argument invalidated? How can you decide?

Minimum-wage Rates

Milton Friedman

Congress has just acted to increase unemployment. It did so by raising the legal minimum-wage rate from $1.25 to $1.60 an hour, effective in 1968, and extending its coverage. The result will be and must be to add to the ranks of the unemployed.

Does a merchant increase his sales by raising prices? Does higher pay of domestic servants induce more housewives to hire help? The situation is no different for other employers. The higher wage rate decreed by Congress for low-paid workers will raise the cost of the goods that these workers produce—and must discourage sales. It will also induce employers to replace such workers with other workers—either to do the same work or to produce machinery to do the work.

Some workers who already receive wages well above the legal minimum will benefit—because they will face less competition from the unskilled. That is why many unions are strong supporters of higher minimum-wage rates. Some employers and employees in places where wages are already high will benefit because they will face less competition from businessmen who might otherwise invest capital in areas that have large pools of unskilled labor. That is why Northern manufacturers and unions, particularly in New England, are the principal sources of political pressure for higher legal minimum-wage rates.

It's anti-Negro

The groups that will be hurt the most are the low-paid and the unskilled. The ones who remain employed will receive higher wage rates, but fewer will be employed. As Prof. James Tobin, who was a member of President Kennedy's Council of Economic Advisers, recently wrote: "People who lack the capacity to earn a decent living need to be helped, but they will not be helped by minimum-wage laws, trade-union wage pressures or other devices which seek to compel employers to pay them more than their work is worth. The more

likely outcome of such regulations is that the intended beneficiaries are not employed at all."

The loss to the unskilled workers will not be offset by gains to others. Smaller total employment will result in a smaller total output. Hence the community as a whole will be worse off.

Women, teen-agers, Negroes and particularly Negro teen-agers will be especially hard hit. I am convinced that the minimum-wage law is the most anti-Negro law on our statute books—in its effect not its intent. It is a tragic but undoubted legacy of the past—and one we must try to correct—that on the average Negroes have lower skills than whites. Similarly, teen-agers are less skilled than older workers. Both Negroes and teen-agers are only made worse off by discouraging employers from hiring them. On-the-job training—the main route whereby the unskilled have become skilled—is thus denied them.

Who is helped?

The shockingly high rate of unemployment among teen-age Negro boys is largely a result of the present Federal minimum-wage rate. And unemployment will be boosted still higher by the rise just enacted. Before 1956, unemployment among Negro boys aged 14 to 19 was around 8 to 11 per cent, about the same as among white boys. Within two years after the legal minimum was raised from 75 cents to $1 an hour in 1956, unemployment among Negro boys shot up to 24 per cent and among white boys to 14 per cent. Both figures have remained roughly the same ever since. But I am convinced that, when it becomes effective, the $1.60 minimum will increase unemployment among Negro boys to 30 per cent or more.

Many well-meaning people favor legal minimum-wage rates in the mistaken belief that they help the poor. These people confuse wage *rates* with wage *income*. It has always been a mystery to me to understand why a youngster is better off unemployed at $1.60 an hour than employed at $1.25. Moreover, many workers in low wage brackets are supplementary earners—that is, youngsters who are just getting started or elderly folk who are adding to the main source of family income. I favor governmental measures that are designed to set a floor under *family income*. Legal minimum-wage rates only make this task more difficult.

The rise in the legal minimum-wage rate is a monument to the power of superficial thinking.

Reading 52

Many economists are concerned over the power of unions in our economy. One of the most articulate of these was the late Edward H. Chamberlin of Harvard University. Here he presents the case that a number of immunities of unions under federal law give labor leaders excessive opportunities to push wages up too fast, to coerce neutrals, and to interfere with the healthy functioning of competitive pressures. Because Chamberlin was father of the theory of imperfect competition, his views gain interest.

Questions to Guide the Reading

Chamberlin argues that excessive power in today's unions does not stem from collective bargaining per se. Would collective bargaining itself be affected if his proposals for curbing union power were adopted?

To what extent does the union power which Chamberlin fears come from the labor market itself? From the existence of high levels of employment? From disorganization or shortsightedness on management's part? From the political climate of the nation?

Can Union Power Be Curbed?

Edward H. Chamberlin

Professor Sumner H. Slichter has pointed out that we live not, as we used to think, in a capitalistic society but in a laboristic one. Certainly most of us have a time lag in our thinking, and the economist's distrust of power has not yet been transferred in any substantial degree to labor. But I do believe that such a transfer is in process. Indeed, the most disturbing thing to my mind is not so much that people are unaware of the significance of this growth in labor union power but that so many seem to think that nothing can be done about it. I do not believe that anything in the field of social policy is inevitable, and we ought to stop saying that it is, however great the difficulties to be overcome.

The belief that nothing can be done about labor union power reduces to the belief that nothing *will* be done about it. This kind of fatalism is particularly evident with respect to the inflationary problem. Creeping inflation, we are told, is inevitable—all we can do is to accept it and learn to live with it.

Cost-push inflation

Now the doctrine that inflation is inevitable is very closely linked with a particular kind

From Edward H. Chamberlin, "Can Union Power Be Curbed?" *Atlantic Monthly*, June, 1959. Reprinted with kind permission of the author and publisher.

of inflation, namely the cost-push type. We know a great deal about how to control inflation of the demand-pull variety by well-established monetary and fiscal techniques. No one believes that such inflation is inevitable, though it may approach inevitability in wartime. If the war years are omitted, prices have risen very little in the United States over the last hundred and fifty years. Years of rising prices have been fewer than those of falling or stable prices, and many of these latter have been years of prosperity.

Inflation of the cost-push variety is held to be inevitable partly because the conventional methods of control are not effective against it. For many reasons, the upward pressure on wages exerted by individual unions is strikingly insensitive to fiscal and credit restraints. And so, when one limits his thinking to fiscal and monetary measures, it is easy to conclude either that nothing can stop the upward cost push or that it can be stopped only at an unacceptable social cost of rising unemployment and lost production. By holding demand in check, the economy is indeed slackened, cost increases are harder to pass on, employer resistance to wage demands is increased, strikes are harder to win, and wage demands are correspondingly reduced. And so economists like to speculate on how high unemployment must go before it begins to act as a brake on wage demands. The great mistake, I think, is in trying to control wage-push inflation by methods which are inappropriate for the job.

It becomes necessary to go back and ask a very simple and fundamental question: What is the source of the problem? If it is excessive power in the hands of labor, the most obvious way to seek a remedy would be to reduce the power, and this is in fact the gist of my proposal. An alternative proposal would be to strengthen management by such devices, for example, as the pooling arrangement among airlines which has recently received so much publicity. Perhaps we might have some of both. But strangely enough I have found in discussing these matters that many who are horrified at the thought of weakening unions have no objection whatever to strengthening management. They would prefer to equalize power at a higher level, for bigger and better struggles, whereas I should prefer a measure of disarmament.

Monopoly is monopoly

Inflation is only one aspect of the general problem. The basis of labor union power is similar to that of any monopoly power—control of a market through collective action—but with the superimposition of decisive elements unique to the labor market.

The monopoly problem is simply one of maximum gain, both by the suppression of internal competition and by closing the path of entry to any from outside who would by their participation tend to break down the monopoly. This is precisely the method of monopoly in both the industrial and the labor areas. The striking difference between them is that monopoly in industry has been recognized as a matter of public concern for a long time and has been subjected, with at least partial success, to a program of regulation; whereas labor monopoly, hidden by the attractive phrase "collective bargaining," has hardly been recognized, let alone brought under control.

The control of monopoly generally involves the application of some standard of fairness, and in industry this standard has usually been found by a reference to competitive markets. Two procedures in applying the competitive criterion have been developed. In the case of public utilities and certain forms of transportation, monopoly is permitted and subjected to direct regulation. Here the lack of alternatives open to the consumer is recognized by imposing the obligation of service on the company. Here too, public commissions, subject to court review, regulate rates and earnings in accord with principles designed to bring about a rough correspondence between earnings in the regulated and in the competitive sectors of the economy, with allowance for such special factors as stability of income, risk, and so forth.

For the great bulk of the industrial area which remains, the attempt is made to preserve competition by forbidding agreements in restraint of trade, forbidding mergers under certain conditions, and outlawing certain specific practices which are regarded as detrimental to healthy competition. The expectation seems to be that enough competition can be preserved to give the public at least a reasonable protection against the abuses of concentrated private power and against the consequences of government regimentation.

The success of these policies may be questioned; I think everyone would agree that there is room for improvement. We get perspective on the policy, however, by comparing the prevailing spirit of American industry with that of Continental Europe, where cartelization is generally accepted and where, since agreements in restraint of trade are not forbidden, all manner of informal and tacit agreements and a generally restrictive mentality dominate the picture. I once heard the contrast put in this form: If a European retailer has an item on his shelf for some months without its being sold, he is likely to raise the price because of the cost he has incurred in keeping it for that time; the American retailer, on the contrary, will lower the price so as to get rid of it and make room for something else. The notion of not engaging too vigorously in price competition is a universal phenomenon in some degree, but a willingness to gain business at a rival's expense is fairly well developed in the United States, and I think the antitrust laws in this country are an important part of the reason why this is so.

Concentration of economic power in the labor field is paradoxically very great, partly because few people are aware of it. It is hidden because the gains which are made, say in terms of wages or so-called fringe benefits, are made immediately, speaking from the employer instead of from the public.

There is a common belief that higher wages come out of profits; and this is often superficially the case as a short-run proposition. Yet such a belief is in direct conflict with a fundamental long-run principle of economics as hoary and as generally respectable as the famous law of supply and demand, namely, the law of cost: that prices tend to conform to cost of production, including a normal allowance for profits. The principle is a rough one, and it ought to be elaborated if space permitted, especially as to the *amount* of profit which it includes. But there is no reason to expect wage increases, any more than increases in the cost of raw materials, to be met out of profits; both are paid in the end by the public in the form of higher prices.

The new despots

Through the law of costs, the power of labor to raise money wages, and so indirectly to raise prices, is fundamentally no different from the power of business to raise prices directly. Monopoly wages, like monopoly prices, are paid in the end by the public; and it is for this reason that there is exactly as much public interest involved in the regulation of monopoly in the labor field as in the field of industry.

Now the problem of industrial monopoly power, even at those times in history when it has been of the greatest public concern, has never been associated with inflation. How is it therefore that such an association is made in the labor field? There are several reasons for this: the practice of wage settlements over wide areas on a pattern basis, so that one increase means many more; the institution of the annual wage increase, augmented by the growing practice of embodying it in long-term contracts; competition among labor leaders to outdo their rivals—and we must include competition from employers in nonunionized areas to do even better, so as to avoid unionization; and finally the fact that wages are more important than profits as an element in prices. The role of union power in cost inflation would seem to indicate that the control of this general inflationary force may be achieved only by putting a damper on thousands of individual wage and price increases.

How then to hold them in check? The decisive elements unique to the labor market which are mainly responsible for the fact that labor has too much power are not a part of collective bargaining per se. They are accretions of power which have developed partly through specific exemptions by Congress and through court interpretations, partly through a failure to understand the problem, but mostly through an uncritical public indulgence which can only be explained by a confused belief that since the labor cause is good, the more power in the hands of labor the better. As a practical matter, it seems to me that progress could be made in reducing union power by attacking directly those accretions which clearly rest upon privileges and immunities of laborers as compared with other citizens, and which it is therefore reasonable and fair to correct on the simple ground of equal treatment for all.

A recent booklet entitled *The Legal Immunities of Labor Unions* by [the late] Dean Emeritus Roscoe Pound of the Harvard University Law School analyzes an impressive list of such immunities. They are treated under the headings of torts (civil wrongs), contracts, restraint of trade, duties of public service, the right to work, racketeering, centralized power, and irresponsibility. Legal immunities are related to economic power, and each such immunity therefore contributes its bit to wage-push inflation. Certainly the appeal of equal treatment for all is a strong one in a democracy. Why should it not apply in this area?

On the more purely economic front, the power accretions are startling. The practice of making a deal with the teamsters to "honor" a picket line has nothing to do with free speech, as the Supreme Court seems to think it has because it involves picketing, and it has nothing to do with collective bargaining. It is simply a power gadget to deprive an employer not only of the services of his own workers who are on strike but of all other goods and services as well. The old legal principle that a service of such vital public necessity as transportation must not be closed or obstructed clearly corresponds to the economic realities. Yet it has not been adapted to developments of recent decades in the transportation field. Most firms in modern times are heavily if not totally dependent for their existence on private trucking. In fact, the teamsters derive most of their power not from the racketeering with which they are ridden but from their control over transportation, including the freedom with which they can choke off this vital service from any specific business enterprise they please.

The threat of potential violence and intimidation through the device of the picket line are powerful factors—so powerful, in fact, that nowadays a firm rarely attempts any operations at all if a strike has been called, although it would be within its legal rights to do so. For all practical purposes the alternative of making a bargain with anyone other than the union has been removed. Even the attempts in the 1959 bus strike in Massachusetts to run a few buses operated by supervisors for school children were successfully blocked by masses of pickets surrounding the buses. Boycotts, hot cargo rules, refusals to work with non-union labor or on materials produced by non-union labor or by the wrong union are used with impunity to close the channels of trade and commerce. These and other privileges and immunities which tremendously augment union monopoly power are unique to the labor market.

Curbing the monarchs

Many of these developments are a logical conclusion of what seems to be the overriding principle that a union's economic power must not be compromised. In the further matter of agreements and alliances, for instance, anything is legal so long as only labor groups are involved. No—there is one qualification of mock seriousness. A union may restrain trade as much as it pleases and combine with others against other unions, against nonunion laborers, against some particular employer, or against the general public, provided only—in the quaint language of the Hutcheson decision —it is acting in its own self-interest.

I have seen a statement by an important labor leader before the Joint Economic Committee of Congress to the effect that even to raise the question of whether unions have too much power is to question their very right to exist. This is the union point of view, and it seems to be widespread. Yet what could be more absurd? Has anyone ever held that to reduce and regulate monopoly power in the business area was to question the right of business to exist?

We need only to make the distinction between collective bargaining and the application of further pressures, to make clear that such pressures may be reduced as the public interest and ordinary fairness require, without imperiling the existence of unions. Should a union be allowed to strangle a business economically by arranging with the teamsters to cut off its transportation? It seems to me we might as well ask if a physically strong customer in a retail shop should be allowed to twist the arm of the shopkeeper in order to drive a better bargain with him.

I suggest as a good general rule that no employer should have brought against him pressures exerted by anyone other than his own employees.[1] To implement such a principle fully may seem too much to hope for, but it should not be overlooked that there is an open-

[1] EDITOR'S NOTE: Since this was written, some tightening up of the restrictions on union power over third parties was passed by Congress in the Landrum-Griffin Act of 1959.

ing wedge in the outlawing of the secondary boycott by Congress in the Taft-Hartley Act. It remains, after closing some of the loopholes which have developed in this prohibition, to make progress in applying the general principle more widely. There seems every reason to think that the questions of alliances in the labor field, interunion relationships, and the extent of single-union control are as much a matter of public concern and of regulation as are intercorporate relationships and agreements in industry.

A national policy of encouraging collective bargaining, adopted in the middle thirties in the belief that labor's bargaining power was weak and needed to be strengthened, has encouraged not merely collective bargaining but the development of a wide power complex. The careless view that labor must have enough power to win may have been understandable when labor was the underdog. But pilots who can close down airlines in negotiating for top salaries of well over $20,000 a year are not underdogs. And when a few hundred workers in New York who merely deliver newspapers after they have been produced can deprive ten million readers of printed news and inflict losses, not only on their employers but on a whole community, estimated at $50 million, it seems clear that the time has come for a re-evaluation of where the power now lies.

As this article is being written (1959), the fast-approaching crisis in the steel industry provides an example on a national scale of where the power lies. However one may judge the demands of the steel workers and wage-price relationships in the industry, the simple fact remains that the nation will be offered its choice between a long-drawn-out strike which would deal a heavy blow to economic recovery or an inflationary increase in costs. Indeed, it may very well get both.

The increase in wages (or fringe benefits) will be inflationary for two reasons: 1) whether at once or after an interval, steel prices will be higher, and so will the prices of all things made of steel; 2) less obvious but much more important, an increase in steel wages (already among the highest) must be followed by other wage increases. This is so because of the pattern phenomenon: if steel workers get more, inexorable pressures are created to bring other wages in the whole structure into line. So the wage-price spiral works not only vertically from wages to prices but horizontally from wages to other wages, and especially so when a key industry like steel is involved. With these considerations in mind, the question of whether or not certain steel companies could increase wages without raising their own prices (whatever the answer) recedes into proper perspective.

The choice between a disastrous closing down of the steel industry and another round of inflation is indeed a hard one, and if unions had less power other alternatives with a measure of concern for the public interest might have a hearing.

Unions have achieved their present position largely through public indulgence, and if the public becomes less indulgent, union power can be curbed. What is needed is a general awakening to the real nature of the problem. In its fundamentals monopoly power is the same whether used by laborers or by businessmen, and it has the same adverse effect on the rest of society, with an inflationary influence to be added in the case of labor. It has been subjected to regulation in business; how much longer will it go unregulated in the labor area? Will the rest of society continue to accept the principle that a labor union's freedom in the pursuit of its own self-interest shall be unrestrained?

International Trade and Finance 5

Tariffs and Free Trade

Reading 53

The advantages of free trade in furthering the international division of labor and thereby raising living standards for both rich and poor nations can be demonstrated by logical argumentation. Frederic Bastiat (1801–1850) fought for this cause with the weapons of satire and wit, and the results were often devastating. In his *Economic Sophisms* he deliberately took the protectionists' case somewhat further than they intended to go and, in so doing, made the whole case teeter.

Questions to Guide the Reading

How closely do the arguments which Bastiat builds into this petition correspond to the most frequently used arguments for tariffs today?

How might the protectionists argue in response to this satire? Does the free-trade case lend itself equally well to this treatment?

Petition of the Candlemakers—1845

Frederic Bastiat

To the Honorable Members of the Chamber of Deputies:

GENTLEMEN,—You are in the right way: you reject abstract theories; abundance, cheapness, concerns you little. You are entirely occupied with the interest of the producer, whom you are anxious to free from foreign competition. In a word, you wish to secure the *national market* to *national labor.*

We come now to offer you an admirable opportunity for the application of your—what what shall we say—your theory? No, nothing is more deceiving than theory;—your doctrine? your system? your principle? But you do not like doctrines; you hold systems in horror; and, as for principles, you declare that there are no such things in political economy. We will say, then, your practice; your practice without theory, and without principle.

We are subjected to the intolerable competition of a foreign rival, who enjoys, it would seem, such superior facilities for the production of light, that he is enabled to *inundate* our *national market* at so exceedingly reduced a price, that, the moment he makes his appearance, he draws off all custom for us; and thus an important branch of French industry, with all its innumerable ramifications, is suddenly reduced to a state of complete stagnation. This rival is no other than the sun.

Our petition is, that it would please your honorable body to pass a law whereby shall be directed the shutting up of all windows, dormers, skylights, shutters, curtains, in a word, all openings, holes, chinks, and fissures through which the light of the sun is used to penetrate into our dwellings, to the prejudice of the profitable manufactures which we flatter ourselves we have been enabled to bestow upon the country; which country cannot, therefore, without ingratitude, leave us now to struggle unprotected through so unequal a contest.

We foresee your objections, gentlemen; but there is not one that you can oppose to us which you will not be obliged to gather from the works of the partisans of free trade. We dare challenge you to pronounce one word against our petition, which is not equally opposed to your own practice and the principle which guides your policy.

Do you tell us, that if we gain by this protection, France will not gain because the consumer must pay the price of it?

We answer you: You have no longer any right to cite the interest of the consumer. For

From Frederic Bastiat, *Economic Sophisms* (G. P. Putnam's Sons, New York, 1922).

whenever this has been found to compete with that of the producer, you have invariably sacrificed the first. You have done this to *encourage labor*, to *increase the demand for labor*. The same reason should now induce you to act in the same manner.

You have yourselves already answered the objection. When you were told, "The consumer is interested in the free introduction of iron, coal, corn, wheat, cloths, etc.," your answer was, "Yes, but the producer is interested in their exclusion." Thus, also, if the consumer is interested in the admission of light, we, the producers, pray for its interdiction.

You have also said, "The producer and the consumer are one. If the manufacturer gains by protection, he will cause the agriculturist to gain also; if agriculture prospers, it opens a market for manufactured goods." Thus we, if you confer upon us the monopoly of furnishing light during the day, will as a first consequence buy large quantities of tallow, coals, oil, resin, wax, alcohol, silver, iron, bronze, crystal, for the supply of our business; and then we and our numerous contractors having become rich our consumption will be great, and will become a means of contributing to the comfort and competency of the workers in every branch of national labor.

Will you say that the light of the sun is a gratuitous gift, and that to repulse gifts is to repulse riches under pretense of encouraging the means of obtaining them?

Take care,—you carry the death blow to your own policy. Remember that hitherto you have always repulsed foreign produce *because* it was an approach to a gratuitous gift, and *the more in proportion* as this approach was more close. You have, in obeying the wishes of other monopolists, acted only from a *half-motive;* to grant our petition there is a much *fuller inducement.*

Labor and nature concur in different proportions, according to country and climate, in every article of production. The portion of nature is always gratuitous. If a Lisbon orange can be sold at half the price of a Parisian one, it is because a natural and gratuitous heat does for the one what the other only obtains from an artificial and consequently expensive one. When, therefore, we purchase a Portuguese orange, we may say that we obtain it half gratuitously and half by the right of labor; in other words, at *half price* compared with those of Paris.

Now it is precisely on account of this *demi-gratuity* (excuse the word) that you argue in favor of exclusion. How, you say, could national labor sustain the competition of foreign labor, when the first has everything to do, and the last is rid of half the trouble, the sun taking the rest of the business upon himself? If then the *demi-gratuity* can determine you to check competition, on what principle can the *entire gratuity* be alleged as a reason for admitting it? Choose, but be consistent. And does it not argue the greatest inconsistency to check as you do the importation of coal, iron, cheese, and goods of foreign manufacture, merely because and even in proportion as their price approaches *zero*, while at the same time you freely admit, and without limitation, the light of the sun, whose price is during the whole day at *zero?*

Reading 54

Some 106 years after Frederic Bastiat published his satirical petition to the French National Assembly, a real-world group of candlemakers offered their serious petition to the Finance Committee of the United States Senate. They were silent on the subject of the sun, but they did argue vigorously, though briefly, on some other grounds for modern-day protectionism.

Questions to Guide the Reading

How does foreign competition in candles differ from, say, new domestic competition in its impact on our economy?

What criteria should our government use to decide whether or not a particular product ought to be given tariff protection?

Assuming that society feels some sort of obligation to a domestic industry being harmed by foreign competition, are there remedies other than those advocated here that might better fulfill this obligation?

Petition of the Candlemakers—1951

Congressional Hearings

February 27, 1951

Re: Extension of the Trade Agreements Act, H.R. 1612

Chairman, Senate Finance Committee,
United States Senate, Washington, D.C.

Sir: This brief is filed in behalf of the candle manufacturers in the United States in protest against an extension of the Trade Agreement Act of 1934 as amended by the House of Representatives, H.R. 1612. In spite of our brief presented in opposition to tariff cuts (which are a matter of record and available to your committee) we have been given the maximum reduction possible up to this point.

The facts upon which we have based our previous briefs are as important and as pertinent as they were when first presented. Rather than take the time of the committee by repetition of the entire argument we are listing the facts (all of which we have previously substantiated) in the hope that this time we will reach some one who has the understanding to interpret these facts intelligently and the power to act in the light of those facts.

1. An industry stemming from Colonial times.
2. A product required in national defense to such an extent as to utilize the full capacity of the industry.
3. High essentiality of labor and materials under war conditions.
4. An overcapacity of more than five to one.
5. Increased labor costs of 25 percent from 1946–50 with labor rates well above those prevailing in competitive countries.
6. A decline in sales of 17.45 percent since 1946.
7. A 63 percent increase in number of manufacturers since 1933.
8. With plants operating one shift, present production well above demand.
9. Full impacts of currency devaluations, abnormal conditions, pending legislation in countries not yet felt in our markets.

The record of imports for last year has shown a steady increase through the first 11 months from 12 countries, most of whom have not supplied candles to the United States for many years if ever. These are the countries mentioned in our earlier briefs from whom we feared this type of low-cost-labor competition. As a result of current untenable conditions one of the oldest manufacturers—representing a substantial percentage of the total candle business—had been forced to close and demolish its plant.

It is evident that the purposes of the act outlined in the preamble are not being fulfilled: "Overcoming domestic unemployment," "increasing purchasing power of the American public," "maintaining a better relationship among various branches of American agriculture, industry, mining and commerce." This country should forgo the trade agreement policy until normal times return during which the benefits or ill effects of this act can be given a fair test. The expanded economy resulting from World War II has precluded any normal business operations and because of the Korean war we are still in an abnormal economy.

Competent legal opinion has proven that the entire act is illegal and unconstitutional. We are requesting outright repeal of the act

From *Trade Agreements Extension Act of 1951, Hearings before the Committee on Finance, United States Senate, on H.R. 1612*, 82nd Cong., 1st Sess. (1951).

at this time. Failing that, we ask that any extension at least carry with it the following recent provisions of the House amendments as well as incorporate the points outlined above.

1. Tie in reductions with parity price levels.
2. Reinstate the peril points empowering the Tariff Commission to fix a point below which the tariff on any item cannot be cut.
3. Reinstate the right of judicial review of grievances and arbitrary decisions which may be imposed upon the citizens by the negotiators.

4. End all tariff concessions to communist countries.

Respectfully submitted.

The Candle Manufacturing Industry
by H. R. Farker

Exchange Rates

Readings 55 and 56

According to classical economics, foreign exchange rates could be stable provided that prices and wages could move flexibly upward and downward to correct any chronic disequilibria in the balance of payments. However, in a modern mixed economy it is rarely possible to engineer downward flexibility of wages and costs without producing great social disorder; and there are grave social objections to engineering inflationary upward movements when such are called for to remove international disequilibria.

In consequence, Professor Milton Friedman, who was introduced in previous readings and as the ideological spokesman for the "Chicago School" of libertarians who espouse reliance on free-market pricing, puts forward the case for floating exchange rates. Many economists of all political persuasions agree with this view. The objections to it and the case for a stable exchange rate are presented by Henry C. Wallich, a Yale professor and *Newsweek* columnist, who was introduced in an earlier reading.

Questions to Guide the Reading

Would international trade, the division of labor, and the process of foreign investment be inhibited if importers and investors had to face the uncertainty of not knowing from day to day what the foreign exchange rate would be? Could speculators be expected to provide a broad market that would promote stability and enable traders to *hedge* their international transactions?

Reading 55

The Case for Flexible Exchange Rates

Milton Friedman

Discussions of U.S. policy with respect to international payments tend to be dominated by our immediate balance-of-payments difficulties. I should like today to approach the question from a different, and I hope more constructive, direction. Let us begin by asking ourselves not merely how we can get out of our present difficulties but instead how we can

From *The United States Balance of Payments, Hearings before the Joint Economic Committee*, 88th Cong., 1st Sess., pt. 3.

fashion our international payments system so that it will best serve our needs for the long pull; how we can solve not merely this balance-of-payments problem but the balance-of-payments problem.

A shocking, and indeed, disgraceful feature of the present situation is the extent to which our frantic search for expedients to stave off balance-of-payments pressures has led us, on the one hand, to sacrifice major national objectives; and, on the other, to give enormous power to officials of foreign governments to affect what should be purely domestic matters.

Foreign payments amount to only some 5 percent of our total national income. Yet they have become a major factor in nearly every national policy.

I believe that a system of floating exchange rates would solve the balance-of-payments problem for the United States far more effectively than our present arrangements. Such a system would use the flexibility and efficiency of the free market to harmonize our small foreign trade sector with both the rest of our massive economy and the rest of the world; it would reduce problems of foreign payments to their proper dimensions and remove them as a major consideration in governmental policy about domestic matters and as a major preoccupation in international political negotiations; it would foster our national objectives rather than be an obstacle to their attainment.

Bringing down tariffs

Suppose that we succeed in negotiating far-reaching reciprocal reductions in tariffs and other trade barriers with the Common Market and other countries. To simplify exposition I shall hereafter refer only to tariffs, letting these stand for the whole range of barriers to trade, including even the so-called voluntary limitation of exports. Such reductions will expand trade in general but clearly will have different effects on different industries. The demand for the products of some will expand, for others contract. This is a phenomenon we are familiar with from our internal development. The capacity of our free enterprise system to adapt quickly and efficiently to such shifts, whether produced by changes in technology or tastes, has been a major source of our economic growth. The only additional element intro-

duced by international trade is the fact that different currencies are involved, and this is where the payment mechanism comes in; its function is to keep this fact from being an additional source of disturbance.

An all-around lowering of tariffs would tend to increase both our expenditures and our receipts in foreign currencies. There is no way of knowing in advance which increase would tend to be the greater and hence no way of knowing whether the initial effect would be toward a surplus or deficit in our balance of payments. What is clear is that we cannot hope to succeed in the objective of expanding world trade unless we can readily adjust to either outcome.

Many people concerned with our payments deficits hope that since we are operating further from full capacity than Europe, we could supply a substantial increase in exports whereas they could not. Implicitly, this assumes that European countries are prepared to see their surplus turned into a deficit, thereby contributing to the reduction of the deficits we have recently been experiencing in our balance of payments. Perhaps this would be the initial effect of tariff changes. But if the achievement of such a result is to be sine qua non of tariff agreement, we cannot hope for any significant reduction in barriers. We could be confident that exports would expand more than imports only if the tariff changes were one sided indeed, with our trading partners making much greater reductions in tariffs than we make. Our major means of inducing other countries to reduce tariffs is to offer corresponding reductions in our tariff. More generally, there is little hope of continued and sizable liberalization of trade if liberalization is to be viewed simply as a device for correcting balance-of-payments difficulties. That way lies only backing and filling.

Suppose then that the initial effect is to increase our expenditures on imports more than our receipts from exports. How could we adjust to this outcome?

Floating rates in history

Floating exchange rates is the method which the United States used from 1862 to 1879, and again, in effect, from 1917 or so to about 1925, and again from 1933 to 1934. It is the method which Britain used from 1918 to 1925 and again from 1931 to 1939, and which Canada used for most of the interwar period and again from 1950 to May 1962. Under this method, exchange rates adjust themselves continuously, and market forces determine the magnitude of each change. There is no need for any official to decide by how much the rate should rise or fall. This is the method of the free market, the method that we adopt unquestioningly in a private enterprise economy for the bulk of goods and services. It is no less available for the price of one money in terms of another.

With a floating exchange rate, it is possible for Governments to intervene and try to affect the rate by buying or selling, as the British exchange equalization fund did rather successfully in the 1930's, or by combining buying and selling with public announcements of intentions, as Canada did so disastrously in early 1962. On the whole, it seems to me undesirable to have government intervene, because there is a strong tendency for government agencies to try to peg the rate rather than to stabilize it, because they have no special advantage over private speculators in stabilizing it, because they can make far bigger mistakes than private speculators risking their own money, and because there is a tendency for them to cover up their mistakes by changing the rules—as the Canadian case so strikingly illustrates—rather than by reversing course. But this is an issue on which there is much difference of opinion among economists who agree in favoring floating rates. Clearly, it is possible to have a successful floating rate along with governmental speculation.

The great objective of tearing down trade barriers, of promoting a worldwide expansion of trade, of giving citizens of all countries, and especially the underdeveloped countries, every opportunity to sell their products in open markets under equal terms and thereby every incentive to use their resources efficiently, of giving countries an alternative through free world trade to autarchy and central planning —this great objective can, I believe, be achieved best under a regime of floating rates. All countries, and not just the United States, can proceed to liberalize boldly and confidently only if they can have reasonable assurance that the resulting trade expansion will be balanced and will not interfere with major domestic objectives. Floating exchange rates, and so far as I can see, only floating exchange rates, provide this assurance. They do so because they are an automatic mechanism for protecting the domestic economy from the possibility that liberalization will produce a serious imbalance in international payments.

False objections

Despite their advantages, floating exchange rates have a bad press. Why is this so?

One reason is because a consequence of our present system that I have been citing as a serious disadvantage is often regarded as an advantage, namely, the extent to which the small foreign trade sector dominates national policy. Those who regard this as an advantage refer to it as the discipline of the gold standard. I would have much sympathy for this view if we had a real gold standard, so the discipline was imposed by impersonal forces which in turn reflected the realities of resources, tastes, and technology. But in fact we have today only a pseudo gold standard and the so-called discipline is imposed by governmental officials of other countries who are determining their own internal monetary policies and are either being forced to dance to our tune or calling the tune for us, depending primarily on accidental political developments. This is a discipline we can well do without.

A possibly more important reason why floating exchange rates have a bad press, I believe, is a mistaken interpretation of experience with floating rates, arising out of a statistical fallacy that can be seen easily in a standard example. Arizona is clearly the worst place in the United States for a person with tuberculosis to go because the death rate from tuberculosis is higher in Arizona than in any other State. The fallacy in this case is obvious. It is less obvious in connection with exchange rates. Countries that have gotten into severe financial difficulties, for whatever reason, have had ultimately to change their exchange rates or let them change. No amount of exchange control and other restrictions on trade have enabled them to peg an exchange rate that was far out of line with economic realities. In consequence, floating rates have frequently been

associated with financial and economic instability. It is easy to conclude, as many have,
that floating exchange rates produce such instability.

This misreading of experience is reinforced
by the general prejudice against speculation;
which has led to the frequent assertion, typically on the basis of no evidence whatsoever,
that speculation in exchange can be expected
to be destabilizing and thereby to increase the
instability in rates. Few who make this assertion even recognize that it is equivalent to
asserting that speculators generally lose
money.

Floating exchange rates need not be unstable exchange rates—any more than the prices
of automobiles or of Government bonds, of coffee or of meals need gyrate wildly just because
they are free to change from day to day. The
Canadian exchange rate was free to change
during more than a decade, yet it varied
within narrow limits. The ultimate objective is
a world in which exchange rates, while free to
vary, are in fact highly stable because basic
economic policies and conditions are stable.
Instability of exchange rates is a symptom of
instability in the underlying economic structure. Elimination of this symptom by administrative pegging of exchange rates cures none
of the underlying difficulties and only makes
adjustment to them more painful.

The confusion between stable exchange rates
and pegged exchange rates helps to explain
the frequent comment that floating exchange
rates would introduce an additional element of
uncertainty into foreign trade and thereby discourage its expansion. *They introduce no additional element of uncertainty.* If a floating rate
would, for example, decline, then a pegged
rate would be subject to pressure that the authorities would have to meet by internal deflation or exchange control in some form. The
uncertainty about the rate would simply be
replaced by uncertainty about internal prices
or about the availability of exchange; and the
latter uncertainties, being subject to administrative rather than market control, are likely
to be the more erratic and unpredictable.
Moreover, the trader can far more readily and
cheaply protect himself against the danger of
changes in exchange rates, through hedging
operations in a forward market, than he can
against the danger of changes in internal

prices or exchange availability. Floating rates
are therefore more favorable to private international trade than pegged rates.

Our current deficit

Though I have discussed the problem of
international payments in the context of trade
liberalization, the discussion is directly applicable to the more general problem of adapting to any forces that make for balance-of-
payments difficulties. Consider our present
problem, of a deficit in the balance of trade
plus long-term capital movements. How can
we adjust to it? By one of the three methods
outlined: first, drawing on reserves or borrowing; second, keeping U.S. prices from rising
as rapidly as foreign prices or forcing them
down; third, permitting or forcing exchange
rates to alter. And, this time, by one more
method: by imposing additional trade barriers
or their equivalent, whether in the form of
higher tariffs, or smaller import quotas, or
extracting from other countries tighter "voluntary" quotas on their exports, or "tieing" foreign aid, or buying higher priced domestic
goods or services to meet military needs, or
imposing taxes on foreign borrowing, or imposing direct controls on investments by U.S.
citizens abroad, or any one of the host of other
devices for interfering with the private business of private individuals that have become
so familiar to us since Hjalmar Schacht perfected the modern techniques of exchange control in 1934 to strengthen the Nazis for war
and to despoil a large class of his fellow citizens.

Fortunately or unfortunately, even Congress
cannot repeal the laws of arithmetic. Books
must balance. We must use one of these four
methods. Because we have been unwilling to
select the only one that is currently fully consistent with both economic and political needs
—namely, floating exchange rates—we have
been driven, as if by an invisible hand, to employ all the others, and even then may not
escape the need for explicit changes in exchange rates.

We affirm in loud and clear voices that we
will not and must not erect trade barriers—yet
is there any doubt about how far we have gone
down the fourth route? After the host of measures already taken, the Secretary of the

Treasury has openly stated to the Senate Finance Committee that if the so-called interest equalization tax—itself a concealed exchange control and concealed devaluation—is not passed, we shall have to resort to direct controls over foreign investment.

We affirm that we cannot drain our reserves further, yet short-term liabilities mount and our gold stock continues to decline.

The final solution

Even all together, these measures may only serve to postpone but not prevent open devaluation—if the experience of other countries is any guide. Whether they do, depends not on us but on others. For our best hope of escaping our present difficulties is that foreign countries will inflate.

In the meantime, we adopt one expedient after another, borrowing here, making swap arrangements there, changing the form of loans to make the figures look good. Entirely aside from the ineffectiveness of most of these measures, they are politically degrading and demeaning. We are a great and wealthy Nation. We should be directing our own course, setting an example to the world, living up to our destiny. Instead, we send our officials hat in hand to make the rounds of foreign governments and central banks; we put foreign central banks in a position to determine whether or not we can meet our obligations and thus enable them to exert great influence on our policies; we are driven to niggling negotiations with Hong Kong and with Japan and for all I know, Monaco, to get them to limit voluntarily their exports. Is this posture suitable for the leader of the free world?

It is not the least of the virtues of floating exchange rates that we would again become masters in our own house. We could decide important issues on the proper ground. The military could concentrate on military effectiveness and not on saving foreign exchange; recipients of foreign aid could concentrate on how to get the most out of what we give them and not on how to spend it all in the United States; Congress could decide how much to spend on foreign aid on the basis of what we get for our money and what else we could use it for and not how it will affect the gold stock; the monetary authorities could concentrate on domestic prices and employment, not on how to induce foreigners to hold dollar balances in this country; the Treasury and the tax committees of Congress could devote their attention to the equity of the tax system and its effects on our efficiency, rather than on how to use tax gimmicks to discourage imports, subsidize exports, and discriminate against outflows of capital.

Demise of gold

A system of floating exchange rates would render the problem of making outflows equal inflows unto the market where it belongs and not leave it to the clumsy and heavy hand of Government. It would leave Government free to concentrate on its proper functions.

In conclusion, a word about gold. Our commitment to buy and sell gold for monetary use at a fixed price of $35 an ounce is, in practice, the mechanism whereby we maintain fixed rates of exchange between the dollar and other currencies—or, more precisely, whereby we leave all initiative for changes in such rates to other countries. This commitment should be terminated. The price of gold should be determined in the free market, with the U.S. Government committed neither to buying gold nor to selling gold at any fixed price. This is the appropriate counterpart of a policy of floating exchange rates. With respect to our existing stock of gold, we could simply keep it fixed, neither adding to it nor reducing it; alternatively, we could sell it off gradually at the market price or add to it gradually, thereby reducing or increasing our governmental stockpiles of this particular metal. In any event, we should simultaneously remove all present limitations on the ownership of gold and the trading in gold by American citizens. There is no reason why gold, like other commodities, should not be freely traded on a free market.

Reading 56

A Defense of Fixed Exchange Rates

Henry C. Wallich

Flexible rates have achieved a high measure of acceptance in academic circles, but very little among public officials. This raises the question whether we have a parallel to the famous case of free trade: almost all economists favor it in principle, but no major country ever has adopted it. Does the logic of economics point equally irrefutably to flexible rates, while the logic of politics points in another direction?

The nature of the case, I believe, is fundamentally different. Most countries do practice free trade within their borders, although they reject it outside. But economists do not propose flexible rates for the States of the Union, among which men, money, and goods can move freely, and which are governed by uniform monetary, fiscal, and other policies. Flexible rates are to apply only to relations among countries that do not permit free factor movements across their borders and that follow, or may follow, substantially different monetary and fiscal policies. It is the imperfections of the world that seem to suggest that flexible rates, which would be harmful if applied to different parts of a single country, would do more good than harm internationally.

The question is, Do we want to look upon the world as quite different from the United States, as hopelessly divided into self-contained units where cooperation and efforts to coordinate policies are doomed to frustration? In that case, flexible rates may be the best way to avoid a very bad situation. But should we not try to establish within the world something that begins to approximate the conditions that prevail within a country, in the way of coordination of policies, freer flow of capital and of goods and so try to achieve the benefits of one large economic area within the world?

Advantages

The proponents of flexible rates argue, in effect, that flexible rates can help a country get out of almost any of the typical difficulties that economies experience. This is perfectly true. If the United States has a balance-of-payments deficit, a flexible exchange rate allows the dollar to decline until receipts have risen and payments fallen enough to restore balance. If the United States has unemployment, flexible rates can protect it against the balance-of-payments consequences of a policy of expansion. We would then have less unemployment. If the United States has suffered inflation and fears that it will be undersold internationally, flexible rates can remove the danger.

All of these advantages are quite clear.

Other countries have analogous advantages. If Chile experiences a decline in copper prices, flexible rates can ease the inevitable adjustment. If Germany finds that other countries have inflated while German prices have remained more nearly stable, flexible rates could help to avoid importing inflation. If Canada has a large capital inflow, a flexible rate will remove the need for price and income increases that would otherwise be needed to facilitate the transfer of real resources.

There are other adjustments, however, that must be made in all of these cases. If a country allows its exchange rate to go down, some price adjustments still remain to be made. Furthermore, each time a country makes this kind of adjustment, allowing its exchange rate to decline, other countries suffer. If the U.S. dollar depreciates, we undersell the Europeans. It could be argued that if the U.S. price levels go down instead of the exchange rate, we also undersell the Europeans, and if because of a declining price level we have unemployment we would be buying still less from them. Nevertheless, there is a difference. A price adjustment tends to be slow and is likely to be no greater than it need be and tends to be selective for particular commodities. In contrast, an exchange rate movement is unpredictable. It can be large—we could easily have a drop of 10 or 20 percent in an exchange

From *The United States Balance of Payments, Hearings before the Joint Economic Committee,* 88th Cong., 1st Sess., pt. 3.

rate. It comes suddenly. And it compels other countries to be on their guard.

Need for discipline

Why, given the attractions of flexible rates, should one advise policymakers to stay away from them? Since the dollar problem is the concrete situation in which flexible rates are being urged today, it is in terms of the dollar that they must be discussed. In broadest terms, *the reason why flexible rates are inadvisable is that their successful functioning would require more self-discipline and mutual forbearance than countries today are likely to muster.* Exchange rates are two sided—depreciation for the dollar means appreciation for the European currencies. To work successfully, a flexible dollar, for instance, must not depreciate to the point where the Europeans would feel compelled to take counteraction. I believe that the limits of tolerance, before counteraction begins today are narrow and that a flexible dollar would invite retaliation almost immediately.

In the abstract, the European countries perhaps ought to consider that if the United States allows the dollar to go down, it is doing so in the interests of all-round equilibrium. They ought perhaps to consider that with a stable dollar rate the same adjustment might have to take place through a decline in prices here and a rise in prices there. In practice, they are likely to be alive principally to the danger of being undersold by American producers if the dollar goes down, in their own and third markets. The changing competitive pressure would fall unevenly upon particular industries, and those who are hurt would demand protection.

The most likely counteraction might take one of two forms. The Europeans could impose countervailing duties, such as the United States also has employed at times. They could alternately also depreciate European currencies along with the dollar or, what would amount to almost the same thing, prevent the dollar from depreciating. This might involve the European countries in the purchase of large amounts of dollars. If they are to peg the dollar, they could minimize their commitment by imposing a simple form of exchanging control that the Swiss practiced during the last war. The Swiss purchased dollars only from their exporters, also requiring their importers to buy these dollars thereby stabilizing the trade dollar, while allowing dollars from capital movements—finance dollars—to find their own level in the market.

The large volume of not very predictable short-term capital movements in the world today makes such reactions under flexible rates particularly likely.

A sudden outflow of funds from the United States, for instance (because of the fear of budget deficits or many other things that could happen), would tend to drive the dollar down. As a result, American exporters could undersell producers everywhere else in the world. It seems unlikely that foreign countries would allow a fortuitous short-term capital movement to have such far-reaching consequences. It would not even be economically appropriate to allow a transitory fluctuation in the capital account of the balance of payments to have a major influence on the current account. Such a fluctuation should not alter the pattern of trade, because the situation is likely to be reversed. Other countries therefore would probably take defensive action to make sure that no industry is destroyed and after several years may have to be rebuilt because of the ups and downs of short-term capital movements.

De-stabilizing speculation

It can be argued that under flexible rates the effects of such a movement would be forestalled by stabilizing speculation on a future recovery of the dollar. This is possible. It is possible also, however, that speculation would seek a quick profit from the initial drop in the dollar, instead of a longer run one from its eventual recovery. Then short-run speculation would drive the dollar down farther at first. In any case there is not enough assurance that speculators will not make mistakes to permit basing the world's monetary system upon the stabilizing effects of speculation.

In the case of countries which import much of what they consume, such as England, a temporary decline in the local currency may even be self-validating. If the cost of living rises as the currency declines, wages will rise. Thereafter, the currency may never recover to its original level.

This points up *one probable consequence of flexible exchange rates: A worldwide accelera-tion of inflation.* In some countries the indi-cated ratchet effect of wages will be at work. If exchange rates go down, wages will rise, and exchange rates cannot recover. In the United States the rise in the cost of imports would not be very important. But the removal of balance-of-payments restraints may well lead to policies that could lead to price increases. The American inflation of the 1950's was never defeated until the payments deficit be-came serious. Elsewhere, the removal of bal-ance-of-payments disciplines might have the same effect. Rapid inflation in turn would probably compel governments to intervene drastically in foreign trade and finance.

It is quite clear that the discipline of the balance of payments has made for a more re-strictive policy in this country than would have been followed in the absence of this discipline. It is quite conceivable that the ab-sence of balance-of-payments disciplines would have strong inflationary effects in some coun-tries. In that case governments would be com-pelled immediately to intervene drastically in foreign trade and finance; in other words, flexi-ble exchange rates would contribute to their own extinction or to exchange control.

Costs of uncertainty

The prospect that flexible rates would greatly increase uncertainty for foreign traders and investors has been cited many times. It should be noted that this uncertainty extends also to domestic investment decisions that might be affected by changing import competition or changing export prospects. It has been argued that uncertainties about future exchange rates can be removed by hedging in the future mar-ket. This, however, involves a cost even where cover is readily available. The history of fu-tures markets does not suggest that it will be possible to get cover for long-term positions. To hedge domestic investment decisions that might be affected by flexible rates is in the nature of things impracticable.

The picture that emerges of the international economy under flexible rates is one of in-creasing disintegration. Independent national policies and unpredictable changes in each

country's competitive position will compel gov-ernments to shield their producers and markets. The argument that such shielding would also automatically be accomplished by movements in the affected country's exchange rate under-rates the impact of fluctuations upon particu-lar industries, if not upon the entire economy. That international integration and flexible rates are incompatible seems to be the view also of the European Common Market countries, who have left no doubt that they want stable rates within the EEC. The same applies if we visualize the "Kennedy round" under the Trade Expansion Act. I think if we told the Euro-peans that, after lowering our tariffs, we were going to cast the dollar loose and let it fluc-tuate, we would get very little tariff reduction. They would want to keep up their guard.

If the disintegrating effects of flexible rates are to be overcome, a great deal of policy co-ordination, combined with self-discipline and mutual forbearance, would be required. The desired independence of national economic policy would in fact have to be foregone—interest rates, budgets, wage and prices policies would have to be harmonized. If the world were ready for such cooperation, it would be capable also of making a fixed exchange rate system work. In that case, flexible rates would accomplish nothing that could not more cheaply and simply be done with fixed rates. It seems to follow that flexible rates have no unique capacity for good, whereas they possess great capacity to do damage.

Wider "points"

A modified version of the flexible rates pro-posal has been suggested. This version would allow the dollar and other currencies to fluctu-ate within a given range, say 5 percent up and down. This "widening of the gold points" is believed to reduce the danger of destabilizing speculation. It might perhaps enlist specula-tion on the side of stabilization, for if the dollar, say, had dropped to its lower limit, and if the public had confidence that that limit would not be broken, the only movement on which to speculate would be a rise. The spectacle of a currency falling below par may induce, according to the proponents, a strong political effort to bring it back.

This proposal likewise strikes me as unworkable. For one thing, I doubt that people would have a great deal of confidence in a limit of 5 percent below par, if par itself has been given up. Political support for holding this second line would probably be less than the support that can be mustered to hold the first. For another, the execution of the plan would still require the maintenance of international reserves, to protect the upper and lower limits. But with fluctuating rates, dollar and sterling would cease to be desirable media for monetary reserves. International liquidity would become seriously impaired. A third objection is that under today's conditions, the complex negotiations and legislation required, in the unlikely event that the plan could be negotiated at all, could not go forward without immediate speculation against the dollar before the plan goes into effect.

Conclusions

It remains only to point out that, even in the absence of a high degree of international cooperativeness, a system of fixed exchange rates can be made to work. It can be made to work mainly because it imposes a discipline upon all participants, and because within this discipline there is nevertheless some room for adjustment. The principal sources of flexibility are productivity gains and the degree to which they are absorbed by wage increases. Wages cannot be expected to decline. But their rise can be slowed in relation to the rate of productivity growth, in which case prices would become more competitive relative to other countries. With annual productivity gains of 2 to 3 percent in the United States and more abroad, it would not take many years to remove a temporary imbalance.

International Liquidity

Reading 57

For a dozen years the United States has had a chronic balance-of-payments deficit. There are several ways of measuring such a deficit. Here a leading economic expert from Harvard, currently serving on Nixon's Council of Economic Advisers, reviews international developments. The author indicates that, although the *deficit* can be nicely covered by heavy American borrowing from the Eurodollar market at high interest rates, still the *dollar* cannot be regarded as being in equilibrium. And at some time in the future it will be desirable to have some measure of *exchange-rate flexibility*. His emphasis on flexibility is all the more important in view of his official position.

Questions to Guide the Reading

If I withdraw money from a Boston bank and put it in the London branch of that same bank and then the Boston headquarters borrows that money for use in the United States this item will be counted as part of the "liquidity" deficit. Does this make any sense?

What will happen when interest rates in the United States need to fall for domestic reasons below the interest rates called for in Europe? Then our private borrowings will have to drop and the "Official Settlements" deficit will shoot upward.

How would you outline a new ideal international order, involving some exchange-rate flexibility and SDRs? Would there be any room at all for gold in your utopia? Would the dollar still be sovereign?

Exchange Flexibility and the Eurodollar Market

Hendrik S. Houthakker

Recent years have been full of turbulence in the foreign exchange markets. So many events have claimed the headlines that our balance of payments has not had the public attention it normally receives. This neglect can hardly be explained by any lack of new developments. Quite the contrary: not only have the usual concepts had unprecedented quantitative magnitudes, but these concepts themselves have been made partly obsolete by structural changes in the international money markets. What I want to do is to set these figures in perspective, to look with some trepidation into the future, and to relate the balance of payments with the public interest.

Let us first look at the recent past. In our official balance of payments statistics two concepts play a central role; one is the "liquidity balance," and the other the "balance on official reserve transactions." The first is intended to measure the change in our total liquid international liabilities and in our official liquid assets (including gold), while the second is confined to the liquid assets of U.S. official institutions and all liabilities to foreign official institutions. Neither of these two concepts gives an entirely adequate picture of our current international transactions, for reasons which I shall discuss below, but for the time being we shall have to use them.

Of these two the liquidity balance has attracted most public attention in the past and when people speak of "the balance of payments" they usually mean the liquidity balance. According to this concept the current year [1969] has seen a serious deterioration in the international transactions of the United States. After having reached a surplus in 1968, for the first time in many years (though with the aid of considerable window dressing), 1969 started with a deficit. Although it is too early to speak with any precision preliminary indications are that the liquidity deficit will be quite large by historical standards.

On the official settlements basis, where we

had also reached a surplus in 1968, this surplus continued into the first two quarters of 1969, but in the third quarter we apparently had a deficit.

Since in earlier years the liquidity deficit and the official settlements deficit had usually moved in a more or less parallel fashion, the picture presented by the 1969 figures is certainly confusing. What is perhaps even more confusing is that in the face of the huge liquidity deficit the dollar has remained strong in the foreign exchange market, while various other currencies were the objects of active speculation.

What is it then that determines the market position of the dollar?

To provide an answer to this question we have to distinguish first between official and private dollar holders. This distinction is especially important since the establishment of the two-tier gold market, already mentioned, which forces private holders to pay a higher price for gold (if they want it) than official holders, who have the privilege of buying gold at the official price from each other. The attitude of official holders towards the dollar is determined not only by economic considerations but also by general foreign policy, national banking laws, or even the desire to influence U.S. policy. This does not mean that economic considerations are unimportant; no doubt the fact that dollars earn interest while gold does not has influenced the behavior of at least some foreign central banks.

In any case the movement of official reserves has not weakened the dollar during the last year and a half. This is no doubt due in part to the fact that we had an official settlements surplus for much of this period, which meant in effect that foreign official dollar holdings were decreasing. To that extent the official settlements balance is therefore a partial indicator of the strength of the dollar. In addition this confidence in the dollar has probably reflected a belief that our own anti-inflationary

From Hendrik S. Houthakker, "Remarks at the Fall Conference of the Financial Analysts Federation," Baltimore, Maryland, October 20, 1969.

policies will work, a growing realization that a rise in the official price of gold is not in the cards, and our rising interest rates.

Eurodollar borrowing

While all has been fairly quiet on the official dollar front, the same can hardly be said about private dollar holdings. During the past year the term Eurodollars, previously familiar only among specialists, has become almost a household word. While estimates of the total volume of the Eurodollar market are perhaps not too meaningful since they contain a great deal of duplication, the expansion in this market can be more accurately judged by the increase in the liabilities of United States banks to their branches abroad. As recently as 1964 these liabilities barely exceeded one billion dollars. They increased fairly steadily to about $7 billion in the fall of 1968, then more rapidly to reach about $14 billion during the summer of 1969, at which point they had become a major source of funds for our domestic banking system.

The recent expansion in liabilities was accompanied by a sharp rise in interest rates. During 1967, Eurodollar rates had fluctuated around a modest level of 5 or 6 percent, but in 1968 they started rising slowly, and in the late spring of 1969 they finally settled to a level of around 11 percent per year, from which they have retreated only a little so far.

The combination of rising liabilities and rising interest rates indicates that the pressure came mostly *from the demand side*, in particular from American commercial banks. The tightening of monetary conditions in the United States would normally have led to increased rates on time deposits and certificates of deposit, two of the main sources of commercial bank liabilities. Since Regulation Q prevented this rise, the banks had to turn to other sources, including the Eurodollar market. Evidently the strong demand for such funds could be satisfied only at increasing rates. Private foreign holders, who constitute most of the supply side in the Eurodollar market, were induced by these high rates to buy dollars and invest them either directly or indirectly with the foreign branches of U.S. commercial banks.

An increase in the foreign liabilities of our commercial banks contributes to a liquidity deficit on the balance of payments. Thus we see, paradoxically, that *as our liquidity deficit increased*, the dollar *has strengthened in the marketplace* because of the creation of additional demand on the part of private foreign holders.[1]

Although these financial movements have assumed a disproportionate role in our balance of payments picture there are several other factors that have been of importance. I shall speak of these in a moment. In the meantime, two points should be noted.

In the first place, the supply of Eurodollars does not come only from private foreigners; some of it comes from private Americans, both corporations and individuals. With Eurodollar interest rates so much above the interest rates on normal short-term investments inside the United States, the incentive to send or leave money abroad has been strong. Unfortunately, we do not know how strong, since the information on transactions of this sort is very sketchy. As a result the liquidity deficit in recent quarters has overstated the increase in our net foreign private liabilities. The liquidity deficit reflects the change in the foreign liabilities of our banks, but it does not reflect the increase in foreign claims by nonbank Eurodollar holders. It is because of this that I said at the beginning of my talk that recent financial developments have made some of our customary concepts obsolete.

The second point I want to make is that the increase in our foreign liabilities (even though it should not be equated with the increase in liabilities of our banks only) has made interest payments a considerable item in our current account. As recently as 1967 the interest paid by commercial banks on their liabilities to foreign branches was probably no more than $200 or $300 million; it is now running at the rate of about $1½ billion a year. And the liabilities to their foreign branches are not the only short-term foreign liabilities of our com-

[1] At the same time our official settlements balance moved into surplus. This came about because the additional dollars demanded by private foreigners for investment in the Eurodollar market came partly out of the reserves of their central banks, and the resulting reduction in our official liabilities counts as a plus on the official settlements concept. It is primarily because of this that the liquidity balance and the official settlements balance have tended to move inversely since the Eurodollar market became *a major factor in our international monetary* transactions.

mercial banks; they also owe large amounts to foreign commercial banks. At the end of July 1969 the dollar liabilities of our commercial banks to private foreigners totaled nearly $28 billion, partially offset by nearly $9 billion of claims. These liabilities had nearly doubled from the end of 1967, but the claims had not increased much.

What we can see in all this is the development of a large-scale international capital market, based on the dollar but not under the control of any individual country. This development is the natural if somewhat belated result of the establishment of convertibility some 10 years ago. It has been accelerated by the more or less fortuitous circumstance of Regulation Q, but some of it was bound to happen in any case.

The clouded crystal ball

Let me now turn to the outlook for the balance of payments. Since many of you are engaged in the difficult art of forecasting share prices you will probably need no convincing that forecasting the balance of payments is a hazardous enterprise, too. It is especially difficult because the balance of payments is the *relatively small difference between two very large quantities,* both of them quite volatile in nature, the inflow and outflow of foreign exchange. Balance of payments projections were hazardous enough when we had to worry mostly about the current account, on which there is at least a great deal of statistical data and economic theory. But as I have just indicated, *the capital account now dominates the situation,* and there we have rather less to go on in our projections.

But if you agree that forecasting is difficult, you will, I think, also agree that it is necessary. Responsible decision-making, in Government, as well as in business, requires us to make the best forecast we can, even though we know that the best forecast is not very good. It is especially important in the case of the balance of payments because *we now stand at a turning point in the international monetary system, where the mechanism of Bretton Woods is in the process of overhaul.* The United States is such a big factor in international finance that the outlook for our balance of payments is inevitably an important input in working towards the necessary improvements in the international monetary system.

Current account. The situation with respect to the current account is relatively simple. *Our exports continue to grow at a fairly steady rate,* which is *determined largely by business conditions abroad.* There is as yet little sign of a slowdown abroad, though it should be realized that our own tight money policy, through its effect on the Eurodollar market, has led to some tightness in other countries as well. A more serious threat to our exports lies in our *domestic inflation, which is further eroding our already difficult competitive position.*

On the import side *the slowdown in our domestic economy has recently shown up in a marked reduction of the growth rate of imports.* Among the "invisible components" of the current account, the earnings on our investments abroad will presumably continue to grow along their steady trend, again assuming there is no slowdown elsewhere. These favorable factors may be offset to some extent, however, by the sharp increase on interest outflows on short-term liabilities, which I mentioned earlier.

Taking all these things together we may perhaps look forward to a modest but not spectacular improvement in the current account.

Capital account. The outlook for the capital account is much cloudier. While our anti-inflationary efforts will almost certainly have a favorable net effect on the current account, it is conceivable that they will have the opposite effect on the capital side, especially in the short run. As far as long-term capital is concerned, the desire of our industry to invest abroad appears to be unabated. The rapid rise in our wage rates and the fall in our output per manhour, temporary though it is likely to be, may have provided further incentives.

The foreign direct investment program [mandatory controls] has been instrumental in increasing the proportion of foreign investment that is financed abroad. The rise in our interest rates relative to those elsewhere has provided incentives in the same direction. As our anti-inflationary policy takes hold our interest rates will possibly decline more than they do abroad. This would decrease the incentive for U.S. corporations to borrow abroad and increase the attraction of our market to foreign borrowers.

The other main component of long-term capital, portfolio investment, is notoriously hard to predict, especially in the case of equities. There are welcome indications that the increased interest of foreign investors in our securities is not a temporary phenomenon, but at the same time it should be recognized that the uncertain outlook for corporate profits (if it does not become an actual fall) is apt to have a dampening effect on our stock market.

On the whole, the long-term capital account will probably not be much help.

The greatest uncertainties, however, are in the area of *short-term capital*, particularly in *private* short-term capital. We have seen how developments in the Eurodollar market, while creating a large liquidity deficit, have been helpful to the official settlements balance and to the technical strength of the dollar. These developments resulted from a tight monetary policy in the face of a strong domestic demand for funds. Now that our policies to restrain inflation are beginning to take effect, the demand for funds will presumably start to become less intense, and at some as yet undetermined point in the future the growth rate of our money supply will presumably come closer to a sustainable long-term trend. If recent history is any guide this will improve our liquidity balance, but the official settlements balance may be adversely affected.

Needed: flexibility in exchange rates

To put these matters in perspective we should note also that our persistent deficit is *the counterpart of persistent surpluses elsewhere.* The most persistent of these, that of Germany, has now been attacked [by 9 percent appreciation of the mark] in a manner that promises considerable relief. In Japan, however, the surplus shows no signs of becoming smaller. These and other surpluses and deficits have persisted so long because the international adjustment process does not function as it was intended to.

It is against this background that we must interpret the study of greater flexibility of exchange rates which was supported by the United States and several other countries at the recent IMF meeting. As far as we can see at the moment *it is doubtful whether present policies, including the control of inflation, will suffice to bring the worldwide pattern of international payments anywhere near balance within the next few years.*

If we want to see the adjustment process working more effectively we need *other* policy instruments. Direct controls are neither a desirable nor, in the long run, an effective means of influencing international transactions. Of the various other instruments that are conceivably available, exchange rates appear to be the most promising.

The reasons for this statement are by now widely familiar and need not be spelled out here. I should, perhaps, make it clear here, however, that *the dollar would remain* the *international standard of value,* so that the exchange rates in question are those of other currencies. It should also be recalled that since the *abrupt* changes of par value envisaged by the Bretton Woods Agreement have turned out to be politically difficult, *ways of making exchange rates adjust more smoothly have to be found.*

The idea of making exchange rates more flexible, while not in itself a radical departure from the Bretton Woods Agreement, is a fairly new one. It was not taken seriously in official and business circles until the almost continuous monetary disturbances of 1968 and 1969 made it clear to most observers that existing arrangements are no longer adequate.

The general concept of greater (but not complete) flexibility includes a number of variants, differing mostly in the degree of discretion that countries would have over the exchange rates of their currencies. It is not my intention to survey the various possibilities here, but I do want to emphasize that the choice between them is not by any means obvious. It is mainly for this reason that the matter before the IMF meeting was not greater flexibility, but a *study of different methods of obtaining greater flexibility.* If any procedure for obtaining more flexibility is ultimately adopted it will have to be a compromise between a number of requirements, and this takes time.

Arguments pro and con

Since greater flexibility is now officially on the agenda, it may be helpful if I discuss a few of the arguments that have been raised in connection with it.

First of all there is the argument that *greater flexibility will weaken "discipline."* By this is meant that if countries can change their exchange rates more easily they will be more tempted to give in to inflationary pressures. It is not easy to see why this should be so. In general countries are opposed to inflation, and try to counteract it, not simply because they wish to hold some arbitrary exchange rate constant but, more fundamentally, because they fear the domestic consequences of inflation. Moreover it is incorrect to think that the exercise of discipline is sufficient to preserve exchange rates at their existing level; appropriate exchange rates do not depend only on relative rates of inflation but on a number of other factors, such as productivity, the growth rate of demand for a country's imports and exports, and others. It is interesting to observe that some of the countries that insist most on the discipline argument have themselves been least able to keep their domestic price level in check. In the case of the United States, where foreign trade plays a relatively minor role in the total economy, there can be no doubt that our determination to control inflation will not be weakened by any improvements in the international adjustment process.

Secondly, there is the argument about sovereignty. *The fixing of par values*, this argument holds, *is a prerogative of each country which cannot be subjected to outside control or to an automatic formula.* Actually the supposed sovereign right of countries to fix their exchange rates had already been limited by the Bretton Woods Agreement. As the International Monetary Fund points out in its recent annual report, "the determination of the rate of exchange for each currency is a matter of international concern." Moreover, the alleged right to fix exchange rates has in fact been rarely exercised freely; nearly all the changes in par value that have taken place in recent years were made under overwhelming pressure of outside forces. It should nevertheless be granted that each country should have some say over its exchange rate, and that for this reason a purely automatic approach to greater flexibility will not be acceptable.

Next there is the *argument about integration*, advanced particularly by the European Economic Community. According to this argument, *greater flexibility of exchange rates would interfere with the more complete economic integration* that is the express goal of the Treaty of Rome. In fact the Common Agricultural Policy has already been disrupted by the changes in par

value that have taken place this year without any benefit of formal procedures for greater flexibility. It appears, however, that the argument puts the cart before the horse. What is needed for full economic integration is a coordination of fiscal and monetary policies which the six Member countries of the EEC have so far not achieved. It is because of this lack of coordination, of which the recent exchange rate problems are merely a symptom, that the Common Agricultural Policy has run into difficulties. There is no reason to think that a common agricultural policy, although not necessarily of the present form, is incompatible* with greater flexibility of exchange rates.

Another argument occasionally advanced against the study of greater flexibility is that the need has disappeared in view of the steps recently taken in Germany to move towards a more realistic parity. While the German measures should lead to a more viable pattern of exchange rates, it would be optimistic to hope that this will eliminate the need for parity changes in the future. We should not postpone the repair of a leaky roof until it starts raining again.

Why seek balance?

I have not yet dealt with the more fundamental question *why* we should want to restore balance in our international payments. At first sight the answer may seem to be obvious, since a balance of payments deficit is often regarded as intrinsically undesirable. There is some merit in this view, but nevertheless it should be recognized that a balance of payments deficit may make a country better off, at least in the short run, *by enabling it to consume or invest more.* Thus if a country imports more than it exports it acquires real resources for immediate use in exchange for promises to pay later. How soon these promises will be exchanged for real resources is normally a choice open to the creditors.

Thus a surplus country which accumulates monetary reserves is in fact forgoing the domestic use of some of its real output for the time being. It is therefore incorrect to argue that a surplus country necessarily makes a sacrifice when it revalues its currency; on the contrary it can thus *recapture* some of the resources that previously were made available to other countries. It is true that by revaluing a country may reduce its exports, but the resources thus freed can be used to augment the standard of living or the capital stock of its residents, as can the additional imports it will be able to buy. *Surplus countries that refuse to let their currencies appreciate are not only impairing the international adjustment process, they may also be shortchanging their own people.*

Of course this is not all there is to it. One important limiting factor on the willingness of countries to incur deficits is the interest they have to pay on their debts. We have seen already that *the interest we are now paying on our short-term liabilities has become a considerable factor in the current account.* It is equally true that surplus countries that accumulate reserves are gaining liquidity and income from interest. Nevertheless it is very important to realize who gains and who loses from misalignment of parities.

Disequilibrium threatens freer trade

There is, however, still another side to the story, which has to do with trade policy. If a country experiences a rapid increase in imports some of its domestic industries may be hurt, for by the very nature of international trade imports and exports tend to be concentrated in a relatively small number of products. In the long run the labor and capital employed in these domestic industries can be shifted to other uses, but in the short run this may be difficult, especially if the industries in question are dominant in particular regions.

These industries will therefore call for protection. While some of the arguments made in favor of protection are untenable, in particular the argument that protection is necessary to maintain the real wages of American labor, the case for protection may then become compelling from a political point of view. *While it is not hard to prove that protective measures in general hurt both the importing and the exporting countries, there is a very real danger that distortions in exchange rates will lead to distortions in trade policy as well.* This is another and very powerful reason why improvements in the exchange rate adjustment process are necessary, and why surplus countries in particular should take an active interest in such improvements.

It is only by a constant willingness to reexamine our policies and institutional arrangements that we can hope to attain the ideal expressed by President Nixon in his inaugural address: "We seek an open world—open to ideas, open to the exchange of goods and people, a world in which no people, great or small, will live in angry isolation."

Reading 58

Most economic experts think the world faces two major problems in international trade. First, there is the American deficit, and, until the 1968 two-tier gold system was established, the resulting gold drain. Second, as will be apparent when the United States finally solves its deficit problem and stops bleeding gold to the rest of the world, world trade grows much faster than the gold mines of South Africa and Russia can spit out gold. Hence, as may have helped precipitate the world Crash of 1929, shortage of international liquidity may throttle world prosperity if we do not introduce new liquidity arrangements, such as "paper gold" in the form of Special Drawing Rights (SDRs) at the International Monetary Fund.

In contrast to most experts, Despres of Stanford, Kindleberger of M.I.T. and Salant of the Brookings Institution argue that the dollar is really stronger than gold. They argue that the United States has been accumulating more long-term assets than she owes; and that the weakness of the dollar is an optical illusion that can be cured by having the United States tell the world it will stop buying gold at $35 per ounce.

Questions to Guide the Reading

If the dollar were in equilibrium, wouldn't short-term dollar securities be a better holding than zero-interest-yielding gold? But what if the dollar is not yet in equilibrium, being *overvalued* and likely to have its parity depreciate relative to other currencies (and perhaps relative to "official gold" in the official tier of the two-tier system)?

Do you think the world would really suffer if once and for all it turned its back on mining gold from the bowels of the earth in order to shove it back into the vaults at Fort Knox or into governments and cellars abroad?

The Dollar and World Liquidity—A Minority View

Emile Despres, Charles P. Kindleberger, and Walter S. Salant

The consensus in Europe and the United States on the United States balance of payments and world liquidity runs about like this:

1. Abundant liquidity has been provided since World War II less by newly mined gold than by the increase in liquid dollar assets generated by United States balance of payments deficits.

2. These deficits are no longer available as a generator of liquidity because the accumulation of dollars has gone so far that it has undermined confidence in the dollar.

3. To halt the present creeping decline in liquidity through central bank conversions of dollars into gold, and to forestall headlong flight from the dollar, it is necessary above all else to correct the United States deficit.

4. When the deficit has been corrected, the growth of world reserves may, or probably will, become inadequate. Hence there is a need for planning new means of adding to world reserves—along the lines suggested by Triffin, Bernstein, Roosa, Stamp, Giscard, and others.

So much is widely agreed.

Four counter propositions

There is room, however, for a minority view which would oppose this agreement with a sharply differing analysis. In outline, it asserts the following counter propositions:

1. While the United States has provided the world with liquid dollar assets in the post-war period by capital outflow and aid exceeding its current account surplus, in most years this excess has not reflected a deficit in a sense representing disequilibrium. The outflow of US capital and aid has filled not one but two needs. First it has supplied goods and services to the rest of the world. But secondly, to the extent that its loans to foreigners are offset by foreigners putting their own money into liquid dollar assets, the US has not over-invested but has supplied financial intermediary services. America's "deficit" has reflected largely the second process, in which the United States has been lending mostly at long and intermediate terms, and borrowing short. This financial intermediation, in turn, performs two functions: it supplies loans and investment funds to foreign enterprises which have to pay more domestically to borrow long-term money and which cannot get the amounts they want at any price; and it supplies liquidity to foreign asset-holders, who receive less for placing their short-term deposits at home. Essentially, this is a trade in liquidity, which is profitable to both sides. Differences in their liquidity preferences (i.e. in their willingness to hold their financial assets in long-term rather

From Emile Despres, Charles P. Kindleberger, and Walter S. Salant, "The Dollar and World Liquidity— A Minority View," *The Economist*, February 5, 1966. Reprinted with kind permission of the authors and publisher.

than in quickly encashable forms and to have short-term rather than long-term liabilities outstanding against them) create differing margins between short-term and long-term interest rates. This in turn creates scope for trade in financial assets, just as differing comparative costs create the scope for mutually profitable trade in goods. This trade in financial assets has been an important ingredient of economic growth outside the United States.

2. Such lack of confidence in the dollar as now exists has been generated by the attitudes of government officials, central bankers, academic economists, and journalists, and reflects their failure to understand the implications of this intermediary function. Despite some contagion from these sources, the private market retains confidence in the dollar, as increases in private holdings of liquid dollar assets show. Private speculation in gold is simply the result of the known attitudes and actions of governmental officials and central bankers.

3. With capital markets unrestricted, attempts to correct the "deficit" by ordinary weapons of economic policy are likely to fail. It may be possible to expand the current account surplus at first by deflation of United States income and prices relative to those of Europe; but gross financial capital flows will still exceed real transfers of goods and services (i.e. involve financial intermediation, lending long-term funds to Europe in exchange for short-term deposits) so long as capital formation remains high in Europe. A moderate rise of interest rates in the United States will have only small effect on the net capital outflow. A drastic rise might cut the net outflow substantially, but only by tightening money in *Europe* enough to stop economic growth; and this would cut America's current account surplus.

4. While it is desirable to supplement gold with an internationally created reserve asset, the conventional analysis leading to this remedy concentrates excessively on a country's external liquidity; it takes insufficient account of the demands of savers for internal liquidity and of borrowers in the same country for long-term funds. The international private capital market, properly understood, provides both external liquidity to a country, and the kinds of assets and liabilities that private savers and borrowers want and cannot get at home. Most plans to create an international reserve asset,

however, are addressed only to external liquidity problems which in many cases, and especially in Europe today, are the less important issue.

With agreement between the United States and Europe—but without it if necessary—it would be possible to develop a monetary system which provided the external liquidity that is needed and also recognised the role of international financial intermediation in world economic growth.

Europe needs dollars

Analytical support and elaboration of this minority view is presented in numbered sections, conforming to the propositions advanced above as an alternative to the consensus.

1. The idea that the balance of payments of a country is in disequilibrium if it is in deficit on the liquidity (US Department of Commerce) definition is not appropriate to a country with a large and open capital market that is performing the function of a financial intermediary. Banks and other financial intermediaries, unlike traders, are paid to give up liquidity. The United States is no more in deficit when it lends long and borrows short than is a bank when it makes a loan and enters a deposit on its books. Europeans borrow from the United States, and Americans are willing to pay higher prices for European assets than European investors will, partly because capital is more readily available in the United States than in Europe, but mainly because liquidity preference in Europe is higher and because capital markets in Europe are much less well organised, more monopolistically controlled, and just plain smaller than in the United States. European borrowers of good credit standing will seek to borrow in New York (or in the Euro-dollar market, which is a mere extension of New York) when rates of interest are lower on dollar loans than on loans in European currencies, or when the amounts required are greater than their domestic capital markets can provide. But when domestic interferences prevent foreign intermediaries from bridging the gap and when domestic private intermediaries cannot bridge it while the public authorities will not, borrowing possi-

bilities are cut, and investment and growth are cut with it.

2. It may be objected that no bank can keep lending if its depositors are unwilling to hold its liabilities. True. But savings can never be put to productive use if the owners of wealth are unwilling to hold financial assets and insist on what they consider a more "ultimate" means of payment. If the bank is sound, the trouble comes from the depositors' irrationality. The remedy is to have a lender of last resort to cope with the effects of their attitudes or, better, to educate them or, if neither is possible, to make the alternative asset, (which, against the dollar, is gold) less attractive or less available. To prevent the bank from pursuing unsound policies—if it really tends to do so—it is not necessary to allow a run on it. The depositors can have their say in less destructive ways, e.g., through participating in the management of the bank of last resort or through agreement on the scale of the financial intermediation.

The nervousness of monetary authorities and academic economists is a consequence of the way they define a deficit and the connotations they attach to it. No bank could survive in such an analytical world. If financial authorities calculated a balance of payments for New York vis-à-vis the interior of the United States, they would impose restrictions on New York's bank loans to the interior and on its purchases of new issues.

The private market has not been alarmed about the international position of the dollar in relation to other currencies or the liquidity of the United States. Although there has been private speculation in gold against the dollar, it has been induced largely by reluctance of some central banks to accumulate dollars. The dollar is the world's standard of value; the Euro-dollar market dominates capital markets in Europe; and the foreign dollar bond market has easily outdistanced the unit-of-account bond and the European "parallel bond." As one looks at sterling and the major Continental currencies it is hard to imagine any one of them stronger than the dollar today, five years from now, or twenty years hence. In the longer run, as now in the short, the dollar is strong, not weak.

3. Since the US "deficit" is the result of liquidity exchanges or financial intermediation, it will persist as long as capital movement is

free, European capital markets remain narrower and less competitive than that of the United States, liquidity preferences differ between the United States and Europe, and capital formation in Western Europe remains vigorous. In these circumstances, an effort to adjust the current account to the capital outflow is futile. The deficit can be best attacked by perfecting and eventually integrating European capital markets and moderating the European asset-holder's insistence on liquidity, understandable though this may be after half a century of wars, inflations, and capital levies.

An attempt to halt the capital outflow by raising interest rates in the United States either would have little effect over any prolonged period or else would cripple European growth. With European capital markets joined to New York by substantial movements of short-term funds and bonds, the rate structure in the world as a whole will be set by the major financial centre, in this instance New York. Interest-rate changes in the outlying centres will have an impact on capital flows to them. Higher interest rates in New York will raise rates in the world as a whole.

The effort is now being made to "correct the deficit" by restricting capital movements. Success in this effort is dubious, however, for two reasons.

Money is fungible

In the first place, money is fungible. Costless to store and to transport, it is the easiest commodity to arbitrage in time and in space. Discriminating capital restrictions are only partly effective, as the United States is currently learning. Some funds that are prevented from going directly to Europe will reach there by way of the less-developed countries or via the favoured few countries like Canada and Japan, which are accorded access to the New York financial market because they depend upon it for capital and for liquidity. These leaks in the dam will increase as time passes, and the present system of discriminatory controls will become unworkable in the long run. The United States will have to choose between abandoning the whole effort or plugging the leaks.

In the second place, it is not enough to restrain the outflow of United States-owned capital. As Germany and Switzerland have found, to keep United States funds at home widens the spreads between short-term and long-term rates in Europe and also the spreads between the short-term rates at which European financial intermediaries borrow and lend, and so encourages repatriation of European capital already in the United States.

4. Capital restrictions to correct the deficit, even if feasible, would still leave unanswered a fundamental question. Is it wise to destroy an efficient system of providing internal and external liquidity—the international capital market—and substitute for it one or another contrived device of limited flexibility for creating additions to international reserve assets alone?

But, it will be objected, the fears of the European authorities about the dollar are facts of life, and the United States must adjust to them. Several points may be made by way of comment.

Europe squeezes itself

In the first place, the European authorities must be learning how much international trade in financial claims means to their economies, now that it has been reduced.

Europe's own capital markets cannot equal that of the United States in breadth, liquidity, and competitiveness in the foreseeable future.

It must be recognised that trading in financial assets with the United States means a United States "deficit"; United States capital provides not only goods and services, but liquid assets to Europe, which means holding dollars. Moreover, the amount of dollars that private savers in Europe will want to acquire for transactions and as a partial offset to debts in dollars, and for other purposes, will increase. This increase in privately held dollars will involve a rising trend in the United States deficit.

Whether householders and banks want to hold dollars or their own national currencies, the effect is the same: both alternatives now frighten the United States as well as Europe. They should not. And they would not if it were recognised that financial intermediation implies a decline in the liquidity of the intermediary as much when the intermediation is being performed in another country as when it is being performed domestically. An annual growth in Europe's dollar-holdings averaging, perhaps, $1½ to $2 billion a year or perhaps

more for a long time is normal expansion for a bank the size of the United States with a fast-growing world as its body of customers. To the extent that European capital markets achieve greater breadth, liquidity, and competitiveness, the rates of increase in these dollar holdings consistent with given rates of world economic growth would of course be lower than when these markets have their present deficiencies. But whatever rate of growth in these dollar holdings is needed, the point is that they not only provide external liquidity to other countries, but are a necessary counterpart of the intermediation which provides liquidity to Europe's savers and financial institutions. Recognition of this fact would end central bank conversions of dollars into gold, the resulting creeping decline of official reserves, and the disruption of capital flows to which it has led.

Let the gold go

Mutual recognition of the role of dollar holdings would provide the most desirable solution. But if, nevertheless, Europe unwisely chooses to convert dollars into gold, the United States could restore a true reserve-currency system, even without European co-operation in reinterpreting deficits and lifting capital restrictions. The decision would call for cool heads in the United States. The real problem is to build a strong international monetary mechanism resting on credit, with gold occupying, at most, a subordinate position. Because the dollar is in a special position as a world currency, the United States can bring about this change through its own action. Several ways in which it can do so have been proposed, including widening the margin around parity at which it buys and sells gold, reducing the price at which it buys gold, and otherwise depriving gold of its present unlimited convertibility into dollars. The United States would have to allow its gold stock to run down as low as European monetary authorities chose to take it. If they took it all, which is unlikely, the United States would have no alternative but to allow the dollar to depreciate until the capital flow came to a halt, or, much more likely, until the European countries decided to stop the depreciation by holding the dollars they were unwilling to hold before. If this outcome constituted a serious possibility, it seems evident that European countries would cease conversion of dollars into gold well short of the last few billions.

This strategy has been characterized by *The Economist* as the "new nationalism" in the United States. It can reasonably be interpreted, however, as internationalism. It would enable the United States to preserve the international capital market and thereby protect the rate of world economic growth, even without European co-operation. The main requirement of international monetary reform is to preserve and improve the efficiency of the private capital market while building protection against its performing in a destabilising fashion.

The majority view has been gaining strength since 1958, when Triffin first asserted that the dollar and the world were in trouble. Between 1958 and 1965 world output and trade virtually doubled, the United States dollar recovered from a slight overvaluation, and the gold hoarders have foregone large earnings and capital gains. Having been wrong in 1958 on the near-term position, the consensus may be more wrong today, when its diagnosis and prognosis are being followed. But this time the generally accepted analysis can lead to a brake on European growth. Its error may be expensive, not only for Europe but for the whole world.

Current Economic Problems 6

Stages of Growth

Readings 59 and 60

To controvert the nineteenth-century Marxian theory of capitalist development, Walt Whitman Rostow presented a five-stage theory of economic growth and development. The "take-off" stage, in which an economy finally moves into accelerated growth and abundance, has captured the public imagination of the readers of this "non-Communist Manifesto."

Every brilliant construction of the imagination must, in a social science like economics, be subjected to the cold confrontation with the statistical facts of historical experience. Here a master economic historian and statistician carefully audits the Rostow thesis.

W. W. Rostow, Yale graduate and Rhodes Scholar, has been a professor at Oxford, Cambridge, and M.I.T. An early adviser to President Kennedy, Dr. Rostow has been a major planner in the State Department and White House, and is now a professor at the University of Texas. Simon Kuznets is a professor at Harvard, having earlier been at Johns Hopkins, the University of Pennsylvania, and the National Bureau of Economic Research. Aside from his seminal works in quantitative economic history and development, Kuznets pioneered the statistical measurement of national income for the United States.

Questions to Guide the Reading

How many hairs does it take to make a beard? By what test can one decide whether there was or was not an industrial revolution in England during the eighteenth century or at any other time? Is it a useful approximation to divide the history of a country into five—or more, or less—distinct stages?

If a dramatic device, such as the take-off, is only approximately valid, might it still be a useful analytical device? Under what conditions could it do more harm than good?

Reading 59

Stages of Growth and the Take-off: Yes

W. W. Rostow

Traditional society

A traditional society is one whose structure is developed within limited production functions, based on pre-Newtonian science and technology, and on pre-Newtonian attitudes towards the physical world. Newton is here used as a symbol for that watershed in history when men came widely to believe that the external world was subject to a few knowable laws, and was systematically capable of productive manipulation.

The conception of the traditional society is, however, in no sense static; and it would not exclude increases in output. But the central fact about the traditional society was that a ceiling existed on the level of attainable output per head. This ceiling resulted from the fact that the potentialities which flow from modern science and technology were either not available or not regularly and systematically applied.

In terms of history then, with the phrase "traditional society" we are grouping the whole

From W. W. Rostow, *The Stages of Economic Growth*, abridged (Cambridge University Press, New York, 1960). Reprinted with kind permission of the author and publisher.

pre-Newtonian world: the dynasties in China; the civilization of the Middle East and the Mediterranean; the world of medieval Europe. And to them we add the post-Newtonian societies which, for a time, remained untouched or unmoved by man's new capability for regularly manipulating his environment to his economic advantage.

To place these infinitely various, changing societies in a single category, on the ground that they all shared a ceiling on the productivity of their economic techniques, is to say very little indeed. But we are, after all, merely clearing the way in order to get at the subject; that is, the post-traditional societies, in which each of the major characteristics of the traditional society was altered in such ways as to permit regular growth: its politics, social structure, and (to a degree) its values, as well as its economy.

Period of transition

The second stage of growth embraces societies in the process of transition; that is, the period when the preconditions for take-off are developed; for it takes time to transform a traditional society in the ways necessary for it to exploit the fruits of modern science, to fend off diminishing returns, and thus to enjoy the blessings and choices opened up by the march of compound interest.

The preconditions for take-off were initially developed, in a clearly marked way, in Western Europe of the late seventeenth and early eighteenth centuries as the insights of modern science began to be translated into new production functions in both agriculture and industry, in a setting given dynamism by the lateral expansion of world markets and the international competition for them. But all that lies behind the break-up of the Middle Ages is relevant to the creation of the preconditions for take-off in Western Europe. Among the Western European states, Britain, favoured by geography, natural resources, trading possibilities, social and political structure, was the first to develop fully the preconditions for take-off.

The more general case in modern history, however, saw the stage of preconditions arise not endogenously but from some external intrusion by more advanced societies. These invasions—literal or figurative—shocked the traditional society and began or hastened its undoing.

The idea spreads not merely that economic progress is possible, but that economic progress is a necessary condition for some other purpose, judged to be good. Education, for some at least, broadens and changes to suit the needs of modern economic activity. New types of enterprising men come forward—in the private economy, in government, or both—willing to mobilize savings and to take risks in pursuit of profit or modernization. Banks and other institutions for mobilizing capital appear. Investment increases, notably in transport, communications, and in raw materials in which other nations may have an economic interest. The scope of commerce, internal and external, widens. But all this activity proceeds at a limited pace within an economy and a society still mainly characterized by traditional low-productivity methods, by the old social structure and values, and by the regionally based political institutions that developed in conjunction with them.

In many recent cases, for example, the traditional society persisted side by side with modern economic activities, conducted for limited economic purposes by a colonial or quasi-colonial power.

The transition we are examining has, evidently, many dimensions. A society predominantly agricultural—with, in fact, usually 75 per cent or more of its working force in agriculture—must shift to a predominance for industry, communications, trade and services.

A society whose economic, social and political arrangements are built around the life of relatively small—mainly self-sufficient—regions must orient its commerce and its thought to the nation and to a still larger international setting.

The view towards the having of children—initially the residual blessing and affirmation of immortality in a hard life, of relatively fixed horizons—must change in ways which ultimately yield a decline in the birth-rate, as the possibility of progress and the decline in the need for unskilled farm labor create a new calculus.

The income above minimum levels of consumption, largely concentrated in the hands of those who own land, must be shifted into the hands of those who will spend it on roads and railroads, schools and factories rather than on country houses and servants, personal ornaments and temples.

Men must come to be valued in the society not for their connection with clan or class, or, even, their guild; but for their individual ability to perform certain specific, increasingly specialized functions.

And, above all, the concept must be spread that man need not regard his physical environment as virtually a factor given by nature and providence, but as an ordered world which, if rationally understood, can be manipulated in ways which yield productive change and, in one dimension at least, progress.

All of this—and more—is involved in the passage of a traditional to a modern growing society.

The take-off

The beginning of take-off can usually be traced to a particular sharp stimulus. The stimulus may take the form of a political revolution which affects directly the balance of social power and effective values, the character of economic institutions, the distribution of income, the pattern of investment outlays and the proportion of potential innovations actually applied. Such was the case, for example, with the German revolution of 1848, the Meiji restoration in Japan of 1868, and the more recent achievement of Indian independence and the Communist victory in China. It may come about through a technological (including transport) innovation, which sets in motion a chain of secondary expansion in modern sectors and has powerful external economy effects which the society exploits. It may take the form of a newly favourable international environment, such as the opening of British and French markets to Swedish timber in the 1860's or a sharp relative rise in export prices and/or large new capital imports, as in the case of the United States from the late 1840's,

Canada and Russia from the mid-1890's; but it may also come as a challenge posed by an unfavourable shift in the international environment, such as a sharp fall in the terms of trade (or a wartime blockage of foreign trade) requiring the rapid development of manufactured import substitutes, as with the Argentine and Australia from 1930 to 1945.

What is essential here is not the form of stimulus but the fact that the prior development of the society and its economy result in a positive, sustained, and self-reinforcing response to it: the result is not a once-over change in production functions or in the volume of investment, but a higher proportion of potential innovations accepted in a more or less regular flow, and a higher rate of investment.

As indicated in the accompanying table, we believe it possible to identify at least tentatively such take-off periods for a number of countries which have passed into the stage of growth.

For the present purposes the take-off is defined as requiring all three of the following related conditions:

1. a rise in the rate of productive investment from, say, 5% or less to over 10% of national income (or net national product [NNP]);
2. the development of one or more substantial manufacturing sectors, with a high rate of growth;
3. the existence or quick emergence of a political, social and institutional framework which exploits the impulses to expansion in the modern sector and the potential external economy effects of the take-off and gives to growth an on-going character.

The third condition implies a considerable

Table 1   Some Tentative, Approximate Take-off Dates

Country	Take-off	Country	Take-off
Great Britain	1783–1802	Russia	1890–1914
France	1830–60	Canada	1896–1914
Belgium	1833–60	Argentina	1935–
United States	1843–60	Turkey	1937–
Germany	1850–73	India	1952–
Sweden	1868–90	China	1952–
Japan	1878–1900		

capability to mobilize capital from domestic sources. Some take-offs have occurred with virtually no capital imports, for example, Britain and Japan. Some take-offs have had a high component of foreign capital, for example, the United States, Russia and Canada.

Whatever the role of capital imports, the preconditions for take-off include an initial ability to mobilize domestic savings productively, as well as a structure which subsequently permits a high marginal rate of savings.

This definition is designed to isolate the early stage when industrialization takes hold rather than the later stage when industrialization becomes a more massive and statistically more impressive phenomenon. In Britain, for example, there is no doubt that it was between 1815 and 1850 that industrialization fully took hold. If the criterion chosen for take-off was the period of most rapid overall industrial growth, or the period when large-scale industry matured, all our take-off dates would have to be set later; Britain, for example, 1819–48.

With a sense of the considerable violence done to economic history, we are here seeking to isolate a period when the scale of productive economic activity reaches a critical level and produces changes which lead to a massive and progressive structural transformation in economies and the societies of which they are a part, better viewed as changes in kind than merely in degree.

Causal process at work

Whatever the importance and virtue of viewing the take-off in aggregative terms—embracing national output, the proportion of output invested, and an aggregate marginal capital/output ratio—that approach tells us relatively little of what actually happens and of the causal processes at work in a take-off; nor is the investment-rate criterion conclusive.

Perhaps the most important thing to be said about the behaviour of these variables in historical cases of take-off is that they have assumed many different forms. There is no single pattern.

The purpose of the following paragraphs is to suggest briefly, and by way of illustration only, certain elements of both uniformity and variety in the variables whose movement has determined the inner structure of the take-off.

By and large, the loanable funds required to finance the take-off have come from two types of source: from shifts in the control of income flows, including income-distribution changes and capital imports; and from the plough-back of profits in rapidly expanding particular sectors.

The shift of income flows into more productive hands has, of course, been aided historically not only by government fiscal measures but also by banks and capital markets. Virtually without exception, the take-off periods have been marked by the extension of banking institutions which expanded the supply of working capital; and in most cases also by an expansion in the range of long-range financing done by a central, formally organized, capital market.

Although these familiar capital-supply functions of the State and private institutions have been important to the take-off, it is likely to prove the case, on close examination, that a necessary condition for take-off was the existence of one or more rapidly growing sectors whose entrepreneurs (private or public) ploughed back into new capacity a very high proportion of profits. Put another way, the demand side of the investment process, rather than the supply of loanable funds, may be the decisive element in the take-off, as opposed to the period of creating the preconditions, or of sustaining growth once it is under way.

What can we say, in general, about the supply of finance during the take-off period? First, as a precondition, it appears necessary that the community's surplus above the mass-consumption level does not flow into the hands of those who will sterilize it by hoarding luxury consumption or low-productivity investment outlays. Second, as a precondition, it appears necessary that institutions be developed which provide cheap and adequate working capital. Third, as a necessary condition, it appears that one or more sectors of the community must grow rapidly, inducing a more general industrialization process; and that the entrepreneurs in such sectors plough back a substantial proportion of their profits in further productive investment, one possible and recurrent version of the plough-back process being the investment of proceeds from a rapidly growing export sector.

The devices, confiscatory and fiscal, for ensuring the first and second preconditions have been historically various. And the types of leading manufacturing sectors which have served to initiate the take-off have varied greatly. Finally, foreign capital flows have, in significant cases, proved extremely important to the take-off, notably when lumpy overhead capital construction of long gestation period was required; but take-offs have also occurred based almost wholly on domestic sources of finance.

Leading sectors

The overall rate of growth of an economy must be regarded in the first instance as the consequence of differing growth rates in particular sectors of the economy, such sectoral growth-rates being in part derived from certain overall demand factors (for example population, consumers' income, tastes, etc.); in part, from the primary and secondary effects of changing supply factors, when these are effectively exploited.

On this view the sectors of an economy may be grouped in three categories:

1. Primary growth sectors, where possibilities for innovation or for the exploitation of newly profitable or hitherto unexplored resources yield a high growth-rate and set in motion expansionary forces elsewhere in the economy.

2. Supplementary growth sectors, where rapid advance occurs in direct response to— or as a requirement of—advance in the primary growth sectors; for example coal, iron and engineering in relation to railroads. These sectors may have to be tracked many stages back into the economy.

3. Derived-growth sectors, where advance occurs in some fairly steady relation to the growth of total real income, population, industrial production or some other overall, modestly increasing variable. Food output in relation to population and housing in relation to family formation are classic derived relations of this order.

In the earlier stages of growth, primary and supplementary growth sectors derive their momentum essentially from the introduction and diffusion of changes in the cost—supply environment (in turn, of course, partially influenced by demand changes); while the derived-

growth sectors are linked essentially to changes in demand (while subject also to continuing changes in production functions of a less dramatic character).

At any period of time it appears to be true even in a mature and growing economy that forward momentum is maintained as the result of rapid expansion in a limited number of primary sectors, whose expansion has significant external economy and other secondary effects. From this perspective the behaviour of sectors during the take-off is merely a special version of the growth process in general; or, put another way, growth proceeds by repeating endlessly, in different patterns, with different leading sectors, the experience of the take-off. Like the take-off, long-term growth requires that the society not only generate vast quantities of capital for depreciation and maintenance, for housing and for a balanced complement of utilities and other overheads, but also a sequence of highly productive primary sectors, growing rapidly, based on new production functions. Only thus has the aggregate marginal capital/output ratio been kept low.

Once again history is full of variety: a considerable array of sectors appears to have played this key role in the take-off process.

What can we say, then, in general about these leading sectors? Historically, they have ranged from cotton textiles, through heavy-industry complexes based on railroads and military end-products, to timber, pulp, dairy products and finally a wide variety of consumers' goods. There is, clearly, no one sectoral sequence for take-off, no single sector which constitutes the magic key. Four basic factors must be present:

1. There must be enlarged effective demand for the product or products of sectors which yield a foundation for a rapid rate of growth in output. Historically this has been brought about initially by the transfer of income from consumption or hoarding to productive investment; by capital imports; by a sharp increase in the productivity of current investment inputs, yielding an increase in consumers' real income expended on domestic manufactures; or by a combination of these routes.

2. There must be an introduction into these sectors of new production functions as well as an expansion of capacity.

3. The society must be capable of generating capital initially required to detonate the take-off in these key sectors; and especially there must be a high rate of plough-back by the (private or state) entrepreneurs controlling capacity and technique in these sectors and in the supplementary growth sectors they stimulated to expand.

4. Finally, the leading sector or sectors must be such that their expansion and technical transformation induce a chain of requirements for increased capacity and the potentiality for new production functions in other sectors, to which the society, in fact, progressively responds.

Reading 60

Stages of Growth and the Take-off: No

Simon Kuznets

The very ease with which separate segments can be distinguished in the historical movement from non-modern to modern economic growth and within the long span of the latter should warn us that any sequence of stages, even if offered as a suggestive rather than a substantive scheme, must meet some minimum requirements—if it is to be taken seriously.

The following requirements are relevant:

(a) A given stage must display *empirically testable characteristics,* common to all or to an important group of units experiencing modern economic growth. This means the specification of modern economic growth; identification of the units that have manifested such growth; and establishment of empirically testable characteristics claimed to be common to those units at the given stage.

(b) The characteristics of a given stage must be *distinctive* in that, not necessarily singly but in combination, they are *unique* to that stage. Mere precedence (or succession) in time does not suffice: given the unidirectional character of growth (by definition), any period is necessarily characterized by larger economic magnitudes than earlier ones and by the structural shifts that accompany such larger magnitudes (particularly a rise in per capita income). Stages are presumably something more than successive ordinates in the steadily climbing curve of growth. They are segments of that curve, with properties so distinct that separate study of each segment seems warranted.

(c) *The analytical relation to the preceding stage must be indicated.* This naturally involves more than saying that the preceding stage is one of preparation for the given. More meaningfully, we need identification (again in empirically testable terms) of the major processes in the preceding stage that complete it and, with the usual qualifications for exogenous factors, make the next (our given) stage highly probable. Optimally, this would permit us to diagnose the preceding stage *before* the given stage is upon us, and thus would impart predictive value to the whole sequence. But even short of this difficult aim, it means specifying the minimum that must happen in the preceding stage to allow the given stage to emerge.

(d) The analytical relation *to the succeeding stage* must be indicated. Here too a clear notion (again in empirically testable terms) must be given of the occurrences in the given stage that bring it to a close—aside from mere passage of time. Optimally, such knowledge would permit us to predict, *before* the given stage is finished, how long it still has to run. But even short of such precision, we should know the essentials that occur during a given stage to bring about its end and clear the ground for the next stage.

(e) These four requirements relate to the common and distinctive characteristics of a given stage, viewed as one in an analytical

From Simon Kuznets, "Notes on the Take-off," paper presented at the International Economic Association's Conference at Konstanz in September, 1960, on "The Economics of Take-off into Sustained Growth." Reprinted with kind permission of the author and St. Martin's Press, Inc., The Macmillan Co. of Canada, Limited, and Macmillan & Co., Ltd., London.

(and chronological) sequence that links successive stages. However, these common and distinctive characteristics may differ among important groups of units undergoing modern economic growth. Consequently, the fifth requirement is for a clear *indication of the universe for which the generality of common and distinctive characteristics is claimed;* and for which the analytical relations of a given stage with the preceding and succeeding ones are being formulated.

Against the background of the requirements just stated, we may consider Professor Rostow's discussion of the common and distinctive characteristics of the take-off stage, and the relations between it and the contiguous stages.

Shortcomings

How distinctive are these characteristics? Do they occur in combination only in the take-off stage and not in any other stage—particularly the preceding transition or preconditions stage and the succeeding self-sustained growth or drive to maturity stage? Professor Rostow is not explicit on this point. Presumably the transition stage does not see a rise in the investment proportion from 5 to 10 per cent or more. Yet much of what Professor Rostow would attribute to the take-off has already occurred in the pre-condition stage. Thus, the agricultural revolution assigned to the precondition stage "must supply expanded food, expanded markets, and an expanded supply of loanable funds to the modern sector"; much of social overhead capital is already invested in transport and other outlays—in the preconditions stage; and, in general, "the essence of the transition can be described legitimately as a rise in the rate of investment to a level which regularly, substantially and perceptibly outstrips population growth." In short, one wonders whether the three specifically stated characteristics of take-off could not be found in the pre-conditions—unless explicit qualifications are attached, e.g., that the investment proportion in that earlier stage must stay below 5 per cent; that the marked agricultural revolution does not immediately call for, and in fact is possible without, a contemporaneous rapid growth in some manufacturing sector; and that investment in overhead capital in transport, etc., is not necessarily accompanied by a rapid growth of one or more modern manu-

facturing sectors. Finally, one should note that [a] characteristic of the take-off mentions both the *existence* and the *quick emergence* of the political, social, and institutional framework favorable to exploiting "the impulses to expansion in the modern sector" as admissible alternatives.

The line of division between the take-off and the following stage of self-sustained growth or drive to maturity is also blurred. Presumably the latter stage is marked by the existence of the proper social and institutional framework—which also exists during the take-off. Presumably this later stage also witnesses the rapid growth of one or more modern manufacturing sectors. Indeed, the only characteristics that are distinctly appropriate to the take-off and not to the next stage are the rise in the rate of productive investment to over 10 per cent of national income or net national product; and the implicit rise in the rate of growth of total and per capita income. But are we to assume that both the rate of investment and the rate of growth of product (total and per capita) level off at the high values attained at the end of the take-off stage? And is it this leveling off, the cessation of the rise in the rate of investment and in the rate of growth, that terminates the take-off stage?

Indictment

Given this fuzziness in delimiting the take-off stage and in formulating its distinctive characteristics; given the distinctiveness only in the statistical level of the rate of productive investment (and the implicit rate of growth), there is no solid ground upon which to discuss Professor Rostow's view of the analytical relation between the take-off stage and the preceding and succeeding stages. At any rate, the brief comments that can be made within the scope of this paper will follow the review of the empirical evidence.

I do not know what "a political, social and institutional framework which exploits the impulses to expansion in the modern sector, etc." is; or how to identify such a framework except by hindsight and conjecture; or how to specify the empirical evidence that would have to be brought to bear to ascertain whether such a framework is in "existence or in quick emergence." It seems to me that the passage just cited defines these social phenomena as a complex that produces the effect Professor Rostow wishes to explain; and then he treats this definition as if it were a meaningful identification.

It is easier to define the characteristic that specifies "the development of one or more substantial manufacturing sectors with a high rate of growth" once "high" is explained. But a review of empirical evidence on this point holds little interest if I am correct in assuming that the major distinctive characteristic of the take-off is a marked rise in the rate of growth of per capita and hence of total income. If the rate of growth does accelerate, some sectors are bound to grow more rapidly than others, as has been demonstrated in Arthur F. Burns' and my own work on production trends—partly in response to the differential impact of technological opportunities (including raw material supplies), and partly in response to the different income elasticities of the demand for various goods. Under these conditions, one or more manufacturing sectors, and one or more sectors of agriculture, transportation, services, etc. are bound to show high rates of growth. The pertinent question is *why* manufacturing —rather than agriculture, transport, or any other rapidly growing industry—should be specified as the leading sector.

In considering this question, the two constitutive characteristics of a leading sector must be kept in mind. First, sector A leads, rather than follows, if it moves not in response to sectors B, C, D, etc. within the country, but under the impact of factors which, relative to the given national economy, may be considered autonomous. The point to be noted is that the autonomous nature of this characteristic, relative to the given national economy, rests upon the origin of the stimulus, not upon the scope of the response. The latter may depend largely upon many other factors besides the stimulus, factors that are part and parcel of a given economy and society.

This brings us to the second constitutive characteristic of a leading sector, the magnitude of its effects; or more specifically, the magnitude of its contribution to a country's economic growth. Sector A may be leading in the sense of responding to an autonomous stimulus, but unless its contribution to the country's economic growth is substantial, it does not "lead" the country's economic growth —no matter how high its own rate of growth.

After all, a thousandfold rise in the production of plastic hula hoops over a decade does not make it a leading industry.

Leadership of sectors, or any other element in the acceleration of the rate of growth can be established only after careful analysis of the particular circumstances preceding and during the period of acceleration—country by country, and by the application of statistical, theoretical, and other tools to the historical evidence.

Negative verdicts

The failure of aggregative data to reveal the characteristics claimed by Professor Rostow as common to the take-off stage, at least in countries that did not experience the drastic and forced transformation associated with Communist revolutions, is disturbing. *It casts serious doubt on the validity of the definition of the take-off as a generally occurring stage of modern economic growth, distinct from what Professor Rostow calls the "pre-conditions" or "transition" stage preceding it and the "self-sustained" growth stage following it.*

The evidence used to test Professor Rostow's scheme is not conclusive. Some non-Communist countries for which we have no data may have experienced a period of growth conforming with Professor Rostow's take-off stage. Also, his scheme may fit the Communist "take-offs," but my knowledge of them is inadequate for checking. *All that is claimed here is that aggregative data for a number of countries do not support Professor Rostow's distinction and characterization of the take-off stage.* On the other hand, the fact that the evidence is confined to aggregative data does not limit their bearing. Economic growth is an aggregative process; sectoral changes are interrelated with aggregative changes, and can be properly weighted only after they have been incorporated into the aggregative framework; and the absence of required aggregative changes severely limits the likelihood of the implicit strategic sectoral changes.

My disagreement with Professor Rostow is *not* on the value and legitimacy of an attempt to suggest some pattern of order in the modern economic growth experience of different countries. On the contrary, I fully share what I take to be his view on the need to go beyond qualitative and quantitative description to the use of the evidence for a large number of countries and long periods, in combination with analytical tools and imaginative hypothe-

ses, to suggest and explain not only some common patterns but also, I would add, the major deviations from them. However, for reasons clearly indicated above, I disagree with the sequence of stages he suggests.

U.S. Growth

Reading 61

Given the spectacular achievements of the American economy in the past, where do we go from here? Having attained the highest standard of living in the world, should we now devote more of our attention and energies to less material concerns than continued economic expansion? Or do the increasing pressures of today's world call for an ever-improving economic performance in the United States? These are not easy questions to answer, for an individual or for a nation.

The difficulty begins when we first talk about measuring economic performance. There are at least two yardsticks that might be used: the yardstick of what we have done compared with what others have done, and the yardstick of what we have done compared with what we would like to do and are technically capable of doing. Given the fact that human wants, even in a rich society such as ours, appear to be insatiable, the second yardstick imposes the tougher measure. Yet recent economic developments in other parts of the world seem to indicate that the former yardstick may also impose a sterner measure in the future than it has in the past.

The strength of this reading is that it forces us to put the *costs* of growth alongside the *gains* from growth. It highlights the "why" type of inquiry that must precede wise choices, and the figures on which it is based are those given in the earlier Reading 49 by Edward F. Denison. Herbert Stein was long the research director of the Committee for Economic Development and is on leave from Brookings Institution to serve on Nixon's Council of Economic Advisers. Denison, already previously introduced, is a senior staff member of the Brookings Institution.

Questions to Guide the Reading

How is it possible in a decentralized, private enterprise economy to formulate an overall growth goal and to translate that goal into an action program? How might a determination by Americans to promote greater domestic growth make itself felt?

Does greater growth inevitably mean a larger role for government in the economy?

How can we construct a balance sheet of gains and costs in any such enlarged role? Didn't the 1960s refute the gloomy view of growth taken here?

Why Growth?

Herbert Stein and Edward F. Denison

The American economy works well. It produces the highest income per capita ever known, and a rate of growth that raises real income per capita by half from one generation to the next. This income, and its increase, are widely distributed. Economic advance has produced a revolutionary reduction in the hours and burdens of work. Americans have great freedom to use their resources and incomes as they choose. The system is highly responsive to the demands of the people, producing with exceptional efficiency, inventiveness and adaptability the particular goods and services for which a private or public demand is expressed. Unemployment remains a problem, but one so reduced in magnitude since the 1930's as to be qualitatively different.

America and the civilization to which it belongs stand at an historic turning point. They confront a critical danger and inspiring opportunities. The danger is indicated by the phrase "cold war." Among the opportunities are to help the billion people of the underdeveloped world realize their aspirations, to reduce nationalist and racialist limitations upon man's freedom and horizons, and to push back the frontiers of human knowledge in many directions. Neither avoidance of the danger nor realization of the opportunities *requires* that the American economy work better, although better economic preformance would make both objectives easier to attain. Insofar as movement toward these more important goals depends upon the availability of economic resources, the American economy as it is and is likely to be can provide them. It would be tragic if the United States should fall prey to the danger or fail to grasp the opportunities because of preoccupation with the idea that it is not rich enough and needs to become richer faster.

Having said this, we can turn to the question of improving the performance of the American economy. We confine our discussion to the relation between the production we can expect from the economy, if it operates near its capacity, and our "needs."

From 1929 to 1957 the total production of goods and services in the United States increased at an average rate of 2.93 per cent per annum. We estimate that if unemployment is kept to about 4 per cent of the labor force, the annual rate of growth from 1957 to 1970 would be 3.27 per cent, and from 1957 to 1980 would be 3.24 per cent. At the estimated rate of growth the Gross National Product would be about $709 billion in 1970 and $972 billion in 1980.

This estimate of future growth assumes that no special measures are taken to accelerate growth other than the reduction of unemployment. It is based on an analysis of the probable contribution to growth that will be made by several factors—the number, hours of work, educational attainment and age-sex composition of the labor force, the stock of capital, the increase of knowledge, and others. It assumes, among other things, that the 1970 labor force will be about 19 per cent larger, and average annual full-time working hours about 5 per cent shorter, than in 1960; that the educational attainment of the labor force will increase sharply; that the capital stock will grow at about the rate indicated by past ratios of saving to national product under prosperous conditions.

Some of these assumptions may turn out to be incorrect. Any estimates of the future may be wrong. We offer ours only as the most reasonable basis we know for considering any policy problems to which an estimate of future growth may be relevant.

The most obvious question to ask about the projected rate of growth is: Will it be enough? In one sense of course the answer is No. The growth of production is the source from which desires for goods and services are satisfied. These desires appear limitless. However fast production may grow, some desires will be left unsatisfied, and many will wish the growth were faster.

However, the rate of growth will not be increased by wishing. Steps will have to be taken to increase it. By and large these steps

From Herbert Stein and Edward F. Denison, "High Employment and Growth in the American Economy," *Goals for Americans* (Prentice-Hall, Inc., Englewood Cliffs, N.J., 1960). Reprinted with kind permission of the authors and publisher.

will involve some cost to someone—otherwise we could assume that they would already have been taken. (Remember that we are discussing the problem of raising the rate of growth above that which would otherwise result at high employment—whatever that rate may be.) The question then is not whether faster growth is desirable but whether it is sufficiently desirable to justify any particular step that might be taken to achieve it.

This question may be concretely illustrated as follows. We estimate that if annual hours of work were to remain at their 1957 level, rather than to decline at the rate we project, our annual rate of growth from 1957 to 1970 would be 3.6 per cent instead of 3.3 per cent. Faster growth is a good thing and reduction of hours of work is a good thing. The question is whether increasing the rate of growth is more important than reducing hours of work. Similar questions can be asked about increasing immigration, or employment of women, or expenditures for education, or taxes for public investment, or tax changes to promote private investment, or expenditures for research.

When the question is put in this way it becomes obvious that the authors of this paper cannot responsibly pretend to answer it. We can try to illuminate the benefits of more rapid growth and indicate the costs of achieving it. But whether the benefits are worth the costs can be answered only by those affected or by those making the decisions. The costs and benefits are not reducible to any common terms that permit their objective measurement and comparison. In the end the decision will have to reflect subjective judgments, and insofar as they are collective decisions they will have to reflect some consensus of subjective judgments.

Whether a collective decision about the rate of growth should be made, through government, is in our opinion a real and serious question. The alternative view is that the desirable rate of growth and the correct means to achieve it are those that would emerge from private decisions. These would inevitably be affected by the action of government in discharging its important functions. But these functions do not include the explicit determination of the rate of growth. We believe that there is much to be said for this position, and we trust that it will receive due weight in public discussion of growth. We do not ex-amine this position here only because it seems more fruitful to use our limited space to indicate what choices are available in the economic system if collective choices are to be made.

How much is growth worth?

If our economy grows at the rate we project, 3.3 per cent per annum, total output (Gross National Product) will be about $710 billion in 1970. If it grows at 4 per cent per annum, GNP in 1970 will be about $780 billion. The value of the higher rate of growth is $70 billion of output in 1970 and corresponding amounts in other years.

How much is this $70 billion worth? Obviously, the answer will depend upon what the $70 billion consists of and what wants it satisfies. If it includes critical defense expenditures, the caloric intake necessary for sustaining the population, the capital assistance that would set the underdeveloped world on the road to growth, then the $70 billion will be of the utmost importance. But anyone can think of possible uses of $70 billion that would be of little importance.

One can conceive of all possible uses of output being ranked in an endless descending series from the most important to the less important, to those of no importance at all, to those of negative value. Ideally, with $710 billion of GNP we would go down from the top of this list through the $710 billion most important uses. If we had another $70 billion of GNP we would take the next most important $70 billion of uses, all of which would be less valuable than any of the first $710 billion. The value of the additional $70 billion would be much less than 10 per cent of the value of the first $710 billion.

It may be that the actual American selection of uses of output does not conform to this pattern. Possibly we select more or less at random from the most important, less important, and unimportant uses. In this case the additional $70 billion of output might be as valuable, dollar for dollar, as the first $710 billion.

There might even be a systematic bias in the process, which causes the less important needs to be satisfied before the more important. If so, the need satisfied by the additional $70 billion of output would be much more important, on the average, than those satisfied by the first $710 billion.

The importance of more rapid growth depends critically upon how well we allocate our output among our needs. This simply means that if we can count on devoting our expected output to satisfying our most urgent needs, additional output will be only as valuable as the satisfaction of our less urgent needs.

As the authors see it, the key current question about the allocation of output relates to the division between private and public uses. There may be limits upon the amount of public expenditure that keep critical public needs from being met, even though much less important private needs are met. Suppose, for example, that we cannot or will not spend more than 20 per cent of the gross national product for public purposes. If the gross national product in 1970 is $710 billion we can have only $142 billion of public expenditures, even though this may leave unmet many public needs more important than the needs satisfied by some of the $568 billion of private expenditures. The value of raising the GNP would then lie in the additional public expenditures it would permit.

It should be understood that in this paper we have made no evaluation of the need for additional public expenditure. Here we are concerned only to explore the implications for economic growth on the hypothesis that a very large increase of public expenditure is necessary.

There are two main possibilities to be considered. One is that we cannot raise tax rates above their present levels, at least without serious effects upon economic growth. The other is that we *will* not raise tax rates. In either case the yield of the existing tax rates sets a limit to public expenditure, and the only way to raise that expenditure would be to increase the yield of the existing tax rates by increasing the rate of economic growth.

Granted a willingness to raise tax rates, it must be recognized that certain patterns of tax increase might tend to retard the rate of growth. But substantial additions to revenue can be obtained without such an effect. This might involve some combination of (a) increases in the beginning rate of individual income tax (b) a broadening of the income tax base by reduction of exemptions and exclusions and (c) increased taxation of consumption.

Such taxation would be burdensome, but this burden is simply that which is implicit in any decision to sacrifice private consumption for public expenditures.

Whether higher public expenditures financed by higher taxes will retard the rate of economic growth depends not only on the character of the taxes but also on the character of the expenditures. If the expenditure increase is heavily weighted with public investment, research, education, and defense programs with a large research content, and if the taxation impinges almost entirely on private consumption, the net effect may be a higher rate of growth.

The argument to this point may be summarized as follows: if the national product is wisely used, the contribution of a higher rate of economic growth would be the satisfaction of less critical needs, not of the most critical needs. But the less critical needs are still worth satisfying, and should not be disregarded. They motivate a large part of the work done in this country.

If this country does not allocate its output to the most important uses, it cannot be sure that any specified rate of growth or level of output will satisfy its critical needs. In this case there are two possibilities. One is to increase the rate of growth, which would probably increase the likelihood that important needs would be met. The other is to become more intelligent in recognizing and responding to vital needs. The latter is essential whatever is done about the former. If we are not wise in the use of our resources, we cannot expect the abundance of our resources always to compensate.

The competition of Soviet growth

Up to this point we have been discussing the value of more rapid growth as a means of satisfying private or public needs for goods and services. In the present state of the world, rapid growth of the American economy may have an additional value.

Let us postulate this situation. The Soviet economy is now growing at a percentage rate higher than ours. If this should continue, the absolute annual growth of the Soviet economy will overtake our growth (it may already have done so). Although there are strong reasons to believe that the Soviet Union will be unable to maintain a growth rate faster than ours once it has achieved a comparable level of technical efficiency, let us nonetheless assume that it will do so. Suppose further that, despite this, the United States is able to maintain an adequate military establishment, provide for necessary public services and sustain a rate of growth of private income that is satisfactory to the American people individually. Would we then regard our rate of growth as adequate?

This is an extremely difficult question to answer. It requires us to project our imaginations into a totally new economic, political and psychological situation. We, our allies, neutral nations, and the Soviet bloc are all deeply affected by the vision of the United States as by far the world's richest and economically strongest country. It is hard to conceive a world in which this would not be true.

But it seems possible that a change to a situation in which the Soviet economy is generally recognized to be growing faster than ours, not only in percentages but also absolutely, not in spurts but steadily, and is approaching ours in total size, could have profound consequences. It could greatly strengthen the confidence of the Russians in their own system, increase the attraction of the Communist system for the independent, underdeveloped countries, worry our allies about their reliance upon us, and weaken our own morale.

These consequences might not follow. Certainly they are paradoxical on their face. They imply that in order to increase the attraction of our system to populations with average per capita incomes of $100 we, with per capita incomes of $2,000, must become still richer faster. They imply that even though we fully discharge our real obligations to our allies, they will lose confidence in us because we do not choose to raise our personal consumption more rapidly. They imply that the rest of the world will not evaluate us by the standards we choose for ourselves but will compel us to be measured by standards made in Moscow.

Moreover no one really knows what the standards are in the production race upon which world opinion is said to hinge. We do not know whether the Soviet GNP is now one-third of ours or two-thirds of ours, because the composition of their GNP is so different from ours. And it is not clear whether the race is in GNP at all, or in steel production, or in butter consumption per capita. Each side presumably wants to race on its own track and to persuade the world that it is the right track. The outcome may depend as much on the persuasion as on the running.

Nevertheless the possibility described cannot be ignored. Accelerating our pace in the production race is probably a positive factor for our national security. How important a factor it is, the authors cannot pretend to say. This is a question the American people will have to decide on the advice of people more expert than we in the politics and psychology of the cold war. If they should decide that it is important, this would, in our opinion, be the strongest reason for a collective decision to increase the rate of growth.

The costs of accelerating growth must still be considered. We do not do *everything* that might promote our national security. Especially, we want to promote our national security in the most efficient way. Somehow we must judge whether a cost of x spent in accelerating growth will yield more in national security than the same cost spent for weapons, or for foreign aid, or for space exploration, or for education, or for reducing racial discrimination, or for tempering nationalism, or for many other things that affect our military, political and psychological position in the cold war.

How might we grow?

On the basis of our estimates, the national product could be raised one per cent above what it would otherwise be in 1970, which would add .1 per cent to the annual growth rate over the next ten years, by any one of the following means:

Double the rate of net immigration during the next decade; or

Curtail by about one-third the reduction that might otherwise be expected in standard annual working hours; or

Reduce by one-eighth the loss of labor resulting from illness, accidents, seasonal fluctuations, excess labor in agriculture, illegal activities, concentrated long-term unemployment, and labor disputes; or

Raise the proportion of gross national product devoted to net investment 1.1 percentage points above what it would otherwise be throughout the next ten years.

This result might also be achieved by an assault on obstacles to the most effective use of resources and on immobility; by an even greater increase in research outlays than is now in prospect; by more effective allocation and organization of the research effort; or by narrowing the gap between the average level of techniques and the best known. The yield from these has not been quantified, but we believe that the effort required to add 1 per cent to the 1970 national product through any of these channels would be major, not trivial.

Increase in education is a major source of long-term growth, but it is already too late to raise 1970 output by lengthening the education of those now attending school.

We of course cannot estimate the effort that the American people might be willing to undertake to increase the rate of growth by these means. Without an extraordinary concerted effort, however, we doubt that the effect would be "big," if by "big" is meant the order of magnitude suggested by an increase from 3 per cent to 4 per cent, or from 4 per cent to 5 per cent. This is not a surprising conclusion. There is no reason to expect an increase

in growth out of proportion to the increase in the forces that produce growth. An increase from 3 per cent to 4 per cent is an increase of one-third; an increase from 3 per cent to 5 per cent is an increase of two-thirds. The authors would not accept this criterion of bigness. We consider differences much smaller than this important and, if achieved by means that are worth their cost, well worth seeking.

Economic growth is a good thing, and it is tempting to elevate any good thing to the state of a goal of national policy. The main point of our paper is that the establishment of such a goal is wise only if the benefits of the "good thing" are worth its costs. We have neither invented nor discovered the costs. In fact, we suppose that consciousness of these costs has weighed in the decisions not to undertake the measures that might have given us more rapid growth in the past.

In closing, the authors repeat what was said at the outset. We do not, in this paper, attempt to decide what the public attitude toward the rate of growth should be. This is a question that the people must decide, referring to the kinds of considerations discussed here but also in the end expressing their own values, their own views of what is worth what.

Reading 62

The previous Stein and Denison reading presents a rather pessimistic appraisal of the goal of growth, perhaps more pessimistic than most economists would agree with. Actually, events of recent years have turned out more optimistically than Stein and Denison envisaged—not merely because full employment was reattained, but also because American productivity in the 1960s has responded remarkably well to vigorous growth programs.

Here Robert M. Solow, professor of economics at M.I.T. and one-time president of the Econometric Society, presents a forceful analysis of our growth potentialities. Point by point he appraises the Denison estimates, isolating the reasons why they seem too low.

Questions to Guide the Reading

What are the principal policy choices that might flow from an acceptance of the Solow estimates on the relative importance of the various factors contributing to our growth record to date?

How important to the American economy are the differences between the "three percenters" and "four percenters" in the debate on growth?

Sources and Outlook for Growth
Robert M. Solow

To me, economic growth means the expansion of the economy's potential output, its capacity to produce. What is produced in a particular quarter or year or decade cannot for long exceed the economy's normal potential or capacity. But it may well fall short if the level of demand is insufficient to buy what the economy is capable of producing.

If we concentrate on economic growth as the growth of capacity to produce rather than the growth of demand, which is an important but separate problem, the foundation of any broad view must evaluate the major determinants of potential output and productivity in an economy, the chances of influencing them and the effectiveness of changes in the determinants on capacity output itself.

Determinants of potential output

Everyone is in broad agreement about the nature of the major determinants of potential output, but there is some disagreement about their relative influence, and recent research has led to some revision of earlier opinions. The main sources of potential output we can name pretty clearly:

1. The first determinant is the number of people available for employment; the number of hours they wish to work; and the level and distribution of skills, education, health and attitudes toward work. I suppose one ought to include managerial and entrepreneurial knowledge and ability as a special kind of labor, or perhaps it deserves a heading to itself.

2. The second broad and important determinant is the size of the existing stock of capital goods and its distribution by age, by industry and by location.

3. The third important determinant is the level of technology. Here one must distinguish between the extent of technological knowledge and the degree to which it can be made effective, because that may depend in large part on the age distribution of the existing capital stock. There is a sense in which the whole civilized world shares the discoveries of modern science and engineering on an equal basis, but an economy saddled with an antiquated stock of capital may be unable to use what in principle it knows.

4. The fourth determinant, I would say, is the terms on which the economy has access to natural resources, whether through domestic production or through imports.

5. The fifth determinant is the efficiency with which resources are allocated to different economic ends; the extent of monopolistic or other barriers to the movement of capital and labor from low productivity to high productivity uses; and the degree of resistance to the introduction of new technology.

If these are the basic determinants of potential output, then the growth of productive capacity is largely limited by the rate at which the basic determinants can be expanded and improved. That, in turn, depends upon the ease with which these determinants themselves can be influenced by conscious policy or fortuitous events, and upon the sensitivity of potential output to changes in the determinants themselves.

Opinions about this have changed drastically over the last century, and even over the last dozen years. The classical economists believed that the ultimate limit to economic growth was given by the finite availability of natural resources. It has always been a source of wonder to me how such intelligent and perceptive men, writing at a time when the industrial revolution had clearly taken secure hold on England, could so underestimate the power of technological progress in offsetting the effects of diminishing returns. Maybe this is a high standard to apply. We still occasionally read dire predictions that we are about to run out of natural resources.

From Robert M. Solow, "Economic Growth and Residential Housing," in *Conference on Savings and Residential Financing, 1962 Proceedings* (United States Savings and Loan League, Chicago, 1962). Reprinted with kind permission of the author and publisher.

Technology and resource scarcity

The truth is, of course, that as certain raw materials become physically scarce, it becomes more expensive to extract them from nature; but this tendency is offset partly by technical progress, partly by investment in improved methods and management, partly by increased reliance on imports and partly by the substitution of cheap raw materials for expensive ones. Even these "partly's" may not add up to the whole. If the offsets are not fully effective, resources can be obtained at somewhat higher cost by digging deeper, using leaner ores, conserving wastes and using heavier equipment. The necessity of devoting more labor and capital to extractive industry is indeed equivalent to a net decline in the productivity of the economy as a whole; but it certainly does not set, as far as we can see, an absolute limit to the growth of the economy.

One way of measuring the effects of resource scarcity is by looking at the long-term trend of raw materials prices relative to finished product prices in general. When one does so, one finds that all raw materials are now about 25% more expensive relative to finished products than they were at the turn of the century, but only 5% more expensive than they were in 1925–1929. More interesting than this very gentle tendency toward increased real cost of raw materials is the wide variety of behavior exhibited by different classes of raw materials. Lumber products have indeed increased rapidly in relative price, almost doubling since 1925–1929, and almost tripling since the turn of the century. This is the way Ricardo presumably expected all raw materials to behave. But there actually may have been some tendency for this trend to moderate in recent years. Mineral construction materials, on the other hand, are cheaper relative to finished goods in general than they were at the turn of the century, though not quite as cheap as they were just before 1914. In any case, the only sound conclusion is that there is much less to natural resource scarcity than meets the eye.

We are a long way from having reliable quantitative answers to the kind of question I am now discussing, but about some gross facts I think we can be fairly confident. I believe, for instance, that it would now be generally accepted that earlier thinking on this subject substantially underestimated the influence of improving the quality of human resources on the economy's capacity to produce.

Educational level and income

This is a particularly tricky area in which to make quantitative inferences, mainly because of the difficulty of imputing observed differences in income at different educational levels in part to differences in native ability and in part to education itself. But if one takes Edward Denison's recent estimates as a fair example, he attributes some 40% of the average annual growth between 1929 and 1957 in national income per person employed to the effects of education in improving the quality of the average man-hour of work. Between 1909 and 1929, he estimates the contribution of education to have been only about a quarter of the annual growth rate in productivity. Notice that this estimate excludes the contribution of education to the advance of knowledge itself.

In other words, had the educational level of the labor force remained stationary where it was in 1929, national income per person employed would have risen not at an average annual rate of 1.6%, as it did between 1929 and 1957, but at something less than 1.0% per year. That is a big difference.

The other big revaluation that has taken place in recent years has to do with the relative importance of capital investment and technical change. The older economists seemed to think of increases in output per man-hour (of constant quality, though they did not often mention that) as being primarily or exclusively a matter of the deepening of capital, of increased capital per worker. Within the last 10 years, research done by Schmookler, Abramovitz, Kendrick and others, including myself, seemed to show that this was not the case. An explanation of the macroeconomic facts appeared to require the conclusion that observed increases in output per man-hour over a 50-year period had only little to do with the increase in capital per worker. The bulk of the explanation, between 85% and 90%, had to come from other sources such as labor quality, technological progress and the like.

Capital investment and economic growth

This downgrading of fixed investment as a source of growth had genuine policy implications. Calculations based on these ideas suggested that substantial rates of growth were obtainable with little or no net investment, and that any visible acceleration of growth through the stimulation of capital formation would require fantastic amounts of investment —although people sometimes forget that with net investment only about half of gross, a 10% increase in the rate of gross investment means in the short run a 20% increase in the rate of net investment.

I finally came to think that this undervaluation, or downgrading, of the importance of capital investment was really a little implausible and that all reasoning like that, including my own, overlooked the fact that at least some technological progress requires being embodied in newly designed types of fixed capital before it becomes effective in production. Investment thus serves the purpose not only of adding to the stock of capital per worker, but also of improving its quality, of carrying new technology into operation.

You could easily devise numerical examples that would convince you that this could make a real difference in the story. When account is taken of "embodied" inventions, the kind of inventions that need new kinds of capital to become effective, then a surge in the rate of capital formation will have bigger effects on potential output than the simple notion of "residual" productivity increase would lead one to expect.

Some rough econometric estimates I once made seem to me to give a plausible figure for the size of the investment effort needed to support a somewhat higher growth rate over the next 10 years. For example, a growth rate of 4% annually in potential GNP between 1960 and 1970, which means a growth rate of some 4½% in realized GNP if 1970, unlike 1960, is a year of full utilization, would require investment in plant and equipment of roughly 11% of GNP as compared with about 9% in the last few years and slightly higher than we had in 1955–1957. This is on the assumption that all technical changes need to be embodied in new fixed capital.

One of the troubles with this whole line of thought is that it is just about impossible to make aggregate data tell anything about the extent to which innovations are of the embodied kind and the extent to which they are disembodied. Denison simply assumes it is half and half, and comes to the conclusion that between 1929 and 1957 less than 10% of the annual growth rate of national income per person employed can be imputed to the increase in reproducible capital per employee, while over a third of the annual growth rate of productivity in the same period can be attributed to the advance of knowledge. My casual guess would be that more than half of technical progress is the embodied kind, but I do not know how to find out.

Capital stock: size, age distribution

The extra "oomph" one gets from investment in this new view comes from the fact that a burst of investment changes not only the size of the capital stock, but also its age distribution. Lowering the average age of the capital stock gives a productivity bonus. But it is not easy to change the average age of a long-lived stock. An increase in plant and equipment investment relative to GNP will eventually move the age distribution of capital as far as it is ever going to move it, and then it will not move it any further. Then the average age remains stationary and the higher growth rate lapses back to what it was when the investment quota was lower, relative to GNP. Output will be forever at a higher level, but the very long-run growth rate will not change. But over a 10- or 20-year period, the change in the investment quota might make a substantial difference.

I might conclude this section by remarking that we probably know least about the contribution to economic growth that could be made by more efficient allocation of resources, the costs of monopoly, restriction and immobility. In some areas—agriculture, perhaps—the costs may be great, and therefore the growth advantage, temporary of course, from removing the restriction may be correspondingly great. But not much is known about the economic costs of monopoly and similar sources of mal-allocation.

I have been dealing at a fairly general level with the trends in ideas about economic growth. When one comes to specific projections of the prospects for economic growth in the United States over the next decade, it turns out that there are at least two schools of thought. They might be described as the three-percenters and the four-percenters. The five-percenter is a dying race.

Three percenters versus four percenters

The most important three-percenter is Edward Denison, whose monumental work I have already cited. Denison estimates that in the absence of a massive policy effort to raise the rate of growth—and the elements of that effort need only be mentioned to scare the pants off you—potential output will grow at something like 3.3% a year over the next decade. Note that this growth rate refers to potential output, not realized output. If, as the evidence seems to suggest, real GNP in 1960 fell 5% or 6% below potential, then the path from 1960 to full employment in 1970 would rise at about 3.8% or 3.9% a year on the average.

The four-percenters are represented by the National Planning Association, the Council of Economic Advisers and apparently John F. Kennedy. They estimate that a moderate policy program favoring economic growth could make potential output rise at something like 4% a year between 1960 and 1970—perhaps even a little faster. And if the path to 1970 winds up at full employment, the actual annual growth rate could exceed 4½%.

No one has yet tried to trace back the difference between the two schools of thought to critical hypotheses or evaluations, and I think it is worth doing. Maybe we ought to begin by laying out the assumptions the two schools hold in common. One would suppose that both schools of thought would at least begin from one piece of common ground: the rate of growth in the past. But even there one finds a vague but important difference in view.

The long-term rate of growth of potential GNP in the United States from 1929 to 1960, or even from 1909 to 1960, is about 3% a year. The three-percenters tend to start from that figure and ask where one might find grounds to hope for an acceleration. But the 15 years since the end of the Second World War have aleady seen a substantial acceleration beyond 3%. Between 1947 and 1960, actual GNP rose at an average rate of 3½%, and rough allow-

ance for the slack existing in 1960 can raise the postwar rate of growth of potential output to 4%. Some of that extraordinarily rapid growth was undoubtedly a consequence of unrepeatable factors: the war itself, and the long depression that preceded it. Even so, the Council of Economic Advisers has estimated that since 1954 or 1955, by which time the legacy of war and depression had probably run its course, potential GNP has been increasing at some 3½% a year.

The four-percenters tend to start from the more recent record, and this explains in part their more optimistic conclusions. But one cannot decide the issue on such grounds. There is no general law of economics or nature which tells you whether the last 50 years or the last 15 years provide a better guide to the next 10 years. No analogies about tails wagging dogs or dogs wagging tails have any explanatory power, because the economy, whatever it is, is probably not a dog. You have to look closer.

Labor force and hours worked

The least controversial element in projections of economic growth for the 1960s is the labor force and the trend of annual hours worked. The three-percenters and the four-percenters are in rough agreement that the labor force will grow at an annual rate of about 1¾% between 1960 and 1970, substantially faster than the 1.3% annual rate recorded between 1947 and 1960. As usual, part of this growth in potential employment will be offset by a continuation of the trend toward shorter hours. The fairly universal conclusion is that annual man-hours at full employment will rise at about 1¼% a year to 1970, compared with ¾ of 1% from 1947 to 1960. This already gives us a leg up toward faster growth of aggregate output during the coming decade. But what actually happens depends, of course, on the path of output per man-hour, and that is the nub of the difference between the two schools of thought.

Between 1947 and 1960, potential GNP per man-hour rose at an annual rate of 3.2% a year—3.8% between 1947 and 1954, and 2.6% between 1954 and 1960. If productivity rises between 1960 and 1970 at the same rate as it did from 1954 to 1960, potential GNP will grow at an annual rate of 3.8% a year in the coming decade. If productivity rises somewhat faster than it did between 1954 and 1960, but slightly less fast than between 1947 and 1960, and considerably slower than between 1947 and 1954—say, at 3% a year or thereabouts—then potential GNP can rise at 4% a year between now and 1970. To bring about this acceleration will cost something, perhaps an increase in the plant and equipment share in GNP from the 9.5% of 1954–1960 (even with 1955–1957) toward the 11.2% of 1947–1954. Indeed, the four-percenters project for 1960 to 1970 a growth in the stock of capital of about 3½% a year, about the rate achieved from 1947 to 1960, and a bit faster than 1954–1960.

The three-percenters, on the other hand, project a rise in output per man-hour at only about 2% a year, roughly the rate observed in the 1929–1960 period, and considerably slower than the postwar, or even the 1954–1960, rate. Correspondingly, Denison, for example, projects capital stock growth at 2.5% a year rather than 3.5%, faster than 1929–1957 (1.9% a year including the Great Depression) but slower than anything observed in the postwar period.

Sources of differences of opinion

To sum up the gross difference of opinion: Starting from the same projection for employment and hours, the four-percenters estimate productivity to rise at a rate of about 0.7% or 0.8% a year faster than the three-percenters do, and this makes the difference between 3.3% and 4.0% in the annual rate of growth of GNP.

Can we track down this difference to more specific hypotheses? We can. The seven-tenths of a point in the growth rate can be accounted for in this way:

a. The one percentage point difference in the estimated rate of growth of capital accounts for about 0.20 to 0.25 point in the rate of growth of GNP.

b. Denison estimates pure technological change to proceed at an annual rate of about 0.2 point below that of the postwar period, and this accounts for about the same difference in the rate of growth of GNP. Optimists expect no such deceleration, and some even hope for a slight increase.

c. The pessimistic projections have investment in education contributing 0.1 point less to productivity growth than in the recent past.

d. By a complicated bit of guesswork, Denison estimates that a much smaller part of the expected decline in hours worked will be offset by automatic improvement in productivity resulting from lessened fatigue and the like; this is enough to account for 0.2 percentage point in the growth of productivity and of output.

I have time for only a few cursory comments on these ultimate components of the difference between a 3% and a 4% growth of potential.

a. There can be no doubt that some part of the postwar spurt of fixed investment was a "make-up" phenomenon, and the rate of growth of the capital stock has slowed visibly in recent years. But the weakness of fixed investment is both cause and effect of the slack that has developed in the economy since 1956, and that slack is remediable by policy.

Even so, the problem should not be blinked. If there is anything to the law of diminishing returns, then extra growth of output through the deepening of capital can be bought only at the expense of a lower profit rate on capital. It is the combined job of fiscal and monetary policy to sweeten that profit rate a little at the margin and to make a somewhat lower profit rate more acceptable by lowering the return on assets alternative to real capital. There might then be difficulties on the side of saving, and this might call for additional policy measures or be taken as a sign that economic growth is not a highly valued social goal.

b. On the rate of pure technological progress, nobody is in a position to speak with authority. There has certainly been an immense increase in research and development expenditure in the postwar period, much of it financed by the federal government and concentrated on industries connected with defense. Whether those outlays have already borne fruit or whether there is more to come, it is difficult to say. But there is perhaps a case for believing that federal policy could contribute to the acceleration of economic growth by an effort to spread into purely civilian industries the kind of technological pressure that seems to have had major results in electronics and space technology.

c. It may be that as time goes on, given the finite number of days in the year, the all but universal diffusion of primary and secondary education, and human impatience, there is an inevitable retardation in the rate at which the quality of the labor force can be improved through education. The unevenness of educational quality from state to state suggests that perhaps something can be done there to pick up the 0.1 point on the growth rate that Denison loses. I am not competent to judge.

d. On this point I think Denison is not so much vulnerable as unconvincing. His assumption is that as late as 1929, when the average employee worked about 2,500 hours a year (between 48 and 49 hours a week), any small reduction in the hours of work was fully compensated by a corresponding increase in productivity because of diminished fatigue, better attentiveness and the like. By 1957, on the other hand, when the average employee worked about 2,050 hours a year, or just about 40 hours a week, he assumes that a further slight reduction in hours was offset to the extent of 40% by the same forces. Extrapolation leads to the conclusion that further reduction in hours will be only about 20% offset and, therefore, more damaging to output.

That some such process is at work is surely true, but Denison himself emphasizes how little is known about the exact relationship. I cannot bring myself to believe that as recently as 1929 the marginal product of an additional hour worked was negative, and I suspect that those European countries which still have a workweek close to 48 hours would be surprised to learn that they could add to output by working less.

Moreover, the reduction in average hours since 1929 has been much sharper in the diminishing agricultural work force than in industry. The average workweek in manufacturing was 44 hours in 1929. It does not matter so much exactly what the degree of offset was in 1929. If the change in the offset was more gradual than Denison suggests, his conclusion would not be so pessimistic.

I conclude that when it is tracked down to its origin, the difference between the three-percenters and the four-percenters is not solidly based. That does not say who is right, but it does suggest the possibility that economic policy need not turn our society on its ear to elicit a growth of potential output near to 4% a year.

Full employment and economic growth

Here I would like to say something about the relation between full employment and economic growth as goals of policy. Does an aggressive full employment policy also stimulate economic growth or retard it?

There are a number of subquestions here which need to be disentangled. The view has recently been expressed in the United Kingdom that some decrease in the average pressure of demand on resources, accompanied by a small increase in the unemployment rate, would be desirable for several reasons and could be engineered without any deterioration in the growth rate and perhaps with some improvement.

I am not sufficiently well acquainted with conditions in the United Kingdom to hold a strong opinion on this subject, but I do not find this view wholly implausible. For one thing, continuous full employment may tend to generate inflationary pressure on prices (whether originating in labor markets or product markets) and recurrent balance-of-payments crises, which require that the upward march of demand be halted frequently.

In turn, the necessary restriction of demand, either through credit tightness or tax policy, may for one reason or another fall heavily on fixed investment. I can easily imagine that this chain of events could make it true that a little extra slack could be engineered without ultimately reducing the growth rate, and perhaps even help it over a decent interval of time.

Secondly, it is often said that a perpetually tight economy builds up immobilities, barriers to the adoption of new technology and resistance to competition. This may be so. What I have observed in the United States is the reverse phenomenon. Too much slack in an economy can build up the same kinds of pressures against innovation, against technological advance, against the mobility of labor and capital from declining to advancing sectors of the economy. In the United States, at least, one even observes an ebb and flow of sentiment for a shortening of the workweek with the business cycle, which relates not to any real preferences for leisure as against income but to a feeling that there is simply not enough employment to go around without a decrease in weekly hours.

Other examples are not hard to find. The movement of labor out of agriculture, for instance, is clearly intimately related to labor market conditions in industry. When urban unemployment is low, the rate of migration out of agriculture is high, and vice versa. Of course the rate of migration is also sensitive to the market for agricultural products. When farmers are doing well, as during the Korean war, even a tight demand for labor in industry will not pull up the migration rate. But that does not contradict my observations.

Growth and economic efficiency

This position that—to quote a recent Report of the Council of Economic Advisers—"a full employment economy can achieve more rapid growth than an economy alternating between boom and recession; for that reason effective stabilization policy is the first step toward a policy of economic growth" has been attacked as theoretically weak and even anti-Schumpeterian. I suppose it is the latter, but not the former.

Joseph Schumpeter argued that the business cycle is the way in which a capitalistic economy makes progress. Eliminate or damp the business cycle, and you slow down the rate of progress. More specifically, of course, Schumpeter had a theory of the bunching of technical innovations. The depression is a way of shaking the unsuccessful or obsolete ones out of the system. Anyone who believes this doctrine believes in strong medicine. The business cycle Schumpeter was thinking of, which is supposed to be necessary for capitalist progress, was not the minor postwar business cycle, but the deeper 10-year major cycle of the 19th century and the prewar years. If that is necessary for economic growth, then the almost worldwide acceleration of growth during the last 15 years becomes very difficult to explain.

Short business cycle and economic growth

Indeed, even the belief that the short business cycle is an indispensable midwife for economic growth is hard to maintain in the face of the postwar history of western European countries. Most of them have experienced faster productivity growth than we have; most of them have shown a sharper acceleration of their prewar trends; and all of them have maintained a consistently tighter pressure of demand and a consistently lower unemployment rate than we have, even allowing for differences in definition and statistical practice.

I have been arguing that steady full employment need not prejudice the growth of potential output. It is a more difficult question whether steady full employment might itself increase the rate of growth. This is once again largely a question of the rate of investment. Despite the fact that plant and equipment spending falls off in recession and rises in recovery, it is logically possible that wiping out the business cycle might not increase the average rate of investment relative to aggregate output. It might be that over a complete business cycle we get all the investment we would get even if the business cycle were not there, only we get it concentrated in periods of high employment, filling in the holes left by periods of low employment.

If, for example, investment were governed simply by the acceleration principle, this would be the case. Nobody can say for sure what the true state of affairs is. I am inclined to believe that the main effect of high-level stability on the volume of investment would be a reduction in the riskiness of investment. It seems plausible that one of the reasons businesses seem to demand a high expected rate of return on new projects is to compensate for the risk of inadequate markets.

The confident expectation of full employment by reducing that risk would probably make for a somewhat lower acceptable average rate of return. In my neoclassical view, that is an important part of the battle to generate higher capacity through the deepening of capital, for, apart from the effects of technical progress, each successive increment to productivity bought in this way involves diminished profitability. If I am right on this, an aggressive full-employment policy would elicit more investment averaged over a cycle than we now have, and this would contribute to economic growth. This argument also suggests that an important part of a fiscal policy designed to add to growth through investment might be an extension of income averaging for tax purposes, more complete loss offsets for corporations and, in this way, some socialization of risk.

Military-Industrial Complex

Reading 63

If the military-industrial complex has a reality, here must be its corporate membership. This list was compiled for the Stanford Research Institute and reported in the press by Professor Murray Weidenbaum of Washington University in St. Louis. Dr. Weidenbaum, who has served as economist for Boeing Aircraft, was appointed assistant secretary of the Treasury by President Nixon.

Questions to Guide the Reading

After World War II, during and after the age of Stalin, the Cold War was marked by Berlin crises; Yugoslavian, Hungarian, and Czechoslovakian departures from orthodoxy; Korean and Vietnam wars; Russian-Chinese tensions; and the Castro revolution in Cuba. Do businesses originate such tensions? Exacerbate them? Do they merely act to take advantage of any public dollar demand for defense wares? What evidence do you think could be useful in evaluating the validity of different points of view?

Who's Who in the Military-Industrial Complex

Murray L. Weidenbaum

Importance of Defense-Space Orders to 35 Major Contractors (fiscal year 1962)

Company	Defense contracts (millions)	NASA contracts (millions)	Total (1) + (2) (millions)	Company sales* (millions)	Ratio of defense-space orders to total sales (3)/(4)
75–100%					
Republic Aviation	$ 332.8	$ 6.9	$ 339.7	$ 295.8	100.00%
McDonnell Aircraft	310.9	68.5	379.4	390.7	97.11
Grumman Aircraft Engr.	303.6	24.6	328.2	357.1	91.91
Lockheed Aircraft	1,419.5	5.0	1,424.5	1,753.1	81.27
AVCO	323.3	1.4	324.7	414.3	78.37
North American Aviation	1,032.5	199.1	1,231.6	1,633.7	75.39
Hughes Aircraft	234.2	9.2	243.4	†	‡
50–74%					
Collins Radio	150.1	3.7	153.8	207.8	74.01
Thiokol Chemical	178.3	0.8	179.1	255.8	70.02
Raytheon	406.6	—	406.6	580.7	70.02
Newport News Shipbuilding & Dry Dock	185.0	—	185.0	267.3	69.21
Martin Marietta	802.7	1.8	804.5	1,195.3	67.31
Boeing	1,132.8	15.6	1,148.4	1,768.5	64.94
General Dynamics	1,196.6	27.9	1,224.5	1,898.4	64.50
Curtiss-Wright	144.6	—	144.6	228.7	63.23
United Aircraft	662.7	34.1	696.8	1,162.1	59.96
Douglas Aircraft	365.6	68.4	434.0	749.9	57.87

From Murray L. Weidenbaum, "Defense-Space Business," *The New York Times*, April 13, 1964, p. 18. © 1964 by The New York Times Company. Reprinted with kind permission of the author and publisher.

Company	Defense contracts (millions)	NASA contracts (millions)	Total (1) + (2) (millions)	Company sales* (millions)	Ratio of defense-space orders to total sales (3)/(4)
25–49%					
American Machine & Foundry	$187.3	$ —	$187.3	$ 415.4	45.09%
General Tire & Rubber	366.1	66.4	432.5	959.8	45.06
Northrop	152.5	1.3	153.8	347.5	44.26
Hercules Powder	181.6	—	181.6	454.8	39.93
Sperry Rand	465.6	2.2	467.8	1,182.6	39.56
Bendix	285.9	19.4	305.3	788.1	38.74
FMC	160.4	—	160.4	506.5	31.67
Pan Amer. World Airways	146.7	—	146.7	503.9	29.11
0–24%					
International Tel. & Tel.	243.6	2.2	245.8	995.5	24.69
General Electric	975.9	23.0	998.9	4,792.7	20.84
Radio Corp. of America	339.6	20.2	359.8	1,742.7	20.65
Westinghouse Electric	246.0	3.4	249.4	1,954.5	12.76
International Bus. Machines	155.5	12.6	168.1	1,925.2	8.73
American Tel. & Tel.	467.7	10.8	478.5	11,742.4	4.07
Ford Motor	269.1	—	269.1	8,089.6	3.33
General Motors	449.0	1.4	450.4	14,640.2	3.08
Standard Oil (New Jersey)	180.1	—	180.1	9,537.3	1.89

* Net sales for fiscal year ending during 1962.
† Not available.
‡ Estimated from other sources to be in excess of 75 percent.
NOTE: In some cases, it appears that the ratio of defense-space orders to total sales in fiscal year 1962 is not an accurate indicator of the actual ratio of military-space sales to total sales.
SOURCE: M. L. Weidenbaum, Stanford Research Institute.

Reading 64

One of the most important contributions of modern economics to public policy is in the area called "cost-benefit" analysis. Instead of deciding issues by anecdotes, hunches, and uninformed emotion, the planner today tries to quantify the advantages and disadvantages of each action.

As a check upon the "military-industrial complex," a group of "whiz kids" were recruited into the Pentagon by President Kennedy—from Ford Motors and the universities. Secretaries of Defense Robert McNamara and Clark Clifford—in contrast to their predecessor and successor, Charles Wilson ("what's good for General Motors is good for the country," that Wilson) and Melvin Laird—fought the generals and admirals with the tools of fact and logic.

Here Alain C. Enthoven, one-time Rhodes Scholar from Stanford and Ph.D. from M.I.T., shows how the computer and judgment led to rejection of the ABM program. (Later President Nixon reversed the decision, counter to the almost universal opposition of informed scientists. The case is important for its own sake, but also for its illustration of general methods.)

Questions to Guide the Reading

Should war matters be decided by the *brain* at all, rather than being matters for the *heart* alone? How could two men, each with accurate computers, possibly come out with answers that do not agree?

What if the ABM would buy extra immunity from (1) a Chinese *first*-strike? From (2) a Soviet *first*-strike? Would that justify our building it at great expense? Would your answer be different if you knew that our building the ABM would cause the Soviets to do likewise, and to regard our action as "provocative"? Suppose submarine Poseidon missiles preserved our retaliatory powers after an enemy first-strike more cheaply than ABM? What decision then? Appraise the Laird argument that an ABM will give us greater "bargaining power" to get the Soviets to be "reasonable."

Cost-Benefit Analysis: Rejecting the ABM by Judgment and Computer

Alain C. Enthoven

It is obvious that our society today faces problems of public policy that are both numerous and exceedingly complex. This is true in foreign relations and defense, and it is true at home in our cities, our universities, and our increasingly polluted air and water. Never has there been a greater need for thorough study, clear thought, and thoughtful reflection. These problems involve both people and things, how people relate to each other and to things, and how things relate to each other and to people. Therefore, they involve both questions of value and questions of physical fact.

The complexity of these problems is increasing. The things involved are more complicated than they used to be. They work faster, fly farther, perform more functions that used to be done by human hands, legs, and brains, and more of them need repairmen with Ph.D.'s in physics. In many ways the people involved are also more complicated.

Two examples of these complex modern problems are national security and the decay of our central cities. One important aspect of the problem is the allocation of resources. Given the resources available to the federal government, how much should be used on defense and how should these resources be allocated among defense programs? These questions can be answered only after the effectiveness and costs of different defense strategies and programs have been estimated and after alternative uses for the resources in other areas have been considered. The problem of relating costs to programs and of measuring the effectiveness of these programs is becoming more complicated, however. This is partly because the *things* involved—long-range missiles, submarines, and tanks—are all derived from an increasingly complex technology that is changing faster and faster. Both the costs and the performance of future weapons are becoming more uncertain. Another reason for the increased complexity is that the people involved in defending our country are having different and greater demands placed on them; the nuclear age imposes constraints on military operations unlike any in the past. Thus, the problem of managing military operations and judging human reactions and behavior under modern political conditions is more difficult than it ever has been.

The problems with our cities primarily concern people. We have poverty and slums in our central cities because of the way people are and because of what they do, and the solution basically lies in changing people—more specifically, their attitudes. But can we change attitudes? I believe we can, since attitudes are a product of environment. Education is the most long-lasting way of changing attitudes, but, given the pace at which the problem worsens, we may not have time to wait for the effects of such a long-term solution.

One of the difficulties in attempting to change people's attitudes toward ghetto Negroes and other minority groups is that many people feel that they have a firm basis for their attitudes or prejudices in their value system. Here is a particular danger point, since some

From Alain C. Enthoven, "Analysis, Judgment, and Computers: Their Use in Complex Problems," *Business Horizons*, Graduate School of Business, Indiana University. Copyright © 1969 by the Foundation for the School of Business, at Indiana University. Reprinted with kind permission of the author and the publisher.

part of the value scheme held by almost all of us can be used to justify a given attitude or prejudice. This is because our value schemes have hidden inconsistencies. One striking example of this is that attitudes stemming from the value many of us place on hard work and individual effort lead to the continuation of ghettos since we tend to assume that hard work and individual effort must lead to prosperity. But the plain fact is that, once in the ghetto, it is extremely difficult to pull oneself out. However, the continuation of the ghetto situation itself is not consistent with other values of ours concerned with justice, equality of opportunity, and alleviation of human suffering. Through analysis we can sort out our values and, with the aid of education, we can change attitudes.

Analysis—servant of judgment

Analysis is the tool the human mind uses for understanding the kinds of problems I have described. The main point is that analysis is the servant of judgment for the solving of both our personal, everyday problems and the problems of large organizations. In no way can analysis be a substitute for judgment; it only focuses judgment on the key issues.

I emphasize that analysis is the servant of judgment, not a replacement for it, because there has been much misunderstanding of this point both by critics of the use of analysis in policy making and by some specialists in analytical method. The critics know that there are many important imponderables in policy issues, and that judgment must play the decisive role in the making of sensible choices. In this they are right. But they are wrong in attacking all uses of analysis; they should be more discriminating in their criticism.

I would say that, in most good analyses of public policy, more than 95 per cent of the important effort is taken up with asking the right question, formulating the problem, gathering relevant data, determining its validity, and deciding on good assumptions.

There is a related point. In the world of operations research and computers, the object of the game is to calculate the best answer—given the assumptions, of course. In the world of public policy there is no best answer to most questions because there is no single universally valid set of assumptions and no agreement on

values. There are good answers and bad answers. As the chief systems analyst for the Defense Department, I always felt that avoiding bad answers was a sufficiently ambitious goal.

Analysis and the ABM

An important debate that occurred several years ago in the Defense Department will clarify my view of analysis and illustrate some other points. In 1965, the Secretary of the Army and the Joint Chiefs of Staff recommended to the Secretary of Defense that he approve the full-scale deployment of an anti-ballistic missile defense of our cities against Soviet attack. Although the initial estimates of the cost of the system were around $10-$20 billion, there was good reason to believe that the eventual costs of such a system would reach $40 billion. But the costs were not the most important question. The decisive issue was whether or not a full-scale ABM defense system, deployed together with the complementary fall-out shelters and air defenses, really would save millions of lives in a nuclear war.

This is an exceedingly complex issue. It involves, among other things, assumptions and judgments about hundreds of technical factors, offensive and defensive tactics, and thousands of calculations. The estimates of the effectiveness of the system must be derived both from data based on test results, about which we can be fairly confident, and from what can be little better than guesses about future enemy technical developments. In the face of this complexity and uncertainty, how could the Secretary of Defense believe anybody's estimates of the effectiveness of the system?

Procedure and result. We had been preparing for this issue for years. We had started with hand calculations and slide-rule and "back of the envelope" work to identify the important variables and how they related to one another. Gradually, as we understood pieces of the problem, we programmed the calculations for a computer so that we could more easily trace the effects of varying one factor or another without having to spend hours doing repetitive calculations. It was important to have done the calculations first by hand; this procedure develops one's understanding of the problem and provides an independent check against error. Then we put the various models together, so that by 1965 we were able to calculate the outcomes of many possible hypothetical wars involving both offensive and defensive forces.

Secretary McNamara saw that the estimates prepared by the Army, concerning the number of American lives saved by the ABM system in case of Soviet attack, gave a very different and much more optimistic picture than the estimates produced by my office. In a way, this was not too surprising since the Army was the main proponent of the system, and I saw my job in part to be the Secretary's prosecutor or interrogator. If a case was to be made against the system, it was my responsibility to do it. So Mr. McNamara asked for a memorandum of points of agreement and disagreement. In other words, if the Secretary of the Army and I disagreed in our estimates, it had to be for reasons that could be stated precisely and explained in layman's language. It could not be that we added differently or used different computers. Mr. McNamara wanted to know what those reasons were so that he could judge them himself.

We finally identified the single most decisive factor in the whole problem, that is, the question of Soviet reaction. The Army's analysis had assumed, implicitly, that *the Soviets would continue to deploy the offensive forces projected for them by our national intelligence estimates, even in the face of a major U.S. ABM deployment.* On that assumption, the ABM system would be very effective. Actually, it was Secretary McNamara himself who first saw the significance of the assumption about Soviet reaction. By now, the calculations done in my office were based on the assumption that the Soviets—like the United States—would react to deployment of an ABM system by deploying more missiles, more payload and multiple warheads, or other devices to overcome the opposing defenses. *And these calculations showed that the ABM would not be effective in protecting our cities from Soviet attack.*

Once the Secretary of Defense and the President made the judgment that the Soviets almost certainly would react to offset the effectiveness of our ABM system, our calculations became the foundation of Secretary McNamara's case against deployment of a full-scale ABM defense of our cities.

So it was by this procedure, an adversary proceeding between opponents who each had a serious and genuine interest in proving their point (a procedure as old as Anglo-Saxon law) through which the Secretary of Defense arrived at an answer to the question of how he could believe anybody's calculations. If my experts and the Army's agreed, given their high competence and opposing motivations, then the calculations were likely to be as reliable as human minds could make them. This, of course, did not guarantee that they were right. Both sides may have accepted—indeed, probably did accept—assumptions that later would turn out to be incorrect, since nobody can predict the future accurately. But at least human minds were on top of the calculations. If mistakes were made, it was because of the inevitable limits on human knowledge about the uncertain future, and not because nobody understood what was really going on inside the computer.

The computer is very useful in dealing with these problems since it allows us to investigate many more laboratory cases and to keep track of all our data and results. The big gain from the computer was in speed of calculation and data handling.

I think our strategic force analysis illustrates another point: *we understand what is going on in our models because we started with simple hand calculations that allowed us to see the important parameters.*

Meaning of judgment. I have refered to "judgment" several times. The word needs some explanation. Judgment is not the same as unsupported personal opinion, nor is it automatically acquired with advancing years and increasing experience. In policy analysis and decisions it is useful to distinguish different kinds of judgment. The first is likelihood or probability judgment.

A second kind of judgment is a value judgment. Is it better to spend so much money on a missile defense that might save so many lives *if* we had a nuclear war, or is it better to spend this money on some other purpose of benefit if we do not have a nuclear war. Analysis can clarify the choices, but the choices themselves are questions of value, properly resolved by the political process.

Computers alone will not enable us to do this. A lot of nonsense is written about computers today. Some of it grossly overstates what computers will do, and some overreacts against the overstatements. Some people allege that computers have mysterious powers that enable them to "tell us what to do." Others fear that users of computers do not know that computers cannot do this. Some people fear that computers are robbing us of our freedom of choice. I believe that public understanding could benefit a great deal from a more precise use of language by everyone concerned with computers.

Computers cannot replace analysts and decision makers since computers are not a substitute for clear hard thinking. Just as analysis should be the servant of judgment, computers should be the servant of analysis. They are a substitute for tedious calculations. They save a great deal of time and, therefore, allow detailed exploration of more alternatives for a given problem or allow more problems to be solved. However, we must continue to investigate a spectrum of alternatives with pencil and paper or we will have lost our chance to understand the problems. In trying to explain all this to a group of naval officers, I once put it this way: "The point is to render unto computers the things that are computers' and to judgment the things that are judgment's. In the end, there is no question that analysis is but an aid to judgment and that, as in the case of God and Caesar, judgment is supreme."

Capitalism to Solve Social Problems?

Readings 65 and 66

Here in Reading 65 a public-spirited businessman, whom we have met before in Reading 14, explores how big business can help solve the social problems of the day. During World War II large corporations like General Electric and duPont did help the government develop the atomic bomb. But can we count on their altruism to solve social problems? What is more important, can they be motivated to do this by the pursuit of profit, while at the same time planning for the public interest is assured?

In Reading 66, Michael Harrington expresses grave doubts that the problem of social reform can be entrusted to private capitalism. Not only will the venture not succeed, but there is also real danger that social goals will be distorted by the working out of private self-interest. Harrington is the author of the book *The Other America,* which can be given much credit for calling attention to poverty in America and stimulating the Kennedy-Johnson war against poverty.

Questions to Guide the Reading

Does the economic miracle of Puerto Rico illustrate the ability of business to solve social problems? Was this not more a case of special tax benefits extended to that island by the government? And does the role of private enterprise in low- and middle-income housing tell us any more than that, where there is no social problem, business can be counted on to meet a commercial market? Finally, how much beyond tokenism have we yet gone in connection with training and hiring "hard-core" unemployed?

How can one set up safeguards so that when business does engage in such tasks as urban renewal the public can be assured that the poor will really benefit? May this not involve an inordinate amount of red tape? Would perhaps a direct operation by public agencies be more efficient in the end? And what is really being accomplished if the government fools itself in thinking that it can save on actual budgetary public expenditure by granting business tax rebates instead? Aren't these tax reductions in effect "back-door expenditures"?

Reading 65

Business Can Help Solve Social Problems

Eli Goldston

In the mixed economy of the United States the traditional function of big business has been to produce, distribute, and sell material goods. That business has performed *this* function better than most other segments of our society have performed their functions is probably more commonly recognized abroad than at home. The element of U.S. society most envied by other countries today is its industrial and commercial management, an envy that even extends to the Soviet Union and its satellites.

Although American business has been developing the most *efficient production* system in history, our religious, academic, and government leaders have not achieved a consensus on the *sharing* of our national income so that poverty does not flourish amid affluence. Until a clear majority of Americans recognizes the gravity of our social problems and makes sufficient funds available to cope with them, no leadership can accomplish very much. But given the determination and the funds, any number of approaches might work. Moreover, the newer attitudes we need are becoming common among *big business leadership,* and private business can now be drawn into participating in the solution of many current social problems.

I predict that American business will increasingly supply many of the physical goods and the services we have obtained, at least since the New Deal era, from public sources. Already there is a perceptible and accelerating *shift* of the administration of proposed solutions for public problems from government bureaucracies to private business enterprises. This superseding of public administration will come through an enhanced attractiveness of these problems as viewed with the traditional profit motivation of business. The entrepreneurial thrust, if encouraged, guided, and controlled by the public agencies of our society, may represent the only permanent solution to the urban problems that have clearly overtaxed the capacity of our public agencies. It offers the best hope that the deprived and neglected parts of our society can be swept into the mainstream of our economy. Of course, instead of the *carrot* of profit motivation, we could try the *stick* of punishment or the persuasion of moral *exhortation* to involve business in social issues. Historically, however, there has been no permanence in the plea or in the stick—only the carrot endures.

These predictions run quite counter not only to the more common notion (shared by an approving left and a deploring right) that big government will learn industrial management and take over business roles, but also to the ethical belief that private profit motivation cannot be used to attain social goals.

Creating an urban-industrial complex

It is useless, in any event, to deplore the expansion of an alliance between industry and government. The alliance is already with us in the so-called "military-industrial complex," which is performing very well the task of arming a technological society. But the tools to *guide* this kind of an alliance must be perfected so that a maximum of social benefit is

From Eli Goldston, "New Prospects for American Business," *Daedalus,* Journal of the American Academy of Arts and Sciences, Winter, 1969. Reprinted with kind permission of the author and publisher.

achieved. We must develop appropriate and controlled incentives that will enable business to deal with such public problems as low-income housing and education; we must find a way to make certain that what is good for business is good for the country. It is often assumed that housing for the poor and schools are "non-market products" that must necessarily be provided by government. Certain products and services must be supplied to all in an ordered society and cannot be metered and charged for—for example, police protection and sanitation. But some of the job can be *contracted out* to private firms, and there are fewer "non-market products" than post-New Deal history leads many to assume.

Handwringers would do well to consider that our cities may never have been so effectively run for the benefit of the majority as at the turn of the century when political bosses in cahoots with utility magnates made City Hall thoroughly *responsive* both to the prosperous resident and to the working-class citizen. The working man was properly recognized as a source of both political power and business profit. There was no talk *then* of alienated voters. And those who criticize business for past reluctance to become involved in social problems, or even to investigate the opportunities for doing so, might compare its performance with that of public agencies. For example, Kenneth Clark [eminent black social psychologist] has said that business offers the best hope for leading us to racial peace, because "business is the least segregated, least discriminatory, most fair of the areas of our society—better than education, religion, unions or government."

This essay does not argue that the profit motive of itself will lead business to socially responsible actions, although it does suggest that professional management of a major firm tends to take a broader and longer view of profitability than the personal owner of a small enterprise. Goal-setting is a public, political function, and it may be more difficult to agree upon goals than to accomplish them once agreement has been reached. My thesis is only that agreed-upon goals may best be realized by using a carefully calibrated system of incentives for private firms. I suggest that the business apparatus is a better social instrument than many realize. The concern of big business executives with the *social responsibility of*

business is more genuine than many current critics believe.

Objectives of business

With the clear focus of business on a public scoreboard where growth in earnings per share is the major criterion, it is easy to understand that earnings growth has become the consuming objective of American business. Four major areas are seen today as places for substantial growth in sales which, it is hoped, will be carried down from higher sales to the real objectives of higher earnings.

1. *New or More Products to the Existing Market.* Color television, electric toothbrushes, home humidifiers, second cars, vacation homes, . . . Marketing, advertising, and selling become even more important as the existing market tends to become saturated, and managers look to new markets and new activities.

2. *New Markets Abroad.*

3. *New Markets Among the Emerging Poor.* Many businessmen who would be inclined to oppose generous relief, a guaranteed minimum wage, or a negative income tax because of Charlie Wilson's "hound-dog philosophy" and their own Horatio Alger upbringing are now beginning to support such proposals. To a considerable extent the civil rights movement has made us all more conscious of the needs of the less affluent. But *business also sees the promise of a vast new market.* Indeed, one of the major marketing interests at the moment is the analysis and segmentation of the Negro market on the theory that no single group in American society will increase its effective total purchasing power more quickly and to a greater extent.

4. *New Activities Once Considered the Province of Government.* The wider opportunities for business growth and profit in areas beyond its conventional operating spheres are just now being realized.

Product. Encouraging a wider ranging view of the business arena is the new "free form" or "conglomerate" enterprise. There is a recently developed idea that top management is really producing not physical products, but financial results. Under this banner, space companies enter the insurance field; investment trusts take management positions in heavy industry; and aircraft companies become comfortable partners of meat-packing firms. More and more, and somewhat to the dismay of the analysts who helped to set the trend in motion, categories of American business are becoming hazy.

If the foregoing picture[1] of the major characteristics of contemporary business is fairly accurate, *strong forces are pushing business to face the major problems of our society*, and ways exist to encourage and control business participation. Today's highly professional manager, eyes focused on profit performance, operating with excellent controls and within strict rules in the glare of a public scoreboard, needing growth opportunities, and not limited by conventional business boundaries, may be the most promising recruit for solution of the crises in our public services.[2]

Finale

For 80 per cent of the world's population, the central problem remains that of producing enough material goods for minimum comfort

[1] See Reading 14 by Goldston.
[2] Three examples of business participation in social-problem areas may offer a guide to the future: the economic miracle of Puerto Rico; the experience of private enterprise in low- and middle-income housing; and current experiments in training and hiring "hard-core" unemployed. The last two examples show the current expansion of business into areas until recently considered public. The first example shows the research, political leadership, as well as the incentives and rules that government must provide if it wants business involvement.

or even survival. For the United States, however, the most optimistic hopes for nineteenth-century technology have been fulfilled. Thus our central problems are to devise a more just distribution of our increasing quantity of material goods; to meet the demand for a better quality of life by expanding vastly the service sector of our economy and by controlling our technology; and to develop a consensus on these and other social values and on their relative priorities. Big business presently foresees in these American problems vast new markets for products and services. Building materials, construction equipment, and contracting services will be needed to rebuild the slums. Teaching machines, classroom materials, and textbooks are required for an expanded and improved educational system. Chemicals and machinery are needed to cut pollution. Fertilizer companies look at backward parts of the United States and underdeveloped nations. Drug firms see expanding sales in disease prevention and population control.

These markets cannot be served by a system of municipal and state government units. As the nation becomes more urbanized and the core city becomes a less significant part of the metropolis, the areas of municipal and state authority increasingly lack any real relationship to the problem areas and service areas. No one would want the federal government to take over all our government functions. An appropriately motivated and guided business structure is able to meet these needs, and every indicator suggests that this development is already well started. It could result in a new and beneficial interplay between the social concern of government, the scholarship of the university, and the know-how of big business.

Reading 66

We Can't Trust the Public Business to Business

Michael Harrington

Many well-intentioned Americans are deceiving themselves and the public when they speak of abolishing the slums. The slums can be abolished, but not in the way they suggest.

A number of programs have been proposed to end the scandal of inhuman housing for the poor. I specifically want to address myself to the theory that some kind of partnership

From Michael Harrington, "Can Private Industry Abolish the Slums?" *Dissent*, January–February, 1968. Reprinted with the kind permission of the author and publisher.

between government and the private sector will solve the problem, because I believe that this theory is an illusion. It will not work.

Although my analysis is radical, it can be documented in the official statements of the United States government.

Nature of gap

The Council of the White House Conference on Civil Rights said that the United States must build 2 million housing units a year, with at least 500,000 especially designed for the poor, if it is going to live up to its responsibilities.

President Johnson proposed building 165,000 low-cost housing units, or 335,000 less than the White House Conference minimum. If past experience is any guide, the actual number constructed will come to a bit over 30,000, or a deficit of 470,000 units.

Moreover, none of the proposals now being discussed come near to the required number. For example, Senator Robert Kennedy's approach is clearly motivated by great compassion, yet it would only provide 400,000 units over seven years through a $1.5 billion tax subsidy to private enterprise.

There can be no creative federalist panacea, enlisting business in a social crusade, that will deal with this problem. The corporate sector, as Mr. David Rockefeller testified with great candor before the Ribicoff Subcommittee, is concerned with making money. Banks, and other business institutions, will only invest funds if they are going to get a return.

Yet the slums are, in business terms, a bad risk. Until August of 1967, the FHA excluded blighted areas from its mortgage insurance programs on the grounds that such undertakings were "economically unsound." I assume that the bloodshed in Detroit motivated the revision of this policy in August 1967. A governmental agency can thus decide, in the name of public social priorities, to make an "uneconomic" investment of money. A private enterprise will not and cannot.

Nor can this problem be dealt with by providing public subsidies to private builders. All such proposals now before the country—from Senators Percy and Robert Kennedy among others—are designed to operate on a publicly supported profit principle. Yet even with this federal support through tax incentives or arti-

ficial interest rates, *every one of these suggestions ends up providing housing for families with incomes well over $4,000 a year.*

There is certainly a need to give governmental support to the housing needs of people with incomes between $4,000 and $8,000. It is one of the great postwar scandals that lavish, but discrete, subsidies have been provided for the homes of the middle class and the rich in the form of cheap, federally guaranteed credit, income tax deductions, and other genteel doles which effectively exclude everyone with incomes of less than $8,000 from the benefits.

But the fact remains that the Kennedy and Percy proposals, if the published reports of their rent levels are correct, would not provide any housing for the poor and the almost-poor. The rents would be too high for, among others, the majority of Negroes in the United States.

And even if some way were found to bring the private sector into the slums, it could not and should not play the leading role. It is precisely the commercial calculus of land value that has exacerbated our crisis and can hardly solve it. As Mayor Lindsay's task force on urban design reported to him, beauty, charm, and history cannot compete with office buildings, and even a venerable structure like the Plaza Hotel will be torn down if present trends continue. *Within the framework of such an "economic" approach, one builds most cheaply and profitably, while social and aesthetic considerations are secondary.*

Who decides?

The issue raised here is simple: Who is going to design the "second America" President Johnson tells us we must build between now and the year 2000? We must construct more housing units than now exist. How? I submit that *businessmen, whatever other qualifications they have, are not competent to design a new civilization and, in any case, have no democratic right to do so.* The fundamental decisions on what America shall look like and what life in it will be like should be made by the people. And this is particularly important in the case of the slum poor, who have been excluded from the making of every important decision in the nation.

In arguing thus, I do not want to suggest that there is no role for the private sector. *It is just that the social and aesthetic choices—those "uneconomic" options—must be democratically planned and, because of the logic of money-making, publicly financed. Then, and only then, can the companies and corporations contract to carry out the public will; but they should not determine it.*

The necessity of such innovation cannot be evaded by magic schemes for "rehabilitation." The worst of our urban slums are criminally overcrowded. To rehabilitate them successfully would mean removing half to three-quarters of the people now living there to new housing. Moreover, the rehabilitation formulas often take the reality of segregation as a given.

Planning against racial discrimination

I believe that our present crisis allows this country a marvelous opportunity to promote racial integration.

In fact if not in theory, our postwar housing has financed segregated, white suburbs. Now that the government has officially recognized that we must more than double the present supply of housing in the next third of a century, there is the possibility of reversing this ugly policy. There should not be one federal cent for "new towns," either outside of or within them, that are not designed to promote racial integration.

And this points up the need for new public institutions of democratic planning. Our postwar housing deficit is not measured in simple terms of our scandalous discrimination in favor of the rich and against the poor; it is a matter of the failure of the democratic imagination as well. Without thought of social or aesthetic consequences, we have proliferated superhighways and suburbs and made slums more miserable, employment more distant for the poor, old age more lonely for those left behind in the central city, and so on.

There is obviously no simple solution to such a complex crisis. But we should spend approximately a billion dollars on finding out what we want to do. This would be a wiser investment than the present Model Cities program.

We cannot go on forever "demonstrating" techniques and leaving the main problem areas untouched.

And in the process of such a massive planning expenditure, every level of American society should be involved in the debate. I do not say this simply out of democratic conviction or populist sentimentality. For I am convinced that *where decisions on public subsidy are made at high levels of expertise, there the priorities of money, rather than those of society, prevail. There is only one way of establishing the social and aesthetic values which will guide the "uneconomic" expenditure of money. That is through democracy.*

Summary

We know that we have to build 500,000 units of housing for the poor every year. We are not doing so.

In market terms, business *cannot* be expected to go into the job of slum eradication because it is a bad risk.

Even if the market terms are modified by federal subsidy, as in various proposals now before the nation, all *the poor and the majority of Negroes would be effectively excluded* from the benefits.

There must, therefore, be an "uneconomic" investment of public funds motivated by considerations of social and aesthetic values rather than by a calculus of private profit.

In this process, the private sector must play a *subordinate* role as the contractor for the popular will. For the basic decisions involved are not susceptible to business priorities and even hostile to them. These are issues in the public sector of American life.

Moreover, the urban crisis *allows* the country a chance to use federal funds to *promote*, rather than, as has been the case until now, to thwart racial integration.

Finally, the enormous undertaking I outline here clearly requires new public institutions for *democratic planning*. There is no other way to design a new civilization.

Reading 67

The automobile is typical of much that is characteristic of modern industrial life. Its mobility has transformed the shape of our cities and countryside. It is one of the largest industries. The exhaust from cars threatens the purity of the atmosphere itself.

Ralph Nader asked in this testimony before Congress whether there had not been treason on the part of scholars in their failure to criticize the present structure of the industry.

Ralph Nader has been a crusader for reform. His early public concern for safety led to an investigation into his private life and character by detectives in the hire of General Motors. Subsequently GM apologized for this invasion of personal privacy and act of intimidation. Nader, who could earn hundreds of thousands of dollars working for a large New York law firm, has chosen to lead a spartan life dedicated to his view of the public interest. He has enlisted the aid of dozens of gifted college and law-school students in preparing unsparing investigations of such regulatory agencies as the FTC. Rarely has one lone-wolf investigator left so large a mark on the development of current society.

Questions to Guide the Reading

Of exactly what crimes has Nader succeeded in convicting the large auto companies? Of being large? Of being interested in maximizing their profits? Exactly what has he spelled out that the courts or the government can do to make the situation better? In Brazil, instead of there being three large auto companies, there are more than seven: Does that mean that we should be surprised that autos sell for twice as much in Brazil as in the United States? If you were a Congressman and had listened to Nader give his testimony, what changes in your voting habits would you determine upon?

The Corporate Monster

Ralph Nader

Mr. Nader. Thank you, Senator Nelson, Senator Morse.

It is a privilege to have the opportunity to discuss with the distinguished members of this [Senate Small Business] committee the growth of auto industry regulatory and planning power, its effect on competition, and the well-being of small business and the consumer. The subject of discussion today is the auto industry and its unchallenged corporate leader, General Motors. This obviously is a vast subject and I regret that General Motors declined the committee's invitation to participate on a panel and afford you and the public the benefit of its decades of experience and information. General Motors is 60 years old this year and one might have expected a greater degree of wisdom from this senior corporate citizen.

Yet on further reflection, perhaps such an expectation is unwarranted. Anthropologists have taught us that the dominant institution in any society not only avoids external scrutiny but strives to strengthen societal controls that insure perpetuation of such an *unexamined status.* In our country, the large corporations are the dominant institution. They comprise the strongest, consistent, generic power in the land. They share a high degree of coordinated

From *Hearings before the Senate Select Committee on Small Business,* U.S. Government Printing Office, 1968.

values. Their power is all the more remarkable in its resiliency and ability to accommodate or absorb other challenging power centers—such as big government and organized labor—in ways that turn an additional profit, erect an additional privilege, or acquire protective mechanisms to ward off new pressures for change or reform.

This process of societal insinuation by large corporate concentrations continues unabated. The description provided by the general counsel and vice president of Ford Motor Co. in 1957 is even more pervasive today, but it is well worth recalling:

"The modern stock corporation," wrote Mr. William Gossett, "is a social and economic institution that touches every aspect of our lives; in many ways it is an institutionalized expression of our way of life. During the past 50 years, industry in corporate form has moved from the periphery to the very center of our social and economic existence. Indeed, it is not inaccurate to say that we live in a corporate society." I want to take note of the implications in Mr. Gossett's statement when contrasted with traditional classical economics and the model of pure competition. Note that he says that industry in corporate form has moved from the periphery to the very center of our social and economic existence.

Need for vigilance

As against this massive presence of industrial, commercial, and financial corporations, bound by a strong sense of common values, world views, and modes of operation, our governmental institutions have neither been able nor willing to even examine systematically what the consequences of the use and selective nonuse of corporate power has been for the public interest. I want to emphasize not only the aspects of abuse of power, Senators, but also the role of the nonuse of power in various contexts.

The last study of corporate America was done by the Temporary National Economic Commission in 1941, and its monumental effort was clipped in the bud by the advent of World War II. The U.S. economy has almost quadrupled since that time and many of the top 200 corporations which now own nearly two-thirds of the manufacturing assets of the land are posting net profits as large or larger than their total sales in 1941. Yet, in the intervening

three decades, there has been no comparable study of concentrated corporate power, equipped with the power of subpena that can take the inquiry beyond the judgments of academicians and company public relations men and into the center of corporate operations. Take the case of the auto industry, for example. The first Government study of the auto industry was done by the Federal Trade Commission in 1939. The Kefauver subcommittee conducted a study in 1957–58. Thus, in the entire history of the automobile industry spanning 65 years or more, there have been only two studies and quite restricted ones at that.

The absence of political vigilance by the organs of Government toward the onrush of corporate collectivism, with the exception of a few aborted Senate inquiries, is fraught with danger to a democratic society. This is the case, no matter how affluent that society has become in the aggregate, because of the gaping injustices affecting minority groups and majority public services. Indeed, the very productiveness of our economic system, a chief referent for corporate apologists, has led, through incaution and indifference, to vast new problems, centering, for example, on the pellmell contamination of soil, air, and water that is taking us toward ecological disaster.

The dreaded corporate state

Ostrichlike, Government organs with real or putative responsibility for securing continual corporate accountability, have failed to alert the public to the facts and, even more, have not even articulated the idealized goals for the populace to strive for on their own. To give an illustration from the auto industry, Senators, it is quite clear that in the early periods of industry, cars could be produced with internal combustion engines that spew forth the traditional emissions. It is just as true that the same production of automobiles multiplied tenfold to twentyfold with the same kind of engine produces a public health problem of the first order of magnitude, so that our ideals or expectations for an earlier period of smaller volume production of the product are quite different for a later period of a similar product but much larger volume of production.

The mark of the contemporary American political and economic system is complicity—active or passive—and the hopeful checks and balances of Government and labor have neither recognized old ills nor new challenges put forth by corporate enterprise. Each segment of the Business, Government and Labor triangle is approaching the mutual similarity of its Euclidian prototype. President Eisenhower's farewell warning to Americans about the "military-industrial complex" is a favorite allusion for liberal jeremiads. But, there has been little recognition of this and other civilian phenomena pertaining to the merger of private and public power. Could the dreaded corporate state be coming on little cat feet quicker than is commonly believed?

Betrayal by the scholars

More basically dismaying is the atrophy of academicians. Without cues and stimuli from public action centers, political economy and the institutional economists have become a memory. Economists who used to think about the great questions of their discipline are gone or retired, replaced by colleagues who work for academic advance by developing myopia that dedicates itself to rigorous trivia.

These concerns are partly why I am so heartened by the statement of Senators Morse and Nelson that:

The public at large should be talking about (corporate concentration) and thinking about it at the same level of concern as is given to war and the arms race, the war on poverty, civil rights and civil liberties, the balance of power and responsibility between Federal and state governments, air and water pollution. Indeed, corporate giantism is not unconnected with any of these topics and is intimately involved in some of them.

This is also true of small business without which much innovation, entrepreneurial risk taking and decentralized economic power are not likely to survive. I might add that, continuing to the present day, the impressive association between basic innovations in our economy and small business firms or individual inventors is really quite startling and I will submit for the record later some of the evidence showing that.

Three points

Before turning to the auto industry, and the challenge to public policy, I wish to make three preliminary points:

1. Limitations of time require that any state-

ment be held to the barest sketch of the problem areas. However, by way of amplification and documentation, I am submitting materials for the hearing record keyed to my testimony.

2. The primary focus of my remarks is on the need for an evaluative framework toward auto company performance in (1) the design and marketing of products and services, and (2) the political and economic environment (or infrastructure) that the industry has developed under the leadership of the dominant firm, General Motors, to secure and further corporate goals.

3. The word "competition" means different things to different people. But, it is clear that it has both quantitative and qualitative features in its operation. Both these features—its scope and its quality—must be taken into account in any evaluation of industry performance.

Moreover, to try and discuss competition, as if it is an isolated phenomenon braced by supply and demand curves, is to fail to come to grips with the political realities of inordinate market power. For example, while the courts must restrict themselves to determining the economic anticompetitive effects of the Government's antitrust case, other decisional forums, such as legislatures, must take a broader assessment of where competition is working, not working, and why. In this way, the political restrictions on antitrust enforcement and the limitations of antitrust action for industrial justice can be disclosed and openly treated.

It is in this broader vein that I wish to discuss corporate planning, regulation, and competition in the auto industry. The type of planning that vectors in different directions, including a type of planning for Government in terms of its antitrust responsibilities. Just as F. A. Hayek, who is considered one of the most conservative economic writers, stated that Government has a function in planning for competition, so have large corporations in this country devoted considerable resources toward planning that Government not plan for competition.

Size of the beast

Turning to the auto industry, getting around on the ground in private transport is America's biggest business. Whether in input-output analysis or simple aggregate data, the automobile industry stands as that private economic activity with the greatest multiplier effect for the rest of the economy. The industry consumed 11 percent of the aluminum, 20 percent of the steel, 35 percent of the zinc, 50 percent of the lead, and more than 60 percent of U.S. consumption of rubber in 1967.

Its capacity for insatiable depletion of public and private pocketbooks can be painful to behold. One out of every six retail dollars goes to buy or provide for motor vehicles.

Over $100 billion a year are expended on new cars, used cars, gasoline, tires, auto repair and replacement parts, auto insurance and finance, the construction and upkeep of roads, and other supportive facilities. Numerous ancillary industries and public services rely on the continuous multimillion volume production of America's most visible industrial art form. It is often said by auto industry boosters that one of every six business establishments is dependent on the purchase and use of motor vehicles. In terms of unused capacity, fuel consumption per passenger, injuries and pollution, and total time displacement of drivers and passengers, automotive travel is probably the most wasteful and inefficient mode of travel by industrial man. Yet automobiles will be here for some time to come and the market structure, conduct, and performance of the industry must command a frontline level of attention.

The domestic automobile industry is composed of four companies, three of whom account for over 97 percent of the domestic car market. General Motors delivered 54.7 percent of the North American-type passenger cars sold in the United States last year. In most of the postwar period, GM's share of the market has consistently been between 50 and 55 percent of the domestic market. (In 1940, GM's share was about 47 percent.)

The dimensions of the world's largest industrial giant require some statistical etching. For 1967, the company's net sales reached $20,026 million, the third highest in its history. Net income was reported at $1,627 million, down from $1,793 million for 1966, and still a distance from its profit record of $2,126 million in 1965. Incidentally, that figure represented 4.7 percent of total U.S. corporate after-tax earnings.

First quarter reports for 1968 point to at least a near record year for sales and profits. Its profit rate is regularly far higher than other auto manufacturers. GM's shares of total domestic automobile manufacture sales and earnings for 1966 were 52 and 69 percent, respectively. For the period 1947–66, GM's profits after taxes averaged 22.7 percent return on net worth, almost twice the 12.2 percent national average. You will note one of the criteria for unreasonable market power by Mr. Turner and Mr. Kaysen is a consistently high level of excessive profits.

This is the most conservative estimate based on GM's accounting practices that understate its income.

The very size and diversity of GM provides an awesome leverage against any competitors. General Motors Acceptance Corp., the company's wholesale and retail financing subsidiary, is alone the single largest seller of short-term commercial paper with outstandings rivaling the U.S. Treasury itself. Motors Insurance Corp., a wholly owned subsidiary of GMAC, is one of the Nation's largest underwriters of physical damage insurance. GMAC has about 80 percent of all GM-financed automobile sales and GM dealers accept such financing not because of its competitive rates, but in part because of coercion or knowing appreciation by the dealer of the consequences under the multifaceted leverage GM has in its franchise agreements. As pointed out in the Senate Antitrust Subcommittee report on administered prices in the automobile industry (1958):

"GM, with its captive finance company, has a double incentive to maintain high automobile prices. As long as new cars are selling in volume, the higher the price, the greater the finance charge [and insurance rates] and hence the profitability of GMAC. Furthermore, in both production and financing, some loss in volume can be counterbalanced by high prices and high finance earnings." I have given other comparisons to show the size of the industry in the testimony which I shall not bother to read.

I also submitted materials relevant to that problem.

Senator Morse. I want to say, Mr. Nader, that I hope you will not desist from reading any of this supporting material that would be of help to this public hearing, because I think your auditors are here because of a great interest in the subject matter. I do not want you to feel that you must save the committee's time.

Mr. Nader. Thank you very much, Senator.

By way of backup here, I have submitted General Motors' organization chart, further statistical data concerning the company and scope of operations, products manufactured by General Motors, distribution of ownership and proxy votes and excerpts from the 1967 annual report of the company. In a time when the word "conglomerate" is describing a rather rapid merger movement in the economy, I might indicate that a glance at the list of the products that General Motors produces indicates that indeed it has been one of the earliest conglomerates.

Senator Morse. All the material just referred to by the witness will be incorporated in the record at this point.

[Hundreds of pages of supporting documents follow.]

Urban and Minority Problems

Reading 68

When someone says that America has solved all its economic problems, he need only be answered by pointing out the extent of our air and water pollution, and the awesome cost of restoring our urban communities to minimum standards of safety, comfort, and beauty.

James Q. Wilson, professor of government at Harvard, points out trenchantly that there is much loose, sentimental, wishful thinking on the issue of urban renewal.

Questions to Guide the Reading

Does the author go too far in minimizing the deterioration that has gone on in the core of the city?

When slums are replaced by modern housing that goes to less impoverished families, is it the poor who are really benefitted?

The War on Cities

James Q. Wilson

President Johnson's special message to Congress on improving the nation's cities was a notable document, both for what it said and what it did not. It was, in many respects, the sanest and most thoughtful presidential statement on "the urban problem" ever issued. It avoided most of those rhetorical absurdities which link the future of Western civilization with the maintenance of the downtown business district; it stressed the primacy of human and social problems over purely physical ones; and it conceded with great candor the dilemmas, contradictions, and inadequacies of past and present federal programs. (Indeed, the first third of the message could easily have been written by any one of several critics of federal urban renewal and public housing programs.) Many of the proposals made by the President were entirely in keeping with a concern for the problems of disadvantaged people

From James Q. Wilson, "The War on Cities," The Public Interest, Spring, 1966. Copyright © National Affairs, Inc. Reprinted with kind permission of the author and publisher.

living in cities. Thus, legislation to bar racial discrimination in the sale or rental of housing, and appropriations to implement the rent supplement program (whereby through direct subsidy the poor are given a better chance to acquire decent housing on the private market) were requested.

But the fundamental problem afflicting federal policy in this area—the problem which this message suggests but does not face—is that *we do not know what we are trying to accomplish.* Do we seek to raise standards of living, maximize housing choices, revitalize the commercial centers of our cities, end suburban sprawl, eliminate discrimination, reduce traffic congestion, improve the quality of urban design, check crime and delinquency, strengthen the effectiveness of local planning, increase citizen participation in local government? All these objectives sound attractive—in part, because they are rather vague—but unfortunately they are in many cases incompatible.

Improving urban design is made harder by efforts to find housing for the poor, for well-designed housing almost always costs more than the poor can afford. A "revitalized" downtown business district not only implies, *it requires* traffic congestion—an "uncongested" Broadway or State Street would be no Broadway or State Street at all. Effective local planning requires *less,* not more, citizen participation—the more views represented, the less the possibility of agreement on any single (especially any single comprehensive) view. Maximum housing choices, unconstrained by discriminatory practices, and reinforced by higher incomes, will give more people the opportunity to join the movement to the suburbs.

American political life has a proven and oft-remarked genius for surviving and even prospering on dilemmas and contradictions. Government maintains the support of potentially hostile groups by letting different federal agencies serve incompatible goals and by encouraging local communities to follow competing policies at federal expense. The new Department of Housing and Urban Development (HUD) stands squarely in this tradition. Under its previous name (the Housing and Home Finance Agency) it subsidized the flight to the suburbs with FHA mortgage insurance, while trying to lure suburbanites back to the central city with subsidies provided by the Urban Renewal Administration. The Public

Housing Administration built low-rent units for the poor while urban renewal was tearing them down. Furthermore, the goals for most programs—especialy urban renewal—were determined at the local level. This meant that urban renewal, in itself simply a tool, was used for very different purposes in different cities—in some places to get Negroes out of white neighborhoods, in others to bring middle-class people closer to downtown department stores, in still other places to build dramatic civic monuments, and in a few places to rehabilitate declining neighborhoods and add to the supply of moderately priced housing. Throughout its life, HHFA could have the best of both worlds —in Washington, its leaders could make broad policy statements which were intended to satisfy whatever critics of the program the administration was most sensitive to; meanwhile, in the hundreds of communities where the actual purposes of our housing programs were determined by the decisions of local governing bodies, many objectives which bore only the loosest relationship to federal policy statements were being pursued.

One can admire a system which so neatly accommodates the tensions of political reality without approving of all its consequences. And these consequences stem, in my view, from the fact that, in thinking about solutions to the "urban problem," we have committed ourselves to certain means before we have made a commitment to any goals. The means have been federally subsidized alterations in the housing stock and in certain other physical equipment (mass transportation, community facilities, and the like). The *a priori* commitment to these techniques has the result that alternative tactics to reach certain goals are not systematically considered, or are considered only as afterthoughts. Surely few would ever have disagreed that the two greatest causes of inadequate housing have been the fact that some people have not been able to afford good housing and that some have, because of race, been denied an opportunity to bid freely for such housing as exists. Yet it was not until last year that HHFA requested of Congress a program that would improve the purchasing power of poor families by direct income subsidies; and it was not until this year that legislation was proposed by the President to bar discrimination in the sale or rental of housing (an executive order by President Kennedy had previously barred discrimination in federally assisted housing, which is about one-fifth of the total).

In the meantime—and continuing right down to the present—local communities are allowed great latitude in deciding how federal funds will be spent on the bread-and-butter programs: urban renewal and public housing. If the Main Street merchants are in power, they can use renewal funds to tear down low-cost housing and put up luxury apartments near the department stores—in effect redistributing income from the poor to the well-to-do while reducing the stock of low-cost housing. If more generous souls are in power, the worst housing is torn down to make room for middle or lower-middle-income housing; the income transfer from poor to not-so-poor is much less, but it is still in the wrong direction. And if the mayor simply is seeking funds with which to run his city in the face of a declining tax base, he discovers that he must join with those who want one of these urban renewal programs because that is about the only way he can get large-scale federal money into his city. He discovers, in short, that he has to hurt his poorest and weakest citizens in order to provide for the general welfare; his only option is to try to do it as humanely as possible. Under any or all of these conditions, urban renewal may or may not produce attractive, well-designed new structures; that is a separate issue. The point is that for almost any legitimate community objective—improving the supply of housing, strengthening the tax base, etc. —urban renewal has in most cases proved to be an unwieldy and costly tool.

What, indeed, is the "urban problem"? The language of crisis with which this subject is normally discussed—"sick cities," "the urban crisis," "spreading blight"—is singularly un-illuminating. I doubt that most residents of most American cities would recognize in such terms a fair description of the conditions in their communities. Since such words are usually uttered or printed in Washington, D.C., or New York City, perhaps the most we can infer is that life is tough in these two places— though the staggering expense the authors of such words are willing to incur in order to live in the very center of these cities suggests that the "crisis" is at least bearable.

Viewed in historical perspective, and taking American cities as a whole, the conditions of urban life have, by most measures, been getting steadily better, not worse. Nationally, the proportion of families under the poverty line—for purposes of argument, let us take that as a family income of $3,000 a year in constant dollars—declined from 31 percent to 19 percent between 1950 and 1963, and the decline was the greatest in the cities of our country, by contrast, about *half* the families still live at or near the poverty line). Since the Second World War, there has been a more or less steady decline in the proportion of housing units that are substandard; this improvement has been greatest in the cities, least in the rural areas. (In 1960, less than 3 percent of the dwelling units in cities of 50,000 population and over were dilapidated by Census Bureau standards.) The "flight to the suburbs" has made most people better off—the middle-income family finds the peace and privacy of a suburban home, the lower-income family takes over the larger, sounder structures vacated in the central city. The proportion of young people who drop out of school before getting a high school diploma has been declining steadily, both absolutely and relatively, for about the last twenty years. Certain forms of violent crime—murder and forcible rape— have declined in rate for the last several decades, though other forms of crime (assault, theft) may have increased (no one knows for certain, because crime statistics are neither completely reliable nor standardized for the changing age composition of the population).

American cities have fully participated in the prosperity of the country—indeed, they have participated more than the rural areas; and this no doubt accounts for the fact that, whatever problems the cities have, people are moving to the cities in very large numbers. But it would be a mistake to try to be unreservedly optimistic about these aggregate trends. Certain classes of people within cities continue to confront problems, and these problems vary with the size and kind of the city in question. Three of these problems are especially noteworthy.

High expectations

First, there is what might be called the "psychological urban problem"—i.e., our expectations are increasing faster than our achievements. As more affluent suburbs spring up, with neat lawns and good schools, the apparent gap between the quality of life in the central city and at the periphery increases. The suburbanites, adjusting rapidly to residential comfort, become more discontented with the conditions that surround the places where they work in the central city, even though these conditions are also (on the average) improving. Those city dwellers who cannot, for reasons of income or race, move to the suburbs, grow increasingly envious of those who can; the prizes of worldly success are held up before their eyes but out of their reach.

Because whites are gaining, in income and housing, faster than Negroes (though they are gaining also), the gap between the two groups is widening.

In addition, the central city has remained the place where important members of the commercial and intellectual elite live. This is the group which, more than any other, sets the tone and provides the rhetoric of public discussion on "urban problems." By habit and tradition, it prizes the cultural amenities of the large central city and it tends to resent the spread of lower-class people into areas where these cultural and commercial institutions are established—even though that spread has been caused by the very increases in freedom and prosperity which the elite itself values. In the resulting distress, we see the conflict between the two major functions of the central city—on the one hand, the maintenance of a highly urbane style of life and of a concentrated and diverse market for the exchange of wealth and ideas; on the other hand, the provision of a place in which the lower classes, especially the immigrant lower classes, are housed, employed, educated, and by slow degrees assimilated to the standards of civility of American society.

The psychological urban problem cannot be solved, it can only be coped with. Indeed, it has been caused precisely because so many other problems *have* been coped with, if not solved. Efforts to lessen the gap between expectations and achievements will, in the short run, only make the discontent produced by that gap more acute. That is one of the inevitable tensions in a society committed to self-improvement.

Technical problems, political solutions

The second kind of urban problem might be called the "technical" problem. By this I mean both that the problems are created because

people are living in highly interdependent, dense settlements in an industrial society and that the solutions to these problems are technically feasible. If the problems are not solved, it is not for lack of knowledge. It might be more meaningful, indeed, to call them "political" problems, inasmuch as the obstacles to their solution are largely political.

These problems result partly from the fact that we are constantly getting in each other's way or otherwise committing various nuisances. We pollute the air with soft coal soot and with hydrocarbons from automobile exhausts; we pollute rivers and lakes with industrial and residential sewage; we congest city streets with cars, and sidewalks with pedestrians. The problems are also in part the result of consuming natural resources—e.g., open space and park land—and of making future generations bear the cost of this consumption. Finally, the "technical" problem is also the result of an imbalance between the costs and benefits of various essential local services—education, police protection, welfare, and the like. Everyone would agree that supplying such services is a common responsibility which one should not be able to escape simply by moving away from the place where such facilities are maintained. Yet this is exactly what many of us do when we leave the central city for the suburbs. If the central city is to continue to perform its traditional function of housing, employing, educating, policing, and supporting the poor and the disadvantaged (and the only alternative is to spread the poor and the disadvantaged throughout the suburbs), then it must be able to tap the taxable wealth of all of us.

What all these problems—nuisances, scarce collective resources, fiscal imbalance—have in common is that they result from a situation in which the costs and benefits of urban life are imperfectly related.

There is no reason in principle why these problems cannot be solved or significantly alleviated. We know, or can discover, techniques for stopping pollution; the crucial task is devising an appropriate combination of legal sanctions, tax policies, and incentives that will make these techniques effective. Open space and other unique natural resources can be conserved by public purchase, by easements, and by tax policies. Those persons who are determined to produce ugliness in parts of the city where ugliness is out of place (and this is not everywhere; every city, like every home, ought to have some place—the equivalent of Fibber McGee's closet—where we can store necessary ugliness) can be restrained by fines, taxes, and laws from carrying on those activities, or can be induced by subsidies to hide the ugliness by appropriate devices. There is nothing very difficult about hiding or getting rid of junked automobiles—provided that the people who are pleased by the absence of junk are willing to share the necessary cost of achieving the result.

Traffic congestion is a somewhat more complicated matter, for it is not obvious in what precise sense it constitutes a problem. Congestion arises because many people want to use limited space; in a sense, as Martin Meyerson and Edward Banfield point out (*Boston: The Job Ahead*), congestion is a means by which we ration access to a scarce resource (i.e., a desirable central city location) just as the price system is a way we ration the enjoyment of most other commodities (e.g., Cadillacs).

But congestion can be reduced if we provide other ways of rationing access besides traffic jams. One way—politically risky, but nonetheless likely to grow in favor—is to assess a charge on automobiles driven into central city locations, the amount of such a charge either to be based on the full cost of accommodating the car (parking space, police and fire protection, road use), in which case it is simply a user charge, or to reflect some penalty cost selected to deter the use of cars rather than merely to finance their accommodation.

The other strategy to deal with congestion is, of course, to subsidize mass transit facilities. The enthusiasm with which this proposal has been embraced by most public spokesmen suggests that their advocacy is based as much on an emotional dislike for automobiles (especially those parts made of chromium) as it is on a sober assessment of the comparative costs and benefits of various transportation programs. There are no doubt communities where the development of this kind of mass transit makes sense, either because of the population densities involved, or the investment already sunk in train tracks and equipment, or both. It is also perfectly clear, as John Meyer, John Kain, and Martin Wohl point out in their comprehensive study, *The Urban Transportation Problem*, that the vast majority of American cities could not possibly support a rail-based system

without staggering subsidies. In fact, most communities would be better served by a mixed transportation plan that relied on a combination of user charges on automobiles entering the central city, high-speed bus service in reserved lanes on existing roadways, and various mechanical devices to regulate the flow of cars on and off expressways. The prosperity that produced the massive shift away from the train and bus and to the private car cannot be reversed by public policy; its effects, however, can be regulated.

The Negroes in the city

The third sense in which there is an urban problem is the most important. It results from the fact that the large central cities are where the immigrant lower classes congregate.

Today, with Negroes constituting the most important part of the urban lower class, the challenge to the central city is greater than ever before, because the Negroes create a unique set of problems. Unlike most previous migrants, they are marked by color. Furthermore, the Negro came originally from a slave culture in which he had no opportunity to acquire a complete range of political, economic, and social skills, and in which his family was subjected to systematic disruption and abuse. Unlike other immigrants—even other colored immigrants, such as the Chinese and Japanese—the Negro began his migration to the central city lacking the relevant skills and experience, and with a weakened family structure. Urbanization, of course, places further strains on community and family ties. The result is a central-city population with little money, few skills, a weakened capacity to cope with large bureaucratic institutions, and high rates of social disorder—crime, broken homes, alcoholism, narcotics addiction, illegitimacy, delinquency, and unemployment.

The argument over the details of the Moynihan Report on the Negro family has to some extent obscured its most important implication, which I cannot believe anyone will reject: if all Negroes were turned white tomorrow, they would still have serious problems. Whether these problems are more the result of a weak family structure, or of the impact of urbanization, or of the past history of discrimination, or of a depressed economic position, is very hard to say. But I suspect that whatever the cause, there are few aspects of this problem which will not be cured—or will not cure themselves—in time.

In time. In how much time? And what does one do in the meantime? I incline to the view that in the long run the acculturational problem of the Negro—i.e., the problem of being unable, as an individual or a family, and as compared with previous migrants to the cities, to cope with the fact of poverty—will be reduced by improvements in income and education; habits will change as class changes, though more slowly. Perhaps I say this because it is easier to think of changing class position than cultural values, though altering the former is hard enough. Perhaps I say it because of the great and obvious differences between middle-class and lower-class Negroes, differences much greater than those between middle-class and lower-class whites. And perhaps I am wrong.

But whatever the strategic factor is, we cannot as yet say we have discovered it. The best that can be said in our favor is that we are perhaps the only free society which has ever tried to change a large racial minority by massively upgrading its condition. The debate about what the goal of "equality" means—whether a random distribution of Negroes throughout the city and the social structure, or a distinctive Negro enclave with guaranteed rights of entry and departure, or some combination of the two—is less interesting to me than the fact that, wherever we want to go, we don't know how to get there. And for the present, the urban Negro is, in a fundamental sense, *the* "urban problem."

If there were no Negroes in our large cities, or if the only difference between Negroes and whites were the accident of skin color, the rate of serious crime in our cities would immediately be cut about a third. The welfare rolls would be cut by a like amount. The population of our state prisons would be cut by more than one-fourth. No one can be sure how many fewer narcotics addicts or alcoholics there would be, but no one could argue the reduction would be negligible. The number of "dilapidated" homes would be further reduced by about 30 percent.

What we don't know

If solutions to the technical problems facing our cities are impeded because our motivation does not yet equal our knowledge, then solutions to our fundamental problems are impeded because our understanding does not yet match our motivation. A dramatic crisis—an epidemic of deaths resulting from smog, for example—will quickly produce the motivation necessary to move swiftly on many of the technical problems. But we have already had our crises with respect to the fundamental problems—Watts, for example—and the result has only been a frantic and futile search for "answers." There is no ready-made knowledge stored up in our universities or foundations on how to prevent a Watts, or even on what causes a Watts. The malaise of lower-class life in the central cities has been a matter of scholarly concern for several decades, but there is not much scholarly wisdom to show for it, except a general—and probably sound—belief that higher incomes, more education, and less discrimination are desirable things. For thirty years, various experiments have been conducted in an effort to reduce juvenile delinquency; although we have occasionally been successful in eliminating gang warfare (primarily by disarming and policing the gangs), no one has been able to reduce the apparent rates of the most common form of delinquency, theft. We know that the rates of certain "private" crimes—murder, for example—cannot be changed no matter what tactics the police may use. We suspect that certain "street" crimes (auto theft, or purse snatching) can be reduced by "saturation" police patrol, but no one knows whether what occurs is actually a reduction or simply a displacement of the crime to other parts of the city—or, if a reduction, whether it can be made permanent. No one is yet precisely certain what effect segregated schools have on Negro children, or how much of the slower rates of learning of these children is the result of family background (which is very hard to change) or of the school experience (which is somewhat easier to change). We do not even know how much narcotics addiction there is, much less what to do about it on any large scale. Above all, we do not know how much urban pathology is in some sense inevitable and how much space, therefore, our central cities must expect to reserve for the derelicts, the alienated, and the unaspiring poor.

One would suppose that we know most about one prerequisite for progress among the lower classes—employment opportunities. Yet, although the debate between the proponents of achieving full employment by stimulating aggregate demand and those who insist that we need structural change (job retraining, family allowances, vocational education, public works) has been raging for a decade or more, neither side has convinced the other. More importantly, *neither* strategy has been seriously tried. Until the war in Vietnam required a greater use of our industrial capacity, the federal government did not attempt as vigorously as it might, through tax and fiscal policies, to create a full employment economy—in part from fear of inflation, in part from a concern over the international balance of payments. Nor have the structuralists tried a program of public works, guaranteed incomes, worker resettlement, and vocational education on a scale sufficient to test the feasibility of eliminating the so-called "pockets of poverty." The war on poverty contains some of the elements of a "structuralist" strategy—for example, the Job Corps as a way of developing skills and motivation, and Project Head Start as a long-term attack on rates of learning—but it will be some time before we know how successful they are and to what extent such methods can be generalized.

Reading 69

The nonwhite population, which is more than 10 per cent of the total number of people in the U.S., gets much less than 10 per cent of the total income. Unemployment of blacks, particularly of black youths, is vastly greater than that of whites. Education and skills are less and wage rates are lower.

What can be done to improve this inequitable and inefficient situation? James Tobin, a realistic liberal and economists' expert, presents a definitive survey.

Questions to Guide the Reading

Confronted with the facts about inequality of education, training, and opportunity for blacks, can you maintain that economic positions reflect genetic inferiority?

Can some measures which aim to help blacks—such as minimum-wage rates—actually hurt him sometimes?

On Improving the Economic Status of the Negro

James Tobin

I start from the presumption that the integration of Negroes into the American society and economy can be accomplished within existing political and economic institutions. I understand the impatience of those who think otherwise, but I see nothing incompatible between our peculiar mixture of private enterprise and government, on the one hand, and the liberation and integration of the Negro, on the other. Indeed the present position of the Negro is an aberration from the principles of our society, rather than a requirement of its functioning. Therefore, my suggestions are directed to the aim of mobilizing existing powers of government to bring Negroes into full participation in the main stream of American economic life.

From James Tobin, "On Improving the Economic Status of the Negro," *Daedalus*, Fall, Journal of the American Academy of Arts and Sciences, 1965. Reprinted with kind permission of the author and publisher.

The economic plight of individuals, Negroes and whites alike, can always be attributed to specific handicaps and circumstances: discrimination, immobility, lack of education and experience, ill health, weak motivation, poor neighborhood, large family size, burdensome family responsibilities. Such diagnoses suggest a host of specific remedies, some in the domain of civil rights, others in the war on poverty. Important as these remedies are, there is a danger that the diagnoses are myopic. They explain why certain individuals rather than others suffer from the economic maladies of the time. They do not explain why the over-all incidence of the maladies varies dramatically from time to time—for example, why personal attributes which seemed to doom a man to unemployment in 1932 or even in 1954 or 1961 did not so handicap him in 1944 or 1951 or 1956.

Public health measures to improve the environment are often more productive in conquering diseases than a succession of individual treatments. Malaria was conquered by oiling and draining swamps, not by quinine. The analogy holds for economic maladies. Unless the global incidence of these misfortunes can be diminished, every individual problem successfully solved will be replaced by a similar problem somewhere else. That is why an economist is led to emphasize the importance of the over-all economic climate.

Over the decades, general economic progress has been the major factor in the gradual conquest of poverty. Recently some observers, J. K. Galbraith and Michael Harrington most eloquently, have contended that this process no longer operates. The economy may prosper and labor may become steadily more productive as in the past, but "the other America" will be stranded. Prosperity and progress have already eliminated almost all the easy cases of poverty, leaving a hard core beyond the reach of national economic trends. There may be something to the "backwash" thesis as far as whites are concerned. But it definitely does not apply to Negroes. Too many of them are poor. It cannot be true that half of a race of twenty million human beings are victims of specific disabilities which insulate them from the national economic climate. It cannot be true, and it is not. Locke Anderson has shown that the pace of Negro economic progress is peculiarly sensitive to general economic growth.

He estimates that if nationwide per capita personal income is stationary, nonwhite median family income falls by .5 per cent per year, while if national per capita income grows 5 per cent, nonwhite income grows nearly 7.5 per cent.

National prosperity and economic growth are still powerful engines for improving the economic status of Negroes. They are not doing enough and they are not doing it fast enough. There is ample room for a focused attack on the specific sources of Negro poverty. But a favorable over-all economic climate is a necessary condition for the global success —as distinguished from success in individual cases—of specific efforts to remedy the handicaps associated with Negro poverty.

The importance of a tight labor market

But isn't the present over-all economic climate favorable? Isn't the economy enjoying an upswing of unprecedented length, setting new records almost every month in production, employment, profits, and income? Yes, but expansion and new records should be routine in an economy with growing population, capital equipment, and productivity. The fact is that the economy has not operated with reasonably full utilization of its manpower and plant capacity since 1957.

The most important dimension of the over-all economic climate is the tightness of the labor market. In a tight labor market unemployment is low and short in duration, and job vacancies are plentiful. People who stand at the end of the hiring line and the top of the layoff list have the most to gain from a tight labor market. It is not surprising that the position of Negroes relative to that of whites improves in a tight labor market and declines in a slack market. Unemployment itself is only one way in which a slack labor market hurts Negroes and other disadvantaged groups, and the gains from reduction in unemployment are by no means confined to the employment of persons counted as unemployed. A tight labor market means not just jobs, but better jobs, longer hours, higher wages. A tight labor market will not only employ more Negroes; it will also give more of those who are employed full-time jobs. In both respects, it will reduce disparities between whites and Negroes.

Labor-force participation. In a tight market, of which a low unemployment rate is a barometer, the labor force itself is larger. Job opportunities draw into the labor force individuals who, simply because the prospects were dim, did not previously regard themselves as seeking work and were therefore not enumerated as unemployed. For the economy as a whole, it appears that an expansion of job opportunities enough to reduce unemployment by one worker will bring another worker into the labor force.

This phenomenon is important for many Negro families. Statistically, their poverty now appears to be due more often to the lack of a breadwinner in the labor force than to unemployment. But in a tight labor market many members of these families, including families now on public assistance, would be drawn into employment. Labor-force participation rates are roughly 2 per cent lower for nonwhite men than for white men, and the disparity increases in years of slack labor markets. The story is different for women. Negro women have always been in the labor force to a much greater extent than white women. A real improvement in the economic status of Negro men and in the stability of Negro families would probably lead to a reduction in labor-force participation by Negro women. But for teenagers, participation rates for Negroes are not so high as for whites; and for women twenty to twenty-four they are about the same. These relatively low rates are undoubtedly due less to voluntary choice than to the same lack of job opportunities that produces phenomenally high unemployment rates for young Negro women.

Duration of unemployment. In a tight labor market, such unemployment as does exist is likely to be of short duration. Short-term unemployment is less damaging to the economic welfare of the unemployed. More will have earned and fewer will have exhausted private and public unemployment benefits. In 1953 when the over-all unemployment rate was 2.9 per cent, only 4 per cent of the unemployed were out of work for longer than twenty-six weeks and only 11 per cent for longer than fifteen weeks. In contrast, the unemployment rate in 1961 was 6.7 per cent; and of the unemployed in that year, 17 per cent were out of work for longer than twenty-six weeks and 32 per cent for longer than fifteen weeks. Between the first quarter of 1964 and the first quarter of 1965, over-all unemployment fell 11 per cent, while unemployment extending beyond half a year was lowered by 22 per cent.

Migration from agriculture. A tight labor market draws the surplus rural population to higher paying non-agricultural jobs. Southern Negroes are a large part of this surplus rural population. Migration is the only hope for improving their lot, or their children's. In spite of the vast migration of past decades, there are still about 775,000 Negroes, 11 per cent of the Negro labor force of the country, who depend on the land for their living and that of their families. Almost a half million live in the South, and almost all of them are poor.

Migration from agriculture and from the South is the Negroes' historic path toward economic improvement and equality. It is a smooth path for Negroes and for the urban communities to which they move only if there is a strong demand for labor in towns and cities North and South. In the 1940's the number of Negro farmers and farm laborers in the nation fell by 450,000 and one and a half million Negroes (net) left the South. This was the great decade of Negro economic advance. In the 1950's the same occupational and geographical migration continued undiminished. The movement to higher-income occupations and location should have raised the relative economic status of Negroes. But in the 1950's Negroes were moving into increasingly weak job markets. Too often disguised unemployment in the countryside was simply transformed into enumerated unemployment, and rural poverty into urban poverty.

Quality of jobs. In a slack labor market, employers can pick and choose, both in recruiting and in promoting. They exaggerate the skill, education, and experience requirements of their jobs. They use diplomas, or color, or personal histories as convenient screening devices. In a tight market, they are forced to be realistic, to tailor job specifications to the available supply, and to give on-the-job training. They recruit and train applicants whom they would otherwise screen out, and they upgrade employees whom they would in slack times consign to low-wage, low-skill, and part-time jobs.

Wartime and other experience shows that job requirements are adjustable and that men and women are trainable. It is only in slack times that people worry about a mismatch between supposedly rigid occupational requirements and supposedly unchangeable qualifications of the labor force. As already noted, the relative status of the Negroes improves in a tight labor market not only in respect to unemployment, but also in respect to wages and occupations.

Cyclical fluctuation. Sustaining a high demand for labor is important. The in-and-out status of the Negro in the business cycle damages his long-term position because periodic unemployment robs him of experience and seniority.

Restrictive practices. A slack labor market probably accentuates the discriminatory and protectionist proclivities of certain crafts and unions. When jobs are scarce, opening the door to Negroes is a real threat. Of course prosperity will not automatically dissolve the barriers, but it will make it more difficult to oppose efforts to do so.

I conclude that the single most important step the nation could take to improve the economic position of the Negro is to operate the economy steadily at a low rate of unemployment. We cannot expect to restore the labor market conditions of the second world war, and we do not need to. In the years 1951–1953, unemployment was roughly 3 per cent, teenage unemployment around 7 per cent, Negro unemployment about 4.5 per cent, long-term unemployment negligible. In the years 1955–57, general unemployment was roughly 4 per cent, and the other measures correspondingly higher. [In the summer of 1966 unemployment finally dipped below 4 per cent. Ed.] But society and the Negro can benefit immensely from tightening the labor market still further, to 3.5 or 3 per cent unemployment.

Increasing the earning capacity of Negroes

Given the proper over-all economic climate, in particular a steadily tight labor market, the Negro's economic condition can be expected to improve, indeed to improve dramatically. But not fast enough. Not as fast as his aspira-

tions or as the aspirations he has taught the rest of us to have for him. What else can be done? I shall confine myself to a few comments and suggestions that occur to a general economist.

Even in a tight labor market, the Negro's relative status will suffer both from current discrimination and from his lower earning capacity, the result of inferior acquired skill. In a real sense both factors reflect discrimination, since the Negro's handicaps in earning capacity are the residue of decades of discrimination in education and employment. Nevertheless for both analysis and policy it is useful to distinguish the two.

Discrimination means that the Negro is denied access to certain markets where he might sell his labor, and to certain markets where he might purchase goods and services. Elementary application of "supply and demand" makes it clear that these restrictions are bound to result in his selling his labor for less and buying his livelihood for more than if these barriers did not exist. If Negro women can be clerks only in certain stores, those storekeepers will not need to pay them so much as they pay whites. If Negroes can live only in certain houses, the prices and rents they have to pay will be high for the quality of accommodation provided.

Successful elimination of discrimination is not only important in itself but will also have substantial economic benefits. Since residential segregation is the key to so much else and so difficult to eliminate by legal fiat alone, the power of the purse should be unstintingly used. I see no reason that the expenditure of funds for this purpose should be confined to new construction. Why not establish private or semi-public revolving funds to purchase, for resale or rental on a desegregated basis, strategically located existing structures as they become available?

The effects of past discrimination will take much longer to eradicate. The sins against the fathers are visited on the children. They are deprived of the intellectual and social capital which in our society is supposed to be transmitted in the family and the home. We have only begun to realize how difficult it is to make up for this deprivation by formal schooling, even when we try. And we have only begun to try, after accepting all too long the notion that schools should acquiesce in, even re-enforce, inequalities in home backgrounds rather than overcome them.

Upgrading the earning capacity of Negroes will be difficult, but the economic effects are easy to analyze. Economists have long held that the way to reduce disparities in earned incomes is to eliminate disparities in earning capacities. If college-trained people earn more money than those who left school after eight years, the remedy is to send a larger proportion of young people to college. If machine operators earn more than ditchdiggers, the remedy is to give more people the capacity and opportunity to be machine operators. These changes in relative supplies reduce the disparity both by competing down the pay in the favored line of work and by raising the pay in the less remunerative line. When there are only a few people left in the population whose capacities are confined to garbage-collecting, it will be a high-paid calling. The same is true of domestic service and all kinds of menial work.

This classical economic strategy will be hampered if discrimination, union barriers, and the like stand in the way. It will not help to increase the supply of Negro plumbers if the local unions and contractors will not let them join. But experience also shows that barriers give way more easily when the pressures of unsatisfied demand and supply pile up.

It should therefore be the task of educational and manpower policy to engineer over the next two decades a massive change in the relative supplies of people of different educational and professional attainments and degrees of skill and training. It must be a more rapid change than has occurred in the past two decades, because that has not been fast enough to alter income differentials. We should try particularly to increase supplies in those fields where salaries and wages are already high and rising. In this process we should be very skeptical of self-serving arguments and calculations—that an increase in supply in this or that profession would be bound to reduce quality, or that there are some mechanical relations of "need" to population or to Gross National Product that cannot be exceeded.

Such a policy would be appropriate to the "war on poverty" even if there were no racial problem. Indeed, our objective is to raise the earning capacities of low-income whites as well as of Negroes. But Negroes have the most to gain, and even those who because of age or irreversible environmental handicaps must inevitably be left behind will benefit by reduction in the number of whites and other Negroes who are competing with them.

Conclusion

By far the most powerful factor determining the economic status of Negroes is the over-all state of the U.S. economy. A vigorously expanding economy with a steadily tight labor market will rapidly raise the position of the Negro, both absolutely and relatively. Favored by such a climate, the host of specific measures to eliminate discrimination, improve education and training, provide housing, and strengthen the family can yield substantial additional results. In a less beneficent economic climate, where jobs are short rather than men, the wars against racial inequality and poverty will be uphill battles, and some highly touted weapons may turn out to be dangerously futile.

The forces of the market place, the incentives of private self-interest, the pressures of supply and demand—these can be powerful allies or stubborn opponents. Properly harnessed, they quietly and impersonally accomplish objectives which may elude detailed legislation and administration. To harness them to the cause of the American Negro is entirely possible. It requires simply that the federal government dedicate its fiscal and monetary policies more wholeheartedly and singlemindedly to achieving and maintaining genuinely full employment. The obstacles are not technical or economic. One obstacle is a general lack of understanding that unemployment and related evils are remediable by national fiscal and monetary measures. The other is the high priority now given to competing financial objectives.

In this area, as in others, the administration has disarmed its conservative opposition by meeting it halfway, and no influential political voices challenge the tacit compromise from the "Left." Negro rights movements have so far taken no interest in national fiscal and monetary policy. No doubt gold, the federal budget, and the actions of the Federal Reserve System seem remote from the day-to-day firing line of the movements. Direct local actions to redress specific grievances and to battle visible enemies are absorbing and dramatic. They have concrete observable results. But the use of national political influence on behalf of the goals of the Employment Act of 1946 is equally important. It would fill a political vacuum, and its potential long-run pay-off is very high.

Reading 70

Daniel Patrick Moynihan is one of the most colorful social scientists of our day. As assistant secretary of Labor in the Kennedy administration, he wrote a controversial report which attributed much of the ills of the blacks to the absence of fathers in so many ghetto homes. Then he became director of the Joint Center for Urban Studies of M.I.T. and Harvard University, and was known as a strong advocate of children's allowances by the federal government. Although a liberal himself, Moynihan became increasingly critical of the social interpretations of liberals. The present trenchant essay may have been partially instrumental in making him acceptable to Nixon's Republican administration. In any case he took leave from Harvard to serve in the White House, and there he has been a strong and effective fighter for the cause of the negative income tax, in the modified form of Nixon's proposed family-allowance system.

Questions to Guide the Reading

Are good intentions enough in the field of economics and the social sciences? How would you contrast the Newark and Detroit situations? The government as employer of last resort does sound noble, but what might some of the problems be if hundreds of hard-core unemployed youths are brought together and made to go through the motions of pretending to do useful work when even they can see the purposelessness of what is being done? Aside from scolding liberals, has Moynihan really new and better suggestions to offer for what are undoubtedly difficult problems?

Race Riots and Poverty

Daniel P. Moynihan

The past is prologue

Nothing that we could say could add to the impressiveness of the lesson furnished by the events of the past year as to the needs and dangerous conditions of the neglected classes in our city. Those terrible days in July—the sudden appearance, as from the bosom of the earth, of a most infuriated and degraded mob; the helplessness of property owners and the better classes; the boom of cannon and rattle of musketry in our streets; the sky lurid with conflagrations; the inconceivable barbarity and ferocity of the crowd . . . the immense destruction of property were the first dreadful revelations to many of our people of the existence among us of a great, ignorant, irresponsible class, who were growing up without any permanent interest in the welfare of the community, of the success of the government . . . of the gradual formation of this class and the dangers to be feared from it, the agents of this society have incessantly warned the public for the past 11 years. (Draft riots in New York, c. 1863)

This description of New York in 1863 could be of Newark or Detroit, or of a dozen other

From Daniel P. Moynihan, "Poverty, Welfare, and Jobs," *Republican Papers*, Melvin Laird (Doubleday & Company, Inc., New York, 1968). Reprinted with kind permission of the author and editor.

American cities in which violence has raged in the streets this summer. But it describes the aftermath of the great Civil War draft riots in which the Irish masses of the city exploded in blind fury at what they perceived to be the injustices of the society in which they found themselves.

The nation was then in the midst of the great crisis of slavery. We are now in the midst of another moment of maximum danger that has evolved from our failure fully to resolve that first crisis, and our unwillingness to see that this second one was developing in an urban setting for which the attitudes, and to some degree the machinery, of American government are desperately ill-suited.

The streets of the Negro slums contain the wreckage of a generation of good intentions on the part of American liberals, and good people generally, who have foreseen this outcome or at least insisted on the urgency of the problems that we must suppose have led to it. Many of our proudest achievements are a ruin as well.

Consideration for liberals

Liberals, to be sure, are not the only people in America who have been hurt and damaged by the violence of this summer. But they, and the poor themselves, are the only ones who deserve much consideration. The racists and reactionaries and so-called conservatives in Congress, the shrewd careerists in the administration who have learned so well how to get along with them while keeping up appearances, and the great indifferent American mass who wanted it that way: for them there need be no sympathy.

When one reads the Democratic chairman of the House Appropriations Committee, describing Mayor Cavanagh of Detroit as "this arrogant man" for daring to suggest that the federal government was not facing up to the needs of our cities, it becomes clear that the leaders of Congress have not only learned nothing from their failure, but that neither do they propose to forgive anyone who warned them against it. They had all but destroyed the legislative program of John F. Kennedy when he was murdered, and only thereafter relented somewhat.

Now that American cities are being assaulted one after another across the land, they appear to have decided against any further display of weakness. These are familiar men in history. They are the ones who lose wars, waste opportunities, squander time and destroy civilizations.

They will commonly do so, while invoking the Chairman's principles of "discipline, self respect . . . law and order." Yet it is not ordained that they should prevail, and in the great crises of the American past they have not. Whether they shall do so now is the issue before the nation.

The outcome is likely to be determined now by persons of good will—who actively desire to see American society continue to succeed, who accept the fact that it has in ways failed, and realize that only great and costly effort can reverse the course of events.

Sources of failure

We liberals must inquire into the sources of our own failure, for surely we have not succeeded in bringing the nation along with us. It is not only useless and tasteless to get into a name-calling contest with our presumed opponents; it is also a sure way to avoid facing the possibility that we have some explaining to do about the sources of the present crisis.

We ourselves have lost battles and opportunities, and with time growing short we would do well to ask "why?"

First, in our concern to protect the good name of the poor, especially perhaps the Negro poor, we have entangled ourselves in positions that have led us into preventing effective action to help them.

Second, in our eagerness to see some progress made we have been all too willing to accept the pathetically underfinanced programs which have normally emerged from Congress, and then to oversell them both to ourselves and to those they are designed to aid.

Third, in our desire to maintain public confidence in such programs, we have tended to avoid evidence of poor results, and in particular we have paid too little heed to the limited capacities of government to bring about social change.

These failings have been accompanied, moreover, by a formidable capacity for explaining them away.

In the aftermath of the Newark riots one could already detect our self-defense system at work. Newark, we were beginning to say, was after all a backward city, doubtless run by the Mafia. Unemployment was high. The mayor was fighting with the poverty program. The police were brutal and corrupt. Newark, we were almost saying, deserved a riot. But Detroit . . . what have we to say after Detroit?

Detroit had everything the Great Society could wish for a municipality; a splendid mayor and a fine governor. A high-paying and, thanks to the fiscal policies of the national government, a booming industry, civilized by and associated with the hands-down leading liberal trade union of the world.

Moreover, it was a city whose Negro residents had every reason to be proud of the position they held in the economy and government of the area. Two able and promising Negro Congressmen are from Detroit. Relations between the Negro community and City Hall could hardly have been better. Detroit Negroes held powerful positions throughout the city administration, and to cap matters, the city was equipped with the very model of a summer task force, with a solid program and a twenty-four-hour watch to avert violence.

Urban under class

How then could Detroit riot? The answer lies in the question, "Who rioted?" The rioting was begun and probably largely continued by *young persons whom sociologists would describe as an urban under class.* They happened in this case to be Negro and American, yet their counterparts are to be found in the slums and in the literature of nations throughout the Western world.

Marx despaired of getting any help for his revolution from persons whose main impulses seemed to be so destructive, both to themselves and the society around them.

Most agree that the life of this stratum of society is profoundly different from that of most working people, and certainly most middle-class people. As one middle-aged Negro declared on television, at the height of the Detroit disturbances, "You don't see a family man out here." He may or may not have been right about that moment, but his understanding was sound: violent and criminal behavior set this group apart from the rest of society.

Where did this under class come from? How

did it form? There does not seem to be any satisfactory answer, save that something like it has always been present in most cities in America, and that there are reasonably good signs by which to detect it. The Children's Aid Society of New York had foreseen the formation of such a class among the Catholic immigrants of the city, and indeed was formed to help the wretched young people—orphans and foundlings—involved. Their first annual report, dated 1854, said:

It should be remembered that there are no dangers to the value of property or to the permanency of our institutions so great as those from the existence of such a class of vagabond, ignorant, and ungoverned children. This dangerous class has not begun to show itself as it will in 8 or 10 years when these boys and girls are matured. Those who were too negligent or too selfish to notice them as children will be fully aware of them as men. They will poison society. They will perhaps be embittered at the wealth and luxuries they never share. Then let society beware, when the outcast vicious, reckless multitude of New York boys, swarming now in every foul alley and low street come to know their power and use it.

A decade or so ago we began to detect the formation of a Negro version of this class growing up in our northern cities. Just as certain, we did little or nothing about it.

The basic conditions that would appear necessary for the formation of such a class have clearly existed in our cities for a generation now. *First, and uppermost, is unemployment.* The Depression has never ended for the slum Negro.

To unemployment, add low wages, add miserable housing, add vicious and pervasive forms of racial discrimination, compound it all with an essentially destructive welfare system and a social scientist would have every ground on which to predict violence in this violent country. Moreover, there were many specific warnings.

1. The increase in welfare dependency. Something like six out of every ten Negro youths reaching eighteen have at some time been supported by the Federal Aid to Dependent Children program.

2. The increase in certain types of crime. For the crimes of burglary, larceny, and auto theft, the Negro crime rate increased 33 per-

cent between 1960 and 1965. White rates also increased but not as much.

3. The missing men in the census count. At least three years ago we began to realize that the number of Negro males enumerated in the 1960 census was far fewer than it should have been. We now know that altogether we missed 10 percent of the Negro population, with a much higher loss rate in young adult males. *Something like one male in six, in effect, had simply dropped out of organized society.*

4. Educational failure. For five years or more, we have known that Negro children were doing very badly even in schools that would have to be described as quite good. For some time we have known that the net results, the failure rates on Selective Service examinations, were horrendous: until recently, something like 56 percent of Negro youth called up for the draft have been failing the mental test—a sixth-grade examination.

5. The steady deterioration of family structure in low-income neighborhoods. *Probably not more than a third of the children of low-income Negro families who now reach eighteen have lived all their life with both their parents.*

This last point is often misunderstood. Probably the best available evidence we have of the increase or decrease in the size of lower-class populations lies in the statistics about family life. Breakdown in family relations among poor persons is a pretty good clue that an under class is forming. Many persons—the more liberal a person is the more likely he will be to react this way—interpret the statement to mean that the plight of the poor is being blamed on the state of their families. In other words, that the poor are to blame for their troubles. But just the opposite is the truth; the state of the families is the best evidence of what is happening to the poor.

Available evidence

It happens that this evidence was available not only for the nation but specifically for Detroit. It would be outrageous and unforgivable at this moment to pretend to understand more than we do, but we do know that these were signs of trouble coming. The Negro community was splitting: on the one hand, there was a large and growing group for whom

progress was real and unmistakable. On the other hand, there was another group for whom things were not working.

Relatively they grew worse off, not just when compared with white society but also when compared with other Negroes.

Negro leaders have naturally and properly wished to draw attention to their great achievements and even greater potential. Trapped in their own decencies, liberals have agreed; and so in a hundred ways, great and small, the problem of the burgeoning urban lower class was concealed.

If there was delinquency in the slums, we told ourselves that well-to-do kids in the suburbs were just as unruly but were never brought to law—which is not true, but which leaves everyone feeling better. If there were fatherless children in the slums, we told ourselves that white middle-class fathers were never at home either—which is true, but has nothing to do with the matter. It also, somehow, leaves those children in the slums needing help and not getting it.

A crucial opportunity

When the new frontier began formulating its programs, these were designed for an essentially different class of person; *the competent, reasonably well-motivated individual who happened to be out of work or out of skills, and who would surely take advantage of opportunities offered him.* Our one crucial opportunity came with the major amendments to the welfare system in 1962, but we did nothing then except to confirm the conventional wisdom that, for example, portrayed the typical mother requiring aid for dependent children as a West Virginia miner's widow. The system was enlarged somewhat but not changed.

Last summer, with something like one New York City child in five living on welfare, Dr. Mitchell Ginsberg of the Lindsay administration declared the system "bankrupt. It was just as bankrupt five years ago, but somehow we could not, would not, see it then."

There has been a massive loss of confidence on the part of Negroes as to white sincerity. Two years ago, during the rioting in Watts, comedian Dick Gregory tried to help calm things. He was shot for his troubles, and told the young man who had done it, "All right;

you shot me. Now go home." Two months ago at a Black Power rally in Washington, Gregory was shouting over and over again: "Watts was legal!"

Our programs might have had far greater impact if only they had been of sufficient size. *The amounts of money going to cities and to the poor increased, but in nothing like the amounts or for the purposes demanded by the situation.*

Anyone who was involved with the establishment of the War on Poverty knows that it was put together by fiscal mirrors; scarcely a driblet of new money was involved. Even an element of fraud entered the picture: the Bureau of the Budget began calculating interstate highway funds as part of the financial aid going to cities.

Such money is of considerable aid to General Motors and the United Automobile Workers, and to the Association of General Contractors, but as for the poor, the best that can be said for it is that it destroys a lot of bad housing.

Here again it was fear of, and after a point too sophisticated a knowledge of, the fiscal conservatism, and also social complacency in the Congress that held us back, that even somehow kept us from telling ourselves the truth.

Huge-sounding bills were passed, but mini-appropriations followed, and after a point both ends of Pennsylvania Avenue were co-operating in this process. Instead of taking what we could get, but insisting that it was not enough, liberals both within and without the administration gave in to an orgy of tub thumping.

It does not automatically follow that we raised hopes out of all proportion to our capacity to deliver on our promises, but if we did, and we *must* have, we have only ourselves to blame.

Ourselves and the federal bureaucracy. *Somehow liberals have been unable to acquire from life what conservatives seem to be endowed with at birth, namely, a healthy skepticism of the powers of government agencies to do good.*

The American national government is a superb instrument for redistributing power and wealth in our society. One person in ten in the United States, for example, now gets a Social Security check every month. But as an instrument for providing services, especially to urban lower-class Negroes, it is a highly unreliable device.

Three recommendations

The more programs, the less impact. The 1966 White House conference "to fulfill these rights" produced a hundred pages of recommendations, which meant that the conference was a failure and a disaster. If it had produced three recommendations, it might have been a success. I shall propose three.

First. The United States government must become the employer of last resort, so that anyone looking for work and not finding it is automatically given a job. Put to work. If this is done stupidly it will turn out to be a WPA, but with just a little administrative energy it can be worked out that such jobs are distributed throughout the labor market, so that in fact they are not visible as such. The government must see to it that everyone looking for work finds work, and correspondingly that those without work have no excuse for their situation.

Second. We have got to get more money directly into the hands of the poor. The best way to do this, or at least the best known way, is through a family (or children's) allowance. The United States is the only industrial democracy in the world that does not have such a system of automatic payments for families who are raising minor children. We are also the only industrial democracy whose streets are filled with rioters each year. The connection may not be direct, or may not exist at all, but then it may.

Such a payment would have the advantage that everyone would get it, not just a special segment artificially defined as below a certain income line or across a certain racial line.

It has worked well all over the world, including Canada, and for $9 billion a year, it would be a sound investment in the future as well as in the present.

Third. We must rebuild, or at least clear, the burnt-out neighborhoods. The federal government has a dozen ways to do this, and it must. Otherwise the ruins remain a symbol of the injustices that led to them. Accompanying such a clearance and rebuilding program, we simply must enact a form of federal reinsurance of small business in such areas. Otherwise they will become deserts.

Reading 71

Minorities—blacks, Mexicans, Chinese and Japanese first-generation immigrants, Jews and occasionally Catholics, and even women—have suffered economic injustices through various forms of open or unconscious discriminations. What was good enough before is good enough no longer. But what needs to be done? At what pace can social changes take place? What strategies and tactics are optimal? Those of Booker T. Washington? Of the NAACP? Of the late Martin Luther King, Jr.? Of the late Malcolm X? Of the black militants?

Dr. W. Arthur Lewis (Sir Arthur Lewis, in recognition of his distinguished scholarly career at the London School of Economics, Manchester University, West Africa, and the United Nations) sets out his provocative view on this matter, based on his experience from his West Indies beginnings to a professorship in the Woodrow Wilson School of Princeton University.

Questions to Guide the Reading

Will nonmilitant blacks ever be accorded success as a result of the author's strategy? Is the segregated slum really "self-selected"? Can black studies impart self-pride? May they shift their focus to the present-day urban and rural scene rather than merely dealing with African and American history? What will happen to black colleges if the best students are drawn off to elite mainly white colleges?

A Black Scientist Urges Participatory Achievement for Black Students

W. Arthur Lewis

When a friend suggested that since I had spent all my adult life in black power movements and in universities, I might make some comments on the highly topical subject of black power in the American university, it did not at first seem to be a good idea. Now that I have come to grips with it I am even more conscious of my folly in tackling so difficult and controversial a subject.

I am also very conscious that my credentials are inadequate, since the black power movements in the countries with which I am familiar differ fundamentally from black power in the United States. My stamping grounds are the West Indies, where I was born, and Africa, where I have worked, and which I shall be visiting for the fourteenth time next month. But in both those places blacks are the great majority of the people—97 per cent in Jamaica, 99 per cent in Nigeria. The objective of the political movements was therefore to capture the central legislature, and the executive and judicial powers. In the United States, in contrast, blacks are only 11 per cent of the population, and have neither claim to nor prospect of capturing the Congress, the executive branch, or the Supreme Court for themselves alone. The objectives have to be different, and the strategy must also be different. Comparison between the colonial situation and the position of blacks in America is bound to mislead if it is suggested as a basis for deciding political strategy.

The fact of the matter is that the struggle of the blacks in America is a unique experience, with no parallel in Africa. And since it is unique, the appropriate strategies are likely to be forged only by trial and error. We are all finding the process a great trial, and since our leaders are going off in all directions at once, a great deal of error is also inevitable. I myself, in venturing onto this ground, claim

From W. Arthur Lewis, "Black Power and the American University," *University, A Princeton Quarterly*, Spring 1969, pp. 8–12. Copyright © 1969 Princeton University. Reprinted with kind permission of the author and publisher.

the protection of the First Amendment, but do not aspire to wear the cloak of Papal infallibility.

Strategy for the American scene

The goals and tactics of black power in America have to be adjusted to the reality of America. Take the issue of segregation. Everywhere in the black world, except among a small minority of American blacks, the fight against segregation has been in the foreground of black power movements. This goes without saying in countries where blacks are the great majority; yet there are situations where a minority may strengthen itself by temporary self-segregation of a limited kind.

All American minorities have passed through a stage of temporary self-segregation: not just the Afro-Americans. Foreigners speak of the United States as a "melting pot" and it may one day be that; but for the present America is really not a melting pot but a welding shop. It is a country in which many different groups of people live and work together side by side, without coalescing. There are Poles, and Irish, and Chinese, and Jews, and Germans, and many other ethnic groups. And their way of living together is set by the clock; there is integration between 7 o'clock in the morning and 5 o'clock at night, when all mingle and work together in the center of the city, in the banks and factories, department stores and universities. But after 5 o'clock each ethnic group returns to its own neighborhood. There it has its own separate social life. There Poles do not marry Italians, even though they are both white Catholics. The neighborhood has its own schools, its own little shops, its own doctors, and its own celebrations. Integration by day is accompanied by segregation by night.

Ethnic self-segregation

It is important to note that this self-segregation is voluntary and not imposed by law. An Italian *can* buy a house in an Irish neighborhood if he wishes to do so, *can* marry an Irish girl, and *can* go to an Irish Catholic Church. Many people also insist that this voluntary segregation is only a temporary phase in the acculturation of ethnic groups. They live together until they have found their feet on the American way of life, after which they disperse. The immigrants from Germany and Scandinavia have for the most part already moved out of segregated neighborhoods. The Irish and the Jews are just in the process, and sooner or later the Poles, the Chinese, and even the Afro-Americans may have dispersed. But in the meantime this voluntary self-segregation shelters those who are not yet ready to lose themselves completely in the American mainstream. Other people believe that there will always be cultural pluralism in America, and that this may even be a source of strength. Whether or not they are right about the long run, there is no disputing that voluntary social self-segregation is the current norm.

The black power movement is therefore fully in the American tradition in recognizing that certain neighborhoods are essentially black neighborhoods, where the black politician, the black doctor, the black teacher, the black grocer and the black clergyman are going to be able to play roles which are not open to them, *de facto*, in other neighborhoods. Many Southern Negroes claim vigorously that blacks are better off in the South than in the North precisely because the Southern white philosophy has reserved a place for a black middle class in the black neighborhoods—for the black preacher or doctor or grocer.

Essentially, what black power is now saying in the North is that the North too should recognize that the middle class occupations in the black neighborhoods belong to blacks, who are not permitted to hold such jobs in Italian, Polish, or other ethnic neighborhoods. The issue is phrased in terms of community power—that is to say, of giving to each neighborhood control over its own institutions—but this is tied inextricably to the distribution of middle class jobs inside the neighborhood. It is unquestionably part of the American tradition that members of each ethnic group should be trained for the middle class occupations in their neighborhoods, and that, given the training, they should have preference in employment in their own neighborhoods.

South Africa versus America

This kind of voluntary self-segregation has nothing in common with the compulsory segregation of other countries. An American neighborhood is not a ghetto. A ghetto is an area where members of an ethnic group are forced by law to live, and from which it is a criminal offense to emerge without the license of the oppressing power. This is what apartheid means in the Union of South Africa. An American neighborhood is not a place where members of an ethnic group are required by law to live; they may in the first instance have been forced to live there by circumstance, but it is soon transmuted, ideally, into a place where members of the group *choose* to live, and from which, ideally, anybody can emerge at any time that he wishes to do so. To confuse this neighborhood concept with apartheid is an egregious error.

The fundamental difference between apartheid and the American neighborhood comes out most clearly when one turns from what happens after 5 p.m. to what happens during the daytime. A neighborhood is a work place for less than half the community. The teachers, the doctors, the police, the grocers—these work where they live. But these people are supported by the labors of those who work in the factories and in other basic occupations outside the neighborhood. Some 50 to 60 per cent of the labor force moves out of the neighborhood every morning to work in the country's basic industries. *So a black strategy which concentrated exclusively on building up the black neighborhoods would be dealing with less than half the black man's economic problems.* The neighborhood itself will not flourish unless the man who goes out of it in the morning brings back into it from the outside world an income adequate to support its institutions.

Day and night

I said earlier that the American pattern is segregation in *social* life after 5 p.m. but integration in the *economic* life of the country during the day. American economic life is dominated by a few large corporations which do the greater part of the country's business; indeed, in manufacturing, half the assets of the entire country are owned by just 100 corporations. The world of these big corporations is an integrated world. There will be black grocery shops in black neighborhoods, but in your

lifetime and mine there isn't going to be a black General Motors, a black Union Carbide, a black Penn-Central Railway, or a black Standard Oil Company. These great corporations *serve all ethnic groups and employ all ethnic groups.* American economic life is inconceivable except on an integrated basis.

The majority of Afro-Americans work not in their neighborhoods but for one of the non-neighborhood corporations or employers, and so it shall be for as far ahead as we can see. The black problem is that while we are 11 per cent of the population, we have only 2 per cent of the jobs at the top, 4 per cent of the jobs in the middle, and are forced into 16 per cent of the jobs at the bottom—indeed into as much as 40 per cent of some of the jobs at the very bottom. *Clearly our minimum objective must be to capture 11 per cent of the jobs in the middle and 11 per cent of the jobs at the top.* Or, for those of us who have a pride in ourselves, it could even be an objective to have 15 per cent of the jobs at the top and in the middle, and only 8 per cent of those at the bottom, leaving the very bottom to less ambitious ethnic groups.

Not all our leaders understand that our central economic problem is not in the neighborhoods, but is in the fact that outside the neighborhoods, where most of us have to work, we are concentrated in the bottom jobs. For if they understood this they could not be as hostile as they are toward the black middle and upper classes. The measure of whether we are winning our battle is in how many of us rise to the middle and the top. When a so-called militant abuses a successful Afro-American for having, by virtue of extreme hard work and immense self-discipline, managed to get to the top in the outside world, instead of devoting his energies to being—in the neighborhood—a social worker, or a night school teacher, or a semi-politician, such a critic is merely being absurd. Rising from the bottom to the middle or the top, in the face of stiff white competition, prejudice and arbitrary barriers, takes everything that a man can give to it. It is our militants who should month-by-month chalk up the score of those who have broken through the barriers, should glory in their achievement, and should hold it up before our young to show them what black men can achieve.

Infiltrating the elite

Now at last I reach my central topic, which is the black man and the university. The road to the top in the great American corporations and other institutions is through higher education. Scientists, research workers, engineers, accountants, lawyers, financial administrators, presidential advisers—all these people are recruited from the university. And indeed nearly all of the top people are taken from a very small number of colleges—from not more than some 50 or 60 of the 2,000 degree-granting institutions in the United States. The Afro-American could not make it to the top so long as he was effectively excluded from this small number of select institutions. *The breakthrough of the Afro-American into these colleges is therefore absolutely fundamental to the larger economic strategy of black power.*

I do not mean to suggest that the most important black strategy is to get more blacks into the best colleges. Probably the greatest contribution to black advancement would be to break the trade union barriers which keep our people out of apprenticeships in the building and printing trades, and prevent our upgrading or promotion in other industries. The trade unions are the black man's greatest enemy in the United States. The number of people who would be at the top, if we had our numerical share of the top, would be small. Our greatest task, in terms of numbers, is to conquer the middle—getting into skilled posts, foremen's posts, supervisory and white collar jobs—through better use of apprenticeships, of the high schools and of technical colleges. I am going to talk about the universities not because this is numerically important, but partly because it has become so controversial, and partly because if we did conquer the top it would make much easier the conquering of the middle—both in our own minds, and in other people's minds, by altering our young people's image of themselves and of what they can achieve.

What can *the good white college* do for its black students that Howard or Lincoln or Fisk cannot do? It can open the road into the top jobs. It can do this only by giving our people that aura of "effortless superiority" which is looked for by people filling top jobs. To put it in unpopular language, it *can train them to become top members of the establishment.*

Aiming high

If it is wrong for young blacks to be trained for the top jobs in the big corporations, for top jobs in the government service, for ambassadorships, for the editorial staff of the *New York Times* and so on—then there is little point in sending them to the best white colleges. On the contrary, if what one wants is people trained to live and work in black neighborhoods, they will do much better to go to the black colleges, of which there are, after all, over 100, which know much better than Yale or Princeton or Dartmouth what the problems of black neighborhoods are, and how people should be trained to handle them. The point about the best white colleges is that they are a part not of the neighborhood side of American life, but of the integrated part of American life, training people to run the economy and the administration in the integrated part of the day before 5 p.m.

But how can it be wrong for young Afro-Americans to be trained to hold superior positions in the integrated working world outside the neighborhood when in fact the neighborhood cannot provide work for even a half of its people? Whether we like it or not, most Afro-Americans *have* to work in the integrated world, and if we do not train for superior positions there, all that will happen is what happens now—that we shall be crowded into the worst paid jobs.

If one grasps this point, that these 50 colleges are the gateway to the superior jobs, then the current attitudes of some of our black leaders to these colleges is not a little bewildering. In its most extreme form what is asked is that the college should set aside a special part of itself which is to be the black part. There will be a separate building for black studies, and separate dormitories and living accommodations for blacks. There will be separate teachers, all black, teaching classes open only to blacks. The teachers are to be chosen by the students, and will for the most part be men whom no African or Indian or Chinese University would recognize as scholars, or be willing to hire as teachers.

Forward or backward look?

Doubtless some colleges under militant pressure will give in to this, but I do not see what

Afro-Americans will gain thereby. Employers will not hire the students who emerge from this process, and their usefulness even in black neighborhoods will be minimal.

I yield to none in thinking that every respectable university should give courses on African life and on Afro-American life. It is, however, my hope that they will be attended mostly by white students, and that the majority of black students in Princeton will find more important uses for their time; that they may attend one or two such courses, but will reject any suggestion that black studies must be the major focus of their programs.

The principal argument for forcing black students to spend a great deal of their time in college studying African and Afro-American anthropology, history, languages and literature is that they need such studies to overcome their racial inferiority complex. I am not impressed by this argument. The youngster discovers that he is black around the age of six or seven; from then on the whites he meets, the books he reads, and the situation of the Negro in America all combine to persuade him that he is an inferior species of *homo sapiens*. By the time he is 14 or 15 he has made up his mind on this one way or the other. Nothing that the college can do, after he reaches 18 or 19, is going to have much effect on his basic personality. To expect the colleges to eradicate the inferiority complexes of young black adults is to ask the impossible. And to expect this to come about by segregating black students in black studies under inferior teachers suggests some deficiency of thought.

The new race pride

Perhaps I am wrong about this. The proposition is essentially that the young black has been brainwashed into thinking himself inferior, so now he must spend four years in some place where he will be re-brainwashed into thinking himself equal. But the prospect that the 50 best colleges in the United States can be forced to take on this re-brainwashing operation is an idle dream. Those who are now putting all their energies into working for this are doomed to disappointment.

We are knocking our heads against the wrong wall. Every black student should learn some Afro-American history, and study various aspects of his people's culture, but the place

for him to do this compulsorily is in the high school, and the best age to start this seriously is even earlier, perhaps around the age of ten. By the time the student gets to a first-rate college he should be ready for business—for the business of acquiring the skills which he is going to be able to use, whether in his neighborhood, or in the integrated economy. *Let the clever young black go to a university to study engineering, medicine, chemistry, economics, law, agriculture and other subjects which are going to be of value to him and his people. And let the clever whites go to college to read black novels, to learn Swahili, and to record the exploits of Negro heroes of the past: they are the ones to whom this will come as an eye-opener.*

This incidentally is very much what happens in African universities. Most of these have well equipped departments of African studies, which are popular with visiting whites, but very few African students waste their time (as they see it) on such studies, when there is so much to be learned for the jobs they will have to do. The attitude of Africans to their past conforms to the historian's observation that only decadent peoples, on the way down, feel an urgent need to mythologize and live in their past. A vigorous people, on the way up, has visions of its future, and cares next to nothing about its past.

It will be obvious to some of you that my attitude to the role of black studies in the education of college blacks derives not only from an unconventional view of what is to be gained therefrom, but also from an unconventional view of the purpose of going to college. The United States is the only country in the world which thinks that the purpose of going to college is to be educated. Everywhere else one goes to high school to be educated, but goes to college to be trained for one's life work. In the United States serious training does not begin until one reaches graduate school at the age of 22. Before that one spends four years in college being educated—that is to say spending 12 weeks getting some tidbits on religion, 12 weeks learning French, 12 weeks seeing whether the History professor is stimulating, 12 weeks seeking entertainment from the Economics professor, 12 weeks confirming that one is not going to be able to master calculus, and so on.

If the purpose of going to college is to be

educated, and serious study will not begin until one is 22, one might just as well perhaps spend the four years reading black novels, studying black history and learning to speak Fanti. But I do not think that American blacks can afford this luxury. I think our young people ought to get down to the business of serious preparation for their life work as soon after 18 as they can.

And I also note, incidentally, that many of the more intelligent white students are now in revolt against the way so many colleges fritter away their precious years in meaningless peregrination from subject to subject between the ages of 18 and 22.

A new self-imposed apartheid?

Let me make my position clear. Any Afro-American who wishes to become a specialist in black studies, or to spend some of his time on such work, should be absolutely free to do so. But I hope that, of those students who get the opportunity to attend the 50 best colleges, the proportion who want to specialize in black studies may, in their interest and that of the black community, turn out to be rather small, in comparison with our scientists, or engineers, accountants, economists or doctors.

Another attitude which puzzles me is that which requires black students in the better white colleges to mix only with each other; to have a dormitory to themselves; to eat at separate tables in the refectory, and so on. I have pointed out that these colleges are the gateway to leadership positions in the integrated part of the economy, and that what they can best do for young blacks is to prepare them to capture our 11 per cent share of the best jobs at the top—one of every nine ambassadorships, one of every nine vice-presidencies of General Motors, one of every nine senior directors of engineering laboratories, and so on. Now I am told that the reason black students stick together is that they are uncomfortable in white company. But how is one to be Ambassador to Finland or Luxembourg—jobs which American Negroes have already held with distinction—if one is uncomfortable in white company? Anybody who occupies a supervisory post, from foreman upwards, is going to have white people working under him, who will expect him to be friendly and

fair; is this going to be possible, after four years spent in boycotting white company?

Nowadays in business and in government most decisions are made in committees. Top Afro-Americans cannot hope to be more than one in nine; they will always be greatly outnumbered by white people at their level. But how can one survive as the only black vice-president sitting on the executive committee of a large corporation if one is not so familiar with the ways and thoughts of other vice-presidents that one can even anticipate how they are going to think? *Blacks in America are inevitably and perpetually a minority. This means that in all administrative and leadership positions we are going to be outnumbered by white folks, and will have to compete with them not on our terms but on theirs. The only way to win this game is to know them so thoroughly that we can outpace them.* Being in one of the best white colleges, where they are molded, gives us this opportunity. For us to turn our backs on this opportunity, by insisting on mingling only with other black students in college, is folly of the highest order.

Black capitalism no panacea

This kind of social self-segregation is encouraged by two myths about the possibilities for black economic progress in the United States which need to be nailed. One is the Nixon myth, and the other, its opposite, is the revolutionary myth.

The first postulates that the solution is black capitalism—to help as many blacks as possible to become big businessmen. To be sure, it is feasible to have more successful small businesses operating inside the protection of the neighborhood—more grocers and drug stores and lunch counters; but I have emphasized that the members of every ethnic group mostly work outside their neighborhood in the integrated economy, buying from and selling to all ethnic groups. In this part of the economy the prospects for small business are bleak.

No doubt a few Negroes, born with the special talents which success in a highly competitive business world demands, will succeed in establishing sizeable and highly competitive concerns. But the great majority who start on this road, whether white or black, go bankrupt in a short time. Indeed, about half of the new white businesses go bankrupt within the first 12 months. To tell the blacks that this is the direction in which they must move is almost a form of cruelty. To pretend that black America is going to be saved by the emergence of black capitalism, competing in the integrated economy with white capitalism, is little more than a hoax.

What revolution can't change

Neither is black America going to be saved by a Marxist revolution. Revolution takes power from one set of persons and gives it to another, but it does not change the hierarchical structure of the economy. Any kind of America that you can visualize, whether capitalist, communist, fascist, or any other kind of ist, is going to consist of large institutions like General Motors under one name or another. It will have people at the top, people in the middle and people at the bottom. Its leading engineers, doctors, scientists and administrators—leaving out a few top professional politicians—are going to be recruited from a small number of highly select colleges. *The problem of the black will essentially be the same—that problem being whether he is going to be mostly in the bottom jobs, or whether he will also get his 11 per cent share of the top and the middle.* And his chance at the top is going to depend on his getting into those select schools and getting the same kind of technical training that the whites are getting—not some segregated schooling specially adapted for him, but the same kind that the whites get as their gateway to the top. Those black leaders who wish us to concentrate our efforts on working for revolution in America are living on a myth, for our problems and needed strategies are going to be exactly the same whether there is a revolution or not. In the integrated part of the American economy our essential strategy has to be to use all the normal channels of advancement—the high schools, the colleges, apprenticeships, night schools: it is only by climbing this ladder that the black man is going to escape from his concentration in the bottom jobs of the economy.

This is not, of course, simply a matter of schooling. The barriers of prejudice which keep us off the ladder still have to be broken down: the task of the civil rights movement is still not completed, and we need all the liberal help, black and white, that we can get to help to keep the ladder clear. We need also to raise our own sights; to recognize that there are now more opportunities than there were, and to take every opportunity that offers. Here our record is good. For as the barriers came down in sports and entertainment our young people moved swiftly to the top in baseball, football, the theatre, or wherever else the road was cleared. *We will do exactly the same in other spheres, given the opportunity.*

The secret is to inspire our young people with confidence in their potential achievement. And psychologists tell us that the background to this is a warm and secure family life. The most successful minorities in America, the Chinese, the Japanese, and the Jews, are distinguished by their close and highly disciplined family, which is the exact opposite of what has now become the stereotype of the white American family, with its undisciplined and uncontrollable children reared on what are alleged to be the principles of Dr. Spock. African families are warm, highly disciplined structures just like Jewish or Chinese families. If black Americans are looking to Africa for aspects of culture which will distinguish them from white Americans, let them turn their back on Spockism, and rear their children on African principles, for this is the way to the middle and the top. Given a disciplined family life and open doors to opportunity, I have no doubt that American blacks will capture one field after another, as fast as barriers come down.

A false choice

The point which I have been trying to make is that the choice some of our leaders offer us between segregation and integration is false in the American context. America is integrated in the day and segregates itself at night. Some of our leaders who have just discovered the potential strength of neighborhood self-segregation have got drunk on it to the point of advocating segregation for all spheres of Afro-American life. But the struggle for community power in the neighborhood is not an alternative to the struggle for a better share of the integrated world outside the neighborhood, in which inevitably most of our people must earn their living. The way to a better share of this integrated economy is through the integrated colleges; but they can help us only if we take from them the same things that they give to our white competitors.

If we enter them merely to segregate ourselves in blackness, we shall lose the opportunity of our lives. Render homage unto segregated community power in the neighborhood where it belongs, but do not let it mess up our chance of capturing our share of the economic world out of the neighborhood, where segregation weakens our power to compete.

Reading 72

The negative income tax is undoubtedly the single most exciting proposal to alleviate poverty of the last decade. We have already learned about it in Reading 21 by James Tobin. In this reading an economic expert on the subject of inequality points out what is wrong about the current system of welfare. He poses some of the choices that confronted President Nixon in 1969 when, after much controversy within his own administration, he finally proposed to Congress a modified negative tax in the form of a family-allowance program. Dr. Lampman is a professor at the University of Wisconsin, affiliated there with the Institute for Research on Poverty. His earlier work on inequality of income at the National Bureau of Economic Research has received much attention. While he was serving on the staff of President Kennedy's Council of Economic Advisers, Lampman was one of those who deserves chief credit for persuading Chairman Walter Heller and President Kennedy to initiate a new and massive attack upon the problem of poverty.

Questions to Guide the Reading

Do the poor consist only of those who are unemployed? Can you list frequent cases in which a family's poverty is permanent, and which, for reasons of age or illness, can never be cured by self-effort? How can one humanely defend a system in which the best thing that a father can do for his family is to leave home? Does it make sense to kill off the incentives of those on relief by making sure that if they earn a new dollar, they will get none of its benefits? Would a negative-income-tax plan help in this situation?

If there are two brothers, both from impoverished backgrounds, and one of them by his own efforts is able to enter into the lower middle classes, do you think that he will resent public assistance to his brother? How can such social backlash be minimized? Why do you suppose President Nixon made at least some pretense of calling for a requirement that recipients of family allowances be available for retraining or employment?

Nixon Tackles Poverty

Robert J. Lampman

The Nixon Administration is considering a radical change in the income maintenance system—a system which was forged in the Great Depression. The historic importance of such a step would rival that of the landmark Social Security Act of 1935. The changes in the wind are:

1. A greatly enlarged role for the federal

From Robert J. Lampman, "Nixon's Choices on Cash for the Poor," Institute for Research on Poverty, University of Wisconsin, May, 1969. Reprinted with kind permission of the author and publisher.

government in federal-state public assistance or welfare programs.

2. A new federal plan to pay income supplements to all poor families with children, including those headed by able-bodied men.

The President's choices have been thrust upon him by a combination of discoveries, events, and changes of attitude of recent years. Among these were:

The discovery and identification of poverty as a national problem and the commitment by President Johnson to eliminate poverty.

The riots in the street and the quiet hunger in the countryside—both of which have been attributed in some degree to the malfunctioning of the welfare system.

The shift from thinking of welfare as a non-enforceable *privilege* over to thinking of it as a *legal right* to certain stated benefits in response to objectively determined needs.

The revolt by state and local taxpayers who see the escalating costs of welfare as too much for them to bear without at least some new sharing arrangement with Washington.

History of our welfare state

To get the President's choices into perspective, it is necessary to look back to the 1930's when the United States moved to play down the importance of state-local welfare programs and to build up a system of income maintenance *dominated by social insurance*, with the key role set for the federal government. Benefits for old-age and short-term unemployment led the list and benefits for survivors were soon added. Later, in Eisenhower's first term, benefits for permanent and total disability were included. Social insurance benefits, including those for "social security" and workmen's compensation, amounted to $30 billion in 1968, and they are an important third layer of protection against the leading hazards to a family's security.

The first layer of protection is, of course, *earnings and property income* made by the family itself. The second is *private insurance*, with or without employer participation. The third is *social insurance*, which establishes contractual rights to income in stated circumstances.

The fourth layer of protection is *categorical*

assistance, for which the federal government in 1935 agreed to share costs with the states, which had in turn, just recently, undertaken to share costs with the local governments. The "categories" of "deserving poor" were identified in 1935 as the old-aged, the blind, and the children in broken homes. Later, the permanently and totally disabled were accorded categorical status.

The fifth layer of protection is non-categorical or *general assistance*, which is taken care of primarily by local government and private charity.

Aid to families with dependent children (AFDC)

The architects of the Social Security Act theorized that the residual role of assistance would gradually wither away with the growth of social insurance and the return to prosperity. This has turned out to be a fair prediction with respect to general assistance and old-age assistance (OAA), but it was a mistaken forecast for aid to families with dependent children (AFDC).

Beginning in the late 1950's AFDC has expanded at an accelerating rate. One minor reason for this expansion is that Congress in 1961 extended the basis for eligibility to include *payments for children with fathers who are unemployed for long periods*. To date, 23 states have taken advantage of the unemployed parent provision (AFDC-UP), but less than ten percent of all the AFDC recipients are in this category. The *largest portion of AFDC benefits go to families broken by a cause other than death of a husband*: divorce, desertion, or illegitimacy. Not only are there proportionately more such family break-ups, but more people in such circumstances apply for and are found eligible for AFDC benefits.

Why this is true is also a complex matter. The Congress has taken steps to liberalize the program through such measures as raising the age limit to include children until they are 21. State legislators and administrators have forced local jurisdictions up to state-wide standards and have backed away from certain ancient devices for keeping down costs, including: "rateable reductions" in benefits, whereby benefits are reduced as the appropriation period wanes; pursuing absent fathers and other "responsible relatives"; establishing an actual budget as a fraction of a "needs budget" for families of given sizes; requiring a family to deplete all of its resources before benefits begin. The courts have also played their part in this liberalization by overruling legislative provisions that have (1) limited eligibility to those who have resided in a state for a year or more and (2) cut off families which have a "man in the house" other than the father. Furthermore, social workers and welfare rights organizations have publicized the availability of welfare and have encouraged families to apply.

As of now, *six percent of all children* under age 18 are receiving AFDC benefits. They comprise *40 percent of the nation's poor children,* and *two-thirds* of all the poor children in families *headed by women.* The typical length of stay on AFDC rolls is a little over two years. Over a fifth of all the children now reaching 18 have been served by AFDC at one time or another during their childhood, making this category of public assistance one of the most important institutions we have for dealing with the needs of children.

The declining numbers of children in poverty (10 million) are gradually approaching the rising numbers on AFDC (4 million). However, the possibilities for further expansion of AFDC cost are still pretty wide open. If the patterns of New York and California were to become general, the number of beneficiaries *would increase by one-half.* And if for all the states the average AFDC benefit were to approach that of the richer states, the national AFDC cost would be half again as high.

It is true that by a 1967 amendment to the Social Security Act, Congress served notice that it wanted to "freeze" the numbers in each state to which it would extend AFDC matching funds. But it is also true that another amendment to the same act required states to adopt an *incentive benefit* formula which would raise the earnings level below which families would be eligible, and hence increase the number of beneficiaries. These amendments, scheduled to go into effect July 1969, lend urgency to some action by President Nixon.

Crisis ahead

The trends discussed above mean that the $3 billion which AFDC is costing us this year could quickly go to $6 billion or more before it levels off. It is a vision like this which

prompts Mitchell I. Ginsberg, Commissioner of Human Resources in New York City, to conclude that "welfare is now almost beyond the power of any city to handle. It is getting too big for a state." It is a vision like this that leads the Advisory Council on Intergovernmental Relations to call for the federal government to take over the *whole* cost of welfare and relieve the state and local governments of their present share of that cost. AFDC's cost, even if it were to rise to $6 billion, would be less than one percent of a $900 billion gross national product. It is curious, then, that it should be such a significant cause of a state and local taxpayer's revolt, and that it should be considered by Governor Nelson A. Rockefeller "the most serious economic paradox of our times," and by President Nixon's Special Assistant Daniel Moynihan "the leading conundrum of American domestic policy."

The excitement is partly due to the fact that, especially if the federal freeze goes into effect, a large fraction of any increase in AFDC costs will come out of badly strained state and local budgets. Another part of it is that any discussion of AFDC in any state legislature or county board is likely to yield equal parts of controversy, outrage, and bitterness and to bring up topics most legislators would prefer to avoid—touching on race (half the beneficiaries are black), religion (family planning), illicit sex, and family responsibility.

A leading cause of the current agonizing about AFDC is the fact that as the number in the program and the average AFDC benefits rise, the disparity between the poor who are on versus the poor who are off the program becomes less and less tolerable. For the most part, a poor child is not eligible for AFDC *unless his father dies or deserts.* This means we have what Yale's economist James Tobin calls "an insane piece of social engineering" which encourages family break-ups. In any event, AFDC is not set up to reach all, or even most, of the children who are poor. If more than a minority of the nation's poor children are to be helped, a new program is needed. President Nixon's proposed tax reform, which raises the income level at which the federal individual income tax begins, is a notable help to many poor and near-poor families. Raising this level from $3,000 to $3,500 (for a family of four, with varying changes for families of different sizes) will add a total of $669 million to their after-tax income. However, none of that extra money will reach families (of four) with less than $3,000 of income.

Toward a negative income tax

Commission after commission has called for a new program which would respond to the needs of all those who are poor for any reason. As long ago as 1964 a President's Task Force on Income Maintenance, of which the present writer was a member, recommended the introduction of a "Tax Adjustment Allowance" for low-income families with children. The Advisory Council on Public Welfare (1966), the National Commission on Technology, Automation and Economic Progress (1966), the Advisory Commission on Rural Poverty (1967), and the Kerner Commission on Civil Disorders (1968), all recommended an extension and reform of welfare to recognize a national interest in the poor in every state and in every category and non-category. Finally, from recent statements by Chairman Ben W. Heineman, it appears that the Commission on Income Maintenance Programs appointed by President Johnson will report this year in favor of a reform aimed both at more nearly uniform nationwide benefits and at eligibility for the non-categorical poor. [It subsequently did.]

All these advisory groups are challenging two tenets of America's conventional wisdom. The first is that *relief should be managed by governments close to home*, where judgment of what is "really needed" and what the taxpayers can "afford to pay" is alleged to be most reliable. This tenet is used to rationalize the wild variations in recipient rates and benefits from one state to the next. It is also used to justify the refusal by some southern counties to distribute food stamps because of a fear that better-fed families will not provide willing workers in the local labor markets. But it is hard to reconcile this tenet with the fact that Chicago may pay the price for Alabama's neglect when migration occurs.

The second tenet being challenged is that *government should not make welfare available to all those who are poor, but only to those who are poor "through no fault of their own."* The notion of the blameless or deserving poor goes back to the enlightenment of 19th century reformers, who sought to save people from the pauperization, the deprivation of civil rights, and the ostracism then accorded indiscriminately to all the welfare poor. The thing most to be avoided, by the lights of American social philosophers from the 17th century on, was encouragement of poverty and idleness. The aim, as Sargent Shriver rather crudely put it in selling the Economic Opportunity Act, is "to convert tax-eaters into tax-payers."

The question of how to do that, however, remains open, with one side saying the poor should suffer scorn and shame, and the other advocating sympathy and "investment" in their future. The Puritan ethic is challenged by a social interest in equality of opportunities. The idea that welfare is giving something for nothing—or worse, that welfare is rewarding the non-performance of parental duties by what George Bernard Shaw called "the barbarous poor"—is challenged by the modern social work proposition that welfare is not a *cause* of misery but merely a *passive receiver* of the failures of individuals and economic and social organizations. Hence, to present-day policy makers, it is at least an open question whether poverty is encouraged or discouraged by a system which denies benefits to needy children because of the category of their parents. Are children of the "undeserving" themselves undeserving of a good chance at life? James L. Sundquist asserts that it is "unsound public policy to deprive multitudes of children of the sustenance they require to grow into healthy and self-sustaining adults, in their own time, in order to punish those of their parents' generation who may be considered to deserve such punishment in our own time."

In summary, President Nixon's arrival in the White House was preceded by the maturing of the social insurance system, a decade of rising cost for AFDC, increasing pressure to change the intergovernmental sharing of the cost for that program, and persistent advice to correct inequities among the poor in the several states and in and out of the categories. Thus, two questions awaited the new president.

Problems and possibilities

A task force appointed by Nixon before he took office suggested that the federal government should strive to reduce disparities of welfare payments in different parts of the nation by (1) requiring all states to pay at least $40 per person per month and then (2) itself providing three-fourths of that minimum and half of the next $40. This scheme would help many of the poorest people in the country and would, it is alleged, slow down the migration into northern cities. It is important to know that 40 percent of the nation's poor are in the South.

However, if the task-force approach were followed, states which now pay low benefits would find themselves confronted with a problem already familiar to high-benefit states like Wisconsin: AFDC benefits for moderate and large-sized families *would exceed the earnings of a fully-employed man at the going wages for low-skill work.* Let me cite an example: a mother and three children living in a state such as Mississippi and having no wages would, under the new approach, get $160 per month or $1,920 per year—and that would be more than many employed men earn in Mississippi. And it is far more than the $500 assistance now available to that mother and her children.

This discrepancy between the incomes of those on and those not on welfare means that, given the regressive nature of state and local taxes, many working-poor men would be contributing through their taxes to the support of broken families who would then have incomes at levels above the amount that they themselves can provide for their own families. As stated by Richard A. Cloward and Frances Fox Piven of the Columbia University School of Social Work, this inequity is an affront to the value of work and tends to drive a wedge of bitterness between the low-income worker and the welfare poor.

In order to avoid this type of inequity and bitterness, [President Nixon has advocated a family allowance plan which will] pay benefits to families headed by able-bodied, working men. A possible compromise is to set the benefit at $1500 a year for a family of four having no other income and to tax all earnings up to $3000 at a 50 percent rate. That is, the $1500 benefit would be reduced 50 cents for each dollar of earnings. Parallel schedules of benefits would, of course, apply for families of different sizes.

That compromise would work all right for the low-income, low-benefit states and would relieve their treasuries of all expense for AFDC

and most general assistance as well. But what about those states that now pay AFDC benefits in excess of $1500 per year to a family of four? One plan is, in effect, to abolish AFDC as a federally-assisted category and to say to the states, "If you want to single out some families and pay them benefits above the $1500 the federal government is paying them, that is your business and you can do as you please with *your* funds." Actually, the $1500 per family is about what the federal share now yields most high-benefit states, so few state treasuries would be adversely affected by adoption of such an overall plan.

But the non-categorical poor would have a new source of aid in every state. Most of the working-poor families now have earnings in the range of $1500 to $2500 and, in the case of a four-person family, would have those earnings supplemented by $750 to $250 under the 50 percent rates schedule. The assumption is that few families now earning in these ranges or above will opt for no earnings and $1500 of benefits. On the contrary, it is expected that *most would continue to work about as much as before* and to take the benefits as additional income rather than replacement income.

Schedule of Benefits for a Family of Four Persons

Pre-allowance income	Net allowance	Post-allowance income
$ 0	$1500	$1500
500	1250	1750
1000	1000	2000
1500	750	2250
2000	500	2500
2500	250	2750
3000	0	3000

A lively argument goes on concerning the likely effect of this plan on wage rates. Some labor leaders fear it would depress wages, while most employers suspect it would make low-income people less eager to work and hence raise the going wage rate. However, the accompanying schedule clearly shows that it is always to the financial advantage of a family to work more. It further shows that any two families having a given rank order in terms of pre-allowance income will always have the same post-allowance order.

[A] two-stage departure by the federal government (aimed at the welfare poor and the working poor) would reduce two of the worst inequities of the present system of income maintenance: the *unequal treatment of equally poor families in different states* and the *unequal treatment of equally poor categorical and non-categorical families within a state*. It would shift much of the burden of helping the poor *from the states to the federal government* at a surprisingly modest addition to total cost. At the same time, the manner of paying this cost would also be shifted from regressive property and sales taxes to the progressive income tax.

Moreover, it would overcome many of the objections to welfare. Disincentives to work would be moderate. Artificial incentives to migrate across state lines because of welfare differences would be reduced. Benefits would be available under a nationwide set of rules administered by a federal civil service. These benefits would be payable under terms that approximate those of social insurance and income taxation, that is, terms that involve the fewest possible demeaning and stigmatizing conditions. Families would, of course, have to report income and family status. But they would not be forced to accept counselling or file suit against relatives.

The direct federal payment would be an innovation not only technically but conceptually as well. It would establish a right to minimum income without prior contract and without determination of blame and it would introduce the notions of horizontal and vertical equity of the progressive income tax into the patchwork of systems we now have for paying out cash to people.

Because the idea is novel, it can undoubtedly be expected to encounter resistance in Congress and with the public. Public opinion polls show the majority of citizens oppose a guaranteed income [favoring instead provision of jobs for all; which explains why President Nixon introduced into his family allowance proposal a requirement that one be available for work or retraining].

It should also be noted that the President's proposal in May of this year to expand the food stamp proposal is, in essence, a negative income tax. Under the proposal, food stamps would be free for families with very low incomes, and would be sold to others at higher costs scaled to rise with the family income.

This scheme embodies the same principle as the sliding scale of cash benefits shown in the table above. Apparently public opinion supports the idea of giving food to the poor.

Criticisms and alternatives

But if the President were to make a proposal for federal payments, it would be shot at not only by those who oppose any and all schemes to spend more on the poor, but also by those who have rival plans. A group of the latter sort favors a *child allowance*, which is employed in 62 other countries. Backers of this plan say it is good policy to pay benefits to all children, rich and poor alike, since this avoids dividing the community between tax-paying non-poor and benefit-receiving poor.

Perhaps the leading objection to the universal child allowance is its cost. To pay $300 per year to each of the nation's 70 million children would cost $21 billion. Withdrawal of income tax exemptions for children would recover $6 billion of revenue. Making the allowance itself taxable would recover another $3 billion at existing tax rates. This would leave $12 billion to be paid for by higher tax rates, a great problem for a tight budget. Such a scheme would produce about $3.5 billion of added income for the poor—little more than the plan discussed above would net them. Perhaps someone can convince the child-allowance enthusiasts that the income maintenance plan discussed here is best thought of as an "income-conditioned child allowance," that it will benefit almost every poor child in America and that it is deserving of their support.

Another, and probably larger, group will criticize the President's plan because it doesn't go far enough and take *everybody* out of poverty. But to set the benefit for zero earnings as high as the poverty line for all the categorical and non-categorical poor would raise the cost enormously. If benefits were reduced a dollar for each dollar of earnings (a 100 percent tax rate), this would undoubtedly succeed in getting many families to opt for the full benefit at no work. On the other hand, a 50 percent tax rate and a full poverty-line benefit would mean that families would be receiving some benefits up to earnings of twice the poverty line, or $7000 for a family of four. Hence, about 40 percent of all families would draw net benefits and would be subject to a 50 percent marginal tax rate plus all existing taxes. With either scheme, those earning enough to disqualify them from benefits would have to pay a total of *over $20 billion in new taxes.*

That is how much it would cost to eliminate poverty this year. *There is no way to do it for less.* It is most unfortunate that many writers have estimated, in error, that it could be done for $10 or $11 billion, which is the size of all the so-called "poverty-income-gap."

Automation and Structural Unemployment

Readings 73 and 74

Every year for the last two decades, popular writers have been hailing a second industrial revolution, in the form of automation. Automation, they confidently predict each year, will soon create mass unemployment as the machine displaces man's muscle power and even brain power. Trained economists know better. As Professor Solow points out, there has not yet been, and there is no statistical evidence suggesting that there is about to be, a cataclysmic quickening of productivity improvement. It is a case of the name for a disease without the disease.

The real debate among professional economists has to do with the relative importance of deficient aggregate demand in explaining the high unemployment rates of the early 1960s versus the importance of "structural" unemployment attributable to the wrong trainings and skills of workers. The successful Kennedy-Johnson tax cuts and fiscal programs controverted the expectations of the pessimistic structuralists by succeeding in bringing unemployment down to the 4 per cent goal. But the fact that America cannot achieve (without encountering sizeable inflation) the 2 per cent unemployment levels of continental Europe, shows that governmental programs to promote skills and improve labor-market mobility are needed complements to high-employment fiscal policy.

Charles C. Killingsworth, of Michigan State University, has been a forceful exponent of the structuralist viewpoint. Robert M. Solow, of M.I.T. and already introduced, helped develop the full-employment program of Kennedy's Council of Economic Advisers.

Questions to Guide the Reading

Why is it more fruitful to concentrate on promoting the purchasing power to create new jobs for unemployed workers than on studying the reason why their former jobs disappeared? Since productivity has improved much during the post-depression years, why aren't we in a greater slump than the 1930s?

How would you buttress expansionary fiscal policies by labor-mobility and educational programs designed to bring down the high-unemployment rates among youths and blacks?

Reading 73

Automation as Threat

Charles C. Killingsworth

Does automation create jobs or does it destroy them? In the view of a great many people, that important question has been conclusively answered, and it is a waste of time to debate it further. Unfortunately, however, there is still strong disagreement as to what that conclusive answer is. The great majority of professional economists today agree that we simply cannot have any such thing as permanent technological unemployment. A prominent economist recently remarked that those who dispute that proposition are simply challenging the main stream of economic thought. On the other hand, voices are heard in the land disputing the proposition that automation creates jobs. Labor leaders, among others, point to such examples as the elimination of tens of thousands of elevator operator jobs in New York City alone as a concrete result of automation, and they view with alarm the appearance of such revolutionary innovations as automatic typesetting.

This sharp conflict between the excessively general assertion and the excessively specific example has seriously hampered the search for solutions to problems of automation and employment.

While it is fashionable to call for more facts and figures on automation, I believe that we already have a considerable body of evidence available to us which can help us to see the nature of the employment problems growing out of automation. This statement undertakes to review that evidence in some detail. I hope to show that the truth of the matter is far more complex than the half-truths that many of us take for granted.

What is automation?

So many definitions of automation have been offered that a number of thoughtful people have concluded that the word has no fixed meaning—that it is simply an emotion-laden slogan which responsible discussion should avoid. Undoubtedly the term is frequently used very loosely, and misused, in popular discussion. But I insist that the word, "automation," is a useful and necessary addition to the language because—in careful usage—it identifies a distinguishable and significant development in modern technology.

The word was originally coined, I believe, simply as a short-cut way of saying, "automatic operation." And that is still an acceptable way to define the word. Many of the more elaborate definitions that have been offered have really attempted to describe particular applications, or particular techniques used to achieve automatic operation. An examination of the fundamental concepts involved in modern automatic systems will, I believe, provide the basis for a more comprehensive and illuminating definition of the term.

The basic elements required for automatic operation are by no means new. And examples of automatic systems of various kinds can be found even in the ancient world. But the explosive growth of scientific knowledge in the last two decades and our successes in applying this new knowledge have greatly affected the elements of automation. Measuring instruments have multiplied in numbers and kinds and they have become incredibly sensitive and reliable. Powered controls have become more versatile and powerful. We have a burgeoning young science of communication and control, called cybernetics, which makes it possible to rig up the measuring instruments to transmit great quantities of information in the form of electric pulses, and to rig up the computer to generate instructions which produce the desired response in the controls. Most significant of all is the development of the computer, which has an infallible memory and the capability to duplicate at lightning speed some kinds of human thought processes.

My definition of automation attempts to go

From *Nation's Manpower Revolution, Hearings before the Subcommittee on Employment and Manpower of the Committee on Labor and Public Welfare,* 88th Congress, 1st Session, Washington, D.C., Part 5.

beyond the comfortably familiar but unillumi-
nating phrase, "automatic operation." My
definition is as follows: "Automation is the
mechanization of sensory, control, and thought
processes." Not all applications of automation
techniques involve all three of these elements;
i.e., sensory, control, and thought processes.
As I will develop further at a later point, automation is a matter of degree. And with all
deference to a number of my respected fellow-
economists, I suggest that those who shrug off
automation as simply another name for technological change reveal a limited understanding
of both terms.

What are the effects of automation on jobs?

Automation, especially in its advanced forms,
fundamentally changes the man-machine relation. Such a change is not unprecedented in
economic history. The assembly line, as it replaced earlier techniques, helped to create
literally millions of simple, repetitive jobs that
could be learned in a few hours or a few days.
Anybody who had two hands, two eyes, and a
capacity to endure monotony could do the
work.

Today we have the electric eye, the iron
hand, the tin ear, and the electronic brain. We
also have the know-how to tie them together
in self-regulating systems that can perform an
enormous variety of jobs. There are two major
results. One is a great reduction in the number
of simple, repetitive jobs where all you need
is your five senses and an untrained mind.
The other result is a great increase in the
number of jobs involved in designing, engineering, programing and administering these
automatic production systems. Industry needs
many more scientists, engineers, mathema-
ticians, and other highly trained people, and
many fewer blue-collar workers.

Table 1 shows what happened between
1957 and 1962 in manufacturing.

Production workers declined by nearly a
million in this period, while nonproduction
workers increased by about a third of a million.
The net change was a reduction of about
600,000 in employment.

Not all of the increase in white-collar employment in manufacturing was due to automation, of course, and not all of the newly
hired employees were scientists and engineers.
But the changing composition of employment
was partly due to automation. Moreover, what

happened from 1957 to 1962 was the continuation of a postwar trend. Throughout the 1920s,
the ratio between production and nonproduction workers fluctuated between narrow limits
at around 19 or 20 percent. The great depression and World War II temporarily affected
the ratio. By about 1951, the prewar ratio of
about one white-collar worker to four blue-
collar workers had been reestablished. But as
automation gathered momentum during the
1950s, the ratio continued to change. It is now
at about 26 percent and the trend is still
strongly upward.

Below the aggregates

In an economy in which so many patterns
are changing rapidly, broad averages and grand
totals may conceal more than they reveal. I
think that this is especially true of the effects
of automation and the concomitant changes of
today. Let us take as an example the figures
showing total civilian employment since 1949.
The figures reveal the persistent upward trend
in total employment—from 58 million jobs in
1949 to more than 68 million in 1963. This
great increase is another piece of evidence
often cited by those who claim that "machines make jobs." But there is another side
to this coin. Unemployment crept upward during the latter part of this period—first two
notches up, then one notch down, and then
another two notches up. In 1951–53, the average was about a 3-percent rate of unemployment. In 1962–63, the average has been almost
double that, or between 5½ and 6 percent.

It is not self-evident from these figures that
any part of this creeping unemployment problem is due to automation or other basic
changes in the patterns of the economy. There
is eminent authority to the contrary. The President's Council of Economic Advisers has repeatedly declared that automation and "structural unemployment" are not responsible for
the gradual creep of unemployment above the
4-percent level of 1957. Their analysis of the
unemployment problem—that it is caused primarily by a lagging growth rate—is the basis
for the administration's emphasis on a large
tax cut as the top-priority item in the program
to "get the economy moving again." Chairman
Walter Heller of the CEA has repeatedly said
that there is a "good prospect" that the tax cut
would reduce unemployment to the 4-percent
level.

Table 1   Employees on Manufacturing Payrolls, First Half Year Averages, 1957 and 1962 (in thousands)

	Total	Production workers	Nonproduction workers
1957	17,223	13,264	3,959
1962	16,589	12,295	4,294
1957–62 change	−634	−969	+335

SOURCE: U.S. Department of Labor, Bureau of Labor Statistics.

I think that it can be demonstrated that the Council is the victim of a half-truth. The lagging growth rate is only a part of the problem, and it may not be the most important part. I think that it is extremely unlikely that the proposed tax cut, desirable though it is as a part of a program, will prove to be sufficient to reduce unemployment to the 4-percent level. Perhaps it is true that in politics you can't get everything all at once. But I feel compelled to say that my analysis leads me to the conclusion that the administration's economic program is seriously incomplete. It gives woefully inadequate attention to what I regard as a key aspect of the unemployment problem of the 1960s; namely, labor market imbalance.

The Council's position on labor market imbalance, quoted above, rests on meticulous and extensive statistical studies. I am sure that the members of the Council, who are scholars of the highest competence and integrity, are willing to go where the facts lead them. The trouble is that their staff studies have not analyzed the figures which, in my judgment, clearly show a growing problem of labor market imbalance.

A new twist

The fundamental effect of automation on the labor market is to "twist" the pattern of demand—that is, it pushes down the demand for workers with little training while pushing up the demand for workers with large amounts of training. The shift from goods to services is a second major factor which twists the labor market in the same way. There are some low-skilled, blue-collar jobs in service-producing industries; but the most rapidly growing parts of the service sector are health care and education, both of which require a heavy preponderance of highly trained people.

It is important to note that all of the im-

provement in the unemployment situation in 1962, as compared with 1950, was concentrated in the elite group of our labor force—the approximately 20 percent with college training. In all of the other categories, which have about 80 percent of the labor force, unemployment rates were substantially higher in 1962 than in 1950. These figures, I contend, substantiate the thesis that the patterns of demand for labor have been twisted faster than the patterns of supply have changed, and that as a result we had a substantially greater degree of labor market imbalance in 1962 than in 1950.

But these figures do not fully reveal the power of the labor market twist. The "labor force" enumeration includes (with minor exceptions) only those who say that they have jobs or that they have actively sought work in the week preceding the survey. *Those who have been out of work so long that they have given up hope and are no longer "actively seeking" work—but who would take a job if one were available—are simply not counted either as unemployed or as a member of the labor force.* The percentage of a given category of the total population that is "in the labor force" (under the foregoing definition) is expressed as the "labor force participation rate." It seems probable that worsening employment prospects for a particular group over a long period would force down the labor force participation rate—i.e., would squeeze a number of people out of the labor market altogether, in the sense that they would give up the continuing, active search for jobs.

Clearly, unemployment at the bottom of the educational scale was relatively unresponsive to general increases in the demand for labor, while there was very strong responsiveness at the top of the educational scale. The percentage unemployment rate for college graduates in 1957 merits close attention. It was an almost incredible 0.6 percent. I have queried the experts in the Bureau of Labor Statistics on this figure, and they assure me that they have no less confidence in it than in the other 1957 figures. Surely a figure as low as that represents what is sometimes called "overfull" employment—i.e., demand which seriously exceeds supply.

Bear in mind that the unemployment rates for the lower educational attainment groups (those with 80 percent of the men) are now higher than in 1950, and that the unemployment rate for college graduates is now substantially lower than in 1950. Also bear in mind that the labor force participation rate figures strongly suggest a large and growing "reserve army"—which is not counted among the unemployed—at the lower educational levels, and that there is no evidence of any such reserve of college-trained men. Finally, bear in mind the differences between the lower end of the educational scale and the upper end in responsiveness to overall decreases in the unemployment rate.

When you put all of these considerations together, I believe that you are ineluctably led to the conclusion that long before we could get down to an overall unemployment rate as low as 4 percent, we would have a severe shortage of workers *at the top* of the educational ladder. This shortage would be a bottleneck to further expansion of employment. I cannot pinpoint the level at which the bottleneck would begin to seriously impede expansion; but, on the basis of the relationships revealed by Table 2, it seems reasonable to believe that we could not get very far below

a 5-percent overall unemployment level without hitting that bottleneck.

Conclusion

The most fundamental conclusion that emerges from my analysis is that automation and the changing pattern of consumer wants have greatly increased the importance of investment in human beings as a factor in economic growth. More investment in plant and equipment, without very large increases in our investment in human beings, seems certain to enlarge the surplus of underdeveloped manpower and to create a shortage of the highly developed manpower needed to design, install, and man modern production facilities.

I would give a considerably higher priority to the stimulation of investment in human beings than I would to such measures as the proposed tax cut. But I would still rate the tax cut as important. Denying that the tax cut is the "ultimate weapon" against unemployment is not denying that it can make some contribution to the reduction of unemployment. After all, even to get below a 5-percent unemployment rate would be a considerable achievement today. But a really effective attack on the complex problem of unemployment requires a whole arsenal of powerful weapons.

And we don't have all the time in the world. Human history has been described as a race between education and catastrophe. In the past dozen years, education has been falling behind in that race.

Table 2   Actual and Relative Unemployment Rates by Educational Attainment, April 1950, March 1957, and March 1962 (males, 18 and over)

| Years of school completed | Unemployment rates | | | |
| | Actual percentages | | Relative[1] | |
	1950	1962	1950	1962
0 to 7	8.4	9.2	154	170
8	6.6	7.5	108	132
9 to 11	6.9	7.3	115	142
12	4.6	4.8	70	75
13 to 15	4.1	4.0	64	65
16 or more	2.2	1.4	34	21
All groups	6.2	6.0	(¹)	(¹)

[1] The relative unemployment rate is the ratio between the percentage unemployment rate for a given educational attainment group and the percentage unemployment rate for all other groups at the same point in time.

Reading 74

Automation No Threat

Robert M. Solow

Whenever there is both rapid technological change and high unemployment the two will inevitably be connected in people's minds. So it is not surprising that technological unemployment was a live subject during the depression of the 1930's, nor that the debate has now revived. The discussion of thirty years ago was inconclusive, partly because there were more urgent things to worry about and partly because economists did not then have a workable theory of income and employment as a whole. They have now. Curiously, the current discussion seems to take place mainly outside of professional economics. That may be because economists feel there are no longer any very important intellectual issues at stake. If that is so, it may be worth stating what the agreed position is.

First, however, one should have an idea of the orders of magnitude involved: how fast is technology changing? After all, an analysis that will perfectly well cover moderate rates of technological progress and moderate increases in the rate may not apply nearly so well if there are catastrophic changes in the role of labor in production. Fortunately this is a fairly straightforward question. Its answer does not depend on what fraction of all the scientists who have ever lived are now alive, or on the number of computers produced and installed last year, or on the existence of an oil refinery with nobody in it, or on any such exotic facts. Any major change in the quantitative relation between output and employment must show up in the conventional productivity statistics. Here productivity means nothing but the value of output per manhour, corrected for price changes. It goes up whenever labor requirements for a unit of final output go down, and by the same percentage. There are productivity statistics for certain industries, for manufacturing as a whole, and for even broader aggregates. It doesn't matter much

which aggregate is selected. What such figures show is easily summarized.

No new industrial revolution

For the private economy as a whole, the average annual increase in output per manhour between 1909 and 1964 was 2.4 percent. But if we divide that long period at the end of World War II, it turns out that the increase was faster after 1947 than before. From 1909 to 1947 productivity rose by 2 percent a year on the average, while from 1947 to 1964 it rose by 3.2 percent a year. Moreover, from 1961 to 1964, productivity rose by 3.4 percent a year.

I said that this was a fairly straightforward question: only *fairly* straightforward because it is not easy to interpret changes in productivity extending over just a few years. Recessions and recoveries have their own productivity patterns and there are erratic fluctuations besides. The 1961–1964 rise, part of a long upswing, is especially suspicious. Still, it is hard to mistake what the figures are trying to say. There was a definite acceleration of the productivity trend about the time of the war.

There may even have been a slight further acceleration after 1961. It is too early to say, and in any case the amount involved is small.

This rough statistical indication is enough. It does not suggest the immediate disappearance of the job as an institution. But what does it say about the possibility of slower, less dramatic technological unemployment, if only a million or so at a time? Popular writing suggests that there are two schools of thought. One claims point-blank that automation necessarily—or at least in fact—"creates more jobs than it destroys." From this it would seem to follow that, if technological progress went at any slower pace than it now does, there would necessarily be more unemployment than there now is. The other school claims that automation necessarily—or at least in fact—destroys more jobs than it creates. So that if technological progress went at any faster pace than it now does, or only just as fast, severe unemployment would be inevitable.

Which school is right? I think the economist's answer has to be that both are wrong or, to be more precise, both are irrelevant. They have simply missed the point. Perhaps the question "Does automation create or destroy more jobs?" is answerable *in principle;* perhaps it is not. What is perfectly clear is that the question is simply unanswerable *in fact.* I doubt that anyone could make a good estimate of the net number of jobs created or destroyed merely by the invention of the zipper or of sliced bread. It would be a fantastically more complicated job to discover the net effect of *all* technological progress in any single year on employment. No one can possibly know; so no one has the right to speak confidently.

The Great Automation Question, as I have phrased it, is not only unanswerable, it is the wrong question. The important point is that, to a pretty good first approximation, *the total volume of employment in the United States today is simply not determined by the rate of technological progress.* Both theory and common observation tell us that a modern mixed economy can, by proper and active use of fiscal and monetary policy weapons, have full employment for *any* plausible rate of technological change within a range that is easily wide enough to cover the American experience.

The European experience

Consider, for example, the West German economy. Output per manhour has been increasing considerably faster there than in the United States—about 6 percent a year since 1950, and 5 percent a year since 1955. While the American *level* of productivity is unsurpassed anywhere, the economy of West Germany has certainly been no less technologically dynamic than our own in the past 15 years. Yet for some time the German unemployment rate has been below 1 percent of the labor force (compared with 5–7 percent here) and there have been 7 to 10 unfilled vacant jobs for every unemployed person. What is even more striking is that this technologically advanced and advancing economy seems to have an insatiable appetite for unskilled labor. Having exhausted the domestic supply, it goes to Italy, Spain, Portugal, Greece and Turkey to recruit workers who have only minimal education and can surely neither read, write, nor even speak German. One has the impression that even an American teenager could find employment in a German factory.

Or take an example on the other side, Great Britain. Their productivity has grown a bit more slowly than ours. The conventional belief is that the British economy offers more resistance to technological progress than most others. The British economy has also had all sorts of other troubles—but the maintenance of high employment has not been one of them. The unemployment rate in Britain is now about 1½ percent. There is even some discussion as to whether the economy might not function a bit more efficiently and smoothly with a slightly higher unemployment rate, say 2 percent.

How capacity grows

Polar examples like these give a strong hint that no simple yea-saying or nay-saying can be the right answer to the question about the likelihood of technological unemployment. The right answer is more complicated and goes something like this: At any one time, we can hope to identify something we can call the capacity output of the economy as a whole. (Sometimes it is called "potential" or "full employment" output; the idea is the same.) This is at best a rough and ready concept. Under stress an economy can produce more than its capacity for quite a while, so capacity output is not a rigid upper limit. Moreover, a modern economy can produce a wide variety of "mixes" of goods and services, heavily weighted with military hardware, or automobiles, or machinery, or food and fiber, or personal services, according to circumstances. When the economy as a whole is operating at or near its capacity, there may be some industries straining their plant and equipment to the limit while others have quite a bit of slack. Nevertheless, under normal circumstances the output-mix changes slowly. We can know what we mean by capacity output and, subject to some error, we can measure it. (In the first quarter of 1965, the country produced a Gross National Product of about $649 billion, annual rate; the Council of Economic Advisers estimated that capacity output was about $25 billion higher.)

The productive capacity of an economy grows fairly smoothly—not with perfect regularity, of course, but fairly smoothly. The growth of productive capacity is determined by an array of basic underlying factors: the growth of the labor force in numbers; changes in the health, education, training, and other qualities of those who work and manage; changes in the number of hours they wish to work; the exhaustion and discovery of natural resources; the accumulation of capital in the form of buildings, machinery, and inventories; and the advance of scientific, engineering and technological knowledge and its application to production. This is one of the important ways in which the level of technology enters our problem. If the rate of technological progress accelerates or decelerates, then the growth of capacity is likely to speed up or slow down with it. The different factors are not entirely independent of one another: new knowledge may require better-trained or differently-trained people or wholly new plant and equipment for its successful application. It is also possible for changes in one of the underlying trends to be offset by changes in another coincidentally or consciously engineered. In any case, they are likely to move with some smoothness, and their net resultant—capacity output—even more so.

The actual output produced by the economy fluctuates more raggedly around the trend of capacity, sometimes above it, sometimes—more often, in the case of the U.S.—below it. When production presses hard against capacity, it is capacity limitations that keep it from going higher. In all other cases, what governs the current level of output is the *demand* for goods and services. Demand is exercised by the interlocked spending decisions of all the final purchasers in the economy: consumers, business firms, all levels of government, and the foreigners who buy our exports. Technological developments play a part here too, among many other determinants of spending decisions. Changes in military technology may cause governments to spend more—or less; the invention of new commodities and new ways to produce old ones may induce industry to

invest in new facilities and consumers to shift their purchases (and perhaps to change the total amount). Of course there are other reasons why the flow of consumption, investment, and government expenditures may vary. So long as capacity pressure is not too strong, bottlenecks not too pervasive, when total demand rises, total output will rise to match it; when total demand falls, total output will fall with it. This doesn't happen instantaneously; inventories provide one buffer. But it happens.

The picture, then, is of a fairly smoothly rising trend of capacity, propelled by some rather deep-seated forces. Moving around it is a much more volatile, unsteady curve of current output, driven by whatever governs aggregate expenditures, including economic policy decisions. Current output cannot be far above capacity for long, but it can drag along below for years at a time. During the first half of this century, the trend of capacity output in the United States seems to have risen on the average at about 3 percent a year. From the end of the Korean War until very recently the rate of growth of capacity was more like 3½ percent a year; and the best evidence seems to be that the current and immediately prospective growth rate of capacity will be in the neighborhood of 4 percent a year, possibly a bit lower now, possibly a bit higher later. The postwar acceleration was mainly a result of the speedup in productivity already mentioned. The current acceleration may draw a little something from a further speedup in productivity, but its main source is the arrival at working age of the first postwar babies.

The triumph of economics over fable

Now the crucial fact is that when output is rising faster than capacity the unemployment rate tends to fall; when output is rising more slowly than capacity—even though it is rising, mind you—the unemployment rate tends to get bigger; and if output rises at about the same rate as capacity, so that the percentage gap between them stays constant, then the unemployment rate stays pretty nearly constant. It is a fairly safe generalization about the past ten years that when aggregate output has risen at about 3½ percent a year between any two points in time, just about enough new jobs have appeared to occupy the increment to the labor force, with nothing left over to reduce unemployment. The tax cut of 1964 is a kind of landmark in American economic policy, the triumph of Economies over Fable. I like to think that it was helped along by the sheer cogency of the arguments for it. But any realist has to give a lot of credit to the fact that, from the middle of 1962 to the middle of 1963, with the economy rising and setting "new records" every quarter, the unemployment rate stuck at about 5.6 percent of the labor force and stubbornly refused to go anywhere, especially not down. Be thankful for small favors; but note also that during that time the GNP corrected for price changes rose only by a little more than 3 percent. The gap between output and capacity was not narrowing; unemployment was not reduced. If it turns out to be right that the growth of capacity during the next few years will be nearer 4 percent annually, then it will take a 4 percent increase in demand every year to hold the unemployment rate constant; what was good enough to keep unemployment level in 1963 may by 1967 not be adequate to stem slowly rising unemployment.

Closer study of the facts suggests a more powerful generalization. On the average, an extra 1 percent growth of real (i.e., price-corrected) GNP in any year has been associated with a reduction in the unemployment rate of roughly one-third of a percentage point. Or, what is the same thing, to get the unemployment rate to fall by one full point from one year to the next requires that real output (real demand) increase by about 3 percent *over and above the increase in capacity*. To see how this works, consider the behavior of the economy since the tax cut.

From the middle of 1963 to the middle of 1964, real GNP gained 5 percent. "Capacity GNP" probably went up by something less than 4 percent. The rule of thumb I have mentioned (which sometimes goes under the name of Okun's Law) would predict a drop in the unemployment rate of something like 4/10 of a percentage point. In fact, the unemployment rate did go down, by 5/10 of a point, from 5.7 percent to 5.2 percent. In the half-year from the third quarter of 1964 to the first quarter of 1965 real GNP gained almost 2½ percent; this is more than one-half of 1 percent over and above the rise in capacity. It should,

therefore, have reduced the unemployment rate by some 2/10 of one point. The unemployment rate actually fell from 5.1 percent to 4.8 percent.

In all honesty I cannot leave the impression that the national economy ticks over like a bit of clockwork, predictable from a few simple rules of thumb. I have picked out a few instances in which the pat relation between output, growth, and unemployment worked just fine. It is not always so. The relation itself is compounded of the effects of changes in demand on hours worked, on the number of people seeking employment, on the short-run ups and downs of productivity itself.

And yet, it's not at all a bad rule of thumb. If I had to predict what would happen to unemployment during the next year I would certainly begin by trying to estimate what is going to happen to the gap between capacity output and aggregate demand.

The moral

What does all this have to do with the question of technological unemployment?

Suppose that a surge of technological progress takes place, whether you call it automation or something less ominous-sounding. Productivity will begin to rise at a faster pace than it used to. So will the trend-line of capacity output. If the demand for goods and services continues to grow only at its old rate, the gap between demand and capacity will get wider. In other words, if the increase in capacity is not matched by an increase in demand, the result will be an increase in unemployment. (All this, mind you, while new records are being set regularly and columnists assure us that the economy is "booming.") You can call this unemployment technological, if you like, but it is not different from ordinary unemployment. *The way to get rid of it is to make sure that demand rises in step with the economy's capacity to produce.*

Recently it has been argued, by Robert L. Heilbroner and others, that analysis like mine is all very well to handle old-fashioned automation. Old-fashioned automation enabled society to produce goods with less labor; fortunately, the displaced labor could transfer into the service or non-good sectors. But the new automation around the corner, argues Heilbroner, will displace labor in the service industries as giant computers take over the white-collar tasks of the economy. That leaves no frontier for labor to escape to, and there is little hope for the system except to give people incomes quite divorced from their work. Will these arguments stand up? I think not. When labor productivity is improved anywhere, that makes incomes potentially higher. Budget studies show that there are characteristic patterns in the way that people will spend higher real incomes. The service industries expanded in the past because services are what people wanted to consume out of increased incomes, and not because they were a haven of escape for the unemployed. If productivity improvements anywhere increase real incomes further, people will again expand their consumptions according to characteristic budget patterns; this includes the distinct possibility that an affluent society will want to expand resources devoted to the public sector, in the form of educational and other collective services. For Heilbroner to be right in thinking that the new automation necessarily would produce unemployment, he must accept the preposterous belief that the American public has become so rich that it has nothing new upon which to spend its higher incomes. Commonsense observation and statistical investigations demonstrate how bizarre such a belief would be either in 1967 or 1997.

I have already mentioned that changes in technology also have an effect on demand. New commodities, new materials, major cost reductions cannot fail to leave a mark on the way in which the public spends its income. (The "public" here includes businesses and governments as well as individual families.) It is possible that any particular burst of technological progress will carry along with it the extra demand necessary to keep extra unemployment from appearing. It is also possible that it will not. It is even possible that a series of innovations should generate a bigger increment to demand than to capacity, and therefore a net reduction in unemployment. The trouble is that nobody can say in advance which will actually be the case. Indeed, as I have suggested, nobody may be able to tell after the fact which has been the case. One

can, of course, say whether unemployment has gone up or gone down. But there are many other influences on employment. Faster growth of the labor force, for example, can also push up the capacity trend; it can also have effects on demand. Except under the best of circumstances, it may prove impossible to identify the particular effects of technical progress and separate them from the effects of other forces.

The moral of this analysis is that such an identification doesn't much matter. Unemployment above the "frictional" level occurs, usually, because total dollar demand fails to keep pace with productive capacity. Whether or not an acceleration of technological progress happens to be among the causes is not all-important. The remedy in any case is to keep total demand moving in step with capacity. And this, governments in the mixed economy do have the fiscal and monetary policies to ensure—if they will use these powers.

New Economics to the rescue

So, as the examples of Germany and Britain confirm, it is possible to have full employment with slow technical progress and full employment with fast technical progress. *But it does not happen automatically.* It requires conscious policy to manage the volume of demand and keep it going at approximately the right pace. (Do not be misled, in this connection, by the case of Germany. The Federal Republic talks the best game of *laissez faire* in the world. At the same time it does dozens of things each one of which would be instantly denounced in the United States as creeping socialism.)

In the modern mixed economy, there is no shortage of instrumentalities for operating on aggregate demand: monetary and credit policy, changes in taxation, adjustments in transfer payments—such as unemployment compensation, family allowances, and social security benefits—and, finally, the direct purchases of goods and services by the government. Since each of these instruments must serve other purposes as well, it may not always be clear exactly what is the best policy. That is what the discussion ought to be about, rather than mere anecdote about the wonders and horrors of modern technology.

The Generation Gap

Reading 75

Increasingly the state pays for higher education. This is as true in California as it is in Britain, as true at the Sorbonne as in Tokyo. But close investigation in all these places shows that it is a myth to think that low-cost college education goes mainly to the poor. Instead of the rich paying for the poor, it turns out in California and elsewhere that the more affluent middle classes get most of the subsidy from higher education—in effect, the workers subsidize the more affluent.

Colin Clark, Milton Friedman, and now E. J. Mishan (Reader at the London School of Economics) have argued that students should be made to pay for their own education, paying back loans from the extra earnings education makes possible; that they should then be able to take any subsidy the state chooses to give and spend it on any university of their choice. The new wrinkle added here is Mishan's belief that this will tame student activism. His text refers primarily to Britain and has been edited here to omit local references. If, however, his analysis is cogent, it should be just as applicable in Asia and America as in Europe.

Questions to Guide the Reading

Does the author show any signs of realizing that his scheme is already partially in effect in such states as California and New York, but that far from ending campus unrest there, those states are active bases for student activism? And is this not also the case at private schools like Harvard and M.I.T., where by and large students do pay high tuition out of their parents' pockets and where there is no shortage of unrest?

Is a private university private property? Who owns Harvard? Who can tell a committee of students or faculty which lawns they cannot meet on? Still, is it wrong for people who stand to make much money in medicine or business to pay back the vocational subsidy given them? What about teaching? Law? Engineering? Physics? Welding?

Rx to Quell the Uprisings: Raise College Tuition and Make Students Borrow

Edward J. Mishan

The 1960s will go down in history as the decade in which the universities first became uncomfortably aware of a growing threat to their cherished independence and to their long heritage of academic freedom, a threat apparently coming from two directions, from the state and, more recently, from the student body. The more popular view is that the danger of state intervention in the affairs of the university is an unavoidable consequence of the unprecedented post-war expansion of current and capital expenditure on higher education and the resulting financial dependence of the universities on the government.

I think this view, which attributes the current malaise ultimately to the extraordinary post-war expansion of higher education, is mistaken—at least if it is taken to imply that the

From Edward J. Mishan, "Some Heretical Thoughts on University Reform," *Encounter*, December, 1968. Reprinted with kind permission of the author and publisher.

independence of the universities cannot be restored while they continue to spend on so massive a scale and to admit students in such large numbers. Indeed, I shall argue that the current threat to the universities can be removed by simple institutional changes—one requiring no more than a switch to a more rational method of accounts that discloses *the full costs of higher education,* the other a change from the present system of student *grants* to student *loans.* Admittedly the latter proposal is no longer novel; but the weight of argument in its favour has not been fully appreciated by the public.

Moreover, the case gathers strength in the circumstances of repeated student excesses and disruption. The proposals, moreover, are immediately practical. Political resistance to proposals for dismantling any existing piece of administrative machinery is always to be anticipated. Inevitably those most centrally involved in the old system seek to defend it. Though social losses of this sort are necessarily incurred in any changeover from one system to another, they are not to be lightly dismissed. In this instance, however, the social gains are substantial enough to enable one to combat political resistance with a clear conscience.

What does a student cost?

Although the arguments in favour of full cost university fees are independent of the actual magnitude, it is of interest to have some idea of the disparity between fees currently charged by [state] universities and the actual costs. The true cost to the university of educating the student is many times the tuition fee, though it is hard to give a precise figure. The total net current expenditure of a typical university obviously includes expenditures on the salaries of the academic staff. But the activities of the academic staff are not wholly devoted to teaching. Part of their time is devoted to independent research. It is sometimes concluded, therefore, that only a proportion of the expenditure on the academic staff should be included in the costs of higher education, this proportion being taken to equal the average proportion of the academics' time that is devoted to teaching or to preparing their lectures.

This proportion is, however, almost impossible to measure. The academic mind tends to be active at all odd hours. The typical don

works at home; he debates with his colleagues; he reads the professional journals, assimilates new facts and ideas and contributes to them himself. He may be paid for his published articles, and may indeed act as correspondent to a newspaper or as consultant to business firms or to the government. Yet all such activities will almost certainly add to his value as a teacher. Certainly the time and effort spent in research are not, in the long run, separable from university education. For the advance of knowledge, which is the purpose of research, is ultimately passed on to the student himself. Though it makes no difference to my proposals, I shall for these reasons continue to use a round figure [several times current tuition charges]. Others, if they wish, can substitute a somewhat lower figure.

An increase of university fees from the present [charge to the true full cost] does not, of course, involve the country in any greater outlay on higher education—though it makes it impossible any longer to conceal from the public, including the student, the full costs to the community of the subsidy being received by the student. But the sums that were once paid to the universities in the forms of grants, and were thus regarded as a direct subsidy to the universities, are now to be paid wholly on a per student capita basis either directly by the central government or by the local authorities.

This financial arrangement is much to be preferred over one in which the central government has used its powers to control fees so as to set them at a figure far below costs. In the process it reduced British universities to complete financial dependence on the state—which is then seen by the public acting as a generous and considerate patron of the spendthrift universities. Allowing the universities to set fees so as to recover the full costs of their services to society would free them at one stroke from their enforced bondage to the state. And once the magnitude of such costs becomes common knowledge, a more informed atmosphere is created in which to debate the crucial issue of loans *versus* grants.

Such a financial arrangement would have a further incidental but by no means minor advantage. It would serve to reform and correct the existing state of affairs in which the universities have no incentive either to ascertain the costs of each of the variety of courses they

offer or to ponder ways and means of economising on these costs. Once the universities
come to depend on their fees to cover the
whole of their teaching expenses, and are
thereby brought into competition with one
another, they can hardly continue to manifest
the present lack of concern.

Inequitable and inefficient

Over the last few years there have been occasional articles and discussions setting out some
of the pros-and-cons of a loans system. We
may begin, therefore, by a brief appraisal of
some of the more common objections.

Perhaps the most fanciful of these is the alle-
gation that loans discriminate against the
marital prospects of the woman student, since
by incurring debt—"mortgaging her future"—
she brings a "negative dowry" to the marriage.
Even in this age of unbridled ambition I find
it hard to picture any one of the young people
I know—male or female, for that matter—
judiciously crossing out one or more names on
a short list in recognition of a so-called negative
dowry. But this is by the way. For, in fact, the
successful woman student who borrows to pay
for her university education does not bring a
negative dowry to her nuptial partner but a
positive dowry. A university training, quite
apart from the status and other inherent advantages it confers, does enhance one's value on
the market. Under the proposed loan scheme,
at least, no student would be inclined to borrow for his education unless he was reasonably
confident that the value of the additional advantages exceeded the cost of the loan. It
might have made more sense to claim instead
that the loan scheme would result in a negative
incentive to bear children until a good part of
the loan was repaid, or until the graduate was
earning more—no bad thing in itself. But if the
difference in the annual earnings as between
the university-trained and the untrained woman
were no less than the annual payments, in the
early years of employment this negative incentive to bear children would be no greater for
the university-trained woman than for the untrained woman—which is, or ought to be, the
issue in equity.

Admittedly, the withdrawal of a free good
(higher education) will not be welcomed by
the student, male or female. But before judging whether the removal of a clear advantage
to one group—in particular that currently enjoyed by the freely educated woman graduate
over the woman without university education—
is socially equitable, it must first be established
that the granting of this advantage was equitable in the first place. As for a system which,
like the present, allows some women to take
up scarce university places only to settle down
afterwards to rear a family it is, on the face
of it, neither fair nor efficient. If the "negative
dowry" of a loans system prevents this happening, it clearly redounds to the credit of
the loans system.

A more specious defence of the existing
system is that in the long run—and provided
the graduate does not emigrate—it pays for itself. Higher education raises the earning power
of the beneficiaries so enabling the government
to recoup its outlays from their consequently
higher tax payments. I do not know if anyone
has troubled to calculate how much additional
tax revenue the government collects as a result
of its expenditure on higher education. But
whatever the sums calculated they would be
relevant *only* if every other borrower of public
funds—or borrower of private funds, for that
matter—were allowed to treat such loans as
free grants in consideration of their investing
the funds profitably thereby raising their tax
liability. I can think of no one who would refuse a sum on these terms. The ordinary
citizen who borrows a capital sum to improve
his material prospects—whether to invest in a
durable good such as a house, or in a capital
asset, or in any equipment that raises the value
of his services to society—has both to repay
the sum with interest and to pay additional
taxes on any subsequent rise in his earnings.
In fact, irrespective of how his education is
financed—whether from a grant of public funds,
from private funds, or from loans—the higher
earnings of the graduate must certainly raise
his tax liability. By switching to a loans system,
however, not only is the taxpayer relieved but,
in respect of his access to investible funds, *the
student is now treated on a par with any other
citizen.*

Not surprisingly, it is also contended that the
loan system would be harder on the poor student who would have to borrow than on the
rich student who would receive the sum as a
gift from his parents or guardians. So long as

our society tolerates inequalities of income the children of the richer members will continue to enjoy some advantages over the children of the poorer members. And if we had thought to remove this particular inequity by a grants system we seemed to have overlooked *the far greater inequity that has resulted.*

The grant system as it currently operates in Britain is manifestly regressive. Only about a quarter of the student population come from working-class families. The remainder are from lower or upper middle-class families. This would be bad enough if the bulk of the taxes collected by the government came from the higher income groups. But today, the greater part of the public revenues is obtained from the taxation of families in the lower income brackets. Ironically, this typically socialist scheme has produced a situation in which *the working classes are effectively financing a predominantly middle-class student population.* On a more fundamental plane, however, there are gross inequities in the meritocracy towards which affluent societies are now moving in response to the democratic ideal of "equality of opportunity."

So long as differences in inherited wealth are the chief causes of large differences in material comfort, then it seems plausible to believe that increasing equality of opportunity tends to equalise individual well-being. With rising standards of material comfort for the bulk of the population, and with inherited wealth being relegated gradually to a minor source of differential earnings—the result partly of heavy taxation but, more importantly, of the spread of technology and the consequent trend of aspiration towards expertise and status rather than to mere claims to wealth—the remaining inequalities from inherited wealth become more tolerable. At the same time, however, the forces released by the greater equalities of opportunity are bringing us face to face with a more basic and less tractable form of inherited inequalities. We are moving into a world in which *men born into talent will be no less fortunate than were men, before the War, born into wealth*—perhaps more fortunate. For the security and status conferred by the training of natural talents cannot so easily be lost by a sudden change of economic climate or expropriated by a new political régime.

But is the man who happens to be born into talent inherently *any more deserving* of the material rewards of this world than the man who happens to be born into money? Indeed, considerations of justice would suggest that talented people receive *smaller earnings* than ordinary mortals to offset in some measure their higher status which, in the meritocracy, contributes to their greater satisfaction. One might go further. If economic considerations were less dominant, it would be clearly more equitable to use whatever funds were available for higher education primarily in improving the minds and the material prospects *of the less talented members of the community.* For the just society is one that acts always to counter the arbitrary distribution of inherited advantages whatever form they take, so contributing towards greater equality of earnings and status.

Yet considerations of economic efficiency are today unquestionably dominant. In a society able to direct only limited resources into higher education and, in pursuit of economic efficiency, allocating these resources among the more promising talents, genetical good fortune becomes compounded by deliberate policy. Indeed, the inequity goes further. For the rest of the community is compelled to finance from their own earnings the vocational training of the privileged group so procuring for its members far higher earnings and status than the taxpayers will ever enjoy.

If we have to pursue economic efficiency, the change to a loans system at least removes the social anomaly whereby the community as a whole is made to finance its privileged student group—in particular when it so happens that the student body as a whole is wealthier than taxpayers as a whole.

There is a proportion of the candidates who are admitted to higher education who would not have elected to apply for it unless it were provided free—certainly not if students, or their families, were expected to pay full costs from their own or borrowed funds. Whether the students in this group are conscientious workers or whether they are content to drift along and settle for a third-class or pass degree, and whatever the future earnings they anticipate, there is no net advantage, on their *own* evaluation, of investing resources in their education. They would not use their own funds, or borrow at the market rate, for the purpose of obtaining a higher education—though, of course, they are content enough to receive it as a free gift from the taxpayer.

No one has estimated how large this group is. But I should be surprised if it were less than a quarter of the wider student body. Their education involves a waste of the country's scarce economic resources. On the other hand, among the several thousand eligible candidates each year who (because of the places taken up by some of the former group) cannot be admitted to the study of the social sciences or of medicine there will be, under the present system, a proportion excluded, the members of which are prepared to pay the full costs of their education, borrowing the money if necessary.

More important yet, there may well be large numbers of school-leavers who at present go straight into the labour force but who if they cannot fully avail themselves of a university education, would be able in their own estimation to profit from two or more years of full-time further education, technical or liberal. The advantage would be enough to make it worth their while paying full costs provided that loans were made available. At present insufficient provision is made for this group which can only hope for part-time technical instruction or extra-mural lectures. Members of this group have no option but to join the labour force and to contribute by their earnings to widen the gap between themselves and the intellectually privileged. Under a loan system, the opportunity to enhance its status and material prospects would be extended to this large group of young people also. A loan scheme would therefore act *to close the rift, encouraged by the present system, between an educated élite and the rest of society.*

The rich and the poor

If the preceding arguments have been assimilated the most common objection to a loan scheme—that it acts to discourage higher education—calls for little additional comment. A switch-over to a system in which students have to pay full fees, borrowing if necessary, will undeniably reduce the attractiveness of a university education as compared with a scheme which offers higher education free. But if society were concerned to make higher edu-

cation yet more attractive, it could be done in many obvious ways: it might, for example, promise a new Jaguar free to every graduate student. Efficiency is not, however, always coterminous with expansion. Having proposed a mechanism whose operation can be justified by reference to *the broad social aim* of economic efficiency, any resulting reduction of the student population must be deemed consistent with that aim.

This much, I think, opponents of a full-cost loan scheme can be made to concede. What apparently they cannot stomach is the further implication of the scheme: that the resulting percentage reduction of students of working-class origin is likely to be higher than the overall percentage reduction. This expected consequence is held to be undesirable in itself and to run counter to current democratic trends. Higher education is envisaged as a ladder of opportunity extended to the nether regions inhabited by working-class denizens enabling some of the more talented among them to climb upwards towards the sunlit pastures of middle-class professionalism. The more of these ladders of opportunity the better. But this belief in the social merit of providing working-class children with the means of escape from a working-class environment is surely a peculiarly middle-class intellectual's view of the aspirations of the working class. Intellectuals are a good deal less envied than they seem to imagine.

In any event the proportion of working-class children—however one defines that category in a society where most people think of themselves as "middle class"—that make the transition to higher income and status via a university training is very small.

I must admit, nonetheless, that this plea for social perspective springs from a personal judgment about the relative importance of this loss to society, and to the working class. But what of the question of principle? Suppose it were universally agreed that although a university education is a good thing in itself it becomes a specially good thing when imbibed by youths of working-class origin. So long as the number of university places are as limited as they will be in the foreseeable future, we can "push" the working-class student only at the expense of the other students. But what is the "ideal" proportion of working-class students? Clearly, economic criteria cannot help us here. I should ask those who favour greater working-class "representation" in the university to disclose the formula they employ to determine this just proportion, and also the social rationale, if any, of the formula. It would be a coincidence if they all agreed, and a greater coincidence yet if the *existing system* had after all managed to produce just the right proportion.

Equality vs. the intellectual elite

There is, in addition to these more enduring advantages of a full-cost fee system, another arising from a more recent social phenomenon. There can be many opinions on the chief causes of student unrest, but one need not analyse them all before proposing remedies.

Certainly, the increased dependence of the universities on public funds has provided an air of specious legitimacy to student demands for more "participation" and control. The general impression, shared by the public and academics as well as students, is that the universities, being financed by the public purse, are *de facto* public property. The affairs of the university are therefore as much the business of the students who are its customers, so to speak, as they are the business of the staff hired to serve in them. Both student and staff are seen, through this distorted vision, to be equally vulnerable—both apparently being dependent on public funds—and the question of apportioning authority between senate, staff, and students seems a proper subject of debate, negotiation, and ultimately of struggle. Any successful defiance of the university authorities by sheer physical pressure of student numbers acts on them like a heady draught. And since agreements, open or tacit, are known to be grounded in expediency rather than in mutually accepted procedures, they are regarded by all as temporary only. An atmosphere grows in which it seems that virtually anything can happen, with publicity always close at hand. In the circumstances, the activities of a faction of extremists ready to take the initiative at a tactical moment, exercises an immoderate influence on the student body.

This question of students' rights along with the occasional rowdyism and incipient violence,

will, I believe, resolve itself once the universities take their place in society as self-supporting and independent institutions, their full costs of research and teaching covered by fees supplemented by their endowment income. As a private corporate body each university will be free to use its revenues as it wishes and without requiring the consent of any public authority. It will make its own rules for regulating the behaviour both of the staff it hires and of the students it chooses to admit.

The legal position at least will be incontestable. The university premises are private property. No part of them can be used by any group without explicit authorisation. Alternatively, the university can hire out its rooms for students' extra-curricular activity on its own terms. Student privileges are those laid down in the regulations of the university, no more, no less. If a student finds them onerous, he is not entitled to break them: he is entitled only to go elsewhere. However, once students are obliged to pay fees from their own resources, with access to loans if necessary, calls by the militants for student solidarity, for "strikes," sit-ins, or sit-outs, will have less appeal. Paying [full] tuition and maintenance costs will provide them with a strong incentive to limit their youthful excesses. In any case, if they do waste money it will not be the taxpayers', it will be their own.

To conclude, the independence of our [state] universities can be completely restored, and without additional cost, simply by allowing them to charge fees that cover their expenditures. This would cost the country no more than it is currently paying.

If the resources available for higher education are limited (and they are), then it is surely *wrong* that only an "intellectual élite" be provided by the rest of the community with the means of raising further their status and earnings, so widening the gap between themselves and the less fortunate members of society. Since the ideal of extending appropriate educational opportunities to all young people is economically impracticable, the only tolerable and viable solution is that of making higher education of some sort available to all at its cost, along with a system of loans for all *bona fide* students unable to meet the costs out of their current resources.

Reading 76

Reading 76

In some circles Galbraith is regarded as a funny but dangerous fellow. From the left, however, he appears as a credulous apologist, who hardly makes up in style for what he lacks in substance and proof. Thus, the notion that there is a technostructure of experts who call the tune in the large corporation is deemed ludicrous by these writers. Who constitutes the technostructure: Robert McNamara at Ford? The Knudsen who replaced a previous whiz kid there, and who in turn was fired by Henry Ford II as the result of a palace coup?

Robert Fitch was a graduate student in economic history at Berkeley when he wrote this piece.

Questions to Guide the Reading

Does the author prove that Galbraith is wrong or only that Galbraith exaggerates? If Galbraith is wrong, does it follow that the pre-Galbraith view of markets is the correct one?

Galbraith as Ideologue of the Status Quo

Robert Fitch

Perhaps it is now time, when America has come to face the complexities of empire, that her best minds begin to shed their innocence. Today the United States carries out *la mission civilatrice* in every part of the globe. The sun never sets on her network of military bases or her multinational corporations. There are revolts, too, on the far frontiers. The generals need troops immediately; more taxes must be raised; the children of the intellectuals—the sensitive ones—will have to put down their books and learn to fire a mortar. The rat-bitten ghetto children will have to wait their turn; the peasants will have to tighten their belts. The social machine is not working well. There's a harsh clatter and roar from the engine room. So many problems. So much misery. So many needs. How can it be changed? Who can even describe it?

There is at least one man among us who feels qualified to describe the way things work. Professor John Kenneth Galbraith's credentials are impressive indeed: he is chairman of the Americans for Democratic Action (ADA), former ambassador to India, professor of economics at Harvard, former head of the Office of Price Administration, a Far Eastern art expert and a novelist both satiric and nostalgic.

Defending the indefensible

The sole asset of men like Galbraith is their ability to develop ideology and present it as social criticism. Republicans don't care much for this sort of thing and they even hate it when it's stood on its head—that is, when social criticism gets developed into ideology—so intellectuals, willy-nilly, get to be Democrats.

And how well we have learned that the structure of the Democratic Party means that any attempt at ideology will produce a monstrosity. At the Party's base is the familiar trade union, black, Jewish, Mexican-American, urban coalition. And at the top are bankers, corporation presidents, oilmen, defense contractors and plantation owners. What sort of Solomon could write a program reflecting the needs of both the share-cropper and the plantation owner, the draft-eligible graduate student and the defense contractor, the automobile manufacturer and the auto worker? It is as if the British Liberal Party, *Action Française*, the Italian Christian Democrats and the South African Nationalist Party had all gone mad and declared a merger.

Galbraith is the only significant producer in a growing market. But the market's product specifications are devilishly narrow. With a stroke of a pen, Galbraith must open the wound and dress it again, titilate the conscience and soothe it. At the end of each paragraph the oilman, the boss, the sophomore and the ordinary citizen must each be able to say: "Ah yes, I see how it works. Now if we will all try a little harder together. . . ."

Paragraph after mellifluous paragraph the magic seems to work. The reader is left with the simultaneous convictions that the status quo is really very decent and that there is also an urgent need for "change." Throughout the entire performance, the reader has the feeling that the author somehow combats all the selfish moguls and ideological troglodytes in Christendom.

What we miss

But a close inspection of the texts shows no advocacy of a more equal income distribution, no plea for full employment, not even a program for closing tax loopholes. What Galbraith does attack are ugly billboards, dirty air, water pollution, insufficient funds for public education, and he says we ought to spend more to see that these problems get solved. This program may put him somewhat to the left of Ladybird, but it is certainly not honest-to-God reformism.

Decent reformism admits, at a minimum, that conflicts of interest exist in society and that consequently the poor and unorganized will have to present a political challenge to the rich and the powerful if they are ever going to achieve their demands. Galbraith, on this fundamental question of power, takes the Democratic Party line: no basic conflicts of interest exist because state power is legitimate and is being exercised for the benefit of all.

Gullible praise

Galbraith's special preeminence in high Democratic Party circles and his notoriety in academic circles stem from his chief ideological discovery: that big business can be beautiful. Prior to Galbraith's popular work, corporate giantism was the dirty little secret of many radicals and a few academic economists. Monopolistic corporations created more embarrassment at the university than the last 30 pages of *Ulysses;* professors admitted their

existence, but preferred to discuss the matter after class. Academic economics is still busy extolling unrestricted competition, free trade, the profit motive and the anarchy of production and distribution. But this world of *laissez-faire* economics, as Galbraith often points out, has pretty well disappeared. It is the wrong apology for the wrong century for the wrong system. Galbraith has a much more salable product.

The theme of monopolistic predominance and its essential benignity carries through all of Galbraith's major work. Most everything else is ancillary. *American Capitalism,* the book which first established Galbraith as an outstanding *advocatus de fide,* argued that political stability in the U.S. was a product of the stalemate between big business and big labor. This was one side of the famous theory of countervailing power. The other side spoke out for the "right" of monopolies to engage in price discrimination. As Galbraith put it: "To achieve price discrimination—to use bargaining power to get a differentially lower price—is the very essence of the exercise of countervailing power."

Galbraith's next important book was the pre-Watts classic, *The Affluent Society,* which showed that political stability in the U.S. had been achieved because the problems of economic equality and insecurity had been largely eliminated. In *The Affluent Society,* Galbraith admitted that monopolized industry tended to produce less than competitive industry, but he side-stepped the issue by righteously pointing out that the U.S. had an unhealthy obsession with production anyway.

In Galbraith's most recent work, *The New Industrial State* (1967), several of the key hypotheses of the prior works have been abandoned, but the defense of monopoly and monopoly power remains as firm as ever. Today the U.S. is stable, Galbraith argues, *despite* the existence of poverty and insecurity (they're "outside" the industrial system) and *because* "big" labor has accepted a subaltern role. (Whatever happened to "countervailing power"?)

It is belief in the permanence of an ideal rather than logical consistency that gives Galbraith's work its unity. In this light, *The New Industrial State* can be seen as Volume Three of a larger opus entitled "Monopoly Without Tears." The overarching theme of the "trilogy" is the endless viability, plasticity and, above all, the desirability (given a few moderate improvements) of the present economic and social order.

The pipedream of the intellectual

To dismiss Galbraith simply as "another Establishment apologist" not only greatly overestimates the craftsmanship of his peers, but it also overlooks what can be learned from observing America's premier "monophile" at work.

Could the monopoly structure of U.S. heavy industry be at the root of persistent unemployment, urban poverty, huge arms budgets and the never-ending crusade against "communism"? Decidedly not, says Galbraith. He admits that some of these ills are consistent with both Marxian-socialist and Smithian-capitalist predications on the consequences of monopoly. But this is precisely why he calls those ideas "the conventional wisdom." For generations the conventional wisdom held that competition was a good thing and monopoly a bad thing. Now that we are living under monopoly capitalism we see how groundless the fears of monopoly were. Monopoly—which Galbraith calls "modern industrialism"—is efficient and humane. Competition is the real villain of the piece.

The New Industrial State acknowledges all the defects of the old system of competitive free-enterprise capitalism. Yes indeed, the author muses, those old-time capitalists—the Fords, Morgans, Mellons and Rockefellers—they were tough old bastards. Union busting, sweating labor, buying up competition, maintaining a vested interest in unemployment—all this was consistent with their solitary goal in life, the accumulation of capital through the pursuit of maximum profits. Galbraith is glad they've all died off and that new men are in power.

Who are the new men of power, who, according to Galbraith, run the modern corporation? They are called the "technostructure." The technostructure is not the top managerial elite, the men whose salaries are set by the ebb and flow of corporate profits. The technostructure is different, and better. First of all it's a lot larger, and that makes an immediate step toward democracy. It's made up of all the engineers and middle-echelon bureaucrats: everyone who brings "specialized knowledge, talent, or experience to group decision making." Second, and most important, since it can't get any of the profits the corporation makes, it doesn't have the old "profit *über alles*" obsession. In fact it seems to be worried mainly about security—the corporation's and its own.

According to Galbraith, now that the technostructure has taken charge and eliminated the profit motive as the single goal of corporate enterprise, it's possible to relax and enjoy "industrialism." The corporations no longer compete against each other: they divide the market and allow everyone to prosper. Nor do they try to hold workers' wages down. Instead, they give the workers a reasonable share of what they want and pass on the increased wage bill to the consumer. This ends the anarchy of the system. The corporations can plan their production schedules with the knowledge that prices will remain constant. And the workers no longer have to fear layoffs. The market is replaced by "planning." We leave the realm of competitive necessity and enter the kingdom of monopolistic "freedom": the Great Post-Keynesian No-Hassle State.

Before we can settle back and enjoy Galbraith's New Order, however, there remains a small problem. Why do corporations and unions still behave very much as they did when the capitalists and their hired managers held sway? Why, to cite only the most obvious example, did 1967 see the highest number of strikes in 14 years? How can "planning" and the demise of the market be reconciled with persistent balance of payments deficits and the export of capital during periods of high unemployment? Or with the go-go mutual funds and the great speculative booms on the stock exchanges?

There are two possible explanations. One is that trade unionists and corporations have not yet learned their Galbraith: they are still burdened with the "conventional wisdom." The other is that *The New Industrial State* represents as faithful a portrayal of America's corporate economy as *Gone With the Wind* did the Southern slave system. Let's examine the latter possibility.

How did the "technostructure" take control of the corporations away from the capitalists in the first place? Galbraith's explanation is that technostructures supply information and capitalists supply capital; and that in a century in which information is scarcer than capital, the technostructure was able to seize power.

It's true, of course, that there is a lot of capital around these days, a lot more than in the 19th century. But big blocs of capital like the $800 million TWA borrowed through the investment banking houses in 1967 aren't to be found in everyone's cookie jar, as the record interest rates indicate. Technical information, on the other hand, while highly prized, is not scarce in the same sense. Nor are the men who provide it. To take an obvious example, in the aerospace industry, which employs over half of all U.S. engineers and scientists, layoffs and unemployment are quite common because of volatility and the competition for government contracts. In fact, technology is changing so rapidly that many engineers are becoming obsolete.

Pawns in the game

Far from constituting the corporate ruling class as Galbraith thinks they do, technicians, according to many experts, are developing into a kind of *lumpenproletariat*. Stanley Hawkins, training coordinator at Lockheed Missile and Space Company, says, "The problem of the unemployed engineer is with us now—the problem of the *unemployable* engineer is approaching with frightening rapidity." Now the technostructure may be as humane and rational as Galbraith thinks it is, but at the moment the technocrats seem to be taking orders from the top, collecting unemployment checks and stretching their coffee breaks, just like the rest of the working class.

If the technostructure doesn't run the corporations, who does? Could it be small groups of rich businessmen similar to those that ran them in the past? Galbraith tries to show that individual wealth no longer plays a role and that the predominance of outside monied interests has vanished. He cites the 35-year-old analysis of "the separation of ownership from control" by Adolph A. Berle Jr., together with a couple of more recent studies by writers equally unable to discover any outside forces controlling corporate management.

The industrial-military complex

Several recent investigators, however, have discovered the outside centers of power that Berle, Galbraith & Company were unable to locate. For example, in 1965 the anti-trust subcommittee of the House Judiciary Committee published a study of 74 important industrial-commercial companies; in this handful of firms 1480 officers and directors held a total of 4428 positions. The report concluded that interlocking directorates are as prevalent today as in 1914 when the Clayton Act, prohibiting interlocking directorates, was passed.

More recently, Fortune reported that in 1966, controlling ownership of 150 of the 500 largest U.S. corporations rested in the hands of an individual or of the members of a single family. And this was admittedly a "very conservatively" drawn estimate, excluding cases in which businessmen—who are known to wield great influence—own less than ten per cent of the voting stock. In practice, Wall Street experts maintain that the holders of five to ten per cent of the stock can prevail over the unorganized mass of stockholders.

With the technostructure back in its accustomed position of supplying technical information to profit-maximizing businessmen, the rest of the corporate landscape also falls back into proper perspective. Corporate "planning"—comfortably eulogized by Galbraith in *The New Industrial State* as a kind of rich man's socialism—instead of replacing the jolts and kicks of the market becomes a series of short-run responses to it.

Take the labor market for example. In *The New Industrial State* wage demands don't lead to bitter class struggles because price increases can always be passed on to the consumer and because labor basically has it made. Within this framework, how can we fit the eight-month-old national copper strike involving nearly 50,000 miners?

In the Galbraithian wonderland of corporate planning, the corporations needn't pay attention to what goes on in the capital market either. The mature corporation has its own "source of capital, derived from its own earnings, that is wholly under its own control. No banker can attach conditions as to how retained earnings are to be used." Were it otherwise, Galbraith admits, bankers would hold the strings of the corporation and tell the technostructure what to do.

In the real world of the American economy, something like this is exactly what does happen. In 1966, for example, about *half* of all the new funds used by corporations for growth came from external sources. In this year alone, bond issues and bank loans were equal to about two-thirds of undistributed profits.

Selling capitalism

Standard Oil of New Jersey, General Electric, Westinghouse, Texaco, Union Carbide—mature corporations all—paid their respects to the bond market to the tune of $200 million or more. Leading all other investment bankers, with $3.8 billion worth of issues, was the old dinosaur of capitalist enterprise, Morgan Stanley. Some of his clients included General Motors, Mobil Oil, U.S. Steel and IBM.

When the investment bankers manage a big bond issue for a corporation, or extend other kinds of credit, they increasingly earn the right to intervene on matters like mergers, financing, granting of stock options, dividends and even advertising campaigns. And with so much emphasis these days upon the stock market "performance," the pressure exerted by the banks for higher profits and dividends grows continually greater.

But even if outside financial interests weren't prodding the corporation to increase its rate of profit; even if the labor market were always stable; and even if one firm's prices weren't another firm's costs, the whole notion of corporate planning "replacing" the market in the U.S. would still be absurd on its face. It is like saying that because two nations' armies follow their respective battle plans and their troops follow orders that the resulting war between them is "planned."

This kind of *post facto* reconciliation of conflicting social forces begins to smell very familiar to the reader with a nose for the ranker side of historical analogy. The "principle of consistency" which Galbraith proclaims from his Procter and Gamble soapbox—"As always reality is in harmony with itself"—smells suspiciously like Hegel's excuse for Frederick William IV: "What is real is rational." And, as Montesquieu pointed out, the Jesuits' apologies for the counterreformation had the same fetid odor: "The Society of Jesus may pride itself on the fact that it was the first to prove to the world that religion and humanity are compatible" (*Esprit des Lois*).

Galbraith is surely in the forefront of those who would do for monopoly capitalism what the Jesuits did for Catholicism—establish its compatibility with humanity. But like all really first-rate ideologists he comes down to earth finally with a political program.

First he disposes of the main alternative system. It's not that socialism is wicked, it's merely *passé*, says Galbraith. The development of technology took control away from the capitalists. Similarly, it is the "technical complexity and planning and associated scale of operations" that has made things too complex for democratic control over the means of production to be exercised today. How could an elective body run a steel factory? It would be impossible. Consequently, socialism is a "spent slogan"; it would result in "social control without success"; it no longer seems "worth the struggle."

So here we are: we can't go forward to socialism; and we can't go backward to competitive capitalism. Monopoly capitalism is all there is.

Problems in the Mixed Economy

Reading 77

Here is a typical illustration of the strengths and weaknesses of contemporary expert forecasting. The reports here for 1969 could be postdated a year without much change: 1969 was actually stronger than most experts thought, but the guessing game for a typical year in the early 1970s poses the same problem.

The actual authors of this official report were Joe W. McLeary and C. S. Pyun.

Questions to Guide the Reading

How good is the fit of the curves in the chart? Can you find data in the *Federal Reserve Bulletin* or other publications to fill in some new points (just as the editor filled in the 1969 point)?

Do the forecasts tell a coherent story? Even if not accurate in their timing, do they perform a useful function? What are your views on the desired compromise between high employment and price inflation?

The Unemployment-Inflation Trade-off: What the Forecasts Imply

Federal Reserve Bank of Atlanta

Compared to 1968, most forecasters predicted a slower economic expansion in 1969. A slower economic expansion is not always good news. But the recent opinion of most economists is that some deceleration in economic activity in 1969 is not only desirable, but is essential if current inflationary price rises are to be checked or reduced. The anticipated slowing of dollar gains and the effects on price advances and unemployment vary considerably, however, according to 11 major business forecasts analyzed by this Bank. The results and some implications of these forecasts are summarized in this article.

In December 1968, when this Bank solicited 1969 economic projections from various individuals or organizations that customarily make forecasts, there was wide agreement among the respondents that the economy would slow down in 1969. There was less agreement on how much deceleration is expected.

Less inflation and more unemployment

Corresponding to their projections of slower economic gains in 1969, most of the forecasters we surveyed also predicted less inflation [for 1969] than occurred in 1968. The median forecast of the rate of price advance was about 3.0 percent, as measured by the GNP implicit price deflator. Although a 3.0-percent inflation rate is historically high, it would represent a full percentage point reduc-

tion from 4.0 percent in 1968. Individual forecasts of overall price rises expected ranged from a low of 2.5 to 4.0 percent. Thus, despite some differences in the actual amount of price increases expected, the forecasters in general see inflation as a continuing problem.

The projections of our respondents seem to imply that they believed reducing or completely eliminating inflation could not be accomplished quickly, even if the rate of economic expansion were to slow down. Moreover, they seemed to believe that a necessary first step in reducing inflation is to accept some increase in unemployment along with the projected slower pace of overall economic activity. Consequently, their median forecast of a smaller rise in prices was coupled with a typical projection of an increase in the unemployment rate to 4.2 percent from the 3.6-percent rate of 1968. Some of the forecasters, however, expect the unemployment rate to stay below 4.0 percent, while others project a rise above the 4.2-percent typical estimate. In most cases, those projecting an unemployment rate on the low side predicted the largest dollar increases in GNP and rate of price advances; those predicting a higher unemployment rate expected smaller increases in GNP and prices.

The treatment by the forecasters of these trade-off relationships between GNP, inflation, and unemployment reflects observable conflicts in trying to achieve, simultaneously, high employment, reasonably stable prices, and a sus-

From "The Unemployment-Inflation Trade-off: What 1969 Forecasts Imply," *Monthly Review*, February, 1969, Federal Reserve Bank of Atlanta. Reprinted with kind permission of the publisher.

tainable rate of economic growth. While most everyone accepts these objectives as desirable goals of the domestic economy, it is also generally recognized that imbalances between these goals may appear frequently. When such conflicts arise, it may be possible to achieve a certain goal only at the expense of not fully achieving others, or of only partially accomplishing several of the objectives.

The existence of an inflation-unemployment trade-off is widely acknowledged, and was implicit in most of the forecasts reviewed. But there was lack of agreement among the forecasters on the amount of slowdown in business activity and increase in unemployment necessary to reduce the inflationary momentum. The 1969 *Economic Report of the President* and *The Annual Report* of the previous administration's Council of Economic Advisers acknowledged these conflicts in goals and labeled the reconciliation of prosperity at high employment with price stability the nation's most important unsolved problem of overall economic performance.

Past trade-offs

Past relationships between the rate of unemployment and price changes undoubtedly influenced the forecasters in their contention that a low rate of unemployment is generally associated with the tendency for price advances to accelerate. The dots in the accompanying chart represent the plottings of the rate of inflation (increase of GNP deflator) for each year from 1950–68 corresponding to the unemployment rate for the same year. The regression lines in the chart represent *an approximation of the average relationships between unemployment and overall price increases.* The lines indicate that to move down the vertical scale toward more stable prices, some increase in unemployment along the horizontal scale is suggested.

The trade-off pattern between prices and unemployment has changed since 1950. The blue line in the chart illustrates the pattern from 1961 to 1968, compared to the black line for the entire period 1950–68. The pattern since 1961 fits extremely well the actual results for each of the years. Since 1965, the unemployment rate has been below 5 percent, and prices have risen over 2 percent per year, as illustrated by the dots representing the years

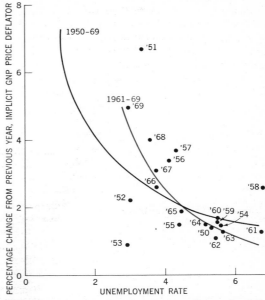

The rate of increase in prices has usually accelerated when unemployment was at a very low level. The black line represents an overall average approximation of this trade-off pattern over the entire period 1950–68. The scatter of dots showing the inflation-unemployment relationships for individual years around this longer-run pattern indicates the lack of a precise statistical fit. On the other hand, the rates of advance in prices and movements in the unemployment rate for each year between 1961–68 are represented remarkably well by the overall pattern for this period—the blue line. These relationships are the implicit basis for most forecasters suggesting that some increase in unemployment must be accepted in order to reduce inflation of 1969.

1965–68. In the early 1960's, when the unemployment rate was above 5 percent, the annual rate of increase in the price level was held below 2 percent.

Although the economic forecasters would surely point out that many other factors besides the level of unemployment may affect short-run inflationary tendencies, they generally concluded that some increase in unemployment is probably necessary to reduce the increases in the price level. If we accept this basic assumption and assume the average pattern of 1961–68 will also hold in 1969, the degree of inflation for various unemployment rates can be calculated. At 4.2-percent unemployment rate predicted by the respondents, prices (GNP deflator) would rise about 2.6 percent (according to our statistical relationship). On the other hand, if the former Council of Economic Advisers' suggestion of an unemployment rate below 4 percent (say 3.8 percent) is realized, then our statistical curve would yield an inflation rate of about 3.8 percent, or higher than the Council's projection of slightly above 3 percent.

Since all the dots for the years 1961–68 do not fall exactly on the regression line, such a mechanical application gives a misleading impression of exactitude. Although the line for 1961–68 shows the average relationships between the rate of unemployment and price changes, the actual rate of price change was greater or smaller than the change indicated by the line. Consequently, even the most mathematically minded forecaster would not expect 1969's performance to follow precisely an estimate based on the average relationship. Moreover, the entire curve depicting the average relationship could shift again as it has in the past. The forecasts show, however, that a major short-run shift is not expected, and the rate of price increases is unlikely to be reduced a full percentage point below last year's increase, without an unemployment rate above 4 percent. Nonetheless, the wide variations in the inflation-unemployment trade-off in the past suggest that whether or not more stable prices can be achieved at low unemployment in 1969 is still an unresolved question.

Smaller consumer gains

Even though most of the respondents expected a smaller rise in consumer spending in 1969, there was a wide divergence in their individual projections.

The divergences in consumption projections stem largely from differences in the assumptions regarding the continuation of the surtax and in their assessment of the efficacy of the fiscal restraints put into effect last July. In general, those projecting the largest increases in consumer spending this year assumed either an elimination of the surtax or a reduction in the surtax rate after July. On the other hand, all of those expecting the smallest gains in consumer spending assumed the full retention of the 10-percent surcharge throughout the year. This latter group appeared also to expect some delayed effects of the earlier fiscal restraints. Most of the forecasters seemed to agree that the exceptionally rapid gains in consumer spending on durable goods last year—particularly on automobiles—will not be repeated in 1969.

Other major sectors

Projections for gross private domestic investment (capital investment, inventories, and residential construction) [involved a] median forecast [of] a 4.6-percent rise over the 1968 level. A few respondents who made projections on business fixed investment generally confirmed the findings of the latest SEC-Commerce Department survey for the first six months of 1969 and the recent McGraw-Hill survey that showed businessmen's plans to increase their plant and equipment expenditures by 6–8 percent in 1969.

The forecasters in general expect a considerable deceleration in the rise in government expenditures this year. [They] expect an increase in the nation's net exports from 1968's $2.4 billion.

Summary of 1969 Forecasts (billions of dollars unless otherwise indicated)

	Low	High	Median
GNP	903.0	920.5	912.5
Personal consumption	560.6	572.2	566.3
Private domestic investment	129.0	135.1	133.4
Government expenditures	209.0	213.6	210.0
Net exports	2.0	6.1	3.7
Wholesale prices*	109.9	112.0	111.0
Consumer prices*	124.5	126.1	125.4
Industrial production Index*	166.0	168.6	167.1
Unemployment rate**	4.0	4.6	4.2

* Index, 1957–59 = 100.
** Percent.

To sum up

Expectations about the performance of the nation's economy vary considerably. In a few instances, forecasters pointed to the danger of an actual economic downturn, or recession; others emphasized fears of continuing rapid inflation. However, the consensus of those persons included in our survey points to a healthy economy in 1969; the expansion will continue but at a slower pace, prices will continue to rise but not as fast, and unemployment, though expected to rise, will remain low.

Those persons who have the courage to engage in the difficult art of economic forecasting know all too well the imprecision of economic forecasts. They have learned from experience that economic relationships can be unstable, and they know that the human behavior behind the decisions establishing these relationships is not precisely predictable. That the economy could continue to expand so vigorously in late 1968, despite earlier predictions of a slowing down, therefore, did not come as a complete shock to the forecasting experts. It was an example of the instability of relationships at work. Neither should it diminish our respect for those persons, the forecasters, who have the courage to make up their minds about the probable course of the nation's economy. Their present uncertainties can be taken as a warning that to be successful, economic policies must be kept flexible.

Reading 78

Every mixed economy in the world has had difficulty in maintaining full employment with reasonable price stability. Every mixed economy has looked for a so-called incomes policy which will solve this dilemma. We know however from the debate between Professors Burns and Eckstein on wage-price guideposts (Readings 79 and 80) that the search for an incomes policy is indeed a difficult one. Why then should we not cut the Gordian knot simply by putting in comprehensive direct wage and price controls? Such is J. K. Galbraith's simple proposal.

Except as an agricultural economist, Dr. Galbraith first came to fame as deputy price administrator in the Office of Price Administration during World War II. Later he wrote a scholarly book on the successes of price and wage control in World War II, but it did not receive as much attention as his more popular works. In *The New Industrial State,* Galbraith confidently prescribes direct controls over wages and prices, arguing in a simple fashion that peace is really no different from war and what worked well during the war will work well now. It is very hard indeed for an editor to find convincing spokesmen for the cause of direct wage and price controls in peacetime situations, except for short emergencies. Fortunately, however, Dr. Galbraith has not changed his opinion since the Korean War and almost with no alterations his testimony before Congress nearly two decades back can be resurrected from earlier editions of this *Readings in Economics* and used to plug a gap. Although Ambassador Galbraith needs no further introduction, it may be noted that he is an expert in Indian art and also a novelist.

Questions to Guide the Reading

If conditions of supply and demand are constantly shifting, what will be the longer-run consequences of freezing relative prices and wages? If established businesses honestly satisfy the letter of the law, with the passing of time will not there be a premium on those who are less honest and more skillful in finding legal loopholes? Underline in pencil those passages in which you think the author is providing proof rather than assertion for what he is saying.

The Need for Direct Plus Indirect Controls

J. Kenneth Galbraith

Control of the wage-price spiral

A complete attack on inflation requires that both causes of inflation—both the *excess of demand,* or spending, and the *wage-price spiral* [cost-push]—be brought under control.

The line of attack on excess spending is obvious. It calls primarily for heavy—very heavy—taxation. It calls also for intelligent economy in expenditures by government. It calls for postponement of business investment. It calls for increased voluntary saving. This means that Americans must be assured for the future, as they have so long been assured in the past, that their dollars are good. They must be assured that the dollar they save instead of spend and put in a bank account or government bonds will have as high a purchasing power in the future as in the present. Nothing will serve this end more effectively than evidence of a strong determination by the administration and the Congress to check inflation.

I should like to make one comment concerning taxes. We shall need higher personal-income taxes and higher corporate-income taxes. We shall certainly have to have more and higher excise taxes. But I especially hope that doctrinaire opposition to the idea of sales taxes will not prevent us from looking carefully at the possibilities of this tax. I would not be in favor of a flat across-the-board levy on food, clothing, and other essentials. I do feel that the sales tax has great possibilities if it is properly designed. The British made extremely effective use of the sales tax in World War II— they called it the purchase tax—as a way of taxing expensive or luxury goods. These are the goods which place the greatest drain on scarce materials, labor, and skills and plant. A sales tax directed toward these goods—toward expensive lines of clothing, for example— can be actually helpful in keeping lower priced lines of goods cheap and abundant. It can also raise a lot of revenue.

The defense against the wage-price spiral— the second of the inflationary forces which work in our economy—are the *direct controls over prices and wages.* These direct controls are not a substitute for a strong fiscal policy; they perform a different task. Taxes and other fiscal measures dry up the excess of purchasing power; wage and price controls keep wages from shoving up prices and prices from shoving up wages. We cannot, under conditions we now face, be sure that any tax or fiscal policy will control the wage-price spiral. No more can we look upon wage- and price-fixing as a defense, in itself, against inflation. *Both* lines of attack are necessary because each deals with a different cause of inflation.

Because the primary purpose of the direct controls is to check the wage-price spiral, the controls we invoke must accomplish that purpose. It is not necessary, however, assuming no one wants control for the sake of control, to do more than necessary to achieve this end. To tie down the wage-price spiral, with reasonable justice and equity, we need to do three things. They are:

1. Effectively *stabilize basic living costs.* This is necessary if wages are to be stabilized.

2. Maintain a *general ceiling on wages and prices* in that part of the economy where wages are determined by collective-bargaining contracts and where prices normally move in response to wage movements. I have reference here to what may properly be called the great industrial core of the American economy—the steel, automobile, electrical goods, construction, transport, and like industries.

3. As a contribution to over-all stability, placing of firm *ceiling prices on basic raw materials.*

Had we approached the problem of controls with a view to having as few of them as possible (though as many as necessary) and had the action been timely, we would have started out along the above lines. It is a system of controls with which, if necessary, we could live for a long time. It would not require a large administrative or enforcement staff.

From *Hearings before the Joint Committee on the Economic Report, 82nd Congress, 1st Session,* pp. 354–356.

Stabilizing the wage-price spiral is the central task of the direct controls. Fixing *all* prices [including] a great many prices that do not need to be controlled provides no guaranty of stable living costs. There is danger that administrative energies will be dissipated over a large number of products when, in fact, the key danger to wage-price stability lies in a relatively *few*—in food, basic clothing, and rents. None of these latter is now securely controlled. While we managed, although not without difficulty, to keep such a general ceiling in effect throughout World War II and for a period thereafter, it is not the kind of regulation which is right for the long pull. In World War II we, in effect, improvised for a particular set of circumstances of *limited duration*. For those circumstances it was the thing to do. We now face a *long* period of inflationary tension. For that a different line of action is called for. Energies should now be concentrated on getting the kind of stabilization program with which we can live, if we must, for a long time. This requires that we control strongly where control is necessary and not at all where it isn't.

The first step is a fundamental attack on living costs. Apart from rent I do not see this as, primarily, a problem in price-fixing. The ceilings, which undoubtedly should be kept on basic clothing and on food, should be viewed as merely an adjunct to more fundamental action. In the case of clothing, for example, a far more effective approach than price-fixing would be to use government allocation powers to direct generous quantities of fiber and textiles into standard low-priced goods—into work clothing, household textiles, children's clothing, and the lower priced lines of men's and women's clothing. These should be made abundant, and so kept cheap. I would not worry if expensive lines of clothing became more expensive and scarce; freedom from ceilings on such clothing should readily be con-

ceded in return for a substantial tax. If we rely on ceilings on clothing we will get too much expensive clothing and not enough of the cheap. We all remember during World War II when gay sports shirts were plentiful and ordinary ones not to be had.

The key to our problem is meat. I very much doubt if present ceilings, even when buttressed by slaughter controls, will hold meat prices even at their present astronomical levels. And even if they should, the attempt to meet the demand at these prices will place a heavy drain on our feed supplies. Rising feed prices will mean higher costs for dairy and poultry farmers, higher milk, poultry, and egg prices, and also more expensive cereals for direct consumption. Barring crop failure and full-scale war, our food position is strong. Could the demand for meat be effectively restrained, feed prices would be easier, and other animal products would be cheaper and more abundant. The necessary steps are not easy. It may be necessary to control here in order to have fewer controls elsewhere. And a policy of minimizing controls may well take more vigor and imagination than one which merely fixes ceilings and hopes for the best.

Action along these commodity lines in the cost-of-living area—coupled with the necessary fiscal policy—will lessen our reliance on price controls as such while greatly increasing our security against inflation. I should not want you to think I am arguing for a soft policy. I regard the threat of inflation as extremely grave. We are currently in much greater danger of demoralization of the economy as a result of inflation than we ever were from the great depression which the Russians were presumed to be counting upon to finish off American capitalism after World War II. It will take a stronger and more sure-footed policy to minimize reliance on ceilings than to multiply them.

Readings 79 and 80

"How to get full employment while preserving reasonable price stability?" That is the question confronting every mixed economy today. In 1962 President Kennedy and his Council of Economic Advisers mapped out the following bold new "incomes policy."

1. Wage rates on the average were to rise only by the same percentage as average labor productivity rose—say 3.2 per cent per year in the mid-1960s.

2. Prices on the average were to be stable, with (a) prices falling in industries enjoying above-average productivity growth, and (b) prices rising in industries of below-average productivity growth.

3. Certain exceptions were to be made—for low-wage hardship cases, for wage incentives in industries needing to recruit greater labor force, etc.

From 1962 to 1965, after some dramatic interventions by Presidents Kennedy and Johnson in the steel and other industries, the guideposts seemed to work well—as witnessed by the unusual pattern of wage moderation and price-cost stability for so sustained an expansion. By 1966 the strength of demand-pull inflation had put greater strains on the guideposts than they could cope with, and they were abandoned.

Arthur F. Burns, long-time professor at Columbia University and head of the National Bureau of Economic Research, was the first chairman of the Council of Economic Advisers under President Eisenhower and is now an advisor to President Nixon and Chairman of the Federal Reserve Board. Otto Eckstein, of Harvard University, served on the Council of Economic Advisers under President Johnson.

Questions to Guide the Reading

Is there room for industrial statesmanship, presidential exhortation, and union responsibility in a competitive society? In a mixed economy do large corporations and national unions have discretionary market power?

Why are stabilizing monetary and fiscal policies indispensable adjuncts to an incomes policy of guidepost type? If you reject guideposts what do you put in their place as an incomes policy to reconcile full employment and price stability?

Reading 79

Wage-Price Guideposts: No

Arthur F. Burns

Let us try to visualize a little more definitely how the CEA's wage-price guideposts, if they were generally and fully respected, would work out in practice.

Wages and prices

Statistical records stretching back into the nineteenth century demonstrate that, although the over-all productivity of our economy occasionally declines, its trend has been steadily upward. If this continues to be true, as we may reasonably suppose, general observance of the guidelines will result in higher wages every year, regardless of the stage of the business cycle or the level of unemployment or the state of the balance of payments. The rise of wages will be the same, on the average, in years of recession as in years of prosperity; but in any given recession the rise of wages could easily be larger than in the preceding years of prosperity. Furthermore, the average wage will tend to rise in any given year by the same percentage in every firm, regardless of its profitability or the state of the market for different kinds of labor.

However, general observance of the guidepost for prices will not freeze individual prices

From Arthur F. Burns, "Wages and Prices by Formula?" *Harvard Business Review*, March—April, 1965. Reprinted with kind permission of the author and publisher.

or the relations among them. What it would tend to freeze is (1) the general level of prices and (2) the ratio of individual prices to unit labor costs of production. The tendency of the price-cost ratio to remain constant will be stronger in some industries than in others. Strictly speaking, the guidepost for prices specifies merely that the ratio of price to unit labor cost of production should not rise; it does not argue against a decline of the price-cost ratio. Hence, firms or industries experiencing a weak demand for their products or keen foreign competition may need to be content with prices that decline relative to their unit labor costs. On the other hand, firms or industries that are favored in the marketplace would be unable to raise prices relative to their unit labor costs even if their incoming orders were many times as large as their production. Nor would they be able to raise prices to compensate for increases in costs of production other than those of labor.

Income shares

The broad effect of these tendencies would be to keep more or less constant the percentage share of the national income—or of national output—going to labor. Changes in the use of capital relative to the use of labor, whether upward or downward, could still have a large influence on the size of the national income but not on the proportion of income accruing to labor. Unless major shifts occurred in the occupational or industrial distribution of employment, any fluctuation in labor's percentage share of the national income would be due primarily to the discrepancy between the movement of over-all productivity in a particular year and the corresponding trend increase. Nonlabor income, in the aggregate, would also tend to be a constant percentage of the national income.

It is well to bear in mind, however, that since profits are only a fraction of nonlabor income, the share of profits in the total national income could either rise or decline. In the postwar period, the amount paid by corporations on account of excises, customs duties, property taxes, licensing fees, and other indirect taxes has risen more rapidly than their net output. If this trend continues, the income share of investors in the corporate sector will

tend to undergo a persistent decline, while that of labor will tend to remain constant.

Throttling of competition

The *fundamental* point of the preceding analysis is that general observance of the guideposts would throttle the forces of competition no less effectively than those of monopoly. The point is important becaue, unlike much of the rest of the world, the rivalry among U.S. business firms is very keen. Even in industries where a few corporations dominate the market —as in the case of automobiles, steel, and aluminum—each corporation competes actively against the others in its industry, against rival products of other industries, and against foreign suppliers. Competition in labor markets is also stronger than casual references to labor monopoly may suggest. After all, only a little over a fourth of the population working for wages or salaries is unionized, and many of the trade unions are weak. By and large, it is competition—not monopoly—that has vast sweep and power in our everyday life. Since free competitive markets would virtually cease to exist in an economy that observed the guidelines, this transformation of the economy merits serious reflection.

To be sure, compliance with the guidelines would be voluntary in the economy we are considering. That, however, may not mean much. For when economic freedom is not exercised, it is no longer a part of life. As far as I can see, an economy in which wages and prices are set voluntarily according to a formula suggested by the government would be almost indistinguishable from an economy in which wages and prices are directly fixed by governmental authorities. In either case—

> ... the movement of resources toward uses that are favored by the buying public would be impeded;
> ... the tendency to economize on the use of what happens to be especially scarce, whether it be materials or labor or equipment, would be weakened;
> ... since prices will no longer tend to equate demand and supply in individual markets, some form of rationing would need to be practiced.

In all likelihood, therefore, a shift from our present market economy to one of voluntary compliance with the guidelines would adversely affect efficiency. It would also adversely affect the rate of economic growth and the rate of improvement of the general standard of living.

Are the guides workable?

This theoretical sketch of how our economy would work if the guidelines were generally and fully observed has blinked institutional factors—such as the adjustments caused by the disappearance of auction markets, the new role of trade unions, and so on. Moreover, our theoretical sketch has tacitly assumed that voluntary compliance with the guidelines is merely a matter of will. Life is not that simple. Even if everyone responded to the government's plea for "cooperation" and sought faithfully to act in accordance with the guidelines, it would frequently be difficult or actually impossible to do so.

There is, first of all, a vast gap in our statistical arsenal. To comply with the guideline for *wages*, businessmen would need to know the trend increase of the over-all output of the nation per man-hour.

Compliance with the *price* guideline would be infinitely harder. For this purpose, every company would need to know the trend increase in the productivity of its own industry and how this increase compares with the trend increase of over-all productivity of the economy. Such information is not generally available, nor is it readily usable.

The productivity indexes now being published, besides being often out of date, lump together a great variety of products. In time, more detailed and more current indexes of productivity will doubtless be constructed, but there are limits to what is statistically feasible. Even if measures of this type become available for each of a thousand or ten thousand industries, much confusion or perplexity will still remain. Better statistics on productivity will reduce these difficulties; however, they cannot possibly remove them.

Other pitfalls and puzzles

Another puzzling problem would be posed by changes in the composition of labor that is used in industry. Consider, for example, the case of a company that has recently decided to employ more skilled workers of different sorts and less unskilled labor.

In view of modern trends that emphasize the use of higher skills, this sort of difficulty would be bound to occur frequently in an economy of voluntary compliance.

Another problem that businessmen and trade-union leaders would need to face is whether the modifications of the guideposts that the Council of Economic Advisers has officially sanctioned apply in a particular case. In assuming, as I have, a general willingness to comply with the guidelines, I have not meant to abstract from human nature entirely. Since the modifications suggested by the Council are phrased in very general terms, men acting in good faith may feel that their situation is precisely the kind of rare case that permits some departure from the guidelines. But will business managers and labor leaders always or even frequently agree in their interpretation of what modifications are permissible? In any event, is it not likely that the modifications will turn out to be numerous, rather than, as now intended by the Administration, relatively few?

In view of these and many other problems that are bound to arise in practice, the guidelines would prove unworkable over a very large segment of industry, even if everyone sought conscientiously to observe them. To deal with this critical difficulty, a new governmental apparatus might need to be established; its function would be to spell out detailed rules and to interpret them in individual cases. Although there is no way of telling just how such an agency would work, it seems reasonable to expect that not a few of its clarifying rules and interpretations would be arbitrary, that its advisory rulings would at times involve considerable delay and thereby cause some economic trouble, and that the rulings themselves would have at least some inflationary bias. These factors inevitably cast a cloud over the preceding analysis of how an economy of voluntary compliance would function, but they hardly make the prospect more inviting.

Specter of controls

I have as yet said nothing about the aspect of guidepost policy that has aroused the most skepticism—namely, the likelihood of general observance on a voluntary basis. In recent years unemployment has been fairly large, and many industries have had sufficient capacity to increase output readily. Under such conditions, upward pressure on prices cannot be great. Even so, the guidelines have been sharply criticized or defied by powerful segments of the business and labor community. The critical test of the inhibiting power of the guidelines will come, of course, when both labor and commodity markets become appreciably tighter—and this test may come soon. If the recent wage settlement in the automobile industry is at all indicative, expectations of a high degree of compliance with the guidelines are hardly warranted. Similar experiments in other countries also suggest that general price stability will not long be maintained through voluntary restraint.

But once the government in power has committed itself to a policy, it may become difficult to move off in a new direction. A strong commitment to the policy of the guidelines inevitably means that any extensive private defiance would, besides frustrating the government's anti-inflation policy, injure its prestige. There is always a possibility, therefore, that failure to comply voluntarily with the guidelines will be followed by some coercive measure. This might initially take the form, as has frequently been proposed, of a review by a governmental board of the facts surrounding the price or wage changes that are being contemplated. The thought behind proposals of this nature is that once the facts are clearly developed, the force of public opinion will ordinarily suffice to ensure "responsible" action by corporations and trade unions.

No one can be sure whether this expectation will be fulfilled. But if it is, the governmental review board will have virtually become an agency for fixing prices and wages. If, on the other hand, the board's reports were flouted with any frequency, the next step might well be outright price and wage fixing by the government. It would seem, therefore, that from whatever angle we examine the guidelines, direct controls pop up dangerously around the corner.

Incipient realities

This danger must not be dismissed as an illusion. Although the guidelines are still in their infancy, they have already hardened. Nor has the evolution of the Administration's thinking concerning the guidelines been confined to a literary plane. In April 1962, only three months after the announcement of the guidelines, the Administration moved sternly to force the leading steel companies to cancel the price increases that they had just posted. This interference with the workings of a private market had no clear sanction in law, and it caused consternation in business circles. Fortunately, a crisis was avoided by a prompt and concerted effort of the Administration, in which President Kennedy himself took the leading part, to restore business confidence.

Since then, the government has been more cautious. But it has continued to expose the need for moderation in the matter of wages and prices, and now and then has even gently rattled its sword. Early in 1964 President Johnson requested the Council to reaffirm the guideposts. He emphasized his commitment to this policy by adding that he would "keep a close watch on price and wage developments, with the aid of an early warning system which is being set up." Last summer, when intimations of a rise in the price of steel appeared in the press, the President lost no time in declaring that such action would "strongly conflict with our national interest in price stability."

Toward sounder policies

As this account of recent history suggests, the guidepost policy may, under the pressure of events, move our nation's economy in an authoritarian direction. The danger may not yet be large, in view of prevailing political attitudes, but it could become serious in a time of trouble or emergency. And this is not the only risk, as I shall presently note. However, the fact that many citizens both within and outside government favor the guidelines must also be considered, for it means that they see smaller risks or larger advantages in this policy than I do.

It may readily be granted that the guidepost policy has the meritorious objective of blunting the power of monopolists to push up the price level. This is the feature of the policy that its proponents often stress. Indeed, they are apt to argue that it matters little in practice whether or not the bulk of the economic community pays any attention to the guidelines—as long as the major corporations and trade unions do so.

But if the guidelines are circumscribed in this fashion, they are still subject to the criticism of interfering with the competitive forces of the markets in which many major corporations actually operate. Moreover, the absence of a precise indication of what firms, industries, or trade unions are covered by the guidelines can create a mood of uncertainty that will militate against compliance. Not least important, the effectiveness of the guidelines in curbing inflation becomes doubtful when their application is restricted. For the very limitation on wage and price increases in the guideline sector of the economy would facilitate increases in the uncovered sector whenever an expansive economic policy generated a monetary demand that grew faster than the supply of goods and services.

Another argument frequently advanced in favor of the guideposts is that if they were in fact respected on a sufficient scale, then profit margins would tend to be maintained and the chances of prolonging the current business expansion would therefore be improved. This consideration is bound to count in men's thinking at a time when our nation is striving to reduce unemployment and to spread prosperity.

We must not, however, become so absorbed in today's problems that we overlook those that will haunt us in a later day. If the guidelines may stretch out the expansion now by helping to maintain the relatively high profit margins of prosperity, may they not at some later time stretch out contraction by serving to maintain the low profit margins of recession?

Let me add, also, that I recognize that the guideline policy was adopted by the Administration only after it had given serious consideration to alternatives. The thought of its economists apparently is that, in general:

1. Monetary and fiscal tools must be used to promote expansion as long as the economy is not operating at full employment.

2. Other devices must therefore be employed (in the absence of full employment) to prevent inflation.

3. Policies aiming to increase competition or to improve productivity cannot accomplish much in the short run or cannot be pushed hard for political reasons.

4. Direct controls of wages and prices cannot and should not be seriously considered under peacetime conditions.

5. Consequently, there is only one major way left for curbing immediate inflation—namely, through devices of exhortation

6. And the guidelines for wages and prices are merely a promising specific application of the technique of exhortation.

Locus of responsibility

Space will not permit me to unravel this complicated argument, but I at least want to suggest why I think it may be faulty. Once the government looks to trade unions and business firms to stave off inflation, there is a danger that it will not discharge adequately its own traditional responsibility of controlling the money supply and of maintaining an environment of competition. In the past our own and other governments have often found it convenient to blame profiteers, corporations, or trade unions for a rising price level. Only rarely have they pointed the finger of blame at their own policies—such as flooding the economy with newly created currency or bank deposits.

To the extent that the government relies on private compliance with its guidelines for prices and wages, it may more easily be tempted to push an expansive monetary and fiscal policy beyond prudent limits. Besides, it may fail to resist strongly enough the political pressure for higher minimum wages, larger trade union immunities, higher farm price supports, higher import duties, more import quotas, larger stockpiling programs, and other protective measures that serve either to raise prices or to prevent them from falling.

One of the major needs of our times is to give less heed to special interest groups and to reassert the paramount interest of consumers in vigorous competition. The political obstacles to reducing artificial props for prices are undoubtedly formidable. However, reforms of this type—supplemented by more stringent antitrust laws, effective enforcement of these laws, and reasonable steps to curb featherbedding—are likely to contribute more to the maintenance of reasonable stability in the general price level than will the guidelines for wages and prices on which we have recently come to rely.

Reading 80

Wage-Price Guideposts: Yes

Otto Eckstein

This economy stands at an extraordinary point in its history. Five years of uninterrupted expansion have brought us great gains. Since the weak business cycle peak of 1960:

Our gross national product is up by 38%,
After tax profits are up 59%,
Income per farm is up nearly 50%,
The spendable income of the typical factory worker family is up 21%,
Employment is up by nearly 7 million, and
Unemployment is below 4%, after 8 long years of substantial excess unemployment.

In the last two years, our real growth has exceeded 5½%, the highest rate of any developed economy in the world. This is a remarkable performance for the most advanced country, which has to be the trailblazer of new technology.

These gains have not just represented greater wealth in the hands of a few. During this expansion,

The number of persons in families below the poverty income line has diminished by 7 million, from over 22% to less than 17% of all Americans.
The number of depressed major labor market areas with unemployment in excess of 7% is down from 25 to just 3—with two of them in Puerto Rico.
The gap between Negro and white incomes has narrowed as Negro income rose from 53 to 56% of white incomes—still too low, but at least well on the path to equality.
And adult Negro unemployment is down from over 9% in 1960 to 5.8% in the last quarter of 1965.
Even the teenage unemployment rate has fallen, from 14% to 11% in the last two years despite an increase in the number of young workers of almost 1 million.

These gains indicate how much is at stake for all Americans in continued, *sustainable* expansion. Prosperity will not solve all our domestic problems. But when firing on all eight cylinders, our economy is a mighty engine of social progress, the greatest man has so far devised.

To the technical analyst, there is little mystery in this record. Fiscal and monetary policies were designed to promote full use of our potential, through expenditure increases and three rounds of tax reduction. The private economy responded to the growth of markets with more efficient operations which produced a high rate of productivity growth. Prudent purchasing, investment and hiring policies helped keep markets in balance. Responsible wage increases generally within the productivity guideposts, and responsible price policies helped preserve our excellent cost and price record. Our balance of trade improved despite rising prosperity and an inevitable expansion of imports. Our goods strengthened their position in foreign markets, as other countries failed to combine prosperity with price-cost stability.

The history of the 1950s

This experience is in sharp contrast to the record of the preceding two short-lived expansions in the 1950's. In those years, the economy's growth was about half of the recent rate. Markets were not allowed to expand to match the economy's rising ability to produce. Slack developed, unemployment increased, and profits became depressed because the operating rates of industry were far below the preferred levels. Yet, the country suffered from creeping inflation, which at least in part must be blamed on cost-push elements. The inflationary experience from 1956 to 1958 was deeply disturbing and gave rise to wide fears that this economy could not prosper unless it also had inflation—

From Otto Eckstein, "Guideposts and the Prosperity of Our Day," *Proceedings of a Symposium on Business–Government Relations,* sponsored by the American Bankers Association, April 1, 1966. Reprinted with kind permission of the author and the ABA.

yet inflation inevitably made expansion unsustainable because of its effect on our international position.

Costs, prices and guideposts in the current situation

This country is determined not to repeat the record of the 1950's. To avoid a repetition of this experience—to allow this society to achieve full use of resources without inflation—the Administration adopted the guideposts for non-inflationary price and wage behavior in 1962. They are a bold and vital innovation—still only imperfectly understood, still in process of evolution, with business, labor and government now learning to live within them. They are a heavy bet that we can measure up to the new opportunities, that private and public leadership can manage their affairs responsibly, so that the American people will obtain the full benefit from the productivity of their labor and of their invested capital.

Innovation is clearly necessary, for history is not at all reassuring. Since World War II every period of full employment was also a period of inflation.

While unemployment was too high and operating rates too low, economic conditions strongly reinforced the guideposts. But today the margins are largely gone. The challenge to public and private policies is greater.

The price-cost record is still good, considering the rapid recent progress. I am sure that few or no observers would have predicted that we could score such gains and reach such levels with industrial prices rising by just 1.4% in the last 12 months, with unit labor costs in manufacturing lower than at the beginning of the expansion and still showing little rise. To be sure there are trouble spots and our price record is no longer perfect. Nonferrous metals have been in short supply in the last 18 months and are sharply up in price. Scattered price increases are now found in most industries and are no longer offset by decreases. More important, farm and food prices are up about 10% in the last 12 months due to low marketings of meat and rising demands. Housewives are keenly aware of their grocery bills and are adding to inflation fears. But the outlook on prices generally remains good despite the great prosperity and the dis-

appearance of margins of unutilized resources. So long as unit labor costs and order-shipments relations show little change, industrial price increases will remain moderate, not of the sort experienced in the creeping inflation of the mid-fifties. Needless to say, the key indicators of excess demand and cost pressures need the closest watching week-by-week.

Federal responsibility to sustain prosperity

All branches of our society, public and private, have their part to play to sustain this great prosperity.

The most important responsibility of the federal government in the present situation is to pursue fiscal and monetary policies that will keep total demand within the economy's capacity to produce. Without such policies, guideposts and other measures cannot succeed. The President has stated clearly in his Economic Report that he "will not hesitate to ask for further fiscal action," that if "additional insurance (against the risks of inflationary pressures) is needed, then I am convinced that we should levy higher taxes rather than accept inflation—which is the most unjust and capricious form of taxation." And he has repeated these views in subsequent statements.

Private responsibilities and guideposts

The main private responsibilities for cost-price stability are these: First, to continue the prudent decision-making that has characterized these last five years; and second, to give full weight to the guideposts.

The general wage guidepost states that the annual rate of increase of total employee compensation (wages and fringe benefits) per manhour worked should not exceed the national trend rate of increase in output per manhour. If wages follow this guidepost, average unit labor costs in the economy will remain stable—the most fundamental for a requisite for price stability.

The general guidepost for prices states that prices should remain stable in those industries where the increase of productivity equals the national trend; that prices can appropriately rise in those industries where the increase of productivity is smaller than the national trend; and that prices should fall in those industries where the increase in productivity exceeds the national trend. In essence, it says that prices can be expected to rise in low productivity industries where labor costs will be rising; that prices should fall in high productivity industries on the basis of their falling labor costs.

Some exceptions to these general guideposts have always been recognized. On the wage side, increases beyond the 3.2% general guidepost may be desirable for an industry to attract its necessary share of the labor force, or to bring up wages if they are near the bottom of the economy's wage scales, or to help defray the human costs associated with productivity boosting changes in work rules. This year's Economic Report adds, "Because the industries in which unions possess strong market power are largely high-wage industries in which job opportunities are relatively very attractive, the first two of these exceptions are rarely applicable."

On the price side, increases beyond the general guideposts "may be appropriate to reflect increases in unit material costs, to the extent that such increases are not offset by decreases in other costs, and significantly impair gross profit margins on the relevant range of products, or to correct an inability to attract needed capital." This year's Economic Report adds "the large firms to which guideposts are primarily addressed typically have ready access to sources of capital; moreover, the profits of virtually every industry have risen sharply and are at record levels as a by-product of the general prosperity of the economy. The second exception is thus not widely applicable in the present environment."

These then are the guideposts. They were first spelled out in the Council's Economic Report of January 1962, and have been repeated each year since then. Both President Kennedy and President Johnson have endorsed them, and in his Economic Report this year the President appealed strongly to business and labor to adhere to their principles.

From confrontation to accommodation

The guideposts, like any new social instrument, are gradually evolving as we accumulate experience and understanding. In their early years the role of the guideposts was mainly educational. They taught business that not all wage increases are inflationary, but only those which exceed the rate of increase of productivity. They taught labor that wages are not only income, but also costs. And they taught all Americans that a rising price level serves no purpose and that a stable price level requires stable unit labor costs and appropriate price decreases to offset necessary price increases.

While the economy had general slack in product and labor markets, this general educational role sufficed. The guideposts were breached occasionally, and sometimes in quite important situations, but the overall record of wages and prices so closely corresponded to the guideposts that one could take deep satisfaction in it.

As the economy approached full utilization of its potential, and particularly when the commitment of resources for Vietnam became large, the government's concern had to be expressed more directly. In the steel negotiations last summer the government helped to achieve a guidepost settlement. And in the several episodes in metal prices last fall and winter the government made its concern with stability of basic industrial prices very clear.

These government interventions created considerable uncertainty and led to some criticism of the guideposts. But I think this was a transitional phase. Both sides have learned a great deal about guideposts: government about operating them without creating unnecessary uncertainty; business about achieving desirable changes of relative prices while following guidepost principles. The two sides have learned from each other and have acquired a finer appreciation of each other's problems and viewpoints.

I doubt that we shall see many more confrontations that make banner headlines. I do expect that business and government will increase their informal contacts, that understanding of price behavior within the guideposts will become general. In other words, I expect that the contribution of guideposts to industrial price stability will continue and even become greater, but through a spirit of partnership and harmony. Of course, for guideposts to play this role, overall fiscal and monetary policy must contain the total demand within the economy's capacity to produce, and the extremes of sectoral imbalance must be avoided.

On the labor side, guideposts have not moved toward sweetness and light within the last few months. To be sure, the labor movement has never endorsed guideposts, and indeed has periodically criticized them throughout their existence. Nonetheless, the guideposts have been a very real factor in a number of important labor negotiations, and I am sure that they will play an increasingly important role.

The present discontent of the labor movement with guideposts is easy to understand. First, the necessity of formulating fair labor standards policy within the guidepost framework—even with some allowance for the low-wage exception—runs counter to labor's normal aspirations. Second, the unwillingness of Congress to repeal Section 14b of the Taft-Hartley Act has reduced the spirit of cooperation in the labor movement. Finally, and most fundamentally, during these five years of expansion the rate of profit per unit of capital has increased substantially more than the rate of wages paid per hour. This disparity is inevitable during a period of cyclical recovery, for profits always fluctuate more than wages: they fall more in recession, rise more in expansion. The guideposts are geared to long-term trends. With wages rising by the long-term productivity trend and prices stable on the average, a cyclical swing in the distribution of income between profits and wages is to be expected.

Now that the economy has completed its cyclical recovery, little further change in the division of income between profits and wages can be expected to occur within the guideposts. This source of friction should therefore disappear. Should the rates of return continue to outstrip wages, it would be evidence that guideposts are not working on the price side.

Labor, like business, understands that the continuation of the five years of uninterrupted progress depends upon the preservation of general price-cost stability. As tempers cool and the risks to prosperity become clear, a rapprochement between labor and the Administration on the guidepost question is the most sensible policy. There is as much need to move from confrontation to accommodation on the labor side as has already occurred on the business side.

If unemployment were pushed back over 5%, and remained there as it did for seven years, there would be no general wage pressures to raise labor costs. And if the operating rates of industry were kept half a dozen points below the preferred rates, there would be little pressure on prices. But we have seen the cost of running the economy at such slack. Our unemployment contributed importantly to many of our social problems. Depressed profits and limited markets retarded the rate of investment in the country's future.

Alternatives to guideposts

The guideposts may fail because of misunderstanding, or inability or unwillingness of private and public leadership to generally abide by them. But make no mistake: we shall all be the worse for it. No incantation of the theories appropriate to an atomistic society of tiny business enterprises and unorganized workers is going to solve this problem. If guideposts are not pleasing, we must turn to alternative approaches. What are the alternatives?

One view occasionally advanced is to relax and enjoy it, suffer a bit of inflation, and reduce the social injustices by tying all forms of income to the rising cost of living. For example, wage contracts would generally contain escalator clauses. Social security would rise by formula, and so on.

This is not only bad, but indeed impossible advice to follow. Our balance of payments cannot stand a rising cost structure at this time. The dollar remains in deficit. We are in the middle of important international negotiations to reform the monetary system, and the United States must deal from strength in these negotiations. A stable price-cost situation is fundamental to our international financial strength. Further, such a situation could easily deteriorate into accelerating inflation.

Another alternative—and the most respectable in academic circles—is to convert the economy to perfect competition through escalated anti-trust policies and other measures. If the economy has cost-push problems, if there is ability to exercise market power to raise prices and wages even when demand does not exceed supply, then break up these concentrations, so it is argued. Now I believe in a firm, solid anti-trust policy. It has played a large role in restraining the growth of monopoly. But it is a wholly unrealistic—and indeed a very radical—counsel to suggest that the gigantic enterprises of our economy should be broken up. This economy relies on our large corporate firms to channel much of its savings into productive investments, to search out new growth opportunities, to make innovations and to operate the large scale productive units which technology requires in many fields. To urge that we break up these enterprises is to propose a change in our economic system far more fundamental than any that has occurred in this century. It would move us into unknown territory which would have new problems that we cannot foresee. It is a solution far more radical than the guideposts. As the Economic Report of 1965 stated, the guideposts "are an attempt to operate our economy as it is—without controls, without wholesale fragmentation of our large, successful enterprises."

Finally, controls are another solution, by direct regulation of wages and prices. The situation today is very far from the sort that would call for this form of intervention. The projected build-up spending for Vietnam still would leave the total commitment of resources at about 1½% of the GNP, hardly an amount that would require putting the entire economy in a strait-jacket.

Some people maintain that even guideposts constitute controls, but this is altogether an unrealistic view. Let me illustrate with an example: During the Korean War the Economic Stabilization Agency had 16,000 employees, and there were other agencies to help them stabilize prices and wages. The entire staff of the Council of Economic Advisers, the agency with the most direct responsibility for giving guidepost advice, is less than 40 people, and it has many other responsibilities. There are no formal reporting requirements on business or labor, no paper work, nothing but a plea to responsible people to consider the national interest in making key decisions.

When you look at the alternatives, guideposts look pretty good.

Readings 81, 82, and 83   Debate on Monetarism

What the Lincoln-Douglas debates were in politics, the 1968 Heller-Friedman debate at N.Y.U. was to modern economics. Both men are eloquent and witty speakers. Each represents a point of view. The audience got its money's worth. But brilliance of the repartee does not make a science. Therefore, reproduced below are not the pyrotechnics of the N.Y.U. debate, but rather the solid and substantive writings of Friedman and Heller—and also a brief Samuelson summing up for an English audience.

We have already met in Readings 32 and 33 by Friedman and Samuelson a discussion of the Quantity Theory of Money and its limitations. Before 1929 most economists thought there was nothing to macroeconomics except the Quantity Theory. Then during the Great Depression of the 1930s, fiscal policy was discovered, and in the extreme form of the Keynesian system it was believed that money did not matter. That this belief still lingers on in England is shown by the Radcliffe Committee Report of 1959, in which scorn was shown for the role of money. Actually, however, post-Keynesians (and for that matter Lord Keynes himself) stressed in an eclectic fashion the vital importance of *both* monetary and fiscal policy.

Professor Friedman has been led by his scholarly studies to reject this eclectic view. The present account summarizes his broad findings on the role of money. Having no hesitation in setting himself up as a target, he insisted that to affect aggregate dollar demand, only money matters—not fiscal policy, not budget policy, not tax-rate policy, and (in other than the shortest-run) not public expenditure policy. At N.Y.U. he said, "I believe . . . the government budget . . . matters a great deal—for some things . . . [for] what fraction of the nation's income is spent through the government . . . [for] the level of our taxes. . . . If the federal government runs a large deficit, that . . . tends to raise interest rates." [But here is Friedman's] "main point— in my opinion, the state of the budget by itself has no significant effect on the course of nominal [i.e., money] income, on inflation, on deflation, or on cyclical fluctuations." No statement could be more clear-cut, but to clarify exactly the sense in which it is money alone that is alleged to matter for inflation and deflation, Friedman explains: "The crucial words . . . are 'by itself' because the whole problem of interpretation is precisely that you are always having changes in monetary policy [and at the same time] changes in fiscal policy. And if you want to think clearly about the two sepa- rately, you must somehow try to separate the influence of fiscal policy from the influence of monetary policy. The question you want to ask yourself is, 'Is what happened to the government budget the major factor that produced a particular change, or is it what happened to monetary variables?' " These quotations, which are from pages 50–51 of the Friedman-Heller debate, are reinforced on pages 60–62 by reference to a November, 1968 statistical study by the Federal Reserve Bank of St. Louis. This Andersen-Jordan study, using multiple-correlation techniques, concluded that GNP changes were sig- nificantly affected by lagged *M* changes, but insignificantly affected by tax- rate changes; and the positive effects of recent public-expenditure changes were washed out by negative effects in the longer run. (See also the Samuel- son Reading 33 for more detailed evaluation of monetarism.)

Walter Heller at N.Y.U. correctly fingered the key contention of "mone- tarism" as against "eclectic post-Keynesianism," saying: "At the outset, let's clarify what is and what isn't at issue in today's discussion of fiscal-monetary policy. The issue is not whether money matters—we all grant that—but whether *only* money matters [for inflation], as some Friedmanites, or perhaps I should say Fieldmanics, would put it." And, in the following passage from Heller's widely read 1966 Godkin Lectures at Harvard, he summarizes the positive case for fiscal policy in affecting aggregate demand over and beyond its associated monetary concomitants.

Heller argues that *both* fiscal and monetary policies count for inflation- deflation analysis. He criticizes automatic reliance on a rigid monetary rule, in which the Federal Reserve keeps some *M* magnitude always growing at some fixed rate—say, 4 to 5 per cent per annum, and does nothing else.

Milton Friedman has already been identified in Reading 32. Dr. Heller is a Regent Professor at the University of Minnesota. From 1961 to 1965 he was chairman of the Kennedy and Johnson Council of Economic Advisers, and is widely regarded as the spokesman for the "New Economics." As a scholar, Dr. Heller is an expert in the field of public finance and co-author of the Heller-Pechman-Friedman plan for automatic tax-revenue sharing by the fed- eral government with the state and localities.

Questions to Guide the Reading

Can you check off those sentences in the Friedman argument which are evidence for the view that it is *only* money that matters for the purpose of appraising the aggregate of inflationary or deflationary spending? Could every one of his allegations be true and still not prove the impotence of fiscal policy or the unimportance of nonmonetary disturbances in creating business instability? If the causal mechanisms of monetarism were true, do you think a strong case could be made for departing from a steady growth in the money supply in favor of a policy of "leaning against the wind"—i.e., expanding money faster when the year ahead looked to be one of too little demand and slowing down money growth when the year ahead looked to be one of too much inflation? What proofs are offered for the assertion that steadiness is the best policy under all circumstances?

Should the wit and eloquence of a speaker be important in judging the merits of his case? Is economics an exact science so that a controlled experiment can be made to see how much (a) fiscal and (b) monetary variables were responsible for the long expansion of the 1960s? Can statistics take the place of controlled experiments? Does correlation prove causation? To get a fair hearing for money, may one have to exaggerate its importance? If M's effects are not perfectly predictable, does Heller agree that a fixed rate of growth of M is the best feasible rule?

Is the debate "much ado about nothing" in view of Dr. Friedman's 1970 statement: "Of the instruments available to the government to affect normal income, I believe that changes in the quantity of money are far and away the most important." But that is a far cry from saying that they are the unique cause.

Reading 81

Monetarism, Yes

Milton Friedman

Long-run money-price relations

There is perhaps no empirical regularity among economic phenomena that is based on so much evidence for so wide a range of circumstances as the connection between substantial changes in the stock of money and in the level of prices. To the best of my knowledge *there is no instance in which a substantial change in the stock of money per unit of output has occurred without a substantial change in the level of prices in the same direction.* Conversely, I know of no instance in which there has been a substantial change in the level of prices without a substantial change in the stock of money per unit of output in the same direction. And instances in which prices and the stock of money have moved together are recorded for many centuries of history, for countries in every part of the globe, and for a wide diversity of monetary arrangements.

There can be little doubt about this statistical connection. The statistical connection itself, however, tells nothing about direction of influence, and it is on this question that there has been the most controversy. It could be that a rise or fall in prices, occurring for whatever reasons, produces a corresponding rise or fall in the stock of money, so that the monetary changes are a passive consequence. Alternatively, it could be that changes in the stock of money produce changes in prices in the same direction, so that control of the stock of money would imply control of prices. The variety of monetary arrangements for which a connection between monetary and price movements has been observed supports strongly the second interpretation, namely, that substantial changes in the stock of money are both a necessary and a sufficient condition for substantial changes in the general level of prices. But of course this does not exclude a reflex influence of changes

From *The Relationship of Prices to Economic Stability and Growth*, 85th Congress, 2nd Session, Joint Economic Committee Print, Washington, D.C.: U.S. Government Printing Office (1958).

in prices on the stock of money. This reflex influence is often important, almost always complex, and, depending on the monetary arrangements, may be in either direction.

The relationship between changes in the stock of money and changes in prices, while close, is not of course precise or mechanically rigid. Two major factors produce discrepancies: changes in output, and changes in the amount of money that the public desires to hold relative to its income.

A wide range of empirical evidence suggests that the ratio which people desire to maintain between their cash balances and their income is relatively stable over fairly long periods of time aside from the effect of two major factors:
(1) The level of real income per capita, or perhaps of real wealth per capita;
(2) the cost of holding money.

The cost of holding cash balances depends mainly on the rate of interest that can be earned on alternative assets—thus if a bond yields 4 per cent while cash yields no return, this means that an individual gives up $4 a year if he holds $100 of cash instead of a bond—and on the rate of change of prices—if prices rise at 5 per cent per year, for example, $100 in cash will buy at the end of the year only as much as $95 at the beginning so that it has cost the individual $5 to hold $100 of cash instead of goods. The empirical evidence suggests that while the first factor—the interest rate—has a systematic effect on the amount of money held, the effect is rather small. The second factor, the rate of change of prices, has no discernible effect in ordinary times when price changes are small—on the order of a few per cent a year. On the other hand, it has a clearly discernible and major effect when price change is rapid and long continued, as during extreme inflations or deflations. A rapid inflation produces a sizable decline in the desired ratio of cash balances to income; a rapid deflation, a sizable rise.

Short-run money-price relations

Over the longer periods considered in the preceding sections, changes in the stock of money per unit of output tend to dominate price changes, allowance being made for the effect of the growth of real income per head. This is less so over the shorter periods involved in the fluctuations we term business cycles, though the general and average relationship is very similar. The reason for the looser connection in such periods presumably is that movements in both the stock of money and in prices are smaller. Over longer periods, these movements cumulate and tend to swamp any disturbance in the relation between desired cash balances, real income, and the cost of holding money; in the ordinary business cycle, the disturbances, though perhaps no more important in an absolute sense, are much more important relative to the movements in money and prices.

There can be little doubt on the basis of this evidence that there is a close link between monetary changes and price changes over the shorter periods within which business cycles run their course as well as over longer periods and during major wartime episodes. But important considerations must be borne in mind if this fact is not to be a misleading guide to policy. [One] has to do with the timing of the changes in the money supply and in income and prices. The generally upward trend in the money supply which accounts for its continuing to rise, though at a slower rate, during most contractions in economic activity as well as during expansions makes it difficult to judge timing relations from ups and downs in the money supply itself. For this and other reasons, we have found it most useful to examine instead the ups and downs in the rate at which the money supply is changing. The rate of change of the money supply shows well-marked cycles that match closely those in economic activity in general and precede the latter by a long interval. On the average, *the rate of change of the money supply* has reached its *peak nearly 16 months before the peak in general business and has reached its trough over 12 months before the trough in general business.*

This is strong though not conclusive evidence for the independent influence of monetary change. But it also has a very different significance. It means that it must take a long time for the influence of monetary changes to make themselves felt—apparently what happens now to the rate of change of the money supply may not be reflected in prices or economic activity *for 12 to 16 months, on the average.* Moreover, the timing varies considerably from cycle to cycle—since 1907, the shortest time span by which the money peak preceded the business cycle peak was 13 months, the longest, 24 months; the corresponding range at troughs is 5 months to 21 months. From the point of view of scientific analysis directed at establishing economic regularities on the basis of the historical record —the purpose for which the measures were computed—this is highly consistent behavior; it justifies considerable confidence in the reliability of the averages cited and means that they cannot easily be attributed simply to the accident of chance variation. But *from the point of view of policy directed at controlling a particular movement such as the current recession, the timing differences are disturbingly large*—they mean that monetary action taken today may, on the basis of past experience, affect economic activity within 6 months or again perhaps not for over a year and 6 months; and of course past experience is not exhaustive; the particular episode may establish a new limit in either direction.

The long time lag has another important effect. It leads to misinterpretation and misconception about the effects of monetary policy, as well as to consequent mistakes in monetary policy. Because the effects of monetary change do not occur instantaneously, monetary policy is regarded as ineffective.

Output relations

Over the cycle, prices and output tend to move together—both tend to rise during expansions and to fall during contractions. Both are part of the cyclical process and anything, including a monetary change, that promotes a vigorous expansion is likely to promote a vigorous rise in both and conversely. Over the longer period, the relation between price changes and output changes is much less clear. Now this seems clearly valid, not only as an expository device but also as a first approximation to reality. What happens to a nation's output over long periods of time depends in the first instance on such basic factors as resources available, the industrial organization of the society, the growth of knowledge and technical skills, the growth of population, the accumulation of capital and so on. This is the stage on which money and price changes play their parts as the supporting cast.

One proposition about the effect of changes in the stock of money and in prices that is widely accepted and hardly controversial is that large and unexpected changes in prices are adverse to the growth of output—whether these changes are up or down. At one extreme, the kind of price rise that occurs during hyperinflation seriously distorts the effective use of resources.[1] At the other extreme, sharp price declines such as occurred from 1920 to 1921 and again from 1929 to 1933 certainly produce a widespread and tragic waste of resources.

So much is agreed. The more controversial issue is the effect of moderate change in prices. One view that is widely held is that slowly rising prices stimulate economic output and produce a more rapid rate of growth than would otherwise occur. A number of reasons have been offered in support of this view. (1) Prices, and particularly wages, are, it is said, sticky. In a market economy, the reallocation of resources necessitated by economic growth and development requires changes in relative prices and relative wages. It is much easier, it is argued, for these to come about without friction and resistance if they can occur through rises in some prices and wages without declines in others. If prices were stable, some changes in relative wages could still come about in this way, since economic growth means that wages tend to rise relative to prices, but changes in relative prices could not, and, of course, there would not be as much scope even for relative wage changes. (2) Costs, and in particular, wages, are, it is argued, stickier than selling prices. Hence generally rising prices will tend to raise profit margins, giving enterprises both a bigger incentive to raise output and to add to capital and the means to finance the capital needed. (3) The most recently popular variant of the preceding point is that costs are not only sticky against declines but in addition have a tendency to be pushed up with little reference to the state of demand as a result of strong trade unions. If the money stock is kept from rising, the result, it is claimed, will be unemployment as profit

[1] However, even open hyperinflations are less damaging to output than suppressed inflations in which a wide range of prices are held well below the levels that would clear the market. The German hyperinflation after World War I never caused anything like the reduction of production that was produced in Germany from 1945 to the monetary reform of 1948 by the suppression of inflation. And the inflationary pressure suppressed in the second case was a small fraction of that manifested in the first.

margins are cut, and also a higher level of prices, though not necessarily a rising level of prices. Gently rising prices, it is argued, will tend to offset this upward pressure by permitting money wages to rise without real wages doing so. (4) Interest rates are particularly slow to adapt to price rises. If prices are rising at, say, 3 per cent a year, a 6 per cent interest rate on a money loan is equivalent to a 3 per cent rate when prices are stable. If lenders adjusted fully to the price rise, this would simply mean that interest rates would be 3 percentage points higher in the first case than in the second. But in fact this does not happen, so that productive enterprises find the cost of borrowing to be relatively low, and again have a greater incentive than otherwise to invest, and the associated transfer from creditors to debtors gives them greater means to do so.

In opposition to this view, it has been argued that generally rising prices reduce the pressure on enterprises to be efficient, stimulate speculative relative to industrial activity, reduce the incentives for individuals to save, and make it more difficult to maintain the appropriate structure of relative prices, since individual prices have to change in order to stay the same relative to others. Furthermore, it is argued that once it becomes widely recognized that prices are rising, the advantages cited in the preceding paragraph will disappear: escalator clauses or their economic equivalent will eliminate the stickiness of prices and wages and the greater stickiness of wages than of prices; strong unions will increase still further their wage demands to allow for price increases; and interest rates will rise to allow for the price rise. If the advantages are to be obtained, the rate of price rise will have to be accelerated and there is no stopping place short of runaway inflation.

Historical evidence on the relation between price changes and output changes is mixed and gives no clear support to any of these positions. All in all, perhaps the only conclusion that is justified is that either rising prices or falling prices are consistent with rapid economic growth, provided that the price changes are fairly steady, moderate in size, and reasonably predictable. The mainsprings of growth are presumably to be sought elsewhere. But unpredictable and erratic changes of direction in prices are apparently as disturbing to economic growth as to economic stability.

Policy implications

Past experience suggests that something like a 3 to 5 per cent per year increase in the stock of money is required for long-term price stability. For cyclical movements, a major problem is to prevent monetary changes from being a source of disturbance. If the stock of money can be kept growing at a relatively steady rate, without erratic fluctuations in short periods, it is highly unlikely if not impossible that we would experience either a sharp price rise—like that during World Wars I and II and after World War I—or a substantial price or output decline—like those experienced from 1920–21, 1929–33, 1937–38.

A steady rate of growth in the money supply will not mean perfect stability even though it would prevent the kind of wide fluctuations that we have experienced from time to time in the past. It is tempting to try to go farther and to use monetary changes to offset other factors making for expansion and contraction. The available evidence casts grave doubts on the possibility of producing any fine adjustments in economic activity by fine adjustments in monetary policy—at least in the present state of knowledge.

There are thus serious limitations to the possibility of a discretionary monetary policy and much danger that such a policy may make matters worse rather than better. Federal Reserve policy since 1951 has been distinctly superior to that followed during any earlier period since the establishment of the System, mainly because it has avoided wide fluctuations in the rate or growth of the money supply. At the same time, I am myself inclined to believe that in our present state of knowledge and with our present institutions, even this policy has been decidedly inferior to the much simpler policy of keeping the money supply growing at a predesignated rate month in and month out with allowance only for seasonal influences and with no attempt to adjust the rate of growth to monetary conditions.[2]

To avoid misunderstanding, it should be

[2] The extensive empirical work that I have done has given me no reason to doubt that the simple policy suggested above would produce a very tolerable amount of stability. This evidence has persuaded me that the major problem is to prevent monetary changes from themselves contributing to instability rather than to use monetary changes to offset other forces.

emphasized that the problems just discussed are in no way peculiar to monetary policy. Fiscal action also involves lags. Indeed the lag between the recognition of need for action and the taking of action is undoubtedly longer for discretionary fiscal than for discretionary monetary action: the monetary authorities can act promptly, fiscal action inevitably involves serious delays for congressional consideration. Hence the basic difficulties and limitations of monetary policy apply with equal force to fiscal policy.

Political pressures to "do something" in the face of either relatively mild price rises or relatively mild price and employment declines are clearly very strong indeed in the existing state of public attitudes. The main moral to be drawn from the two preceding points is that *yielding to these pressures may frequently do more harm than good.* The goal of an extremely high degree of economic stability is certainly a splendid one; our ability to attain it, however, is limited; we can surely avoid extreme fluctuations; we do not know enough to avoid minor fluctuations; the attempt to do more than we can will itself be a disturbance that may increase rather than reduce instability. But like all such injunctions, this one too must be taken in moderation. It is a plea for a sense of perspective and balance, not for irresponsibility in the face of major problems or for failure to correct past mistakes.

Reading 82

Both Fiscal and Monetary Policy, Yes

Walter W. Heller

The new look in fiscal policy

Reorienting policy targets and strategy to the economy's full and growing potential yielded new norms for stabilization policy, especially in its fiscal aspects.

Gap-closing and growth. This, rather than the smoothing of the business cycle became the main preoccupation of policy, its broader guide to action. As we put it in our January 1962 *Annual Report:* "The mandate of the Employment Act renews itself perpetually as maximum levels of production, employment, and purchasing power rise through time. The weapons of stabilization policy—the budget, the tax system, control of the supply of money and credit—must be aimed anew, for their target is moving."

Fiscal drag. The moment the upward-moving target was recognized, three things became clear.

First, the traditional thinking that tended to identify prosperity with a rising economy often gave the wrong signals to fiscal policy, calling for a cut-off of its stimulus long before the production gap was closed, long before full employment was reached. Part of the critical barrage that greeted Kennedy's tax-cut proposal early in 1963 was based on this failure to distinguish between the *direction* of the economy, which was up, and its *level*, which was still far below its capabilities.

Second, the vaunted "built-in flexibility" of our tax system, its automatic stabilizing effect, is a mixed blessing. True, it cushions recessions, which is good. But left to its own devices it also retards recovery by cutting into the growth of private income, which is bad—at least until the production gap is closed and inflation threatens.

Third, in a growth context, the great revenue-raising power of our Federal tax system produces a built-in average increase of $7 to $8 billion a year in Federal revenues (net of the automatic increase in transfer payments). Unless it is offset by such "fiscal dividends" as tax cuts or expansion of Federal programs, this automatic rise in revenues will

From Walter W. Heller, *New Dimensions of Political Economy,* which constituted the Godkin Lectures at Harvard University (Harvard University Press, Cambridge, Mass. 1966), pp. 64–66, 68–70, 79, 116. Copyright © 1966 by the President and Fellows of Harvard College. Reprinted with kind permission of the author and publisher.

become a "fiscal drag" siphoning too much of the economic substance out of the private economy and thereby choking expansion.

Fiscal dividends. A central part of the job of fiscal policy is precisely this delicate one of declaring fiscal dividends of the right size and timing to avoid fiscal drag without inviting inflation. In an overheated economy, the fiscal drag that develops when fiscal dividends are *not* declared is a welcome antidote to inflation. When recession threatens, an extra dividend is appropriate. But in normal times we must close the fiscal loop by matching the annual $7 to $8 billion of revenue growth with tax cuts, increased expenditures (including social security benefits), and more generous support to state and local governments.

Full-employment (or high-employment) surplus. As part of the reshaping of stabilization policy, then, our fiscal-policy targets have been recast in terms of "full" or "high" employment levels of output, specifically the level of GNP associated with a 4-percent rate of unemployment. So the target is no longer budget balance every year or over the cycle, but balance (in the national-income-accounts, or NIA, budget) at full employment.

•

New performance

Operationally, training our sights on specified full-employment targets led to several significant changes in fiscal strategy.

First, it became more activist and bolder. Feeding fiscal stimulus into a briskly rising economy—typified by the Berlin defense build-up without a tax increase in 1961 and, even more, by the huge tax cut in 1964—is now seen as a prudent response to the needs of an expanding economy that is still operating well below its full potential.

Second, it follows that fiscal strategy has to rely less on the automatic stabilizers and more on discretionary action responding to observed and forecast changes in the economy—less on rules and more on men.

Third, under the new approach, not only monetary policy but fiscal policy has to be put on constant, rather than intermittent, alert. Since 1961, there have been almost continuous official consideration and public debate over tax cuts and expenditure increases to stimulate the economy or, since late 1965, tax increases

or expenditure cuts to curb inflation. Clearly, the management of prosperity is a full-time job.

In part, this shift from a more passive to a more active policy has been made possible by steady advances in fact-gathering, forecasting techniques, and business practice. Our statistical net is now spread wider and brings in its catch faster. Forecasting has the benefit of not only more refined, computer-assisted methods, but of improved surveys of consumer and investment intentions. And the advances made in strategic planning and systematic analysis in business are building a better base for forecasting the inventory and capital-spending sector of the GNP.

At the same time, the margin for error diminishes as the economy reaches the treasured but treacherous area of full employment. Big doses of expansionary medicine were easy—and safe—to recommend in the face of a $50 billion gap and a hesitant Congress. But at full employment, targets have to be defined more sharply, tolerances are smaller, the line between expansion and inflation becomes thinner. So in a full employment world the economic dosage has to be much more carefully controlled, the premium on quantitative scientific knowledge becomes far greater, and the premium on speed in our fiscal machinery also rises.

The decline of the doctrinaire

But the record of the 1961–1966 experience in putting modern economics to work is not to be read solely in the statistics of sustained expansion or in critics confounded. An important part of the story is a new flexibility in the economic thinking of both liberals and conservatives. Both have been dislodged from their previously entrenched positions, their ideological foxholes, by the force of economic circumstance and the impact of policy success.

It is an escape from dogma. It is a realization that, in President Kennedy's words, "What is at stake in our economic decisions today is, not some grand warfare of rival ideologies which will sweep the country with passion, but the practical management of a modern economy."

The promise of modern economic policy, managed with an eye to maintaining prosperity, subduing inflation, and raising the quality of life, is indeed great. And although we have made no startling conceptual breakthroughs in economics in recent years, we *have*, more effectively than ever before, harnessed the existing economics—the economics that has been taught in the nation's college classrooms for some twenty years—to the purposes of prosperity, stability, and growth. As we have seen, we cannot relax our efforts to increase the technical efficiency of economic policy. But it is also clear that its promise will not be fulfilled unless we couple with improved techniques of economic management a determination to convert good economics and a great prosperity into a good life and a great society.

Reading 83
Monetarism Pure and Neat, No

Paul A. Samuelson

Monetary policy seems to have been underrated by British economists in recent decades. Now there seems to be a real danger that financial opinion is veering to the opposite extreme of a crude monetarism. And that would be a pity.

Rediscovery of money

The new impetus appears, in the first instance, to be an import from America. Money was, so to speak, "rediscovered" in my country around 1950. We are all post-Keynesians now. And that means, among other things, that we believe national income can be significantly affected by monetary as well as fiscal policy.

I believe this. Walter Heller, chief economic adviser to Presidents Kennedy and Johnson, believes it. Paul McCracken, newly appointed as chairman of Nixon's Council of Economic Advisers, believes in the potency of both tools of policy—monetary as well as fiscal.

I could go down the list of our experts. Professor Tobin of Yale. Professor Modigliani of M.I.T. All are agreed on this eclectic position.

The new prophet

All? Well, almost all. Professor Milton Friedman is an exception. His is a voice that says the rate of growth of the money supply is vastly more important than any changes in tax rates or fiscal expenditures. And Friedman's voice is like the voice of ten.

Like Billy Graham, Dr. Friedman has been making converts throughout the land. The Federal Reserve Bank of St. Louis has seen the light. Senator Proxmire's Joint Economic Committee has requested the Federal Reserve to keep the money supply growing within the range of 2 to 6 per cent per year.

At the First National City Bank in New York and the Harris Trust Company in Chicago, vice presidents prepare their forecasts on the basis of the New Quantity Theory of Money.

Within the academic community, Professors Allen Meltzer of Carnegie, Karl Brunner of Ohio State, Richard Seldon of Cornell, Phillip Cagan of the National Bureau of Economic Research and Columbia, all play up the importance of money.

At the distance of 3,000 miles, all this might look like the general American position and the wave of the future. In my view it is neither of those.

The brute facts

Let me review the evidence, very briefly—all too briefly.

First, the current strength of the American economy is indeed greater than was predicted by those who believed that fiscal restraint in the form of the 10 per cent mid-year tax surcharge would greatly slow up our rate of growth.

It is naive to infer from this that fiscal potency is nil, or that the discrepancy is explicable in terms of the New Quantity Theory, or the old one for that matter.

For every monetarist who predicted pretty much what happened, I can give you one who predicted greater current weakness than did

Abridged from Paul A. Samuelson, "Don't Make Too Much of the Quantity Theory" *London Sunday Telegraph*, December, 1968. Reprinted with kind permission of the publisher.

the fiscal enthusiasts; and another who declared that the divergences between growth rates of alternative definitions of the money supply make all predictions difficult. (The same diversity of analysis held for the slowdown following the 1966 "money crunch": some of the greatest errors in 1967 forecasts were made by Chicago economists. And, in 1970, one can add that 1969 forecasts by monetarists showed the same wide errors of estimate as other methods.)

Finally, there is the appeal to authority. None of the non-Chicago authorities have succumbed to the disease of monetarism. Not even one governor of the Federal Reserve Board can endorse its monism, and usually you can find one in seven in favour of anything.[1]

When Professor Friedman formulates his system in generality—with the velocity of cir-

[1] Paradoxically, the "Keynesians" on the Federal Reserve Board—Sherman Maisel and George Mitchell—are the advocates of having the agents of the Open-Market Committee replace chief reliance on "interest-rate and orderly-market-targets" by greater reliance on "aggregative" targets dealing with the M supply. I, as a Keynesian eclectic, also favor this—while rejecting pure "monetarism."

culation of money a function of the rate of interest and all the rest—it coincides with the post-Keynesianism of the Tobin-Modligliani type. When he speaks less guardedly, the consensus is rudely shattered.

It was in connection with such less-guarded utterances that Professor Tobin once properly remarked—Proving that "Money does not matter" is false only proves that "Money does matter," not that "Money alone matters."

I may reverse the Tobin syllogism to point out the fundamental and fatal *non sequitur* of the Radcliffe Committee—Proving that "It is not money alone that matters (and matters in a simple quantity-theory proportionality)" does not at all establish the proposition that "Money does not matter."

Britain does seem in need of greater recognition that monetary and credit policies count, and can count for much.

But why should it be necessary to go overboard and import crude monetarism?

Gresham's Law does operate in the realm of ideology: "Strong ideology drives out weak —among the gullible, that is." But why fall into such company?

Reading 84

The number-one economist in the Nixon Administration is Paul McCracken, chairman of the Council of Advisers and E. E. Day University Professor at the Graduate School of Business Administration at the University of Michigan. Harvard-trained, Dr. McCracken perceived late the light from Chicago. The views expressed here represent the peak of Dr. McCracken's monetarist phase, from which some recession could be noted in his official utterances.

Questions to Guide the Reading
If fiscal and monetary variables swing greatly in system swings like 1921 and 1933, can we suppose that periodic lunacy is the real course of major business cycles? Did a majority of Congress, and all on the Federal Reserve Board, lose their senses for reasons of (a) sunspots, (b) random exogenous shocks, (c) mass hysteria? How can you reconcile the phrase "massive monetary blood-letting" with the actual historical fact that the "monetary base," the high-powered money described in Reading 29 and which monetarists hope to control, was in fact made to grow throughout the 1931–33 period when the overall M supply languished? Did bank failures have something to do with all this?

If "monetary policy establishes the level of business activity," why did McCracken and Nixon ask Congress to extend the tax surcharge to fight inflation (thereby differing in counsel from Dr. Friedman)? Can one be a monetarist without believing in monetarism? How did gradualism—so to speak, coarse rather than fine tuning—work out in the 1969 inflation?

Government Errors Destabilize the Essentially Stable Private Economy

Paul McCracken

High on the list of deficiencies which economists share with Americans generally is *inattention* to the lessons of history. While we use statistics and other raw material of experience prodigiously, we are not much inclined to read the minutes of earlier meetings in order to gain some historical perspective about how we got to where we are. This is a pity because the record of our experience with the operation of economic policy provides us with some useful, and even surprising, lessons.

As we examine this record, one conclusion stands out sharply. *Fiscal and monetary policies have themselves been a major source of erratic movements in the economy,* and the first requirement for improving our economic performance is that these policies themselves be operated in a more even-handed and steady manner. Far from automating fiscal policy, this view of the problem will, if it is correct, require considerably more sophistication and precision than we have yet applied to the task.

Inherent stability

The prevailing concept about the nature of the problem of economic instability is itself a manifestation of our disinclination to examine history. We have tended to assume that ours is an economy with *strong indigenous tendencies to ricochet from boom to bust,* from overheating to unemployment, unless these inherent tendencies are neutralized by stabilizing economic policies. Our strategy, then, would be for these policies to zig or zag vigorously as the economy zags and zigs.

There is a good deal of historical evidence to suggest that this conception of the problem is close to being 180 degrees off course. It would be more in accord with the evidence of history to say that *we have had an economy with an impressive capacity to follow a course of vigorous and orderly expansion*—except when it has been deflated by a miscarriage of economic policy. Suppose that we explore this a bit to see whether it seems to square with the facts of history.

For several reasons it is useful here to begin with the pre-1929 era, specifically the four decades from 1889 to 1929. The period has certain natural advantages for our point. Annual data are reasonably available. We did not even have a central banking system for two-thirds of these years. During most of these four decades the federal budget was equal in magnitude to about 3 percent of GNP, so its inherent capacity to keep an erratic economy on a short leash would have been severely limited. In any case the concept of fiscal policy had not even been invented at this time. Thus we have here a segment of history during which we should be able to observe the private economy "in the raw" before the instruments of economic stabilization were really available to exert their "restraining" effects on its natural instability.

The National Bureau of Economic Research has decreed that there were twelve identifiable cyclical swings in this span of four decades. And there were eight years during which real output fell below that of the previous year. When we examine the data more closely, however, we discover some interesting things. The median decline for the recedence years was only 2.6 percent in real output. And in eight of the twelve recessions real output in the year containing the low point of the recession was higher than that for the year containing the previous peak.

The four more serious recessions were 1894, 1908, 1914, and 1921. The recession of 1908 was clearly associated with a major monetary panic, and the collapse of 1921 arose out of an overly expansionist set of policies through 1919, followed in 1920 by a drastic reversal of both monetary and fiscal policies. The remarkable thing here is not that there was a 1921 recession but that our economic system even survived this massive fiscal and monetary whipsaw.

Here clearly what we are observing is not an economy with some endemic case of the shakes, inherently tending to dash from the cellar to the penthouse. It is a record of sur-

From Paul McCracken, "Economic Policy and the Lessons of Experience," in *Republican Papers,* Melvin Laird (ed.), (Doubleday & Company, Inc., New York, 1968). Reprinted with kind permission of the author and editor.

prisingly orderly and sustained expansion, except when our foot was pressed too heavily on the accelerator or on the brake (often in quick succession).

The great twenties

The final decade of this period (i.e., 1922 to 1929) is particularly instructive here. Indeed, it is one of the ironies of history that this vastly underrated economic performance tends so often to be characterized as the era that landed us in the ditch of the Great Depression. Actually it was a period that lived up well to the Employment Act of 1946. Real output rose at the average rate of 4.7 percent per year and each year saw a rise. The price level was steady. And the unemployment rate averaged 3.6 percent.

This good economic performance was no accident. The money supply rose quite steadily at the average rate of 5.1 percent per year, and fiscal policy was also turning in an impressive performance. The *full employment surplus* (the difference between federal outlays and the receipts that the revenue system would produce at full employment) for fiscal years 1923 to 1930 apparently ranged from a low of about $0.7 billion in 1926 and 1929 to a high of just under $1 billion in 1930. The full employment surplus, in short, varied within a narrow range that was equal to roughly 0.3 percent of GNP. Thus the calibration of fiscal policy (which is, of course, analytically superior to actual surpluses as a measure of fiscal policy) shows a remarkable stability, with a full employment surplus of somewhat less than 1 percent of GNP during this period.

Washington-made depression

Though it has required about three decades to get the point in focus, we do now see that the Great Depression itself was also the result, particularly in the critical 1931 to 1933 phase, of our doing things wrong in the field of public policy virtually whenever there was an opportunity to do so. And we also now see that the catastrophe had nothing to do with any inherent or natural tendency of our economic system to operate at underemployment levels. What we had here was a massive monetary blood-letting. By 1933 the full-employ-

ment money supply would have been roughly 50 percent above actual levels, and our zeal for economic masochism had enabled us to accomplish the extraordinary feat of extinguishing 40 percent of our banks. (We had 25,000 banks in 1929, and we emerged in 1933 with about 15,000.)

Fiscal policy was also afflicted with its full share of gremlins in this unhappy period. The full employment surplus moved from a deficit to a modest surplus in the critical 1932–33 period, a "wrong" swing of close to 2 percent of GNP. And the swing in the full employment surplus from a deficit of roughly $2½ billion in 1936 to a surplus of less than $1 billion in 1937 (a perverse swing equal to about 4 percent of GNP) was certainly a major source of the downturn in 1937 that began before we had regained full employment—a downturn of great conceptual significance because it raised questions about the ability of our economy to sustain reasonably full employment.

Eisenhower economics

The long-sustained period of abnormally high employment from late 1957 to mid-1965 is, of course, another illustration of an *aberration* in our economic performance whose sources can be traced *to economic policy*. The glacial pace of monetary expansion from 1956 through 1959 (excluding a brief interlude early in 1958) was certainly a major factor. The money supply (including time deposits) from the end of 1955 to the end of 1959 was allowed to increase at the rate of 3.1 percent per year, considerably short of that required for the economy to keep on a growth path consistent with reasonably full utilization of our productive resources.

Fiscal policy also was allowed to wander off course in a major way. In the recedence phase fiscal policy actually was working well. The full employment surplus was declining rapidly to a $1–2 billion level by the end of 1958, and this contributed to the brevity of the decline and the strong subsequent upswing. At this point things began to develop less favorably. The full employment surplus then rose from this $1–2 billion annual rate at the end of 1958 to the $14 billion zone two years later. Monetary policy also turned severely restrictive as the money supply from mid-1958 to mid-1960 was permitted to increase at the rate of

2.4 percent per year—wholly inadequate for an economy whose basic capacity was rising then 3½–4 percent each year. Subjected to these fiscal and monetary drags, the economy faltered in 1960 before it achieved full employment. The administration's failure to provide leadership for a 1958 tax reduction cost the economy another recession (and its own party the White House in 1960). Here is a major lesson for the Republicans in the realities of political economy.

At the same time it must be remembered that this was an era of inflation-mindedness. The price level was rising at the rate of more than 3 percent per year. Of even greater significance was the surge of inflationary expectations, and decisions about things ranging from investments to the size of wage increases were being distorted accordingly. While fiscal and monetary policies did become too restrictive, a stern disinflationary policy was then in order, and it made a major (and underappreciated) contribution to the orderly subsequent expansion.

The new boosters

So much for a history that to some must seem ancient. Fortunately in recent years, some feel, the forces of darkness that produced these aberrant results have been dispersed. With the new economics we have ushered in an age of enlightenment. Since 1961, we have been told (about as often in lyric poetry as in prose) that the economic performance has been truly remarkable. Now it has been a better performance than we saw in the late 1950s. From 1960 to 1966 real output grew at the average annual rate of 4.8 percent per year—quite impressive for an economy whose long-run growth rate has been about 3½ percent. Moreover, there has been no recession since 1961 (though the expansion suffered a prolonged interruption in late 1962 and early 1963, and a recedence in the first half of 1967). And we had a major tax decrease in 1964 that clearly helped the economy to regain full employment somewhat over a year later.

Now it is not easy to gain perspective on the new economics. For one thing the precise substantive content of the phrase is astonishingly difficult to identify. There is certainly very little in its literature about objectives of economic policy that is new. Let me quote a sentence: "Government must use all practicable means to promote high levels of production and employment, and to contribute toward achieving an expanding and widely shared national income earned in dollars of stable buying power." The author of this sentence, which might have come even from New York's junior senator [Robert Kennedy], was actually a spokesman seemingly more benevolently disposed toward the Johnson administration—namely, the last Republican President in his 1957 Economic Report.

Nor have there been major innovations in the instruments of economic policy. The guidelines were a logical extension of increasing official attention before 1962 to the wage-price problem, but by 1967 they seemed to have a tenuous hold on official affection. There was a large tax reduction in 1964 that was needed and effective, equal in magnitude to 2.1 percent of 1965's GNP (the year in which the full reduction became effective). We have had, however, other tax cuts of similar relative magnitude. A decade earlier the $7.4 billion tax reduction was equal to 2.0 percent of 1954's GNP, and it was in the face of a substantial deficit in the budget. Moreover, it was made with the economic situation in mind—this according to no less a "new economist" than Secretary of the Treasury George M. Humphrey. Indeed, one of the best performances in tax reductions (or for fiscal policy generally) was in the mid-1920s when in three steps the revenue producing capability of the federal tax structure was reduced by $1.6 billion [by Republican Andrew Mellon]. Moreover, the full employment surplus from 1922 to 1929 was kept remarkably steady, moving within a quite narrow range. Indeed, by this important measure *fiscal policy was operated more expertly in the 1920s than in the 1960s.*

Post hoc, ergo . . .

For a time the main basis for claiming that our capacity to execute policy has improved dramatically in recent years has been simply the improved performance of the economy. This better performance must mean that policies have also been different and better. Undoubtedly our policy capabilities have improved. Hopefully we learn a few things as we go along. What needs far more critical evaluation, however, is precisely this basic premise that our performance in recent years has been so superior that it is out of context with our historical experience. This is not so obvious as it may seem. The average annual rate of growth in the 1920s was equal to that since 1960—4¾ percent per year in both cases. And we did at least that well for a period that was twice as long from 1895 to 1907 (both cyclical "peak" years).

The real point here, however, is something more fundamental than a crude comparison of growth rates. That the growth capability of the economy was going to be unusually high in the 1960s was determined less by the new economics than *by the birth statistics* following the war that made a rapid subsequent rise in labor force ineluctably certain. We are now in a period when the annual increments to the labor force are almost double their numbers

Average Annual Increase in the Labor Force (in thousands)

Period	Number
1950–60	810
1960–65	1,010
1965–75*	1,520

* Cf. "U. S. Economic Growth to 1975: Potentials and Problems," Joint Economic Committee (89th Congress, 2d Session, 1966), p. 11.
SOURCE: Basic data from Department of Labor.

in the 1950s, and there is some evidence [from Nicholas Kaldor] that the rate of growth in productivity is also favorably affected by the higher rate of growth in output made possible by the more rapidly enlarging labor force. The test of policy is how the economy operated relative to this more rapidly rising potential. And here the record since 1960 is simply not superior. In the low quarter of 1961, according to the Wharton index of capacity, the economy's operating rate was 80.5 percent. This was within a percentage point of the figure at the low point in 1949 and again in 1958, but it was below the 85.2 percent in the third quarter of 1954. The 1961 recession, in short, did not bring the economy's operating rate to a level unusually low by historical standards. Moreover, after the first year's improvement of the operating rate into early 1962, there was no further gain until the

second quarter of 1964. After the low point in 1961 the economy required sixteen quarters to accomplish a gain in its operating rate that required only four quarters in the post-1958 period—in both cases starting with about the same relative shortfall from par.

The reason why

When we realize this, the absence of a recession in the 1960s also takes on a somewhat different meaning. It arose in part out of the *unusually long, drawn-out path of the return to full employment,* and when full employment was finally achieved in the final quarter of 1965, some of the old problems again became visible. And they have been exacerbated by an *unusually erratic* course of policy in 1966 and 1967.

In 1965 as the economy was re-entering the zone of full employment fiscal and monetary policies should have become less expansive. Instead, they became more so. The rate of monetary expansion in 1965 accelerated from an 8.4 percent annual pace in the first half to a 10.6 percent rate in the second half. And the $8.6 billion full employment surplus (at an annual rate) in the first half of 1965 shifted to a small deficit in the second half—a $9 billion swing in the wrong direction.

Federal Reserve crimes coming and going

Then came the ill-fated January 1966 Budget Message, with its egregious underestimate of outlays, which immobilized fiscal policy and made it impossible to establish the case for a 1966 tax increase. Faced with an accelerating economy, the *Federal Reserve panicked in 1966 and jammed hard on the brakes.* There was an almost classic response. With the usual lag of two or three quarters, the economy in 1967 faltered—with enough weaknesses to have produced a recession except for rapidly rising federal outlays (heavily for national security). During 1967, as if to cancel one error with another, the Federal Reserve allowed the money supply to increase at a 12–14 percent rate—twice the economy's growth capability. And we now confront a budget for FY 1968 in a state of fundamental disequilibrium—with a prospective deficit that may be in the $20 billion range. These policies now expose us to a baleful combination of upward pressures on the price level, floundering credit markets, a major disequilibrium in our balance of payments and demands for direct controls. Some may be tempted to conclude that those now in charge of policy are simply less expert practitioners of economic policy than their predecessors in the early 1960s. Not necessarily. *Those in the early 1960s had a far easier task than they readily admit.* The disinflation of 1958–60 had established the basis for an orderly expansion. What then happened to be needed were expansive policies—which are also popular.

The real point is more fundamental. Departures from the full employment growth path have had their origins primarily in the erratic management of economic policy, and this has its manifestations in the era of the new economics as well as earlier. The first great hope for a steadier course of economic expansion is, therefore, a steadier and more even-handed management of economic policy.

A monetarist, I—almost

It is opened up by the fact that the *relationship between the money supply and GNP is fairly stable through time.* During the last decade the ratio of the money supply to GNP averaged 43.3 percent, and only 1958 of the eleven years from 1957 to 1967 turned in a ratio deviating from this average by more than one percentage point.[1] If we calibrate monetary ease or tightness by the rate of monetary expansion, we have an unambiguous measure. A more rapid rate of monetary expansion is an easier monetary policy than a policy permitting a slower expansion. Thus monetary policy was tightening in 1966 because the rate of monetary expansion was reduced, *not because interest rates were rising.* And monetary policy became easier in the second half of 1965 *because the rate of monetary expansion was allowed to accelerate,* even though interest rates were also rising.

Since the economy is not apt to stray far from the trail being blazed earlier by the pace of monetary expansion, we must then be careful in our use of such concepts as "easier fiscal policy and tighter credit policy." A tighter

[1] Even on a first difference basis, lagged quarterly changes in the money supply explain statistically about 44 percent of the changes in GNP.

monetary policy in the sense of a reduced pace of monetary expansion is apt to slow the economy even if fiscal policy is eased in the sense of reducing the full employment surplus. *Indeed, we could almost say that monetary policy establishes the level of business activity, and fiscal policy influences such financial matters as money and capital market conditions and the level of interest rates.*

Now this is not to say that a change in fiscal policy has *no* effect on the level of business activity. It can *help* to activate an expansion or to cool off an overheated economy. The effect of, for example, an easier fiscal policy may work itself out through a reduced propensity to hold money (*though the ongoing tolerances here are small*), or it may force or enable the pursuit of a more rapid monetary expansion.

Fine tuning out, gradualism in

Much of the discussion in recent years about strengthening the capability of policy to stabilize the economy has been in terms of introducing greater flexibility—e.g., giving the President limited power over tax rates. These proposals have merit. Most important ones would require approval of the Congress, however, and the Congress has seemed fully capable of restraining its enthusiasm about these suggestions. Moreover, the theory of strategy often implied here is that the primary task of policy is to dash about quelling uprisings whose origins are in the private economy. This is based on a faulty premise, and it is too crude and primitive a strategy for the modern economy.

Since a major source of departures from the path of vigorous and orderly growth and reasonably full employment has been the fitful and spasmodic behavior of fiscal and monetary policies, the most fundamental requirement for orderly movement along the full-employment growth path is that fiscal and monetary policies themselves pursue a more steadfast course. It is here that the greatest gains are to be had, and fortunately this does not involve colliding with any great constitutional issues such as the doctrine of the separation of powers. Moreover, it is worth repeating that this is not a recommendation for abdication to automaticity. It is a call for learning to operate these instruments of policy with more sophistication and exactitude, and within substantially narrower tolerances, than in the past.

If we can keep expenditures in reasonably close balance with revenues that the tax system will generate at full employment, and if the course of monetary expansion also moves more steadily along the full employment growth path, we can reasonably expect that the economy will come even closer to a course broadly consistent with utilizing all of our "plans, functions, and resources . . . to promote maximum employment, production, and purchasing power."

Reading 85

If an ignoramus in economics says that the current economic system cannot be interpreted as a rational scheme, that is nothing. But if one of the greatest analytical economists of our era says this, she is worth listening to. Joan Robinson, Professor of Economics at Cambridge University, won fame young as one of the inventors of the theory of imperfect competition. She consolidated her worldwide reputation by becoming one of the leading contributors to the Keynesian macroeconomic literature. Perhaps the most searching criticism of the Marxian system of economics has come from her pen, and in recent decades Mrs. Robinson has been an important pioneer and critic of growth models. For any of these accomplishments she might well be awarded the Nobel prize in Economics.

Professor Robinson dislikes inequality. If in the past inequality of wealth was often excused on the grounds that it was needed to get people to save so that society could make progress through new capital formation, she believes the excuse is no longer valid. To her the part of the national income which goes to property owners as income is not only undeserved but also performs no modern function. Capital would more or less easily maintain itself in a system without private property, she believes, and would be allocated among new uses—or could be made to be reallocated by some nudges from rational collective planners. She does not agree that the owners of capital are providing a useful function in the way they funnel out the aggregate between different ventures of uncertain worth.

At one time or another Joan Robinson has discerned superior merit in the eastern European organization of society and that of Northern Korea and mainland China. But Professor Robinson wears the yoke of no political party; she is a stern moralist who scolds wrongdoers in Moscow, Washington, Delhi, and if she thinks they deserve it—in Peking.

Questions to Guide the Reading

The long Keynes quotation, which comes from the *Economic Consequences of the Peace* (1919), is beautiful in its prose, but were any of the major problems that plagued the capitalistic countries after World War I connected importantly with the danger that capitalists would consume and not save? What is the point of the quotation?

The Ford Foundation or the National Science Foundation has to make difficult decisions as to which scientists and institutions to give financial backing. Many small- and big-town bankers claim that they are in a similar position, arguing that no government planning body could substitute for the thousands of decentralized decisions that are being made all the time to determine into what directions the aggregate of societies existing and new capital will go. Is there merit in this contention? Would Mrs. Robinson agree? What kind of evidence would we need to decide whether Mrs. Robinson or, say, Friedrich Hayek were right in this matter.

Critique of Capitalism and the Mixed Economy

Joan Robinson

It is impossible to understand the economic system in which we are living if we try to interpret it as a rational scheme. It has to be understood as an awkward phase in a continuing process of historical development.

No doubt in every age economic life has been a scene of conflict and compromise, defended by rationalizations that did not fit with experience. Fifty years ago, Sunday-school children were taught to sing:

> The rich man in his castle,
> The poor man at his gate,
> God made them high and lowly
> And ordered their estate.

In this century, the conflicts are more acute, the compromises more uncertain and the rationalizations more unconvincing because history has been going on so fast.

Keynes described the capitalist economy before 1914:

Europe was so organized socially and economically as to secure the maximum accumulation of capital. While there was some continuous improvement in the daily conditions of life of the mass of the population, Society was so framed as to throw a great part of the increased income into the control of the class least likely to consume it. The new rich of the nineteenth century were not brought up to large expenditures, and preferred the power which investment gave them to the pleasures of immediate consumption. In fact, it was precisely the inequality of the distribution of wealth which made possible those vast accumulations of fixed wealth and of capital improvements which distinguished that age from all others. Herein lay, in fact, the main justification of the Capitalist System. If the rich had spent their new wealth on their own enjoyments, the world would long ago have found such a regime intolerable. But like bees they saved and accumulated, not less to the advantage of the whole community because they themselves held narrower ends in prospect.

The immense accumulations of fixed capital which, to the great benefit of mankind, were built up during the half century before the war, could never have come about in a Society where wealth was divided equitably. The railways of the world, which that age built as a monument to posterity, were, not less than the Pyramids of Egypt, the work of labour which was not free to consume in immediate enjoyment the full equivalent of its efforts.

Thus this remarkable system depended for its growth on a double bluff or deception. One the one hand the labouring classes accepted from ignorance or powerlessness, or were compelled, persuaded, or cajoled by custom, convention, authority, and the well-established order of Society into accepting, a situation in which they could call their own very little of the cake, that they and Nature and the capitalists were co-operating to produce. And on the other hand the capitalist classes were allowed to call the best part of the cake theirs and were theoretically free to consume it, on the tacit underlying conditions that they consumed very little of it in practice. The duty of "saving" became nine-tenths of virtue and the growth of the cake the object of true religion. There grew round the non-consumption of the cake all those instincts of puritanism which in other ages has withdrawn itself from the world and has neglected the arts of production as well as those of enjoyment. And so the cake increased; but to what end was not clearly contemplated. Individuals would be exhorted not so much to abstain as to defer, and to cultivate the pleasures of security and anticipation. Saving was for old age or for your children; but this was only in theory—the virtue of the cake was that it was never to be consumed, neither by you nor by your children after you.

In writing thus I do not necessarily disparage the practices of that generation. In the unconscious recesses of its being Society knew what it was about. The cake was really very small in proportion to the appetites of consumption, and no one, if it were shared all round, would be much better off by the cutting of it. Society was working not for the small pleasures of today but for the future security and improvement of the race—in fact for "progress."

Writing in 1918, Keynes thought that the war had smashed this system up, but it staggered to its feet again. Not the war, but the great slump of the thirties struck the mortal blow. It is painful to reflect that, if a British government after 1931 had known how to make full employment by peaceful means, the Nazis would have had no appeal. But full employment, in the democratic countries, had to wait for a new war, and ever since, cold and hot wars have made a great contribution to maintaining it. The Western world learned by the collapse of the market economy (from which the Soviet Union was immune) that the cake was already large and that when it is not cut it dries up and crumbles away. But we have no philosophy to guide us in sharing it out. The old hymn throws the glamour of feudalism over inequality. It did not say:

> The rich man in his board room
> The poor man in his slum.

Now what story are the children to be told?

It is impossible to imagine the huge accumulation that made modern industries possible without the 'double deception' of bitter exploitation on the one side, and devoted profit seekers on the other. Social justice and political equality would have strangled the system before it could grow. The institutions and the habits of mind built up during the period when the surplus was being squeezed out survive after they have ceased to be useful and have not yet been replaced.

The notions of *laisser faire*, that business men know what is best, are contradicted by the evident need for planning to maintain 'a high and stable level of employment.' The notion that property confers obligations to justify privilege is contradicted by the separation of ownership from control in modern business. The notion that governments have only to see fair play between employers and employed is contradicted by the requirements of control over money incomes and prices. The notion that the free play of supply and demand produces a viable system of international trade is contradicted by the payments crises from which no country is immune for long.

These contradictions arise from the need to readjust the organization of Society to the fantastic capacity for production of material wealth that the application of science to technology has made possible.

Such problems arise within the Western industrial nations. Meanwhile, their situation in the world has changed still more dramatically. They are now rivalled by socialist nations which have installed modern industry far more rapidly than they did themselves and surrounded by a third world where misery is growing faster than wealth. These internal problems, however, are matter enough for us here.

Changing the distribution of wealth

Keynes' description of capitalists who "were allowed to call the best part of the cake theirs . . . on the tacit underlying condition that they consumed very little of it" applied to the old-style entrepreneur managing a business that he had built up from his own resources. There are still sometimes great fortunes acquired by individual tycoons and there are still family businesses which have not yet become public companies or been absorbed into one of the great amalgamations. In the main, industry and trade are now dominated by *managerial capitalism*, that is by companies nominally owned by a shifting population of shareholders and actually run by salaried staff.

Rentier income

The principle of limited liability enabled managerial capitalism to grow up over the last hundred years. An owner of wealth can spread his risks by holding shares in many companies about whose business he knows nothing except what may affect their value on the Stock Exchange. His rights as an owner of a company concern him only in cases of emergency. The return on shares, from his point of view, is merely an alternative to interest on a loan, and his role in business is simply that of a *rentier*, just as much as though his wealth were placed in gilt-edged government bonds or derived from rent of land.

Unearned income. Rentier property, as a social institution, provides a number of conveniences. It pays a premium on savings designed to carry purchasing power forward to a time when family needs will be greater. It provides for widows and orphans in the middle class. It provides endowments for many worthy institutions. The returns which insurance companies and pension schemes get on their funds improve the terms that they can offer. For the most part, however, its function is only to provide what the Inland Revenue rightly describes as *unearned income* to the heirs of entrepreneurs and to contribute taxes to the exchequer, just as rent from land provides unearned income to the heirs of feudalism.

The stock exchange. Amongst possible placements from which rentier income can be derived, shares issued by limited liability companies of all kinds are particularly attractive, especially in a period of chronic inflation. But a share is a *share* in the fortunes of a company. In the hurly-burly of competition individual fortunes cannot be foreseen. Moreover taxation distorts relative yields in a complicated way, and the market as a whole is liable to swing up and down with changes in level of rates of interest (which, as we have seen, are connected with the international financial situation), with waves of sentiment and with the interpretation that it puts upon political events. Dealing in shares is by no means a simple matter. A great apparatus of jobbers, brokers, advisers and financiers has been created to assist the rentier in placing his wealth. The game of spotting winners then develops as a by-product that swallows up the original purpose for which the institution was created. This game is not easy and it can be lucrative. It therefore attracts a great deal of high-class brain power from more constructive activities.

Redundancy. The contribution which the capital market makes to providing finance for industry is very small in relation to the resources that go into keeping up the whole affair. The existence of the market facilitates raising finance by new issues, but this is a minor part of the finance which industry absorbs, since the greater part is provided from retained profits.

For its hierarchy of managers, a company takes on a life of its own, like a college or a regiment; their loyalty is to the company as such rather than to the shareholders. From their point of view the distribution of dividends is a necessary evil; the proper use for profits is investment to enlarge the operation of the company.

In this way we have drifted unconsciously into a highly peculiar economic system. The net earnings of a company belong to its shareholders. They receive them either in the form of dividends or in the form of the rise in the value of shares corresponding to the earning power of additional investments financed by retained profits. They are free to spend these capital gains for consumption. In so far as they do not spend them, the system so to speak credits them with saving. The wealth generated by technical progress, capital accumulation, work and business acumen, thus drops into the laps of rentiers while they sit at home or occupy themselves with other tasks.

The old excuse for the existence of a wealthy class—that they are necessary to provide savings—has worn extremely thin. On the contrary, it is their consumption which is a draft upon the nation's resources.

The excuse that the stock exchange provides a good guide to profitability and so channels finance to where it can best be used, was never convincing and it was laughed out of court by Keynes' description of the manner in which the market operators, like those who go in for a newspaper competition to select the most beautiful film star, make their gains by "anticipating what average opinion expects average opinion to be."

Ownership and control

To a certain extent, the divorce between ownership and control has softened the rigour of laisser-faire capitalism. The managers must pursue profits for their firm to survive and grow, but good reputation and humane labour relations may also be their object. Equally, so may be an easy life and long weekends.

The freedom of managers is, however, circumscribed by the legal fiction that the shareholders own the company. The group of rentiers who, at any particular moment, hold the company's shares regard them merely as an eligible placement for a fraction of their private wealth. They see no objection to selling their holdings to anyone who offers favourable terms. Thus when, for good reasons or bad, the stock exchange value of a company falls below the potential profitability of its real assets, it is in danger of a *take-over bid* from another company or an individual tycoon who can buy up the business behind its own back, throw out the board of directors, prune the management and switch to a more profitable, though not necessarily a more admirable, line than was being pursued before.

The market (especially in England) values shares more by dividends than by earnings. Thus, to make itself less tempting for a take over by keeping up its *valuation ratio* (the stock exchange value of the shares over the value of the earning assets based on expected profitability) the management must pay out more dividends than they would like.

The nation as rentier

In spite of its drawbacks, managers generally value the freedom that this peculiar system gives them. For the most part, they dislike the idea of being nationalized or even of being financed by a public body which would have a right to supervise them. The great financial institutions such as insurance companies, which actually own a great deal of industry, lean backwards not to interfere. In principle, there is no reason why the state should not also enjoy ownership without control where management by private enterprise is considered preferable. A budget surplus *above the line*, that is on income account, instead of being used to check the growth of the national debt could be used to buy industrial shares.

In a period when there is continuous economic growth in real terms (cancelling out the falling value of money) through rising productivity, when land, labour and capital each receive fairly constant overall shares in net national income, the total of private property is growing, but the prospect of a long run rise in the value of any particular company is highly speculative so that it is heavily discounted in its present value. If, for the sake of argument, we suppose that a good lot were taken over, they could each be bought at market price, and the value of the lot would be certain to rise, giving a fair profit to the nation (not to mention the unfair profit due to inflation). Rentier consumption would be *pro tanto* stabilized, and its erstwhile growth could be de-devoted to public expenditure, public saving through a budget surplus, or reduction of taxes on earned income. This is not so much a programme as an illustration of the nature of rentier wealth.

The corresponding proposal to take over property in land has often been advocated. The longer it is put off, the greater the un-earned increment of private wealth.

Inherited wealth

The large fortunes built up during the process of accumulation that Keynes described, as well as those inherited from feudalism, have left a permanent legacy of great inequality of property. It perpetuates itself, for one finds it easy to make money if one has some, and next to impossible if one has not.

Progressive taxation. Inequality is not accepted by the democratic conscience and has to be combated by taxation. The apparatus of taxation is expensive; whatever criteria of taxable capacity are devised are necessarily somewhat arbitrary and set up meaningless distortions in the values of different kinds of property; a great deal of highly expert manpower is devoted to advising rentiers and businessmen on legal tax avoidance (not to mention the other kind); the legislative, administrative and legal apparatus of the country is burdened with the task of making the tax system fair, or appear fair, as between equal incomes, and the definition of income for tax purposes has developed an elaborate body of theology which is a constant source of dispute. In short, the whole affair is a great nuisance.

In spite of all, inequality remains. Progressive taxation has made scarcely a dent in it.

Standards of life. Inequality in post-tax income and capital gains gives rise to inequalities in consumption which makes it very hard to persuade the trade unions that incomes policy is on the level.

Families with high incomes cannot be prevented from spending them on what they most need, and so the two-tier system of health and education services is perpetuated, and contributes to perpetuating inequality.

A drastic remedy. The concept of the nation as rentier points the way out of this situation. Concentrations of private property could be wiped out in a generation of confiscatory death duties (leaving a reasonable life interest to widows and orphans, and buttressed by equally heavy taxation on gifts). The titles to property could be handed over in the form in which it exists, to be held like any other endowment of a trust, and the income from it devoted to public purposes. This would not merely check the growth of rentier income, as nationalization with compensation does, but take a large bite out of it. In particular, the reduction of fee-paying demand would make it possible to unify and improve the health and educational services.

Salaries. There is another source of inequality also connected with the share of profit in the proceeds of industry—the high salaries and perquisites of business executives. They, even more than the pay of skilled workers, are subject to wage drift in the competition between firms for the best men. They subject education, research and the learned professions to a brain drain which has to be answered by setting up comparable salary scales—infecting the republic of letters with demoralizing commercialism.

This could be checked by the Inland Revenue refusing to allow, as costs for tax purposes, salaries above a certain multiple of the average wage. There would of course be a great outcry about *incentives*, but incentives are relative. "The game can be played just as well for lower stakes once the players are used to them."

Why not? The obstacles to such schemes are neither technical nor legal. They lie in the political opposition that could be rallied against them at home and the threat of flights of capital and capitalists to more congenial shores. (In the Common Market they could not be attempted until the whole of Christian Democracy was converted to the idea.)

The main obstacle, all the same, to eliminating functionless wealth is lack of imagination in developing ideas and institutions appropriate to an economy that has got over the hump of heavy accumulation and needs to find a rational way of enjoying the benefit.

Reading 86

Usually men believe what is believed by the system which they are born into. The author argues here that since the Industrial Revolution it has been common in our society to accept as axiomatic the mentality of the market mechanism. In his view this has shaped our every thought and institution. But, he goes on to argue, there is nothing at all natural about this market-dominated view of the world. Societies did not have it in earlier centuries. Anthropologists observe that non-Western societies respond to a different drumbeat. Polanyi believes that in the near future we shall see a fundamental transformation away from the ideology of laissez faire.

In America, the word "liberal" means somebody who is a little bit left of center; for example, a Roosevelt New Dealer or Kennedy New Frontiersman. Still farther to the left of a liberal would be a "radical" or a "communist." In contrast to a "liberal" is a "conservative" or even a "reactionary." But in English history and in the history of ideas generally, "liberalism" stands for a philosophy which believes in letting the market handle things and keeping the role of government severely limited. Thus the Manchester-School free-traders of the nineteenth century were "liberals" par excellence. The author here adheres to this non-American tradition. Therefore the editor has in almost every place substituted, without calling attention to the fact, the expression "laissez faire" for "liberal" or "liberalism."

Karl Polanyi, born in Hungary, taught at Columbia University before his recent death. He is the author of *The Great Transformation*, and his important essays that integrate economics with the other social sciences have been edited by George Dalton under the title *Primitive, Archaic and Modern Economies* (Anchor Books, Doubleday & Company, Inc., New York, 1968).

Questions to Guide the Reading

Does the author perhaps exaggerate in asserting that markets have become important only since the Industrial Revolution? Were not markets much like ours already present in the classical world, with vestiges remaining even in the Middle Ages?

Would a believer in the Marxian economic and materialistic determination of history agree with Polanyi that only in the market society does the economic factor become primary in determination of social ideology? Do you think there is anything pathological or schizophrenic in having a man come home at night from work, and then enter, so to speak, a new and different world? Might that not be a pleasant and normal, rather than disorganizing, mode of behavior? Since Karl Polanyi obviously does not like the tyranny of a government bureaucracy, should this perhaps predispose him toward a less critical view of a mixed economy in which much of the task of economic organization is done through market mechanisms? If he were alive today, what would he think of the move toward more use of market pricing in the communist countries of eastern Europe? Since the time that his essay was written (1947), has the previous order decayed in the fashion which he had been prophesying? How do you account for your answer?

Our Obsolete Market Mentality

Karl Polanyi

The first century of the Machine Age is drawing to a close amid fear and trepidation. Its fabulous material success was due to the willing, indeed the enthusiastic, *subordination of man to the needs of the machine.* [Laissez-faire] capitalism was in effect man's initial response to the challenge of the Industrial Revolution. In order to allow scope to the use of elaborate, powerful machinery, we transformed human economy into a self-adjusting system of markets, and cast our thoughts and values in the mold of this unique innovation.

Today, we begin to doubt the truth of some of these thoughts and the validity of some of these values. Outside the United States, [laissez-faire] capitalism can hardly be said to exist any more. How to organize human life in a machine society is a question that confronts us anew. Behind the fading fabric of competitive capitalism there looms the portent of an industrial civilization, with its paralyzing division of labor, standardization of life, supremacy of mechanism over organism, and organization over spontaneity. Science itself is haunted by insanity. This is the abiding concern.

No mere reversion to the ideals of a past century can show us the way. We must brave the future, though this may involve us in an attempt to shift the place of industry in society so that the extraneous fact of the machine can be absorbed. The search for industrial democracy is not merely the search for a solution to the problems of capitalism, as most people imagine. It is a search for an answer to industry itself. Here lies the concrete problem of our civilization. Such a new dispensation requires an inner freedom for which we are but ill equipped. We find ourselves *stultified* by the legacy of a market-economy which bequeathed us oversimplified views of the function and role of the economic system in society. If the crisis is to be overcome, we must recapture a more realistic vision of the human world and shape our common purpose in the light of that recognition.

Industrialism is a precariously grafted scion upon man's age-long existence. The outcome

From Karl Polanyi, "Our Obsolete Market Mentality," *Commentary*, vol. 3, February, 1947, pp. 109–117. Reprinted from *Commentary*, by permission; copyright 1947 by the American Jewish Committee.

of the experiment is still hanging in the balance. But man is not a simple being and can die in more than one way. The question of individual freedom, so passionately raised in our generation, is only one aspect of this anxious problem. In truth, it forms part of a much wider and deeper need—the need for a new response to the total challenge of the machine.

Our condition can be described in these terms: Industrial civilization may yet undo man. But since the venture of a progressively artificial environment cannot, will not, and indeed, should not, be voluntarily discarded, the task of adapting life *in such a surrounding* to the requirements of human existence must be resolved if man is to continue on earth. No one can foretell whether such an adjustment is possible, or whether man must perish in the attempt. Hence the dark undertone of concern.

Meanwhile, the first phase of the Machine Age has run its course. It involved an organization of society that derived its name from its central institution, *the market*. This system is on the downgrade. Yet our practical philosophy was overwhelmingly shaped by this spectacular episode. Novel notions about man and society became current and gained the status of axioms. Here they are.

As regards *man*, we were made to accept the heresy that his motives can be described as "material" and "ideal," and that the incentives on which everyday life is organized spring from the "material" motives. Both utilitarian liberalism and popular Marxism favored such views.

As regards *society*, the kindred doctrine was propounded that its institutions were "determined" by the economic system. This opinion was even more popular with Marxists than with liberals.

Under a market-economy both assertions were, of course, true. *But only under such an economy*. To overcome such doctrines, which constrict our minds and souls and greatly enhance the difficulty of the life-saving adjustment, may require no less than a reform of our consciousness.

Market society

[Laissez-faire] economy, this primary reaction of man to the machine, was a violent break

with the conditions that preceded it. A chain-reaction was started—what before was merely isolated markets was transmuted into a self-regulating *system* of markets. And with the new economy, a new society sprang into being. The crucial step was this: labor and land were made into commodities, that is, they were treated *as if* produced for sale. Of course, they were not actually commodities, since they were either not produced at all (as land) or, if so, not for sale (as labor). Yet no more thoroughly effective fiction was ever devised. By buying and selling labor and land freely, the mechanism of the market was made to apply to them. There was now supply of labor, and demand for it; there was supply of land, and demand for it. Accordingly, there was a market price for the use of labor power, called wages, and a market price for the use of land, called rent. Labor and land were provided with markets of their own, similar to the commodities proper that were produced with their help. The true scope of such a step can be gauged if we remember that labor is only another name for man, and land for nature. The commodity fiction handed over the fate of man and nature to the play of an automaton running in its own grooves and governed by its own laws.

Nothing similar had ever been witnessed before. Under the mercantile regime, though it deliberately pressed for the creation of markets, the converse principle still operated. Labor and land were not entrusted to the market; they formed part of the *organic structure* of society. Where land was marketable, only the determination of price was, as a rule, left to the parties; where labor was subject to contract, wages themselves were usually assessed by public authority. Land stood under the custom of manor, monastery, and township, under common-law limitations concerning rights of real property; labor was regulated by laws against beggary and vagrancy, statutes of laborers and artificers, poor laws, guild and municipal ordinances. In effect, all societies known to anthropologists and historians restricted markets to commodities in the proper sense of the term.

Market-economy thus created a new type of society. The economic or productive system was here entrusted to a self-acting device. An institutional mechanism controlled human beings in their everyday activities as well as the resources of nature. This instrument of material welfare was under the sole control of the incentives of hunger and gain—or, more precisely, fear of going without the necessities of life, and expectation of profit. So long as no propertyless person could satisfy his craving for food without first selling his labor in the market, and so long as no propertied person was prevented from buying in the cheapest market and selling in the dearest, the blind mill would turn out ever-increasing amounts of commodities for the benefit of the human race. Fear of starvation with the worker, lure of profit with the employer, would keep the vast establishment running.

In this way an "economic sphere" came into existence that was sharply delimited from other institutions in society. Since no human aggregation can survive without a functioning productive apparatus, its embodiment in a distinct and separate sphere had the effect of making the "rest" of society dependent upon that sphere. This autonomous zone, again, was regulated by a mechanism that controlled its functioning. *As a result, the market mechanism became determinative for the life of the body social.* No wonder that the emergent human aggregation was an "economic" society to a degree previously never even approximated. "Economic motives" reigned supreme in a world of their own, and the individual was made to act on them under pain of being trodden under foot by the juggernaut market. Such a forced conversion to a utilitarian outlook fatefully warped Western man's understanding of himself.

This new world of "economic motives" was based on a fallacy. Intrinsically, hunger and gain are no more "economic" than love or hate, pride or prejudice. No human motive is per se economic. There is no such thing as a *sui generis* economic experience in the sense in which man may have a religious, aesthetic, or sexual experience. These latter give rise to motives that broadly aim at evoking similar experiences. In regard to material production these terms lack self-evident meaning.

Evidence from anthropology and history

Aristotle was right: man is not an economic, but a social being. He does not aim at safeguarding his individual interest in the acquisi-

tion of material possessions, but rather at ensuring social good will, social status, social assets. He values possessions primarily as a means to that end. His incentives are of that "mixed" character which we associate with the endeavor to gain social approval—productive efforts are no more than incidental to this. *Man's economy is, as a rule, submerged in his social relations.* The change from this to a society which was, on the contrary, submerged in the economic system was an entirely novel development.

The evidence of facts, I feel, should at this point be adduced. *First,* there are the discoveries of primitive economics. Two names are outstanding: Bronislaw Malinowski and Richard Thurnwald. They and some other research workers revolutionized our conceptions in this field and, by so doing, founded a new discipline. The myth of the individualistic savage had been exploded long ago. Neither the crude egotism, nor the apocryphal propensity to barter, truck, and exchange, nor even the tendency to cater to one's self was in evidence. But equally discredited was the legend of the communistic psychology of the savage, his supposed lack of appreciation for his own personal interests. (Roughly, it appeared that man was very much the same all through the ages. Taking his institutions not in isolation, but in their interrelation, he was mostly found to be behaving in a manner broadly comprehensible to us.) What appeared as "communism" was the fact that the productive or economic system was usually arranged in such a fashion as not to threaten any individual with starvation. His place at the campfire, his share in the common resources, was secure to him, whatever part he happened to have played in hunt, pasture, tillage, or gardening. Here are a few instances: Under the *kraalland* system of the Kaffirs, "destitution is impossible; whosoever needs assistance receives it unquestioningly" (L. P. Mair, *An African People in the Twentieth Century*, 1934). No Kwakiutl "ever ran the least risk of going hungry" (E. M. Loeb, *The Distribution and Function of Money in Early Society*, 1936). "There is no starvation in societies living on the subsistence margin" (M. J. Herskovits, *The Economic Life of Primitive Peoples*, 1940). In effect, the individual is not in danger of starving unless the community as a whole is in a like predicament. It is this absence of the menace of individual destitution that makes primitive society, in a sense, more humane than nineteenth-century society, and at the same time less "economic."

The same applies to the stimulus of individual gain. Again, a few quotations: "The characteristic feature of primitive economics is the absence of any desire to make profits from production and exchange" (R. Thurnwald, *Economics in Primitive Communities*, 1932). "Gain, which is often the stimulus for work in more civilized communities, never acts as an impulse to work under the original native conditions" (B. Malinowski, *Argonauts of the Western Pacific*, 1922). If so-called economic motives were natural to man, we would have to judge all early and primitive societies as thoroughly unnatural.

Secondly, there is no difference between primitive and civilized society in this regard. Whether we turn to ancient city-state, despotic empire, feudalism, thirteenth-century urban life, sixteenth-century mercantile regime, or eighteenth-century regulationism—invariably the economic system is found to be merged in the social. Incentives spring from a large variety of sources, such as custom and tradition, public duty and private commitment, religious observance and political allegiance, judicial obligation and administrative regulation as established by prince, municipality, or guild. Rank and status, compulsion of law and threat of punishment, public praise and private reputation, insure that the individual contributes his share to production. Fear of privation or love of profit need not be altogether absent. Markets occur in all kinds of societies, and the figure of the merchant is familiar to many types of civilization. But isolated markets do not link up into an economy. The motive of gain was specific to merchants, as was valor to the knight, piety to the priest, and pride to the craftsman. The notion of making the motive of gain universal never entered the heads of our ancestors. At no time prior to the second quarter of the nineteenth century were markets more than a subordinate feature in society.

Thirdly, there was the startling abruptness of the change. Predominance of markets emerged not as a matter of degree, but of kind. Markets through which otherwise self-sufficient householders get rid of their surplus neither direct production nor provide the pro-

ducer with his income. This is only the case in a market-economy where *all* incomes derive from sales, and commodities are obtainable exclusively by purchase. A free market for labor was born in England only about a century ago. The ill-famed Poor Law Reform (1834) abolished the rough-and-ready provisions made for the paupers by patriarchal governments. The poorhouse was transformed from a refuge of the destitute into an abode of shame and mental torture to which even hunger and misery were preferable. Starvation or work was the alternative left to the poor. Thus was a competitive national market for labor created. Within a decade, the Bank Act (1844) established the principle of the gold standard; the making of money was removed from the hands of the government regardless of the effect upon the level of employment. Simultaneously, reform of land law mobilized the land, and repeal of the Corn Laws (1846) created a world pool of grain, thereby making the unprotected Continental peasant-farmer subject to the whims of the market. Thus were established the three tenets of economic liberalism, the principle on which market economy was organized: that labor should find its price on the market; that money should be supplied by a self-adjusting mechanism; that commodities should be free to flow from country to country irrespective of the consequences—in brief, a labor market, the gold standard, and free trade. A self-inflammatory process was induced, as a result of which the formerly harmless market pattern expanded into a sociological enormity.

These facts roughly outline the genealogy of an "economic" society. Under such conditions the human world must appear as determined by "economic" motives.

Under capitalism, every individual has to earn an income. If he is a worker, he has to sell his labor at current prices; if he is an owner, he has to make as high a profit as he can, for his standing with his fellows will depend upon the level of his income. Hunger and gain—even if vicariously—make them plow and sow, spin and weave, mine coal, and pilot planes. Consequently, members of such a society will *think of themselves* as governed by these twin motives. In actual fact, man was never as selfish as the theory demanded. Though the market mechanism brought his dependence upon material goods to the fore, "economic" motives never formed with him the sole incentive to work. In vain was he exhorted by economists and utilitarian moralists alike to discount in business all other motives than "material" ones. On closer investigation, he was still found to be acting on remarkably "mixed" motives, not excluding those of duty toward himself and others—and maybe, secretly, even enjoying work for its own sake.

However, we are not here concerned with actual, but with assumed motives, not with the psychology, but with the *ideology* of business. *Not on the former, but on the latter, are views of man's nature based.* For once society expects a definite behavior on the part of its members, and prevailing institutions become roughly capable of enforcing that behavior, opinions on human nature will tend to mirror the ideal whether it resembles actuality or not. Accordingly, hunger and gain were defined as economic motives, and man was supposed to be acting on them in everyday life, while his other motives appeared more ethereal and removed from humdrum existence. Honor and pride, civic obligation and moral duty, even self-respect and common decency, were now deemed irrelevant to production, and were significantly summed up in the word "ideal." Hence man was believed to consist of two components, one more akin to hunger and gain, the other to honor and power. The one was "material," the other "ideal"; the one "economic," the other "non-economic"; the one "rational," the other "non-rational." The Utilitarians went so far as to identify the two sets of terms, thus endowing the economic side of man's character with the aura of rationality. He who would have refused to imagine that he was acting for gain alone was thus considered *not only immoral, but also mad.*

Economic determinism

The market mechanism, moreover, created the delusion of economic determinism as a general law for all human society. Under a market-economy, of course, this law holds good. Indeed, the working of the economic system here not only "influences" the rest of society, but determines it—as in a triangle the sides not merely influence, but determine, the angles. In Maine's famous phrase, "contractus" replaced "status"; or, as Tönnies preferred to put it, "society" superseded "community"; or,

in terms of the present article, *instead of the economic system being embedded in social relationships, these relationships were now embedded in the economic system.*

While social classes were directly, other institutions were indirectly determined by the market mechanism. State and government, marriage and the rearing of children, the organization of science and education, of religion and the arts, the choice of profession, the forms of habitation, the shape of settlements, the very aesthetics of private life—everything had to comply with the utilitarian pattern, or at least not interfere with the working of the market mechanism. But since very few human activities can be carried on in the void; even a saint needing his pillar, the indirect effect of the market system came very near to determining the whole of society. It was almost impossible to avoid the erroneous conclusion that as "economic" man was "real" man, so the economic system was "really" society.

Yet it would be truer to say that the basic human institutions abhor unmixed motives. Just as the provisioning of the individual and his family does not commonly rely on the motive of hunger, so the institution of the family is not based on the sexual motive. Sex, like hunger, is one of the most powerful of incentives when released from the control of other incentives. That is probably why the family in all its variety of forms is never allowed to center on the sexual instinct, with its intermittencies and vagaries, but on the combination of a number of effective motives that prevent sex from destroying an institution on which so much of man's happiness depends. Sex in itself will never produce anything better than a brothel, and even then it might have to draw on some incentives of the market mechanism. An economic system actually relying for its mainspring on hunger would be almost as perverse as a family system based on the bare urge of sex.

To attempt to apply economic determinism to all human societies is little short of fantastic. Nothing is more obvious to the student of social anthropology than the variety of institutions found to be compatible with practically identical instruments of production. Only since the market was permitted to grind the human fabric into the featureless uniformity of selenic erosion has man's institutional creativeness been in abeyance.

No protest of mine, I realize, will save me from being taken for an "idealist." For he who decries the importance of "material" motives must, it seems, be relying on the strength of "ideal" ones. Yet no worse misunderstanding is possible. Hunger and gain have nothing specifically "material" about them. Pride, honor, and power, on the other hand, are not necessarily "higher" motives than hunger and gain. Our animal dependence upon food has been bared and the naked fear of starvation permitted to run loose. Our humiliating enslavement to the "material," which all human culture is designed to mitigate, was deliberately made more rigorous. This is at the root of the "sickness of an acquisitive society" that Tawney warned of. And Robert Owen's genius was at its best when, a century before, he described the profit motive as "a principle entirely unfavorable to individual and public happiness."

The reality of society

I plead for the *restoration of that unity of motives* which should inform man in his everyday activity as a producer, for the reabsorption of the economic system in society, for the creative adaptation of our ways of life to an industrial environment.

On all these counts, laissez-faire philosophy, with its corollary of a marketing society, falls to the ground. It is responsible for the splitting up of man's vital unity into "real" man, bent on material values, and his "ideal" better self. It is paralyzing our social imagination by more or less unconsciously fostering the prejudice of economic determinism. It has done its service in that phase of industrial civilization which is behind us. At the price of impoverishing the individual, it enriched society. Today, we are faced with the vital task of *restoring the fullness of life to the person, even though this may mean a technologically less efficient society*. In different countries in different ways, classical [laissez-faire] liberalism is being discarded. On Right and Left and Middle, new avenues are being explored. British Social-Democrats, American New Dealers, and also European fascists and American anti-New Dealers of the various "managerialist" brands, reject the liberal [laissez-faire] utopia. Nor should the present political mood of rejection of everything Russian blind us to the achieve-

ment of the Russians in creative adjustment to some of the fundamental aspects of an industrial environment.

On general grounds, the Communist's expectation of the "withering away of the state" seems to me to combine elements of liberal utopianism with practical indifference to institutional freedoms. As regards the withering state, it is impossible to deny that industrial society is complex society, and no complex society can exist without organized power at the center. Yet, again, this fact is no excuse for the Communist's slurring over the question of concrete institutional freedoms. It is on this level of realism that the problem of individual freedom should be met. *No human society is possible in which power and compulsion are absent, nor is a world in which force has no function.* [Laissez-faire] philosophy gave a false direction to our ideals in seeming to promise the fulfillment of such intrinsically utopian expectations.

Freedom in industrial society

The breakdown of market-economy imperils two kinds of freedom: some good, some bad.

That the freedom to exploit one's fellows, or the freedom to make inordinate gains without commensurable service to the community, the freedom to keep technological inventions from being used for the public benefit, or the freedom to profit from public calamities secretly engineered for private advantage, may disappear, together with the free market, is all to the good. But the market economy under which these freedoms throve also produced freedoms that we prize highly. Freedom of conscience, freedom of speech, freedom of meeting, freedom of association, freedom to choose one's job—we cherish them for their own sake. Yet to a large extent they were *byproducts* of the same economy that was also responsible for the evil freedoms.

The existence of a separate economic sphere in society created, as it were, a gap between politics and economics, between government and industry, that was in the nature of a no man's land. As division of sovereignty between pope and emperor left medieval princes in a condition of freedom sometimes bordering on anarchy, so division of sovereignty between government and industry in the nineteenth century allowed even the poor man to enjoy freedoms that partly compensated for his wretched status. Current skepticism in regard to the future of freedom largely rests on this. There are those who argue, like Hayek, that since free institutions were a product of market-economy, they must give place to serfdom once that economy disappears. There are others, like Burnham, who assert the inevitability of some new form of serfdom called "managerialism."

Arguments like these merely prove to what extent economistic prejudice is still rampant. For such determinism, as we have seen, is only another name for the market mechanism. It is hardly logical to argue the effects of its absence on the strength of an economic necessity that derives from its presence. And it is certainly contrary to Anglo-Saxon experience. Neither the freezing of labor nor selective service abrogated the essential freedoms of the American people, as anybody can witness who spent the crucial years 1940–43 in these States. Great Britian during the war introduced an all-round planned economy and did away with that separation of government and industry from which nineteenth-century freedom sprang, yet never were public liberties more securely entrenched than at the height of the emergency. In truth, we will have just as much freedom as we will desire to create and to safeguard. There is no *one* determinant in human society. Institutional guarantees of personal freedom are compatible with any economic system. In market society alone did the economic mechanism lay down the law.

What appears to our generation as the problem of capitalism is, in reality, the far greater problem of an industrial civilization. The eco-nomic [libertarian] is blind to this fact. In defending capitalism as an economic system, he ignores the challenge of the Machine Age. Yet the dangers that make the bravest quake today transcend economy. The idyllic concerns of trust-busting and Taylorization have been superseded by Hiroshima. Scientific barbarism is dogging our footsteps. The Germans were planning a contrivance to make the sun emanate death rays. We, in fact, produced a burst of death rays that blotted out the sun. Yet the Germans had an evil philosophy, and we had a humane philosophy. In this we should learn to see the symbol of our peril.

Among those in America who are aware of the dimensions of the problem, two tendencies are discernible: some believe in elites and aristocracies, in managerialism and the corporation. They feel that the whole of society should be more intimately adjusted to the economic system, which they would wish to maintain unchanged. This is the ideal of the Brave New World, where the individual is conditioned to support an order that has been designed for him by such as are wiser than he. Others, on the contrary, believe that in a truly democratic society, the problem of industry would resolves itself through the planned intervention of the producers and consumers themselves. Such conscious and responsible action is, indeed, one of the embodiments of freedom in a complex society. But, as the contents of this article suggest, such an endeavor cannot be successful unless it is disciplined by a total view of man and society very different from that which we inherited from market economy.

Readings 87 and 88

Capitalism has changed, claims England's Andrew Shonfield. Economic planning by governments underlies the post-World War II production miracles of Germany, France, Japan, the Netherlands, Italy, Sweden, and Europe generally. Only Britain has failed. And, according to Shonfield, the United States could use considerably more planning.

Agreeing that the mixed economy differs from old-fashioned capitalism, Charles P. Kindleberger nevertheless argues that Shonfield exaggerates the role that planning has played in the Common Market and other miracles.

Andrew Shonfield is director of studies at the Royal Institute of International Affairs, London; C. P. Kindleberger is professor of international economics at M.I.T.

Questions to Guide the Reading

Must planning involve a sacrifice of personal freedoms? Can one distinguish fiscal and monetary policies from "planning"? What would you recommend for the United States?

Reading 87

Modern Capitalism

Andrew Shonfield

The advanced industrial countries of the Western world have during the 1950s and early 1960s enjoyed an extended period of prosperity for which it is impossible to find a precedent. Three major factors can be identified which are responsible for the distinctive economic flavour of the postwar period.

First, economic growth has been much steadier than in the past. It has not been completely even, but the recessions, when they have come, have been very mild and shallow by historical standards. In several countries they have resulted in nothing more than the temporary slowing down of a continuing advance. There has been no halt or reversal. In others, where production has fallen back in recessions, these interruptions have been short-lived and have had relatively little effect on the level of employment.

Secondly, the growth of production over the period has been extremely rapid. It is true that in the United States there have been periods in the past, notably from 1900 to 1913, when the average rate of economic growth was even higher than in the 1950s. But the American case was exceptional in the postwar Western world. It was accompanied by many features which had no parallel elsewhere— notably a rising level of unemployment and a declining level of business investment, measured as a proportion of the national product. In Western Europe the pace of economic advance after the middle of the century was much faster, as well as being less interrupted, than in any known comparable period of peacetime history.

Thirdly, the benefits of the new prosperity were very widely diffused. In the conditions of full employment and rising demand for labour established in almost all areas of Western Europe during the 1950s, average wage earnings rose as fast as, or faster than, the national product. In the United States too consumption rose fairly steadily and the upward trend was barely interrupted even by business recessions. What distinguished Western Europe was the deliberate effort to widen the spread of consumer benefits, by means of welfare services and pension schemes, to those members of society who cannot rely on automatic gains as a result of the rise in wage-earnings.

Pre-Kennedy doldrums

It is noteworthy that this diffusion of rising incomes over the population as a whole has not reduced the flow of savings required to support a high level of investment. On the contrary, Western Europe has set aside a larger proportion of its resources for investment than ever before. Again the United States is different: there the rate of investment was somewhat lower than in the period of expansion immediately preceding the First World War. One of the aims of the Democratic Administration which took office in 1961 was to raise the level of American investment, with the help of fiscal incentives and the promise of sustained economic expansion uninterrupted by serious recessions.

The evidence suggests that a continuing 'recession psychology' in the United States has been a major reason for the contrast between American and West European economic ex-

From Andrew Shonfield, *Modern Capitalism* (published under the auspices of the Royal Institute of International Affairs by Oxford University Press, New York and London, 1965). Reprinted with kind permission of the author and publisher.

perience in recent years. Analysis of the actual recessions which have occurred since the war suggests that they have been aggravated in the United States by government financial policies. There have been more recessions in the United States than in Western Europe, and they have been allowed to go further before the government intervened decisively to boost demand.

There is an alternative explanation of the postwar contrast between North America and Western Europe, which sees the latter as enjoying an exceptional and transient expansion while the former is closer to the long-term economic norm. An important school of economic historians argues on the basis of the experience of the past century that the favourable conditions from 1950 onwards reflected a 'long upswing' (of about ten years' duration) of a kind which has been seen regularly, alternating with downswings of about equal duration, in the past. On this view there has been no decisive change of trend in the Western capitalist world leading to a sustained high rate of economic growth. The reason why appearances suggest that there has been is that a number of extremely favourable conditions have fortuitously combined to accelerate the expansion of the 1950s; the lucky combination is unlikely to endure.

How the West grew

Two powerful economic forces have played a major part in raising the tempo of economic growth in the West. They are: (1) the sustained expansion of international trade, and (2) the great building boom of the 1950s. Some economists, among whom Simon Kuznets and Arthur Lewis are outstanding, maintain that these are transient phenomena; both residential building and international trade in manufactured goods are believed to have been subjected to a species of forced growth, which will be matched by a markedly slower rate of expansion later on.

[My] central thesis is that there is no reason to suppose that the patterns of the past, which have been ingeniously unravelled by the historians of trade cycles, will reassert themselves in the future. To begin with, the advent of full employment, and its conscious pursuit in the advanced industrial countries as an act of policy, have added a new dimension to international trade. When countries are operating constantly at the margin of their available resources, their imports of manufactured goods tend to rise faster than their domestic output of manufactures. This tendency is particularly marked during a period of rapidly advancing technology.

The distinctive features of the new era of capitalism which has opened since the end of the Second World War are first, the conscious pursuit of full employment, and secondly, the accelerated pace of technological progress. The latter has made possible a high and steady increase from year to year in output per manhour. This process will continue and may accelerate.

The early stages of the new capitalism were sustained in several countries with the help of ample supplies of additional labour moving into industry. The 1960s show a marked change in the trend. This has reinforced the emphasis on technological innovation in general and on higher education in particular.

Thus far the argument has tried to show only that continuing prosperity and uninterrupted growth on the scale of recent years are possible in the future. The underlying conditions in the second half of the twentieth century are more favourable than at any time in the history of capitalism. The more interesting question, however, is whether success is probable. The answer to this depends very largely on political will and skill: specifically on the management of the institutional apparatus which guides Western economic life.

Keynes to the rescue

There is an alternative approach which sees this whole issue as a technical problem, and one that was solved some time ago as a result of the advance in economic techniques. Once Keynes showed how an economy should be handled when it produced the recurrent signs of debility, there was little more to it, it is averred, than following the instructions in the new guide book. You might find yourself with a little more inflation than you had bargained for, but you could always rely on having plenty of economic growth.

Control over the business cycle, which owes so much to Keynes's work, has been one of the decisive factors in establishing the dynamic and prosperous capitalism of the postwar era. Indeed, it is probably the single most important factor in this change. So many other developments flow from it, notably the reduction of business risks and the incentive to speed up the process of investment. My point is only that if the change from old-style capitalism to the new style had depended solely on a process of intellectual conversion to the system of economic doctrines developed by Keynes, it is unlikely that it would have got as far as it has. Moreover, the future would by now be looking highly uncertain. After all, there have been many occasions since the war when we have seen people in authority, who believe themselves to have penetrated the truths of Keynesian economics, being guided in an emergency by quite other, and often contradictory, policies.

What is characteristic of the postwar period is that a variety of independent forces have combined to increase the available powers of control over the economic system and at the same time to keep the volume of demand constantly at a very high level. Governments have therefore been given time to learn how to intervene with increasing skill, without causing disaster in the course of educating themselves.

There is indeed an element of paradox in the fact that the two nations which had earliest and most readily absorbed the Keynesian message—Britain and the United States—were also the least successful among the Western capitalist countries in managing their economies after the Second World War. This contrast would itself be sufficient to suggest that the purely intellectual change, which is popularly labelled the 'Keynesian revolution', is not the decisive factor. Something more is evidently required than a knowledge of techniques. On the continent of Europe during the period immediately following the war, the Keynesian message was not generally accepted. Yet there were other more powerful factors which allowed these countries to avoid any serious cyclical fluctuations and to maintain a significantly higher rate of economic growth than either Britain or the United States.

The miraculous Common Market

This success of the continental Europeans was so glaring that by the early 1960s it had become a significant factor in both British and American domestic politics. At any rate both countries embarked on policies which were intended to mark a deliberate break with the past, while copying some feature, real or imagined, of the European experience. In Britain the effort was concentrated on avoiding 'stop-go' measures, which had interfered with an even rate of growth; the formula adopted was economic planning on the French model which, by making progress more even, would also, it was expected, make it more rapid. In the United States, after the Democratic Administration took office in 1961, following eight years of Republican rule, the whole focus of economic policy shifted: it came to concentrate on the objective of full employment, which was to be achieved by deliberately pushing up the demands on the country's productive apparatus.

It is worth noting that when the United States came to set itself its new objective, it did not turn to Britain for its model, despite the fact that the British had successfully maintained a state of full employment, without interruption, for two decades. It was the experience of continental Europe in the 1950s which beckoned to the Americans. What had been achieved there was the combination of full employment with a high rate of growth and international competitive power which had notably eluded the British.

I shall try to identify the characteristic institutional features of the economic order which has gradually emerged in postwar capitalism. There are big differences between the key institutions and economic methods of one country and another. The differences are often the subject of sharp ideological cleavages. Yet when the total picture is examined, there is a certain uniformity in the texture of these societies. In terms of what they do, rather than of what they say about it, and even more markedly in terms of the pattern of their behaviour over a period of years, the similarities are striking. This may be because nations exchange their experiences nowadays, including the intimate experiences of management both in the public sphere and in business, more actively than ever before. That may also be one of the reasons why the design of the pattern has become clearer in the 1960s than it was in the 1950s.

Shape of things to come

Some of its outstanding features may be usefully listed:

1. There is the vastly *increased influence* of the *public authorities* on the management of the economic system. This operates through different mechanisms in different countries: in one the control of the banking system is decisive, in another it is the existence of a wide sector of publicly controlled enterprise. In all of them the government's expenditure has been enormously enlarged and determines directly a large segment of each nation's economic activities.

2. The *preoccupation with social welfare* leads to the use of public funds on a rising scale, most notably to support people who do not earn, either because they are young and being educated or old and retired. Public welfare policies, of course, have a long history in several European countries; what is, however, characteristic of the postwar period is the steady advance of social welfare measures over wide areas of the Western world. This is most obviously reflected in the fact that education and pensions together have been absorbing an increasing proportion of the national income of the advanced capitalist countries. (Again a proviso must be made about the United States in the 1950s.)

3. In the private sector the *violence of the market has been tamed*. Competition, although it continues to be active in a number of areas, tends to be increasingly regulated and controlled. The effort to secure an enlarged area of predictability for business management, in a period in which technological change is very rapid and individual business investments are both larger in size and take longer to mature, has encouraged long-range collaboration between firms. Governments in their anxiety to increase the area of the predictable for purposes of economic planning have encouraged firms within an industry to evolve agreed policies on the basis of their common long-range interests. The classical market of the textbooks in which firms struggle with one another and disregard any possible effect that their actions may have on the market as a whole has become more remote than ever.

4. It has now come to be taken for granted, both by governments and by the average person in the Western capitalist countries, that *each year should bring a noticeable increase in the real income per head of the population.* The accepted procedure of annual wage claims in most countries reflects this expectation. It is, in fact, capable of being fulfilled, at any rate for a long time to come, as a result of the accelerated pace of technological innovation in industry. But to secure the full benefits of the enlarged industrial potential requires new forms of organization, (*a*) in the sphere of research and development, and (*b*) for the training of workers and generally for the more efficient deployment of scarce resources of skilled manpower. A conscious effort has begun to be applied in both fields since the late 1950's. The purpose of (*a*) is to reduce the time span from the inception of novel ideas to their development into usable models ready to be absorbed into the process of production; while (*b*) aims to reduce the bottlenecks caused by the shortage of trained labour capable of responding to new technology. There is increasing realization that in a full employment economy, rapid technical progress can be sustained only if there is an active public policy designed to speed up the transfer of people from jobs in which they are established to new forms of employment.

5. The characteristic attitude in large-scale economic management, both inside government and in the private sector, which has made itself increasingly felt during the postwar period, is the *pursuit of intellectual coherence*. Its most obvious manifestation is in long-range national planning. Lengthening the time horizon used in making economic decisions also means extending the range of data that have to be studied in the present; more current facts become relevant. Thus the framework of systematic analysis has to be extended in two dimensions. Techniques and institutions, different in the various countries and varying in efficiency, have been developed to meet the demand for both explicitness and coherence in those economic decisions which have a significant impact on national production or public welfare. Once again the motive is at least partly the desire, in the face of greatly accelerated change, to try to reduce the area of the unpredictable to a manageable series of clear alternatives.

Last questions

Finally, how far are the methods being adopted for the efficient management of the new capitalism compatible with the ideas and practice of traditional parliamentary democracy? How much of the original objective of government by popular consent can be sustained in a system in which the sphere of active government has been greatly enlarged and is likely to become more so?

Reading 88

The Best Laid Plans

Charles P. Kindleberger

It is somewhat ironic that Shonfield's book was published in January, 1966, after the United States had assumed the growth lead over Japan and the nations of North America and Europe. Part of his thesis is that traditional capitalism is flawed for purposes of growth because it relies on government only to stabilize demand and on the market to produce the supply response, whereas under "modern" capitalism it is necessary, above all, to plan, coordinate or organize supply through government or through governmental surrogates. Like Baum and Luethy, who wrote off French economic vitality prematurely only to have the patient flex his muscles before their books reached print—a point which Shonfield does not miss—the author falls victim to printer's lag, and his ideas are in some part overtaken by the fast pace of events.

Thesis

Shonfield's major theme is that modern capitalism needs government and centralization. (Incidentally, he fails to note that what modern socialism seems to need, judging from Yugoslav and Soviet experience, is decentralization.) Adam Smith is stood on his head. People do not know their best interest. Markets are "violent," and "market prices generally fail to measure either social costs or benefits." Enterprise needs "tutelary" (a favorite word of his) direction.

Government, on the other hand, has produced the dazzling performance of capitalism since World War II, in all but the United States and Britain, by its activity as an entrepreneur, by guiding private enterprise and by both stimulating technical change and producing coherence in disparate private decisions.

Planning is all, even though in some environments it is disguised as anti-planning. The period since 1945 is not a Kuznets cycle, in which a burst of energy sparked by technological change produces a once-and-for-all reallocation of resources and dies away. The very nature of the system has changed, and growth is built in on a permanent basis. This overstates the thesis perhaps, but not by much.

Antithesis

If Shonfield had been content to say that the horizons of households, firms and governments had been extended in time one could hardly fault him.

On all sides, it is clear that the short-run profit maximizer, interested in separate, discrete "deals," has been superseded by (or converted to) the manager calculating returns over extended periods, and that this changes the nature of capitalism. Maximizing profits at low rates of implicit interest over the long run is indistinguishable from maximizing survival.

If supply bottlenecks or undesirable social consequences of present action can be foreseen by government, governmental steps may be taken. Government, having in mind the future consequences of present action, is readier today to intervene in the public interest. In

From Charles P. Kindleberger, "The Best Laid Plans." Reprinted from *Challenge*, The Magazine of Economic Affairs, a publication of Challenge Communications, Inc., May–June, 1966. Reprinted with kind permission of the author and publisher.

limited areas there are external economies and diseconomies, where market prices do not reflect social values; in a world of pollution, overcrowding and aggressive commercialization, it is clearly not true to maintain that man always advances the common welfare in pursuit of his own interest.

One can even go further and say that the governmental problem changes, from the macroeconomic or aggregative steps required in an economy with unemployment, to the difficult micro as well as macro problems under full employment. But Shonfield wants to say more. He wants to insist on the inescapable necessity of some elusive technique called planning.

I applaud the attention to supply. Keynesians have been right about the United States up to now and, during the 1950s, about Belgium, but they are totally wrong about England, for example. So are the anti-Keynesians. The point is not that there has been too little, or too irregular or too much demand. What they have slighted or ignored is supply.

But Shonfield is certainly not right in implying that all supply problems are basically the same. In France it was the structure of industry; in Italy structural unemployment; in Britain the immobility (and occasionally the intransigence) of labor. German rapid growth until 1965 was helped by the inflow of refugees and later immigrants who provided a peculiarly mobile labor force. In the United States, enterprise did respond quickly to demand, though pockets of poverty have remained. It is hard to generalize about the nature of the bottlenecks and social problems; and even harder about the therapy that will cope with them.

False synthesis

To attempt such generalization leads to error. Shonfield is persuaded that the wide-ranging intervention of governments and monopoly banks in European capital markets is a source of strength. He refers derisively to the "grossly inefficient structure of American Banking," and hankers after a system in which the Reconstruction Finance Corporation was the allocator of capital, like the "Caisse" in France or the "Kreditanstalt fuer Wiederaufbau" (plus the "Lastungsausgleichfond," which he neglects) in Germany. (He even hints that the United States went off the track in scrapping

NRA, and has a good word to say for the Nazi industrial associations.)

Students of the subjects will have a hard time with his views on capital markets on both sides of the Atlantic. What is a reasonable test of the efficiency of capital markets: the level of rates, the spread between lenders' and borrowers' returns, the need to depend on profits for investment? By any of these tests, the Shonfield verdicts would be reversed.

Semantics of planning

An interpretation which gives me great trouble is implied in the reference to Sweden's "central planning." But Swedish policy is distinguished first by its short-run stabilization of demand through investment reserves, and second by its governmental assistance to labor and capital markets. This is making private markets work better, not replacing them. Resources are not directed so much as made more mobile. There is no "coherence" imposed on resource allocation, even though such might logically follow from the investment reserve scheme. Similarly in Austria, which grew with nationalized industry but with no plan, it is hardly a point for planning that Austrian socialists "have come to see" the need for planning. The task is rather to explain why the Austrian economy grew so rapidly without it.

Planning in Shonfield's usage, turns out to be merely intervention. He insists that this is not so: *ad hoccery* is excluded. The case is not persuasive. Planning focuses on key industries here, structural objectives there, factor markets in this setting, allocating capital in that. In France planning has weak statistics but strong action; in the Netherlands it is the contrary. It may have been that planning was a dirty word as capitalism is an O.K. word in the United States, but if the first condition is going to be changed, we must know what we mean by planning if it is O.K., and this is not made clear.

This sounds uniformly negative. It is not meant to be. The book is rich in information, historical insights, suggestive asides and good writing. It is the standard revenge of the economist who writes mouthfilling jargon to accuse the fluent economist of lack of rigor. Shonfield will have to suffer from the envy of his less articulate brethren, as Galbraith and Rostow have done. But while I envy his prose style, I really differ with Shonfield's analysis.

The new era

European growth at 8 to 10 per cent a year from 1950 to 1963 cannot be sustained. It was the consequence of a backlog of demand, a technological backlog to be made up in investment, and excess supplies of labor on the Continent, not to mention the useful start of the Marshall Plan. Once the excess labor supply runs out, as it has done, supergrowth is over, and there is nothing that planning can do to restore it.

This is partly so because the interruption of growth, to hold down prices, alters the expectations of enterprise that demand will expand each year in five, not only four out of five.

There is not a risk of overinvestment whereas previously the only possible error was from underinvestment. Governments may plan and push, haul, nudge, apply body-English in trying to make enterprise conform to the plan, but without the same effect when demand and supply are expanding in unison with a mobile labor supply. Italy has been trying now for 18 months to restimulate private investment— with all the apparatus of which Shonfield makes so much, and with planning too—and is finding it difficult indeed.

It would be pleasant to subscribe to his central thesis, that the patterns of the past will not reassert themselves. But while it is true that government will respond to any lapse from growth with more speed and understanding than ever before in history, I cannot adhere to the view that the major danger for European growth stems from lack of international monetary reserves. The era of European supergrowth after World War II is over already, and one of the first victims of the change is this highly useful and stimulating book.

Reading 89

More than a billion people living in China and eastern Europe believe in the doctrines of Karl Marx. Yet these doctrines are rarely given much emphasis in the economics courses taught in the West. Is this because of prejudice? Or fear? Or boredom?

Whatever the cause of this neglect, Dr. Robert Heilbroner, brilliant freelance writer and professor of economics at the New School for Social Research, believes it is unjustified. One of the most memorable chapters from his exciting book *The Worldly Philosophers* (which has sold more than a million copies and is available in paperback from Simon and Schuster) is devoted to Marxian economics. Any student who wishes to pursue the subject further will want to read the little book on Marxism by Joan Robinson and also the book from which Reading 90 on imperialism was taken, *Monopoly Capitalism* by Paul Baran and Paul M. Sweezy (Monthly Review Press, New York, 1968).

Dr. Heilbroner is correct in believing that the crucial point in Marx's theory of exploitation involved his view that if it costs only two hours of a day's work to produce the output needed for a man's minimum subsistence, he need be paid no more than two-eighths of what his labor produces when he works an eight-hour day. A modern economist would have to say that this pivotal point involves the Achilles heel of the Marxian theory of exploitation: if the average worker has a marginal productivity four times the minimum of subsistence, under competitive capitalism that is what employers would have to pay him. If you cannot describe correctly how the motor of a car operates when it is idling, you are unlikely to be able correctly to explain its dynamic laws of motion. This is a crude analogy to drive home the point that if it is indeed true that Marx's view of what determines exploitation of wages and the distribution of income at a moment in time is faulty at the core, then his attempt to portray the dynamic laws of motion of capitalistic development are also likely to be fatally flawed. In 1890 one did not need to have the apparatus of the Marxian system of economics to perceive that monopolies were forming in the advanced nations, and that the problem of the business cycle was far from being solved under capitalism. So Heilbroner's enthusiasm for the correctness in the beginning of Marxian predictions is not necessarily a powerful test for the correctness of the Marxian notions of surplus value and the labor theory of value. Hence, one is less than surprised that the development within this century, and particularly since 1929, of (1) managed macroeconomics of the mixed economy, of (2) the welfare system of redistributive taxation and social security programs, and of (3) antitrust controls on the powers of monopoly are not particularly illuminated by the Marxian categories.

Questions to Guide the Reading

Since 1953 when Heilbroner wrote, there has been much greater interest in the pre-Manifesto writings of Marx dealing with social alienation of the worker. Does this fit in with the current generation gap and with emphasis on "alienation"? Can a man be a good long-run prophet and still misjudge badly whether there will be a revolution next year or in the next decade? Can a man be a good prophet for a thirty-year span but then find that subsequent history is running against his expectations? If like Marx you reject the Malthusian stress on diminishing returns, why should you believe in a subsistence wage? By how much could a reserve army of the unemployed—of let us say 3 million out of a labor force of 75 million—depress average wages if modern technology is such that employment of even 75 million new men would not lower labor productivity (marginally reckoned or on an average basis) by more than 10 per cent and if wages are now a dozen times physiological subsistence? Henry Carey, a famous American economist in the decades before Marx, believed in a labor theory of value; but, unlike Marx, he deduced from that theory that the improvement of technology would have to result in a *vast increase* in the real wage rate. Has the 1870–1970 experience in America, Europe, Japan, and Africa been more along the lines of Henry Carey or of Karl Marx?

Marxian Economics—A Survey

Robert L. Heilbroner

The *Manifesto* opened with portentous words: "A spectre is haunting Europe—the spectre of Communism. All the powers of old Europe have entered into a holy alliance to exorcise this spectre: Pope and Tsar, Metternich and Guizot, French Radicals and German police-spies."

The specter certainly existed: 1848 was a year of terror for the old order on the Continent. There was a revolutionary fervor in the air and a rumble underfoot. For a moment— for a brief moment—it looked as if the old order might break down. In France the plodding regime of Louis Philippe, the portly middle-class king, wrestled with a crisis and then collapsed; the king abdicated and fled to the security of a Surrey villa, and the workingmen of Paris rose in a wild uncoordinated surge and ran the Red Flag over the Hôtel de Ville. In Belgium a frightened monarch offered to submit his resignation. In Berlin the barricades went up and bullets whistled; in Italy

From Robert L. Heilbroner, *The Worldly Philosophers* (Simon and Schuster, Inc., New York, 1953), pp. 127–131, 146–163. Copyright 1953 by Robert Heilbroner. Reprinted by permission of Simon and Schuster, Inc. and William Morris Agency, Inc.

mobs rioted; and in Prague and Vienna popular uprisings imitated Paris by seizing control of the cities.

"The Communists disdain to conceal their views and aims," cried the *Manifesto*. "They openly declare that their ends can be attained only by the forcible overthrow of all existing social relations. Let the ruling classes tremble at a Communist revolution. The proletarians have nothing to lose but their chains. They have a world to win."

The ruling classes did tremble and they saw the threat of communism everywhere. Nor were their fears groundless. In the French foundries the workmen sang radical songs to the accompaniment of blows from their sledge hammers, and Heinrich Heine, the German romantic poet who was touring the factories, reported that "really people in our gentle walk of life can have no idea of the demonic note which runs through these songs."

But despite the clarion words of the *Manifesto*, the demonic note was not a call for a revolution of communism; it was a cry born only of frustration and despair. For all of Europe was in the grip of reaction compared with which conditions in England were positively idyllic. The French government had been characterized by John Stuart Mill as "wholly without the spirit of improvement and . . . wrought almost exclusively through the meaner and more selfish impulses of mankind" and the French had no monopoly on such a dubious claim to fame. As for Germany, well, here it was, the fourth decade of the nineteenth century, and Prussia still had no parliament, no freedom of speech or right of assembly, no liberty of press or trial by jury, and no tolerance for any idea which deviated by a hair's breadth from the antiquated notion of the divine right of kings. Italy was a hodgepodge of anachronistic principalities. Russia under Nicholas I (despite the Tsar's onetime visit to Robert Owen's New Lanark) was characterized by the historian De Tocqueville as "the cornerstone of despotism in Europe."

Had the despair been channeled and directed, the demonic note might have changed into a truly revolutionary one. But as it was, the uprisings were spontaneous, undisciplined, and aimless; they won initial victories and then, while they were wondering what next to do, the old order rocked invincibly back into place. The revolutionary fervor abated, and where it

did not, it was mercilessly crushed. At the price of ten thousand casualties, the Paris mobs were subdued by the National Guard, and Louis Napoleon took over the nation and soon exchanged the Second Republic for the Second Empire. In Belgium the country decided that it had better ask the king to stay after all; he acknowledged the tribute by abolishing the right of assembly. The Viennese and Hungarian crowds were cannonaded from their strongholds, and in Germany a constitutional assembly which had been bravely debating the question of republicanism broke down into factional bickering and then ignominiously offered the country to Frederick William IV of Prussia. Still more ignominiously, that monarch declared that he would accept no crown proffered by the ignoble hands of commoners.

After the crisis

The revolution was over. It had been fierce, bloody, but inconclusive. There were a few new faces in Europe but the policies were much the same.

But to a little group of working-class leaders who had just formed the Communist League, there was no cause for deep despair. True, the revolution for which they had entertained high hopes had petered out and the radical movements pocketed throughout Europe were being more ruthlessly hounded than ever before. But all that could be regarded with a certain equanimity. For according to their understanding of history, the uprisings of 1848 were only the small-scale dress rehearsals of a gigantic production that was scheduled for the future, and of the eventual success of that catastrophic spectacle there could be not a shadow of a doubt.

The league had just published its statement of objectives and called it the *Communist Manifesto*. But for all its slogans and its trenchant phrases, the *Manifesto* had not been written merely to whip up revolutionary sentiment or to add another voice of protest to the clamor of voices that filled the air. The *Manifesto* had something else in mind: a philosophy of history in which a communist revolution was not only desirable but demonstrably *inevitable*. Unlike the Utopians, who also wanted to reorganize society closer to their desires, the Communists did not appeal to men's sympathies or to their addiction to build castles in the air. Rather, they offered men a chance to hitch their destinies to a star and to watch that star move inexorably across the historical zodiac. There was no longer a contest in which one side or the other ought to win for moral or sentimental reasons or because it thought the existing order was outrageous. Instead there was a cold analysis of which side *had* to win, and since that side was the proletariat, their leaders had only to wait. In the end, as necessarily as two and two made four, they could not lose.

The *Manifesto* was a program written for the future. But one thing would have surprised its authors. They were prepared to wait—but not for *seventy* years. They were already scanning Europe for the likeliest incubator of revolt. And they never even cast a glance in the direction of Russia.

Two remarkable men

The *Manifesto*, as everybody knows, was the brain child of that angry genius, Karl Marx. More accurately, it was the result of collaboration between him and his remarkable companion, compatriot, supporter, and colleague, Friedrich Engels.

They are interesting, and, of course, enormously important men. The trouble is, they are no longer just men; Marx the human being is obscured behind Marx the Figure; and Engels behind the shadow of Marx. If we are to judge by a count of worshipping noses, Marx must be considered a religious figure to rank with Christ or Mohammed, and Engels thus becomes a sort of Saint Peter or a John. In the Marx-Engels Institute in Moscow, scholars have pored over their works with all the idolatry they ridicule in the antireligious museums down the street; but while Marx and Engels are canonized in Russia, they are still crucified in much of the world.

They merit neither treatment, for they were neither saints nor devils. Nor is their work either Scripture or anathema. It belongs in the great line of economic viewpoints which have successively clarified, illuminated, and interpreted the world for us, and like the other great works on the shelf, it is neither without flaw nor devoid of merit. The world has been preoccupied with Marx the Revolutionary. But had Marx not lived there would have been

other socialists and other prophets of a new society. The real and lasting impact of Marx and Engels is not their revolutionary activity, none of which bore too much fruit during their own lifetimes. It is with Marx the Economist that capitalism must finally come to grips. For the final imprint he made on history was his prediction that capitalism must inevitably and necessarily collapse. On that prediction, on that "scientific" prognostication, communism has built its edifice.

The new-new testament

What was Marx's prognosis for the system that he knew? The answer lies in that enormous work *Das Kapital—Capital*. With Marx's agonizing meticulousness, it is remarkable that the work was ever finished—in a sense it never was. It was eighteen years in process; in 1851 it was to be done "in five weeks"; in 1859 in "six weeks"; in 1865 it was "done"—a huge bundle of virtually illegible manuscripts which took two years to edit into Volume I. When Marx died in 1883 two volumes remained: Engels put out Volume II in 1885 and the third in 1894. The final (fourth) volume did not emerge until 1910.

There are twenty-five hundred pages to read for anyone intrepid enough to make the effort. And what pages! Some deal with the tiniest of technical matters and labor them to a point of mathematical exhaustion; other swirl with passion and anger. This is an economist who has read *every* economist, a German pedant with a passion for footnotes, and an emotional critic who can write that "capital is dead labour, that vampire-like, only lives by sucking living labour" and who tells us that capital came into the world "dripping from head to foot, from every pore, with blood and dirt."

And yet one must not jump to the conclusion that this is merely a biased and irascible text inveighing against the sins of the wicked money-barons. It is shot through with remarks which betray the total involvement of the man with his theoretical adversary, but the great merit of the book, curiously enough, is its utter detachment from all considerations of morality. The book describes with fury, but it analyzes with cold logic. For what Marx has set for his goal is to discover the intrinsic tendencies of the capitalist system, its inner laws of motion, and in so doing, he has eschewed the easy but less convincing means of merely expatiating on its manifest shortcomings. Instead he erects the most rigorous, the purest capitalism imaginable and within this rarefied abstract system, within an imaginary capitalism in which all the obvious defects of real life are removed, he seeks his quarry. For if he can prove that the best of all possible capitalisms is nonetheless headed for certain disaster, it is certainly easy to demonstrate that real capitalism will follow the same path, only quicker.

And so he sets the stage. We enter a world of perfect capitalism: no monopolies, no unions, no special advantages for anyone. It is a world in which every commodity sells at exactly its proper price. And that proper price is its *value*—a tricky word. For the value of a commodity, says Marx (and Smith and Ricardo before him), is the amount of labor it has within itself. If it takes twice as much labor to make hats as shoes, then hats will sell for twice the price of shoes. The labor, of course, need not be direct manual labor; it may be overhead labor which is spread over many commodities or it may be the labor which once went into making a machine and which the machine now slowly passes on to the products it shapes. But no matter what its form, everything is eventually reducible to labor, and all commodities, in this perfect system, will be priced according to the amount of labor, direct or indirect, which they contain.

In this world stand the two great protagonists of the capitalist drama: worker and capitalist—the landlord has by now been relegated to a minor position in society. They are not quite the same protagonists we have met earlier in similar economic tableaux. The worker is no longer the slave to his reproductive urge. He is a free bargaining agent who enters the market to dispose of the one commodity he commands—labor-power—and if he gets a rise in wages he will not be so foolish as to squander it in a self-defeating proliferation of his numbers.

The capitalist faces him in the arena. He is not a bad fellow at heart, although his greed and lust for wealth are caustically described in those chapters which leave the abstract world for a look into 1860 England. But it is worth noting that he is not money-hungry from mere motives of rapacity: he is an owner-entrepreneur engaged in an endless race against his fellow owner-entrepreneurs; he

must strive for accumulation, for in the competitive environment in which he operates, one accumulates or one gets accumulated.

Cherchez la profits

The stage is set and the characters take their places. But now the first difficulty appears. How, asks Marx, can profits exist in such a situation? If everything sells for its exact value, then who gets an unearned increment? No one dares to raise his price above the competitive one, and even if one seller managed to gouge a buyer, that buyer would only have less to spend elsewhere in the economy—one man's profit would thus be another man's loss. How can there be profit in the *whole* system if everything exchanges for its honest worth?

It seems like a paradox. Profits are easy to explain if we assume that there are monopolies in the system which need not obey the leveling influences of competition or if we admit that capitalists may pay labor less than it is worth. But Marx will have none of that—this is to be *pure* capitalism which will dig its own grave.

He finds the answer to the dilemma in one commodity which is different from all others. That commodity is labor-power. For the laborer, like the capitalist, sells his product for exactly what it is worth—for its value. And its value, like the value of everything else that is sold, is the amount of labor that goes into it—in this case, the amount of labor that it takes to "make" labor-power. In other words, a laborer's salable energies are worth the amount of socially necessary labor it takes to keep that laborer alive. Smith and Ricardo would have agreed entirely: the true value of a workman is the wage he needs in order to exist. It is his subsistence wage.

So far, so good. But here comes the key to profit. The laborer who contracts to work can only ask for a wage which is his due. What that wage will be depends, as we have seen, on the amount of labor-time it takes to keep a man alive. If it takes six hours of society's labor to maintain a workingman, then (if labor is priced at one dollar an hour), he is "worth" six dollars a day. No more.

But the laborer who gets a job does not contract to work only six hours a day. That would be just long enough to support himself. On the contrary, he agrees to work a full eight-hour, or in Marx's time a ten- or eleven-hour, day. Hence he will produce a full ten or eleven hours' worth of value and he will get paid for only six. His wage will cover his subsistence which is his true "value," but in return he will sell the value which he produces in a full working day. And this is how profit enters the system.

Exploitation

Marx called this layer of unpaid work "surplus value." But it is quite devoid of moral indignation. The worker is only entitled to the *value* of his labor-power. He gets it in full. But meanwhile the capitalist gets the full value of his workers' whole working day, and this is longer than the hours for which he paid. Hence when the capitalist sells his products, he can afford to sell them at *their* true value and still realize a profit. For there is more labor-time embodied in his products than the labor-time for which he was forced to pay.

How can this state of affairs come about? It happens because the capitalists monopolize one thing—*access to the means of production themselves.* If a worker isn't willing to work a full working day, he doesn't get a job. Like everyone else in the system, a worker has no right and no power to ask for more than his own worth as a commodity. The system is perfectly equitable and yet all workers are cheated, for they are forced to work a longer time than their own self-sustenance demands.

Does this sound strange? Remember that Marx is describing a time when the working day was long—sometimes unendurably long— and when wages were, by and large, little more than it took to keep body and soul together. The idea of surplus value may make little sense in a world where the sweatshop is very largely a thing of the past, but it was not merely a theoretical construct at the time that Marx was writing. One example may suffice: at a Manchester factory in 1862 the average workweek for a period of a month and a half was 84 hours! For the previous 18 months it had been 78½ hours.

Laws of motion

But all this is still only the setting for the drama. We have the protagonists, we have their motives, we have the clue to the plot in the discovery of "surplus value." And now the play is set in motion.

All capitalists have profits. But they are all in competition. Hence they try to accumulate and so to expand their scales of output, at the expense of their competitors. But expansion is not so easy. It requires more laborers and to get them the capitalists must bid against each other for the working force. Wages tend to rise. Conversely, surplus value tends to fall. It looks as if the Marxian capitalists will soon be up against the dilemma faced by the capitalists of Adam Smith and David Ricardo—their profits will be eaten away by rising wages.

To Smith and Ricardo the solution to the dilemma lay in the propensity of the working force to increase its numbers with every boost in pay. But Marx has ruled out this possibility. He doesn't argue about it; he simply brands the Malthusian doctrine "a libel on the human race"—after all, the proletariat, which is to be the ruling class of the future, cannot be so shortsighted as to dissipate its gains through mere unbridled physical appetite. But he rescues his capitalists just the same. For he says that they will meet the threat of rising wages by introducing laborsaving machinery into their plants. That will throw part of the working force back onto the street and there, as an Industrial Reserve Army, it will serve the same function as Malthus' teeming population: it will compete wages right back down to their former "value"—the subsistence level.

But now comes the crucial twist. It seems as though the capitalist has saved the day, for he has prevented wages from rising by creating unemployment through machinery. But not so fast. By the very process through which he hopes to free himself from one horn of the dilemma, he impales himself on the other.

For as he substitutes machines for men, he is simultaneously substituting nonprofitable means of production for profitable ones. Remember that in this never-never world, no one makes a profit by merely sharp bargaining. Whatever a machine will be worth to a capitalist, you can be sure that he paid full value for it. If a machine will yield ten thousand dollars' worth of value over its whole life, our capitalist was charged the full ten thousand dollars in the first place. It is only from his living labor that he can realize a profit, only from the unpaid-for hours of surplus working time. Hence when he reduces the number or proportion of workers, he is killing the goose that laid the golden egg.

And yet, poor fellow, he has to. There is nothing Mephasthelean about his actions. He is only obeying his impulse to accumulate and trying to stay abreast of his competitors. As his wages rise, he *must* introduce laborsaving machinery to cut his costs and rescue his profit margin—if he does not, his neighbor will. But since he must substitute machinery for labor, he must also narrow the base out of which he gleans his profits. It is a kind of Greek drama where men go willy-nilly to their fate, and in which they all unwittingly cooperate to bring about their own destruction.

For now the die is cast. As his profits shrink, each capitalist will redouble his efforts to put new laborsaving, cost-cutting machinery in his factory. It is only by getting a step ahead of the parade that he can hope to make a profit. But since everyone is doing precisely the same thing, the ratio of labor (and hence surplus value) to total output shrinks still further. The rate of profit falls and falls. And now doom lies ahead. Profits are cut to the point at which production is no longer profitable at all. Consumption dwindles as machines displace men and the number of employed fails to keep pace with output. Bankruptcies ensue. There is a scramble to dump goods on the market and in the process smaller firms go under. A capitalist crisis is at hand.

Not forever. As workers are thrown out of work, they are forced to accept subvalue wages. As machinery is dumped, the stronger capitalists can acquire machines for less than their true value. After a time, surplus value reappears. The forward march is taken up again. But it leads to the same catastrophic conclusion: competition for workers; higher wages; labor-displacing machinery; a smaller base for surplus value; still more frenzied competition; collapse. And each collapse is worse than the preceding one. In the periods of crisis, the bigger firms absorb the smaller ones, and when the industrial monsters eventually go down, the wreckage is far greater than when the little enterprises buckle.

The inevitable collapse

And then, one day, the drama ends. Marx's picture of it has all the eloquence of a de-

scription of Damnation: "Along with the constantly diminishing number of the magnates of capital, who usurp and monopolize all advantages of this process of transformation, grows the mass of misery, oppression, slavery, degradation, exploitation; but with this too grows the revolt of the working-class, a class always increasing in numbers, and disciplined, united, organized by the very mechanism of the process of capitalist production itself . . . centralization of the means of production and socialization of labour at last reach a point where they become incompatible with their capitalist integument. This integument bursts asunder. The knell of capitalist private property sounds. The expropriators are expropriated."

And so the drama ends in the inevitable overthrow which Marx had envisioned in the dialectic. The system—the pure system—breaks down as it works upon itself to squeeze out its own source of energy, surplus value. The breakdown is hastened by the constant instability which arises from the essentially planless nature of the economy, and although there are forces at work which act both to prolong and to hasten its end, its final death struggle is inescapable. And if the pure system is unworkable, what possible hope can there be for the real system, with all its imperfections, monopolies, cutthroat tactics, and heedless profit seeking?

For Adam Smith, the capitalist escalator climbed ever upward, at least as far as the eye could reasonably see. For Ricardo that upward motion was finally stalled by the pressure of mouths on insufficient cropland, which brought a stalemate to progress and a windfall to the fortunate landlord. For Mill the vista was made more reassuring by his discovery that society could distribute its product as it saw fit, regardless of what "economic laws" seemed to dictate. But for Marx even that saving possibility was untenable. For the dialectic told him that the State was only the political ruling organ of the economic rulers, and the thought that it might act as a neutral body, as an impartial third force which might balance the claims of its conflicting members, would have seemed little else but sheer wishful thinking. No, there was no escape from the inner logic, the inexorable development of a system which would not only destroy itself but which, in so doing, would give birth to its successor.

The new society

As to what that successor might look like, Marx had little to say. It would be "classless," of course—by which Marx meant that the basis for an economic division of society based on property would be removed once society owned all the means of production of goods. Just how society would "own" its factories; what was meant by "society"; whether there would or could be bitter antagonisms between the managers and the managed, between the political chieftains and the rank and file—none of this did Marx specify. During a transitional period there would be a "dictatorship of the proletariat"; after that, "pure" communism itself.

Marx, it must be kept in mind, was not the architect of communism. That task would fall to his successor, Lenin. *Das Kapital* is the Doomsday Book of capitalism, and in all of Marx there is almost nothing which looks beyond the Day of Judgment to see what lineaments paradise may present.

Evaluations

What are we to make of his apocalyptic argument?

There is an easy way of disposing of the whole thing. Remember that the system is built on value—labor value—and that the key to its demise lies in that special phenomenon called surplus value. But the real world consists not of "values" but of real tangible prices. Marx must show that the world of dollars and cents mirrors, in some approximate fashion, the abstract world that he has created. But in making the transition to a price-world from a value-world, he lands in the most terrible tangle of mathematics. In fact he makes a mistake.

It is not an irreparable mistake and by going through an even worse tangle of mathematics one can make the Marxist equations come out "right"—one can, that is, explain a correspondence between the prices that really obtain in life and the underlying values in labor-time. But the critics who pointed out the error were hardly interested in setting the scheme aright and their judgment that Marx was "wrong" was taken as final. When the equations were finally justified, no one paid much attention. For regardless of its mathematical purity, the Marxian rigmarole is at best a cumbersome and difficult framework and an unnecessarily laborious method of getting at the required understanding of how capitalism works.

But while we might be tempted to toss the whole analysis to one side because it is awkward and inflexible, to do so would be to overlook its values. Marx, after all, did not strip capitalism down to its barest essentials merely to indulge his bent for abstract argument. He did so because he believed that in the simplicity of a theoretical world the mechanics of the actual world would lie clearly exposed; because he hoped that the very starkness of his model world would highlight tendencies hidden in real life.

And so it did. For all its clumsiness, Marx's model of the capitalist world seemed to *work*, to display a kind of life of its own. Given its basic assumptions—the *mise en scène* of its characters, their motives and their milieu—the situation it presented *changed*, and changed in a way that was foreseeable, precise, and inevitable. We have seen what these changes are: how profits fell, how capitalists sought new machinery, how each boom ended in a crash, how small businesses were absorbed in each debacle by the larger firms. But all this was still within the framework of an abstract world: now Marx applied his findings on paper to the real world about him—the actual world of capitalism, he said, must also display these trends.

Prophecy and fact

He called the trends the "laws of motion" of a capitalist system—the path which capitalism would tread over future time. And the astonishing fact is that almost all these predictions have come true!

For profits *do* tend to fall in an enterprise economy. The insight was not original with Marx, nor do profits fall for the reason he gave—we can dispense with the idea of exploitation contained in the theory of surplus value. But as Adam Smith or Ricardo or Mill pointed out—and as any businessman will vouchsafe—the pressures of competition and rising wages will serve quite as well. Impregnable monopolies aside (and these are few), profits are both the hallmark of capitalism and its Achilles' heel, for no business can *permanently* maintain its prices much above its costs. There is only one way in which profits can be perpetuated: a business—or an entire economy—must grow.

But growth implies the second prediction of the Marxist model: the ceaseless quest for new techniques. It was no accident that industrial capitalism dates from the Industrial Revolution, for as Marx made clear, technological progress is not merely an accompaniment of capitalism but a vital ingredient. Business *must* innovate, invent, and experiment if it is to survive; the business that rests content on its past achievements is not long for this enterprising world. It is interesting to note that recently one large chemical company announced that sixty per cent of its income came from products that were unknown ten years ago; and although this is an exceptionally inventive industry, the pattern is typical.

The model showed still two more tendencies for capitalism which have also come to pass. We hardly need document the existence of business cycles over the past ninety years nor the emergence of giant business enterprise. But we might remark on the daring of Marx's prediction. When *Das Kapital* appeared, bigness was the exception rather than the rule and small enterprise still ruled the roost. To claim that huge firms would come to dominate the business scene was as startling a prediction in 1867 as would be a statement today that fifty years hence America will be a land in which small-scale proprietorships will have displaced giant corporations.

It was, all things considered, an extraordinary bit of foresight. And note this: all these changes, vast and portentous as they were, could not have been unearthed purely by examining the world as it appeared to Marx's eyes. For these are historical changes, slow in their unfolding and stretched out over time; as real, but as unnoticeable, as the growth of a tree. It was only by reducing the world to a microcosm and then by observing that microcosm in its speeded-up life span that this drift of the future could be apprehended.

It was not, of course, exact. Marx thought that profits would not only fall *within* the business cycle, which they do, but that they would display a long downward secular trend; this does not appear to have taken place. Marx did not stop to consider that the economic particles with which he played had feelings and volitions and consciences that could also

change and that they would not therefore behave with the imperturbable predictability of the particles under a chemist's microscope. But for all its shortcomings—and it is far from infallible, as we shall see—the Marxist model of how capitalism worked was extraordinarily prophetic.

But everything that Marx had predicted so far, was after all, innocuous. There remained the final prediction of the model; for as the reader will remember, in the end Marx's "pure capitalism" *collapsed*.

Alienation

Let it be said at the outset that this prediction as well cannot be lightly brushed aside. In Russia and Eastern Europe capitalism has disappeared; in Scandinavia and Britain it has been partially abandoned; in Germany and Italy it drifted into fascism and emerged from its bath of fire in less than perfect health. Indeed, almost everywhere except in the United States capitalism is on the defensive; and while wars, brute political power, exigencies of fate, and the determined efforts of revolutionaries have all contributed their share, the grim truth is that its demise has largely been for the very reason Marx foresaw: it broke down.

Why did it break down? Partly because it developed the instability Marx said it would. A succession of business crises, compounded by a plague of wars, destroyed the faith of the lower and middle classes in the system. But that is not the entire answer—we too have had our wars and depressions, and capitalism here is very much alive. Something else spelled the difference between survival and destruction: European capitalism failed not so much for economic as for *social* reasons.

And Marx predicted this too!

For Marx recognized that the economic difficulties of the system were not insuperable. Although antimonopoly legislation or anti-business cycle policies were unknown in Marx's day, such activities were not inconceivable: there was nothing inevitable in the *physical* sense about Marx's vision. The Marxist prediction of decay was founded on a conception of capitalism in which it was *socially* impossible for a government to set wrongs aright; intellectually, ideologically, even emotionally impossible. The cure for capitalism's failings would require that a government would have to rise above the interests of one class alone—and that, as Marx's doctrine of historical materialism revealed, was to assume that men could free themselves from the shackles of their immediate economic self-interest.

And it is just this lack of social flexibility, this bondage to shortsighted interest, which weakened European capitalism. For one who has read the works of Marx it is frightening to look back at the grim determination with which so many nations steadfastly hewed to the very course which he insisted would lead to their undoing. It was as if their governments were unconsciously vindicating Marx's prophecy by obstinately doing exactly what he said they would. When in Russia under the Tsars all democratic trade-unionism was ruthlessly stamped out, when in England and Germany monopolies and cartels were officially encouraged, the Marxist dialectic looked balefully prescient indeed. Even today, when one considers that in France or Italy or Greece capitalist governments still cannot collect the taxes they levy on their own business communities, when one inspects the enormous gulf between rich and poor and sees evidence of the indifference of the former for the latter, then one has the uneasy feeling that the psychological stereotypes which Marx cast in his historical drama were all too truly drawn from life.

The mixed economy

And it is these very facts which give us the clue as to why capitalism has worked in the United States. We have had our share of reactionaries and revolutionaries. But capitalism here has evolved in a land untouched by the dead hand of aristocratic lineage and age-old class attitudes. Hence we have faced up to the economic problems of capitalism with social attitudes that sprang from a less hardened heritage: attitudes of experiment and adaptation, a healthy disrespect for too much power, public or private, and a social flexibility that has prevented the development of brittle and die-hard class structures.

The result has been a Marxist impossibility. Here is a capitalist government that actually prosecutes monopolies! Here is a nation in which almost no one thinks of himself as a proletarian; upper-class America has sometimes kicked its lower classes around, but it has not *despised* them. Here is a business community in which "public relations" have come to be a paramount concern—in which, that is, business is engaged in explaining and justifying its place in society. How incomprehensible to a Marxist that one of our biggest motor companies should give ninety per cent of its earnings to a philanthropic fund and then divest itself of all control over that fund!

It is in these attitudes that the answer to Marxian analysis lies. Marx was not so much "wrong" in his economic vision as he was wrong in assuming that his psychological and sociological preconceptions were fixed and unalterable. The laws of motion which his model of capitalism revealed may still be visible in American capitalism—indeed, they are—but they are faced with a set of remedies which spring from social attitudes quite beyond his imagination. To Marx, the capitalist class was as incorrigibly chained to the ruthless search for profit as the working class had been, for Malthus, to sex. For Marx, a government was as inevitably a tool of the capitalist class as a revolutionary proletariat was inevitably a product of factory life. There was reason to form such ideas in the dark atmosphere of England in the 1860's—let us not forget that the world Marx knew, economically and politically, was cruel, cold, and doctrinaire. In too much of Europe it never quite lost that unhealthy cast—and the result for European capitalism was catastrophic. But in the New World new attitudes have emerged: the idea of democracy, the idea of an impartial government seeking to reconcile divergent interests, the idea of a class *struggle* without a class *war*. Our government has often been tinctured with class interest; it has rarely been tainted with it. All this would have seemed only a wishful fantasy to Marx.

The fact is that capitalism was capable of developing in almost totally divergent social directions. The tragedy is that for much of the world—and for all of the communist world—the stereotypes with which Marx set his plot into motion, the grasping Manchester mill-owner and the untractable regimes of 1848, are still taken as true likenesses of capitalism everywhere.

But shorn of its overtones of inevitable doom, the Marxist analysis cannot be disregarded. It remains the gravest, most penetrating examination the capitalist system has ever undergone. It is not an examination conducted along moral lines with headwagging and tongue-clucking over the iniquities of the profit motive—this is the stuff of the Marxist revolutionary but not of the Marxist economist. For all its passion, it is a dispassionate appraisal and it is for this reason that its somber findings must be soberly considered.

Marxism: science or ideology?

To repeat an earlier statement: it is with Karl Marx the Revolutionary that the world has been preoccupied, with Marxism as an intolerant force for the enslavement of free opinion. Certainly that is the immediate battle. And yet it is not with Marx the Revolutionary that capitalism must finally contend. It is with Marx the Economist, Marx the finicky scholar who laboriously sought to prove, through the welter of surface distraction, that the essence of capitalism is *self*-destruction. The answer to Marx lies not so much in pointing out the injustices of communism as in demonstrating that in a social atmosphere of which Marx never dreamed, capitalism can survive and flourish.

Karl Marx pronounced his sentence of doom on capitalism in 1867; the system was diagnosed as the victim of an incurable disease, and although no timetable was given, it was presumed to be close enough to its final death struggle for the next-of-kin—the Communists—to listen avidly for the last gasp that would signal their inheritance of power. Even before the appearance of *Das Kapital*, the deathwatch had begun, and with each bout of speculative fever or each siege of industrial depression, the hopeful drew nearer to the deathbed and told each other that the moment of Final Revolution would now be soon at hand.

But the system did not die. On the contrary, it seemed to emerge from each attack of weakness with renewed strength and to rebound from each crisis with a vigor that dismayed the critics. True, many of the Marxist laws of motion were amply verified by the march of events: big business did grow bigger and recurrent depressions and unemployment did plague society. But along with these confirmations of the prognosis of doom, another highly important and portentously phrased Marxist symptom was remarkable by its absence: the increasing misery of the proletariat.

For Marx had believed that with the protean struggle of the system to maintain itself, the working classes would be relentlessly ground underfoot, and that when the final death throes of capitalism were at hand, their revolutionary tempers would have snapped. With a kind of grim justice, the cruelties of capitalism would have brought into being its own executioner.

And that simply failed to happen. On the contrary, a British Committee on Depression which convened to look into the slump of 1886 reported that "there is no feature in the situation which we have been called upon to examine, as satisfactory as the immense improvement which has taken place in the condition of the working class." And this was not just the patronizing cant of class apologists: conditions were better, enormously better. In 1840, according to the calculations of Arnold Toynbee, the wage of an ordinary laborer came to eight shillings a week, while his family necessaries of life cost him fourteen shillings; he made up the difference by begging, stealing, sending his children to the mills, or simply by drawing in his belt. But by 1875, although necessaries had gone to fifteen shillings and a little over, his wages had nearly drawn abreast. *For the first time* he was making enough to keep body and soul together—a sorry commentary on the past, but certainly a hopeful augury for the future.

And not only had wages gone up, but the very source of surplus value had diminished: hours were far shorter. At the Jarrow Shipyards and the New Castle Chemical Works, for example, the workweek had fallen from sixty-one to fifty-four hours, while even in the sweated textile mills, the stint was reduced to only fifty-seven hours. Indeed the mill-owners complained that their wage costs had risen by better than twenty per cent. But while progress was expensive, it paid intangible dividends. For as conditions ameliorated, the mutterings of 1848 died down. "You cannot get them to talk of politics so long as they are well employed," testified a Staffordshire manufacturer on the attitude of his working force.

Revisionism and indifference

Even Marx and Engels had to recognize the trend. "The English proletariat is becoming more and more bourgeois," mourned Engels in a letter to Marx, "so that this most bourgeois of all nations is apparently aiming ultimately at the possession of a bourgeois aristocracy and a bourgeois proletariat *as well as a bourgeoisie*."

Clearly, Marx was premature in his pronouncement of impending doom. For the Faithful, of course, the unexpected turn of events could be swallowed in the comforting knowledge that "inevitable" still meant inevitable, and that a matter of a generation or two came to little in the grand march of history. But for the non-Marxist surveyors of the scene, the great Victorian boom meant something else. The world appeared full of hope and promise and the forebodings of a dissenter like Karl Marx seemed merely the ravings of a discontented radical. Hence the great intellectual bombshell that Marx had prepared went off in almost total silence; instead of a storm of abuse, Marx met the far more crushing ignominy of indifference.

Reading 90

Few Marxists are to be found in the economics departments of American universities. The late Paul Baran, professor of economics at Stanford, was one of the rare exceptions. His earlier book, *The Political Economy of Growth* (Monthly Review Press, New York, 1957), is critical of capitalistic colonialism and enjoys considerable audience abroad. Dr. Sweezy, trained at Exeter, Harvard, and the London School of Economics, has written a definitive work on Marxian economics, *The Theory of Capitalist Development* (Oxford University Press, New York, 1942), and is the editor of the *Monthly Review*.

The present excerpt was selected by the surviving author. The chapter from which it is taken claims much more than that America's attitude toward the Cuban revolution is primarily determined by the pecuniary interests of Standard Oil and other large corporations that hope to profit from a nonrevolutionary colony.

Questions to Guide the Reading

Had Cuba never offered a foothold for American business, would the American public still have been unconcerned to have a self-styled Marxist-Leninist government 90 miles from our shores? Is opposition to the Soviet Union and to what was regarded as expansion of the communist sphere of interest attributable only, or even primarily, to threatened loss of profits? Reversing roles, does the U.S.S.R. hope to get material economic benefit from Cuba? Is Russia interested primarily in helping the peasants of Cuba? In all this do power politics, nationalism, balance of power, and xenophobia play important roles? How can one test the validity of conflicting theses?

U.S. Business Interests Abroad: A Modern Marxist's View

Paul Baran and Paul M. Sweezy

It is often said that capitalism cannot exist without foreign trade and that every advance of socialism means a constriction of capitalism's trading area. Hence, the argument continues, for the leading capitalist countries, even if they are not threatened by powerful internal socialist movements, the struggle against socialism is quite literally a struggle for survival.

From Paul Baran and Paul Sweezy, "Monopoly Capital: An Essay on the American Economic and Social Order," *Monthly Review Press*, New York, 1968, pp. 193–203. Copyright © 1966 by Paul M. Sweezy. Reprinted with kind permission of the author and publisher.

Put in this form, the reasoning from capitalist interests involves a *non sequitur*. It is true that capitalism is inconceivable without foreign trade, but it is not true that socialist countries are unwilling or unable to trade with capitalist countries. Hence the spread of socialism, taken by itself, does not imply any reduction of the trading area open to the capitalist countries. One can even go further. Bourgeois economists never tire of repeating that the more industrially developed a country is, the greater its potential as a trading partner. Since underdeveloped countries industrialize more rapidly under socialism than under capitalism, the leading capitalist countries, on this argument, should welcome the spread of socialism in the underdeveloped parts of the capitalist world. That they do not but instead resist it tooth and nail must be explained on other grounds.

The problem is in reality much more complex and can only be fruitfully posed in quite different terms. Capitalist governments do not, in general, trade with each other. Most trade in the capitalist world is carried on by private enterprises, mainly by large corporations. What these corporations are interested in is not trade as such but profits: the reason they and the governments they control are opposed to the spread of socialism is not that it necessarily reduces their chances of importing or exporting (though of course it may), but that it does necessarily reduce their opportunities to profit from doing business with and in the newly socialized area. And when account is taken of the fact that for corporations in the leading capitalist countries, profit rates from doing business with and in the less developed and underdeveloped countries are generally higher than domestic profit rates, the reason for the vehemence of opposition to the spread of socialism in precisely those areas will be appreciated.

We advisedly use the general term "doing business with and in" rather than the more limited "buying from and selling to." The international relationships and interests of the typical giant corporation today are likely to be diverse and extremely complex, much more so than mere exporting or importing. There is perhaps no better way to make this clear than by summarizing the world-wide scope and character of what is unquestionably the leading United States "multinational corporation"— Standard Oil of New Jersey. The facts and figures which follow are taken from official publications of the company.[1]

In terms of dollar assets, Jersey Standard is the largest industrial corporation in the United States, the total at the end of 1962 amounting to $11,488 million. Aggregate revenues for the same year were $10,567 million and net income (profit) $841 million. It is only when these figures are broken down geographically, however, that the crucial importance of foreign operations becomes clear. As of the end of 1958, the percentage distribution of assets and profits by regions was as follows:

	Assets	Profits
United States and Canada	67	34
Latin America	20	39
Eastern Hemisphere	13	27
Total	100	100

While two thirds of Jersey's assets were located in North America, only one third of its profits came from that region. Or to put the point differently, Jersey's foreign investments were half as large as its domestic investments but its foreign profits were twice as large as its domestic profits. The indicated profit rate abroad is thus four times the domestic rate.

That Jersey's operations are truly worldwide can be gathered from the facts that in 1962 the company sold its products in more than a hundred countries and owned 50 percent or more of the stock in 275 subsidiaries in 52 countries. Summarizing by regions, we find that Jersey had 114 subsidiaries in the United States and Canada, 77 in Europe, 43 in Latin America, 14 in Asia, 9 in Africa, and 18 elsewhere.

The tremendous variety and scope of Jersey's foreign operations might lead one to suppose that over the years the company has been a large and consistent exporter of capital. Nothing could be further from the truth. Apart from a small initial export of capital many years ago, the expansion of Jersey's foreign assets has been financed from the profits of its foreign operations. Moreover, so great have been these foreign profits that after all foreign expansion needs have been taken care of, there have still been huge sums left over for

[1] *Notice of Special Stockholders' Meeting* (October 7, 1959); *Form 10-K for the Fiscal Year Ended December 31, 1962* (filed with the Securities and Exchange Commission pursuant to Section 13 of the Securities Act of 1934); and *1962 Annual Report*.

remittance to the parent company in the United States. Separate figures on the amount of these remittances from foreign profits are not published, but an idea of the orders of magnitude is conveyed by the following figures for 1962. In that year, as already noted, total profits were $841 million. Of this sum, $538 million were paid out as dividends to stockholders, the vast majority of whom are residents of the United States. The remaining $303 million were added to the company's investments, at home and abroad. Elsewhere in the same Annual Report that records these figures we learn that profits from operations in the United States in 1962 were $309 million. This figure, it will be seen, is $229 million less than the amount of dividends paid. In other words, approximately 40 percent of dividends paid to stockholders plus whatever net investment was made in the United States during the year were financed from the profits of foreign operations. In a word: Standard Oil of New Jersey is a very large and consistent *importer* of capital.

At this point, however, we must pause and ask whether Standard Oil of New Jersey is really an ideal type which helps us to distill the essence of capitalist reality, or whether on the contrary it may not be an exceptional case which we should ignore rather than focus attention on.

Up to the Second World War, it would have been correct to treat Standard Oil as a sort of exception—a very important one, to be sure, exercising tremendous, and at times even decisive, influence on United States world policy. Nevertheless in the multinational scope and magnitude of its operations not only was it far ahead of all the others; there were only a handful which could be said to be developing along the same lines. Many United States corporations of course had large interests in import and export trade, and quite a few had foreign branches or subsidiaries. In neither respect, however, was the situation much different in 1946 from what it had been in 1929. Indeed, direct foreign investments of United States corporations actually declined from $7.5 billion to $7.2 billion, or by 4 percent, between these two dates.[2] Most of

the giant corporations which dominated the American economy in those years were, in the words of *Business Week*, "domestically oriented enterprises with international operations" and not, like Standard Oil, "truly world oriented corporations." [3]

A big change took place during the next decade and a half. To quote *Business Week* again, "In industry after industry, U.S. companies found that their overseas earnings were soaring, and that their return on investment abroad was frequently much higher than in the U.S. As earnings abroad began to rise, profit margins from domestic operations started to shrink. This is the combination that forced development of the multinational company." [4] As a result, of course, foreign direct investments of American corporations shot up—from $7.2 billion in 1946 to $40.6 billion in 1963, a more than fivefold increase in the years since the Second World War.[5] Parallel to this growth in foreign investments has gone an increase in the sales and profits of foreign branches and subsidiaries. In manufacturing (excluding petroleum and mining), sales of such affiliates amounted to $18.3 billion in 1957 (the first year for which figures are available) and to $28.1 billion in 1962, an increase of 54 percent in six years.[6]

Some idea of the growing relative importance of these foreign operations of American corporations may be gathered from Table 1, which presents data on the sales of foreign manufacturing affiliates, total domestic manufacturing sales, and nonagricultural merchandise exports. (See p. 432 for Table 1.)

It would of course be preferable to compare the foreign and domestic sales and exports of those corporations which have foreign branches or subsidiaries; and it would be still better if we could include the profits of these corporations from foreign and domestic operations

[3] "Multinational Companies," *Business Week*, April 20, 1963. It is interesting to note that in the United States the business press is often far ahead of the economics profession in recognizing, and even trying to analyze, the latest developments in the capitalist economy.

[4] *Ibid.*

[5] *Survey of Current Business*, August 1964, p. 10.

[6] Fred Cutler and Samuel Pizer, "Foreign Operations of U. S. Industry: Capital Spending, Sales, and Financing," *Survey of Current Business*, October 1963, p. 19.

[2] United States Department of Commerce, Office of Business Economics, *U.S. Business Investments in Foreign Countries: A Supplement to the Survey of Current Business*, Washington, 1960, p. 1.

Table 1 Growth of Foreign and Domestic Manufacturing Sales and Merchandise Exports, 1957–1962 (billions of dollars)

	Sales of foreign manu- facturing affiliates	Total domestic manu- facturing sales	Merchandise exports (excluding foodstuffs)
1957	18.3	341	16.8
1958	n.a.	314	13.8
1959	21.1	356	13.7
1960	23.6	365	16.6
1961	25.6	368	16.9
1962	28.1	400	17.3

n.a. = not available
SOURCES: Foreign sales, Fred Cutler and Samuel Pizer, "Foreign Operations of U. S. Industry," *Survey of Current Business,* October 1963; domestic sales and exports, *Economic Indicators,* current issues.

respectively. If such data were available, we could form a very clear picture of the degree of involvement of the United States giant corporations in foreign activities. But even the figures presented in Table 1 bear eloquent testimony to the rapid growth of that involvement. In the six years beginning with 1957, the sales of foreign affiliates grew by 54 percent, while total domestic manufacturing sales expanded only 17 percent and non-agricultural exports hardly changed at all.

So much for the record of recent years. If we look ahead, we find that American corporate business, far from regarding its expansion abroad as having come to an end, is relying heavily for its future prosperity on the continued penetration of other countries' economies. "America as the 'land of opportunity' is beginning to lose that title in the eyes of many U.S. businessmen," says a Special Report in *U.S. News & World Report.*[7] And the Report goes on to tell why:

These businessmen increasingly are deciding that markets abroad—not those in this country—offer the

[7] "For New Opportunities: Now, the Word Is 'Go Abroad,'" *U. S. News & World Report,* June 1, 1964. In order to gather material for this report, "members of the International Staff of *U. S. News & World Report* talked with scores of U. S. firms abroad. Added material was gathered from corporations in the U. S. heavily engaged in the foreign field."

biggest potential for future growth. The feeling grows that the U. S. market, while huge, is relatively "saturated."

It is overseas that businessmen see the big, untapped market with hundreds of millions of customers wanting—and increasingly able to buy—all kinds of products and services.

To go after this market, U. S. firms are building and expanding factories all around the world. Since 1958, more than 2,100 American companies have started new operations in Western Europe alone.

All types of businesses—from autos to baby foods —predict a glowing future for markets outside the U. S.

It thus appears both from the record of the past and from the plans and hopes for the future that American corporate business has irrevocably embarked on the road long since pioneered by Standard Oil. Standard is still the model of a multinational corporation, but it is no longer an exception. It simply shows us in the most developed form what the other giants either already are or are in the process of becoming.

As it happens, the recent history of Standard Oil of New Jersey also supplies us with a textbook example of why multinational corporations are profoundly hostile to the spread of socialism. Before the Cuban Revolution, Jersey was heavily involved in Cuba in several ways. It owned refining facilities on the island and operated an extensive distribution system, involving altogether properties valued at $62,269,000.[8] In addition, Jersey's Cuban subsidiary bought its crude from Creole Petroleum, Jersey's Venezuelan subsidiary, at the high prices maintained by the international oil cartel. The company therefore reaped profits in two countries and on three separate operations—sale of crude, refining of crude, and sale of finished products. As a result of the Revolution, the company's properties in Cuba were nationalized without compensation, and Creole lost its Cuban market. More than $60 million in assets and all three sources of current profit were lost in one blow—and without in any way involving exports from or imports to the United States.

It might be argued that if Jersey and the United States government had pursued different policies toward Cuba, the revolutionary regime would have been glad to continue

[8] Standard and Poor, *Standard Corporate Descriptions,* July 24, 1961.

buying oil from Venezuela, which after all is the nearest and most rational source of supply. This is no doubt true—but with a big proviso. The revolutionary regime would have been glad to continue buying oil from Venezuela, but it would not have been glad to continue paying prices and meeting terms of payment dictated by Standard Oil. And since it could turn to the Soviet Union as an alternative source of supply, it was no longer obliged to go on submitting to the cartel's terms. Hence to remain in the Cuban market, Jersey would at the least have had to cut its prices and offer better credit terms. This not only would have meant less profits on sales to Cuba but would have threatened the whole structure of cartel prices. Jersey and Washington decided instead to make war on the Cuban Revolution.

That what is at stake in the conflict between the United States and Cuba is not trade between the two countries is confirmed by Cuba's relations with other capitalist countries. Long after the socialization of the Cuban economy, the Havana government was vigorously promoting its trade with Britain, France, Spain, Canada, Japan—in short, with any country willing and able to do business with Cuba. It is true, of course, that Cuba's capacity to export and import has been seriously curtailed by the disorganization and other difficulties of the early years of the change-over to socialism, but there seems to be no reason to doubt the Cubans' own contention that in a few years the island will be a much better trading partner than it was under the old neo-colonial regime. Nor is there any reason to doubt that the United States could capture a major share of the Cuban trade if the blockade were called off and normal relations re-established between the two countries.

But this is not what really interests the giant multinational corporations which dominate American policy. What they want is *monopolistic control* over foreign sources of supply and foreign markets, enabling them to buy and sell on specially privileged terms, to shift orders from one subsidiary to another, to favor this country or that depending on which has the most advantageous tax, labor, and other policies—in a word, they want to do business on their own terms and wherever they choose. And for this what they need is not trading partners but "allies" and clients willing to adjust their laws and policies to the requirements of American Big Business.

Against this background, one can see that Cuba's crime was to assert, in deeds as well as in words, her sovereign right to dispose over her own resources in the interests of her own people. This involved curtailing and, in the struggle which ensued, eventually abrogating the rights and privileges which the giant multinational corporations had previously enjoyed in Cuba. It was because of this and not because of a loss of trade, still less because of any irrational fears or prejudices, that the corporations and their government in Washington reacted so violently to the Cuban Revolution.

It might perhaps be thought that since Cuba is a small country, the violence of the reaction was out of all proportion to the damage suffered. But this would be to miss the main point. What makes Cuba so important is precisely that she is so small, plus the fact that she is located so close to the United States. If Cuba can defect from the "free world" and join the socialist camp with impunity, then any country can do so. And if Cuba prospers under the new setup, all the other underdeveloped and exploited countries of the world will be tempted to follow her example. The stake in Cuba is thus not simply the exploitability of one small country but the very existence of the "free world" itself, that is to say, of the whole system of exploitation.

It is this fact that has dictated the Cuban policy of the United States. The strategy has been to damage and cripple the Cuban economy in every possible way, with a threefold objective. First, it is hoped that the Cuban people will sooner or later become disillusioned with their revolutionary leadership, thus setting the stage for a successful counter-revolution. Second, the peoples of the underdeveloped countries are to be taught that revolution does not pay. And third, the burden of supporting the Cuban economy thrown on the rest of the socialist camp, and especially on the Soviet Union as its economically most developed member, is to be maximized so that these other socialist countries may be induced to use their influence to restrain any new revolutions which might place further burdens on their already overstrained economies.

Reading 91

The mixed economies of the advanced west are increasingly turning to some reliance on economic planning; and the countries behind the Iron Curtain are increasingly turning to some reliance on market pricing. Although they are still far from meeting on common ground, the differences between them are narrowing down and becoming as much quantitative as qualitative.

Jan Tinbergen, professor of economics at Rotterdam University and 1969 Nobel prize co-winner (with Norway's Ragnar Frisch), has been one of the leaders of economic planning within the government of the Netherlands. He is also one of the world's leading economists. Here he and his collaborators take an objective view of countries to the right and left of the Dutch economy.

Questions to Guide the Reading

Can you see how the discussion here reinforces the testimony of Readings 94 and 95 by Bergson? Similarly, how does it fit in with the Reading 87 by Shonfield?

The Twain Shall Meet: Convergence of East and West

J. Tinbergen, H. Linnemann, and J. P. Pronk

Numberless times every day, most of us either participate in, or observe, an exchange in which one person asks, "How *are* you?" and another rejoins, "How are *you*?" A question has been answered with a question. No information has been exchanged; but then none was really desired or expected, and the parties walk away satisfied that a social obligation has been punctiliously discharged.

A prominent psychiatrist identified this interaction as one of the most common everyday examples of ideology: that is, the habitual use of language without any appreciation of, or concern with, meaning. It represents nothing more than a ritualistic exercise, and no one would be more upset than the parties to this little game if a third individual were to stop them and point out that they had failed to communicate.

It is always dangerous to attempt to penetrate ideological screens—whether personal and individual (like the myth that we are really interested in our neighbor's welfare) or political and economic. Yet the requirements of human welfare as well as respect for the truth-value of language require that this be done, and so the authors will make so bold as

to try to cast some doubt on the central, and perhaps most pernicious, ideological stumbling block of our epoch: the proposition that the existing communist and western socioeconomic systems cannot possibly be reconciled and that the main cause of east-west conflict is rooted in structural differences.

Far from subscribing to this notion, we hold that, economically if not culturally and psychologically, the two systems are not very far apart and that, moreover, a strong converging influence can be discerned. In order to examine the validity of this proposition it is first necessary to review the major characteristics of the eastern and western socioeconomic orders.

The fundamental economic aim of the east is frequently stated as the elimination of exploitation, defined more specifically as the abolition of an unearned income for those who are able to work. The ultimate goal of the west is often formulated as the maximization of well-being, to be realized by increasing mass consumption and achieving equity in distribution.

Terminological differences notwithstanding, these aims appear more alike than inveterate ideologues on both sides care to admit. Thus

From J. Tinbergen, H. Linnemann, and J. P. Pronk, "The Meeting of the Twain," *Columbia Journal of World Business*, Summer, 1966. Reprinted with kind permission of the authors and publisher.

the elimination of exploitation in essence produces a change in income distribution and, viewed in this light, can thus be regarded as a high-priority western aim. True, the west has pursued this aim by different methods than the east; but it has nonetheless managed to fashion an aftertax income structure that compares favorably with that of communist countries. At the same time a western aim—high average consumption—is increasingly becoming a main objectives for the eastern economies. The existing differences in level must be understood partly as a result of historical circumstances rather than ideological goals. The communists were late starters in the race for industrial supremacy.

But if the two blocs seem reasonably close with respect to ultimate welfare aims, they have always appeared to diverge sharply on the means—both qualitative or institutional (e.g., property rights, degree of centralization, market structure) and quantitative (e.g, volume of investment, strength of material incentives, incidence of taxation)—to attain these goals. Both types of systems have been changing, however. Let us now take a closer look at what has been going on.

Structure of Soviet planning

The tasks of the Soviet government planning apparatus consist of drawing up plans for different periods of time, up to twenty years. Among these the annual plan is certainly the most significant. This specifies output figures —several thousand in fact, although the number is now declining. The plan also specifies investments, foreign trade, and until recently gave precise directions as to which factory was to supply which other factory. In the late Fifties, some 6% of all production was planned at the all-Union level, 71% at the Republic level and 23% at the local level. There is also planning for consumption; but since rationing was abolished some years ago, this is indicative only. As to agriculture, only those deliveries that must be made to the non-farm sector are planned.

National income concepts introduced

In the early phases of Soviet planning, targets were not formulated in macroeconomic terms but in quantities of the main commodities.

Later on, money was introduced as a common denominator and in recent years national income concepts have been increasingly used, though these are defined differently from comparable western concepts. Growth rates in capital goods industries have been considerably in excess of those in consumer goods industries; but while output in the former was 70% greater than in the latter from 1929 to 1940, it is only 7% larger today.

The planning procedure has traditionally followed this succession of steps:

1. Formulation of some general targets by the government;
2. Scrutiny of the consistency of these targets by Gosplan;
3. Announcement of these targets to all lower levels;
4. Preparation of draft plans by single factories, shops, etc.;
5. Fitting together of such draft plans by higher levels, while consulting various types of agencies (lower authorities, research agencies, sector authorities, group organizations), recontacting each until the discrepancies disappeared; and finally,
6. Fixing the plan.

Planning such as this has always been a process of trial and error, involving a large number of subsequent revisions in the light of new evidence. The natural conclusion—to decentralize a larger portion of the decisions—was only slowly accepted. However, current arrangements provide that fewer items will be planned at the center and more at lower levels, down even to the single factory.

How much freedom for the manager?

Recently there has been considerable discussion of the kinds of decisions that ought to be made at the factory level and the ways in which enterprise performance should be measured. In the last few years a number of clothing and footwear factories have been given the right to confer with the department stores selling their products on the styles and qualities desired by customers. Comments on this experiment are generally favorable and it is being extended to other areas of the economy. Such steps no doubt reinforce the power of the individual managers.

Some Soviet experts go beyond this and urge that all managers be freed to improve productivity by concentrating on making a profit. The use of profit as a paramount "success indicator" and as a substitute for commands issuing from the center presupposes, of course, that prices realistically reflect the relative scarcity of products. This raises certain questions as to the market. So far this institution has been used in the Soviet Union or, for instance, in Poland, only in a very limited way—mainly for a portion of agricultural production. Some authorities that favor decentralizing to the extent of expanding the private sector nevertheless balk at making the market a price-fixing institution. Only in Yugoslavia has the free market been given broad scope, and the results have not been entirely beneficial.

If long-contained centrifugal forces are modifying the pyramidal shape of Soviet-bloc industrial organization, centripetal tendencies are clearly knitting together the atomism long characteristic of the western socioeconomic order. Take the matter of planning. Planning was present in some large western enterprises but was virtually absent at the government level before 1914. The two wars and the great depression brought government intervention, and this in turn necessitated greater coordination and more planning. In periods of stress or war the scope of this planning was vastly expanded to take in the detailed allocation of scarce resources. During the postwar reconstruction, a number of countries maintained some central planning, mainly to furnish indirect guidance to the economy (e.g., United Kingdom, the Netherlands, Norway, and France, soon followed by the United States). Some of these activities were stimulated by the Marshall Plan. While the main emphasis of planning in most of these countries was on employment policy, balance of payments equilibrium, income distribution, and price stability, French planning went beyond this to concern itself with development aims. Later the responsibility to plan for development was accepted by Italy, Sweden, Denmark, and Belgium as well, and in the past few years we have witnessed an increased use of sectorwise development planning: direct intervention in the public sector and indirect (via monetary and fiscal policy) in the private economy.

Retreat from the market

We have also observed a persistent decline in the strength of purely market forces. Central governmental regulation of industry has intensified. Large cartels have developed, limiting competition within branches of industry, although not so easily between branches. Managerial freedom with respect to labor and working conditions has been checked. The freedom to spend has been reduced by progressive taxes and market pricing has been eliminated in many unstable markets, such as agriculture and mining. Decisions on the main issues of socioeconomic policy are often made by central organizations of employers and employees or by the government in close contact with these organizations.

Convergence in agriculture

Turning now to agriculture, we discern similar lines of east-west convergence, though the picture is not so clear as in industry. The Soviets have always had enormous difficulty centralizing agriculture. One obstacle is, of course, peasant psychology. Another is the fact that the space-consuming nature of agricultural production does not lend itself to centralized control. Yet the Soviet-bloc countries persevered. Collective and state farms were organized, machine and tractor stations set up, and forced deliveries of a portion of crops at fixed prices insisted upon. The system failed to generate enough production. The Soviets shifted gears, began opening up large virgin areas with the help of mass-production techniques. This arrangement also did not work. Finally, the machine and tractor stations were abolished, while in Poland and Yugoslavia collective farms were abandoned. The Soviet bloc has now loosened its control over agriculture and numerous incentives have been introduced. Prices of forced deliveries have been raised; supplementary deliveries to the authorities at better prices introduced; and sales directly to the public, at prices set by the market, allowed. Farmers in collective farms still have their private plot, the significance of which was recently emphasized by the authorities, and specialized state farms for vegetables and fruits have their own trade channels.

What about the west? Although western agriculture is still overwhelmingly in private hands, there is a strong though slow tendency toward larger units, where increasing returns to scale can be realized. Almost all agricultural markets are now considered inherently unstable and hence are regulated by national or international plans. Moreover, considerable support is given to agricultural prices in many western countries.

The communists discover trade

The impression of converging lines of development is further confirmed by a brief look at the evolution of the trade policies of the two systems. As long as the Sovet Union was the only communist-ruled country, the degree of centralization in decisions on the interregional division of labor in the eastern world was relatively high, the main decisions being taken only in Moscow. After World War II the scene changed. Even though the Soviet Union had overwhelming power to impose its will, formal and, increasingly, actual power to decide was partly handed over to the "people's democracies" of Eastern Europe. China early followed its own course. Soviet experience in governing a "socialist economy" played a considerable part, however, in shaping the other countries' policies and thus even the small countries strove to become as self-sufficient as their mentor and guide.

One argument in favor of self-sufficiency was that planning can be more consistent; another was that national independence can be furthered. The creation of steel industries everywhere is a well-known consequence of that view. Trade was considered a secondary device to get rid of surpluses and remedy the worst shortages, and in the beginning trade agreements were negotiated only after the national plans had been drawn up. Gradually the importance of international exchange was recognized and some coordination envisaged, resulting in the creation of Comecon (Council for Mutual Economic Cooperation). Until 1963, however, trade agreements were kept in bilateral equilibrium. Finally, the communists discovered that multilateral equilibrium would guarantee higher living standards for all concerned, and in 1963 they stopped insisting on bilateral balancing. Even so, a large portion of trade between the communist countries is still strictly bilateral, as is the case in Western Europe. In 1964 an International Bank was created. While planning is still primarily considered an individual country affair, some supranational planning can already be found. Interesting enough, the communist-ruled world is as little internationally minded as the western world, or probably even somewhat less.

In the western world international trade has always been given considerable emphasis. But while many economists and some governments have advocated free trade, most governments stuck to some degree of protection—partly for fiscal reasons, partly in order to protect their economies against sudden changes in competitive power, or partly for nationalistic reasons. Thus each nation considered it vital to produce a minimum of indispensable consumer goods within its borders. The two world wars tended to reinforce national isolation. After World War II Western European countries first followed a policy of trade and payments control —which often resulted in bilateral equilibria. Under OEEC trade was increasingly multilateralized and trade impediments reduced. EEC and EFTA continued the process of reduction of barriers among their members. The criterion of the international division of labor applied is free competition, which for many industries is almost identical with comparative advantage. This is not true for trade with the outside world, however, since external tariffs are considerable for some types of goods, particularly EEC agricultural products. In recent years proposals envisaging some supranational planning have been getting serious attention within EEC.

Having discussed some of the main institutional changes, we turn next to the shifting role of the quantitative economic policies of both east and west.

Probably the most important quantitative means (or instrument) of eastern socioeconomic policy has been the level of investment expenditures. Subsumed under this category are material investments (in fixed capital goods and inventories) and education (or investment in human beings) in its broadest sense. The proportion of Soviet-bloc national income devoted to material investment (measured according to western definitions, for reasons of comparison) has been estimated at about 25%, nor has this percentage varied greatly. Education expenditures and other measures of educational activity (enrollment figures) have also been high, matching the U.S. in most areas and exceeding it in resources devoted to scientific and technological instruction.

The West speeds up investment

The investment picture has changed more radically in the west than in the east. For decades the proportion of national income saved was estimated at 11% to 12% (average over cycles) in the United Kingdom and the United States. In Continental Europe it may have been somewhat higher, say 15%. After World War II, Europe began investing up to 20% and Japan almost 30% (net) of their national income. Education expenditures also increased as a percentage of national income or on a per capita basis. Educational levels in Western Europe seem to be lower than in the United States or the Soviet Union. In recent years, economists have taken to estimating the impact of education on productivity. Denison calculates that, for the United States, of an average rate of increase in product per capita of 1.6% (over the period 1929–1957), some 0.6% is the result of increasing educational attainment.

No doing without incentives

Another vital quantitative means are incentives and the distribution of income. Having no understanding of the economic function of income inequality, the Soviet authorities first attempted to equalize income by decree. Only exyperience taught them that this could not be done without disrupting the relationship between the supply of and demand for labor of different quality, and thus interfering with the rapid economic growth which they believed they had to achieve. In the Thirties, therefore, they reimposed payment according to productive contribution, which was then announced as a socialist wage policy in contradistinction to the communist wage policy of payment according to need. Egalitarian principles were, from that moment on, denounced as dilettantism and petty-bourgeois. This important change constituted one of many further steps meant to create material incentives to further productive effort, to replace pure command or an appeal to idealism, which only works under special circumstances and with a minority of people. The problem still exists to some extent, as is illustrated by the recent contention (1962) that in Poland wages in the machine industry were too equal.

There are now a variety of incentives for managers, workers, and peasants. Both managers and workers share, but at different rates, in the additional income obtained from plan overfulfilment. Various types of premiums have been introduced and some experimenting goes on, remarkably parallel with western experiments. Thus, at one time piece rates were considered a good stimulus, but the Soviets came to feel in 1962 that they were going too far in this direction and reimposed time rates in a number of occupations. Premiums were tried at the individual level and later with groups of varying size.

As the results of more education begin to show up, the supply of qualified labor is being increased and that of unskilled people reduced, thus changing the equilibrium rates for the various occupations. This has made it possible to attain greater wage equality. Thus, in 1960, the degree of inequality (the average absolute deviation from mean income) was estimated to be the same as in 1930, before egalitarian wage scales were abandoned.

Income distribution in western countries was very unequal in the 19th century but has gradually become more equal, despite the fact that unearned income has never been eliminated. Instead of all-out nationalization, the west has slowly increased the size of the public sector (now perhaps 20% or 25% of all means of production), and introduced increasingly progressive income and estate taxes. Aftertax income inequality has probably fallen to 0.55 (again expressed as the average absolute deviation from the mean), about the same as that achieved in the east.

Incentives have always played a large role in western societies and again are very similar in nature to those evolved in the east. Recently, the west has been giving its youth greater incentive than previously to continue their education; apart from the growing scholarship program, financial assistance to students has expanded considerably. A powerful incentive to entrepreneurs, with less desirable side effects, is capital gains, a natural consequence of private ownership. Of late, some attempts have been made in western countries to limit these gains by capital gains taxes.

Even an interest charge!

Another set of quantitative means deal with pricing, to which we have already alluded, and investment criteria. As is well known most Soviet-bloc prices are set by central government agencies and are based on the labor theory of value. This means that capital-intensive goods such as electricity are priced low and labor-intensive goods, high. It has only been recently that the eastern countries have begun to take into account the cost of capital. Now, however, this CPSU (Communist Party of the Soviet Union) program refers to profit as an element of correct pricing while Hungary and Poland have even gone so far as to impose interest charges. The chief criterion for a capital charge is now the recoupment period, that is, the ratio of additional investments to their cost savings. In Poland and Hungary a uniform upper time limit is applied in all industries, with corrections for differences in gestation period and the life of the equipment. Since the other eastern countries have not accepted this concept, their capital allocations will probably be less than optimal.

Tax policies

The last quantitative instrument we will consider is taxation. The main difference between the eastern and western tax structures is that direct taxes play a much larger part in the latter countries than in the former. In the west they are a substitute for what public ownership of the means of production accomplishes in the east: the reduction of unearned income. These taxes have been introduced mainly under socialist pressure; their disadvantage is that they require a complicated administration and may reduce incentives to higher production, although if policy is well formulated, this drawback may be overcome.

Another difference between east and west is that the former distinguishes between consumer and producer goods for tax purposes while the latter differentiates more between necessities and luxuries. However, this distinction is somewhat blurred, since the communist countries do vary "turnover tax" rates for different consumer goods.

Communist Economics

Readings 92 and 93

Anyone who comes back from the dead is bound to be of great interest. Yugoslavia is the one case of a country which joined the Stalinist camp of communism, but which under the leadership of Tito succeeded in doing what Hungary and Czechoslovakia did not—namely, going its own way. This does not mean that Yugoslavia became capitalistic. Rather it has retained its own version of communism. This version is of extraordinary interest as a hybrid, seeming to combine some of the features of capitalism with those of communism. The profit motive is given considerable scope and much of planning is decentralized.

In Reading 92 a distinguished correspondent for the *New York Times* reports upon a particular example of the Yugoslavian new way. In Reading 93 Professor Lindblom of Yale University develops the theme that it is in non-laissez-faire societies that the most exciting rediscoveries of the market mechanism have been taking place.

Questions to Guide the Reading

If profit sharing works, why not go all the way back to laissez-faire capitalism? Does the cooperative movement in Yugoslavia have anything to offer to the present generation of college students who are attracted by notions of "participatory democracy" and who often look to the Israeli kibbutz for a possible pattern of social reorganization?

Obviously, laissez faire would be unthinkable without reliance on the mechanism of market pricing. But it is more remarkable that this same market mechanism is becoming increasingly popular with those who believe in a planned and collectivist society. Libermanism in Soviet Russia is only one indication of this renewed interest.

Does rediscovery of the market mean that communism really does not work? Do you understand what a *shadow price* is (i.e., a price that is used for accounting or planning purposes even though nobody's income may get determined by it)? Why should there be a problem of allocative efficiency in a socialistic society: will not the philosophy "from each according to his ability, to each according to his need" render such niceties unnecessary? Is it possible that the developing countries like India, which have neither the widespread reliance on markets of the United States nor the central collectivist planning of the Soviet Union, would be getting the worst of all worlds?

Reading 92

Profit Rears Its Head in Yugoslavia

Anthony Lewis

KORCULA, Yugoslavia—Zivan Filippi is 29 years old, a native of the island of Korcula, a graduate of Zagreb University. He also spent a year at the University of Nottingham, England, where he studied literature and wrote a paper on Saul Bellow's exotic early novel, "Henderson the Rain King."

When he is not talking about literature or the history of Korcula, Mr. Filippi could be mistaken for a product of an American management training course. He speaks the language of the sales chart.

He and four other Zagreb graduates, also Korculans, returned here a few years ago and decided to go into the hotel business. At that time the island had only one hotel.

As permitted by President Tito's economic reforms, the group formed what Mr. Filippi calls "an enterprise"—perhaps avoiding the word company because of its capitalist ring.

Each put in the equivalent of $80, a symbolic investment that was all they had.

From a Belgrade bank the young men borrowed $300,000—on the advantageous terms of 5 per cent for 25 years. (Half a dozen other Yugoslav banks were possible sources of money, and the loan might have been arranged abroad.)

One of the founding group was an architect and drew the plans. The first section of the hotel was built between March and July, 1967 —111 days, Mr. Filippi says proudly.

Last year a second section was finished. The Hotel Bon Repos, as it is called, now has 500 beds. This summer it filled "45,000 bed nights," as Mr. Filippi put it, nearing capacity. The appeal is strictly to mass tourism. The architecture is undistinguished Mediterranean egg-crate, but for $6.50 a day in a double room the tourist gets balcony, private shower

From Anthony Lewis, "Individual Initiative in Communist Yugoslavia," *The New York Times*, September 5, 1969. Reprinted with kind permission of the author and publisher.

and toilet, and full board. Mr. Filippi tours Europe each winter to drum up block bookings.

Expansion plans

The enterprise is about to add 700 more beds to the Bon Repos in new wings, and then to build a new hotel of 350 beds, The Korkyra, by 1971. It has already sold 200 rooms in The Korkyra for 1971 to a West German travel agency.

At the moment the hotel owes $1-million to banks. It has annual revenue of $350,000 but is not yet making a profit. If and when it does, it may invest the surplus in new facilities or decide to pay higher salaries—to, for example, Mr. Filippi, assistant manager.

Such major decisions, under the Yugoslav system of worker management in each business, are taken by the staff as a whole. Actually, as elsewhere, the views of the top men usually prevail.

The story of the Hotel Bon Repos has been told at some length because it is so remarkable by the economic standards of either East or West—remarkable in the scope afforded for individual initiative.

Under orthodox Soviet Communism, there would of course be central planning and central control, with all the familiar deadening effects. And in the complicated economy of the United States these days, with the vast power of established business, it is not exactly easy for a group of young men to put a significant business together as Mr. Filippi and his friends have.

Independence of business decision seems to be characteristic of the Yugoslav system. The shipyard at Vela Luka, at the other end of this island, uses engines from Sweden, Fiberglas from an American-owned plant in Rotterdam and resin from Austria.

Examples of competition abound. Two travel agencies operate in Korcula. Next door to the supermarket is a small general store. There is one restaurant operated by the commune of Korcula, and there are others run by private families.

The price of all this for President Tito and his colleagues is a complicated life.

If business is independently managed and must compete, for example, some will fail: there are bankruptcies and court-appointed receivers in Yugoslavia. Other businesses have cut wages as much as 50 per cent in an effort to survive. In short, there are conflict and uncertainty—which some people think are the necessary accompaniments of economic progress but which make some people unhappy.

Experimenting communist

For Tito there is the added pressure of his evident desire to retain the status of a good Communist. Over all the years of conflict with the Soviet Union he has tried, in periodic phases, to restore good relations. That is why, recently, he has soft-pedaled criticism of the Czech affair and why he is now receiving Soviet Foreign Minister Gromyko.

Thus, from time to time, Tito will warn against "capitalist" tendencies. But in fact there is no exact parallel for the economic system now being attempted here. It is an experiment that any open-minded society should be interested to observe.

Reading 93

The Rediscovery of the Market

Charles E. Lindblom

What is the significance of the great debate, already several years old, on the appropriate role of profits in the planned economies of Communist Europe?

One interpretation of this sea change in Communist thinking is that Communism is turning capitalist. Since imitation is the sincerest form of flattery, many Americans are

From Charles E. Lindblom, "The Rediscovery of the Market," *The Public Interest*, Number 4, Summer, 1966. Copyright National Affairs, Inc. Reprinted with kind permission of the author and publisher.

delighted to accept this interpretation. But the Communists do not see their reforms in this light; and Professor Liberman, whose name is foremost in the Soviet debate over the profit motive, has explicitly denied that Communist use of the profit motive is capitalistic. On his side of the argument there is some weighty evidence: namely, the existence of profit-oriented *socialist* enterprises all over the world—e.g., municipally-owned public utilities in the U.S., the nationalized industries of Britain and Western Europe, and the socialized enterprises of many developing nations (like Hindustan Machine Tools of India).

Indeed, the significance of the reforms has little to do with the antithesis capitalism-socialism. The new and growing use of profitability criteria in Communist enterprises can better be understood as a phase in *a world-wide rediscovery of the market mechanism.*

Markets for planners

Now, capitalism and the market mechanism are not the same thing. Understandably, they are often confused with each other, because it was under capitalist auspices that the market mechanism first became, on a vast scale, the organizer of economic life. But the market mechanism is a device that can be employed for planned as well as unplanned economies, and for socialism and communism as well as capitalism. Today the market mechanism is a device both for the organization of the relatively unplanned sectors of the American economy and for such central planning as is practiced in the United States. In Britain and Scandinavia, it organizes both the private and the socialized sectors of the economy. In Yugoslavia it serves as an overall coordinator for an economy of publicly-owned enterprises. In many underdeveloped countries it is a powerful tool of development planning. It is this market mechanism rather than capitalism that the U.S.S.R. and its satellites are trying to employ—precisely to improve their planning.

Except for a convulsive attempt between 1918 and 1921, Soviet policy has never questioned the practical usefulness of money and prices. This does not mean, however, that the Soviet Union has heretofore made much use of the market mechanism. By the market

mechanism, we mean the use of money and prices in a very particular way: *prices and price movements are employed—instead of targets, quotas, and administrative instructions —to give signals to producers with respect to what and how much they should produce; and prices on labor and materials consumed are set to reflect the relative value of these inputs in alternative uses to which they might be put.*

It is the possibility of using a pricing process to evaluate alternative possibilities and to cue producers accordingly—whether to suit the preferences of individual consumers in the market or the preferences of central planners, whether to administer the resources of an advanced economy or to guide the developmental choices of an underdeveloped economy—that has struck a new note in Communist economic policy, in the economic reorganization of Western Europe, and in the economic development of the nations still in early stages of growth. The significance of the development, of which Communist reforms are only a part, can be appreciated in the light of its own history.

Adam Smith and laissez faire

Most people who know anything at all about the market mechanism seem not to have advanced beyond Adam Smith's view of it. He saw it as *an alternative* to government control of economic life. He was concerned about inefficiency and other defects of mercantilism; and, to speak anachronistically, he thought he had found in the market mechanism a *substitute for incompetent planners.* His specific insights were profound. He saw the possibility that resources could be systematically allocated in response to human needs as a by-product of "selfish" individual decisions simply to buy or to sell. He saw that prices established by consumers in their trading with producers could establish a set of signals that could direct the productive processes of the whole economy. He saw that competitive bidding for inputs would establish a market value for them that would make possible a comparison of their productivities in alternative uses. He saw that a comparison of input prices and output prices, that is, of the money cost of production with money receipts, could control the flow of resources into each of their alternative possible uses. Finally, he saw that the market mechanism was for all these reasons an extraordinarily powerful device for decentralizing economic decisions. In all this, however, his vision was limited: the market mechanism was always a private enterprise market and always an alternative to planning.

Market socialism

It was not until the development, over a century and a half later, of the theory of market socialism that any significant number of people perceived the possibilities of using the market mechanism in a completely socialized economy. Even today the idea of market socialism remains esoteric. In 1920, Ludwig von Mises published his now famous challenge to the socialists to indicate whether they had any system in mind for the actual administration of economic affairs in a socialist order. It was a challenge that many socialists brushed aside, believing that they could cross that bridge when they came to it. But a few socialists, conspicuous among them the late Oskar Lange, turned back to the 1908 work of the Italian economist Barone, to construct a model of a socialist economy that would practice a systematic and decentralized evaluation and allocation of its resources. They showed that prices could be manipulated by government in such a way as to reflect the values that consumers put on consumer goods and services, and also to reflect the values of inputs in alternative uses. Their discussion of the pricing process under socialism clarified the useful functions that prices can perform. If, for goods and services in short supply, prices are systematically raised by government pricing authorities, the high prices can be taken as signals for increased production, while being at the same time at least temporary deterrents to consumption. Similarly, if prices are systematically lowered for goods in overabundant supply, the low prices can be taken as signals by producers to curtail supply, and by consumers to increase consumption.

Lange's 1936 exposition of these possibilities made it clear that prices could be systematically regulated to perform the signalling and evaluating functions even in the absence of those competing private sellers whose rivalry sets prices in a private enterprise economy. Moreover, his exposition demonstrated that prices so set permit a systematic comparison of alternative patterns of allocation, a comparison that would not be possible without prices of this kind.

If the development of the theory of market socialism made it clear that the market mechanism could serve socialism as well as capitalism, it nevertheless did not much interest the socialists of Western Europe or the planners of Communist Europe. For the market socialist had developed a model of a socialist economy that left very little room for central planning. Their socialist market mechanism was designed, as was the market mechanism of classical economics to serve the preferences of individual consumers rather than the priorities of central planners. As in a capitalist economy, in this kind of market socialism the consumer remained sovereign—at a time when most socialists, planners, and Communists were looking for ways to *effect collective purposes and national goals, rather than individual preferences.* Although socialist theory considered harnessing the market mechanism to centrally determined priorities, it did not construct a persuasive case as to how it could be done.

In the Communist countries, the possibilities of market socialism were underrated for still other reasons. Communist ideology was antagonistic to the very idea of the market, hence inevitably to market socialism. Academic and professional Soviet economics was also antagonistic to the orthodox tradition in economic theory out of which the theory of market socialism sprang. Finally, with respect to formal planning and resource allocation, the overwhelming concern of Soviet policy was "balance" rather than what economists call optimality. Optimality involves a careful evaluation of returns to production in alternative lines. To Soviet planners, however, the need for big allocations to steel, electric power production, and national defense seemed obvious. Speaking very roughly, all that remained to be done was to insure that allocations for the rest of the economy were roughly consistent with, or in balance with, the crudely calculated but obviously necessary allocations to these high priority sectors. And even this formal interest in balance was secondary to their interest in the crude growth of physical output.

The market mechanism for centrally determined objectives

If the market mechanism was ever to be of any use for central planning, it had to be shown that prices could be set to reflect centrally determined values, and not merely individual consumer values. In the economics of the West, it has in fact long been clear that they can do so. For example, a subsidy to maritime shipping lines or to airmail carriers is a way of raising the price received by those who provide these transport services, thus signalling them to increase their production of the services. Similarly, a tax on liquor is a way of depressing the price received by manufacturers and distributors, hence a way of signalling them to restrict output. The result of these interventions—either subsidies or taxes—is to achieve a price that reflects both individual consumer preference *and* the preferences of governmental authorities.

A government can go even further—and in wartime often does. It can completely eliminate the effect on price of individual consumer demands so that producers respond to a price set entirely by government. This can be done either through the imposition of a legal price or by exclusive government purchase of commodities and services, after which government agencies either consume the purchased goods and services themselves or, in the case of consumer goods, redistribute them in some way to consumers.

Using the market mechanism in this way is an alternative to direct administrative control —to targets, quotas, physical allocations, specific instructions, etc. It is not always a good alternative, but it often is, since it is a way of manipulating incentives powerfully while leaving the actual decision—to produce or consume more or less—in the hands of the agency or enterprise whose price has been altered. Hence, a general virtue of the market mechanism as an instrument of central direction is that it permits extraordinary decentralization of detailed decision making.

To understand the possibility of subordinating the market mechanism to governmental rather than to individual choice, it is essential to distinguish between actions in which governments signal their production targets through prices, and actions in which they intervene in the market mechanism to alter the results without, however, actually using prices systematically as such a signalling device. To raise agricultural prices, for example, in order to stimulate agricultural production is a way of employing the market mechanism for the achievement of a centrally-determined goal of high agricultural production. On the other hand, to raise agricultural prices as part of a complex process of restricting farm output (as in the U.S.) is an entirely different kind of operation, in which direct administrative controls (such as acreage quotas) replace the market mechanism. Or again: depressing the price received by a manufacturer by imposing a tax on his output is a way of implementing a central decision to discourage consumption of the commodity, whereas the general imposition of legal maximum prices to control inflation has the effect of interfering with the market's ability to reflect either collective or individual choices and will ordinarily give rise to rationing, or to some other administrative device for the allocation of goods and services.

Perhaps it is the easy confusion of miscellaneous intervention in the pricing process (which the Communist economies have always practiced) with the skillful use of pricing to implement central planning of production that has contributed to Communist indifference to the latter. In any case, the Western demonstration that the market mechanism could be used to implement central priorities did not significantly affect Communist policy until certain other developments occurred. Even as late as 1950, the model of market socialism seemed to be consigned to a limbo of interesting irrelevancies. Ideological barriers were still strong; so also was the obstacle of fundamental ignorance in Soviet economies about the pricing process.

Yugoslavia

The Yugoslav economy was the one sensational exception to Communist indifference to the market mechanism. Yugoslav Communism was indigenous, not imposed by the U.S.S.R. as in the satellites generally. Political relations with the Soviet Union were such that in Yugoslavia independence in economic policy came to be valued rather than feared. Moreover, Yugoslav intellectuals and politicos had closer ties with their counterparts in the West than did any of the other Communist countries. Whatever the reasons, in 1952, recoiling from the inefficiencies of detailed administrative control over the economy, Yugloslavia brought into being a greatly decentralized market socialism. The change of direction, taken together with the rapid growth that ensued, excited much interest in the Communist world. The significance for Communism of the Yugoslav venture was greatly diminished on one score, however. For when the Yugoslavs abandoned detailed administrative control over the market mechanism they also went a long way toward consumer sovereignty as a replacement for the central direction of the economy. Hence, in the eyes of Communists elsewhere the Yugoslavs had largely abandoned central planning itself.

New freedom for economic inquiry

New possibilities for economics were opened up by Stalin's death in 1953. Soviet economists, engineers, and administrators could finally look with some freedom at the lessons to be learned from foreign experience with the market mechanism. One especially noteworthy gain for economic analysis was the lifting of Stalin's capricious ban on mathematical economics (input-output analysis, and linear programming, etc.).

Soviet mathematical economics, reaching back to work originating in the 1930's but not then pursued further, demonstrated independently of Western economics that pricing can be made useful to the planning of resource allocation even in the absence of any actual exchange between a buyer and seller. If we consider all the alternative combinations of end products that an economy can choose from, and all the alternative combinations of inputs that might be used to produce any given output, we see that there are vast possibilities of substitution—of one end product for another, and of one input for another. These possibilities of substitution can be represented by "substitution ratios"—and these substitution ratios can be expressed as a system of prices. (In the absence of any actual transaction in which a real price would be set, they are often called "shadow prices".) *Pricing turns out, therefore, to be implicit in the very logic of rational choice among alternative uses of resources.*

This discovery clearly removes certain tradi-tional ideological objections to market pricing, for it makes clear that *pricing is not a capitalist invention but a logical aid to rational calculation even in circumstances far removed from capitalist buying and selling.* Whether in fact the discovery has yet achieved this consequence for Soviet thought is not certain, however; for Soviet mathematical economists have, on the whole, drawn the inference, not that the market mechanism might now be more openly examined, but that such pricing as might be achieved through the market mechanism can in principle now better be achieved through further mathematical analysis and electronic computation.

The "in principle" is crucial, since a prodigious amount of information needs to be gathered and processed in order to substitute computers for actual markets; and so far the accomplishment is beyond the capacity of economists, Soviet or Western. Nor can it be said with confidence that there is any way to gather and test the required information except by putting consumers or planners in the position of actual choice in a real market. Still, the exploration of the practical mathematics of resource allocation is far from its maturity.

The rising concern for allocative efficiency

In any case, the discovery of "shadow pricing" did not of itself overcome Communist disinclination to exploit the market mechanism. A final consideration was the growing complexity of the Soviet economy, with complexity outstripping admittedly growing Soviet competence in planning. The economy became more complex for at least two reasons: with the rising standard in living, the demand of consumers for varied and higher-quality consumer goods came to be more pressing; and with technological advance, alternative production possibilities became more numerous and complex. Soviet policy makers could no longer be satisfied with the simple mobilization of large quantities of capital, and the attendant mobilization of agricultural labor, for industry. As one student of the Soviet economy has written:

The Soviet economy again appears to be at a turning point. It is clear, as the debate shows, that it is becoming more and more difficult to plan *everything* centrally. The Soviet economy has grown not only in size, but in sophistication in concern for the consumer. As a result, campaigns and storming can no longer solve all the problems that arise. There are simply too many sectors which need attention. They can not all be manipulated from the center. It has been estimated that, if the economy continues its present growth, by 1980 the planning force will have to be thirty-six times its present size.

It is especially noteworthy that the older Communist concern for "balance" is, in the face of this new complexity, no longer thought sufficient. It is increasingly difficult to find some clear superiority of one pattern for a few key industries over another alternative pattern. And that being so, Communist countries can no longer be satisfied with merely balancing the outputs and inputs of all other industries to satisfy a prior commitment to a few key programs. In short, consistency in an economic plan is no longer enough; optimality in a plan is now becoming a pressing objective. Hence, finally, the new interest in the market mechanism.

Raymond P. Powell and Richard Moorsteen document still another hypothesis to explain the new Soviet interest in improved resource allocation ("optimality"). The Soviet Union, they suggest, has been exhausting the possibilities for rapid growth through indefinitely larger and larger capital investment; it must now either find an alternative source of growth—i.e. a better allocation of resources—or resign itself to a lower growth rate.

The rediscovery of the market in the West

Outside the Communist orbit, an appreciation of the usefulness of the market mechanism has been most conspicuously on the rise since World War II. With good reason, the market was under great attack in the depression of the '30's, the severity of disillusionment with its usefulness nowhere more vivid than in the American NRA, an attempt at partial displacement of the market in favor of private and public administrative controls. But in the late '30's, Keynesian economics began to hold out the promise of ending depressions by improving rather than eliminating the market mechanism; and Western governments, learning the lesson, have in recent years sustained higher levels of employment than used to be thought possible. Similarly, taxation and transfer payments, as well as provision of subsidized public goods like education, have attacked problems of inequality in income distribution—such problems can therefore no longer motivate

proposals to disestablish the market mechanism. The result is that, in the West, the market mechanism is in better repute than ever before, as is indicated in the decline of socialist opposition to the market mechanism both on the continent and in Britain, where after World War II socialists deliberately subjected their newly nationalized enterprises to market controls rather than to the battery of administrative controls they had once contemplated. And the great event in Western European development in recent decades has been a substantial move toward unification, not through common government, flag, army, or language, but through the Common *Market*.

The developing nations

As a group, the underdeveloped nations of the world are lagging in their understanding of the usefulness of the market mechanism. Abstractly, they should be eager to exploit every possibility for economic advance; in fact, they stand in a kind of backwater.

One reason is that their leaders and intellectuals are often prisoners of a once exciting but now stifling orthodoxy. Some of them are prisoners of early Marxian doctrine on planning, the very orthodoxy from which European Communism is escaping. Others are prisoners of English socialism of the style and date of Harold Laski, or even of earlier versions of English socialism—in either case antagonistic to the market mechanism. But times change: although Nehru was a prisoner of both, his daughter may turn out to be a prisoner of neither.

Another reason is, oddly enough, the insistence of the United States, the World Bank, and other lenders that underdeveloped countries formulate national economic plans in order to qualify for aid. They mean by a plan a balanced and consistent set of investment outlays. The effect is to divert some of the best brains in these countries away from high priority questions of growth strategy to the construction of reconciled investment programs reminiscent of those the Communist countries are trying to leave behind as inadequate. In India, for example, *the question of the size and internal consistency of the five-year plans overshadows in public discussion, and in the attention it receives from experts in Indian government, many more rewarding questions of growth strategy,* including such questions as how the market mechanism might be employed to hold out incentives to farmers to raise food production or how it might ration scarce foreign exchange in such a way as to substantially raise the level of economic achievement.

To be sure, just how much the underdeveloped economies should count on the market mechanism is subject to much dispute. The point being made here is only that the underdeveloped countries themselves do not well understand the issues, and have often not tumbled to the fact that, for many of the specific developmental problems they face, they can employ the market mechanism in tandem with other methods of controlling and planning economic development.

The prospect that the underdeveloped countries may take a new view of the market mechanism as an instrument of development planning is, of course, greatly enlarged by what they now see developing in Communist Europe. For even if they do not intend to follow the Communist path to development, the evidence that Western and Communist economies alike are finding the market mechanism useful is certain to impress them.

Furthering development

How they can best employ the market mechanism depends upon the particulars of their circumstances. But on a few counts a general usefulness of the market mechanism for these economies can be predicted. First, they all suffer desperately from a shortage of administrative skills and organization: they are not very competent in executing *any* kind of plan, economic or otherwise. Even the best of their civil services have developed procedures and traditions more suitable to keeping the peace than to stimulating economic development. Hence, on this score alone, they need the market mechanism more than do the advanced countries of the world.

Secondly, most of them have accumulated a mixed bag of administrative interventions in the market mechanism, such as price controls and exchange allocations, which have undercut the serviceability of the market mechanism without putting any positive administrative program in its place. To impose, for example, maximum prices on food grains in order to hold down the price of food in towns and cities saps the farmer's incentive to produce more. It takes away the monetary incentive and puts nothing in its place—it destroys one mechanism of development without substituting another.

Thirdly, while the development of an economy through administrative techniques furiously engages the energies of a planning elite, participation in development through the market mechanism is open to everyone and, indeed, typically engages most of the adult population. Cueing, signalling, rewarding, and penalizing through the market mechanism are methods of drawing on the largest possible number of responses—and, in addition, a method of extricating a traditional peasantry from older institutions and habits of life that retard development.

Fourthly—and here is a consideration of enormous importance to most underdeveloped countries—they need the market mechanism because they cannot take the route to rapid development that the Soviet Union took from the 1920's to the '60's. Foreswearing in that period any hope for skillful allocation of their resources, the Soviets instead counted on achieving growth through restricted consumption and massive investment. Their strategy worked because the restriction of consumption was in fact possible. It was possible for two reasons: the standard of living was high enough to permit forced savings, and the Soviet government was willing and able to use compulsion. In many underdeveloped countries, neither of these conditions holds; in some, only one does. In many cases, the surplus over and above what is essential to consumption is much smaller than in the Soviet case, where development proceeded from an already advanced stage of early industrialization and food availability. And in ever more cases neither effective systems for tax administration nor other instruments of compulsion are sufficient to gather the savings that are hypothetically available. Hence, except to the extent that capital assistance from abroad can take the place of forced savings and investment, these underdeveloped countries cannot successfully imitate the older Soviet pattern. They need to understand, as even the Soviet Union in its new condition is coming to understand, the indispensability of a judicious use of the market mechanism for efficient use of the limited resources they can command.

... That the market mechanism can be serviceable to planned and unplanned economies alike, to public and private enterprise alike, to collective and individual choice alike, is a discovery the significance of which may soon dwarf what we have seen of its consequences so far. Although disputes will remain, and although different countries will choose different combinations of the market and other forms of organization of economic life, the market mechanism is now everywhere coming to be recognized as a fundamental method of economic organization which no nation can ignore and which every nation can well afford to examine freshly.

Reading 94

International comparisons of growth rates are invariably tricky: the statistics are hard to come by and easy to play with. Yet the vaunted growth of the Russian economy in the last two decades has caused considerable concern in the United States. There are Cassandras and Polyannas alike among the interpreters of the data showing that the Soviet Union is growing at a faster rate than we are.

What does the best recent scholarship suggest on the ability of the Russians to maintain their higher growth rate and to pass us as the world's greatest industrial power? Abram Bergson, professor of economics at Harvard University, is one of the best known of the American economists specializing in Russian affairs, and the passing years have conformed remarkably well with his predictions.

Questions to Guide the Reading

What are the most reasonable assumptions to make now about the likelihood that (1) the Soviet Union will accelerate its current growth rate and (2) the United States will decelerate its growth rate?

What difference does it make whether the Soviet Union catches up to the United States in gross national product by, say, 1999?

The U.S.S.R.'s Growth Race

Abram Bergson

As the 1962 Cuban episode showed, Khrushchev, in seeking to "bury us," is prepared to vary his tactics as circumstances permit. But in the economic field he has pursued steadfastly the imperative he inherited from Stalin: by outpacing the U.S.A. economically, the U.S.S.R. must eventually supplant us as the world's first industrial power. How are the Russians progressing in their "economic competition" with us? What are their future prospects?

Stalin died March 5, 1953. For the years that followed, through 1961, the Soviet government claims that the U.S.S.R. increased its national income at an average rate of 9.7 per cent a year. Independent Western calculations, however, place the correct figure at somewhere around six per cent, which is still a rapid pace.

From Abram Bergson, "The Great Economic Race," *Challenge*, March, 1963. Reprinted with kind permission of the author and publisher.

While it is certainly not unprecedented in Western experience, the Soviet growth rate compares favorably enough with that of the U.S. for recent years—about 2.7 per cent over the last few cycles.

In expanding their output in recent years, the Russians have been able to rely only to a very limited extent on increases in *employment* of labor. Industrial expansion has been achieved principally through increases in *output per worker*. Moreover, available population projections indicate that employment is not apt to increase any more rapidly in the coming years than it has in the recent past. In fact, there is a good chance that the rate of increase will decline. In hourly terms, however, the Soviet government might avoid such a trend if it should decide to postpone the promised reduction in the workweek to 35 hours by 1964–68. It follows that the growth in output will depend, as it has in the recent past, primarily on productivity increases. What are the prospects for such increases?

Any serious appraisal must consider, to begin with, that, because of the limited amount and quality of natural resources, production in the U.S.S.R., as elsewhere, is subject to diminishing returns. While these limitations will be felt throughout the Soviet economy, in the years ahead they are especially apt to be felt in agriculture—for the U.S.S.R. in terms of soil and climate is not nearly as well endowed agriculturally as its great land surface might suggest. The Russians' recent experience in farming is a dramatic reminder of this fact. I refer, in particular, to the already reduced returns on the vast new acreage cultivated during 1955–58. Thus, in Tselinnyi Krai, the heartland of this acreage, even dubious official figures show that the grain harvest, which was not especially high to begin with, has steadily declined. It was 14.3 million tons in 1958, 13.9 million in 1959, 12.9 million in 1960 and 10.3 million in 1961.

Borrowed technology and planning inefficiencies

Furthermore, in expanding their output lately, the Rusians have still been able to borrow new technology from the West and to extend to industry in general borrowed technology which previously had been used only in advanced enterprises. This "advantage of backwardness," however, is no longer as important as it was in the Thirties, and as the Soviet economy continues to advance, its role will decline even further. Of course, the U.S.S.R. now has a large corps of scientists and engineers of its own, one which can even stand comparison with that of the U.S.A. In addition, the Soviet government is devoting large and increasing sums to research. Therefore, as opportunities to profit from foreign technology dwindle, self-generated innovation will be something of an offset.

Closely related to but not the same thing as the state of technology is "economic efficiency." To weigh from this standpoint the impact of the extraordinary changes in economic organization, principles and procedures that have occurred since Stalin is a difficult task. But by all accounts the Soviet planning system still leaves much to be desired with respect to economic efficiency. And the succession of reforms at least attests to the fact that the government is seriously concerned with exploiting such "hidden reserves." Moreover, the government has also seen fit recently to allow Soviet economists a degree of discretion to explore and debate alternative techniques that was unheard of under Stalin. Even branches of "bourgeois" economic theory, such as "input-output analysis" and "linear programing," are no longer beyond the pale.

By implication, even though it is faced with diminishing returns from natural resources and slowing technological progress, the U.S.S.R. may still be able to avoid a reduced rate of productivity increase by raising economic efficiency. In trying to accomplish this through their planning system, however, the Russians will be treading new and as yet unexplored ground, and how much they will be able to achieve still remains to be seen.

As output has expanded, so too has variety, and partly for this reason the task of planning has become more complex. Accordingly, the Russians may have to improve their economic organization even to hold their own with regard to efficiency, to say nothing of raising it.

Agricultural wage

I have been referring to the efficiency of the economic system generally. In the agricultural sector, chiefly because of the use of the state farm in the execution of the new lands program, the notorious collective farm is no longer as important as it once was, but it is still predominant. And avowedly the government will continue to rely heavily on it in the coming years. When we consider the U.S.S.R.'s adverse natural endowment, we can see that the Soviet collective farm is not quite as inefficient as is often supposed, but future gains in this regard should be modest.

There are indications, however, that the government at long last is preparing the ground for the transformation of the collective into state farms. Among other things, in place of their customary cooperative shares, collective farm members are increasingly being paid a money income of a sort very much like the money wage of state farm employees. Because of differences in capital and quality of land, the comparison of state farm and collective farm productivity is a complex matter. Soviet economists probably are correct, however, in maintaining that the state farm is often superior to the collective farm, particularly in the growing of grain. But to what extent the higher productivity would survive the conversion of the collectives into state farms, especially if the conversion is abrupt, is another matter.

In general, how much progress will be realized regarding agricultural efficiency will depend very much on the prudence and restraint exercised with regard to farm policy and administration. These are qualities which the arbitrary and impatient Soviet government has thus far found it difficult to realize.

Accelerating capital growth

One of the principal reasons for the rapid rise of labor productivity in the past has been the authoritarian political control exercised over the volume of capital investment. One must be highly optimistic to suppose that this will not persist.

Indeed, given such control, one might wonder whether through its exercise alone the government could not offset or more than offset any and all forces making for a slowdown in the growth of the economy. But it should be borne in mind that the Soviet stock of fixed capital already is growing at an extraordinary rate—in the Fifties by some 11 per cent per year. Even maintaining this high tempo, to say nothing of increasing it, will be a difficult

task. This could not be accomplished merely by maintaining the present share of national income devoted to new capital investment. Rather the government would have to continually raise this share.

While this important fact is still not always understood, it becomes obvious when one considers that capital stock has been growing much more rapidly than output and that this is the chief reason that it has been possible to increase output at a rapid pace to begin with. As we saw, the growth in the employment of labor has only been modest.

Thus, in order for the capital stock to expand as in the past, the share of income going to capital investment would have to rise even if in the future output continued to grow at the past tempo. If output should slow down because of retarding forces elsewhere, the rate of investment would have to rise still more.

This leads to the conclusion that the share of national income available for consumption would have to fall. If the rate of growth of income should be maintained or not decline much, total consumption could still increase, for even a declining share of a growing pie can increase absolutely. There might also be an increase in per capita consumption. But the

National Income Projections: U.S. and U.S.S.R. (as % of U.S. National Income, 1960)

	U.S. with annual increase of		U.S.S.R. with annual increase of	
	3.0 %	4.0 %	5.0 %	6.0 %
1960	100.0	100.0	48.0	48.0
1970	134.4	148.0	78.2	86.0
1980	180.6	219.1	127.3	153.9

gains in the latter would have to be modest and no doubt would only seem more so to a people who have waited so long and have lately been led by their government to expect so much as have the Russians.

Thus suppose even that there should be no retarding forces elsewhere, so that with the capital stock growing no more rapidly than before, output should continue in the future to grow at six per cent. If allowance is made for the investment needed currently to assure this continued expansion of the capital stock by 11 per cent, according to a crude calculation, consumption per capita during the Sixties might rise by 2.3 per cent, or $9 to $12 a year, from the 1960 level of, say, $400 per capita. This would be respectable progress, but the result would hardly be the affluence that has been promised. If because of retarding forces elsewhere output should tend to grow less rapidly than six per cent, consumption would increase still less.

Consumption prospects

In deciding its future investment policy, the Soviet government must consider such possible consequences. As we may judge from the continuing stress on "heavy" compared with "consumer goods" industries, it already has determined to increase further the rate of investment, but how much is a momentous matter which it no doubt will decide currently only in the light of the circumstances of the time.

Reference has been to consumption exclusive of communal services, particularly education and health care. What of the latter items? How these might vary in the future is conjectural, but for purposes of the above calculation they are taken to increase proportionately with national income. Hence, with their inclusion in consumption, this category might grow somewhat more rapidly than was indicated. Actually, under its new program the party has committed itself to expand sharply the scope of communal services in the coming years. Among other things, housing in time is to be supplied free of charge instead of (as is now done) at a nominal rental. But such rearrangements would be purely financial and could not affect at all the underlying realities of the matter, particularly the total supply of consumer goods and services of all sorts that will be made available.

For purposes of the hypothetical calculation, I also assume that defense outlays will increase proportionately with national income. Should they fail to do so, there would necessarily be additional productive resources available for either consumption or investment, as the government might wish. And resources available for these purposes would only be greater if at long last defense expenditures were curtailed absolutely. In short, for the U.S.S.R., defense outlays are onerous, and it can only gain economically from disarmament. On the record to date, however, there is little basis to suppose that the Soviet government might determine its future policy on disarmament simply on this basis.

In sum, we can hardly foresee with any accuracy the future course of the Soviet economy. But it should be difficult for the Russians in the coming years to maintain the six per cent growth rate in output they have realized since Stalin. Still we must assume that they will continue to outpace the U.S.A., at least for some years to come, but most likely the margin by which they do so will tend to diminish.

In any event, if the Russians ever are to achieve the economic superiority over the U.S. that they seek, it will not be soon. This emerges clearly enough from the hypothetical projections of national income in the two countries as shown in the preceding table. All figures, including those for the U.S.S.R., are expressed as percentages of the U.S. national income in 1960.

We must not underestimate the Soviet economic challenge, but it is not quite as serious as many in the West have supposed.

Reading 95

In the mid-1960s Russian administrators and economists rediscovered the price system. Centralized decision making could scarcely cope with the million and one variables that had to be resolved each month. In consequence, profitability began to replace purely physical and technical quotas. Nevertheless, there was a tendency for westerners to exaggerate the degree of change in the Russian ideology and practice.

Professor Abram Bergson was introduced as author of the previous reading. One of his numerous books and monographs on the Soviet economic system has been his study for the nonprofit RAND Corporation. That study earned the supreme compliment of being translated by the Russians to help their bureaucrats understand their own system.

Time has also confirmed the predictions made here. The slowdown observed earlier in the final table seems to have continued in 1966–1970.

Questions to Guide the Reading

To run an economic system optimally, is it not enough to replace the motive "production for profit" by the goal "production for use"? Why is the problem of economic organization so much more complicated than this? Why does profitability have a role to play even in a system that is not run for private profit? If consumers are to have a range of free choices and if production is still to be organized with efficiency, why does pricing have a role to play?

Planning and the Market in the U.S.S.R.

Abram Bergson

Recently announced decisions of the Soviet government to reform its planning system have been greeted in the West as a momentous international event. The changes being made are surely not quite as dramatic as this assumes, but the government is reorganizing, often in novel ways, its proverbially centralized arrangements for industrial planning, and it has good reason to do so.

To refer only to bare essentials, the agency at the lowest bureaucratic level in Soviet industry and hence the one immediately in charge of operations is the *predpriiatie*, or enterprise. Under centralized planning, enterprise management has not been subject to control from above to quite the minute degree often supposed, but its authority has been severely limited. Under the new program, such authority is to be expanded. This will occur through a reduction in the number of the enterprise's plan targets that must be approved by superior agencies, and also in other ways. Thus, in utilizing available wage funds, enterprise management previously was much constrained by targets for wage payments, for employment and for average earnings for different categories of workers. Now management will be subject to only one such target, for total wages paid to all workers. Within the limits of the total fund assigned it, the management may employ labor as it wishes. Scales

of basic wage rates for different categories of workers, however, will continue, as in the past, to be determined primarily by superior agencies. Dismissals of workers presumably will still require, as they have since 1958, the consent of the trade union factory committee.

Again, decisions on capital investments hitherto have been especially centralized, but through charges to profits and depreciation, each enterprise is now to establish a "fund for the growth of production," which it may use with some discretion to finance modernization, automation and various other capital investment projects. Since, for industry generally, funds for the growth of production are expected to finance about 20 per cent of state capital investment in 1966, the additional authority gained at this point could be of some consequence.

Enterprise management is also to be allowed greater discretion in some other, related ways. Thus, it may now decide whether and to what extent piece (rather than time) work is to be employed in determining wages; it has more authority than before in respect to custom production, and so on.

Targets and incentives

Plan targets in the USSR constitute at once standards of performance, in effect, "success

From Abram Bergson, "The Current Soviet Planning Reforms," in Alex Balinky et al., *Planning and the Market in the USSR* (Rutgers University Press, New Brunswick, N.J., 1967). Reprinted with kind permission of the author and publisher.

criteria," for enterprise management, but necessarily not all targets can have equal weight. Interestingly, then, not only are targets approved by superior agencies being reduced in number. To some extent they are also being changed in character, and apparently also in their relative importance. Among other things, targets for output, including unfinished goods and stocks, which were previously stressed are to give way to one for "realized production," or sales. Contrary to many reports, profits have long been calculated in the USSR, but now the target for profits is also to become an important test of performance.

Along with success criteria, changes are also being made in arrangements for managerial bonuses. These affect managerial behavior under Soviet socialism hardly less than elsewhere. Thus, bonuses, which hitherto have been based chiefly on performance relatively to the plan target for output, or a variant thereof, are henceforth to depend primarily on performance relatively to the plan targets for sales and profits.

Then, too, such managerial bonuses, together with some premia for workers generally, are now to be paid out of a new "fund for material encouragement," which is to be maintained to a considerable extent through charges from profits. Appropriations will depend not only on sales and profits, but on other indicators of performance, including "profitability," a Soviet euphemism for the rate of return on capital. Regarding sales and profits, what will count is performance relatively not only to the plan but to pre-plan levels. The government is also establishing new arrangements for rewarding the introduction of new products, and hopes to heighten interest in satisfactory performance generally through diverse changes in procedures for financing of housing, nurseries, and the like, that are administered by the enterprise.

Last but not least, the changes in success criteria are to be accompanied by revisions in financial and price-fixing practices. According to a strange but long-standing policy, new capital hitherto has been made available to enterprises for the most part in the form of interest-free grants from the government budget. In future, however, enterprises will have to pay out of their profits a charge, typically 6 per cent, on their capital. The enterprises will also have to finance their capital needs increasingly through repayable loans. A firm which enjoys an especially favorable position regarding natural resources may also be subjected to a fixed "rental" payment.

For the rest, the manner in which price-fixing practices will be changed is still under study. Apparently, industrial wholesale prices, which usually are fixed to allow a standard mark-up over average branch cost, but which for the most part have not been changed since July 1, 1955, are at long last to be up-dated. In the process, the prices presumably will also be altered to allow for the novel charges on capital, and rental payments.

In sum, in industrial planning the Soviet government is scarcely dismantling wholesale its system of centralized planning, as sometimes has been suggested in the West, but it is adapting this system measurably in the direction of decentralization and increased use of market-type controls.

Bad effects of centralization

Why is the government at long last initiating such changes?

The USSR, it has been reported,[1] is "going through a crisis as profound, if not as eye-catching, as capitalism's crisis in the 1930's." Though eye-catching, this is hardly accurate, but the government is manifestly concerned about the onerous responsibilities which under centralized planning superior agencies in the bureaucratic structure must bear. Subject to approval at the highest level, such agencies must among other things determine in essentials the volume and direction of capital investment. They also have major responsibilities for the coordination of myriads of plan targets, and for the control of current factor inputs, especially of materials, fuel, power and machinery that are required to implement the plan.

With such responsibilities, the superior agencies understandably find it difficult to cope, and one must read partly in this light complaints that lately have become commonplace even in the USSR, such as this:

because of the absence of equipment, there are now about 1.5 million square meters of deserted productive floor space. In the textile department of the Kursk Synthetic Fiber Kombinat more than

[1] *The Economist,* March 19, 1966, p. 1100.

3000 square meters of floor space have been empty since 1960. In the "Tadzhiktekstilmash" Factory around 5000 square meters of productive floor space ... have been idle for more than two years because of the lack of specialized equipment.

The government understandably is now seeking to lighten responsibilities of superior agencies. Since managers of enterprises have often complained of the "petty tutelage" to which they are subject, it is also hoped that the authority transferred to them will be exercised more effectively than it was by their superiors.

The government has no less reason to reform managerial success criteria, however, for within their limited sphere enterprise managers also act wastefully, and curiously they are even impelled to do so by the success criteria that have prevailed. Even with a "visible hand" replacing an "invisible" one, as it has turned out, what is good for the individual enterprise is by no means always good for the country.

Thus, the infamous "safety factor" which is also a familiar theme in the USSR: Enterprise managers of necessity are allowed to negotiate with superior agencies regarding their plan targets, and in doing so seek to limit their assignments. In this way they hope more easily to earn bonuses for plan fulfillment. To the same end, the managers also hesitate to overfulfill targets, for fear that subsequent goals will only be made the higher.

In trying especially to fulfill the target for gross output, managers also often find it possible, and even expedient, to stress inordinately goods that bulk large physically. Alternatively, where gross output is calculated in value terms, emphasis may be placed rather on products that have relatively high ruble prices, but such prices too have their limitations, so the resulting assortment again may be strange. Thus the unending reports of difficulties of the Soviet consumer in shopping for particular items: for example, in buying large-size boy's shoes, as distinct from small-size men's shoes; of shirt as distinct from bandage cloth; of small-size as distinct from large-size electric bulbs, and so on.

Almost inevitably short-cuts are also taken regarding quality: as in the RSFSR, where among products examined by inspectors of the Ministry of Trade in the first half of 1962, 32.7 per cent of the clothing articles, 25 per cent of the knitwear, and 32.6 per cent of the leather shoes were rejected or reclassified in a lower quality category; or in the Ukraine where 20 to 25 per cent of the clothing and knitwear examined by the Ministry of Trade during 1963 had to be condemned as defective; or as where a factory manufacturing tractor parts found it advantageous to overfulfill its output goal by 60 per cent while lowering the quality of its products and so reducing their useful life by 40–50 per cent. In order to fulfill the current target for output, managers also hesitate to introduce new products, and find it profitable to abuse their machinery.

Reasons for change

The foregoing deficiencies in centralized planning are hardly new; they had already become manifest in the early five year plans under Stalin. Why is the government only now taking any consequential action to alleviate them? Reform might have been in order long ago, but it has become especially so lately because of the ever-increasing complexity of the task with which the cumbersome system of industrial planning must grapple.

The complexity is also greater because the government's own aim is no longer simply to produce steel and then more steel, as it was in essentials under Stalin. In his famous attack on Gosplan men in "steel blinkers" Khrushchev, of course, meant to urge not merely a greater use of plastics, but a more flexible outlook on alternative industrial branches generally. Despite their criticism of him, Khrushchev's successors probably will hesitate to abandon altogether this particular policy. Moreover, the government, which in the face of crop shortages has been importing about 20 million tons of grain since mid-1963, is also more attentive to consumers than it was under Stalin. For the dictator, food shortages did not even preclude exports. And the task of directing economic activity has become the more intricate because, though still not affluent, the consumers themselves have become more choosy; as witness the quite new phenomenon in the USSR of overstocks of consumers' goods of less desirable sizes, styles, and so on.

If prevailing priorities reflect a greater awareness of alternatives, this must be due partly to another development which has also been favorable to economic reform in other ways as well. The government has now found it expedient to allow economists generally to explore [economic] questions. In doing so, the economists are even permitted to use forms of analysis, especially of a mathematical sort, formerly regarded as bourgeois, and so tabu.

The invigorated economics that has quickly emerged not surprisingly has itself been a factor in the equation indicating economic reform. Thus, much of the Soviet criticism of planning procedures is to be found in the writings of Soviet economists themselves.

Scarcely less momentous than these developments, however, has been another: as reported, the rate of economic growth has declined; and markedly, according to both Soviet official and Western calculations, though the former as usual seem inflated:

Even the reduced rates are still respectable, but the decline must be disconcerting for proponents of a social system whose asserted economic superiority is held to be observable, above all, in its ability to generate rapid growth. And, still worse, the rival capitalist system in the West lately has itself shown unexpected capabilities in this regard, first in Western Europe and most recently even in the United States. To "overtake and surpass" the advanced capitalist countries economically can no longer seem the easy task that the ebullient Khrushchev assumed not so long ago.

By all accounts, economic growth has declined in the USSR for diverse reasons, and among these some of the most important, such as those causing the continued stagnation in

| | Real national income, average annual % increase | |
	Soviet official data	Western data
1950–58	10.9	7.0
1958–59	7.5	4.2
1959–60	7.7	4.9
1960–61	6.8	6.8
1961–62	5.7	4.3
1962–63	4.1	2.6
1963–64	9.0	7.2
1964–65*	6.0	3.0

* In 1966–70, the slowdown observed earlier seems to have continued.

agriculture, are remote from deficiencies in industrial planning. By repairing these deficiencies, however, the government hopes to assure an increasingly effective use of productive factors in industry, and on this basis to offset more successfully retarding forces affecting the economy generally.

The government is not about to restore capitalism, and Soviet economists have rightly criticized commentators, both in China and the West who have suggested as much, but it may not be easy to confine the market to limits now being observed. Another characterization of the current reforms also suggested, therefore, may not really be amiss: "creeping capitalism." It will be fascinating to see how in the years ahead the government grapples with its complex problem of planning organization.

Reading 96

The idea that communism represents one monolithic approach to economics or politics has been shaken to its roots by the variations among the European communist societies and, above all, by the patterns of events in the People's Republic of China. Moscow and Peking are at odds over the correct interpretation of Karl Marx in today's world; but they also pursue sharply different paths to solve their distinctive problems.

The Communist China case has relevance that goes well beyond the argument that we need to look closely at alternative systems so as to understand our own system better. China's example, if it were to prove successful in lifting large numbers of people out of centuries of poverty, would have appeal for other poor countries gripped by the urgency of new expectations. This article tells in outline form what the Communists faced when they came to power, what they did with their power, and what problems they have encountered. Because the situation is so constantly in flux and because data on the

Chinese experience are so hard to come by, this article needs to be read less for specifics on today's China than for an analysis of the overall strategy of a made-in-China brand of communism.

Questions to Guide the Reading

What considerations might communist leaders take into account in deciding upon the relative priorities as between agriculture and industry?

What principal lessons emerge from this account of Chinese experience? To what extent are the problems here unique to communism and to what extent are they inherent in all attempts at rapid economic growth in underdeveloped lands?

The Economy of Communist China

A. Doak Barnett

While political power in Communist China, as in all totalitarian societies, has become an end in itself—in fact, if not in theory—it is also much more than that. It is the tool to shape society into the Communists' image of the millennium, the weapon with which to achieve their vision of China as a powerful, industrialized state. From the start, therefore, the leaders have placed high priority on the need for rapid, planned, state-controlled, economic development and have used their power to this end.

The economy which the Chinese Communists inherited in 1949, however, was not only one of the poorest and least developed of any major nation, it was also in a shambles after years of disunity and war. Both industrial and agricultural production had dropped to low levels. Transport was disrupted. Inflation was rampant.

Economic reconstruction

The Communists' first task, therefore, was to rehabilitate the inherited economy, to get existing farms and factories working again, to repair transport, revive trade and control inflation.

China's first plan was modeled closely on Stalinist experience. Moreover it draw heavily on Soviet technical assistance and depended fundamentally on imports of capital goods from Russia (for which, however, the Chinese have had to pay). "The Soviet Union of today is the China of tomorrow," Peking proclaimed and its first plan, like Stalin's, called for over-all state planning under tight central control, rapid industrialization with a primary focus on heavy industries and high levels of state investment requiring enforced consumer austerity.

The struggle to achieve daily, weekly, monthly, quarterly and annual production or construction goals soon became a new way of life for millions of Chinese. Prodded to fulfill and overfulfill quotas by the ever-present cadres and the entire party and government apparatus, the Chinese worker entered a new world of "socialist competition," a world obsessed by numbers, figures and statistics, all designed both to demonstrate the inexorable progress of economic growth and to spur each worker to do a little more.

Before long, results began to be visible. Not only did the wheels of existing industries move faster, but also new factories dotted the countryside and new rail lines crisscrossed its open spaces. Factories and mills producing steel, machine tools, chemicals, cement and an impressive range of heavy manufactured goods, from trucks and tractors to generators and

From A. Doak Barnett, "Communist China—Continuing Revolution," *Headline Series* (Foreign Policy Association, New York), No. 153, May–June, 1962. Reprinted with kind permission of the author and publishers.

electronic equipment, rose not only in the older established centers of foreign-built industry, such as Manchuria, Shanghai and Tientsin, but also in remote cities in central, northwest and southwest China—and even in Inner Mongolia and Sinkiang. These burgeoning symbols of the growth and spread of industrialism in China became the show places for foreign visitors, and to the Chinese Communists themselves they provided reassuring symbols of economic development. These signs of progress were visible, tangible and impressive. The high price paid for them by the masses of Chinese people in overwork, underconsumption and regimentation was not so readily observable.

First plan accomplishments

Without doubt, Communist China was able, during 1953–57, to initiate an extremely significant process of economic growth. After 1953 it was able to build its economy at a rate as high or higher than that achieved by any other important underdeveloped nation—and higher than the rate achieved by the Soviet Union in its early years.

The most spectacular progress during the first plan period was in heavy industries. In some, including steel, the rates of growth suggested that in time Communist China might be able to achieve, in certain key industries most crucial to modern industrial power, output levels comparable to or surpassing those of important industrial nations such as Britain and Japan (only in absolute terms, however; in per capita terms China will long remain far behind).

The rate of total economic growth, measured in gross national product (GNP), was also extremely impressive during this period. Independent estimates by qualified economists in the West indicate that during 1953–57 the average annual increase in China's GNP may have been 7 or 8 percent, a rate about double India's during the same period (Japan's rate at that time, though, was comparable to China's and probably somewhat higher).

Lag in agriculture

Peking's emphasis on heavy industry was lopsided, however. Agriculture was seriously neglected, especially in the state's investment policies, and a persistent lag in farm output created continuing and growing problems for the regime. The Chinese Communists did foster many projects for irrigation and flood control, and tried to improve agricultural methods in simple ways, but their main response to the problem was to step up efforts to organize and control the peasants—to insure that, come what may, the state would obtain the grain and other farm produce needed to support China's economic plans.

In 1953 Peking established nationwide state control and rationing of grain. From then on it slowly increased the pressures on the peasants to join various types of farm organizations designed to prepare the way for collectivization. And then in 1955–56 came the big push that organized the peasants into roughly three-quarters of a million full-fledged collectives (called "higher state agricultural producers' cooperatives"), carried out with remarkable speed and efficiency.

Shortcomings and shifts in planning

Despite their pride in what had been achieved during the first plan, Peking's leaders began to show increased anxiety and dissatisfaction with economic trends during the final year of the plan. The year 1957 was not a good one and the regime had to cut back in many fields. The new collectives were encountering numerous problems. Per capita consumption actually declined from the level of 1956. The last payment from past Soviet loans was received—it was only $10 million—and there was no indication that more financial aid would be forthcoming to help China pay for needed industrial imports. In addition, China was obligated to repay all past loans and interest. Peking was forced to reduce its over-all budget, and state investments were cut 10 percent below 1956. It appeared, in fact, as if Communist China's entire development program might be losing momentum.

This was the context in which Peking's leaders pondered new solutions to existing problems. Those who favored a relatively cautious approach lost out. The "radicals" took charge. The approach they dictated called for bold, even reckless, policies based on the premise "it is not technique but man" that counts. To speed up the process of growth, the entire population, male and female, would be mobilized, recharged with ideological fervor and set to work on new tasks developing both agriculture and small-scale industry (the latter to supplement, not replace, continued construction of large-scale modern industry). The important thing would be manpower and morale, not technique or material incentives. This would be a new, unprecedented road to modernization and communism, differing significantly from the Stalinist model which guided China's First Five-Year Plan.

"Great leap forward"

The new policies first began to unfold during the winter of 1957–58. Over 100 million peasants reportedly were set to work on huge state-directed water control projects. In early 1958, "the great leap forward" was officially announced. The original production targets for 1958, and for the entire second plan period, were soon torn to shreds. The regime projected unprecedented growth rates and set literally fantastic targets. A startling new program was pushed to construct small-scale industries throughout rural China—industries using maximum labor and minimum capital. "Back yard steel furnaces" sprouted everywhere. Suddenly, instead of rural underemployment, there was actually a labor shortage in the countryside. City people were sent to the villages to work and everyone was prodded to work harder, but there were too many things for even China's huge population to do.

In the fall of 1958, only a few months after the first experimental commune was established, the entire countryside was quickly communized during a hectic campaign in which the collectives were merged into about 26,000 communes. These new units took over the functions of local government, mobilized and allocated labor like military command posts giving orders for the day, and undertook to manage almost every conceivable activity within their respective areas—not only agriculture, but also local industry, commerce, finance, education and military affairs. A big push was made to promote communal living, partly to make a rapid stride toward the ultimate goals of communism, partly to release more manpower and womanpower for production. Com-

mon mess halls, nurseries, old people's homes and service industries were established to release woman from household duties.

Everybody was worked to the point of exhaustion. The peasants went into the fields in large organized teams to do "close-planting" and "deep-plowing," agricultural techniques that acquired almost mystic significance. They were assigned by the millions to hundreds of thousands of new rural "factories" (many of them little more than handicraft establishments). The pace of work was accelerated until Communist China's leaders were compelled to caution local cadres to see that people were given time for adequate sleep.

Breakdown of planning

Although Peking provided the motive power behind all of these developments, central planning became almost meaningless for many of the hectic programs in the countryside, and the national statistical system went haywire. This was a guerrilla warfare approach to economic development. Local cadres were like low-level commanders, on their own; higher authorities demanded results, but how the cadres achieved them was largely their problem. They had to do their best and then report the results to the chain of command. Under relentless pressures from above, they did make great efforts—and sent in glowing reports, many of them grossly exaggerated. As a result, Peking was badly misinformed, so much so that at first it published incredible figures indicating that both grain and steel output had more than doubled in 1958 alone. It soon became necessary to backtrack and scale these figures drastically downward.

The great leap continued, at least in the official view, through 1960, but actually the pace began to slacken even during 1959. While some small-scale rural industries were successful, many were so inefficient and wasteful they had to be abandoned. The back yard steel furnaces were a notable failure; most of their output was unusable. Close-planting and deep-plowing proved to be no panacea; in some instances, in fact, their effects were harmful. The lack of effective central planning, or even statistical control, resulted in many serious dislocations and imbalances. The transportation system, overloaded and disorganized, developed crippling bottlenecks. The communes proved unable to plan and administer all of their new responsibilities. Through poor management, labor and resources were allocated in ways which damaged production. The peasants, treated like conscripts in a production army and deprived of almost all material incentives, began to drag their feet. And despite the millions of man-days invested in water control projects, the regime was still unable to control floods and droughts. Old man weather, one of the greatest tyrants of all throughout China's history, struck once again with natural disasters during three successive years, starting in 1959.

Steel versus grain

Looking at the great leap in retrospect, perhaps nothing highlights its successes and failures more clearly than the results achieved in two key commodities—steel and grain. Steel output skyrocketed from 5.35 million tons in 1957 to a claimed 18.45 million in 1960, a phenomenal achievement which seemed to put the regime way ahead of its original plans. By contrast, however, it is estimated by well-qualified Western analysts that although grain output did rise from 185 million tons in 1957 to perhaps 200 or 210 million in 1958 (Peking's claim, even the revised one, of 250 million is not credible), it then dropped to roughly 190 million in 1959 and in 1960 was probably again close to 185 million. In grain production, therefore, Communist China probably ended its great leap about where it started—but in the meantime China's population had grown by perhaps as much as 30 to 40 million.

Over-all growth, measured in GNP, is more difficult to judge, but independent estimates by Western experts suggest that it too followed a similar pattern. According to one such estimate, Communist China's rate of annual growth in GNP zoomed from about 5 percent in 1957 to 17 or 18 percent in 1958, dropped to roughly 12 percent in 1959, slumped still further to perhaps 4 percent in 1960, and during 1961 was very low indeed.

These facts, trends and problems forced Peking to re-examine its policies and to make a major retreat from the great-leap policies and the communes.

Changes in communes

Since the Chinese Communist party Central Committee meeting of January 1961, the pressure has been relaxed. Prime emphasis, moreover, has shifted from industry to agriculture. Every effort is now being made to increase agriculture output and to regularize and normalize the economy. The communes, while preserved as administrative units, have been radically changed—at least for the present. Many commune functions, including allocation of labor and distribution of income, have been shifted down to the production brigades (equivalent to the old collectives), and some have been decentralized even further to the small production teams. Numerous steps have been taken to try to restore the morale of individual peasants and create some incentives for them to increase output. Once again peasants have been allocated small private plots for their own use and rural trade fairs have been reopened so they can market the produce of these plots.

Many communal dining halls have been closed down and participation in numerous other communal activities, once compulsory, has now been made voluntary. The number of local commune industries has declined, and allocation of labor and resources to them has been minimized. At the national level, industrialization appears to be marking time. A sizable number of industries closed down during 1961 for varying periods of time, in some cases to service and repair machines suffering from the attrition of years of almost uninterrupted operation, in others because of raw-material shortages. New investment in heavy industrial construction appears to have been drastically cut. Special emphasis is being placed on industries producing goods which support agriculture—fertilizers, tractors and farm tools. Consumer goods industries are being encouraged, but they are also suffering from serious shortages of agricultural raw materials.

Unresolved problems

The events since 1958 clearly demonstrate that there is no miraculous formula for quickly solving the problem of increasing agricultural production in China. The struggle to solve it will be long and arduous. Investment in the rural sector of the economy will have to be increased . and farm techniques improved. And the atti-. tudes and feelings of the peasantry cannot be completely overlooked.

The continuing growth of China's population will also be difficult to ignore, as the Chinese Communists have done so far except for one short period toward the end of the first plan period when they briefly pushed birth control. Estimated to be close to 700 million already (specific estimates vary; some are above 700 million, some below), China's population could reach a billion by the 1980's if the present annual increase rate of perhaps 2 percent is not reduced. Conceivably Peking, with its great totalitarian power over people's lives, might be able to accomplish something in birth control if it really tried. But apparently the party does not wish to limit population—and consequently the labor force—at the present stage.

The problem of importing essential capital goods for industrialization has also become increasingly difficult. In 1960 Communist China incurred a deficit of over $300 million in its balance of payments with the Soviet Union. The Russians agreed to give the Chinese five years to pay this off, but an obligation of these dimensions, added to debts already incurred, will impose definite limits on Peking's ability to buy more machines and equipment from the Soviet Union. The need to purchase huge quantities of food from the West—in both 1961 and 1962—has already forced China to cut substantially its imports of industrial goods from Western Europe. Both of these trends portend increased difficulties in obtaining what is needed from abroad for China's continuing industrialization.

Problems such as these will probably make it extremely difficult for the Chinese Communists to get their economic development program into high gear again. Nevertheless one can be sure they will try. They might, in fact, be willing to pay a high price and take substantial risks to reaccelerate their industrialization drive whenever they decide that the time is ripe for a new push.

The Future?

Reading 97

In the midst of the Great Depression, the most important economist of this century was able to glimpse into the future. Decades before J. K. Galbraith, Keynes foresaw the "affluent society." Although Keynes knew that laissez faire could not be counted upon to do so, he was optimistic that macroeconomic policies could secure full employment and rapid growth for the mixed economy. Keynes gave Marx his fatal rebuttal. Under affluence, economics would cease to be Man's master and become his useful servant. That is the vision of Lord Keynes, genius and economist.

Questions to Guide the Reading

Do men need the goad of economic scarcity to keep life from becoming dull? William James once spoke of the need for "a moral equivalent of war"—e.g., the Peace Corps or the vigorous battle against poverty, which was to engage the energies bred into man by the evolutionary struggle for existence. Can you construct a "moral equivalent" for economic scarcity? Foreign aid? Adult cultural enrichment?

Economic Possibilities for Our Grandchildren (1930)

John Maynard Keynes

I

We are suffering just now from a bad attack of economic pessimism. It is common to hear people say that the epoch of enormous economic progress which characterised the nineteenth century is over; that the rapid improvement in the standard of life is now going to slow down—at any rate in Great Britain; that a decline in prosperity is more likely than an improvement in the decade which lies ahead of us.

I believe that this is a wildly mistaken interpretation of what is happening to us. We are suffering, not from the rheumatics of old age, but from the growing-pains of over-rapid changes, from the painfulness of readjustment between one economic period and another. The increase of technical efficiency has been taking place faster than we can deal with the problem of labour absorption; the improvement in the standard of life has been a little too quick; the banking and monetary system of the world has been preventing the rate of interest from falling as fast as equilibrium requires. And even so, the waste and confusion which ensue relate to not more than 7½ per cent of the national income; we are muddling away one and sixpence in the £, and have only 18s. 6d., when we might, if we were more sensible, have £1; yet, nevertheless, the 18s. 6d mounts up to as much as the £1 would have been five or six years ago. We forget that in 1929 the physical output of the industry of Great Britain was greater than ever before, and that the net surplus of our foreign balance available for new foreign investment, after paying for all our imports, was greater last year than that of any other country, being indeed 50 per cent greater than the corresponding surplus of the United States. Or again—if it is to be a matter of comparisons—suppose that we were to reduce our wages by a half, repudiate four-fifths of the national debt, and hoard our surplus wealth in barren gold instead of lending it at 6 per cent or

more, we should resemble the now much-envied France. But would it be an improvement?

The prevailing world depression, the enormous anomaly of unemployment in a world full of wants, the disastrous mistakes we have made, blind us to what is going on under the surface—to the true interpretation of the trend of things. For I predict that both of the two opposed errors of pessimism which now make so much noise in the world will be proved wrong in our own time—the pessimism of the revolutionaries who think that things are so bad that nothing can save us but violent change, and the pessimism of the reactionaries who consider the balance of our economic and social life so precarious that we must risk no experiments.

My purpose in this essay, however, is not to examine the present or the near future, but to disembarrass myself of short views and take wings into the future. What can we reasonably expect the level of our economic life to be a hundred years hence? What are the economic possibilities for our grandchildren?

From the earliest times of which we have record—back, say, to two thousand years before Christ—down to the beginning of the eighteenth century, there was no very great change in the standard of life of the average man living in the civilised centres of the earth. Ups and downs certainly. Visitations of plague, famine, and war. Golden intervals. But no progressive, violent change. Some periods perhaps 50 per cent better than others—at the utmost 100 per cent better—in the four thousand years which ended (say) in A.D. 1700.

This slow rate of progress, or lack of progress, was due to two reasons—to the remarkable absence of important technical improvements and to the failure of capital to accumulate.

The absence of important technical inventions between the prehistoric age and comparatively modern times is truly remarkable. Almost everything which really matters and

From John Maynard Keynes, *Essays in Persuasion* (Macmillan and Co., London, 1933). Reprinted with kind permission of Rupert Hart-Davis Limited.

which the world possessed at the commencement of the modern age was already known to man at the dawn of history. Language, fire, the same domestic animals which we have to-day, wheat, barley, the vine and the olive, the plough, the wheel, the oar, the sail, leather, linen and cloth, bricks and pots, gold and silver, copper, tin, and lead—and iron was added to the list before 1000 B.C.—banking, statecraft, mathematics, astronomy, and religion. There is no record of when we first possessed these things.

At some epoch before the dawn of history—perhaps even in one of the comfortable intervals before the last ice age—there must have been an era of progress and invention comparable to that in which we live to-day. But through the greater part of recorded history there was nothing of the kind.

The modern age opened, I think, with the accumulation of capital which began in the sixteenth century. I believe—for reasons with which I must not encumber the present argument—that this was initially due to the rise of prices, and the profits to which that led, which resulted from the treasure of gold and silver which Spain brought from the New World into the Old. From that time until to-day the power of accumulation by compound interest, which seems to have been sleeping for many generations, was re-born and renewed its strength. And the power of compound interest over two hundred years is such as to stagger the imagination.

Let me give in illustration of this a sum which I have worked out. The value of Great Britain's foreign investments to-day is estimated at about £4,000,000,000. This yields us an income at the rate of about 6½ per cent. Half of this we bring home and enjoy; the other half, namely, 3¼ per cent, we leave to accumulate abroad at compound interest. Something of this sort has now been going on for about 250 years.

For I trace the beginnings of British foreign investment to the treasure which Drake stole from Spain in 1580. In that year he returned to England bringing with him the prodigious spoils of the *Golden Hind*. Queen Elizabeth was a considerable shareholder in the syndicate which had financed the expedition. Out of her share she paid off the whole of England's foreign debt, balanced her Budget, and found herself with about £40,000 in

hand. This she invested in the Levant Company—which prospered. Out of the profits of the Levant Company, the East India Company was founded; and the profits of this great enterprise were the foundation of England's subsequent foreign investment. Now it happens that £40,000 accumulating at 3¼ per cent compound interest approximately corresponds to the actual volume of England's foreign investments at various dates, and would actually amount to-day to the total of £4,000,000,000 which I have already quoted as being what our foreign investments now are. Thus, every £1 which Drake brought home in 1580 has now become £100,000. Such is the power of compound interest!

From the sixteenth century, with a cumulative crescendo after the eighteenth, the great age of science and technical inventions began, which since the beginning of the nineteenth century has been in full flood—coal, steam, electricity, petrol, steel, rubber, cotton, the chemical industries, automatic machinery and the methods of mass production, wireless, printing, Newton, Darwin, and Einstein, and thousands of other things and men too famous and familiar to catalogue.

What is the result? In spite of an enormous growth in the population of the world, which it has been necessary to equip with houses and machines, the average standard of life in Europe and the United States has been raised, I think, about fourfold. The growth of capital has been on a scale which is far beyond a hundredfold of what any previous age had known. And from now on we need not expect so great an increase of population.

If capital increases, say, 2 per cent per annum, the capital equipment of the world will have increased by a half in twenty years, and seven and a half times in a hundred years. Think of this in terms of material things—houses, transport, and the like.

At the same time technical improvements in manufacture and transport have been proceeding at a greater rate in the last ten years than ever before in history. In the United States factory output per head was 40 per cent greater in 1925 than in 1919. In Europe we are held back by temporary obstacles, but even so it is safe to say that technical efficiency is increasing by more than 1 per cent per annum compound. There is evidence that the revolutionary technical changes, which have so **far** chiefly affected industry, may soon be attacking agriculture. We may be on the eve of improvements in the efficiency of food production as great as those which have already taken place in mining, manufacture, and transport. In quite a few years—in our own lifetimes I mean—we may be able to perform all the operations of agriculture, mining, and manufacture with a quarter of the human effort to which we have been accustomed.

For the moment the very rapidity of these changes is hurting us and bringing difficult problems to solve. Those countries are suffering relatively which are not in the vanguard of progress. We are being afflicted with a new disease of which some readers may not yet have heard the name, but of which they will hear a great deal in the years to come—namely, *technological unemployment*. This means unemployment due to our discovery of means of economising the use of labour outrunning the pace at which we can find new uses for labour.

But this is only a temporary phase of maladjustment. All this means in the long run *that mankind is solving its economic problem*. I would predict that the standard of life in progressive countries one hundred years hence will be between four and eight times as high as it is to-day. There would be nothing surprising in this even in the light of our present knowledge. It would not be foolish to contemplate the possibility of a far greater progress still.

II

Let us, for the sake of argument, suppose that a hundred years hence we are all of us, on the average, eight times better off in the economic sense than we are to-day. Assuredly there need be nothing here to surprise us.

Now it is true that the needs of human beings may seem to be insatiable. But they fall into two classes—those needs which are absolute in the sense that we feel them whatever the situation of our fellow human beings may be, and those which are relative in the sense that we feel them only if their satisfaction lifts us above, makes us feel superior to, our fellows. Needs of the second class, those which satisfy the desire for superiority, may indeed be insatiable; for the higher the general level, the higher still are they. But this is not so true of the absolute needs—a point may

soon be reached, much sooner perhaps than we are all of us aware of, when these needs are satisfied in the sense that we prefer to devote our further energies to non-economic purposes.

Now for my conclusion, which you will find, I think, to become more and more startling to the imagination the longer you think about it.

I draw the conclusion that, assuming no important wars and no important increase in population, the *economic problem* may be solved, or be at least within sight of solution, within a hundred years. This means that the economic problem is not—if we look into the future—*the permanent problem of the human race*.

Why, you may ask, is this so startling? It is startling because—if, instead of looking into the future, we look into the past—we find that the economic problem, the struggle for subsistence, always has been hitherto the primary, most pressing problem of the human race—not only of the human race, but of the whole of the biological kingdom from the beginnings of life in its most primitive forms.

Thus we have been expressly evolved by nature—with all our impulses and deepest instincts—for the purpose of solving the economic problem. If the economic problem is solved, mankind will be deprived of its traditional purpose.

Will this be a benefit? If one believes at all in the real values of life, the prospect at least opens up the possibility of benefit. Yet I think with dread of the readjustment of the habits and instincts of the ordinary man, bred into him for countless generations, which he may be asked to discard within a few decades.

To use the language of to-day—must we not expect a general "nervous breakdown"? We already have a little experience of what I mean —a nervous breakdown of the sort which is already common enough in England and the United States amongst the wives of the well-to-do classes, unfortunate women, many of them, who have been deprived by their wealth of their traditional tasks and occupations—who cannot find it sufficiently amusing, when deprived of the spur of economic necessity, to cook and clean and mend, yet are quite unable to find anything more amusing.

To those who sweat for their daily bread leisure is a longed-for sweet—until they get it.

There is the traditional epitaph written for herself by the old charwoman:—

Don't mourn for me, friends, don't weep for me
    never.
For I'm going to do nothing for ever and ever.

This was her heaven. Like others who look forward to leisure, she conceived how nice it would be to spend her time listening-in—for there was another couplet which occurred in her poem:—

With psalms and sweet music the heavens'll be
    ringing,
But I shall have nothing to do with the singing.

Yet it will only be for those who have to do with the singing that life will be tolerable—and how few of us can sing!

Thus for the first time since his creation man will be faced with his real, his permanent problem—how to use his freedom from pressing economic cares, how to occupy the leisure, which science and compound interest will have won for him, to live wisely and agreeably and well.

The strenuous purposeful money-makers may carry all of us along with them into the lap of economic abundance. But it will be those peoples, who can keep alive, and cultivate into a fuller perfection, the art of life itself and do not sell themselves for the means of life, who will be able to enjoy the abundance when it comes.

Yet there is no country and no people, I think, who can look forward to the age of leisure and of abundance without a dread. For we have been trained too long to strive and not to enjoy. It is a fearful problem for the ordinary person, with no special talents, to occupy himself, especially if he no longer has roots in the soil or in custom or in the beloved conventions of a traditional society. To judge from the behaviour and the achievements of the wealthy classes to-day in any quarter of the world, the outlook is very depressing! For these are, so to speak, our advance guard—those who are spying out the promised land for the rest of us and pitching their camp there. For they have most of them failed disastrously, so it seems to me—those who have an independent income but no associations or duties or ties—to solve the problem which has been set them.

I feel sure that with a little more experience we shall use the new-found bounty of nature quite differently from the way in which the rich use it to-day, and will map out for ourselves a plan of life quite otherwise than theirs.

For many ages to come the old Adam will be so strong in us that everybody will need to do *some* work if he is to be contented. We shall do more things for ourselves than is usual with the rich to-day, only too glad to have small duties and tasks and routines. But beyond this, we shall endeavour to spread the bread thin on the butter—to make what work there is still to be done to be as widely shared as possible. Three-hour shifts or a fifteen-hour week may put off the problem for a great while. For three hours a day is quite enough to satisfy the old Adam in most of us!

There are changes in other spheres too which we must expect to come. When the accumulation of wealth is no longer of high social importance, there will be great changes in the code of morals. We shall be able to rid ourselves of many of the pseudo-moral principles which have hag-ridden us for two hundred years, by which we have exalted some of the most distasteful of human qualities into the position of the highest virtues. We shall be able to afford to dare to assess the money-motive at its true value. The love of money as a possession—as distinguished from the love of money as a means to the enjoyments and realities of life—will be recognised for what it is, a somewhat disgusting morbidity, one of those semi-criminal, semi-pathological propensities which one hands over with a shudder to the specialists in mental disease. All kinds of social customs and economic practices, affecting the distribution of wealth and of economic rewards and penalties, which we now maintain at all costs, however distasteful and unjust they may be in themselves, because they are tremendously useful in promoting the accumulation of capital, we shall then be free, at last, to discard.

Of course there will still be many people with intense, unsatisfied purposiveness who will blindly pursue wealth—unless they can find some plausible substitute. But the rest of us will no longer be under any obligation to applaud and encourage them. For we shall inquire more curiously than is safe to-day into the true character of this "purposiveness" with which in varying degrees Nature has endowed almost all of us. For purposiveness means that we are more concerned with the remote future results of our actions than with their own quality or their immediate effects on our own environment. The "purposive" man is always trying to secure a spurious and delusive immortality for his acts by pushing his interest in them forward into time. He does not love his cat, but his cat's kittens; nor, in truth, the kittens, but only the kittens' kittens, and so on forward for ever to the end of cat-dom. For him jam is not jam unless it is a case of jam to-morrow and never jam to-day. Thus by pushing his jam always forward into the future, he strives to secure for his act of boiling it an immortality.

Let me remind you of the Professor in *Sylvie and Bruno:—*

"Only the tailor, sir, with your little bill," said a meek voice outside the door.

"Ah, well, I can soon settle *his* business," the Professor said to the children, "if you'll just wait a minute. How much is it, this year, my man?" The tailor had come in while he was speaking.

"Well, it's been a-doubling so many years, you see," the tailor replied, a little gruffly, "and I think I'd like the money now. It's two thousand pound, it is!"

"Oh, that's nothing!" the Professor carelessly remarked, feeling in his pocket, as if he always carried at least *that* amount about with him. "But wouldn't you like to wait just another year and make it *four* thousand? Just think how rich you'd be! Why, you might be a *king*, if you liked!"

"I don't know as I'd care about being a king," the man said thoughtfully. "But it *dew* sound a powerful sight o' money! Well, I think I'll wait—"

"Of course you will!" said the Professor. "There's good sense in *you*, I see. Good-day to you, my man!"

"Will you ever have to pay him that four thousand pounds?" Sylvie asked as the door closed on the departing creditor.

"*Never*, my child!" the Professor replied emphatically. "He'll go on doubling it till he dies. You see, it's *always* worth while waiting another year to get twice as much money!"

Perhaps it is not an accident that the race which did most to bring the promise of immortality into the heart and essence of our religions has also done most for the principle of compound interest and particularly loves this most purposive of human institutions.

I see us free, therefore, to return to some of the most sure and certain principles of religion and traditional virtue—that avarice is a vice, that the exaction of usury is a misdemeanour, and the love of money is detestable, that those walk most truly in the paths of virtue and sane wisdom who take least thought for the morrow. We shall once more value ends above means and prefer the good to the useful. We shall honour those who can teach us how to pluck the hour and the day virtuously and well, the delightful people who are capable of taking direct enjoyment in things, the lilies of the field who toil not, neither do they spin.

But beware! The time for all this is not yet. For at least another hundred years we must pretend to ourselves and to every one that fair is foul and foul is fair; for foul is useful and fair is not. Avarice and usury and precaution must be our gods for a little longer still. For only they can lead us out of the tunnel of economic necessity into daylight.

I look forward, therefore, in days not so very remote, to the greatest change which has ever occurred in the material environment of life for human beings in the aggregate. But, of course, it will all happen gradually, not as a catastrophe. Indeed, it has already begun. The course of affairs will simply be that there will be ever larger and larger classes and groups of people from whom problems of economic necessity have been practically removed. The critical difference will be realised when this condition has become so general that the nature of one's duty to one's neighbour is changed. For it will remain reasonable to be economically purposive for others after it has ceased to be reasonable for onself.

The *pace* at which we can reach our destination of economic bliss will be governed by four things—our power to control population, our determination to avoid wars and civil dissensions, our willingness to entrust to science the direction of those matters which are properly the concern of science, and the rate of accumulation as fixed by the margin between our production and our consumption; of which the last will easily look after itself, given the first three.

Meanwhile there will be no harm in making mild preparations for our destiny, in encouraging, and experimenting in, the arts of life as well as the activities of purpose.

But, chiefly, do not let us overestimate the importance of the economic problem, or sacrifice to its supposed necessities other matters of greater and more permanent significance. It should be a matter for specialists—like dentistry. If economists could manage to get themselves thought of as humble, competent people, on a level with dentists, that would be splendid!

DATE DUE

GAYLORD			PRINTED IN U S A